THE ROUTLEDGE COMPANION
TO SOUND STUDIES

The Routledge Companion to Sound Studies is an extensive volume presenting a comparative and historically informed understanding of the workings of sound in culture, while also mapping potential future directions for research in the field. Experts from a variety of disciplines within sound studies cover such diverse topics as politics, gender, media, race, literature and sport. Individual sections consider the importance of sound in an increasingly mediated world; the role that sound media play in the construction of experience; and the ways in which sound has been theorized to produce a distinctive sensory contribution to knowledge.

This wide-ranging and vibrant collection provides a rich resource for scholars and students of media and culture.

Michael Bull is Professor of Sound Studies at the University of Sussex. His works include *Sounding Out the City: Personal Stereos and the Management of Everyday Life* (2000) and *Sound Moves: iPod Culture and Urban Experience* (Routledge 2007). He has just completed a monograph on *Sirens* and is presently writing a monograph on *Reinterpreting the Sounds of World War 1*. He is the co-founding editor of the journals *Senses and Society* and *Sound Studies* (both with Routledge) and is editor of the book series *The Study of Sound*.

THE ROUTLEDGE COMPANION TO SOUND STUDIES

Edited by Michael Bull

Routledge
Taylor & Francis Group

LONDON AND NEW YORK

First published 2019 by Routledge

2 Park Square, Milton Park, Abingdon, Oxfordshire OX14 4RN
52 Vanderbilt Avenue, New York, NY 10017

Routledge is an imprint of the Taylor & Francis Group, an informa business

First issued in paperback 2020

British Library Cataloguing-in-Publication Data
A catalogue record for this book is available from the British Library

Library of Congress Cataloging-in-Publication Data
A catalog record has been requested for this book

ISBN: 978-1-138-85425-3 (hbk)
ISBN: 978-0-367-65974-5 (pbk)

Typeset in Bembo
by Sunrise Setting Ltd, Brixham, UK

CONTENTS

Contents

Contents

LIST OF FIGURES

LIST OF CONTRIBUTORS

Tom Artiss teaches in the Department of Sociology, University of Cambridge, where he completed his doctorate in 2014. His dissertation, "*A Social Life of Songs: Inuitization and Music in Nain, Labrador*", explores the ways in which Western music inflects and reflects modern Inuit identities. Current research extends to radio and affect in Canadian indigenous communities.

Frauke Behrendt is Principal Lecturer in Media Studies at the University of Brighton and Deputy Head of School for Research and Enterprise in the School of Media. She is also the founding director of the Centre for Digital Media Cultures. Behrendt led the EPSRC-funded research project "*Smart e-Bikes – Understanding How Commuters and Communities Engage With Electrically-Assisted Cycling*", the "*Intelligent Transport Solutions for Social Inclusion*" project, and the research on the *NetPark* project.

Karin Bijsterveld is Professor of Science, Technology, and Modern Culture at Maastricht University, the Netherlands. She is author of *Mechanical Sound: Technology, Culture, and Problems of Noise in the Twentieth Century* (MIT, 2008), co-editor of the *Oxford Handbook of Sound Studies* (2012, with Trevor Pinch), co-author of *Sound and Safe: A History of Listening Behind the Wheel* (Oxford UP 2014, with Eefje Cleophas, Stefan Krebs & Gijs Mom), and editor of a special issue on *Auditory History in The Public Historian* (2015). Her book *Sonic Skills* is forthcoming (Palgrave, 2018).

Carolyn Birdsall is Assistant Professor of Media Studies at the University of Amsterdam. Her publications include *Nazi Soundscapes: Sound, Technology and Urban Space in Germany, 1933–1945* (Amsterdam University Press, 2012) and *Sonic Meditations: Body, Sound, Technology* (edited with Anthony Enns, Cambridge Scholars Press, 2008). Birdsall's current research examines the early history of radio sound archiving in and beyond Europe.

Amanda Cachia has curated over forty exhibitions, many of which highlight disability politics in contemporary art. She is an Assistant Professor of Art History at Moreno Valley College in Riverside, California, and director of the new Moreno Valley College Art Gallery, scheduled to open in autumn 2018. She completed her PhD in Art History, Theory, and Criticism at the University of California, San Diego, in spring 2017.

Thomas F. Carter is an anthropologist who has conducted international research on a range of issues within sport. He currently leads the social science postgraduate provision of Masters courses in the School of Sport and Service Management at the University of Brighton. He has conducted ethnographic fieldwork in the US, Ecuador, and Wales with extensive fieldwork being conducted in Northern Ireland and Cuba. He is the author of two books: *The Quality of Home Runs* (Duke University Press, 2008) and *In Foreign Fields: The Politics and Experiences of Transnational Sport Migration* (Pluto Press, 2011). *The Quality of Home Runs* won the North American Society for the Sociology of Sport's Outstanding Book Award for 2009.

Yiu Fai Chow is Associate Professor at the Department of Humanities and Creative Writing, Hong Kong Baptist University. His publications cover gender politics and creative practices, including *Caring in the Time of Precarity: A Study of Single Women Doing Creative Work in Shanghai* (Palgrave Macmillan, forthcoming, 2019) and *Sonic Multiplicities* (co-authored, University of Chicago Press, 2013). Chow is also an award-winning writer in lyrics and prose.

Alex W. Corey is Lecturer on History & Literature at Harvard University and Program Coordinator of the Futures of American Studies Institute at Dartmouth College. Prior to joining History & Literature, they served as Manager of the Laboratory for Race and Popular Culture at CU Boulder, where they completed their PhD in English. They are currently working on a book project titled *Beyond the Blues: Music, Gender, and Black Modernisms*, which explores how the gendering of sound led into and emerged out of the twentieth-century problem of the colour line in the United States.

Blake Durham is a DPhil student at Worcester College, University of Oxford. His research focuses on musical circulation through comparative ethnographic analysis of licensed and unlicensed spheres of musical exchange.

Tim Edensor is the author of *Tourists at the Taj* (Routledge, 1998), *National Identity, Popular Culture and Everyday Life* (Berg, 2002), *Industrial Ruins: Space, Aesthetics and Materiality* (Berg, 2005), *From Light to Dark: Daylight, Illumination* and *Gloom* (Minnesota, 2017) as well as the editor of *Geographies of Rhythm* (2010). Tim has written extensively on national identity, tourism, industrial ruins, walking, driving, urban materiality, and landscapes of illumination and darkness.

Nina Sun Eidsheim is Professor of Musicology and Special Assistant to the Dean of the UCLA Alpert School of Music. As a scholar and singer she investigates the multisensory and performative aspects of the production, perception, and reception of vocal timbre of twentieth- and twenty-first-century music. Current monograph projects include *Sensing Sound: Singing and Listening as Vibrational Practice* (Duke University Press, 2015) and *Measuring Race: The Micropolitics of Listening to Vocal Timbre and Vocality in African-American Popular Music* (Duke UP, forthcoming). She is also co-editing the *Oxford Handbook of Voice Studies* (Oxford UP, forthcoming) and a special issue on voice and materiality for the journal, *Postmodern Culture*. In addition, she is the principal investigator for the UC-wide, transdisciplinary research project entitled *Keys to Voice Studies: Terminology, Methodology, and Questions Across Disciplines* and recipient of the Woodrow Wilson National Career Enhancement Fellowship (2011–12), Cornell University Society of the Humanities Fellowship (2011–12), the UC President's Faculty Research Fellowship in the Humanities (2015–16), and the ACLS Charles A. Ryskamp Fellowship (2015–16).

David Goodman teaches American history at the University of Melbourne. He is the author of *Radio's Civic Ambition: American Broadcasting and Democracy in the 1930s* (Oxford University Press, 2011). His recent publications have been on American broadcasting history and he is completing a book on the local debate about US entry into World War 2.

Mark Grimshaw-Aagaard is the Obel Professor of Music at Aalborg University, Denmark. He has published widely across subjects as diverse as sound, biofeedback in computer games, virtuality, the Uncanny Valley, and IT systems and also writes free, open source software for virtual research environments (WIKINDX). Mark is series editor for the Palgrave Macmillan series *Studies in Sound*, and his books include the anthologies *GAME Sound Technology & Player Interaction* (IGI Global, 2011) and *The Oxford Handbook of Virtuality* (Oxford University Press, 2014), and, with co-author Tom Garner, a monograph entitled *Sonic Virtuality* (Oxford University Press, 2015). A two-volume anthology, *The Oxford Handbook of Sound & Imagination*, is due in 2018 from Oxford University Press.

Julian Henriques is Professor, convenor of the MA Scriptwriting and MA Cultural Studies programmes, and director of the Topology Research Unit in the Department of Media and Communications, Goldsmiths, University of London. Prior to this, Julian ran the film and television department at CARIMAC at the University of the West Indies, Kingston, Jamaica. His credits as a writer and director include the reggae musical feature film *Babymother* (1998) and as a sound artist on "*Knots & Donuts*" (2011) at Tate Modern. Julian researches street cultures and technologies and has published *Changing the Subject* (Routledge, 1998), *Sonic Bodies* (Bloomsbury Press, 2011) and *Sonic Media* (forthcoming).

Bennett Hogg is a composer, improviser, and musicologist whose recent work is concerned with sound/music and place, and sound/music and nature. From 2012–14 he was PI of "*Landscape Quartet*", and an AHRC-funded project focussed on participative sound art in natural environments, and in 2014 held a six-month Austrian Science Fund fellowship at Kunst Universität, Graz, working as a co-investigator on the "*Emotional Improvisation*" project, led by Dr Deniz Peters. His academic writing tends to come from a phenomenological orientation, but he has also drawn on psychoanalytic theories, and other hermeneutic theories. His creative practice covers a broad range of musics, from experimental environmental sound works, through electroacoustic composition, free improvisation, a more "conservative" voice in instrumental composition, and Northumbrian folk music. He is currently Senior Lecturer in Music at Newcastle University.

David Howes is Professor of Anthropology and Co-Director of the Centre for Sensory Studies at Concordia University, Montreal. He is also the Director of the Concordia Centre for Interdisciplinary Studies in Society and Culture (CISSC) and an Adjunct Professor in the Faculty of Law, McGill University. David is the general editor of the new Sensory Studies series from Bloomsbury, as well as a founding editor of the journal *The Senses and Society*. David has edited the four volume *Senses and Sensation: Critical and Primary Sources* compendium (Bloomsbury, 2018), *A Cultural History of the Senses in the Modern Age, 1920–2000* (Bloomsbury, 2018) and *Ways of Sensing: Understanding the Senses in Society* (Routledge, 2014) with Constance Classen.

Martyn Hudson is lecturer in Art and Design History at Northumbria University. He is the author of the books *The Slave Ship, Memory and the Origin of Modernity* (Routledge, 2016), *Ghosts, Landscapes and Social Memory* (Routledge, 2017), *Species and Machines: The Human Subjugation of*

Nature (Routledge, 2017), *Centaurs Rioting in Thessaly: Memory and the Classical World* (Puncum Books, 2018), and *Critical Theory and the Classical World* (Routledge, forthcoming). His research focuses on aesthetic forms and their relation to social theory and philosophy and particularly on the visual and aural cultures of capitalism.

Meri Kytö is an ethnomusicologist and a cultural researcher studying articulations of privacy and domestication in urban spaces. She is a postdoctoral researcher in music studies at the University of Tampere, Finland.

Thor Magnusson is a Lecturer in Music at the University of Sussex. His work focusses on the impact digital technologies have on musical creativity and practice, explored through software development, composition, and performance. He is the co-founder of ixi audio, and has developed audio software, systems of generative music composition, written computer music tutorials, and created two musical live coding environments. As part of ixi, he has taught workshops in creative music coding and sound installations, and given presentations, performances, and visiting lectures at diverse art institutions, conservatories, and universities internationally.

James G. Mansell is Associate Professor of Cultural Studies in the Department of Culture, Film and Media at the University of Nottingham, UK. He is the author of *The Age of Noise in Britain: Hearing Modernity* (University of Illinois Press, 2017) and co-editor of *The Projection of Britain: A History of the GPO Film Unit* (BFI Books, 2011).

Shannon Mattern is an Associate Professor of Media Studies at The New School in New York. She is author of *The New Downtown Library: Designing With Communities* (Minnesota University Press, 2006), *Deep Mapping the Media City* (Minnesota University Press, 2013), and *Code and Clay: Data and Dirt: Five Thousand Years of Urban Mediation* (Minnesota University Press, 2017).

Paul Nataraj is a practicing sound artist and sound studies researcher. His sound works have been featured on BBC Radio three and internationally. He completed his doctorate at the University of Sussex in 2018.

Louis Niebur is Associate Professor of Musicology at the University of Nevada, Reno. His research fields include avant-garde and popular music of the postwar era, including music in radio, television and film, and the significance of popular music to LGBTQ communities, particularly as it has shifted between live music, the jukebox, and the disc jockey in the context of queer spaces. He is author of *Special Sound: The Creation and Legacy of the BBC Radiophonic Workshop* (Oxford University Press, 2010).

John M. Picker is Lecturer in Comparative Media Studies/Writing at the Massachusetts Institute of Technology. He is the author of *Victorian Soundscapes* (Oxford University Press, 3003) and recent chapters in *The Sound Studies Reader* (Routledge, 2012), *Sounds of Modern History* (Berghahn Press, 2016), and *The Auditory Culture Reader* (Bloomsbury Press, 2015).

Jonathan Pieslak is Professor at The City College of New York where he specializes in research on the cultural dimensions of terrorism and political violence, with a specific focus on music. (www.jonathanpieslak.com)

Ben Powis, PhD, is a Lecturer in Football Studies at Southampton Solent University. His research interests include the sociology of disability sport, the embodied experiences of visually impaired people in sport and physical activity and investigating the significance of sensuous sporting experiences.

Richard Cullen Rath is Associate Professor of History at the University of Hawai'i at Mānoa. He is the author of *How Early America Sounded* (Cornell University Press, 2003) and is currently working on two books, one an introduction to the history of hearing and the other comparing the rise of print culture in the eighteenth-century Atlantic world to the rise of internet culture today. He has also written three award-winning articles on music, creolization, and African American culture. Recently he has published articles on the sonic dimensions of wampum, media, and the senses in the Enlightenment, and the open source digital future of the humanities. In addition to writing, he is presently leading a collaborative digital arts and humanities initiative at the University of Hawai'i. Rath is also a musician who has found ways to use music to "do" history and American studies whenever possible.

Ian Reyes is Associate Professor of Communication Studies in the Harrington School of Communication and Media at the University of Rhode Island, where he teaches audio production, media theory, and cultural criticism. His research on the intersections of media, markets, and cultures appears in publications including *Journal of Popular Music Studies*, *The Senses & Society*, *Journal of Marketing Management*, and *Consumption Markets & Culture*.

Tom Rice is a Senior Lecturer in Anthropology at the University of Exeter. He specializes in researching auditory culture. He has written numerous articles and book chapters and in 2013 published an ethnographic monograph on listening practices in the hospital setting entitled *Hearing and the Hospital: Sound, Listening, Knowledge and Experience* (Sean Kingston Publishing). As well as writing and teaching on sound, Rice has produced audio pieces including *The Art of Water Music*, a documentary for BBC Radio 4 on the relationship between music and water, and *Govindpuri Sound*, a programme for the BBC World Service about the sound environment of a Delhi slum.

Hillegonda Rietveld is Professor of Sonic Culture at London South Bank University, and was Editor of *IASPM Journal*, the journal of the International Association for the Study of Popular Music. In addition to publication work on electronic music by artists such as Kraftwerk and Brian Eno, as well as on game music with a co-edited special issue on the subject for *GAME: The Italian Journal of Game Studies* (2017), she has published extensively on electronic dance music cultures, including a co-edited special issue, 'Echoes of the Dubdiaspora', for *Dancecult: Journal of Electronic Dance Music Culture* (2015); the co-edited collection *DJ Culture in the Mix: Power, Technology, and Social Change in Electronic Dance Music* (2013); and the monograph *This is Our House: House Music, Cultural Spaces and Technologies* (1998).

Alexander Russo is Associate Professor in the Department of Media and Communication Studies at The Catholic University of America in Washington, DC. He is the author of *Points on the Dial: Golden Age Radio Beyond the Networks* (Duke University Press, 2010), as well as articles and book chapters on the technology and cultural form of radio and television, sound studies, the history of music and society, and media infrastructures.

Justin St. Clair is Associate Professor of English at the University of South Alabama. He is the author of *Sound and Aural Media in Postmodern Literature: Novel Listening* (Routledge, 2013).

Holger Schulze is Full Professor in Musicology at the University of Copenhagen and principal investigator at the Sound Studies Lab. He serves as curator for the Haus der Kulturen der Welt Berlin and as founding editor of the book series *Sound Studies*. His research focus is the cultural history of the senses, sound in popular culture, and the anthropology of media. He was invited Visiting Professor at the Musashino Art University in Tokyo, at the Leuphana Universität Lüneburg, at the Berlin University of the Arts, and the Humboldt-Universität zu Berlin. He is Associated Investigator at the cluster of excellence Image Knowledge Gestaltung at the Humboldt-Universität zu Berlin and Vice Chair of the European Sound Studies Association. He writes for *Neue Zeitschrift für Musik, Seismograf, Merkur, Freitag, TEXTE ZUR KUNST, Positionen*. Book publications: *Intimität und Medialität* (Avinus Verlag, 2012), *Gespür* (Textem Verlag, 2014), *Sound as Popular Culture* (MIT Press, 2016, ed.), *The Sonic Persona* (Bloomsbury Press, 2018).

Jacob Smith is founder and director of the Master of Arts in Sound Arts and Industries, and Professor in the Department of Radio/Television/Film. He is the author of *Vocal Tracks: Performance and Sound Media* (University of California Press, 2008), *Spoken Word: Postwar American Phonograph Cultures* (University of California Press, 2011), *The Thrill Makers: Celebrity, Masculinity, and Stunt Performance* (University of California Press, 2012), and *Eco-Sonic Media* (University of California Press, 2015). He writes and teaches about the cultural history of media, with a focus on sound and performance.

Christabel Stirling teaches in the Music Department at the University of Oxford.

Marie Thompson is a Lecturer of Media, Sound and Culture at Lincoln School of Film and Media, University of Lincoln. She is the author of *Beyond Unwanted Sound: Noise, Affect and Aesthetic Moralism* (Bloomsbury, 2017) and co-editor of *Sound, Music, Affect: Theorizing Sonic Experience* (Bloomsbury, 2013). Marie is the academic lead of the University of Lincoln's Extra-Sonic Practice (ESP) research group.

Neil Verma is Assistant Professor of Sound Studies in Radio/Television/Film at Northwestern University. He is author of *Theater of the Mind: Imagination, Aesthetics, and American Radio Drama* (University of Chicago Press, 2012), winner of the Best First Book Award from the Society for Cinema and Media Studies. He is co-editor of *Anatomy of Sound: Norman Corwin and Media Authorship* (University of California Press, 2016), winner of the Kraszna-Krausz Best Moving Image Book Award. Verma has published articles in such journals as *Critical Quarterly, The Journal of American Studies, The Journal of Sonic Studies, RadioDoc Review* and *The Velvet Light Trap* and contributed chapters to several edited volumes. He is Co-Network Director for the Radio Preservation Task Force at the Library of Congress, and founder of the Great Lakes Association for Sound Studies (GLASS). Recently, Verma won a grant from the National Endowment for the Humanities to develop digital tools for analysis of archival voice recordings. He holds a PhD in History of Culture from the University of Chicago, where he also won a Harper-Schmidt Postdoctoral Fellowship, serving in the Society of Fellows in the Liberal Arts from 2010–14.

Salomé Voegelin is an artist and writer engaged in listening as a socio-political practice of sound. Her work and writing deal with sound, the world sound makes: its aesthetic, social, and political realities that are hidden by the persuasiveness of a visual point of view. She is the author of *Listening to Noise and Silence: Towards a Philosophy of Sound Art* (Continuum, 2010), and *Sonic Possible Worlds: Hearing the Continuum of Sound* (Bloomsbury, 2014), and together with Thomas

Gardner she has co-edited *Colloquium: Sound Art-Music* (ZeroBooks, John Hunt Publishing, 2016). As an artist she works collaboratively with David Mollin (Mollin+Voegelin) in a practice that engages words, things, and sound and focusses on invisible connections, transient behaviour, and unseen rituals. Salomé is a Reader in Sound Arts at the London College of Communication, UAL.

Tim Wall is Professor of Radio and Popular Music Studies at Birmingham City University. He researches into the production and consumption cultures around popular music and radio. His recent publications have included the second edition of *Studying Popular Music Culture* (Sage, 2013), and articles and chapters on a diverse range of subjects, including music radio online, punk fanzine, the transistor radio, personal music listening, popular music on television, television music histories, jazz collectives, Duke Ellington on the radio, and *The X Factor*. He is currently working on a monograph on the history of jazz broadcasting on BBC radio.

Cara Wallis is Associate Professor in the Department of Communication at Texas A&M University. She studies the social and cultural implications of emerging media technologies, with a particular focus on how uses and understandings of technology both reproduce inequitable power relations and open up spaces for individual and collective agency and thus, social change. She is the author of *Technomobility in China: Young Migrant Women and Mobile Phones* (NYU Press, 2013), which is an ethnographic exploration of the use of mobile phones by young rural-to-urban migrant women working in the low-level service sector in Beijing. She is currently completing a book on social media use in China.

INTRODUCTION: SOUND STUDIES AND THE ART OF LISTENING

There is a wonderful moment in a documentary I watched some years ago about the role of television in American presidential campaigns in the 1950s. Adlai Stevenson was the democratic candidate in 1956 and had been allocated a television advisor – who was to orchestrate the presentation of his campaign for the then new medium. Throughout the campaign Stevenson who wasn't interested in television never spoke to the advisor. Then one evening the advisor was called to Stevenson's hotel room. This he thought was the moment when he could make a contribution to the campaign. On entering the room Stevenson pointed to the television in the room and said: "You're the television guy, aren't you? How do you switch this thing on!" Stevenson lost to Eisenhower in the election of that year.

Despite the recent rapid growth of sound studies, it is still a relatively new "discipline" and when asked what my area of research is – on telling the questioner that I am a Professor of sound studies – I sometimes receive a quizzical look followed by an enquiry as to whether I study music, sonic design, sonic technologies, cultures that use sound in particular ways or whether I engage in some other form of sonic sub-cultural analysis or something more esoteric? In truth, I still haven't worked out a one sentence answer that will suffice. Historians, anthropologists, geographers, musicologists and media academics normally do not have these problems – their fields of study are roughly understood within and outside of the academy. In terms of sound studies any perceived ambiguity lies in the very interdisciplinary nature of the subject and the role that sound plays in the disciplinary interests of a wide range of writers who focus upon the sonic. For example, the contributors to this volume come from a wide range of disciplines – as ethnomusicologists, geographers, literary theorists, urban theorists, sociologists, media theorists and more. What primarily joins them together is an interest in sound either as a major focus within their research or as a significant element within it. This eclectic and inherently interdisciplinary aspect of the study of sound has come together under the term "sound studies" with only a handful of contributors to this volume referring to themselves professionally as "sound studies" scholars. This disciplinary coming together through the study of the sonic provides an enormous range and diversity of intellectual enquiry and subject matter as evidenced in the chapters that follow. In parallel to this breadth and diversity, the study of sound also produces a range of theoretical, methodological and cultural challenges that are also explored in many of the entries to this volume, thus pointing to the future directions that sound studies will take as it reaches a level of maturity. Whilst sound has been studied for many years within a wide variety of disciplines within the arts, social sciences and sciences – the term "sound studies" itself is relatively new and is indeed not uncontested (Grimshaw-Aagaard in this volume). Despite this sound studies has gained wide recognition within the academy over the last ten years and has been enormously successful in its own right. It is a successful "work in progress" as evidenced by the wave of publications, journals, research projects and indeed university courses that now go under the name of "sound studies". In terms of publishing we have seen a series of books retracing the complex and often highly divisive histories of sounds (Birdsall 2012; Cockayne 2007; Picker 2003; Rath 2003; Smith 2007); historical and philosophical accounts of sound (Erlmann 2011; Grimshaw and Garner 2015; Schwartz 2011); the changing character and nature of the voice (Connor 2000; Petmann 2017; Ree 1999); new analysis of the nature of architectural and urban sounds (Bijsterveld 2016; Blesser and Salter 2007; Thompson 2002); the history and nature of technological sounds (Katz 2010; Sterne 2003; Schmidt-Horning 2015; Suisman and Strasser 2009; Taylor 2015; Tosoni and Pinch 2016); as well as work on a plethora of sonically based technologies (Bull 2000, 2007; Goggin 2006; Henriques 2011). In addition to this there has been much work highlighting the relationship between violence and sound (Johnson and Cloonan 2009; Daughtry 2015; Gilman 2016; Pieslak 2009); religious sounds (Hirshkind 2006; Pieslak 2015); sound and race (Stoever 2016); together with new theoretical interventions on the nature of the sonic (Kane 2014). In addition to the many anthologies of sound and auditory culture there is a flowering of academic journals which include *Sound Effects; Interference; Sound Studies* and *The Journal of Sonic Studies* that provide a diverse platform for new work in the field.

This focus upon sound is partly the result of a re-evaluation of the breadth and meaning of cultural sensory experience more broadly coupled with a move away from a largely unreflective, visually based epistemology that had dominated academic discourse in the social sciences, arts and humanities until relatively recently. This has also been accompanied by a "sensory turn" in the academy that had as its genesis a theoretical and empirical evaluation of "embodiment" as a focus of research which in its own way attempted to overcome the traditional mind-body dualism inherent in Western thought since the Greeks (Csordas 1990). These two strands – the nature of cultural experience and sensory embodiment – often overlap but are not necessarily reducible. For example, studying the role of sound within the BBC Radiophonic Workshop in the UK need not be a study of sensory embodiment (Niebur 2010). Sound studies is a broad church, theoretically, methodologically and empirically as the present volume testifies.

Whilst recognising the diverse nature of sound studies, *The Routledge Companion to Sound Studies* focuses largely upon the study of sound within media and culture with the meaning of the "cultural" broadly conceived to incorporate elements of history, sociology, anthropology and associated subjects. It is therefore located firmly in the social sciences and humanities and primarily concerns itself with the study of sound in society and hence is largely "culturalist" in orientation. Murray Schafer, for many the leading voice within sound studies (he referred to it as soundscape studies), argued that "the home of soundscape studies will be the middle ground between science, society and the arts. From acoustics and psychoacoustics, we will learn the physical properties of sound and the way sound is interpreted by the human brain. From society we will learn how man behaves with sounds and how sounds affect and change his behaviour. From the arts, particularly music, we will learn how man creates ideal soundscapes for that other life, the life of imagination and psychic reflection" (Schafer 1979: 4).

Whilst this volume primarily concentrates on the second of Schafer's subjects, this does not imply that the study of acoustics or the aesthetics of sound understood through compositions or other artefacts are not discussed – indeed the reader will see a certain amount of shadow boxing going on by contributors in this volume in relation to the above areas of study. The artistic and aesthetic elements of the study of sound are foregrounded in Routledge's recently published volume on *Sounding Art* which concentrates primarily upon the aesthetics of sound. The editors of that volume point out that "Sound Studies includes, potentially, the investigation of all sounds, whereas the study of sounding art focusses upon the artistic and/or aesthetic applications of sound" (Cobussen, Meelberg and Truax 2017: 2). However, despite this separation there exists a communality of intellectual heritage between the two areas as evidenced by the commonality of bibliographic citations in both volumes.

In the remaining pages of this introduction I deal with potential developments within sound studies in the coming years and some of the challenges that scholars of sound might engage with. Sound studies is in rapid transition culturally, methodologically and theoretically as recognized by many of the authors in the present volume. As it develops and grows it is necessary to take stock of its own theoretical, methodological and cultural foundations. Jonathan Sterne recently argued that sound studies should "be grounded in a sense of its own partiality, its authors' and readers' knowledge that all the key terms we might use to describe and analyse sound belong to multiple traditions, and are under debate" (Sterne 2014: 4). In order to achieve this critical self-evaluation Sterne replicates C. Wright-Mills' invitation to sociologists in the 1960s to exercise their "sociological imagination" by invoking sound scholars to cultivate their own "sonic imaginations" in order to "rework culture through the development of new narratives, new histories, new technologies, and new alternatives" (Sterne 2014: 6).

The authors in the present volume largely follow Sterne's advice and in the remaining pages of this introduction I reflect upon a range of issues surrounding the range and scope of what it means to "listen" or more accurately to focus upon the question: when we "listen" what is it that we "hear"?

In 2003 when writing the introduction to the first edition of *The Auditory Culture Reader* myself and Les Back called for the need to develop strategies of "deep listening" that was indebted in part to the innovatory work of Murray Schafer. Now fifteen years later what constitutes just such a "deep listening" might well now be contested. Nowhere is this questioning more apparent than in the relationship of sound studies to race. In 2016 Jenny Stoever published *The Sonic Color Line: Race and the Cultural Politics of Listening* that provocatively challenges sound studies to consider "whiteness as an auditory construction" (Stoever 2016: 18). Stoever, a scholar specializing African American literature, music and history, investigates the complex relationships that exist between sound, race and technology in order to "excavate a century of aural genealogies and a politics of racialized sound to reveal the dynamic relationships between racial ideologies, the development of sound media, and the modern listening practices that shape (and are shaped by) them" (Stoever 2016: 4). Stoever stresses both the advantages of sound studies for an interdisciplinary scholar like herself whilst simultaneously criticizing, what she takes as an unreflective approach to race and listening. She describes the attraction of sound studies in the following terms:

> Learning to listen differently to race, gender, power, place, and history brought me to "sound studies," not the other way around; however, the fields, methodological freedom greatly enabled my scholarship in African American literature, music, and history…I meet sound where, when, and in what form I find it, not as an object of study, but as a method enabling an understanding of race as an aural experience with far reaching historical and material resonance.
>
> *(Stoever 2016: 18)*

The methodological implications of Stoever's embrace of sound studies will be addressed in a later section of this volume. Suffice to say that Stoever obliges us to rethink the cultural and sonic significance of the written word when it comes to analysing the role of race in culture. This point is echoed in the work of Anna Maria Ochia Gautier whose analysis of the sonic nature of 19th-century Columbian culture required "an acoustically attuned exploration of the written archive" (Ochia Gautier 2014: 16).

However, the adoption of sound studies by Stoever and others comes with an attendant criticism as she argues that sound studies has itself failed to interrogate the complex, diverse "whiteness" of its own central categories. Stadler (2015) and Stoever (2016) argue that "whiteness" remains a largely unrecognized or compartmentalized category in much sound studies work. The development of ontological theories of sound discussed in Part I of this volume appear to relegate forms of cultural listening and affect to epiphenomena which could be interpreted, unwittingly, as relegating notions of cultural "difference" to the level of the periphery of experience. Stadler claims that notions of race continue to shape listening practices throughout many parts of the world and that when sound studies does turn its attention to race and difference it is often carried out through a liberal politics of "representation" and "inclusion". These authors make the serious argument, in line with Jonathan Sterne's injunction to question one's own foundational concepts, that sound studies needs to confront the "underlying whiteness of the field" rather than "conform to the neo-liberalist project of 'giving voice to the voiceless' or recovering 'lost' sounds" (Stoever 2016: 6). Whilst there is indeed a recognition of the historical nature of diverse listening positions within culture in the literature on listening within sound studies there is little analysis of the ways in which listening itself becomes racialized. Indeed, even the most notable work in the field tends to compartmentalize or join together differences in listening under the general rubric of class, gender and race whilst hermetically sealing off the epistemological nature of "listening" from further interrogation.

In the remaining pages of this introduction I engage through a diverse range of examples ranging from listening to popular culture, to the past, to cities, to trains, to sirens and to data in the spirit of Jonathan Sterne's plea for the use and development of our sonic imagination in order to ask what it is that we hear when we listen through the use of one's own sonic imagination. In doing so, I will critically engage with my own form of shadow boxing with the work of Murray Schafer.

Listening to the past: writing sound and sound as sound

The authentic instrument movement of the 1960s spearheaded by David Munrow, Nikolas Harnoncourt, Trevor Pinnock and others sought to reproduce original performance practices through a meticulous re-interpretation of pre-classical texts and the reconstruction of musical instruments to their "original" state so that performances would sound as close as possible to the "originals" from the 16th, 17th and 18th centuries. In doing so it was hoped that classical performers and audiences would open their ears to the sounds of period performances by clearing away the playing and listening practices of the 19th and 20th centuries informed by Romanticism and the technical innovations that had made classical instruments smoother and capable of greater virtuosity. This desire to authentically recreate the listening practices of the past was criticized by Pierre Boulez, the French composer and conductor who, when asked what he thought of re-creating period performances, commented that audiences listened with "modern ears" thus appearing to discount the possibility of re-creating an historical authenticity of musical listening practices.

Notions of historical specificity and cultural contextuality in relation to listening practices extend beyond the domain of music and filter into a wide range of listening practices and related sonic methodologies that are used to access and understand the sonic in society. Whilst the period instrument movement recreated the sounds of the past through the creation of "period" instruments, methodologically much historical research into the sounds of the past is necessarily reliant upon written documentary data although the development of sonic archaeology is now attempting to generate new ways of listening to the ancient past. Through the use of rigorous historical methodologies historians have been able to cast light upon the sonic worlds of the past. This reading of the sonic does not preclude the development of new methodologies orientated to "sound as sound" as against reading sound through print. However, the historian Mark Smith has forcefully argued for the importance of written records for the historian:

> Among the most important questions guiding historical acoustemology are: is print capable of recording sound? Or must we insist on trying to re-create that same sound – that same cannon boom using salvaged cannon and gunpowder from the period – to reproduce what some perceive as a wholly accurate echo, one that our listening ears can reliably hear and say, yes, that's the sound of the past?
>
> *(Smith in Novac and Sakakneeny 2015:56)*

Smith appears to make the same point as Pierre Boulez in terms of what it means to "listen" to the past in the present. According to Smith, if we were to recreate battle scenes from the American War of Independence using similar weaponry on the same terrain then, whilst it might technically produce similar sounds it would not replicate the experience of battle at the time. These are not merely questions of methodology, but also questions of epistemology and cultural specificity.

This is not merely a defence of the historians' use of written data but a questioning of the use of sonic data reproduced on tape and other forms of archival databases. These issues extend into the significance of "actual" recordings of events – in historical archives or reproduced in audio/visual documentaries. Recordings for example are potentially a valuable form of data, yet the data does not "speak" for itself as Karin Bijsterveld notes:

> Studying cultures of sound implies an interest in the oft taken-for-granted ways in which people give meaning to the sounds they are surrounded with, in how they routinely act upon and use these sounds, and in how that has changed over time. But how can we get access to what is taken for granted in past and contemporary worlds (Bijsterveld 2016:100).

Traditionally the distinctiveness of sound tended to lie in its temporal and spatial nature, its specificity and immediacy. With the advent of recording technologies such as the phonograph in the late 19th century up until the advent of digital technologies in the 21st century, sounds can now be increasingly captured for research purposes. Whilst we cannot hear the voice of Michelangelo, we can now hear the voices of the famous and infamous; the voices of the dead, the sounds of air-raid sirens in London in 1942, the recorded music of Caruso to David Bowie and the voices of ordinary people embedded in radio programs from the 1920s onwards. The ability to store sonic data has expanded our ability to fix the sounds of the past and present within our research methodologies. However, this ability to abstract out the sonic from a broader sensory range of experience poses its own problems. These are problems of specificity, cultural contextualization and meaning. The 20th and 21st centuries have seen a dramatic change in the sonic environment through the development of a range of acoustic technologies such as telephones, microphones, loudspeakers, phonographs, radios, tape recorders, compact discs, cellular phones, MP3 players, digital voice mail and talking computers that have transformed what it means to study and understand sonic experience. These technologies provide wonderful opportunities to the researcher whilst still posing newly configured issues of specificity, cultural contextualization and meaning for the sonic researcher as Mark Smith noted: "recordings are inherently ahistorical and, as such, not only fail to communicate which constituencies heard what and how and why;

they also lull unwitting listeners into thinking that what they are hearing is freighted with the same meaning as the sound (or silence) in its original context" (Smith 207: 59).

Listening to popular culture

Cobussen, Meelberg and Truax in their introduction to *The Routledge Companion* to Sounding Art recognize that of the thirty-nine entries that go to make up their volume that there was, "a fairly limited range of types of music discussed here, but hopefully it will be easy to extrapolate these ideas in a diversity of directions" (Cobussen, Meelberg and Truax 2017: 5). Looking through the name index of the volume confirms the editor's observation. Most entries go to the composer John Cage, followed by Pierre Schaeffer and Murray Schafer, whilst the only other composers that are mentioned are Stockhausen, Varese, Xenakis and Boulez. Culturally, all members of what might be considered the musical avant-garde with virtually no mention made of the music that most people listen to, perform and move to. The question to ask here is whether an epistemology of listening practices based upon the above writers and composers preclude or discourage the study of listening practices in more popular forms of music? The issue is complicated if we filter this question of epistemology through Bourdieu's understanding of "habitus" and "cultural capital" whereby subjects orientate themselves culturally and hierarchically to a range of social practices and evaluations.

If we take the Bourdieu approach, and if we accept that avant-garde musical practices have taken centre stage in sound studies then the conclusion that might be drawn is that whilst there is nothing inherently "exclusionary" about using the listening practices of Cage et al., the cultural formation of those who enact such epistemologies of "listening" led them to study and work within the cultures of the avant-garde? Alternatively, it might be argued that there is something in the epistemology of listening as articulated by Cage et al. that lends itself to studying the margins of musical experience rather than its centre. The response to these two separate yet linked questions is a mixed one. In order to think about them it is useful to recap on the foundational role played by Cage and Schafer in the epistemology of listening employed by many sound studies scholars. Murray Schafer produced an innovative toolkit for the study of sound enabling scholars to listen and hear the world in fresh, innovative and useful ways. The articulation of concepts such as soundscape, signal, soundmark, keynote sounds and flat line sounds enabled researchers to place sounds within time and space like never before. These concepts were articulated in the World Soundscape Project based at Simon Fraser University in Canada which studied the soundscape of Vancouver and other European, usually rural soundscapes. In developing his schema Schafer drew upon the work of Cage, especially on his Dadaesque 4'33" work in which Cage questioned the very relationship between music and sound – as audiences listened to the sounds of themselves and the world beyond the salon for 4'33" whilst the pianist remained silent. This radical rupture between what had traditionally been considered as music and the sounds of the natural and social environment became central to sound studies. Performers/composers/theorists produced their own intellectual "soundmark" within the field of sound studies and revolutionized what is understood to be the relationship between sound, music, culture and nature. Yet, this very radicalness has resulted in a paradoxically narrow cultural focus in terms of music use and listening practices. Several of the entries in the present volume deal with aspects of the popular in culture and indeed those scholars of sound working within the fields of culture and history often deal with the sounds of the everyday. Whilst the present volume deals with a broad spectrum of cultures of sound that includes the "popular" and not merely the "avant-garde" it remains the case that it references the composers John Cage and Murray Schafer more than any other composer/musician as do most sound studies books on the topic. This might imply that the use of these foundational figures does not hinder the more general study of the popular in music and culture. That whilst the focus of these figures necessarily drifted to the cultural edges of society – this was a contingent, not a necessary movement. This is a conclusion that I am broadly in agreement with, with one or two caveats.

A critical reading of Schafer for example finds a largely negative evaluation of popular and everyday modes of music listening:

> In stressing low-frequency sound popular music seeks blend and diffusion rather than clarity and focus…Such music (Mozart, Beethoven) also demands great concentration. That is why silence is observed at concerts where it is performed…Thus the concert hall made concentrated listening possible, just as the art gallery encouraged focused and selective viewing. It is a unique period in the history of listening and it produced the most intellectual music ever created. It contrasts vividly with music designed for outdoor performance, such as folk music, which does not demand great attention to detail, but brings into play what we might call peripheral hearing, similar to the way the eye drifts over an interesting landscape.
>
> *(Schafer 1979: 117)*

Schafer appears to consign the music produced and consumed in the late 20th century to a distraction – a form of passive consumption of distracted listening very much in the manner of Adorno's work on forms of musical reception. Many of the entries in the present volume engage with a range of sonic practices with greater creativity by unpacking a range of different ways in which we experience the sonic, noise and music both cognitively and physically. My own work on Walkman and iPod use demonstrates the way in which users can operationalize intense, active and analytical modes of concentrated listening in everyday practices one moment whilst displaying more relaxed modes of listening at other times (Bull 2000, 2007).

However, we also need to go further than this to Schafer's notion of what it is to listen itself – there are many different ways in which we might listen and Schafer certainly provides a blueprint, a schema for one very specific form of listening. Schafer understands the historical derivation of certain forms of listening practices – the listening position of an audience for example and the rise of concert going. This historical form of listening is however paradoxically replicated in the position of the audience who listen to Cage's 4'33" whereby the audience remains inert, silent – actively involved in decoding the sounds that they hear – a disembodied, objective form of listening far removed from many everyday forms of listening. There is a similarity between Schafer and Theodor Adorno here in terms of their dismissal of the "popular" and their elevation of aspects of the avant-garde as the true harbingers of cultural authenticity – it was once said of Adorno that the reader couldn't imagine him dancing to music. In the present volume work authors chart new ways of working with, consuming and producing forms of the sonic experience that breaks down these distinctions between the popular and the avant-garde, the cognitive and the physical.

The second issue lies in the breakdown of the distinction between music and sound – a core element within sound studies. This very breakdown of the distinction between music and sound whilst highly productive analytically has also produced attendant issues concerning listening practices in everyday life. It is interesting that a largely "anti-urbanist" thinker such as Schafer was favourably disposed to the work of the Futurists who in their celebration of urban noise and the technologies of war represented the antithesis of Schafer. Yet Schafer was in agreement with their dissolving the distinction between sound and music. In this light, the Russian avant-garde composer Arseny Avraamov's Symphony of Factory Sirens of 1922 fits paradoxically into the cultural remit of sound studies despite the use of factory and urban sounds disliked by Schafer. The point to be made here is not the focus upon the work of Auraamov per se, but the neglect of other more popular forms of listening practices. For example, a striking comparison could be made of the way in which people experienced the music of arch conservatism, the powerfully yet moving National Anthem of the Union of Soviet Republics sung by millions both in Russia and elsewhere then and more recently. This should not represent an either /or of the study of sound and music but an embracing of both modes. Yet the culturally broadening out of the subject should not be understood in isolation to the epistemological basis of sound studies. It is not merely a broadening out of the subject that is required but a critical and reflective development of the subject of listening itself.

Listening to the city

In 1908, the American author O. Henry published a short story entitled *The Voice of the City*. In it the author poses the problem of relating the personal experience of urban sonic experience to a more generalized understanding of what the city – in this instance, New York – sounded like. The author recalls his own experience of reciting in class as a young boy: "the children used to chant their lessons. The manner of their delivery was a singsong recitative between the utterance of an Episcopal minister and the drone of a tired sawmill" (Henry 1935: 1). He then asks whether anybody is able to grasp the composite sound of New York. In the story, he rather futilely goes from person to person; a policeman, a bartender, a newspaper seller and a poet, asking what sounds they think of when they think of the sound of New York. Each respondent doesn't understand this impossible question but falls back on describing the sounds of their workplace experience. O. Henry might have had greater luck with his question in the highly mediated and technologized New York of the 21st century. In my own study of iPod users, one user described walking around New York with his iPod on, "I have a dedicated playlist called 'NY state of mind'. This includes a lot of New York rap music and NY/east coast jazz. Something with NY in the lyrics, but also the sophistication, edge and energy of the place" (Bull 2007: 37). The sounds and meanings of the city, for this person at least, are experienced through the products of the culture industry (music and iPod) as a form of privatized and largely fictionalized cosmopolitanism.

The paradox of O. Henry's question as to what it means to "listen to the city" – the individualized, the geographically and culturally localized, the structural and overarching have all taken their place within sound studies from the pioneering work of CRESSON, sound artists, urban theorists, novelists and cultural theorists. Despite this urban orientation in much work that goes under the title sound studies, it remains the case that in its origins sound studies appeared as largely anti-urban in its understanding of urban sound and the technologies that contributed to its "noisiness" and that this position was reflected in its very theorization and conceptualization of sound. Here the work of Schafer is central. Culturally, Schafer draws upon a wide range of literature to locate his understanding of the sounds of the city drawing upon Thoreau, Hesse, Tolstoy, Hardy, Mann Turgenev, Gorky, Virginia Woolf, Stendhal, Zola, Dickens to discuss the reception of sounds within developing urban culture. These voices in the main, as Schafer recognizes, are largely class based yet more importantly are frequently anti-urban in nature, with writers such as Charles Dickens being an instrumental mover in noise abatement legislation in London in the 19th century. Whilst recognizing their class orientation, Schafer is very much in tune with these anti-urban sentiments which form an important element in the development of his own sonic conceptual framework through which to understand sound.

The largely negative evaluation of urban culture at the dawn of the 20th century as one of "sensory overload" fitted a specific intellectual trajectory both within urban culture and in artistic circles at the time. These cultural considerations seep into some of the theoretical and methodological tools through which we are invited to understand the sonic. Schafer is very much at home with the normative nature of sound in his work. Environments are characterized as either "Hi-fi" or "Lo-fi" in orientation with Hi-fi being characterized as one "in which discrete sounds can be heard clearly because of the low ambient noise level…sounds overlap less frequently; there is perspective –foreground and background" whereby "Lo-fi" are ones in which "individual acoustic signals are obscured in an over-dense population of sounds"(Schafer 1979: 43).In Schafer's evaluation "Hi-fi" equates as "good" whereby "Lo-fi" is invariably "bad". The industrialized soundscape in Schafer's work had reached levels of sonic pollution that had "reached an apex of vulgarity in our time" (Schafer 1979: 3).

Dominant in Schafer's theoretical framework is the ability to listen with fresh ears – the development of "clean hearing" coupled with a normative aim to reaffirm the role of music/sound as a "search for the harmonizing influence of sounds in the world about us" (Schafer 1979: 6). This normative understanding of urban "noise" has produced mixed results in terms of our orientation to the sounds of the city. Whilst noise abatement campaigns in Western cities have proved a valuable foil to the unfettered imposition of unwanted and sometimes dangerous levels of sound in urban environments, they themselves have often predicated on cultural notions of the public and the private – for example Dickens was annoyed with the sounds of street musicians that impinged upon his study as he was writing, often about the poor of the city.

Schafer is keenly aware of the problem of noise in everyday life as he is with the supposed culprit which for him are the very technologies that inform daily life, transportation and communication technologies:"the lo-fi soundscape originates with sound congestion…the Electric Revolution added new effects of its own and introduced devices for packaging sounds and transmitting them schizophonically across time and space to live amplified or multiplied audiences" (Schafer 1979: 71). Anyone who lives underneath the flight path of a major airport or who lives nearby a major urban road will recognize Schafer's concerns.

Yet it is instructive to look at the cultural omissions in Schafer's work. Whilst he cites writers who at best are sceptical about much urban development, there is no mention of authors such as Thomas Pynchon, Don DeLillo, Beckett or even earlier novelists such as Joseph Roth who engaged with the complex sensory and technological mix of the modern in a manner that doesn't hark back to the pre-modern – but takes the modern at face value and who largely embrace it. For example, Carlo Levi's wonderful description of being immersed in the sounds of 1950s Rome during the Feast of St John in the Piazza Navona being a case in point:

> From afar, you can sense a sort of throbbing and shrilling in the air, and that alone begins to tug you towards a different world. The closer you come to the Piazza Navona, the greater the throbbing becomes…Everyone has their own whistle and everyone is blowing their own, trying to drown out the others…And as my whistle grew louder, stronger and more determined, I realized that the sound issuing from my little instrument was enveloping me like a compact atmosphere and that in this sonorous atmosphere, as if within an invisible suit of armour, I grew more and more to be part of the crowd surrounding me; and yet at the same time, I was increasingly isolated from it… Perhaps this explains the great popularity of the deafening little engines of the Vespa and the Lambretta that create a transparent but impenetrable wall of sound, transporting us out into the world while isolating us from it.
>
> *(Levi 2004: 29–30)*

In a similar vein Joseph Roth describes the multiple sounds of urban cosmopolitanism of Marseilles in the 1920s: "I love the noise of Marseilles, first the outriders, the heavy church bells, the hoarse whistles of steamers, the melody of the birdsong dripping from the blue heights. Then follows the main body – the infantry –of everyday sounds, the shouts of people, the tooting of vehicles, the jingling of harnesses, the echo of footsteps, the tapping of hooves, the barking of dogs. It's a procession of noise" (Roth 2004: 56).

Levi and Roth both in their own way give voice to O. Henry's question as to what is it we hear when we listen to the sounds of the city. Their writings provide one side of a dialectic in which urban sounds are experienced as intoxicating and pleasurable rather than as polluting and unpleasant. Sound studies today increasingly embraces both sides of the dialectic in asking what is it that we are opening up our ears to when we listen to the city?

Listening to trains

As a child one of my main pleasures was to climb atop the local railway bridge with friends and listen out for the sounds of the arrival of the next steam train. What I remember most was the speed of the oncoming train and the smoke from its engine which engulfed us in dense cloud as it passed beneath us. I remember a visceral pleasure in this – shared with my friends. Beyond this I never thought that much about trains and rarely travelled on them until I left home to go to university. Trains like other technologies are subordinate clauses in the march of cultural history deriving their meanings from power, economics, cultural and perhaps more personal experiences. At various times we have listened to and understood the locomotive through the prism of leisure, noise pollution, industrialization, imperialism, progress and so on. It all depends upon what we a listening out for.

Popular song often refers to the "clickety-clack" of trains, revelling in and mirroring the rhythmic attraction of the moving train. The Kingston Trio's song "Fast Freight" of 1958 is rather typical. It goes like this: "Clickety-clack/ Hear the whistle blow, Hear the whistle blow" (Fast Freight. The Kingston Trio 1958). *Fast Freight* represents a common cultural theme of escape as the singer sings of wishing to escape from the hum-drum mundane life he's leading. The sound of the train representing the sound of freedom, of a world beyond routine, full of possibilities. The Russian ballet dancer Rudolf Nureyev also dreamt as a young man of escape from his home town of Ufa, situated on Russia's Asian border in the Ural Mountains. He describes sitting on the surrounding hills listening to the sounds of the trains which could be heard many miles distant and dreaming of the cosmopolitan allure of their destinations. He dreamed of the train as a bridge between himself and Moscow, Leningrad, Paris and London: "In my mind I'd travel by those trains…in the night I'd wake up hearing the wheels tapping the time of the distance" (Foy 1991).

Trains are frequently located culturally, economically and technologically as transformative, as representing the essence of modernity (Wolmar 2010). Railroads have been perceived as "diminish(ing) and expand(ing) space. The dialectic of this process states that this diminution of space (i.e., the shrinking of transport time) causes an expansion of transport space by incorporating new areas into the transport network" (Schivelbusch 1977: 43). Trains represent everything from the mundane (the daily commute), the exotic (holiday travel from Brighton to the Rocky Mountains) to the exceptional (supplying weaponry, resources and troops in wars from the Crimean War onwards).

The meanings attached to listening itself is dependent on values, purpose, interest and knowledge. For example, Murray Schafer hears a poverty of contemporary sounds and the allure of the American Frontier in the sound of the train: "By comparison with the sounds of modern transportation, those of the trains were rich and characteristic: the whistle, the bell, the slow chuffing of the engine at the start…The sound of travel have deep mysteries…The trains whistle was the most important sound in the frontier town, the solo announcement of contact with the outside world" (Schafer 1979: 81). Whilst supposedly the white European settlers of the West heard the civilizing sounds of the railway, groups in London at around the same period of time were concerned with rail travellers developing "railway spine" if they used trains frequently. Railway travel differed significantly from earlier coach travel whereby shock was intermittent not continual: "this is a feeling of what is 'no longer felt', or the blurring together of individual jolts into a 'continuous vibration' (Trower 2012: 97). Just as those who were concerned with "railway spine" were largely silent about Britain's use of the railway in its imperialist expansion, so the American settlers were silent on the role of train expansion in the resettlement of Native American tribes so as to facilitate the laying of railway tracks between 1840 and 1880 or the railroads role in the opening up of the Great Plains for commercial hide trading which saw the extinction of Bison, a Native American livelihood, over the subsequent years. There are virtually no American Indian accounts of the coming of, or the sound of the railways. This silence extends to indigenous accounts of the development of the railway line in the jungle of the Congo between Madadi and Kinshasa during the 1880s used to transport rubber back into the bludgeoning industries of 19th-century Europe. The novelist Joseph Conrad sailed for the Congo on a ship that carried the first batch of rails for the new railway there. His experiences of those forced to work in the building of the railroad became translated into his novel *The Heart of Darkness*:

> A slight clinking behind me made me turn my head. Six black men advanced in a file toiling up the path. They walked erect and slow, balancing small basket full of earth on their heads, and the clink kept time with their footsteps. I could see every rib, the joints of their limbs were like knots in a rope, each had an iron collar on his neck and all were connected together with a chain whose bights swung between them, rhythmically clinking.
>
> *(Conrad 2014: 26)*

The rhythmic clinking of their chains paralleling the clickety-clack of the train enslaving them. Conrad commenting later about the writing of *The Heart of Darkness* observes "that sombre theme had to be given a sinister resonance, a tonality of its own, a continued vibration that, I hoped, would hang in the air and dwell on the ear after the last note had been struck" (Conrad 2014: xviii). Adam Hochschild has argued that Conrad's was the only Western authorial voice to give testament to the European scramble for Africa at the end of the 19th century and the genocidal practices it encompassed. These colonial vibrations mentioned by Conrad also have physical, historical and cultural resonances. The German genocide of the Herero people in German Southwest Africa at this time, orchestrated by Herman Goring's father, reappeared and were later transferred by Goring himself onto the Jews of Europe in the "Final Solution" (Hochschild 1999).

"Fast Freight" is a song about stowaways on freight trains escaping the shackles of the mundane everyday. To stowaway on a "passenger train" presented more difficulties – hence the mystique of the freight train amongst the poor or disadvantaged. The song is also about speed measured rhythmically through the sound of the "clickety-clack". Speed itself representing modernity – "faster and faster" (Gleick 1999). This distinction between "passenger" and "freight" as does the notion of "speed" breaks down in 1943 as the railways of Central Europe were used to facilitate the extermination of European Jewry. Those few who survived both the transportation and the camps very rarely mention the clickety-clack of the trains – rather they mention the sounds of baying dogs and the harsh shouts of the guards, the "crying and yelling all night long…the sounds of utter despair" (Cole 2016: 104). There were 430,000 Hungarian Jews transported in 127 trains, 200 to each cattle tuck, to Auschwitz representing "an experience radically at odds with visions of international train travel as the high point of European modernity…the train was a site of death" (Cole 2016: 102). The transports were slow, often shunted into sidings to allow for the transportation of goods, soldiers and civilians. The German, Hungarian and Polish civilians who travelled purchased their tickets to known destinations, often return tickets. European Jewry were forced to purchase their tickets by the Deutche Reichsbahn – to an unknown destination – one way. For those who survived, many never travelled on a train again.

Listening to the sirens

The varied phenomena of sirens have proved a popular source of analysis and discourse in a range of disciplines as broad as those that embody this volume. It is an appropriate topic with which to close this introduction in relation to the question concerning the relationship between hearing and listening. Sirens in their material manifestation have been discussed in relation to the sirens we hear in our streets daily – those of the police and ambulance services, or in terms of an urban aesthetic as they become incorporated into the sounds of the city as in the music of Varese or in their role as signifying conflict within city populations as in their frequent use in Hip Hop music (Osborne 2007). In addition to this siren have been interpreted as embracing both the seductive and destructive understanding of sound as embodied in Greek myth and more generally in subsequent moments in popular culture. This in contrast to the more material warnings of destruction and danger embodied internationally in a whole range of sirens from World War Two. These two strands of siren meanings are filtered through a range of ideologies embodying the "Cold War" nuclear warnings in cities around the world to those that represent the "feminine" as "Siren" in popular culture from "Film Noir" and beyond (Fleeger 2014; Levy 2006; Miklitsch 2011; Peraino 2006).

Dominant in our understanding of sirens are their role in Greek myth through the Odyssey and beyond whereby the Sirens represented the seductive, yet fatal allure of song perceived intermittently to be embodied in some notion of the "feminine". This despite their non-materiality in the Odyssey, Odysseus merely hears the Sirens as an acoustic presence – not a physical one. This history of the materialization of the acousmatic is told elsewhere. Theoretically the Sirens of Greek myth became a central plank to a more generalized critique of Western culture in Max Horkheimer and Theodor Adorno's *Dialectic of Enlightenment* that extended to Sloterdijk's treatment of technology and space in which he bemoans the industrialization of the siren from the mythical to the material:

> This choice of name plays with the insight that sirens can trigger archaic feelings among those that hear them, but it distorts this with wicked irony by associating the siren with a forced alarm. The most open form of listening was thus betrayed by terror, as if the subject were only close to its truth when running to save itself. At the same time, this renaming of the siren voice inappropriately coarsens it, instrumentalzing it for the most brutal mass signals. Sirens of this kind are the bells for the industrial and world War age. They do not mark the sonosphere in which a joyful message could spread. Their sound carries the consensus that everything is hopeless to all ears that can be reached
>
> *(Sloterdijk 2011: 500)*

Despite the interest shown in the cultural, philosophical and aesthetic nature of sirens both mythical and material, little attention has been paid to one important materialization of the siren: air-raid sirens, despite their periodic yet prominent role in the sonic practices, organization and ideologies of the 20th and 21st centuries. The rest of this section concerns itself with air-raid sirens in order to highlight the extent to which practices of listening need to be culturally and historically situated and then interrogated beyond the practice of listening itself in order to gain greater understanding of the phenomena.

I begin with a personal observation that occurred in Paris around lunchtime on the 9th January 2015. I had just left my accommodation in the Marais district of Paris near the Cathedral of Notre-Dame when the two-tone sounds of police sirens ubiquitously appeared to be everywhere; above and beyond them I heard the eerie sound of air-raid sirens. These sirens are tested on the first Monday of each month in Paris – they exist to warn the inhabitants of Paris of terrorist attacks and impending natural disaster. However, this was a Wednesday – although the time of day was the correct one for a siren trial. The everyday sounds of the street became infused with the multiple sounds of sirens. Yet cars and buses continued their noisy path through the crowded streets. Those of us on the street, perhaps unconsciously caught in a time loop, looked skywards – isn't this where danger was meant to come from? Others scanned their smartphones for information whilst others went into cafés to listen to radios and enquire. None of us had been trained to respond to the sounds of air-raid sirens – to decipher their potential meaning and act upon them. Daughtry, in his recent analysis of the sounds of the Iraq war, argued that "a sounds salience and emotional charge depends upon the life histories of people who hear it, and upon the comparative backdrop against which they listen to the sounds that are emplaced in a particular time and location" (Daughtry 2015: 38). The sounds of the "air-raid" sirens appeared in this instance to be out of time and out of place in the bustle of Parisian daily life. I learned subsequently that the journalists of the satirical magazine Charlie Hebdo have been murdered by Islamic terrorists in another district of Paris – already dead by the time the sirens began.

Air-raid sirens warn those who hear their sounds, yet what is it that the listener hears? On the one hand they represent an ominous reminder of "total war" and impending death from the sky; a truncating of space between the victim and the increasingly sophisticated technologies of death available. They also represent an ideology of sonic protection against the threat of destruction. Sirens, in the main, are static constructions, as static as the subject populations who are to be attacked. The speed with which total war is visited upon unsuspecting victims has accelerated from the 474 kilometres per hour of the B29 that dropped the first atomic bomb on Hiroshima to the 6.7 kilometres per minute of a contemporary intercontinental missile that obliterates everything in its path. They are not called weapons of mass destruction for nothing.

In peacetime Paris, the concept of total war – of indiscriminate killing – had returned – not with the sophisticated weaponry developed from World War One onwards, but with the discrete – traditional Kalashnikov. The localized brutality of killing was met with a public/global sonic warning system – as the Parisian air was filled with the abstract sonic warnings of a country unknowingly at "war". By 2015 the sounds of air-raid sirens installed in World War Two had lost their clarity of meaning – the city carried on largely as before.

The sound and delivery of air-raid sirens have remained largely unchanged until recently when they have transformed into smart phone apps in Mexico, Israel and elsewhere where they have most frequently morphed from the warning of a man-made apocalypse to one of the natural world – to warn populations of earthquakes, tsunamis and typhoons.

Air-raid sirens originally were dominant in the cities of the world in World War Two and subsequently in the Cold War world where they acted as dummy runs for the apocalypse. Air-raid sirens represent, in the main, sonic instruments of the State re-inscribing the soundscape of a city – placed throughout the city – high up on the roofs of buildings or on lamp-posts so that all could ideally hear with subject populations becoming a part of a negative collectivity juggling fear, hope and community (Birdsall 2012).

They are also a by-product of governments' attempts to command the air, the development of aviation itself and the ability to develop bombs and missiles that could attack and destroy cities from London to Hanoi. Sirens are the state's response to their own Dialectic of Enlightenment (Horkheimer and Adorno 1972). They are a Fordist technology, the Muzac of human and eco-logical destructiveness – primarily functioning and sounding the same wherever they are placed, and moreover evoking similar responses, despite any cultural differences represented by the cities and inhabitants of London, Coventry, Berlin, Dresden, Tokyo and Hiroshima.

Sirens of war therefore are not to be understood in isolation, but as a response to the struc-tural, political and technological abolition and transformation of space which has resulted in the negation of any notion of safety zones beyond the immediate and traditional notion of "theatre" of war.

On the ground, air-raid sirens demanded a training of the sensibilities with responses to air-raid sirens being understood as individual, collective and institutional. Subject populations learnt how to listen, not just in order to interpret the meaning of the air-raid sirens, but also to listen out for the sounds of aircraft and direction of exploding shells. City dwellers learnt how to wait, experiencing time in new ways – for example, estimating the length of time it took to run to the nearest air-raid shelter. Daily life was reorganized with the feelings of fear, expectation and resignation incorporated into the everyday.

Whilst air-raid sirens had warned those in cities to seek shelter, in air-raid shelters, bunkers, basements and tube stations with some success during the early parts of World War Two in Europe this became increasingly less so as the war continued and more cities were subject to intense bombing. The scale of attacks also rendered the sounding of alarms problematic as wave after wave of bombers might bomb a city such as Hamburg for several days:

> In the confusion of the evening, the air raid alarms had been set off at 9.30 p.m.,
> followed by the all clear at 10, and then set off again at 12.33. The Hamburg police
> logged their 319th air raid alarm of the war at 12.51 a.m.
>
> *(Taylor 2004:3)*

The intended clarity of the air-raid signal was rendered increasingly impossible in the continued "carpet" bombing of cities like Dresden, Hamburg and Tokyo. On the ground air-raid sirens frequently gave confused warnings as wave after wave of bombers flew over confusing lookouts and radar systems before the sirens themselves became silenced in the destruction.

Adorno frequently referred to the destruction wrought on Hiroshima by the dropping of the atomic bomb in his post war writings. The sirens sounded when three planes, one of which was the Enola Gay which carried the atomic bomb, were seen in the sky followed by the all-clear given moments before the blast that killed the inhabitants of Hiroshima in the blink of an eyelid. The sounding of the air-raid sirens would have made no difference either way. The power of the bomb rendering the air-raid siren redundant. Whilst sirens have increasingly become nor-malized the air-raid siren is emblematic of how it is necessary to look beyond the actuality of, the presence of any particular sound to delve into the social, historical, political, economic and ideological contexts within which we listen.

There follow six Parts of the *Routledge Companion to Sound Studies*. These Parts should not be viewed as fully discrete – yet intimately connected and overlapping.

References

Bijsterveld, K. T., 2016, Ethnography and Archival Research in Studying Cultures of Sound. In J. G. Papenburg and H. Schulze (Eds.), *Sound as Popular Culture Research Companion* (pp. 99–109). Cambridge, MA: MIT.

Birdsall, C., 2012, *Nazi Soundscapes: Sound, Technology and Urban Space, 1933–1945*, Amsterdam: Amsterdam University Press.

Blesser, H. and Salter, L., 2007, *Spaces Speak, Are You listening?* Cambridge, MA: MIT Press.

Bull, M., 2000, *Sounding Out the City: Personal Stereos and the Management of Everyday Life*, London: Berg.

Bull, M., 2007, *Sound Moves: iPod Culture and Urban Experience*, London: Routledge.

Bull, M. and Back, Les, 2003, *The Auditory Culture Reader*, London: Berg.

Cobussen, M., Meelberg, V., and Truax., B., 2017, *The Routledge Companion to Sounding Art*, London: Routledge.

Cockayne, E., 2007. *Hubbub, Filth, Noise and the Stench of England*, New Haven, CT: Yale University Press.

Cole, T., 2016, *Holocaust Landscapes*, Oxford: Oxford University Press.

Connor, S., 2000, *Dumbstruck. A Cultural History of Ventriloquism*, Oxford: Oxford University Press.

Conrad, J., 2014, *The Heart of Darkness*, London: The Folio Society.

Csordas, T., 1990, "Embodiment as a paradigm for anthropology", *Ethos*, 18(1): 5–47.

Daughtry, J. M., 2015, *Listening to War. Sound, Music, Trauma, and Survival in Wartime Iraq*, Oxford. Oxford University Press.

Erlmann, V., 2011, *Reason and Resonance: A History of Modern Aurality*, New York: Zone Books.

Fleeger, J., 2014, *Mismatched Women: The Siren's Song through the Machine*, Oxford: Oxford University Press.

Foy, P., 1991, Rudolf Nureyev: A Documentary, DVD, London: Arthaus.

Gilman, L., 2016, *My Music, My War*, Middletown: Wesleyan University Press.

Gleick, J., 1999, *Faster: The Acceleration of just About Everything*, London: Little Brown.

Goggin, G., 2006, *Cellphone Culture: Mobile Technology and Everyday Life*, London: Routledge.

Grimshaw, M. and Garner., T, 2015, *Sonic Virtuality: Sound as Emergent Perception*, Oxford: Oxford University Press.

Henriques, J., 2011, *Sonic Bodies: Reggae Sound Systems, Performance Techniques, and Ways of Knowing*, London: Bloomsbury.

Henry, O., 1935, The *Voice of the City and other Stories*, New York: Limited Editions Club.

Hirshkind, C., 2006, *The Ethical Soundscape: Cassette Sermons and Islamic Counterpublics*, New York: Columbia University Press.

Hochschild, A., 1999, *King Leopold's Ghost*, London: Pan Books.

Horkheimer, M. and Adorno, T., 1972 *The Dialectic of Enlightenment*, London: Penguin.

Johnson, B. and Cloonan, M., 2009, *Dark Side of the Tune: Popular Music and Violence*, Farnham: Ashgate Press.

Kane, B., 2014, *Sound Unseen: Acousmatic Sound*, Oxford: Oxford University Press.

Katz, M., 2010, *Capturing Sound: How Technology Changed Music*, Berkeley, CA: University of California Press.

Levi, C., 2004, *Fleeting Rome: In Search of la Dolce Vita*, London: John Wiley.

Levy, I. 2006, *Sirens on the Western Shore. The Western Femme Fatale, Translation, and Vernacular Style in Modern Japanese Literature*, New York: Columbia University Press.

Miklitsch, R. 2011, *Siren City. Sound and Source Music in Classic American Noir*, New Jersey: Rutgers University Press.

Niebur, L., 2010, *Special Sound: The Creation and Legacy of the BBC Radiophonic Workshop*, Oxford: Oxford University Press.

Ochia Gautier, A. M., 2014, *Aurality: Listening and Knowledge in Nineteenth-century Columbia*, Durham, NC: Duke University Press.

Osborne, R. 2007, *The London Consortium Static*, Issue 6 – Alarm, Alarms on Record.

Peraino, J., 2006, *Listening to the Sirens: Musical Technologies of Queer Identity from Homer to Hedwig*, Berkeley: University of California Press.

Petmann, D., 2017, *Sonic Intimacy: Voices, Species, Technics*, Palo Alto, CA: Stanford University Press.

Picker, J., 2003, *Victorian Soundscapes*, Oxford: Oxford University Press.

Pieslak, J., 2009, *Sound Targets*, Bloomington: Indiana University Press.

Pieslak, J., 2015, *Radicalism and Music: An Introduction to the Music Cultures of al-Qaida, Racist Skinheads, Christian-affiliated Radicals, and Eco-animal Rights Militants*, Middletown: Wesleyan University Press.

Rath, R. C., 2003, *How Early America Sounded*, Ithaca: Cornell University Press.

Ree, J., 1999, *I See a Voice: Deafness, Language and the Senses – A Philosophical History*, London: Harper Collins.

Roth, J., 2004, *The White Cities: Reports from France 1925–39*, London: Granta Books.

Schafer, R. M., 1979, *The Soundscape: Our Sonic Environment and the Tuning of the World*, Rochester, VT: Destiny Books.

Schivelbusch, W., 1977, *The Railway Journey: The Industrialization of Time and Space in the Nineteenth Century*, Berkeley: University of California Press.

Schmidt-Horning, S., 2015, *Chasing Sound: Technology, Culture and the Art of Studio Recording from Edison to the LP*, Baltimore: John Hopkins University Press.

Schwartz, H., 2011, *Making Noise: From Babel to the Big Bang and Beyond*, New York: Zone Books.

Sloterdijk, P., 2011, *Bubbles Spheres 1 Microspherology*, South Pasadena: Semiotexte.

Smith, M., 2007, *Sensing the Past: Seeing, Hearing, Smelling, Tasting and Touching History*, Berkeley: University of California Press.

Novac, D. and Sakakneeny, M. (Eds.), 2015, *Keywords in Sound*, Durham, NC: Duke University Press.

Stadler, G., 2015, On whiteness and sound studies, *Sounding Out!* Soundstudiesblog.com.

Sterne, J., 2003, *The Audible Past: Cultural Origins of Sound Reproduction*, Durham, NC: Duke University Press.

Sterne, J., (Ed.), 2014, *The Sound Studies Reader*, London: Routledge.

Stoever, J., 2016, *The Sonic Color Line, Race and the Cultural Politics of Listening*, New York: New York University Press.

Suisman, D. and Strasser., S. (Eds.), 2009, *Sound in the Age of Mechanical Reproduction*, Philadelphia: University of Pennsylvania Press.

Taylor, F., 2004, *Dresden: Tuesday, 15th February, 1945*, London: Harper Collins.

Taylor, F., 2015, *Coventry: Thursday 14th November 1940*, London: Bloomsbury Press.

Thompson, E., 2002, *The Soundscape of Modernity*, Cambridge, MA: MIT Press.

Tosoni, S. and Pinch, T., 2016, *Entanglements: Conversations on the Human Traces of Science, Technology and Sound*, Cambridge, MA: MIT Press.

Trower, S., 2012, *Senses of Vibration: A History of the Pleasure and Pain of Sound*, New York: Continuum Press.

Wolmar, C., 2010, *Engines of War: How Wars Were Won and Lost on the Railways*, London: Atlantic Books.

PART I

Introduction:
sonic epistemologies and debates

Some years ago, I interviewed a young American man who lived in the UK. During the interview he described driving down a motorway in his automobile listening to music on his sound system. This was not the normal sound system we find in automobiles however. He had a very expensive and powerful amplifier fixed to the chassis of the car and twenty-three speakers placed throughout the driving compartment. He described driving at speed down the motorway to music as loud as he could bear. After a few miles the sound was so intense he had to stop on the hard shoulder. As he exited the car he described having to lean against the side of the car, unable to stand as his whole body felt like "jelly." The experience was described as intensely pleasurable, indeed exhilarating. The meanings attached to this simple account are multiple. My American interviewee had belonged to an automobile club in the US whose whole raison d'être was to maximise the volume of sound in automobiles. The meaning attached to such activity was sub-cultural in nature whereby members learnt how to experience intense sonic listening practices in automobiles as well as showing off the sophistication of their auto sound systems. These experiences are partially learnt even though the physical response – the jellied body – is largely pre-conscious and bodily in nature. The experience itself is dependent upon forms of technological sonic capability and the legal framework within which it is acceptable to drive under these conditions. My respondent was at pains to point out that he was a considerate driver and that he would not drive through town listening thus as he considered it to be both a dangerous and anti-social activity in such spaces. Thus, the example combines a cocktail of body, sound, culture, desire, and technology in the explanatory mix of the behaviour. This matrix of sonic, and indeed the sensory factors involved in explaining, understanding and theorising such experience, lies at the heart of this Part.

The relationship between the making of and the experiencing of sounds informs many of the entries in this Part as does the very remit of sound studies itself. This Part produces a lively debate from within its contributors who interrogate the nature and meaning of the sonic from a variety of theoretical viewpoints. Epistemologically, the question arises, to what extent does the experience of sound as a sensory experience differ from an understanding of what constitutes experience more generally as articulated throughout the Western philosophical tradition per se? If as the philosopher Thomas Nagel argued that the history of knowledge resembles an epistemological graveyard in which successive generations of thinkers have attempted to leap from the subjective nature of knowledge – that which I experience in some way – to the "objective" –

that which in some sense might be considered 'true' beyond that immediate experience – then in the very act of leaping from the "subject" to the "object" the thinker necessarily falls into an epistemological abyss. Nagel merely highlights the dualism of much thought – between subject and object, mind and body, and so on. These dichotomies were articulated in Greek philosophy over two thousand years ago in the metaphysics of Plato and in the empiricism of Aristotle. Plato's Theory of the Forms and his "simile of the cave" are well known. Suffice to note that for Plato, the empirical world of the inhabitants of the cave is represented by the shadows created by their campfire. They had no notion of the sunlight that created the flickering shadows. Plato proceeds to reject the simply empirical – which includes the sensuous world in favour his theory of "forms" which represent unchanging concepts, such as the form of a triangle that is not subject to change in contrast to notions of physical beauty, for example, which are located in the transitory and the cultural – hence representing, for Plato, mere shadows and as such do not represent "true" knowledge. The desire to prove forms of universal truths are deeply embedded in Western philosophical thought, including notions of the universal nature of space and time which is considered an instrumental foundation to all experience within which any particular place and time is necessarily subordinate to the universal. Universalisms have taken many forms, from the mathematical work of Russell and Whitehead to the general laws of linguistics articulated in the work of de Saussure and Chomsky. In a world of universals, local knowledge, local customs, local places are mere variants of the universal and are subordinate to them.

Universalism has come to sound studies in the form of a post-Deleuzian ontology which, just as in neuro-anthropology, has questioned the cultural significance of a range of differences (Bull and Mitchell 2016). Brian Kane in a recent critique of sonic ontology critiques the position of Cristof Cox whom he feels articulates this post-Deleuzian position in his theory of sonic experience: "The metaphysics of the actual and the virtual entails a specific view about culture and nature. Appearances, or the 'diversity' of empirical things, 'are the products or manifestations of material intensive "differences" that operate at the micro-level of physical, chemical, and biological matter but that remain virtual, unapparent at the level of actual, extensive things'" (Kane 2015: 4). Kane thus articulates and critiques the relationship between the pre-conscious and the conscious and thus cultural in the work of Cox and others.

Most entries in this part understand sonic experience through some notion of the cultural although not exclusively so, and hence can be read as articulating the complex relationship between notions of the ontological and the empirical within sound studies.

The part begins with Holger Schulze who describes the history of sound as theory as an "unfinished project." He provides the reader with a wide-ranging historical and conceptual analysis of what it is we hear when we are hearing. He begins by pointing to the scientific heritage of the study of sound, to the work of Helmholtz, Fletcher, and Baranek who investigate the physiology of the ear in relation to the science of soundwaves and points to the importance of this scientific framework in the creation of materialist notions of sound as matter. He contrasts this position to the more common sonic narratives that are embodied in the later work of Schafer, Attali, and a range of soundscape artists who reaffirm, in a variety of ways, the importance of the listening subject. Whilst sound scholars might re-evaluate historical narratives that provide a hierarchy of the senses in which one sense, or set of senses, are pitted against the others, Shulze argues that we need to situate sound within a more general sensory mode of investigation that recognises the body/subject as increasingly the site of much sonic research. Equally, he argues that the science of sound should not transcend our understanding of the social meanings attached to sound – sound as pressure waves is not identical to their cultural manifestation. Affect, he argues, is both a cultural and cognitive phenomena, not merely a response to a uniform vibration as argued by a range of Deleuzian-inspired ontologists of sound. Schulze, as such, is interested in actual listening practices, the phenomenology of sound, body and corporal resonance, but also in forms of sonic imagination as articulated through the work of Eshun and others. This leads Schulze to argue for the development of specifically sonic methodologies in order to enable us to understand the complex nature of experiencing the sonic within society. He cites the creation and use of sound walks and sound installations in support of Voeglin's idea that "research on sound needs to be conceptualized, performed, and presented foremost in the realm of the sonic" (Voeglin in this volume). In providing this historical narrative Schulze provides a conceptual framework that enables the reader to situate the more detailed and specific theoretical debates within sound studies that go to make up the remainder of this first part of the Handbook.

Mark Grimshaw-Aagaard argues that it is common for scholars of sound studies to investigate sound from the position of its use, role, and meaning in culture while tacitly assuming that sound is as defined in physics and acoustics. Opposed to this standard definition of sound as a sound wave he instead argues for a definition of sound as a perception (more fully articulated in Grimshaw and Garner 2015). By focussing upon sound as perception, Grimshaw-Aagaard is able to cast light upon a variety of sonic experiences that need not necessarily be vibrational in origin. Grimshaw-Aagaard argues that sound studies are at its strongest when it investigates the roles of memory, knowledge, reason, experience, emotion, mood, and so on in order to understand the ways in which sonic perceptions are formed.

This recognition of the centrality of society, culture, and the individual's relationship to the social is the starting point of David Howes' contribution in this Part. Howes, a scholar of anthropology and the senses, delivers an impassioned defence of a multi-sensory, historically situated account of the "embodied" subject, arguing that the senses are made, not given, and that all perception represents a cultural act. In arguing thus, Howes, like Kane, is contrasting his work against the work of Ingold and those scholars of sonic ontology for whom vibration or sound more generally underpins the idea of a unified pre-reflective sensory perceptual system. Howes forcefully reminds the reader of the importance of cultures of perception in relation to both sound and the indeed the body.

Nina Sun Eidsheim continues and develops the cultural perceptions of Howes by focussing upon inter-sensoriality in relation to sound, body, and voice, arguing that the discrete investigation of the senses within their respective disciplines often prevents a richer investigation of the phenomena. She illustrates this point through an intriguing range of empirical examples. In the pursuit of the inter-sensorial Sun Eidsheim promotes what she refers to as methodological experimentation: "What I propose herein is to move from binary to simultaneous and concurrent conceptualizing and experiencing of phenomena to which we now refer as sound, body, or voice."

The aesthetics of sound weaves in and out of sound studies, revisiting the social and philosophical elements of the nature of judgement. We noted in the introduction to this volume Schafer's preoccupation with an ethics of listening that tended to be anti-urban in nature together with sound studies' reliance on the work and thought of John Cage and Pierre Schaffer who took listening subjects into specialised cultural and performance spaces – either with a preference for listening to the sounds of the world attentively or culturally situating sonic practices aesthetically within what might be considered the realm of the avant-garde. Verma in distinction to these preoccupations discusses how the philosophy of aesthetics has been more easily framed within vision than with sound. In terms of looking and listening practices, audiences were more likely to accept cubism in art, for example, than the twelve tone works of Schoenberg. Verma argues that sound studies needs to articulate an aesthetics of bodily experience rather than focussing merely upon the cognitive. This point returns us to the intense listening practices that stem from attentive music listening practices embodied in the Romantic movement of the 19th century and now embodied in the close listening practices of those subject to John Cage's 4.33 where audiences could literally hear a pin drop. A listening mode that became increasingly disembodied and analytical – despite Cage's experience of listening to his own body in the anechoic chamber!

Annabel Stirling continues Verma's pursuit of bodily and cultural experience by focussing upon affect, rather than the aesthetic and as such approaches bodily affect from a complementary perspective. Stirling moves away from the culturally rarefied atmosphere of listening to 4.33 to the use of Rock and Roll to discuss sound, affect, and politics. She discusses trancing and altered states of consciousness in order to ask what music feels like as distinct from what it sounds like? She argues that if sound studies scholars investigate a range of music practices empirically and sub-culturally that they will discover that affect can be both individual and collective. New affect theories, she argues, lack empirical grounding for their essentialist ontology. Rather they rely upon pre-existing theories as a way of articulating sonic experience in novel ways. Stirling argues that affect does not just work on a Deleuzian pre-mediated level. Her own rich ethnographies of Lucky Cloud Parties demonstrate how "musical affectivity is contingent upon the precise ways in which it is encultured." Affect, in other words, is culturally pre-disposed and affect theories underplay the empirical at their peril.

References

Bull, M. and Jon Mitchell (eds) 2016, *Ritual, Performance and the Senses*, London: Bloomsbury Press.

Grimshaw, M. and Garner, T., 2015, *Sonic Virtuality: Sound as Emergent Perception*, Oxford: Oxford University Press.

Kane, B., 2015, Sound studies without auditory culture: a critique of the ontological turn, *Sound Studies*, pp. 2–21, Vol. 1.

1

SOUND AS THEORY 1863–2014: FROM HERMANN VON HELM-HOLTZ TO SALOMÉ VOEGELIN

Holger Schulze

Sound can be looked at. Yes, you just read this sentence: *Sound can be looked at.* Yet, what can be seen of sound are mainly translations of the pressure waves – out of which any sound actually consists – into scores, diagrams, into sonograms. One sees the effects these pressure waves can take onto other objects, fluids, gases, onto elastic materials, onto the connected limbs of mechanical or electromechanical artifacts. As indirect as they are, these effects of sounds provide the contemporary forms of *Anschauung*, of *theoria* on sound in the early 21st century. Sound *is* vision these days as sound production, sound analysis, and sound technology are effectively operated mainly via the somewhat strange detour of visual displays. Should there be a natural order of the senses? A vast army of thinkers does affirm this assumption. They actually form the canonical literature of Western philosophy and theory, surely not only starting with Aristotle, Jean-Jacques Rousseau, Immanuel Kant and definitely not ending with Ferdinand de Saussure. These *logocentrists* did assume, implied or explicated in their writings, that a natural order of the senses does exist. According to this logocentric sensory anthropology the higher senses are situated closer to the visual perception of arguments and mathematical equations – and lower senses hence closer to seldomly reflected passions, affects, to momentary, idiosyncratic, and entangling impulses, to lust or to longing. More recently though a series of – as I like to call them – *audiopietists* (Schulze 2007) emerged like R. Murray Schafer, like Walter J. Ong or like Joachim-Ernst Berendt who argue as well for a natural order of the senses – though simply reversed: the higher senses are, for them, closer to individual affects and to intimacy, to passions, and to corporeal sensibilities – the lower senses though closer to the supposedly dry and alienating operations of writing and reading, measuring, and calculating. As a countermovement, this reversal of a normative sensory order is quite understandable, at times it could even be considered a kind of subversive or trickster move. Yet, the main fallacy of claiming a stable order of the senses regardless of historical and cultural transformations is truly not corrected by just claiming a different order as stable. Moreover, such audiopietists are not seldomly connecting their mission to anti-modernism and anti-urbanism, to an elitist disregard for popular and everyday cultures, even to technophobia and Luddism. Effectively, the mission of audiopietism is to promote the *audiovisual litany* that Jonathan Sterne did deconstruct so strikingly once and for all (Sterne 2012a: 8).

Thinking about sound is inextricably relying on thinking about the senses. It relies on notions about the plasticity, the mingledness, and the idiosyncrasies shaping sensory and sonic experiences. Theoretical approaches to sound therefore can take very different shapes and forms – outside the well-known approaches to *theoria*, sticking to a traditional logocentrist or an anti-traditional audiopietist order of the senses. Such efforts to theorize sound underwent various transformations and experiments in the last 150 years: one can observe timid retractions of once experimental ambitions and submissions to hegemonial research paradigms as well as renewed revolutionary ambitions to finally eliminate institutional and methodological restrictions. These efforts took place to foster the progress in researching sounds as well as in operating with sounds, all in order to expand the research field and its research methods. The history of *sound as theory* is thus explored in this chapter as a transdisciplinary and unfinished research project. A project that in itself generated the vivid and largely heterogeneous research field which now bears the name of *sound studies*. In its research culture fundamentally contradicting approaches and methods, positions on the role of the arts, of design, of scientific research, of empirical methods, and of new hermeneutic, post-hermeneutic, new digital or post-digital approaches coexist and complement each other. This very multitude of conflicting approaches and competing methods actually constitutes a proper research field: in contrast to an esoteric school, in which all disciples mainly affirm and elaborate on the genius of one early sage, his holy words, and a selection of holy scriptures. Dissent is how research operates and progresses.

1863–1954:

Theories of sound

A *theory of sound*, if you intended to invent it anew – how would you start conceptualizing this? With a focus on specific sounds and experiences of hearing maybe? With going out in the field and collecting characteristic sonic experiences in common and not so common situations? Maybe even with travelling all over the globe and looking for the most remote and most unusual sonic experiences in a wide array of cultures and subcultures? Such an approach would be considered rather characteristic for globalized, mediatized, and commodified research in the early 21st century with its focus on material, specific, and empirically recognizable tiny situations – moreover integrating aspects of globalization, mediatization, and individualization. In contrast to such an approach, research on sound in the 19th century did start, unsurprisingly, at a radically different point, focusing on substantially different questions, intending to achieve a different goal. In those times of electrification, of imperial nationalism, and excessive colonialism, at the climax of a bourgeois concept of territorializing all aspects of life, history, space, and existence, the research cultures of those times were as well-tailored to contribute to this process of industrialization, of commodification, and of capitalization.

The audio technology present today, all these amplifiers and compressors, surround sound systems, hearing aids, the mixing desks, the effect tools, the sound processing software suites: in these artifacts the historical sound theory, stemming from the aforementioned 19th-century efforts of European and American science imperialism and their historical framework of epistemology and social as well as economic order is still manifest. *Theories of Sound* from this period did materialize, quantify, and objectify sound in order to support the major process of capitalization and commodification. These theories present themselves to us as the one and only, the exclusive, and the only actually useful and profitable way of storing, transmitting, presenting, and reflecting sounds. Studies by Hermann von Helmholtz, by Harvey Fletcher, or by Leo Beranek can serve thus as appropriate entry points into this historical and impactful specimen of theorizing sound. Their research, covering over one century, colonizes if you will the whole range of corporeal aspects of aural listening: listening *by the ear.* Their research tries and succeeds in quantifying aural and auditory sensations; it succeeds in materializing the before often imma-terialized process of listening; and it *almost* succeeds in establishing a language that speaks about sounds for once not in terms of the unspeakable or the imaginary – but in terms of corporeal sensations, of bodily events.

Hermann von Helmholtz's research is one starting point. His research focused on a mate-rialization of the ear, its functioning, its means and materials for signal transduction from the surrounding and intruding air into the body, into the nerve net, and the brain (for example Helmholtz 1863). The experiments and the models invented and crafted by Helmholtz are impressive still today, for he managed to conceptualize sound as one coherent signal that could be transduced through carriers and channels inside a humanoid body. This alone qualifies as a major theoretical step in the history of any *theory of sound*. With this new, scientific entity and model it actually became possible to describe sound as a material phenomenon – not merely an imaginary or at best supernatural event beyond any comprehension of humanoid mortals. With the physiological and sensorial research by Helmholtz and his disciples such as Wilhelm Wundt and later researchers such as Carl Stumpf or Hermann Ebbinghaus, the sacred areal of the human body and its behaviour concerning sensory perception and auditory phenomenol-ogy were joyfully profanized to become a research field of its own. Without Helmholtz's crucial first step no research on perception and on auditory cognition as it is present today would have been possible.

A second crucial step in the history of any theory of sound can be found in the research of Harvey Fletcher (Fletcher 1929). Fletcher, being principal investigator for the *AT&T Bell Telephone Laboratories* in the late 1920s and early 1930s, conducted research on the limitations and the potential of speech recognition. Yet, the status of AT&T as an aspiring monopoly at that time almost necessarily corrupted this research (cf. Sterne 2012b: 43–45). The goal was *not* speech recognition in general, but how to minimize the transmitted quality of sound, and hence to maximize the profits from transmitting sounds: "Where AT&T could once bill for one call, it could now bill for four – with minimal modifications of infrastructure and no price increase" (Sterne 2012b: 45). The capitalization of sound is therefore an inbuilt constituent of any sound research following this approach.

A third and final step then is to be detected in the massive research of Leo J. Beranek on concert hall acoustics and room acoustics in general (Beranek 1954, 2004). Developing military- and network-technology with *Bolt, Beranek and Newman* (BBN), Beranek made serious efforts not only to materialize and to quantify a *theory of sound* but to formalize and to proceduralize the measuring, the evaluating, and hence the design or redesign of concert hall venues. His research thus follows quite consistently Jonathan Sterne's descriptions of modern sound dis-courses: discourses that engage in the materializing, the commodifying, the processing, and the applying of sound as data. Subsequent acoustic theories of the present are relying thoroughly on exactly these theories and their epistemological as well as ideological framework. The history of auditory cognition, of room acoustics and of the acoustics in telecomunications studies is not thinkable without these studies. And yet, if one relies *solely* on these approaches the description of sonic experiences remains strangely hollow, empty, and insufficient. Their authors would then probably be claiming: This is exactly the intention. In the framework of logocentric research and its imperialist, territorializing urge in the 19th and early 20th century, the colonization of the white areas on the map of knowldge is the main goal. Yet, the map of the mind, of affect, and of experience was hardly imaginable at that time. The whole sphere of individual and idiosyncratic experiences around and with sound was necessarily excluded from research. Research on sound had to neglect and ignore any individual assimilation and idiosyncratic affectation by the sonic. Only if it could be considered a sufficiently general effect of sound, preferably with physical and quantifiable results, then it could be researched. The life of sensibilites was taken out of sound research. This is the exact point where a *theory on sound* seemed to come in handy.

1977–1994:

Theories on sound

Only a few decades ago – quite recently in the *longue durées* of cultural history – sound became an analytical object that could be researched by cultural theory. The first prominent theories on sound emerged in the 1970s – supposedly in the aftermath of the first soundscape movement following the writings and compositions by R. Murray Schafer on the one side (Schafer 1977, 1967) and on the other side following the massive distribution of commodified devices for sound recording and sound reproduction into all areas of everyday life. Still impactful and strongly contested is the long reflection by Jacques Attali on the economy of music he titled *Bruits* or *Noise* in 1977, written just before Punk broke. The prognostic qualities of this book are still unmatched, especially concerning the dynamics of the music industry and various institutional dispositives of containing violence, aggression, and resistance in the form of harmonizing organizations. Attali's essay marks an audacious and highly complex effort to analyse Western societies in the course of written history by their *sonic practices* and their *auditory dispositives*: two concepts that the more recent sound studies are founded upon (Sterne 2003; Back & Bull 2003; Schulze 2008; Bijsterveld & Pinch 2011; Papenburg & Schulze 2016). To be perfectly clear, it was *not* Jacques Attali who did actually introduce these two concepts; yet he argues and he thinks in this essay in a way that tacitly takes these two concepts as *implicit* starting points. As in this paragraph:

> Eavesdropping, censorship, recording, and surveillance are weapons of power. The technology of listening in on, ordering, transmitting, and recording noise is at the heart of this apparatus. The symbolism of the Frozen Words, of the Tables of the Law, of recorded noise and eavesdropping – these are the dreams of political scientists and the fantasies of men in power: to listen, to memorize this is the ability to interpret and control history, to manipulate the culture of a people, to channel its violence and hopes. Who among us is free of the feeling that this process, taken to an extreme, is turning the modern State into a gigantic, monopolizing noise emitter, and at the same time, a generalized eavesdropping device. Eavesdropping on what? In order to silence whom?
>
> *(Attali 1985: 7)*

Attali assumes here a so-called "hearing perspective" (Auinger & Odland 2007) to society, to history and technology, to politics, and to cultural developments. He interprets these aspects and strata of culture following audible and auditory effects, through dispositives and practices. Though his main reference for analysis is one from the visual arts: an excerpt from the large painting *The Fight between Carnival and Lent* (1559) by Pieter Bruegel the Elder. Exactly this move is one of his major and quite clever rhetoric tricks. Attali introduces his readers into *sonic thinking* by refering to an example of *visual* thinking they might more easily digest. In accepting this visual yet eminently *artistic* example for once, a reader then can become more inclined to accept other artistic examples as arguments: for instance *sonic* artistic examples. Hence, Attali does not widen an imagined gap between the visual and the sonic as an audiopietist would do, but he bridges the gap by connecting both sides via the artistic approaches, inhabiting both areas at once. Therefore not an scholarly or even a scientific argument provides a route into more complex reflections of sensory experiences, but artistic practices and aesthetic experiences. This rhetoric figure will evolve over time to a crucial and prolific element in sound studies.

But what about actual sonic examples? Examples of *sonic* experience and *corporeal* sound events? Again, wouldn't these provide the obvious empirical material for any *theory on sound*? You might have guessed already: not so much for the early history of sound theory. Of all, it was a philosopher of science and technology who dared to focus largely on an actual phenomenology of sounds: the phenomenology of *Listening and Voice* (1976). A work that is still one of the most inspiring and thought-provoking concerning the voice and its sounding – and yet largely underrated in the field of sound studies. Ihde takes his readers onto a journey of various phenomena in experiencing sound "doing a phenomenological investigation" (Ihde 2007: xix) of *radical empiricism* (James 1912) in order to incorporate the *auditory dimension* into phenomenology. Hence, he presents in his book an "anthropological-archaeological-historical set of variations" (Ihde 2007: 263). His descriptions of everyday listening situations, of listening habits and individual reflections on listening and sounding provide an immensely inspiring introduction into the actual academic *practice* of phenomenological and anthropological writing about sounding and listening. Any research in sound studies intending to work about actual sonic experiences and specific listening situations and sound practices can start with this seminal volume by Ihde.

Yet, tracking the actual effects and affects of sonic experiences: what could be the result of such a study? Klaus Theweleit explored this in various studies since the 1970s, not always focused solely on sound – but consistently analysing corporeal, personal, social, and cultural effects of intensified sensory and sonic experiences and the individual tricks and detours on how to deal with those, for instance in one of his major works, *Buch der Könige. Volume 2x & 2y: Orpheus am Machtpol – Recording Angels' Mysteries* (1994). For Theweleit the impact of sound is corporeal – and as such it is personal, intimate, social, and global at the same time. The body experiences and it records sounds, in every cell and nerve being worn out or anticipating specific sonic experiences:

> The muscular system is a registry of auditory pleasures (and horrors). Tones have a physical precipitation. [...] certain parts of the cell structure of my body have changed after they recorded certain musics. I react differently then; differently not only to certain musics; also differently to certain people and different to states of reality in general, with which I have to deal with.[1]
>
> *(Theweleit 2007: 30; transl.: HS)*

Here the hearing perspective is in full effect: the corporeal resonance on sonic experience is the main perspective Theweleit assumes here. This approach channels already the approach of *sonic materialism* (Kim-Cohen 2009; Cox 2011; Schrimshaw 2013; Schulze 2016) which should become a major thread in sound studies years after. Yet, could there be another, an even more materialist, even more sensorially thought relation between sound and theory? A relation that actually would have been unthinkable in the research dispositives of the 19th and most of the 20th century? Not a small number of researchers at that time (and obviously still today) included in their personal, ostensibly *non-professional* (yet highly instructive) practice the knowledge of musicians, of singers, of composers, arrangers, of dedicated listeners, and sound aficionados; though at this time it would have seemed a rather weird if not lunatic concept to do research on sound and to present its results via the means of actual sound practices: *sound on theory*.

1967–2005:

Sound on theory

Researchers of sound are guided, and all too often imprisoned, by the epistemological frameworks and the institutional restraints that make research possible in a given cultural environment and a historical era. Hence research publications represent and reproduce foremost the historical idiosyncrasies and cultural inhibitions from where they originated. There are, though, selected efforts by researchers to break out of these prisons and to expand or even exchange the main epistemological concepts and the arsenal of recognized research methods. In the field of sound most of the researchers discussed in this chapter actually contributed to this transformation: a few of them are not even researchers in a traditional sense – or they would not have been given access to research environments due to their gender, their race, their social status, or their erratic sensibilities and idiosyncratic heuristics. Stunningly enough this was also true for researchers who decidedly refused to publish their research results in academic writing, presenting a verbal argument, supported by visualizations or diagrammatic representations. As these researchers published mainly *sound pieces, soundwalks, sound installations*, or *concepts for sound performances*, they would have had a hard time entering the globalized institution of research in the sciences or humanities. This was true for the core period of establishing modern European and North-American research cultures in the 19th and early 20th century. In this period the modern, territorializing desire of establishing national research cultures lead to a neglect, all too often even to a malevolent, condescending disrespect for all methods not exclusively adhering to acknowledged models of proof and presentation in academia. This disrespect towards artistic approaches, though, represents apparently a repressed desire.

As most of the traditional *theories of sound* emerged out of highly idiosyncratic sensibilities and inclinations of their leading researchers, these sensibilities and desires had to be hidden and camouflaged in their academic publications. This repressed desire finally returned even more impactful in the form of *Artistic Research* or *Aesthetic Research*. These forms of expanded research confront academic institutions in the sciences and the humanities with a substantial methodological and existential critique. Starting out with the avant gardes of the 20th century, artistic research has transformed in recent decades from an essayistic provocation to a very much more respected, and in some cases even institutionalized, area of research. Hildegard Westerkamp proposed for instance a quite impactful, and radically individualistic and corporeal approach to research in her prolific concept of *Soundwalk* (1974):

> Start by listening to the sounds of your body while moving. They are closest to you and establish the first dialogue between you and the environment. If you can hear even the quietest of these sounds you are moving through an environment which is scaled on human proportions. In other words, with your voice or your footsteps for instance, you are "talking" to your environment which then in turn responds by giving your sounds a specific acoustic quality.
>
> *(Westerkamp 1974)*

Effectively, Westerkamp transforms the relation of a researcher to her research subject – and thus the role of the researcher is completely reconceptualized. The researcher is not anymore an anonymous entity, exhaustively erudite, omniscient, and calmly evaluating various hypotheses and models in objective deliberation. This fiction of objectivity which researchers learn to indulge in very early in their education, this imaginary is lightheartedly rejected. Westerkamp assumes in contrary a researcher who is an empirical person of a certain gender and race, age and social status, physical stature and idiosyncratic corporeal abilities as well as cultural inhibitions: an approach that later was expanded to a proper ethnographical research method in the *Sensory Memory Walk* (Järviluoma & Vikman 2013) and effectively inspired manifold research into the corporeal ubiquity of sound (Henriques 2011; Kassabian 2013). This epistemic quality of an irreducible constellation made of corporeal, affective, and conceptual idiosyncrasies has become a major mark in the artistic theories, the *Künstlertheorien* (cf. Lehnerer 1994) of two other highly influential sound artists: Maryanne Amacher and Pauline Oliveros. Maryanne Amacher operated in her workgroups *City-Links* (1967–88) as well as in *Intelligent Life* (1981–2009) directly in the physical material of a given location: the walls and the floors, the cables and the furnitures, people lingering and working there, appliances, machines, and computers connected to the electrical grid. Her soundworks are indeed physiologically and auditorily extremist explorations of what sounding and listening are capable of in our cultures:

> When played at the right sound level, which is quite high and exciting, tones in this music will cause your ears to act as neurophonic instruments that emit sounds that will seem to be issuing directly from your head. [...] Produced interaurally, these virtual sounds and melodic patterns origiante in ears and neuroanatomy, not in your loudspeakers.
>
> *(Amacher 1999: booklet)*

You, the listener, become the location of sound reproduction and hence the field of artistic fieldwork. A parallel endeavour motivated the artist, composer, sonic thinker, and performer, Pauline Oliveros. In her work she moved more and more to a kind of sound piece that can be regarded as meditating exercises in which a listener *is* the actual performer: A researcher's listening habit and her or his idiosyncrasies here also consitute the actual research field (Oliveros 2005). In contrast to more widely known artists and sonic thinkers like Max Neuhaus, Alvin Lucier, and John Cage, all of these researchers managed to actually leave traditional ties in institutional frameworks behind. They expanded their soundworks into artistic operations consisting of *Sound On Theory*. Following this major step of incorporating artistic practices into sound research, an even more daring move into the unknown of theory had become possible: *Sound* could now even be considered *as theory* itself.

1998–2014:

Sound as theory

"You are not censors but sensors, not aesthetes but kinaesthetes. You are sensationalists. You are the newest mutants incubated in wombspeakers". (Eshun 1998: 1)

With *More Brilliant Than the Sun* by Kodwo Eshun, published in 1998, a whole different period of writing and publishing sound theory has begun: "Far from needing theory's help, music today is already more conceptual than at any point this century, pregnant with thought-probes waiting to be activated, switched on, misused" (Eshun 1998: 003).

Whereas for over one century any writing about music or sound that dared to indulge in sensory subtleties and complex affects while experiencing or creating sound events was doomed to be defamed as unscientific and merely lyrical, some more chauvinist researchers even cursed it as being *uneducated*, *confused* and *effeminate*. This quite scary repression of sentiment and sensibility in theories about sound now finally seems to have vanished, step by step.

There is no distance with volume, you're swallowed up by sound. There's no room, you can't be ironic if you're being swallowed by volume, and volume is overwhelming you. It's impossible to stay ironic, so postmodernism, all the implications of that go out of the window, simultaneous with Benjamin and all the modernist arguments, all those go out of the window as well. So not only is it the literary that's useless, all of the traditional theory is pointless. All that works is the sonic plus the machine that you're building. So you can bring back any of those particular things if you like, but it better work. And the way you can test it out is to actually play it. (Eshun 1998: 188f.)

With Eshun's effort to establish a writing of *sonic fictions*, of highly idiosyncratic and often erratic, yet thoroughly convincing and plausible narrations and constructions around sonic artifacts of any kind, it became clear that this form of writing actually has to be regarded as the core of any writing, researching and theorizing around sound: To unravel the sensory and imaginary impact of a specific specimen of organized sounds – in a characteristic and culturally as well as historically contextualized situation (Schulze 2013). Sound *is* theory and sound *as* theory is written in *sonic fictions*.

"The African drumchoir complexifies the beat into distributed Polyrhythmachines, webbed networks of poly*counter*contra*cross*staggered rhythms that function like the dispersed architecture of artificial life by generating emergent consciousness". (Eshun 1998: 5)

With this concept Eshun convincingly exchanged the whole framework for any future or past theory *of* or *on* sound: Any effort of crafting such a theory now must be read as just one specimen of academic writing styles. The epistemic model of sonic fiction is a performatively radical constructivist one: It assumes that all verbal, diagrammatic or algorithmic representations of sonic experiences are highly idiosyncratic edifices fuelled by the imagination of a group of researchers, their projections, memories, obsessions, and fears. Most of these – probably also in this and all other chapters of this volume – do rather schematically reflect their highly personal, historical, and cultural limitations of constructing an epistemic reality. Therefore the physicalist models of Hermann von Helmholtz represent foremost his avoidance of speaking about affects and immersion; in a similar and very personal way as the musical performances and recordings by Sun Ra and his ensembles represent among others his afrofuturist perspective onto the creation of sound, life and interaction; in a way close to the works by Pauline Oliveros that represent a way of being affected by sound and by intense sensory experiences in a meditating situation. In the framework of sonic fiction all of these cultural artifacts belong obviously to quite different social meshworks with differing goals, different regulations for articulation as well as different categories for evaluating artifacts. Yet all of these examples share an ambition to embody a certain historically and culturally quite specific and idiosyncratic *hearing perspective* (Auinger & Odland 2007).

This concept of the *hearing perspective* and the artistic research around it is the logical consequence of proposing *Sound As Theory*. The works by Sam Auingeer and Bruce Odland represent this artistic approach to theory at its best. Since the early 1990s they work on a series of installations, performances, and sound art pieces that explore what they and many other sound artists call *sonic thinking* (Herzogenrath 2017; Schulze 2017b) or *sonic epistemologies* (Cobussen, Meelberg & Schulze 2013). This approach, supported by many other sound artists and sonic thinkers such as Brandon LaBelle (LaBelle 2006, 2010) or David Toop (Toop 2010), Kaffe Matthews or Ulrike Sowodniok (Sowodniok 2013, 2016), Jeremy Woodruff or Salomé Voegelin (Voegelin 2010a, 2010b, 2014), starts with the assumption that research on sound needs to be conceptualized, performed, and presented foremost in the realm of the sonic, the audible, the sensible itself – and not in translations into neighbouring realms of alphanumeric codes, logocentric hermeneutics or refined abstractions crafted from philosophical concepts. The sonic experience and an approach of radical empiricism to it is the first material, the first empirical ground to work in *Sound As Theory*. The main research goal for sonic thinking is hence:

> to make sense of the sound environment we live in by listening with attention, hearing, exploring, and attempting to understand the cultural waveform as a language. […] These sounds are often shut out of our mental picture of a space as *noise*. By listening to and studying these noises, they become useful sound sources.
>
> (Auinger & Odland 2007)

Sound is in this area of research not anymore interpreted as representing something external to it – as it was in the earlier specimen of *theory of sound* and *theory on sound*. Sound is the material in which research is operating and in which the results of this research are presented. These results are not – as in the approach of *sound on theory* – easily repressed as being *only art/only music*. But the findings of these sound artists and sound researchers, these sonic thinkers are being acknowledged as the research they are, starting with authors such as Seth Kim-Cohen or Christofer Cox who affirm their relevance, their impact and their groundbreaking character. Especially in the writings by Salomé Voegelin the interweaving of sensory fictions, sonic performativity and acoustic knowledge has reached an impressive apex:

> at an open window sounds my simultaneity with my environment. Singing birds, humming traffic, the clanking of scaffolding being taken down and the spinning of the washing machine sound simultaneous with my hands tapping the keyboard and the movements of my cotton jumper. I experience an equivalence of inside and out that engages me in the environment. I write about it through taking part in it: from my equivalence into the environment.
>
> By contrast when I go to the British library with all its air tight, windowless quietness, I hear painfully only myself, cut off from my surroundings, pursuing scholarly research that does not link me to the sound world out there, I write with a closed off self-referentiality.
>
> Sitting at my window the relationship of myself writing is with a world out there and my inhabiting of that world, and it is as that inhabiting self that I write about the sound of that world.
>
> (Voegelin 2011)

What in the writings by Hermann von Helmholtz needed still to be neglected and psychologically separated into a less meaningful, profane and too materialist part of the researcher's actual everyday life, can be found reintegrated in Voegelin's writings. Research on sound is happening *in* sound. The repressed forms of knowledge and epistemic, the sensory and the material, the visceral, and the dynamically plastic can be included in reseach (Schulze 2017a). Sound theories can be listened to. Sound theories are sounding.

Note

1 "[D]ie Muskulatur ist eine Registratur auditiver Lüste (und Schrecken). Die Töne haben ihren körperlichen Niederschlag. […] bestimmte Teile der Zellstruktur meines Körpers haben sich verändert nach der Aufnahme bestimmter Musiken. Ich reagiere anders; nicht nur anders auf bestimmte Musiken; auch anders auf bestimmte Leute und anders auf die Zustände des Wirklichen überhaupt, mit denen ich zu tun habe" (Theweleit 2007: 30).

References

Amacher, M. (1999). *Sound Characters (Making The Third Ear)*. New York, NY: Tzadik Records.

Attali, J. (1985). *Noise: The Political Economy of Music*. Minneapolis. MN: University of Minnesota.

"Auinger, S. & Odland, B. (2007). "Hearing Perspective (Think with Your Ears)." In C. Seiffarth, C. & M. Sturm (Eds.), *Sam Auinger Katalog*. Wien: Folio Verlag.

Back, L. & Bull, M. (Eds.) (2003). *The Auditory Culture Reader*. Oxford: Berg Publishers.

Beranek, L. (1954). *Acoustics*. New York, NY: McGraw Hill.

Beranek, L. (2004). *Concert Halls and Opera Houses: Music, Acoustics, and Architecture*. New York, NY: Springer Publishing.

Bijsterveld, K. & Pinch, T. (2011). *The Oxford Handbook of Sound Studies*. New York, NY: Oxford University Press.

Cobussen, M, Meelberg, V. & Schulze, H. (2013). "Towards New Sonic Epistemologies." *Journal of Sonic Studies* 3, Vol. 4.

Cox, C. (2011). "Beyond Representation and Signification: Toward a Sonic Materialism." *Journal of Visual Culture* 10, *No. 2*, 145–161.

Eshun, K. (1998). *More Brilliant Than the Sun. Adventures in Sonic Fiction*. London: Quartet Books.

Fletcher, H. (1929). *Speech and Hearing. With an Introduction by H.D. Arnold*. New York, NY: D. Van Nostrand Company, Incorporated.

Helmholtz, H. (1863). *Die Lehre von den Tonempfindungen als Physiologische Grundlage für die Theorie der Musik*. Braunschweig: Friedrich Vieweg und Sohn.

Henriques, J. (2011). *Sonic Bodies. Reggae Sound Systems. Performance Techniques, and Ways of Knowing*. New York, NY: Bloomsbury.

Herzogenrath, B. (Ed.) (2017). *Sound Thinking – Vol. 4 of the book series Thinking Media*. New York, NY: Bloomsbury Publishing.

Ihde, D. (1976/2007). *Listening and the Voice: Phenomenologies of Sound*. New York, NY: State University of New York.

James, W. (1912). *Essays in Radical Empiricism*. New York, NY: Longman Green and Co.

Järviluoma, H. & Vikman, N. (2013). "On Soundscape Methods and Audiovisual Sensibility." In: *The Oxford Handbook of New Audiovisual Aesthetics*. Edited by John Richardson, Claudia Gorbman & Carol Vernallis. Oxford: Oxford University Press, 645–658.

Kassabian, A. (2013). *Ubiquitous Listening: Affect, Attention, and Distributed Subjectivity*. Berkley, CA: University of California Press.

Kim-Cohen, S. (2009). *In the Blink of an Ear: Toward a Non-Cochlear Sonic Art*. New York, NY: Bloomsbury Publishing.

LaBelle, B. (2006): *Background Noise. Perspectives on Sound Art*. New York, NY: Bloomsbury Publishing.

LaBelle, B. (2010). *Acoustic Territories. Sound Culture and Everyday Life*. New York, NY: Continuum.

Lehnerer, T. (1994). *Methode der Kunst*. Würzburg: Königshausen & Neumann.

Oliveros, P. (2005). *Deep Listening: A Composer's Sound Practice*. New York, NY: iUniverse, Inc.

Papenburg, J.G. & Schulze, H. (Eds.) (2016). *Sound as Popular Culture. A Research Companion*. Cambridge, MA: The MIT Press.

Schafer, R. (1967). *Ear Cleaning. Notes for an Experimental Music Course*. Toronto/Canada: Berandol Music Limited.

Schafer, R. (1977). *The Soundscape. Our Sonic Environment and the Tuning of the World*. New York, NY: Knopf.

Schrimshaw, W. (2013). "Non-cochlear sound: On affect and exteriority." In: *Sound, Music, Affect. Theorizing Sonic Experience*. Edited by Ian Biddle & Marie Thompson. New York, NY: Bloomsbury Publishing, 27–44,

Schulze, H. (2007). "Die Audiopietisten. Eine Polemik," *Kultur und Gespenster* 2 (2007), H. 3: "Dokumentarismus – die Inszenierung des Authentischen." Hamburg: Textem Verlag, 122–129.

Schulze, H. (Ed.) (2008). *Sound Studies: Traditionen – Methoden – Desiderate. Eine Einführung*. Bielefeld: transcript Verlag (Sound Studies Series Volume 1).

Schulze, H. (2013). "Adventures in Sonic Fiction. A Heuristic for Sound Studies." *Journal of Sonic Studies* 3, Vol. 4.

Schulze, H. (2016). "Der Klang und die Sinne. Gegenstände und Methoden eines sonischen Materialismus." In: *Materialität. Herausforderungen für die Sozial- und Kulturwissenschaften*. Edited by Herbert Kalthoff, Torsten Cress & Tobias Röhl, München: Wilhelm Fink Verlag, 413–434.

Schulze, H. (2017a). *The Sonic Persona. An Anthropology of Sound*. New York, NY: Bloomsbury Publishers.

Schulze, H. (2017b). "How To Think Sonically? On the Generativity of the Flesh." In: *Sonic Thinking: A Media Philosophicaal Approach*. Edited by Bernd Herzogenrath –Vol. 4 of the book series *Thinking Media*. New York, NY: Bloomsbury Publishing.

Sowodniok, U. (2013). *Stimmklang und Freiheit. Zur auditiven Wissenschaft des Körpers*. Bielefeld: Transcript Verlag.

Sowodniok, U. (2016). "Voce in libertà." *The Senses & Society* 11, no. 1.

Sterne, J. (2003). *The Audible Past: The Cultural Origins of Sound Reproduction*. Durham & London: Duke University Press.

Sterne, J. (2012a). *The Sound Studies Reader*. London: Routledge.

Sterne, J. (2012b). *MP3 – The Meaning of a Format*. Durham & London: Duke University Press.

Theweleit, K. (2007). *Übertragung. Gegenübertragung. Dritter Körper. Zur Gehirnveränderung durch die Medien. Internationale Flusser Lecture*. Köln: Verlag der Buchhandlung Walther König.

Toop, D. (2010). *Night Leaves Breathing*. RTE Radio Ireland 27 October 2010.

Voegelin, S. (2010a). *Listening to Noise and Silence. Towards a philosophy of Sound Art*. New York, NY: Continuum.

Voegelin, S. (2010b). *Sound Words: A Blog about Sound and Words*. New York, NY: Tumblr. soundwords. tumblr.com

Voegelin, S. (2011). *Writing*. June 10, 2011, 10:16 pm. http://soundwords.tumblr.com/post/6395471901/ writing

Voegelin, S. (2014). *Sonic Possible Worlds. Hearing the Continuum of Sound*. New York, NY: Bloomsbury Publishing.

Westerkamp, H. (1974). "Soundwalking," *Sound Heritage* III, No. 4 (also in: *Autumn Leaves, Sound and the Environment in Artistic Practice*, Ed. Angus Carlyle, Double Entendre, Paris, 2007, 49).

2

WHAT IS SOUND STUDIES?

Mark Grimshaw-Aagaard

Introduction

I consider myself a sound studies researcher and yet I do not consider myself a sound studies researcher. To explain this paradox: the object of study in my research is sound and yet I do not fit easily within the sound studies bracket as defined in numerous descriptions of sound studies as a research field and as an academic pathway. Still, in my professional life, I find myself regularly labelled as someone who "does sound studies," whose work should be viewed through the distorting prism of sound studies. Categories and definitions, descriptive or normative, and in any field but, perhaps, particularly so in the humanities, do matter because they are useful tools for politicians and administrators and analysts and reviewers to, among other uses, formulate policies and decisions of inclusion and exclusion. This essay, therefore, is part rumination on what precisely sound studies is, part discussion of what sound is, and, ultimately, part suggestion that sound studies could be redefined to include what, if one holds to nominative determinism, should be the core object of study.

What is sound studies?

In this section, I survey attempts to define sound studies as a field of academic study and discourse. As with many relatively new fields of study, it can be difficult to accurately pin down when the term started to be used, when the field began to aggregate, and some future academic archaeologist will, no doubt, be able to trace the genesis of the field, as the foci of inquiries from diverse disciplines began to coalesce into a recognizably distinct body of work, much further into the past than I would care to. What interests me here are the attempts to define the field that have been provided since the start of the century, that point in time I would cautiously define as marking the beginning of sound studies proper.

Michael Bull and Les Back, in the introduction to *The Auditory Culture Reader* (2003), implicitly acknowledge that the field of sound studies has yet to be defined in their hope that the chapters of the anthology should "provide an integrated picture of what sound studies should look like" (Bull & Back 2003, 3). A further indication of this acknowledgement is that the editors at least twice use scare quotes in the introduction *viz.* "'sound' studies" (Bull & Back 2003, 3–4). What is demonstrated in the anthology is that, whatever "sound studies" should look like," it is *not* the study of sound per se. The field is better described as *auditory culture*, as stated in the anthology's title, in that the contributions range from listening through to studies of sound's use and function in culture and society. Throughout, that sound is a sound wave is an assumption not questioned.

In 2004, Trevor Pinch and Karin Bijsterveld provided what is, to the best of my knowledge, the first succinct definition of sound studies in the journal *Social Studies in Science*: "Sound Studies is an emerging interdisciplinary area that studies the material production and consumption of music, sound, noise, and silence, and how these have changed throughout history and within different societies" (Pinch & Bijsterveld 2004, 636). What is particularly telling here is the mission statement of the journal: to encourage "submissions of original research on science, technology, and medicine. The journal is multidisciplinary, publishing work from a range of fields including: political science, sociology, economics, history, philosophy, psychology social anthropology, legal and educational disciplines."[1] It should be noted that, until 1975, *Social Studies in Science* was titled *Science Studies*. The definition that Pinch and Bijsterveld provide, then, is a justification for the relationship of music, sound, noise, and silence, and the study of their production and consumption, to the broader field of science and technology studies and, therefore, to the remit of the journal. The authors also wish to demonstrate how the methods and methodologies of science and technology studies can be of use to sound studies: "What S&TS can contribute is a focus on the materiality of sound, its embeddedness not only in history, society, and culture, but also in science and technology and its machines and ways of knowing and interacting" (Pinch & Bijsterveld 2004, 636).

In 2012, the field had matured enough to warrant the publication of two substantial anthologies whose titles explicitly state this maturation of the field. *The Oxford Handbook of Sound Studies* (Pinch & Bijsterveld 2012) adheres, in the main, to the science and technology studies track and this should come as no surprise as the editors are the two authors behind the article in *Social Studies in Science* mentioned above. In describing the process of transduction as turning "sound into something accessible to other senses" (Pinch & Bijsterveld 2012, 4), they state that: "[N]ow that technologies of transduction are everywhere, we would like to foreground their appropriation and consequences in science, society, and culture as important topics for study" (Pinch & Bijsterveld 2012, 4). Sound studies, thus, deals with "technologies for storing, manipulating, and transferring sound and music ... and new ways of measuring, conceptualizing, and controlling sound" (Pinch & Bijsterveld 2012, 5). Following on from this technological bent, sound studies also investigates interaction with sound and the role of technology in aiding or enhancing that interaction (for example stethoscopes and hearing aids/prostheses). The field is interdisciplinary and the editors list a number of contributing disciplines and other fields: acoustic ecology; sound and soundscape design; anthropology of the senses; history of everyday life; environmental history; cultural geography; urban studies; auditory culture; art studies; musicology; ethnomusicology; literary studies; science & technology studies; cultural history; anthropology of medicine and the body; media studies; film studies; and game studies (Pinch & Bijsterveld 2012, 6–7).

Jonathan Sterne, in *The Sound Studies Reader* (2012), defines sound studies thus:

> Sound *studies* is a name for the interdisciplinary ferment in the human sciences that takes sound as its analytical point of departure or arrival. By analyzing both sonic practices and the discourses and institutions that describe them, it redescribes what sound does in the human world, and what humans do in the sonic world.
>
> *(Sterne 2012, 2)*

He goes on to state that:

> Sound studies' challenge is to think across sounds, to consider sonic phenomena in relationship to one another – *as types of sonic phenomena rather than as things-in-themselves –*

whether they be music, voices, listening, media, buildings, performances, or another other [sic] path into sonic life.

(Sterne 2012, 3)

Importantly for Sterne, "[n]ot all scholarship about or with sound is 'sound studies,'" and "[s]ound studies has an essential 'critical' element" (Sterne 2012, 4–5); sound studies, therefore, is not itself production of sound or any form of sound practice. As with Pinch and Bijsterveld, Sterne provides a long list of academic professions and disciplines feeding off and into sound studies:

[H]istorians, philosophers, musicologists, anthropologists, literary critics, art historians, geographers ... media studies, disability studies, cinema studies, cultural studies, gender studies, science and technology studies, postcolonial studies, communication studies, queer studies, American studies and on and on.

(Sterne 2012, 3)

If the definitions provided above, along with the explanatory argumentation and justification, have anything in common it is that they avoid sound itself as the object of study. This is somewhat surprising given the inclusion and prioritization of that very word in the term *sound* studies. One would assume, confronted with a newly defined field of academic inquiry termed sound studies, that the object of study in the field is sound. Yet, it is not. As Sterne states: "Sound studies ... takes sound as its analytical point of departure or arrival." Yet, for "one of the field's central concepts" (Sterne 2012, 7), sound is notable by its absence.

This omission of the study of sound itself from sound studies is, in fact, noted and lamented by Sterne when he briefly queries what sound is: "Does sound refer to a phenomenon out in the world which ears then pick up? Does it refer to a human phenomenon that only exists in relation to the physical world? Or is it something else? The answer to the question has tremendous implications for both the objects and methods of sound studies" (Sterne 2012, 7). Reading the chapters in the anthologies listed above, one must assume that most if not all of those who "do sound studies" hold to the view that sound is a vibration (within the auditory range) that travels through a medium, as does Sterne in his introduction (despite having asked the questions above). The study of *sound* is therefore the province of acousticians and not of sound studies and this view is borne out by the dearth of analysis of sound (as opposed to analysis of the use and effects of sound artefacts through history and in society and culture that are hallmarks of the writings of sound studies scholars). Sterne himself acknowledges an unease with the term sound studies by suggesting that it might be better called "'auditory culture' to reflect the degree to which sound is a sensory problem" (see Bull & Back above) and because one path into sound studies "assumes the physicality of sound and then considers its cultural valence" (Sterne 2012, 7).

While I disagree that "sound is a sensory problem" (as I make clear below), I do agree with Sterne that the question of what sound is "has tremendous implications for both the objects and methods of sound studies." Although I do not suggest that sound studies concerns itself only with the metaphysical and the abstract, in many ways my stance on sound studies echoes that of Claudia Abbate's (2004) views on musicology: "[why is] the academic discourse devoted to music ... comfortable with the metaphysical and abstract and uninterested in the systems that bring music into ephemeral phenomenal being" (Abbate 2004, 513). There is plenty of debate outside sound studies as to what sound *is* and so I use the following section to survey a number of extant definitions of sound – not only the acoustic definitions (yes, there are at least two of them) – with a view to finding a definition that can provide the core object of study and so provide a sound foundation to sound studies.

What is sound?

It is neither my intention here to list all extant definitions of sound nor to expand in great detail upon those I do present; I and others have done this elsewhere (for example Pasnau 1999; Casati & Dokic 2005/2010; Nudds & O'Callaghan 2009; Grimshaw & Garner 2015; Grimshaw 2015). I use this section, then, to discuss the standard western definitions of sound (that is, those in the field of acoustics and having general currency) to question the fundamental assumption within sound studies that sound is thus defined and need not be discussed further, to discuss some other relevant definitions of sound, and to briefly present a definition of sound that I believe has more relevance and use to sound studies than that tacitly assumed.

I mentioned above that there are in fact two definitions of sound (possibly three depending on one's interpretation of the wording) to be found in the acoustics standards. The first is the familiar one that the 10th edition of *The Concise Oxford Dictionary* defines as "vibrations which travel through the air or another medium and are sensed by the ear." Both this definition and the second definition are more fully stated in American National Standards Institute (ANSI) documentation: sound is either "(a) Oscillation in pressure, stress, particle displacement, particle velocity etc., propagated in a medium with internal forces (for example elastic or viscous) or the superposition of such propagated oscillation" or "(b) Auditory sensation evoked by the oscilla- tion described in (a)."[2] However, even acousticians doubt the correctness of these definitions: when I asked an acoustics colleague to clarify the wording, clarification came there none, but rather a denial of the validity of the definitions: "[the] definition [is] out of scope for most of the purposes I know [the definition] is only operational for some purposes [...] It is therefore necessary to use domain-specific definitions."[3] One wonders if even an acoustician is willing to dispute the standard acoustic definitions of sound (including one that underpins the popular and apparent scientific consensus of what sound is), and to such a strong degree, should not sound studies scholars also reconsider their basic assumptions as to what sound is and turn their attentions to this subject?

I have my own views regarding the standard definitions. For example, the ANSI definitions have the following footnote: "Not all sounds evoke an auditory sensation, for example ultra- sound and infrasound. Not all auditory sensations are evoked by sound, for example tinnitus." With some simple word substitution from the definitions, one can arrive at the curiously pat- aphysical statements that a) not all sounds evoke a sound and b) not all sounds are evoked by sound. If one does indeed accept that not all sounds evoke an auditory sensation, then one must assume that either dogs do not hear a sound but respond to something else when a high- pitched dog whistle is used or that what they hear cannot be defined as sound simply because we humans are unable to sense such doggy sounds. Further incoherence can be found in numerous examples of downright sloppy use of the term sound in numerous articles and textbooks on physics and acoustics where, for example, sounds arrive at the ear and are then transported (as sound) to the brain or that the brain translates vibrations in a medium into sound (for these and other examples see for example Pasnau 1999; Grimshaw 2015).

One other objection I would like to raise to the standard definitions of sound is that they neither explain various auditory phenomena nor do they support the phenomenology of our everyday hearing. One famous anomaly is the McGurk Effect in which an audio recording taken from a video recording of someone's mouth articulating the syllable "baa" is superimposed on a video of the same mouth articulating the syllable "faa." When a subject is played the first video the syllable "baa" is heard as expected. But, when played the second video, the subject hears "faa." How is it possible to hear two different sounds while sensing the same sound wave (sound), to have different auditory sensations evoked by the same oscillations (or to have different sounds evoked by the same sound if one takes the pataphysical approach)? Either what we hear is not sound or, if what we hear is indeed sound, then sound is neither of the ANSI definitions.

Phenomenologically speaking, the location of the sound we hear can be quite variable in that, depending on context and other factors, we experience sound as either being dynamic, and thus in accordance with the notion of sound as a moving waveform in a medium (the sound is coming from the left loudspeaker – it can be dynamic too in another sense such as panning the sound from the left to the right loudspeaker), or being static (I hear the sound of her voice over there). Equally, we also quite naturally equate sound sources with sounds in our everyday language. Gaver (1993) provides a good example: a researcher running a hearing experiment plays an audio recording and asks a subject to describe what has been heard; the subject responds "a single-engine propeller plane flying past"; the researcher, frustrated, asks the question again stressing this time that the subject must not interpret the sound; the subject still responds "I hear a plane"; irritated, the researcher retorts "you didn't hear an airplane, you heard a quasi-harmonic tone lasting approximately 3 seconds with smooth variations in the fundamental frequency and the overall amplitude"; "no I didn't, I heard a plane" the subject insists (Gaver 1993, 286–287). Human experience resists scientific objectification and therefore, if one wishes to study sound as the object of our hearing (and thus its use and effect in technology, culture, and society), one must define sound as something other and more than the standard definitions. In my view, acousticians do not study sound; rather, they study acoustic waves and these are the objects of an auditory sensation that is only a part of what results in the sound that we hear.

In the western world there have, of course, been definitions of sound that pre-date those of modern acoustics. That early proponent of atomism, Democritus (active in the 5th and 4th centuries BC), suggested that sound was a stream of particles emitted by a thing and, interestingly, the basis for this idea has found a new lease of life in quantum physics with the concept of the phonon (Gabor 1947) and this leads to the interesting notion that sound has mass and can therefore be deflected by gravity (Unnikrishnan 2005) – perhaps the long lists of disciplines and fields contributing to sound studies given above should also include quantum physics. However, there are also several definitions of sound that attempt, philosophically or phenomenologically, to describe sound in ways that account for our everyday experience of hearing (particularly the question of our experience of the location of sound).

Among the more recent definitions, in appealing to the veridicality of our perception, Pasnau (1999) is among those claiming that sound is the property of an "object that 'makes' them ... objects *have* sounds" (Pasnau 1999, 316) because "we do not hear sounds as being in the air; we hear them as being at the place where they are generated" (Pasnau 1999, 311). Others (following Aristotle's claim in *De Anima* that "sound is a particular movement in air" [quoted in O'Callaghan 2009, 27]), argue that sound is an event and that this event causes periodic motion in the medium (O'Callaghan 2009, 37) and that "[s]ounds are events that take place near their sources, not in the intervening space" (O'Callaghan 2009, 48). Yet others describe sound as both object and event. For Scruton (2009), sounds are secondary objects and pure events; sound is "an object of attention" (Scruton 2009, 50) that, in being such a secondary object, does not undergo change (for example when broadcast or recorded), and is a pure event because it does not happen to anything – there is thus "a virtual causality in sound that has nothing to do with the process whereby sounds are produced" (Scruton 2009, 64). In failing to demonstrate "a causal mechanism linking our neurological processes with the supposed subjective effect – the world of our perception" (Riddoch 2012, 14), the standard acoustic definition of sound does not account for the "worldly phenomena" that are sounds. Riddoch instead proposes two categories of sound: cochlear sound (those sounds involving sound waves); and non-cochlear sound (sounds produced by cross-modal effects such as synaesthesia, infrasonic sounds, and auditory imagination).

The question *where is sound?* is a fascinating one to ponder not least because it forms the basis for several of the definitions presented above. If we can answer the question satisfactorily, then presumably one has taken the first step towards defining sound. Nevertheless, while the question is a good one and should be asked, I believe asking it first places too much emphasis on the necessity of sound waves to sound (that is, sound as not defined according to acoustic definitions). Find the source of the sound wave and there will be found sound, and so all of the above definitions (with the exception of Riddoch's non-cochlear sound) presume a causal connection from sound to sound wave. Yet, we are quite capable of experiencing sound (frequently so) as being at or issuing from somewhere other than the sound wave source as evidence from, for example, the cinema (*viz.* synchresis [Chion 1994]) and the ventriloquist's dummy (for example Warren, Welch, & McCarthy 1981) demonstrates all too clearly. There are other problems with the definitions discussed above. For instance, Scruton bases his definition on studies of music perception (a rather singular mode of sonic expression) and insists that humans alone are able to perceive order in sound (for evidence to the contrary, see for example Patel, Iversen, Bregman, & Shulz 2009)[4] while O'Callaghan, in defining sound as an event bringing "a medium into *periodic* motion" (2009, 37 italics mine), ignores that vast majority of sound waves that arise from a medium in *inharmonic* motion.

In the book *Sonic Virtuality* (Grimshaw & Garner 2015), Tom Garner and I proposed another definition of sound: sound is an emergent perception that arises primarily in the auditory cortex and that is formed through spatio-temporal processes in an embodied system. This is a definition that accounts for the many objections Garner and I had to current definitions of sound including being able to account for the human factor in our experience of sound, the imagining of sound, and the localization of sound (the question *where is sound?*).

Regarding the imagination of sound (also known as auditory imagination or aural imagery), Garner and I were keen to have a concept of sound that allowed us to explain the imagination of sounds as sounds in themselves (this mirrors some of Riddoch's thinking above). There is plenty of evidence from neuroscientific studies to suggest that such sonic imagination plays a large part in our multi-sensory experience of the world whereby the brain, for example, is capable of "filling in the gaps" left by absent sound wave stimuli if the context demands it and so such imagined sound should be a part of any holistic conception of sound (see for example Hoshiyama, Gunji, & Kakigi 2001; Hughes et al. 2001; Kraemer et al. 2005; King 2006). Furthermore, we were interested in the possibility of extracting sound from the brain. That is, neurally decoding the brain wave activity of the emergence of sound as a perception and then using this imagining of sound to create digital audio and, ultimately, to produce sound waves. To do this, one needs a conception of sound as perception and to be able to identify the relevant brain wave activity. While it has yet to be achieved with sound, such neural decoding has achieved success with visual imagery and speech perception and there are plans to attempt it with musical imagery (for example Nishimoto et al. 2011; Pasley et al. 2012; Thompson, Casey, & Torresani 2013) and therefore the possibility to do likewise with sound, for instance, to be able to "think" sound into a Digital Audio Workstation, has important consequences for our future design of technology and our interaction with it.

On the question of localization of sound, rather than first use the answer to that question to drive the formulation of our definition, we used our definition itself as the means to answer the question. This allowed us to account for our experience of synchresis, for example, and so the localization of sound is not a process of *finding* the sound wave source but of *placing* the sound out into the world where it makes *cognitive* sense to locate it. This is a form of cognitive offloading (such a concept being found in theories of Embodied Cognition [see for example Wilson 2002]) and, in addition to using it to explain effects such as synchresis, I have since used this notion of sound localization to explain the role of sound in presence in virtual worlds such as computer games (Walther-Hansen & Grimshaw 2016; Grimshaw 2017).

Sound studies and sound studies

Here is an important link to sound studies: a conception of sound as an emergent perception that, to return to Sterne, could have, if not "tremendous implications," at least some implication "for both the objects and methods of sound studies" but that also helps to explain how to bring sound in as a core object of study to sound studies while at the same time maintaining some insularity from acoustics and like subjects (that study the physics and sensations of sound waves).

As stated in my introduction, it is not my intention to redefine sound studies but to suggest that it could be redefined should those with a vested interest in sound studies wish to do so. My main contention is that sound studies should hold true to its title and therefore have at its core the study of sound. This does not mean that sound's relationships to, uses in, effects on, and roles in forming technology, society, and culture should be ignored; far from it as these are important topics. But a conception of sound that is perceptually based has use-value to sound studies because sound as a perception, being formed from bottom-up processes (that is sensation) and/or top-down processes (that is cognition), is formed not only from sound waves (if they are present at all) but also from memory, knowledge, reason, experience of physical spaces, expectation, emotion, mood, imagination, and so on. Studying how that perception is formed, therefore, provides a rich vein of research into society and culture as well as into the individual as a product of society and culture. Finally, a conception of sound as emergent perception allows for a proactive approach to be included in sound studies whereby the development and design of technology is informed by an analysis of knowledge about that perception.

Notes

1 http://sss.sagepub.com/
2 American National Standard, *Acoustical Terminology*. ANSI/ASA S1.1-2013.
3 Personal email communication, 1st September 2015.
4 And one must draw attention again to the ANSI definitions of sound that are strictly human-centered. Ultrasound (in the ANSI definition, a sound not producing an auditory sensation) is defined as being above the upper human hearing limit (c.20kHz) and so, despite many dogs having perfectly serviceable hearing up to c.45kHz, any pressure wave fitting the primary ANSI definition but that nevertheless lies within the 20-45kHz range does not produce an auditory sensation. Similarly, cats have a hearing range of up to c.80kHz and are often used experimentally to inform about the *human* auditory system. All of this is absurd.

References

Abbate, C. (2004). Music: Drastic or gnostic? *Critical Inquiry, 30*(3), 505–536.
Bull, M., & Back, L. (Eds.). (2003). *The Auditory Culture Reader*. Oxford: Berg.
Casati, R., & Dokic, J. (2005/2010). Sounds. *Stanford Encyclopedia of Philosophy*. Retrieved on May 15, 2016, http://plato.stanford.edu/entries/sounds/.

Chion, M. (1994). *Audio-vision: Sound on Screen.* C. Gorbman, Trans. New York, NY: Columbia University Press.

Gabor, D. (1947). Acoustical quanta and the theory of hearing. *Nature, 159,* 591–594.

Gaver, W.W. (1993). How do we hear in the world? Explorations in ecological acoustics. *Ecological Psychology, 5*(4), 285–313.

Grimshaw, M. (2015). A brief argument for, and summary of, the concept of sonic virtuality. *Danish Musicology Online – Special Issue on Sound and Music Production,* 81–98.

Grimshaw, M. (2017). Presence through sound. In C. Wöllner (Ed.), *Body, Sound and Space in Music and Beyond: Multimodal Explorations.* Aldershot: Ashgate.

Grimshaw, M., & Garner, T.A. (2015). *Sonic Virtuality: Sound as Emergent Perception.* New York, NY: Oxford University Press.

Hoshiyama, M., Gunji, A., & Kakigi, R. (2001). Hearing the sound of silence: A magnetoencephalographic study. *NeuroReport, 12*(6), 1097–1102.

Hughes, H.C., Darcey, T.M., Barkan, H.I., Williamson, P.D., Roberts, D.W., & Aslin, C.H. (2001). Responses of human auditory association cortex to the omission of an expected acoustic event. *NeuroImage, 13,* 1073–1089.

King, A.J. (2006). Auditory neuroscience: Activating the cortex without sound. *Current Biology, 16*(11), 410–411.

Kraemer, D.J.M., Macrae, C.N., Green, A.E., & Kelley, W.M. (2005). Musical imagery: Sound of silence activates auditory cortex. *Nature, 434*(7030), 158.

Nishimoto, S., Vu, A.T., Naselaris, T., Benjamini, Y., Yu, B., & Gallant, J.L. (2011). Reconstructing visual experiences from brain activity evoked by natural movies. *Current Biology, 21,* 1641–1646.

Nudds, M. & O'Callaghan, C. (Eds.). (2009). *Sounds & Perception.* Oxford: Oxford University Press.

O'Callaghan, C. (2009). Sounds and events. In M. Nudds and C. O'Callaghan (Eds.), *Sounds & Perception* (pp. 26–49). Oxford: Oxford University Press.

Pasley, B.N., David, S.V., Mesgarani, N., Flinker, A., Shamma, S.A., & Crone, N.E., et al. (2012). Reconstructing speech from human auditory cortex. *PLoS Biology, 10*(1).

Pasnau, R. (1999). What is sound? *The Philosophical Quarterly, 49*(196), 309–324.

Patel, A.D., Iversen, J.R., Bregman, M.R., & Shulz, I. (2009). Studying synchronization to a musical beat in nonhuman animals. *The Neurosciences and Music III—Disorders and Plasticity: Annals of the New York Academy of Sciences,* 459–469.

Pinch, T., & Bijsterveld, K. (2004). Sound studies: New technologies and music. *Social Studies of Science, 34*(5), 635–648.

Pinch, T., & Bijsterveld, K. (2012). New keys to the world of science. In T. Pinch and K. Bijsterveld (Eds.), *The Oxford Handbook of Sound Studies* (pp. 3–35). New York, NY: Oxford University Press.

Riddoch, M. (2012, September 9–14). *On the Non-Cochlearity of the Sounds Themselves.* Paper presented at International Computer Music Conference.

Scruton, R. (2009). Sounds as secondary objects and pure events. In M. Nudds and C. O'Callaghan (Eds.), *Sounds & Perception* (pp. 50–68). Oxford: Oxford University Press.

Sterne, J., ed. (2012). *The Sound Studies Reader,* New York: Routledge.

Thompson, J., Casey, M., & Torresani, L. (2013, December 9–10). *Audio stimulus reconstruction using multi-source semantic embedding.* Unpublished poster presented at *Neural Information Processing Systems workshop on Machine Learning and Interpretation in Neuroimaging,* Lake Tahoe, USA.

Unnikrishnan, C.S. (2005). On the gravitational deflection of light and particles. *Current Science, 88*(7), 1155–1159.

Walther-Hansen, M. & Grimshaw, M. (2016, October 4–6). Being in a Virtual World: Presence, Environment, Salience, Sound. In *Proceedings of the 11th Audio Mostly Conference.*

Warren, D.H., Welch, R.B., & McCarthy, T.J. (1981). The role of visual-auditory "compellingness" in the ventriloquism effect: Implications for transitivity among the spatial senses. *Perception & Psychophysics, 30*(6), 557–564.

Wilson, M. (2002). Six views of embodied cognition. *Psychonomic Bulletin & Review, 9*(4), 625–636.

3

EMBODIMENT AND THE SENSES

David Howes

The four cases presented below highlight some of the many issues raised by foregrounding sound and the power of hearing as both object of study and means of inquiry – a theoretical and methodological move which has been integral to the "sensory turn" in the humanities and social sciences. The sensory turn, which commenced in the 1990s, may be seen as an outgrowth of the corporeal turn of the 1980s, when "embodiment" emerged as a paradigm for research in the human sciences (Csordas 1990; Bynum 1995). More on this presently.

The anthropologist Paul Stoller recounts an incident from his fieldwork among the Songhay people of Niger, where he apprenticed himself to a healer. The healer had been called to the bed of a sick man who was the victim of a curse. The healer determined that a sorcerer had taken possession of the man's double and was slowly devouring him from within. To prevent the man from dying, the healer had to find and liberate the patient's double. He prepared a remedy to be applied to the man's joints and sensory orifices, then led Stoller on a search that took them to the edge of the village. They came to the crest of a dune where there was a large pile of millet seed husk. The healer bent to sift through the pile, then abruptly stood up and cried out "Wo, wo, wo, wo …" He asked Stoller:

> "Did you hear it?"
> "Hear what?" I asked dumbfounded.
> "Did you feel it?"
> "Feel what?" I wondered.
> "Did you see it?"
> "What are you talking about?" I demanded.

The healer then enjoined him: "You look but you do not see. You touch, but you do not feel. You listen but you do not hear. Without sight or touch … one can learn a great deal. But you must learn how to *hear* or you will learn little about our ways" (Stoller 1989: 115).

Among the Suyà (also known as the Kisêdjê) people of the Mato Grosso region of Brazil, boys and girls are fitted with ear-discs upon reaching puberty. In addition to the ear-discs, adult men are permitted to wear lip-discs. These adornments, or extensions of the ear and mouth, symbolize the importance attached to "hearing well" and speaking as well as singing clearly. The largest lip-discs are reserved for the chiefs and this reflects their preogative to engage in "everybody listen talk" or "plaza speech" during the communal rituals which take place at night. The figure of the chief contrasts with that of the witch. Witches are distinguished by their tendency to mumble (or "perverted speech"), their poor hearing (which explains their anti-social ways) and their extraordinary vision which enables them to "see things" that are invisible to the eyes of more cultured individuals. The sensory profile of the chief also contrasts with that of women. Suyà women do not wear lip-discs (only ear-discs), and their principal role at Suyà feasts is "as audience and suppliers of food rather than as singers" (Seeger 1975: 215).

In early China (the China of the Warring States Period, 475–221 BCE), the senses were typically classified in a fivefold manner, much as in ancient Greece (Vinge 2009). However, there was some diversity of opinion as to which bodily organs counted as senses. Most lists include the eyes, ears, mouth, nose and body (or form), but some iterations leave out one or other of these body parts, while others continue with, for example, "trust, awe and peace" (that is emotions).

Significantly, in view of the highly bureaucratic nature of Chinese court society, the most common model of the sensorium depicted the five senses as five "officials" with the "heart-mind" (xin) as their ruler.

> Ear, eye, nose, mouth, and form, each has its own contacts [lit. "receptions" or "meetings"] and does not do things for the others. Now, these are called the heavenly officials. The heartmind dwells in the central cavity and governs the five officials. Now this is called the heavenly ruler.
>
> *(Xunzi quoted in Geaney 2002: 19)*

The idea here is that the senses are intelligencers of the ruler, with priority attached to the offices of hearing and sight. Interestingly, one way in which a ruler would gauge the state of his realm was by summoning musicians from each of its territories and checking whether their instruments (as well as local folk songs) were attuned to the five notes of the Chinese musical scale. If all of the provincial orchestras and songs were in tune (according to the ruler's ear), there would be harmony; if not, there was danger of discord (Tame 1984: 15–16).

The power of music as a medium for rulers to gauge the state of the realm, or express and wield power, is further attested by the following excerpt from the "Record of Music" (*Yueji*) in the *Book of Rites*:

> So it is that when [proper] music is in place then logic is clear, the ears and eyes are perspicacious and acute, blood and material force *(qi)* attain harmony and equilibrium, cultural environments and customs change [gradually], and all under heaven is tranquil.
>
> *(quoted in Brindley 2006: 1)*

Finally, an English play from the early seventeenth century gives an amusing insight into the ex-centricity of the senses, or conflict of the faculties, in the early modern period. It is entitled *Lingua, or the Combat of the Tongue, and the Five Senses for Superiority* (Tomkis 1607). The play (a comedy) begins with the outsider persona of Ladie Lingua (the tongue and faculty of language) protesting that she is no less worthy than the five senses and should be included in their circle. She trickily sparks dissension within the ranks of the pentarchy by concealing a robe and crown for the five to discover and fight over. The sensorium quickly breaks down into warring sense organs, each proclaiming its own importance as the most worthy of the senses. Common Sense steps in to umpire the debate, commanding each sense to "present their objects" and arguments for why they should be considered the most worthy. Olfactus presents the pleasing smell of flowers, but in counterargument it is observed that every good smell has its contrary, and in any event "he smelleth best that doth of nothing smell." Tactus proffers the hand, "the instrument of instruments," and further argues that his skinfulness is "the eldest, and biggest of all the rest." His *coup de grace* is to assert

> Tell me what sense is not beholding to me;
> The nose is hot or cold, the eyes do weep;
> The ears do feel, the taste a kind of touching,
> That when I please, I can command them all,
> And make them tremble when I threaten them.
> (Tomkis n.p.)

Tactus's argument is later undone when the others conspire to tickle him. And so it goes with each of the senses: that is, each sense plays up his most distinctive, only to be humbled by his peers. How did the dispute end? What did Common Sense decide? The answer is best left to a later point in this essay when we are in a better position to appreciate the intricacies of the judgment of Common Sense.

There are four major implications I would like to draw from a consideration of these cases. The first has to do with the discrimination or individuation of the senses. Different cultures divide the senses differently and the bounds of sense cannot be assumed in advance. Which senses are counted, and what counts as a sense (for example emotions as well as perceptions in some cases, or speech as well as hearing) is contingent on culture and history. Even the conventional (Western) distinction between cognition and perception, or mind and the senses, can be elided (for example in Buddhism the mind is regarded as a sense on a par with the other five). This underscores the importance of focussing on the relations *between* the senses, rather than analysing them individually, one-at-a-time (for example Goldstein 2004), and has implications for the very definition of "sound studies" or "auditory culture" (we use the terms interchangeably). Sound studies must be seen as a branch of sensory studies, which treats the sensorium *as a whole* as its object of study.

Second, each culture should be approached on its own sensory terms. This entails attending to its sensory priorities and developing an awareness of the culture's own techniques of perception or "ways of sensing" (Howes and Classen 2013). Put another way, the senses are made, not given; perception is a cultural act, not simply a psychophysical phenomenon. The cultural modulation of perception is apparent in Stoller's bewilderment at how the Songhay healer used his senses. Stoller lacked the requisite technique to hear the sound of the patient's double being released. It is also manifest in the different models of the sensorium which different cultures embrace, whether it be the five officials of early Chinese epistemology, or the bestiary of the senses in medieval Christianity – which regarded the eagle as an emblem of sight, the spider of touch and so on (Classen 1998), or the "computational" theory of vision and the other senses that prevails today (Nudds 2014).

Third, sensory values are social values, and how the senses are conditioned is intimately tied to the condition of different groups within society. For example, the condition of women and the condition of witches in Suyà society reflects the differential moral value and development of the senses of hearing, speech or singing and sight (women listen but do not sing; the witch's vision is overdeveloped, their hearing and speech underdeveloped). The ear- and lip-discs worn by the Suyà socialize the senses. They are constant reminders of the moral value attached to hearing and speaking/singing. Significantly, the Suyà term *m-ba*, "to hear" also means "to understand." The centrality of aurality to Suyà epistemology and ceremonial life led their ethnographer to propose that: "the Suyà village [with its central plaza and huts arranged in a circle] can be likened to a concert hall, its annual round equated with a concert series" (Seeger 1987: 65). Singing, according to Seeger, created "a certain kind of settlement, in which sounds revealed what vision could not penetrate": it coordinated collective action, mediated gender relations and imprinted its structure on the experience of space, time and personhood (ibid. 140).

Fourth, while the senses complement each other and normally work in concert, they may also conflict. On a quotidian level, this is evidenced by the way a stick in water may look crooked to the eye but feel straight to the touch. On a ritual level, the Suyà practice of staging their ceremonies at night has the effect of accentuating the role of the 'other' senses, most notably hearing and speaking/singing, relative to sight. On an epistemological level, it is exemplified by the personification of the senses in Lingua and their "combat" for superiority. One way of summing up the foregoing discussion would be to say that the sense of the senses is in their use, that perception is best understood in terms of performance rather than psychophysics.

The suggestion that perception is best understood as performance might seem to bring the approach advocated here into line with the position of Tim Ingold, who insists that perception is a "skill" (Ingold 2000). Ingold has emerged as a dominant voice within sensory anthropology, and has attracted numerous disciples (for example Hsu 2008; Pink, in Pink and Howes 2010) ever since publishing a scathing (if unfounded) critique of the anthropology of the senses in *The Perception of the Environment* (Ingold 2000: chs. 9, 14), which drummed out the voices of a host of earlier theorists and ethnographers, including Edmund Carpenter (1973), Marshall McLuhan (1964), Paul Stoller (1989), Anthony Seeger (1975, 1987), Constance Classen (1993), Steven Feld (1982) and Alfred Gell (1995), as well as the present writer (Howes 1991). Ingold dismisses the contribution of these "sensuous scholars" (Stoller 1997) because their accounts of the senses fail to cohere with the dictates of the "phenomenology of perception" according to Maurice Merleau-Ponty, which insists on the subjectivity of perception and "prereflective unity" of the senses, and the "ecological psychology" of J.J. Gibson, which treats the senses as "perceptual systems" and limits their operation to picking up on the pre-given "affordances" of the environment.

In an oft-cited article entitled "Against Soundscape," Ingold goes further and in one fell swipe dismisses the whole (interdisciplinary) field of sound studies (insofar as it is predicated on R. Murray Schafer's concept of the soundscape) and visual culture (insofar as it is primarily focussed on the interpretation of images). He argues that sound "is not the object but the medium of our perception. It is what we hear *in*. Similarly, we do not see light but see *in* it. … [e.g.] When we look around on a fine day, we see a landscape bathed in sunlight, not a lightscape" (Ingold 2007: 11). It is all so simple the way Ingold puts it. Too simple actually.

What is missing from Ingold's account is any sense of the social organization of the senses and perception. This is because he prides himself on being a post-social anthroplogist. The social is dissolved into "a field of relations," and Ingold insists that "relations among humans, which we are accustomed to calling 'social', are but a subset of ecological relations" (Ingold 2000: 5). His work starts "from the premise that every living being is a particular nexus of growth and development within a field of relations. Skills of perception and action indeed emerge within these processes of ontogenetic development" (Ingold, in Ingold and Howes 2011: 314). Ontogeny is not only privileged over phylogeny on this account, it is all there is. Indeed Ingold's focus on the individual obliterates any sense of the social just as his preoccupation with "activity" prevents him from paying much, if any, attention to structure (never mind reflection). As discussed elsewhere, Ingold's idea of "the environment" is equally impoverished, from a sensorial perspective: his environment is "one in which you can look, listen, and are always on the move, but not taste or smell" (Howes 2005).[1]

The crux of Ingold's argument is that hearing involves "an experience of sound" and seeing involves "an experience of light" *tout court*. A poke in the eye belies this argument, since it causes one to "see stars" independent of any light source. (The equivalent experience in the auditory realm would be feeling infrasonic vibrations.) However, even if one did accept Ingold's premise, the fact is that the experience of light (and shadow and darkness, I would add) is conditioned by culture, and imbued with social values. For example, there is the premium attached to *hygge* (a warm, cozy light) in Danish society (Bille and Sørensen 2007), the value attached to "shimmering" light in Australian aboriginal cultures (Deger 2007) or the salience ascribed to shadows in Japanese culture (Tanizaki 1977). None of these instances of the cultural construction of light in different traditions matter to Ingold because his approach is purely psychophysical. A further problem has to do with his insistence on the "prereflective unity" and "interchangeability" of the senses (following Gibson and Merleau-Ponty). Indeed, Ingold posits that vision, understood as "a mode of active, exploratory engagement with the environment ... has much more in common with audition than is often supposed, and for that matter also with gustation and olfaction" (Ingold, in Ingold and Howes 2011: 314; Ingold 2000: ch. 14). However, it is only in the most abstract (and uninteresting) sense that this proposition is true. Of course all the senses are "active, exploratory modes of engagement with the environment." This even goes without saying. The real question is *how*, and that is where the cultural conditioning of the senses intervenes.

Let me flesh out what is meant here by "the cultural conditioning of the senses" by drawing on my research in Papua New Guinea. Among the Kwoma of the Middle Sepik River region of Papua New Guinea, social status is the precondition of what and how far one can see. Each year, in the context of the yam harvest ceremony, the initiated men stage a ritual which involves them making a stupendous din with various instruments (the sacred flutes, bullroarers, etc.) within the screened-off confines of the men's house. The sounds produced are said to be the voices of the spirits. Women and uninitiated men, who hear these sounds from the other side of the screen, believe their ears and are frightened of the spirits whereas the men inside know the secret of the sounds' human origins because they alone are able to see as well as hear. If this secret were exposed it would undermine the men's authority as the guardians of the spirits and sole intercessors with the supernatural. The mens' anxieties as regards the bases of their authority is expressed in a myth which relates how the women were the ones who first discovered the flutes and kept knowledge of them from the men. They kept the flutes in a tree-house and commanded the men to bring them food while they played on and on – until the day the men, tired of being abused by the women, by an act of treachery, toppled the tree-house and seized the flutes. The men have lorded their control of the means of communication with the spirits over the rest of society ever since. (The women are now the ones who must prepare food and bring it to the men ensconced in their men's house.) Here we see a situation where it is precisely the split between seeing and hearing, and the non-interchangeability of these two sensory registers, that undergrirds the structure of Kwoma society (Howes 2003: ch. 5).

Consideration of the Kwoma case suggests that, contrary to Ingold, what a properly sensory anthropology calls for is *more reflexivity*, not less; more attention to relations of *intersensoriality*, not (some putative) unity or interchangeability; and, above all, more awareness of the *indissociability* of the social and the sensible (Laplantine 2015), not just "the environment" or "landscape." In his critique of soundscape, Ingold makes much of what he calls the "prototypical concept of landscape." This concept commends itself to his way of thinking because "it is not tied to any specific sensory register – whether vision, hearing, touch, smell or whatever. In ordinary perceptual practice these registers cooperate so closely, and with such overlap of function, that their respective contributions are impossible to tease apart" (Ingold 2007: 10). In point of fact, the concept of landscape is a product of a particular painterly style (the so-called picturesque) which originated in the eighteenth century. It is not "prototypical." Rather it is thoroughly historical and ineluctably beholden to sight. This is precisely what inspired Schafer and others to embrace the concept of soundscape as an antidote to the visualism of the idea of landscape, and use it as a means to open up other sensory dimensions of the environment for investigation.

Probing deeper, we can see how Ingold's inability to "tease apart" the respective contributions of the senses (an "impossibility" which he projects onto all humanity) is an effect, an artifact, of his prior *abstraction* of the operation of the senses from their embeddedness – or *emplacement* – in a given social context. For example, the Kwoma do discern and enforce a separation between vision and hearing in certain ritual contexts (i.e. the yam ceremony). Or again, when Ingold affirms: "I *am*, at once, my tasting, my listening, and so forth" (Ingold, in Ingold and Howes 2011: 321), he is legislating for all humanity again, without the least trace of any reflexivity as to the particularity of his own experience. There exist other subject positions (for example that of women), but Ingold is too self-centred to recognize this.

Ingold's abstract, purely psychophysical, radically individualist, post-social approach to the study of the senses and perception is not a sensible paradigm for research. Compare Constance Classen's position in "Foundations for an Anthropology of the Senses," which is attuned to sensory diversity both across and within cultures. She writes:

> When we examine the meanings associated with various sensory faculties and sensations in different cultures, we discover a cornucopia of potent sensory symbolism. Sight may be linked to reason or to witchcraft, taste may be used as a metaphor for aesthetic discrimination or for sexual experience, an odour may signify sanctity or sin, political power or social exclusion. Together, these sensory meanings and values form the *sensory model* espoused by a society, according to which the members of that society "make sense" of the world, or translate sensory perceptions and concepts into a particular "worldview." There will likely be challenges to this model from within the society, persons and groups who differ on certain sensory values, yet this model will provide the basic perceptual paradigm to be followed or resisted.
>
> *(Classen 1997: 402)*

Following Classen, we come to see how the senses are constructed and lived differently in different societies, giving rise to different models – and the practices which support them. Such models frequently have a cosmological dimension, according to Classen (1998), which leads her to speak of "sensory cosmologies" (rather than "worldviews"). By way of example, in the early modern period, in a pattern that had its roots in ancient Greece (Vinge 2009), each of the senses was held to operate through a different medium or element. In *Lingua*, for example, the chief reason for dismissing Ladie Lingua's petition to be counted a sense was that this would go against the fivefold division of the cosmos, or elementary structure of the universe:

> The number of the *Senses* in this little world is answerable to the first bodies in the great world: now since there be but five in the Universe, the four elements and the pure substance of the heavens [i.e. the aether], therefore there can be but five Senses in our *Microcosm*, correspondent to those, as the sight to the heavens, hearing to the air, touching to the earth, smelling to the fire, tasting to the water; by which five means only the understanding is able to apprehend the knowledge of all corporal substances.

On this account, the medium of hearing is air (not sound), earth is the medium of touch, fire of smell, water of taste and the aether (not light) is the medium of sight. The composition of the body and senses manifests the same multimodal, quintessential structure as the composition of the universe. (This elemental understanding of perception would be lost on Ingold, who blindly cleaves to his own ontology.) It follows that the senses act outwardly through their "correspond-ing" medium or element. This extramissive understanding of how the senses function is the inverse of the intromissive or mentalist ideology of same that dates from the seventeenth century and was first and most forcibly articulated by John Locke (see Howes and Classen 2013: vh.6).

This idea of sensory "correspondence" was also foundational to the epistemology and ritual life of early China. According to the "Theory of the Five Elements" (or "Evolutive Phases"), each of the principal elements of Fire, Wood, Earth, Metal and Water corresponded to a different musical note, colour, odour, taste, season and direction. For example, the musical note *chih* and colour red, a smoky scent, bitter taste, season of summer and direction of south all corresponded to the element of Fire. These correspondences inflected all aspects of daily life – from diet to colour of apparel, and from the perfumes that were worn to the orientation of living space in different seasons – in the Emperor's court (itself a microcosm of the universe). Great importance was attached to maintaining the proper relations between sensations, and this was tied to main-taining the proper relations between persons.

> Heaven and Earth have their patterns, and people take these for their patterns ... [Among these patterns are] the five tastes, manifested in five colors and displayed in the five notes. When these are in excess, there ensue obscurity and confusion, and people lose their nature. That is why they were made to support that nature...There were ruler and minister, high and low ...There were husband and wife ... There were father and son, elder and younger brother...
>
> *(cited by Wang 2000: 184)*

As this quote makes clear, sensory relations were mapped onto social relations. "Thinking and living according to the established pattern of cross-modal associations provided a potent model for the maintenance of orderly and interdependent relationships within society" (Howes and Classen 2013: 163–4).

Ingold's "ecological psychology" may be faulted not only for its inattention to the sociology and cosmology of sensation, but also for its failure to theorize the mediumship of the senses. He treats auditory perception as "an experience of sound" and visual perception as "an expe-rience of light" without regard to how these experiences are modulated by cultural schemas. Consider Renaissance painting. True, without light one could not see a painting, but more to the point is how a painting structures perception. In *Ways of Seeing*, John Berger convincingly argues that the technique of linear perspective, which emerged during the Rernaissance, and which centres everything in the eye of the spectator, contributed to the growth of individu-alism. "The visible world is arranged for the spectator as the universe was once thought to be arranged for God" (Berger 1972: 16). The spectator became the unique centre, and this had the effect of prying the individual loose from the hierarchized, communal structure of the medieval social order.

Ingold is dismissive of readings such as Berger's:

> We should not be fooled by art historians and other students of visual culture who write books about the history of seeing that are entirely about the contemplation of images [with no mention of light]. Their conceit is to imagine the eyes are not so much organs of observation as instruments of playback, lodged in the image rather than the body of the observer. It is as though the eyes did our seeing for us, leaving us to (re)view the images they relay to our consciousness.
>
> *(Ingold 2007: 10)*

Ingold's rejection of media studies (visual, auditory, etc.) here prevents him from seeing how media, such as painting, which are best viewed as "extensions of the senses" (following McLuhan 1964) *modulate* the perception of the social and physical environment. In place of Ingold's theory of the transparency of light and psychophysics of sight, we need a theory of the *mediatory* role of media, which is precisely what the field of sound studies and visual culture have to offer. We become what (and, more importantly, how) we behold, to rejig the old adage.

McLuhan's media-centric theory of perception is a far more sensible approach than Ingold's, though it too has its problems. For example, its technological determinism, its essentialist construction of the senses,[2] its bipolarism (as if everything turned on whether the ear or eye is the dominant modality). Contrary to McLuhan's "Great Divide" theory of the differences between oral (read: aural) and literate (read: visual) mentalities and societies, it has been shown that there is as much sensory diversity within the category of "oral societies" as there is between oral societies and literate societies (Classen 1993). This is why we prefer the concept of "ways of sensing," with its emphasis on cultural practice, to McLuhan's media-driven concept of the "sense-ratio" (Howes and Classen 2013).

One point on which we must nevertheless agree with Ingold in his diatribe against the art historians is his critique of their exclusive focus on visual images. A more relational, intersensorial approach, attuned to practice and context, is called for, even when it comes to the interpretation of a painting. For example, it has recently come to light that paintings were sung to in the Renaissance. The singing was integral to the experience of viewing (Stowell 2016). It is important to attend to these patterns and practices of intersensoriality if we are to arrive at an understanding of the "period sensorium" (see further Classen 2017). Most studies stop at the "period eye."

The same critique could be levelled at sound studies. Its exclusive focus on sound may prove counterproductive. In *Sensing Sound: Singing and Listening as Vibrational Practice* (2015), Nina Sun Eidsheim exposes the limitations of the paradigm of music as sound by rethinking music as a "practice of vibration." She was brought to this position by studying the vocal performance of Juliana Snapper, the underwater opera singer. Snapper's practice sparked in Eidsheim a shift in focus from pre-fixed definition to issues of transmission, transduction and transformation. In *Eye h(Ear): The Visual in Music* (2013), Simon Shaw-Miller relates how the modernist embrace of "absolute music," conceived as "pure sound," actually had the effect of interpellating the visual in countless complex ways (from the centrality of the score and musical notation to the site (and sight) of the concert hall which took the place of the concert hall or tavern). His aim is "to claim music for art historians" (of all people!). In both these works, music is reconceptualized as intersensorial practice.

In this essay, the emphasis has been on arriving at an understanding of sensory diversity in history and across cultures. But there is also intra-cultural diversity, or the question of subaltern sensoria, as when Classen cautions: "There will likely be challenges to [the sensory model] from within the society, persons and groups who differ on certain sensory values, yet this model will provide the basic perceptual paradigm to be followed or resisted" (Classen 1997: 402). What of women's senses, for example? The reader will no doubt have noticed that both among the Suyà of Brazil and the Kwoma of Papua New Guinea, women's sensory role seems limited to listening and preparing food for the men. Is that it? The Suyà ethnography is silent on this score, and the Kwoma ethnographic record is not much better. However, I can offer a few precisions regarding how the division of the senses and the division of the sexes intersect. One thing that struck me during my fieldwork among the Kwoma is that women had elaborated their powers of touch to a remarkable degree through their continuous production of net bags (billum). This female hypertactility (or feminine dexterity) stands in contrast to how men control the aural universe through their mastery of the flutes and other instruments, and also control the visual universe through their production of paintings and sculptures. In effect, the sensory model of Kwoma society is structured on a visual scaffolding (through the use of screens). It is a highly exclusionary, fractured society, with little or no transparency, only enmity between the nine autonomous villages which make it up. Significantly, women must move to the village of their husband upon marriage, while the men stay put. Through marrying out the women, the women literally weave the society (such as it is) together. This profoundly social fact is also reflected in the weave of the netbags they produce and gift to their husbands and brothers. The male gaze divides and fractures, the female touch integrates. Women's skill at weaving complements the men's skill at painting, and it is the interrelationshp of the two socially distinct skill sets that constitutes the fabric of Kwoma society (Howes 2003: ch. 5).

Ladie Lingua's petition in the court of Common Sense presents another example of what Classen calls resistance to the sensory model. The five senses in *Lingua* are all male, she is the only female, so this battle of the senses was also a battle of the sexes. She stated her case well (as one would expect of the tongue). For example, she points out that she alone is able to represent things which are not present, only to be called out by the others for her propensity to prevaricate. In the end, Common Sense (in a very tactical move) awarded the crown to Visus and the robe to Tactus (as representatives of Commoditie or "well-being" and Necessity respectively), while distributing consolation prizes to the other three senses. Common Sense goes on to invoke the argument from design (that is the quintessential structure of the universe) to scuttle Ladie Lingua's position, and concludes: "wherefore we judge you to be no *Sense* simply; onely thus much we from henceforth pronounce, that all women for your sake, shall have six *Senses,* seeing, hearing, tasting, smelling, touching, and the last and feminine sense, the sense of speaking." (It is apparent from other references that what Common Senses means by "speaking" is really only chattering or prattling.) Ladie Lingua is nonplussed at being dubbed "half a sense" and seeks retaliation by drugging the five senses, but her plot is foiled. It seems that a sixth (that is a supernumerary) sense is the best the second sex can expect, until a female playwright comes along and rewrites the script.[3]

At the beginning of this essay it was noted that the sensory turn of the 1990s could be seen as an outgrowth of the corporeal turn of the 1980s, when "embodiment" emerged as a paradigm for research. Some further clarification is necessary by way of closing. The embodiment paradigm sought to overcome the longstanding split between body and mind in the Western tradition, and gave rise to such concepts as the "mindful body" and "embodied mind." This stress on unity or integration proved to be a bit much, and accordingly fractured as the sensory turn unfolded and shifted attention to analysing the relations *between* the senses (relations which are not always harmonious, and can be oppositional). The sensory turn also introduced more complexity and reflexivity into the conversation by taking media as "extensions of the senses" seriously and by introducing the notion of "emplacement," or "the sensuous interrelationship of body-mind-environment" (Howes 2005: 7). The point is that perception can only meaningfully be studied in context – that is, in some environment (a point which the embodiment paradigm tends to overlook), and that the senses "mingle" with the world (Serres 1985). Perception does not simply go on in the head. Rather, "the perceptual is *cultural and political*" (Bull et al. 2006), and the meaning or import of the senses is in their use.

Acknowledgments

This essay is a product of an ongoing program of research sponsored by the Social Sciences and Humanities Research Council of Canada and the Fonds de Recherche du Québec – Société et Culture.

Notes

1 Ingold is an action man, not an ideas man. Indeed, he scorns any suggestion that there is an ideational component or "prior design" to the production of artifacts (see Ingold 2007). This is why we say there is no room for reflection in his "activity theory" (as it is sometimes called). Other absences include how there is no reference to gender, class or race (all staple topics in *social* anthropology) in *The Perception of the Environment*, just as there is no mention of taste or smell or texture. His book would be more accurately called *The Misperception of the Environment*. It is a testimony to the poverty of phenomenology (see Howes and Classen 2013).
2 That is to say, McLuhan attributes certain intrinsic qualities to sound and "acoustic space," but they remain just that, attributions. They are variable, not essential, across cultures. McLuhan's ideas about sound were of a piece with those of the hip culture of his day (see Ford 2013).
3 Actually, already in the seventeenth century, there was such a playwright, Margaret Cavendish, who penned many other works as well (see Classen 1998: ch. 4).

References

Berger, John. 1972. *Ways of Seeing*. London: BBC Books.

Bille, M. & Sørensen, T. F. 2007, "An Anthropology of Luminosity. The Agency of Light," *Journal of Material Culture*, 12(3): 263–284.

Brindley, Erica. 2006. "Music, Cosmos and the Development of Psychology in Early China," *T'oung Pao*, 92: 1–49.

Bull, Michael et al. 2006. "Introducing Sensory Studies," *The Senses and Society* 1(1): 5–7.

Bynum, Caroline 1995. "Why All the Fuss About the Body? A Medievalist's Perspective," *Critical Inquiry*, 22(1): 1–33.

Carpenter, Edmund. 1973. *Eskimo Realities*. New York: Holt, Rinehart and Winston.

Classen, Constance. 1993. *Worlds of Sense: Exploring the Senses in History and Across Cultures*. London and New York: Routledge.

_____. 1997. "Foundations for an Anthropology of the Senses," *International Social Science Journal*, 153: 401–412.

_____. 1998. *The Color of Angels: Cosmology, Gender and the Aesthetic Imagination*. London and New York: Routledge.

_____. 2017. *The Museum of the Senses: Experiencing Art and Collections*. London and New York: Bloomsbury.

Csordas, Thomas. 1990. "Embodiment as a Paradigm for Anthropology," *Ethos*, 18(1): 5–47.

Deger, Jennifer. 2007. *Shimmering Screens: Making Media in an Aboriginal Community*. Minneapolis, MN: University of Minnesota Press.

Eidsheim, Nina Sun. 2015. *Sensing Sound: Singing and Listening as Vibrational Practice*. Durham, NC: Duke University Press.

Feld, Steven. 1982. *Sound and Sentiment: Birds, Weeping, Poetics, and Song in Kaluli Expression*. Philadelphia, PA: University of Pennsylvania Press.

Ford, Phil. 2013. *Dig: Sound and Music in Hip Culture*. New York: Oxford University Press.

Geaney, Jane 2002. *On the Epistemology of the Senses in Early Chinese Thought*. Honolulu: University of Hawaii Press.

Gell, Alfred. 1995. "The Language of the Forest: Language and Phonological Iconism in Umeda." In E. Hirsch and Michael O'Hanlon, eds., *The Anthropology of Landscape*. Oxford: Clarendon, 232–254.

Goldstein. E. Bruce. 2004. Sensation and Perception. Belmont: Wadsworth Publishing.

Howes, David. ed. 1991. *The Varieties of Sensory Experience: A Sourcebook in the Anthropology of the Senses*. Toronto: University of Toronto Press.

_____ 2003. *Sensual Relations: Engaging the Senses in Culture and Social Theory*. Ann Arbor, MI: University of Michigan Press.

_____ ed., 2005. *Empire of the Senses: The Sensual Culture Reader*. Oxford: Berg.

Howes, David and Classen, Constance. 2013. *Ways of Sensing: Understanding the Senses in Society*. London: Routledge.

Hsu, Elizabeth. 2008. "The Senses and the Social: An Introduction," *Ethnos*, 73(3): 433–443.

Ingold, Tim. 2000. *The Perception of the Environment: Essays on Dwelling, Livelihood and Skill*. London: Routledge.

_____. 2007. "Against Soundscape." In A. Carlyle, ed., *Autumn Leaves*, Double Entendre: Paris, 10–13.

Ingold, Tim and Howes, David. 2011. "Worlds of Sense and Sensing the World: A Reply to Sarah Pink and David Howes," *Social Anthropology*, 19(3): 313–331.

Laplantine, François. 2015. *The Life of the Senses: Introduction to a Modal Anthropology*, trans. Jamie Furniss. London: Bloomsbury.

McLuhan, Marshall. 1964. *Understanding Media: The Extensions of Man*. New York, NY: New American Library.

Nudds, Matthew. 2014. "The Senses in Philosophy and Science: From Sensation to Computation." In David Howes, ed. *A Cultural History of the Senses in the Moderrn Age, 1920–2000*. London and New York: Bloomsbury.

Pink, Sarah and Howes, David. 2010. "The Future of Sensory Anthropology/The Anthropology of the Senses," *Social Anthropology*, 18(3): 331–340.

Seeger, Anthony. 1975. "The Meaning of Body Ornaments: A Suya Example," *Ethnology*, 14: 211–224

———. 1987 *Why Suyà Sing: A Musical Anthropoogy of an Amazonian People*. Cambridge: Cambridge University Press.

Serres, Michel. 1985. *Les cinq sens*. Paris: Flammarion.

Shaw-Miller, Simon. 2013. *In Eye h(Ear): The Visual in Music*. Farnham: Ashgate.

Stoller, Paul. 1989. *The Taste of Ethnographic Things: The Senses in Anthropology*. Philadelphia, PA: University of Pennsylvania Press.

———. 1997. *Sensuous Scholarship*. Philadephia, PA: University of Pennsylvania Press.

Stowell, Steven. 2016. *The Spiritual Language of Art: Medieval Christian Themes in Writing on Art of the Italian Renaissance*. Den Haag: Brill.

Tame, David. 1984. *The Secret Power of Music*. Rochester, VT: Destiny Books.

Tanizaki, Jun'ichirō. 1977. *In Praise of Shadows*. New York, NY: Leete's Island Books.

Tomkis, Thomas. 1607. *Lingua, or the Combat of the Tongue, and the Five Senses for Superiority*. Ann Arbor, MI: Early English Books On-Line. http://quod.lib.umich.edu/e/eebo/A62894.0001.001?view=toc [accessed 1 September 2016].

Vinge, Louise. 2009. The Five Senses in Classical Philosophy and Science. In David Howes, ed., *The Sixth Sense Reader*. Oxford: Berg.

Wang, A. 2000. *Cosmology and Political Order in Early China*. Cambridge: Cambridge University Press.

4

MULTISENSORY INVESTIGATION OF SOUND, BODY, AND VOICE

Nina Sun Eidsheim

Introduction

In colloquial terms, western thought and language tend to treat the sound of the voice, the material voice, and what the voice produces as the same. As classicist Shane Butler notes, these ambiguities can be traced back to at least as early as ancient discussions of the *phōnē* and *vox*, the two principal Greek and Latin words for "voice."[1] This chapter addresses two problems associated with these ambiguities which have consequently shaped sensorial experience and understanding to align with these and related phenomena. First, academia is splintered into areas of specialization. As Tomie Hahn has pointed out, research has historically been divided by the senses: to bring out the differences, we can note that ethnomusicologists, for instance, observe through listening; dance scholars specialize in physical and tactile inquiry; and musicologists observe through reading manuscripts.[2] Because each field builds not only on the premise of an artificially separated segment of a rich phenomenon but also on the inherent diffuseness of definitions, each discrete area of research is limited in its efforts to capture the phenomenon at hand. Second, both scholarly investigation and everyday experience of most phenomena are built upon a naturalized cultural and social sensorial framework, and this framework separates the senses. It is through these imprecise perspectives that processes of knowledge creation are set into motion and subsequently become established. And, it is such an iterative process that has defined these scholarly fields for themselves and in opposition to one another.

In this chapter, then, I will offer a discussion of the ways in which the cultural and socio- sensorial framework creates and inadvertently sets limits on knowledge development. I will posit that the limited frame of reference used to investigate voice and sound often artificially separates them from the body specifically and materiality generally. What is notable here is not only the initial separation itself, but also that the very separation and the subsequent field-specific process of inquiry confirm and reinforce this partition. In short, this separation prevents richer understanding of sound and voice as potentially distinct phenomena, and of their relationship to each other.

The three terms I discuss below—or, more precisely, the categories represented by each term—which relate to and, at times, co-create one another in their distinction and separation are sound, body, and voice. First, I discuss how each of these terms leads to a funnel of privileged methodologies that, as a direct result of the research methods selected, draws out each object's distinctions. This process of discernment takes place at the expense of identifying commonalities and convergences. Second, I also recognize that the observation which identifies any given category is created through a culturally constituted sensorium. This sensorium was formed as a result of attunement to particular concerns and values, and hence it has organized, privileged, highlighted, and muted certain aspects of experience and its conceptualization. Finally, I suggest a methodological starting point that can lead to an understanding of interconnectivity between the three phenomena, while also deepening a particular understanding of each phenomenon's multidimensionality. Thus, drawing on organizational behaviorist Justin M. Berg's work on creativity as well as examples of my own work, I make a case for methodological experimentation in inquiries into voice, sound, and body. Doing so, I suggest, leads not only to increased understanding of the interconnectivity between sound, body, and voice, but also to a deepening understanding of each object and concept. Ultimately, in the long view, such research can contribute incrementally to our understanding of how sound and voice each do what they do when they evoke emotion and meaning for people.

Sound, body, and voice definitions as "primal marks"

What kind of information do we access when we examine phenomena that are divided into sound, body, and voice? The premise of this chapter is that we access rich phenomena from a partial point of view, and, in our case, that the process through which this partial view comes into relief is determined by the definition of the phenomena into sound, body, or voice. In other words, investigation into the phenomenon is limited to an already partial point of observation and experience before the methods of inquiry have even been selected.

According to Berg's theory of the "primal mark"—that is, "the first bit of content [researchers] start with as they generate ideas, which anchors the trajectory of novelty and usefulness"— the imprint at the starting point is crucial. Indeed, in his formulation, "the beginning shapes the end in the development of ideas."[3] In his work on creative ideas, Berg has identified the challenge of developing ideas that are both "novel" and "useful." In other words, if an idea's novelty value is high, it is often not very useful. If a primal mark's usefulness factor is high, the ideas it generates are generally higher in usefulness than in novelty, and vice versa. Berg, however, suggests the process of mitigating potential tradeoffs between the novel and the useful by integrating familiar and new material (hence balancing the primal mark) and generating ideas that are both useful and novel.

Considering Berg's framework in relation to humanistic research, an inquiry based on the set pairing of a definition of the object—such as sound, body, or voice—and the scholarly fields and methodologies that are required by the definition of the object functions as a "primal mark." That is, in such a setting, the primary mark is first and foremost set by a given usefulness factor—for which, for our purposes, Berg's "familiarity" factor seems more appropriate. We can think about conventional pairings of defined objects and methodologies commonly used as familiar. Here, the primal mark is familiar through and through, and will most likely not yield a high novelty factor.

For me, the lack of the primal mark's novelty in this formula is encapsulated in the classic question: "If a tree falls in the forest and no one is there to hear it, does it make a sound?" A leading question which also defines the object at hand, it offers no room for novelty. While people generally pose this conundrum in order to raise issues about reality and observation, it is a closed-ended question and its premise is set by the socio-cultural separation of the sensorium into distinct phenomena that appeal to either audition, vision, tactility, olfaction, or taste. To adapt Clifford Geertz's terminology, the question moves without examination from a thick event (the falling of a tree) to the experience as relayed through a sensorium (audition). By offering a definition of the phenomenon, the question and its attendant assumed methodologies set up the inquiry's primal mark. As Berg proposes, "the final novelty and usefulness of ideas depends on the seeds that are planted near the very beginning of creative tasks," with the limiting seeds planted by the falling tree question confining our inquiry to its sonorous dimensions.[4]

Not only this particular philosophical question but, if we reflexively follow the conventions of a given field, research questions in general can foreclose the possibility of introducing novel dimensions into the mix. For example, in questions posed through the framework of sound, the researcher would ask about volume, etc. and get out her decibel meter. If her questions are posed through the more specific framework of music, it is assumed that the event is made up of sounds and silences which together create some type of form by virtue of starting at a particular point and ending at a different one—even if what she observes is that the music goes on forever, that is, that it breaks the general rule. Within a music framework, the multifaceted event of a falling tree would be rendered *music*, and a leading set of questions and corresponding skillsets would be set out in order to locate the music in the phenomenon. From the outset, the specific vocabulary would establish a music world, and possibly a sound world. It could establish a music world by asking about the range of the *pitches*, the musical texture, the form, and the timbre. It could further strengthen the definition of the falling tree event by connecting it to music history. For example, an uncontroversial history of music would tie such a composition to John Cage's 4'33", and would discuss the free-falling sounds with a defined musical space. The analytical tools would be drawn from practices that deal with this type of music. And, in the end, we would have created our piece of music.

If our question were posed through the framework of voice, we would also search for the sound, but would ask a different set of detailed questions. Considering the sonorous dimensions of the tree's voice, how many phrases did it produce? What is the syntax of the phrases? Do we hear any resemblance to a given language? How would the event be noted so that a voice could reproduce it? Personifying the tree, we could further ask about the phrase's meaning. Moreover, metaphorizing voice, we could ask about the subjectivity expressed through the tree's voice, made evident in its decision to fall.

Posing our question through the framework of the bodily, we could go in at least two different directions: materiality generally, and body movement (dance/choreography) as one specific sub-area. As materiality, we could investigate the weight, length, and circumference of the tree and calculate the force with which it hits the ground. We could consider the composition of bodies in space with the tree in place and after its fall. Furthermore, we could consider the effect of the impact on surrounding growth and the length of time it would take before the cleared area was covered again by small growth.

While the above assessments may seem like caricatures, their considerations are not far removed from the process (and its associated research steps) of conceiving of a falling tree as sound. In isolation, none of the above approaches—considering a falling tree through music, body, or voice—begins to address the richness of the phenomenon in question. The same applies to rich phenomena that are indexed as music, sound, singing, and listening. Sound, body, and voice are phenomena that unfold across time and space, and are materially specific and relational. Scholarly approaches take live, complex phenomena and project them into a linear framework that fails to account for their fullness; this framework also, to some extent, misdirects the knowledge we develop about their specifics. As the linear model becomes the framework through which a phenomenon is experienced, it is truncated, not unlike the above descriptions that might have been read as caricatures. Specifically, each of these models—and, I do believe that an unambiguous definition of sound, body, and voice is basically only a model—deals only in an isolated "channel" of the sensorium. Sound, in the specific iteration of music and voice, is treated as dealing in audition. Body is treated as dealing in tactility. Again, these modes of the sensorium are, first, culturally constructed, and, second, artificially separated from one another for the purposes of research and for their usefulness factors.

From familiarity to the novelty of a sensorium challenge

If the establishment of disciplines creates ready-made familiar "primal marks" that result in blindness to new knowledge, why would we not simply move away from such a model? Each discipline's specific goal is to create an area of expertise and depth. Each discipline also seeks comprehensiveness. But achieving comprehension also tends to create isolation. A common graduate student comprehensive exam format is a prime example: it defines what is inside a given area and what is outside it, and mandates the building of thorough knowledge of a subject inside the circle. In the case of rich phenomena from which concepts such as sound, body, and voice may be parsed, we are not only talking about a theoretical reading list and knowledge of those texts and their discursive relations. We're also talking about a set of socio-culturally formed sensory systems and the ways in which the senses create sensory systems. In fact, the "correct" sensorium is taught from the very first entry into language and concepts, and is part of any pre-school curriculum. In the cultural context of the writing of this chapter, this sensorium is formed, reinforced, and known to be reality through processes such as basic repeated questions and responses: "How do we hear?" "We hear with our ears." Thus, scholarly discourse is always already informed by the culturally tuned sensorium. This perspective is isolating in terms of the creation of knowledge, which operates in a binary and linear fashion.

What I propose herein is to move from binary to a simultaneous and concurrent conceptualization and experience of the phenomena which we have historically referred to as sound, body, or voice. This can be accomplished by integrating primal marks "that combine new and familiar" content and perspective.[5] Instead of paths of inquiry that rely on one of the senses (as defined by a particular culture) to the exclusion of others, I am committed to a research approach which recognizes that the singular paths are always already a reduction of the phenomenon of, for example, the falling tree. I encourage the use of a set of research strategies and processes that can recognize the three-dimensional, non-linear, non-binary reality of the falling tree phenomenon—or, for that matter, sound, body, and voice—at once. Thus, the kind of attention or discernment I wish to promote is the realization that experiencing and living sound, body, and voice is to live simultaneously in three dimensions. In effect, the two dimensions within which the binary operates are always already reductive, restricting our ability to interact with and comprehend any given phenomenon. What I conceive as multisensory relational materiality multiplies the available paths. Not only does it expand knowledge, but it offers the capacity to increase scholarly cross-fertilization as well as broaden community.[6] It has been my experience that, when a researcher is able to perceive the event of the falling tree as an unnamed whole, the potential to recognize the validity and depth of knowledge of each specialized path becomes available, while openness to other, sometimes opposing knowledge is maintained. This process of uncertainty and self-exposure to a non-expert mind may be contrasted with binary thinking, in which the likelihood of creating a universe of limited, and hence diminished, reality increases. When we take that route, we create isolation and restrict our ability to move forward in both research and everyday experience. Within sound studies, how may we start to interact with complex events beyond the primary mark and its default familiarity, set by a given discipline? And, if we are confined within the already partial and limited perspectives of the sensorial system within which we have been cultivated and through which we experience the world, how might we forge a way toward a balance between the familiar and the novel?

The foundation of this new balance is built on acknowledging that each scholarly perspective is an isolated and limiting path, providing only primal marks, the value of which is already secured—that is, the outcomes will fall within known territories. Adding the perspectives to one another can allow them, together, to account for a fuller story. Recall that, in Berg's conceptualization of this process, familiarity and novelty may be combined. However, introducing novelty and open-ended outcomes stands in opposition to the ways in which scholarly discourses are formed, defined, and traditionally carried out. It is not necessarily the case that one discounts the research of another outright. However, the boundaries of a given field are normally used to establish "relevant" knowledge for that field. Thus, while research within other scholarly areas is not directly dismissed by a given field, it is not taken into account in a serious way, because it is understood that it does not intersect.[7] While not discounted, though, stories are most commonly hermetically sealed. In other words, a line of research is defined by its avoidance of overlap with another line of research, specifically the definition of the object—definitions in opposition such as sound, body, and voice are classic examples—and its attendant epistemological circumference. Even when the object may seem linguistically the same (as, say, *voice*), the fields distinguish themselves from each other by dealing in particular sub-definitions of the object (say, voice as text, language, performance, organ, mechanical vibration, and so on).

If the method itself creates the evidence that proves or develops knowledge only in expected areas, and the resulting object is predefined by a chosen methodology, then—practically—how can we move beyond the confines of that which is defined by the culturally entuned sensorium? For Berg, as the concept of the "primal mark" suggests, it is the starting point of idea generation that sets the course for the types of ideas that it is possible to generate. Like a painter's first brushstrokes, which shape the trajectory of the painting, the starting point of idea generation opens a pathway for some ideas and precludes the testing of others. In an experiment, Berg asked participants to begin with a given object and create a product that would be helpful in a job interview. When given a three-ring binder, Berg's study participants came up with ideas which were deemed obvious by an independent panel. When the starting point was the concept of an in-line skate for rollerblading, the resulting idea was a watch that would show the passing of time through a changing physical element (such as skates). The user can feel the passing of time by squeezing the watch. However, while the first invention's use value was low because it was too familiar, the second invention would arguably be considered equally unhelpful because it was too novel. By asking the participants to refine the product and adding a familiar element—photos of a series of objects commonly used in job interviews—to the process, the mix between novel and useful was balanced. The new iteration was a pen that, through small buttons, automatically changes position to mark the passing of time. This generated idea was informed by both the novel and the familiar.

How may we adapt the framework of balance between the familiar and the novel to the simultaneous deepening of knowledge? And, how may we cultivate outside-the-box insights when the definitions and the sensory modes of the categories sound, body, and voice are derived from a culturally dependent sensorium, a system akin to a primal mark? In music and voice research, for example, within the western classical music tradition and musicology, voice has not primarily been considered in its sonorous form, but rather as text and as predictable performances of compositions. And, when music or sound generally, and voice specifically, are considered in their sonorous aspects, their auditory form is dependent on a limited material iteration.

If we examine conventional approaches to the voice, we may conclude that the study of the voice as libretto, score, and the transmission of sound through air is the musicological equivalent of Berg's three-ring binder. Like Berg, I do not advocate for a dismissal of traditional and proven, productive methodologies. Instead, with him, I seek a balance between the familiar and the novel. In this situation, examples of the familiar could include the recognition of voice as a performance of a composition. The novel could take the form of an unusual case study which a researcher may reject because it does not fit within the methodological scheme. Or, as Berg's examples demonstrate, it could take the form of a forced and unexpected starting point, such as asking the researcher to create a cartoon that expresses an analysis of the vocal work, rather than a traditional written exposition.

As Berg notes, in order to access a broader picture and push into creativity—here meaning creativity in relation to research—any given approach will of course cease to offer novelty. Thus, as we choose a relatively unfamiliar perspective or instrument within a given context, we also must be prepared to detect the moment when that which once offered novelty no longer contributes to a balance between the familiar and the new. It is important to point out that we do not seek to replace one approach with another, but rather to supplement the existing approach and to devise fresh combinations. In this way, even commonly used approaches can yield new information when put into conversation with new ones. At the core of the matter, we are looking for something that will disrupt the convention of one or a few paths only, not as a replacement, but as an addition. What was once novel will, with adaptation, become familiar and be integrated into the norms of the field. Within a continuing productive approach, the process of including novel primal marks is iterative. Recall that in order to create a balanced primal mark, there must be at least two differing factors. Therefore, what was once novel could, at some point in the process, begin to serve as the familiar.

The equilibrium between Wagner and underwater singing

In the early 2000s, I failed to act on an exclusive invitation to witness a performance of Juliana Snapper's underwater *Five Fathoms Opera Project*.[8] While she had been a longtime friend, and a singer and artist I greatly admired, soprano and performance artist Snapper's projects took me some time to get around to. When I did engage with underwater opera work, though, it demonstrated to me the balance between the familiar and the novel in musicology, sound, and voice studies. I dismissed this project because it flew in the face of everything I knew about singing generally, and classical singing in particular. In addition, its dramatic presentation underwater was even more fantastical than Baroque opera. My internal list of reasons for rejection reads like a laundry list: Snapper sang in a place that was unconducive to singing; she transformed the music by singing in such a different materiality; she was in a separate material space from her audience. These reasons made it difficult to study her work in a traditional sense—a context in which her work would be rejected. However, by taking it on, I learned a lot about what our current methodologies are good at, but also about the aspects of sound, body, and voice which they naturalize. Moreover, in taking it on, an agenda was set for me in regards to adopting a predetermined and novel starting point.

If the notion that voice and music occupy a textual or conventional sonorous analysis constitutes our three-ring binder, then the in-line skate Snapper offers is the idea that sound, music, and voice are realizations of an unrepeatable intermaterial vibrational relationship in which the body is a central player. Through Snapper's work I stood at the trailhead of an exciting journey, a journey that tasked me with keeping traditional aspects in mind while also finding new questions and pursuing peculiarities. On the one hand, Snapper's repertoire was anchored in the classical canon: she sang compositions by Hanns Eisler and Richard Wagner. On the other hand, her interpretation and staging were unlike any I'd heard before. In this way, she provided balance between the familiar, in the form of well-known repertoire, and the novel, in the form of the staging: submerged in water. Had Snapper simply staged this type of repertoire in a concert setting—or, at this point in the history of site-specific art, anywhere within the medium of air—it would have been akin to the three-ring binder, and that start to the challenge would have led the researcher to pursue familiar questions. However, when the singer is underwater, extremely basic questions become novel—questions so basic that they are often not asked in relation to performance of classical repertoire immediately arose: "How can Snapper sing?"; "How does she get oxygen?"; "Does, or how can, the audience hear Snapper?"; "Why is she doing this?" Moreover, while these questions might lead to basic investigations of singing, they also address profound issues at the heart of sound, body, singing, and listening.

What Snapper's underwater opera project invoked, for both audience and researcher, was a primal mark that did not distinguish between sound, body or material, and voice, and that assumed they worked together, as a complex. The dissolution of distinct categories—singers, compositions, listeners, material transmissions, and meaning-making—was also part of this primal mark. Such a starting point raised questions about the material separation between audience and singer when the audience is not submerged in water with Snapper, or a shared materiality when the audience is underwater with her. This led me to investigate sound and voice from physics and mechanical engineering perspectives, applying insights from these fields to an aesthetic context. What I found was that events of voice, sound, and hearing are always already the result of a specific relational configuration between the vibration of the material vocal apparatus, the produced sound, the material that transmits the sound (such as air, water, or metal), and the listening body's material configuration in relation to that transmitting material.[9]

In other words, what Snapper's "in-line skate" effect both exposed and offered as a fruitful area for investigation was the naturalization of what we believe we know about sound and voice sonically, and the ways in which we take the sensorium and the data we derive from it for granted, in its naturalized formulation. Once sound and voice have been denaturalized in terms of their realization in air, and once they are always already not only implicated in body (materiality) but realized through a material relationality, none of the previous analytical models are sufficient in themselves. Therefore, through her provocative series of performances, Snapper provides an in-line skate that no longer allows for traditional considerations. We cannot return to our tried-and-true analytical models without keeping this added perspective in mind. Thus, Snapper's stagings raise basic questions and provocations that, at least for the time being, feature a novel primal mark, but are bathed in the familiar in terms of repertoire and musical practice.

Also key to this project's primal mark is how it assists us in expanding our inquiry beyond the socio-culturally formed sensorium. While not undoing centuries of refinement, by expanding the definition of singing beyond aurality to include tactility and materiality, the study of song is pushed into new sensorial territory, gathering in aspects of the sensorium that are not normally addressed in relation to singing. Thus, by providing such a strong primal mark, Snapper challenges her audience and researchers to experiment beyond their sensory or field-specific "go-to" methodologies which have already naturalized the sensorium and the corresponding sense.

Specifically, Snapper's underwater opera project set me on an unexpected research journey that led me, in the end, to introduce basic physical principles to serve as novelty marks in regards to sound. By bringing traditional repertoire into an unfamiliar materiality, Snapper exposes the contingent materiality of air itself, and of the bodies that hear within it. Through her project, she opens a space within which we may rediscover the material relationality between the so-called source and its listeners, since sound and voice, if heard, are ultimately realized through the materiality of the listener. In this way, an underwater opera project which consists of standard repertoire sung in an utterly unfamiliar setting offered a productive primal mark, balancing familiar and novel, in areas ranging from the types of questions provoked by the project to the methodological approaches it suggested. The blending of these two paths into a rich primal imprint allowed for a deepening of my understanding of sound, body, and voice not only as co-producing categories, but also as distinct characters.

Conclusion

Even if I needed time to take her venture seriously due to its strong novelty factor, the invaluable in-line skate aspect of the primal mark was offered by Snapper herself. While Berg's study was published in 2014 and I only learned about it a year later, on looking back I see that we consistently search for projects that present a novelty factor, and there is no shortage of this type of work in the musical and artistic worlds. However, if a potential research project does not present the recommended balance between the familiar and the novel, how may we *devise* so-called in-line skates? To think through phenomena that include sound, body, and voice, I often use, and have also taught, the same series of exercises which play with and take advantage of the fact that we experience the world through a socio-culturally constructed sensorium. While I often view this naturalization as limiting my experience of the world, contrary to common sense, that very rigidity may also be exploited to offer novelty.

My series of exercises is simple. It asks researchers, who I conceive as practitioners, to purposefully apply and exercise senses that are not commonly associated with the object or medium under scrutiny. Thus, the exercises scramble the culturally spun logic of the sensorium by crossing wires, so to speak. For example, instead of asking how to *describe* a given sound in the expected vein—"it sounded loud; the note ascended; it is made by an alarm or a computer"—I suggest the researcher ask herself: if I were to take in this phenomenon as something other than sound perceived through audition, how would it look, taste, smell, and feel? Or even, multiplying a given sensorial path, we could ask: what would it sound like as another sound? This deliberate cross-sensory approach acknowledges that although music consists of sound waves and falls within a socio-cultural context known to appeal primarily to hearing, the full range of senses interacts and converges in intricate ways, never operating in isolation. In this way, the aspects of the sensorium that are surgically divided by the question about the falling tree can again be related to each other. Through a multiplicity of sensory entry points, akin to dual vision compared to monovision, the phenomenon's complexity is given consideration. As the visual analogy highlights, what closing one eye when aiming provides in terms of accuracy (which we can compare to specialization within a field), opening a second eye adds in depth and complexity. In the same way, a rich primal mark is devised from two or more points of view. An examination of the event of the falling tree through questions that inquire along multiple sensory paths will offer means to increase our understanding of the complexity of the event that led to its sound. Similarly, multisensory investigation of phenomena that have historically been studied through a single sense can increase our knowledge of their complexity, hence serving our research, disciplines, and general understanding of sound, body, and music.

Notes

1 For a nuanced discussion of the etymological and philosophical history of the term "voice," see Shane Butler, "What Was the Voice?" *The Oxford Handbook of Voice Studies* (New York: Oxford University Press, in press).

2 Tomie Hahn, 2007. The Body Articulate—Dance Notation and Ethnography. In the Society for Ethnomusicology's Annual Meeting. Columbus, OH (October 25, 2007).

3 Justin M. Berg, "The Primal Mark: How the Beginning Shapes the End in the Development of Creative Marks," *Organizational Behavior and Human Decision Processes*, 125 (2014) 1.

4 Ibid.

5 Ibid.
6 For an in-depth discussion of this, see Nina Sun Eidsheim, *Measuring Race: The Micropolitics of Listening to Vocal Timbre and Vocality in African-American Music* (Duke University Press, forthcoming).
7 Note that interdisciplinary research sometimes does, and sometimes does not, challenge the situation described here.
8 To read in detail about this project, see Eidsheim, *Sensing Sound: Singing and Listening as Vibrational Practice* (Duke University Press, 2015).
9 See Ibid., 1–95; 154–186.

5

THE RETURN TO SOUND AESTHETICS

Neil Verma

In this chapter I follow three lines of thinking on the role of aesthetics in sound studies over the past two decades, asking how the term binds together problems, areas, and projects. The first section considers the rhetorical function of aesthetics, the way its invocation is a signpost for scholars. The second explores how sound studies prompts a rethinking of the concept of the aesthetic, something widely understood to involve the category of beauty as conceptualized through a set of mutually supporting historical intellectual movements (18th-century Western philosophy, academic music appreciation, bourgeois values), a usage of the term currently waning but unlikely to dwindle completely. The third is to show how sound has played a role in the shift from an aesthetics of value to a "media aesthetics," from a theory rooted in judgment to a theory with an agnostic approach to the merits of individual works, drawing instead from critical theory, media studies, and classical theories of *aesthesis* to consider how sound media (in both their individual specificity and their common mediality) shape how we encounter and process sense-experience in the first place.

I will argue that when it comes to sound studies, these lines of thinking share a point of convergence. In their approaches, contemporary scholars in all of these lines stress the need to preserve a robust sense of sound's embeddedness within social, cultural and political life, which aesthetics is often accused of ignoring. This is the keynote of the literature: an anxiety that opening the question of aesthetics is liable to force a decoupling with the social, thus betraying a general worry about such a cleavage. Aestheticians seem to take sounds and put them in a kind of museum, away from contexts, disobeying the precept that sound is fundamentally social. As Michael Bull and Les Back (among others) have argued, the tendency to objectify and universalize phenomena – a hallmark of "aesthetic" engagement, to many – is a symptom of misleading distance-based "visual epistemologies" that have guided Western thought for too long (Bull and Back 2003: 4–5). It makes sense, then, to approach sound aesthetics with suspicion, as something that might render social ramifications moot and betray "the sonic" by imputing a boundary between the inner and the outer, the private and the public, that sound itself will not brook. To speak of aesthetics is stressful because it raises the unhappy possibility that those who study "sound" as object and those who study "listening" as an activity might not be able to cooperate as well as they might wish to. Aesthetics thus reminds us of the vexed (but also generative) ways in which the motley group of writers and creators that Jonathan Sterne calls "sound students" ground their critiques (Sterne 2012: 4–5).

Insisting on social, political, or cultural dimensions to aesthetic phenomena, or fretting about the failure to do so, is not unique to sound studies, but rather represents a time-honored gesture in modern thought. In her reading of Kant, Hannah Arendt emphasized that Kant's insistence that judgments of beauty necessarily involve a claim to universal validity (when we say something is beautiful, we are not merely finding it "agreeable" but also believing that others should, too), which compels us to recognize that others have the same faculty as we. Aesthetics is thus a kind of judgment that exists in the presence of others (Arendt 1982). For Walter Benjamin, it was urgently necessary to politicize art to confront the reactionary aesthetics of fascism that valorized war, and this held true for sound media as for other forms in the age of mechanical reproducibility (Benjamin 2002). For Pierre Bourdieu, art and aesthetics were socially instituted through a field of critics, dealers, patrons and others; art moved in a field of cultural production, it existed in states of decipherment by those socially sanctioned to ascribe value within that field (Bourdieu 1994). Art appreciation was a way of understanding classes, capital and how they interact through symbolic value and cultural capital, a perspective that has held sway across the humanities over the past generation.

Since the 20th century, the direction of this thinking has altered somewhat. Rather than recuperating purportedly autonomous art into the social, writers are beginning to approach aesthetic analysis as itself a form of political activity amenable to reflexive humanist analysis. Jacques Rancière has argued that aesthetic thought is profoundly political in that it involves the "delimitation of spaces and times, of the visible and the invisible, of speech and noise, that simultaneously determines the place and the stakes of politics as a form of experience" (Rancière 2004: 8). For him, aesthetic acts matter for how they form experience, while also showing an ability to reconfigure subjectivity. Aesthetics is a way of isolating practices behind artwork, but it is also about the modes of perception, regimes of emotion, categories and other ideas whereby that same artwork can be heard and spoken about: "These conditions make it possible for words, shapes, movements and rhythms to be felt and thought as art" (Rancière 2001: x). Aesthetics is political for Rancière not just because it reflects shared sensibilities but also because it distributes the sensible according to a *regime*. Attempting an account of that process is like background noise of sound studies nowadays, which is preoccupied with the power of aesthetics and the aesthetics of power.

The rhetoric of aesthetic return

Because aesthetics involves a set of questions about experience, feeling, taste, and cultural value that are less frequently debated between the disciplines in which sound students are often trained – philosophy, literature, art, critical theory, ethnomusicology, performance studies, cinema & media studies, history, sociology, cultural studies, music – and more hotly disputed within them, a "definitive" entry on aesthetics in sound studies will elude this chapter as surely as it eludes the field itself. Artist Leonard Koren's study of the word as it appears in recent discourse produces a dizzying range: in ordinary speech we use "aesthetics" to refer to superficiality, artistic style, taste, theory of beauty, decadence, a particular creative practice, a cognitive mode, or a language shared by arts communities (Koren 2010). Sound scholars employ most of these usages, from identifying unique signatures (art writers speak of "Cagean aesthetics") to emphasizing cognitive modes (musique concrète writers discuss the "aesthetics" of reduced listening).

If we follow Koren's lead and isolate the "natural meanings" of the term rather than relying on rigid definitions, then another thing to account for is what has been called an "aesthetic turn" in sound studies in recent years. Over the past decade, "aesthetics" has provided writers a point of reference with which they bring sound studies to bear on subjects ranging from "brostep" culture to feminist electronic music, from practices of 1970s film sound design to discourses surrounding South Asian singing, from the role of improvisation in Black radical tradition to analysis of the responses of users to simulated soundscapes (D'Errico 2014; Rodgers 2010; Beck 2016; Moten 2003). Yet it is unclear just when aesthetics took on this prominence, or which scholarly figure we should associate with it. When it comes to opening up areas in sound studies, acoustic ecology has R. Murray Schafer, sound art has Alan Licht, Brandon LaBelle and Douglas Kahn, film sound has Rick Altman and Michel Chion, political economy has Jacques Attali, radio has Michele Hilmes, cultural history of technology has Jonathan Sterne, listening has Pauline Oliveros, and so on. Sound aesthetics, by contrast, seems to have no bright point of origin, let alone a set of positions recognized by all interlocutors with a stake in the question. In light of this, historically locating *the* aesthetic turn is less important than identifying what underlying logic governs the tendency of aesthetics to return in particular circumstances.

Indeed, aesthetics "returns" for all the authors I just mentioned, each of whom has made contributions to the topic, ranging from Attali's dialectic of "music" and "noise" and Licht's taxonomy of the sound arts to Sterne's influential study of the cultural underpinnings of audile techniques associated with sound reproduction (Attali 1984; Licht 2009; Sterne 2004). Yet these, and others, are not quite taking on aesthetic disciplinarity directly. One candidate for that role is Horkheimer and Adorno's 1944 "Culture Industry" essay, often used as a touchstone by writers in this area. In that essay, however, the term aesthetics arises less than a dozen times in 11,000 words, usually nested among characteristically adornian negations – "impoverishment," "barbarity," "broken promise," etc. This is no accident. For Horkheimer and Adorno, aesthetics had been reduced to "style," which is little more than obedience to social order (Horkheimer and Adorno 1994: 128–31). Whatever you make of that assertion, to consider it a turn *toward* aesthetics is perverse since its burden is precisely to explore how any aesthetics worthy of the name has been obviated. As Miriam Hansen observed, in the culture industry critique, "The primacy of (industrial) technology prevents, or at least seriously restricts, the development of technique in the aesthetic sense, understood as 'conscious free control over the aesthetic means'" (Hansen 2012: 215). It is a theory of the absentia of creative practice in mass culture, a stillbirth. That is because "aesthetics" is used here mostly as the armature on which a challenge to interwar theory was mounted. The culture industry critique is not about sound aesthetics. Rather, it uses the example of sound aesthetics, and others, as a mediating phenomenon through which to rethink critical theory under capitalism at a particularly salient historical inflection point.

While the substance of Horkheimer and Adorno's essay may move through our subject negatively, like a shadow, its parallel use of aesthetics in a "mediating" role is a canny way of thinking about why the subject tends to return in discourse every now and then. Rather than a take-it-or-leave-it intellectual terrain, the term "aesthetics" signposts disciplinary breaks, cracks, interventions, and disjunctures. That is surely the case in recent years. Shawn VanCour, for instance, has written of new interest in aesthetics among radio scholars, where the term is understood as "analysis of narrative structure and broadcast genres, methods of spatial and temporal representation, styles of vocal performance, and experiential qualities of radio listening" (VanCour 2013). VanCour argues that aesthetic questions have been raised since at least the 1930s by a variety of thinkers, some of whom were already associated with the term (gestalt theorist Rudolf Arnheim) and others whose work at first seems antithetical to it (social researchers Hadley Cantril and Paul Lazarsfeld). These roots of the current aesthetic turn, moreover, suggest that we renew our interest in the day-to-day work of radio creators, emphasizing "the processes through which particular sets of programming forms and production styles are consolidated, and connecting them to the larger modes of production." In this way, aesthetics connects objects of study to historical approaches to encourage radio studies to reorient around production studies methods that follow "below the line" media work. Aesthetics leads, marvellously, not toward the bloodless world of sonic forms, but instead toward the people behind them and the stories they tell about their material practices, alongside detailed observations of how those agendas coalesce into media products.

Other authors have considered aesthetics in order to expose contradictions among scholarly approaches that have broad ramifications for the field. In a tour-de-force essay in the first issue of the *Sound Studies* journal, for instance, Brian Kane has challenged what he calls the "onto-aesthetic" position of writers such as Christoph Cox and Greg Hainge, showing how their preference for sound art that seems to disclose the condition of sound media – to emphasize material support, following a sense of aesthetics linked with critic Clement Greenberg – is problematic (Kane 2015). While it is possible for art to call attention to its medium or sonic mode according to a set of criteria established by culturally contingent factors manifested as a symbolic system shared by critics, it is not also possible for one sonic art piece to *be* more sonic than another in an ontological sense. Robert Morris's *Box with the Sound of Its Own Making* (1961), Alvin Lucier's *I am Sitting in a Room* (1969) and Susan Philipsz's *Lowlands* (2010) all have different ways of aesthetically disclosing their use of recording media, and these may be found more or less meritorious according to different hierarchies of value, but none is more or less "sonic" than the others. Kane has a larger objective in his excursus, too; here he is using the relation between aesthetics and ontology to rebalance the level between "disciplines" that approach sounds as isolated objects, and auditory culture studies, which reveals how contingent value systems give sounds an "ontographic" status that never fully transcends context. Just as aesthetics is a framework for VanCour to make proposals about a production studies approach to historiography, for Kane a confrontation with the relation between ontology and aesthetics opens out to a methodological assertion about the constitutive role of auditory culture, thereby promoting an idea of sound culture studies as a "field" rather than a "discipline."

The argument also represents an effort to protect ontology and aesthetics from one another, to introduce a sense of social contingency between the two that is often neglected by those who focus on "sound" over "listening" to the point of reifying one or the other. However, that argument is not designed to provide something very much on the mind of Cox, Hainge and others who critically study of sound art – the vestigial imperative to assess the merits of artwork. One thing that the onto-aesthetic regime is good at, after all, is fusing an older sense of aesthetics as an arbiter of value with an aesthetics focused on material supports of particular works. It may be that poor ontology can be derived from Greenberg's argument for medium-specificity in which artistic "purity" is only a condition that results when the individual arts "have been hunted back to their mediums" where they are "isolated, concentrated, and defined," but his model at least adduces a modern sensitivity to the traditional set of elitist criteria for assessing its excellence (Greenberg 1940: 305). Whatever else he wanted from art, as Seth Kim-Cohen has emphasized, "What Greenberg wanted was quality" (Kim-Cohen 2009: 5). And the problem of what to do with the aesthetics of quality, a definition that dominated Western thought for two centuries, presents challenges today.

Sound and modern thought

For many, sound aesthetics is a contradiction in terms because aesthetics suggests irreducibly visible experiences linked to the fine arts (Kristeller 1951). Like the notion of the fine arts itself, this idea has historical roots in philosophy, in which aesthetics seems elusive because it is a modifying subcategory crossing relatively organized fields – according to the *Stanford Encyclopedia of Philosophy*, aesthetics is (emphasis added) "a *kind* of object, a *kind* of judgment, a *kind* of attitude, a *kind* of experience and a *kind* of value" – where the logic of kindedness frequently rests on the common denominator of visual experience (Shelley 2015).

It did not start out that way. Aesthetics (in its philosophical sense) was inaugurated by Alexander Baumgarten in the 18th century, who adopted this term to describe a field that would assess something that was predominantly textual, with poetry and eloquence. Philosophers who followed this early foray moved to natural phenomena for their preferred examples as the discourse took up the problem of taste. In his *Critique of Judgment* (1790) Kant employed visual instances of sublime natural vistas (mountains, hurricanes, volcanoes) to elaborate his well-known theory, following the work of Edmund Burke. Kant also broadened the perimeter of aesthetic inquiry to incorporate painting, sculpture, and architecture. In his typology of the fine arts, the sound art of music is at the low end, beneath arts that "address themselves to the eye" (Kant 1987: 196-201). For Kant, visual arts involved the movement from determinate ideas into sensations, whereas sonic arts involved the movement from sensations into indeterminate ideas. Not only are they going the wrong way, they are going to the wrong place. Moreover, the unbounded nature of sound undermines the disinterestedness of the auditor's pleasure, which is what vouchsafes the system that sets aesthetic judgment off from other kinds of judgments for Kant. Because the ear lacks an eyelid, music is like a perfume thrust upon us, which is something quite different from an image at which we might elect to gaze upon or turn away from in contemplation. The latter experience had a seriousness of purpose more significant to Kant and many who followed him.

In the 19th century a variety of thinkers would alter this hierarchy, beginning with the rise of a scholarly tradition in musical appreciation among Romantic critics such as Eduard Hanslick and others responsible for elevating Beethoven, Schumann, and Brahms to their current status as masters. Meanwhile aesthetic philosophers began to express an emphatic preference for music and its effects. For Walter Pater, the obliteration of the distinction between form and content that characterized music was the condition to which all arts ought to aspire (Pater 1986: 86). For Schopenhauer, music lacked a mimetic relationship with the world; sound copies not the world of appearances, but the will that subtends it (Schopenhauer 1969: 255–70). Around the kernel of this insight, Nietzsche elaborated a system of aesthetic understanding in his *Birth of Tragedy* (1872), which put sound squarely in a "Dionysian" role. Where images were dreamlike, individuated and Apollinian, sound was intoxicating, painful, primal, yet metaphysically comforting by conveying unindividuated oneness. A rebirth of this spirit was coming through German music (embodied by Wagner) fusing with the tragic hero: "Tragedy absorbs the highest ecstasies of music," Nietzsche predicts. "So that it truly brings music, both among the Greeks and among us, to its perfection" (Nietzsche 1967: 125). Seeking a rebirth of a fantasized classical mythopoetics, Nietzsche provided an aesthetic language that bridged music and sound studies, as the concept of the Dionysian would remain a touchstone for such divergent authors as Attali and Schafer well into the 20th century.

Today, however, many writers look upon this tradition warily, either because it is inept in analysing the works with which they engage, or because it harbours sinister undertones. Salomé Voegelin has argued that Kant's best-remembered aesthetic model (that of the sublime) cannot hold up to sound, which does not admit the sense of vast scale over which reason may triumph, since no sound is greater than the act of listening to it (Voegelin 2014: 117–119). Matt Sakakeeny has argued that in its development of the aesthetics of appreciation, the idea of music as "organised sound" (Edgard Varèse's term) has been inextricably linked with imperialism. "Music" (aesthetic) and "sound" (nonaesthetic) were set apart from one another, recapitulating imperial racial stratifications that writers justly abhor. "Aesthetic distinctions of music and sound" such as those associated with Hanslick, he writes, "were entangled with western scientific standards that worked in tandem to either affirm or deny the humanity of others" (Sakakeeny 2015: 117).

Theorist Jean-Luc Nancy has raised a related point, noting that the 19th-century fascination with the "ineffable intimacy" of music that began with Schopenhauer was imbricated with the rise of European fascism, which perversely turned a musical sensibility into a mode of signification (Nancy 2007: 49–59).

One writer who has wrestled with the legacy of this tradition is Joanna Demers, in her work on electronic music. Acknowledging academic wariness about aesthetics, Demers points to the rhetoric of distinction touted by many listeners when it comes to institutional electroacoustic music, electronica, and sound art. Where academics tend to fall into "Kantian" or "Marxist" camps that focus (respectively) either on the objective autonomy of "beauty" or on the social forces subtending that sense of autonomy, experimentalists that Demers considers tend to hold both views at once. The field "clings to notions of aesthetic superiority and autonomy from market forces even as it regards aesthetic experience as inseparable form culture" (Demers 2010: 141). The heart of Demers's argument is that music itself has changed, and aesthetics must change with it. "Whereas in art music listeners are expected to pay full attention to the music and ignore almost everything else around them, listening to electronic music, dance music, and popular forms is a composite of sensory experiences" that includes movement, distraction, and other experiences (Demers 2010: 152). To meet this sort of music, she proposes "aesthetic listening," a mode that permits intermittent focus, external sensory stimuli and appreciation of non-musical sounds. In the past, "musical listening" focused on understanding slowly building formal codes of themes, harmonies, and melodies, but experimental electronic music does not request the intense focus that those codes require, as it tends to repeat small units over long periods of time. For this reason, Demers proposes a reinvention of the term aesthetics that rejects ineffable intimacy while also preserving a sense of aesthetics as the proper register for the pleasure afforded by the work.

Demers provides a picture of sound that is full of bodies, systems, and groupings, a hive of human activity that any aesthetic analysis ought to highlight rather than bracket. If anything is affecting aesthetics these days, it is surely new ideas about sensing sound. Perhaps the most vivid articulation comes from Nina Eidsheim. In her work on the voice and listening, Eidsheim displaces the notion of sound as an external object (a "figure of sound") and replaces it with a sense of sound as an unfolding phenomenon passing through a series of interactions, what she calls an "intermaterial vibrational practice." Each sounding that occurs is a unique, unrepeatable, unfolding event happening to a body; therefore there is no external musical event to which we can address inquiry, as each body experiences unfolding in its own way, sometimes with radically different results. Eidsheim's "organological" model also looks to music as a set of interacting relationships between human and nonhuman vibrating materials that transmit or transduce mechanical energies, aiming to move discussion of music "out of the orbit of the knowable and the potentially meaning making, to the material and always already relational" (Eidsheim 2015: 157). Together, Demers and Eidsheim propose new forms of music and of listening that vastly complicate what had once been a relatively straightforward intellectual habit of knowledge through appreciation. It is not that judgments of merit are impossible in the new framework. It is much worse than that – they are uninteresting. Writers working in this idiom, it is no surprise, require another sense of the "aesthetic" altogether.

Toward a media aesthetics

My first monograph explored the use of sonic technical details (distance, volume, sound effects, sound design) as well as formal narrative ones (structure, narration, genre) in a large body of classic American radio plays, drawing on both close listening, focusing on specific moments and details, and distant listening, focusing on how formal features worked broadly across programs over time. To me it was intuitive to capture these attributes with "aesthetics," which I put into my subtitle – *Imagination, Aesthetics and American Radio Drama*. Ever since, I have been asked to name the "greatest" radio plays in the period or to defend programs such as *Dimension X* or *The Strange Dr. Weird* from the accusation of kitsch. The question leaves me torn. On the one hand, I feel eager to put forward the works of Norman Corwin, Wyllis Cooper, and Lucille Fletcher as meaningful art. On the other hand, I have an equally powerful impulse to reject the task of doing so. Kitsch is beside the point; what matters is how these plays reveal cultural sensibilities at the level of the senses, and what they say about the society that produced them. Political values and social expectations circulate through aesthetic choices in this medium as saliently as they do through the manifest subject matter of the plays.

I am not the only sound studies scholar torn between making the case for a sound art of canonical importance, while feeling ambivalent about doing so because the effort shortchanges a broader cultural historical endeavour. From the forgoing sections, it is clear that sound studies has a fraught relation with the legacy of aesthetic philosophy. Increasingly, many writers are beginning to circumnavigate that legacy, particularly those trained in cinema studies and English, where a series of movements, ranging from post-structuralism and media archaeology to New Aestheticism, have come together over the past thirty years to form what we might think of as a "media aesthetics" model in the humanities. Writers in this idiom focus on sensory encounters with sound works or the devices that bear them, and often write about the historical specificity of media as well as the proposal of a state of "mediality" conditioning aesthetic interactions. Writers fixate on particular devices or platforms – the phonograph, the tape recorder, music sampler, or MP3 – providing rich explorations of how we engage with sound and media devices by exhibiting sensitivity to stylistics and the unique capacities of media products, as well as exploring the interplay of affect and sensation that characterizes interactions with sound through one technology over another.

In abandoning the fine arts as such, what I am calling the "media aesthetics idiom" affords more lateral thinking than modes that rely on appreciation or stylistics, something proven repeatedly over the last decade. Alexander Weheliye's work is an excellent example, tracing how sound technologies and Black popular music shaped one another since the 19th century. He writes, "The phonograph – both as an object and a mechanic ensemble – and many of the culturotechnological formations after it – intimate a prima facie crossroads from and through which to theorize the intricate codepedency of blackness and the modern, since this apparatus, in its catechristic naming, technological capabilities, and cultural discourse directs our ears and eyes to the grounds of blackness's materialization and figuring in the West" (Weheliye 2005: 45). For Weheliye, working in the idiom of aesthetics makes it possible to draw together the practices of beatmatching from DJ culture to give a fresh way of understanding W.E.B. Du Bois's seminal *Souls of Black Folk*, as the sensibilities that surround one media practice daringly open up those of another. Aesthetics is also a touchstone in Jacob Smith's recent *Eco-Sonic Media*, a book dedicated to excavating the forgotten history of ecologically green sound technologies. From the aesthetic links between trained roller canaries and discs of trained bird callers to a study of the "dark ecology" aesthetic of radio narratives, Smith shows the history of low-carbon media and provides an aesthetic road map about how to study it (Smith 2015). Scan recent edited collections in sound studies and you will find many examples of media aesthetics sensibilities – a seriousness about engaging at the level of sense-experience, theoretical work on technology, a sense of embeddedness in cultural history, disinterest in canonization of works or performances – to explore music technologies, games, creators, platforms, and devices (Gopinath and Stanyek 2014; Smith and Verma 2016; Théberge, Devine and Everett 2015).

Where does the media aesthetics paradigm come from? Historical texts in its deep roots include Lucretius's *De Rerum Natura*, Lessing's *Laocoon* and Hume's *Enquiry Concerning Human Understanding*, all of which focus more closely on the nature of sense-experience than on what assessments we make of them. It would be difficult to see the approach growing if not for the rise of media theory since McLuhan, the return of phenomenology in the last decade, the rise and retreat of cultural studies, or the debates between determinism and social construction of the 1980s and 90s. One overlooked lineage I would like to highlight comes from recent work on critical theory (Buck-Morss 1992; Hansen 1999). In their engagements with Walter Benjamin's pivotal "Art in the Age of Mechanical Reproducibility" essay, Susan Buck-Morss and Miriam Hansen have drawn out Benjamin's then-atypical model of aesthetics that focuses closely on how technology can give form to experience. In an age preoccupied with elitist taste, Benjamin turned back to the Greeks. For Aristotle, *aesthesis* had little to do with sublime vistas. Instead, it meant sense-perception as distinct from thought, ascribing to this type of feeling "an interdependent cognitive value to sensory ways of knowing" in the words of Caroline Frick (Aristotle 1991; Frick 2010: 91). This is the oldest meaning of the term, and according to Hansen, Benjamin reaches for it for a reason, circumnavigating the lineage of aesthetic thinking rooted in 18th-century philosophy:

> The aesthetic can no longer be defended in terms of the idealist values of the few that make it complicit with the suffering of the many, nor even in terms of style and artistic technique; rather, the political crisis demands an understanding of the aesthetic that takes into account the social reception of *technology*, the effects of sensory alienation on the conditions of experience and agency.
>
> *(Hansen 1999: 312)*

On Hansen's account, Benjamin believed that the senses cannot escape technology, the apparatus already having become part of subjectivity in the "second fall" of modernity, and puts his energies into how to reorganize its effects around collective innervation.

In a later essay "Why Media Aesthetics?," Hansen writes a series of questions that clarify the urgency that impelled Benjamin's thinking:

> Benjamin recast the more orthodox Marxist question of false consciousness in terms of his un/timely theory of "anthropological materialism": How is consciousness, whether false or critical, produced and reproduced in the first place? What is the effect of industrial-capitalist technology on the organization of the human senses, and how does it affect the conditions of experience and agency, the ability to see connections and contradictions, remember the past, and imagine a (different) future? How can the alienation inflicted on the human sensorium in the defense against technologically induced shock (what Susan Buck-Morss has called *anaesthetics*), the splitting of experience into isolated sensations, affects, and sound bites, be undone or, rather, transformed? What kind of understanding—and practice—of art and aesthetics would be needed toward that goal?
>
> *(Hansen 2004: 393)*

These are the questions that lead to what Hansen calls Benjamin's "gamble" on cinema as a utopian medium, one with the potential to ameliorate distortions of consciousness. It is telling that Hansen refers to the "sound bite" as something in need of transformation in her quote. In sound studies nowadays, there are many who look to sound media for such an opportunity, seeking in the use of sonic devices, performances, and artifacts the chance for opening new ways of organizing sense-experience against dominant regimes of bits and bites. Perhaps the shift toward a media aesthetics paradigm is neither wholly felicitous nor likely to eclipse the aesthetics of value. But thanks to this way of thinking, aesthetics is a surprisingly hopeful area of sound studies nowadays, a mode of analysis that believes that transformation – big transformation – is possible according to writers who embrace aesthetics as integral to social mission, for those who, like Benjamin, are ready to gamble on sound as a way of feeling and knowing.

References

Arendt, H. (1982) *Lectures on Kant's Political Philosophy*, Chicago: University of Chicago Press.

Aristotle (1991) *De Anima*, trans. R. D. Hicks, Buffalo, NY: Prometheus Books.

Attali, J. (1984) *Noise: The Political Economy of Music*, trans. Brian Massumi, Minneapolis, MN: University of Minnesota Press.

Beck, J. (2016) *Designing Sound: Audiovisual Aesthetics of 1970s American Cinema*, New Brunswick, NJ: Rutgers University Press.

Benjamin, W. (2002) "The Work of Art in the Age of Mechanical Reproducibility" (Second Version) in his *Selected Writings Vol. 3: 1935–1938*, trans. Edmund Jephcott, Howard Eiland et al., Cambridge, MA: Belknap Press, pp 101–133.

Bourdieu, P. (1994) *The Field of Cultural Production: Essays on Art and Literature*, New York, NY: Columbia University Press.

Buck-Morss, S. (1992) "Aesthetics and Anaesthetics: Walter Benjamin's Artwork Essay Reconsidered," *October* 62 1:3–41.

Bull, M. and L. Back (2003) "Introduction: Into Sound," in M. Bull and L. Back (eds) *The Auditory Culture Reader*, New York, NY: Berg, pp 1–18.

Demers, J. (2010) *Listening Through the Noise: The Aesthetics of Experimental Electronic Music*, New York, NY: Oxford University Press.

D'Errico, M. (2014) "Going Hard: Bassweight, Sonic Warfare and the 'Brostep' Aesthetic," *Sounding Out: The Sound Studies Blog*, accessed 10 June 2016, https://soundstudiesblog.com/2014/01/23/

Eidsheim, N. (2015) *Sensing Sound: Singing & Listening as Vibrational Practice*, Durham, NC: Duke University Press.

Frick, C. (2010) "Senses," in W.J.T. Mitchell and Mark B.N. Hansen (eds) *Critical Terms for Media Studies*, Chicago, University of Chicago Press, pp 37–71.

Gopinath, S. and Stanyek, J. eds (2014) *The Oxford Handbook of Mobile Media*, Oxford: Oxford University Press.

Greenberg, C. (1940) "Towards a Newer Laocoon," *Partisan Review* 7:4 pp 296–310.

Hansen, M. (2012) *Cinema and Experience: Siegfried Kracauer, Walter Benjamin and Theodor W. Adorno*, Berkeley, CA: University of California Press.

———— (1999) "Benjamin and Cinema, Not a One-Way Street," *Critical Inquiry* 25:1 pp 306–343.

———— (2004) "Why Media Aesthetics?" *Critical Inquiry* 30:1 pp 391–395.

Horkheimer, M. and Adorno, T. (1944) *Dialectic of Enlightenment*, trans. John Cumming, New York, NY: Continuum.

Kane, B. (2015) "Sound Studies Without Auditory Culture: a Critique of the Ontological Turn," *Sound Studies: An Interdisciplinary Journal* 1:1 pp 2–21.

Kant, I. (1987) *Critique of Judgment*, trans. Werner S. Pluhar, Indianapolis, IN: Hackett.

Kim-Cohen, S. (2009) *In the Blink of an Ear: Toward a Non-cochlear Sonic Art*, New York, NY: Bloomsbury.

Koren, L. (2010) *Which Aesthetics do You Mean?: Ten Definitions*, Point Reyes, CA: Imperfect Publishing.

Kristeller, P. (1951) "The Modern System of the Arts," *Journal of the History of Ideas* 12:4 pp 496–527.

Licht, A. (2009) "Sound Art: Origins, Development and Ambiguities," *Organised Sound* 14:1 pp 3–10.

Moten, F. (2003) *In the Break: The Aesthetics of the Black Radical Tradition*, Minneapolis, MN: University of Minnesota Press.

Nancy, J-L. (2007) *Listening*, trans. Charlotte Mandell, New York, NY: Fordham University Press.

Nietzsche, N. (1967) *The Birth of Tragedy and the Case of Wagner*, trans. Walter Kaufmann, New York, NY: Random House.

Pater, W. (1986) *The Renaissance: Studies in Art and Poetry*, New York, NY: Oxford University Press.

Rancière, J. (2004) *The Politics of Aesthetics*, trans. Gabriel Rockhill, New York, NY: Bloomsbury.

_____ (2001) *Aisthesis: Scenes from the Aesthetic Regime of Art*, trans. Zakir Paul, New York, NY: Verso.

Rodgers, T. (2010) *Pink Noises: Women on Electronic Music and Sound*, Durham, NC: Duke University Press.

Sakakeeny, M. (2015) "Music," in David Novak and Matt Sakakeeny eds, *Keywords in Sound*, Durham, NC: Duke University Press.

Schopenhauer, A. (1969) *The World as Will and Representation*, Vol. 1, trans. EFJ Payne New York, NY: Dover.

Shelley, J. (2015) "The Concept of the Aesthetic," in Ed. Edward N Zalta, *The Stanford Encyclopedia of Philosophy* (Winter 2015 Edition) http://plato.stanford.edu/archives/win2015/entries/aesthetic-concept/ accessed 5 June 2016.

Smith, J. (2015) *Eco-Sonic Media*, Oakland, CA: University of California Press.

Smith, J. and N. Verma (eds) (2016) *Anatomy of Sound: Norman Corwin and Media Authorship*, Oakland, CA: University of California Press.

Sterne, J. (2004) *The Audible Past: Cultural Origins of Sound Reproduction*, Durham, NC: Duke University Press.

_____ (2012) "Sonic Imaginations," in ed. J. Sterne *The Sound Studies Reader*, New York, NY: Routledge, pp 1–18.

Théberge, P., Devine, K., and Everett, T. eds, (2015) *Living Stereo: Cultures and Histories of Multichannel Sound*, New York, NY: Bloomsbury.

VanCour, S. (2013) "New Directions in Media Studies: The Aesthetic Turn," *Antenna: Responses to Media and Culture* http://blog.commarts.wisc.edu/2013/02/11/new-directions-in-media-studies-the-aesthetic-turn/, accessed 4 June 2016.

Voegelin, S. (2014) *Sonic Possible Worlds: Hearing the Continuum of Sound*, New York, NY: Bloomsbury.

Weheliye, A. (2005) *Phonographies: Grooves in Sonic Afro-Modernity*, Durham, NC: Duke University Press.

6

SOUND, AFFECT, POLITICS

Christabel Stirling

Introduction: what is affect good for?

The "turn to affect" in the humanities and social sciences has sparked an epistemological upheaval over the last decade. In this chapter I ask: how have sound and music been brought into articulation with affect theories? Sound's ability to alter our bodily states—to invade us physically in ways that first become perceptible as atmosphere, vibe, or sensation—is hard to ignore. As Goodman puts it, sound has a "seductive power to caress the skin, to immerse, to soothe, beckon and heal, to modulate brain waves and massage the release of certain hormones" (Goodman, 2010: 10). Yet sound can also induce "diminished intellectual capacity, accelerated respiration and heartbeat, hypertension [and] neurosis" (ibid). In this overview, I engage theoretically and ethnographically with the implications of a turn to affect in sound and music studies. I ask, paraphrasing Mazzarella (2009), what sonic/musical affect might be "good for": what is the socio-political power of sonically incited affect, not only as a concept but as a tangible, lived experience? And how might one go about researching it empirically?

Before turning to these issues, it is useful to consider the sorts of definitions and modes of thinking that the turn to affect has brought into being. What *is* affect? And why has it surged into fashion across so many disciplines? In the introductory paragraphs, I address these questions in relation to dominant paradigms in the new affect theories. By "new" I distinguish the recent wave of work on affect from its foundations in historical social-psychological literatures (see Blackman, 2012).

The turn to affect is concerned with how bodies and bodily matter participate in the ongoing construction of the social and, ultimately, politics and the political. The first point to note here is the specific emphasis on *bodies*. Affect is taken to refer to those elements of experience "over which humans have the least control [such as] hormonal flows, especially of adrenaline; breathing… and those absolute intensities, which cannot be contained within a logic of signification" (Gilbert, 2004: 11). Affect, then, points towards corporeal states, sensings, and auras, rather than to "their manifestation or interpretation as emotions" (Hemmings, 2005: 551). Significantly, this shift towards the body and physiology is seen by those advocating it as a counter-force to the logocentrism of poststructuralism. By attending to the non-verbal, non-conscious dimensions of living—the motor mechanisms of the body that are felt to be in excess of "the speaking subject" (Blackman & Venn, 2010)—new affect theorists are keen to stress the limits of discourse, signification, and meaning, thus largely opposing the linguistic models of experience characteristic of much poststructuralist and deconstructionist work (Gilbert, 2004; Massumi, 2002). A primary aim of the new affect paradigm, then, is to search for "vocabularies other than those that rely on language as their master-metaphor" (Gilbert, 2004: 14), thereby moving away from the "textual" as a primary theoretical touchstone (Gregg & Seigworth, 2010).

A second key dimension of the turn to affect is its focus on what are held to be the "impersonal" qualities of bodily states, as opposed to the "personal" nature of emotions (see Leys, 2011, for a critique). Turning away from the interiorized, subject-oriented understanding of emotions found in psychoanalysis, affects are conceived as "impersonal" in the sense of being trans-subjective, shared, contagious, and tied to non-intentional, "pre-personal" forces. Affects are thus supposedly irreducible to notions of experience associated with the individual subject (Clough, 2007). The conceptual distancing of affect from emotion is, then, simultaneously a rejection of the individualizing, psychologizing, and in some traditions linguistic ways in which psychoanalysis approaches bodily, psychic, and social matters. As Gilbert notes, "this is not to dispute the importance of the Lacanian framework for understanding social phenomena. But it is to insist that such [social] phenomena possess dimensions that exhaust explanatory possibilities, in particular when [they] are irreducibly collective in character" (Gilbert, 2004: 14). New affect theorists are thus sceptical of psychoanalytic concepts of the bounded, autonomous individual subject, tracing instead the affective connective tissue that binds subjectivities to other bodies, socialities, places, technologies, and worlds (Blackman, 2012; Clough, 2007).

A third introductory point to note is the preoccupation amongst new affect theorists with how bodily states are transmitted, facilitated, or "engineered" as patterns of influence that animate social and political connectivity between humans and nonhumans. Affect theorists are thus resolutely anti-structural in their theorization of the social. Instead, sociality is conceived as inherently mobile and dynamic, constantly forming and re-forming through the associations and suggestions that unfold between human and nonhuman bodies. The question for these theorists is then not so much "what is a body?" but "what can a body do?" (Deleuze & Guattari, 2004). How does affect enliven the potential for action, relation, and encounter between humans, animals, and machines? What kinds of social matrices might ensue in a milieu where subjectivities are defined not by individuated ideologies and identities, but by their "capacities to affect and be affected"? (Blackman & Venn, 2010: 9). A third central feature of the new paradigm is therefore that it explores how affective encounters between human and nonhuman bodies mediate the social and political. What comes to the fore is a decentring not only of the logocentrism of poststructuralism and the individualism of psychoanalysis, but of the Kantian-Hegelian location of the human subject at the heart of experience.

Having introduced key aspects of the new affect theories, I next point to how they can be brought to music and sound. I then extend this discussion by referencing my own and others' ethnographic work, suggesting that when scrutinized empirically through sound and music, affect emerges as something conceptually quite different to how it is portrayed in the new paradigm. Finally, I highlight the sorts of socio-political openings that sound and music portend, focusing on how musical and sonic affect can mediate social stratifications and forms of power. A revised understanding of affect, I argue, is central to any analysis of sonic or musical publics, and therefore also to sonic or musical politics.

Sound, music, and affect

If new affect theories have tended to exclude music and sound (Kassabian 2013b: 179), sound studies and recent musicology are equally culpable of absenting affect and the body from accounts of sonic experience. Following Gilbert's (2004) diagnosis of the linguistically oriented poststructuralist turn in cultural studies, the postmodern and poststructuralist turns in musicology might be added to the list of epistemologies that elevate semiotics and representation over affect and sensation. This is not to minimise the importance of such work. Clearly, the deconstruction of "structural listening" played a crucial role in destabilising the ideology of the "music itself", demonstrating that music and sound can have multiple meanings (Subotnik, 1988; Dell'Antonio, 2004). But it had little concern with bodily matters. Indeed, it is only recently that musicologists have begun fully to engage with what music and sound feel like as well as what they mean (Cook, 2013; Cusick, 2008). Surprisingly, given that it is a younger discipline, sound studies also betray a certain logocentrism. Influential sound theorist Kim-Cohen, for instance, builds his sonic anti-essentialism around Derrida's semiotic concept of *différance* and Peirce's "thirdness", scarcely mentioning the body in his call for a "non-cochlear" sonic art (Kim-Cohen, 2009).

In contrast, certain areas of interdisciplinary music research pay close attention to questions of affect, albeit in very different terms to the new affect theories. Particularly notable are the sub-disciplines of music psychology and music and consciousness studies, which explore physiological processes such as mimetic desire and rhythmic entrainment (Clarke & Clarke, 2011), as well as trancing, dissociation, and altered states of consciousness (Becker, 2004; Herbert, 2011). Other precursors to a sonic affective turn include theories of corporeality in music philosophy (Kivy, 1989; Meyer, 1956); aspects of popular music studies—for example, Dyer's notion of "whole-body eroticism" in disco (Dyer, 1979) and Frith's concept of "physical sympathy" when listening to soul singers' vocalizations (Frith, 1996: 192); the emphasis on Lacanian *jouissance* in writings on electronic dance music (for example Gilbert & Pearson, 1999); and the auto-ethnographies and aural psycho-geographies of sound studies scholars who document the experiential aspects of sound installation art (for example Voegelin, 2010). This diverse body of work provides some starting points for thinking about sound, music, and affect. However, the focus remains mainly on individual experiences and behaviours, neglecting how affect operates in social or collective realms of living.

Additional studies addressing sound, music, and affect come from the sociologists Bull (2000, 2007) and DeNora (2000). Working ethnographically, both writers find highly original ways to talk about music and sound's physical effects, although again not in the terms of new affect theories. Bull's accounts of iPod/mobile music listeners illuminate music's ability to affectively "empower" individuals as they traverse the city, augmenting their physical and cognitive capacities (Bull, 2007: 41). In turn, DeNora focuses on music as a "technology of the self" (DeNora, 2000: 46), tracking how "people mobilize music for the doing, being and feeling that is social experience" across a range of public and private settings (DeNora, 2000: 49). Particularly striking is the resemblance between DeNora's work and the Deleuzian strand of affect theory, given her focus on how music extends and curtails "what the body can do" (DeNora, 2000: 103). Criticising semiotic musicology, DeNora roots her analysis firmly in music's affective agency: its power to modulate states of mood, well-being, energy, and action. Moreover, to avoid any reincarnation of the "music itself", she invokes Gibson's concept of "affordance" (Gibson, 1966) as a means of highlighting "the collaborative dimension of how music's effectiveness is achieved" (DeNora, 2000: 96). For DeNora, music's ability to move us from one bodily state to another is, then, not "caused" by musical sound, but results from the relational "partnership" that arises between music's acoustic ingredients on the one hand, and the potentials that such ingredients "afford" to particular "situated users" on the other (ibid: 96).

The uptake of Gibson's "affordance" by music scholars such as DeNora and also Clarke (2005) provides fertile ground on which to begin theorizing sound and affect. For one thing, it offers a way of talking about music and sound's physical properties as agential, but not essential:

not reducible to the "object itself". In this way, sonic materials can be seen to "afford" particular affective and practical "potentials" (for example dance-ability), while the manner in which those "potentials" are actualized remains contingent on the encultured listening subject and the context of their encounter (cf. Born 2010a). But more than this, "affordance" opens up unprecedented routes in the music disciplines for thinking about how sonic properties such as rhythm, pitch, texture, and timbre can inspire and modulate a body's capacity to *act, do*, and *become*. It is, then, the closeness of the relations between touching, feeling, and doing that makes "affordance" such a useful concept (cf. Sedgwick, 2002). In this light, "affordance" provides two key tenets for a theory of sonic affect. The first is the notion of sound-subject-context contingency (DeNora, 2000: 43). What matters, in short, are not only the potential capacities that a sound "affords" but the radically variant ways in which those potentials can be realised depending on who encounters them and in what circumstances. The second is the emphasis that affordance places on sound's relationship to action. By stressing sound's materiality, "affordance" shifts the focus away from any semiotic probing for immanent meanings to the sensory, tactile, and textural motivators of affect, practice, and performance.

Where affordance is less effective conceptually is as a basis for understanding musical and sonic socialities. DeNora's own primary concern is with how music functions as a resource for modulating psychological states of being—that is, with music's links to subjectivity and identity at an individual level (DeNora, 2000: 130). But affordance is less useful for understanding the socio-political implications of musically animated affective contagion and other rapid, non-conscious processes, or for examining how music and sound can afford collective experiences that affirm, entrench, or destabilise normative social hierarchies. For all its significance, then, it is necessary to look beyond this sociological work to comprehend how music and sound influence socio-corporeal relations, and to what political ends.

New affect theories

The obvious place to look for a conceptual vocabulary that moves beyond the individual to address how affect mediates the social and political is the new affect theories. To my knowledge, the first writer to bring affect theory to music and sound was Grossberg. In an early paper on rock and roll, Grossberg rejected the idea of a split between "signification" and "materiality", noting that "[i]t is not that rock and roll does not produce and manipulate meaning but rather that meaning itself functions in rock and roll affectively" (Grossberg, 1984: 233). Rock and roll, he argued, is not a semiotic "text", but a set of "networks" through which pleasure, desire, and "strategic empowerment" are made "possible and important for its audiences" (ibid: 227–8). Moreover, such networks of empowerment—or "affective alliances" (ibid)—are, he suggested, potentially generative of oppositional strategies that are "removed from the hegemonic affective formation" (ibid: 235–7, 240). As early as 1984, Grossberg thus not only broke with linguistic Althusserian concepts of "ideology", invoking instead a "flat-ness" between the discursive and material that prefigured his turn to Deleuze (Grossberg, 2010: 323). He also recognised music's "affective alliances" as inherently social and political, implicated in the reconfiguring of embodied social boundaries and power relations. Pursuing Grossberg's work in the early 2000s, and drawing again on music, Gilbert then advocated a Deleuzian "shift" in cultural studies, referencing Williams's "structures of feeling" (Williams, 1977) as well as Deleuze to point to the intertwining of the discursive and material (Gilbert, 2004: 12–13). Through this anti-dualistic approach, Gilbert argued for the "sociality" of musical affect—its social, cultural, and structural-historical mediation (ibid). At the same time, like Grossberg, he recognised that affective investment in music could itself potentially "re-structure" the social by mobilising groups into counter-hegemonic political positions. As becomes clear later, this work is crucial both for its relationality and its socio-political grounding.

Moving into music and sound research, Goodman's *Sonic Warfare* (2010) was also among the first to engage with sound and the affective turn. In contrast to Grossberg and Gilbert, Goodman explores the deployment of sound as a "weapon" to affectively manipulate and deceive populations in late capitalism via machineries such as sonic branding and the Mosquito Anti-Social Device (Goodman, 2010: xvi, 146). Most significant, here, is Goodman's attunement to the "ambivalence" of sonically induced affect (cf. Hemmings, 2005): its ability to generate repetitive, pestering, and overpowering experiences via the implantation and arousal of embodied memories, and thus its alignment with stasis and fixity as much as novelty and change. Further developments have arisen with the flurry of work on sound and affect that has emerged in Goodman's wake (Thompson & Biddle, 2013; Kassabian, 2013b; Jasen, 2016). In their 2013 edited volume, Thompson and Biddle provide the first comprehensive introduction to sound, music, and affect theory, tracing dominant and marginal antecedents to the current affective turn, and locating a genealogy of affect in the history of musical aesthetics. Like Goodman, Thompson and Biddle raise the issue of affect's "ambivalence", problematizing—through a discussion of affect's role in boundary rituals—the constant theorization of affect as transformative (for example Massumi, 2002), when, as they put it, "[musical] affect... provides no such always-already radicalizing dynamic" (Thompson & Biddle, 2013: 7, 13). Their statement finds support in chapters by Kassabian and Jarman, who, developing Goodman's work, examine how music and sound are increasingly commoditized and distributed according to "a logic of affect"—for example in Sleep Apps, Compilation CDs ("Smooth Classics for Rough Days") and listening technologies such as Moodagent (Kassabian, 2013a; Jarman, 2013: 184).

This recent sound/music-based work is therefore attentive to the collective, relational nature of affect—the ways in which sonically generated affects "extend beyond the individual towards the bodies of others" (Thompson & Biddle, 2013: 8). Kassabian, in particular, develops an important sonically derived theory of "distributed subjectivity"—a "nonindividual" subjectivity in which bodies and subjects are strengthened and impeded by the "ubiquitous musics" that hail from cafés, games consoles, smart phone apps, and even clothing (Kassabian, 2013b). Yet while this engagement with the social and bio-political aspects of musical affect is welcome, concerns are raised by the lack of empirical grounding for key arguments. Indeed, the majority of writers mentioned tend to import pre-existing affect theories into their work as a way of articulating sonic experience in novel ways. Goodman, for example, adopts the Deleuzian concept of affect as "pre-personal" (Deleuze & Guattari, 2004) as a means of suggesting that people's individual histories and social identities have no bearing on how, whether, or by what they are affected. The consequences are manifest in universalizing claims scattered throughout his book, such as that "certain frequencies... produce an affective tonality of fear", or that infrasound "arouses anxiety" and "[makes] you shake" (Goodman, 2010: 66, 189). In short, by assuming that affect is "pre-personal"—that it does not need a subject to register—Goodman implies that sonic materials can affect the body in ways that are unmediated by personal history, socio-cultural milieu, genre, and situation. Sound thus becomes a "force" like gravity, and the body becomes "dumb matter" (DeNora, 2000; Blackman, 2012: 17). The effect is a re-emergence of the essentialist ideology of the music or sound "itself"—an archaic approach that is in marked friction with empirical work like DeNora's that goes to great lengths to illustrate the sound-subject-context "partnership" by which music's efficacy is achieved.

If others such as Jarman and Kassabian are sceptical of the notion that particular frequencies induce particular affects in listeners, their work is nonetheless speculative. While this is perfectly reasonable, it lacks the kinds of empirical insights that could fuel further conceptual development in new affect theories. Instead, they and other contributors to Thompson and Biddle's volume tend to adhere to one or other variant of affect theory, presenting the editors with what they call a dilemma of "definition": "Where does one draw the line between affect and emotion? Are we following a Freudian or Deleuzian/ Guattarian trajectory?" (Thompson & Biddle, 2013: 23). This body of work thus reveals the limits of purely theoretical approaches: by continually returning to abstract philosophical ideas to explain affect's social and political power, these theorists risk advocating a politics that may be unviable—"a theatre of concepts the power of which… is matched only by their powerlessness to transform" (Stengers, 2011: 380). Thus, while conceptual work is vital for enlivening our intellectual paradigms, it must also be put to work and recalibrated through an engagement with the empirical, rather than simply "followed" (Born, 2010b). As Grossberg notes, "a better understanding of the present is the condition of possibility for a better [political] imagination. Imagination involves empirical labour" (Grossberg, 2010: 322).

Building on this, I next want to show how ethnographic work enables theoretical developments beyond those pioneered by new affect theorists. Along with my own fieldwork, I refer to other ethnographers of sound, music, and affect: *inter alia*, Henriques's (2010) work on affect and/as the spread of vibrations in Kingston's dancehall scene; Hirschkind's (2006) ethnography of sermon tapes and affective listening practices amongst Muslims in Cairo; Overell's (2012) research on "brutal belonging" in Japan and Australia's grindcore scenes, which develops the key ethnographic observation that "[p]ower relations mediate affect", and, specifically, that "gender identity… enables or restrains scene-members' ability to experience [such] brutal belonging" (2012: 216–7); and Stokes's (2010) analysis of Turkish popular music, which draws on Berlant's (1997) concept of "intimacy" to emphasise the life-affirming potentials that music's "affective alliances" afford amidst sectarian clashes. Importantly, in all of this ethnographic work, musical affect in some ways articulates and is articulated by the social.

Transforming new affect theories

The key aspect of new affect theory that I wish to contest is its tendency to conceptualize affect as "pre-personal" or pre-mediated, which is to say, in excess of the ideologies and intentionalities of individual subjects. The popularity of this stance is attributable to neo-Deleuzian affect theorists such as Massumi (2002), who have projected ontological Deleuzian concepts onto the empirical. For Massumi, a sociality flowing out of "pre-personal" affective intensities that operate autonomously to individuated ideologies is not a potential or "virtual" realm as it was for Deleuze, but a persistent empirical reality—one that he "proves" in a series of questionable laboratory-style experiments (Massumi, 2002: 25). Rather than testing the feasibility of Deleuze and Guattari's political ontology in a rigorously empirical and historically situated manner, Massumi thus takes their concepts verbatim. The same can be said of cultural geographers Amin and Thrift (2013). By using artistic practice to "tap into the pre-personal plane", they argue, new modalities of belonging can be forged that do not begin with the individual subject and identity (Amin & Thrift, 2013: 72, 158). Again, "pre-personal" ontologies are empirically assumed, and invented philosophical concepts become a basis for politics.

In my ethnography, passages into the Deleuzian plane of "pre-personal" affect and bodily anomaly did not make themselves apparent in any substantial way. On the contrary: the personal histories, psyches, and social positionalities of encultured subjects frequently emerged as resilient, working to align affective experience with fixity and "stickiness" (Ahmed, 2004) rather than change. Asserting that the pre-personal can be invoked or "engineered", as Massumi and others do, is thus problematic. As feminist, queer and critical race affect theorists put it, to claim that it is possible to summon a set of milieus in which experience is detached from individuated iden-tities (gender, race, or any pre-existent "we") is to undermine affect's role in the reproduction of social oppressions—its tendency to circulate along already existing lines of social and cultural investment, and thereby to perpetuate or entrench social relations of domination (Berlant, 1997; Blackman, 2012; Brennan, 2004; Hemmings, 2005). While Massumi does, notably, acknowledge the existence of socio-historical stability and inertia, he attributes this to an apparently dif-ferent mechanism: embodied "habit" (Massumi, 2002). Meanwhile, the virtual, pre-individual Deleuzian concept of "affect" is treated as an empirical constant through which such rigid, subject-bound, socially conditioned "habits" can be escaped (ibid: 236). In short, the claim by neo-Deleuzians that pre-subjective delirium and fluidity are empirically immanent, brought into existence through "experimentation", implies a world in which the territorializing dimen-sions of history, social identity, institutionalization, and ideology are avertable. My ethnography suggests otherwise.

In making this argument, it is not, however, my intention to suggest that affect is fully determined by the social, or that it resides purely "within" the physiological body, immune to suggestion and imitation (Brennan, 2004). Such a perspective does not allow for the question of how we become open to change: how a person's prior sense of self and sense of "we" can be overturned and permanently altered by a musical or sonic encounter. What I specifically object to, rather, is the unmediated manner in which neo-Deleuzian theorists depict such moments of change. In fieldwork, affective difference and suggestibility certainly did manifest, but not via a radically autonomous, indeterminate body. Rather, such processes tended to arise out of a porous merging of old and new: a psychic-somatic attunement in which robust musical-affective habits became flexible, sometimes temporarily, sometimes on a long-term basis, creating open-ings into emergent socialities in which new socio-musical bodily habits were formed. Thus, against Massumi, habitual affects are not the closure or "blockage" of some vital unmediated "becoming" (Massumi, 2002), but rather can be the very condition of possibility for change. Sonically embodied habits can become "un-stuck" and susceptible in ways that shift normative hierarchies; while suggestible affects can solidify, at times "becoming-stuck" and entrenching wider social divisions (Blackman, 2012). Affect's confounding, transformative capacities are not, then, the result of an unruly, unmediated logic, but evolve out of a multiplicity of intersecting histories, habits, and stabilities. This importantly nuances the socio-political potentials that are at stake in discussing musical affect.

To illustrate my position, I will now give three ethnographic examples. All relate to a par-ticular musical assemblage—the London Lucky Cloud parties.[1] In the first example, I show how sonic affective attachments can become ingrained at a bodily level, working to entrench social relations of difference. In the second, I illustrate the conditions under which such attachments can slide and mutate, overturning generic preconceptions and enlisting people into new soci-alities. In the third, I trace how such moments of "sliding" may gradually become stable again, but in this particular instance, in a way that is socially and politically transformative, working to connect a socially emergent assemblage.

★ ★ ★

Rooted in the principles of the late David Mancuso's New York Loft parties (see Lawrence, 2003), the Lucky Cloud parties privilege high-fidelity audio, social experience and egalitar-ian musical practices. Records are played through Klipschorn speakers and other audiophile equipment with the level of sound not exceeding 100DB—a paradigm that enables highly detailed musical reproduction but at a volume where people can still dance and talk comfortably without shouting. There is no mixing or other technical intervention, orienting the focus towards the dancers and dancefloor rather than the DJ/their skill. And musical selections— which are generically expansive, but which tend to fall into the rare groove/disco/deep house continuum—are rigorously "programmed" for their perceived ability to take the listener on a dramatic sonic-psychic journey or trip, aided for some by psychedelics and empathogens. The parties can thus loosely be defined by their kinetic and sociable dancefloor energy; their anti-hierarchical, anti-egoist ethos; and their seamless, holistic musical aesthetic, which aims to trace the emotional contours of an evening.

One of my experimental methods for researching affect was to invite participants to musical events with which they were unfamiliar or socially affectively disconnected from. In so doing, the aim was to test these individuals' affective thresholds: their ability to attune to, or "make sense" of sonic social spheres that were not their own. In one case, I invited Simon[2]—a 30-year-old man whose musical biography revolved around Britpop, ambient, noise, and dub music—to participate in the Lucky Cloud parties. His initial response was one of genuine interest and openness. Though he confessed to having held a disdain for house music, garage, and disco for much of his adult life—an antipathy rooted in teenage perceptions of these genres as "townie", "commercial", and "cheesy"—he felt that these "embarrassing preconceptions", which, he admitted, were classed and gendered in undertone, were behind him. After a number of hours on the Lucky Cloud dancefloor, however, Simon professed that he was unable to sink into the vibe of the party, and described feeling isolated from the affective contagion palpably germinating around him. He attributed this in part to the bias that he had held against house and disco as a teenager, which, he felt, continued to endure "in his body", if not in his intellect, impeding his ability to "tune in". But another obstacle for Simon was what he referred to as the "bodily pressure" from those around him to achieve affective communion through dancing and physical movement. In the musical spheres to which he had become attached (particularly ambient and dub), collective musical pleasure is accessed through bodily stillness, introversion and controlled transfixion, rather than psychosocial communication—a distinction moderated by the use of mild psychoactive substances like marijuana rather than empathy-enhancing psychedelics. Finally, he felt discomfited by the low volume of sound at Lucky Cloud, having acclimatized to a certain "sonic dominance" (Henriques, 2010) in his own "affective alliances", where the sheer immersive power of sound precludes socializing through talking.

Simon's experience illustrates how musical affectivity is contingent upon the precise ways in which an encultured, historicized subject comes into relation with an encultured, historicized musical "event"—how music's affective capacities are sound-subject-context contingent (Born, 2010a; DeNora, 2000). Further, in this case, Simon's inability to attune to the sonic affective atmosphere around him was not only tied to personal history and socio-cultural location, but to socio-historical processes of genre formation (Born, 2005, 2011; Overell, 2012). As Simon himself reflected, his orientation away from the sounds, genres, and social vibes prevalent at the Lucky Cloud parties had to do with an inability to detach from his early experiences of disco and house—experiences that were, in turn, marked by the reified gendered and classed connotations that these genres had accrued for him via the historical context of their emergence, particularly their reputation for producing women-friendly, pan-sexual, musically anti-elitist spaces. The point, then, is that multiple histories—personal, social, cultural, institutional—enter into sonic affective experiences; and, in this instance, they did so in a way that affirmed pre-existing sonic affective dispositions and generic biases. Simon was not, then, able to simply overcome prior differences by succumbing to a "pre-personal" affective register. Rather, his affective attachments and disassociations manifested as "sticky" (Ahmed, 2004), corporeally ingrained, and enduring in the face of socio-musical influence. What thus emerges is an affective mechanism analogous to

Hirschkind's "somatic learning" (Hirschkind, 2006: 76): a training and inculcation of the body by historically and socially mediated sounds. Not only did Simon's affective robustness engender an experience of repetition and stability; it also affirmed prior socio-cultural differences and ideologies at a corporeal level.

Sonic affective attachments do not always manifest as "sticky", however. They are not, that is, reducible to "blockage", social reproduction, or physiological automatism (Massumi, 2002). On the contrary, under certain conditions, such attachments can "slide", become flexible and vulnerable, sometimes working to introduce elements of uncertainty into socio-musical formations. This became apparent in fieldwork when tracing out the individual histories of those collectivized by the Lucky Cloud parties. It transpired that of the many Lucky Cloud participants that I interviewed, most hailed from radically divergent and often incongruent personal and socio-musical pasts, each one punctuated by "turning points", "epiphanies", and the breaking of embodied, psychic, and social habits. In other words, the affective attachments that these individuals shared towards the Lucky Cloud assemblage did not simply reflect or reproduce a shared set of socio-cultural histories, ideologies, and tastes, but were preceded by incidental and often-unforeseen personal routes and paths. The question is, how had these particular encultured and historical individuals, who had travelled such different socio-musical trajectories, come to aggregate around a shared musical sphere as a distinctive "affective alliance"? What had facilitated their individual-collective openness? And why was Simon unable to experience a similar openness?

The case of one Lucky Cloud participant, Danny, is illuminating. Danny, also in his early 30s, shared a similar musical biography to Simon. Growing up as a metal head and drum 'n' bass head, Danny had "absolutely abhorred" house and UK garage, seeing these genres as "tacky" and "handbag". For him, it was the emergence of dubstep in the early 2000s—a genre that blended UK garage with the darker edges of dance music—that created an interstice in his sonic affective register. Dubstep's innovative aesthetic amalgam opened Danny's psyche/body to UK garage for the first time, amplifying his capacity to affect and be affected, and thereafter turning him onto deep house, disco, and rare groove. As he described, the feeling of "being on the edge" that dubstep's emergence engendered was coaxed by the spaces and atmospheres that he subsequently "discovered" in the disco and house scene—particularly the contagious energy that "propagated" from one body to another across the Lucky Cloud dancefloor (Henriques, 2010). It was, in his words, a "massive turning point" that he "couldn't have foreseen", and constitutes an instance of how robust sonic affective attachments can become flexible, overturning not just personal-somatic orientations and tastes, but, in this case, a gendered and classed generic-affective bias against so-called "handbag" musics like garage. This example, then, illustrates how an historical event—in this case, the emergence of a genre—can create a crack in the genres of normative socio-musical life, a fissure in a person's psycho-affective index. In such a moment of "suspension", what happens next may be uncertain and unstable, but it is not random or a-subjective; it is contingent upon the specificity of a person's socio-musical-affective history. That is to say, habit and invention, stasis and change, repetition and difference emanate out of the same processes, each oriented by intersecting personal and socio-cultural histories, the history or path-dependency of genre, and the movement of historical conditions. Knowing which prevails and why is not something that can be decided in advance, but requires empirical research.

In the final example, I reflect on the social and political implications of the sonic affective processes I have just described. The moment of affective "suspension" experienced by Danny during the advent of dubstep made perceptible something important: namely, his capacity to diverge, to create, to make a connection where one did not exist previously. This is what Stengers, after Deleuze and Guattari (2004), calls the capacity to resist: "[not] to denounce or to criticize but to construct" (Stengers, 2005: 122). In this vein, I want to suggest that sound and music's potential to engender moments of affective "openness", to divert the socio-historical trajectories in which a person's life-making practices are cast, to trigger shifts in a person's affective register that move them into new kinds of collectivity where new social alliances can be forged, are what endow sonic affect with a socio-political capacity. At the Lucky Cloud parties, a significant proportion of those collectivized have, at some point in their lives, lived through a personal and/or socio-musical-affective "suspension": an interruption that opened them to the possibility of "something else"—of making connections that confounded previously embedded sonic attachments, selves, socialities, and hierarchies; of living and loving otherwise. Largely for this reason, the sociality summoned into being by the parties is one that is refractive of numerous social identity formations, namely sexuality, class, age, nationality, and gender. As one interviewee, Cora, put it:

> The [Lucky Cloud] parties are unique, because… people are all different ages, sexualities, backgrounds… some of them have kids, and bring [their kids] earlier in the night, so… there's this whole close-knit community of people that you wouldn't really find anywhere else. A lot of them I see away from the parties too.

Where this stance differs from new affect theories is in its emphasis that such sonic affective "openness" is not anomalous or pre-mediated, but contingent upon multiple, often-constraining histories. It is noteworthy, for instance, that while aggregating an unusually diverse demographic, the Lucky Cloud parties are also predominantly white, with only a small number of ethnic minorities regularly in attendance. This "whiteness" in turn has to do with complex histories regarding the relative lack of genealogical tie between black British communities and black American-originating musics such as disco, house, and jazz—histories that, for now at least, appear relatively defiant. Moreover, it would be naïve to think that sound and music's ability to generate emergent socialities is solely contingent upon affect. The reason that the Lucky Cloud parties are significant as opposed to, for instance, the London electronic dance music scene generally, is because of the highly specific protocols, rituals, and histories that prefigure it as an assemblage—its commitment to egalitarianism and community-building via the legacy of Mancuso; its accessible modes of publicity and ticketing; its anti-corporate ethos, which places the crowd at the centre of importance; its inclusion of children for the first few hours—all of which *combine* with the affective dimensions of sound quality, musical "programming", social and spatial atmosphere to configure a socially atypical and anti-normative coalition of people.

The bringing into existence of a new social public is only part of the socio-political question, however. It also matters how people relate to one another on a microsocial level. A second way that sonically incited affect plays a key role at the Lucky Cloud parties, then, is by "sticking" the heterogeneous group of people that aggregate together. That is, the diverse social groups that gather on the Lucky Cloud dancefloor do not simply bifurcate into socially distinct micro-publics, as is often the case at club nights, but affectively encounter and attune to one another. One way this is achieved is through the cyclic repetition of certain tunes—tunes that have, over time, become ingrained in the personal histories and psyches of the regulars who make up the majority of the crowd. These "Classics", as they are known, function as "affective anchors", heralding an explosion of jubilant energy as soon as they become audible, pulling people from all corners of the room into a shared sonic-bodily familiarity. As well as affirming musical affinities, the "Classics" help to forge powerful social bonds by affectively grouping people of different ages, sexual orientations, nationalities, gender identities, and class positions together; binding them through their implicit corporeal-collective attachment to particular records. As Danny described:

> One of the first [Lucky Cloud] parties I went to, I heard Tamiko Jones "Can't Live Without Your Love". The room literally exploded with this… almost *spiritual* energy! […] In the next year or so, I heard that tune and some other [Classic] tunes again… And each time, that same energy would re-appear and spread across the room, and each time… I felt as though the loose friendships I was making were sort of made stronger… Just by getting to know the tunes […] and feeling that shared, kind of instant elation with other people around you.

This, then, is an example of how repetitive-habitual sonic affects—when collectively embodied or shared by a counter-hegemonic social assembly—can simultaneously be transformative. Through the collective investment of embodied psycho-corporeal memories in "Classics" such as Tamiko Jones "Can't Live Without Your Love" and Karma "High Priestess", music and sound, in this assemblage, help build affective and social alliances that not only contradict certain pre-existing social hierarchies, but that also spiral outwards from the events themselves in the form of enduring friendships and solidarities (cf. Born, 2011; Grossberg, 1984). As an empirical example, this importantly demonstrates that, contrary to Massumi, affective repetition and "habit" do not necessarily act as an imposition to novelty and change, but can themselves be collectively empowering and life-changing (cf. Stokes, 2010: 3–5).

* * *

In sum, two key insights emerge with regards to what sonic/musical affect might be "good for". The first relates to the bringing into existence of subjectivities and socialities that are *emergent*, and that might be in contradiction with existing power structures (Born, 2011). Through the example of Danny, I have shown how music and sound, by virtue of the vibes and social spaces that they generate as well as sounds, can create a "suspension" of social subjective continuities that may, for a specific person or people, open up connections that were not previously perceptible. When combined with a musical event's multiple other mediations (publicity, promotion, policing…), such affective "openings" *may* bring people into association in ways that put existing social orders into question. Recognising, however, that pluralism, difference and co-presence mean little if the encounters that manifest between bodies continue to legitimize relations of hostility and domination, the second insight relates to the nature of the social relations that are brought into play within a specific sonic social space. Through the example of "Classics", I have shown how music has the capacity to engender channels of affective and psychic communion between socially heterogeneous individuals who may not otherwise encounter one another. By rousing what Gilbert calls affective "collective retentions" (Gilbert, 2013: 688), the "Classics" take on an adhesive function by binding a not-quite-pre-existent collectivity together. In so doing, they provide the means through which to encounter difference in rewarding, non-verbal ways, while also offering opportunities for group life that potentially re-organise prevailing social divisions and disconnections.

Conclusion

The implications of using music and sound to research affect are considerable. Conceptually, affect emerges as an ambivalent "threshold condition" (Blackman, 2012) that is personal, socio-cultural and historical, as well as psychically volatile. It is thus a mechanism capable of cementing social relations of difference as well as transmuting them. Crucially, however, I have argued that even where it is socially transformative, affect is not pre-personal in origin. Rather, it is pre-disposed by multiple personal, social, cultural, and institutional histories, with their variant temporalities. The questions that follow are thus not simply "what can a body do?" but who or what—at any given time—is able to become affectively open to new connections, why, and to what social and political ends? This approach differs significantly from dominant affect theories. On the one hand, it suggests a need to move beyond the reification of movement advocated by neo-Deleuzians, who preclude the reality of stasis and hierarchy. On the other hand, it diverges, if only marginally, from feminist, queer, and critical race affect theorists, whose work occasionally borders on social reductionism. Instead, it seems necessary to look to new paradigms that advocate a generative relationship between empirical research and conceptual development (Born, 2010b: 27–28). In Born's (2005) theory of music's social and material mediation, for instance, which emerges from what she calls a "post-positivist empiricism" with inventive conceptual effects (Born 2010b: 28), socio-historical conditions are understood to inherently intervene in affective experience—not in a way that is causal or deterministic, but in a way that refuses a conceptualization of "becoming" as random. Instead, suggestibility and emergence are seen to radiate out of history, as—in Lefebvre's words—"possibilities, uncertainties, opportunities and probabilities" (Lefebvre, 2003: 66). These writers thus provide the basis for a conceptual framework that comes closer than any contemporary affect theory to accommodating sonic affect's contradictory, but not haphazard social and political effects.

Notes

1 See www.loftparty.org/about.html.
2 All names have been changed to protect the privacy of my participants.

References

Ahmed, S. (2004) *The Cultural Politics of Emotion*, Edinburgh: Edinburgh University Press.
Amin, A. & N. Thrift (2013) *Arts of the Political: New Openings for the Left*, Durham, NC: Duke University Press.
Becker, J. (2004) *Deep Listeners: Music, Emotion and Trancing*, Bloomington, IN: Indiana University Press.
Berlant, L. (1997) *The Queen of America goes to Washington City: Essays on Sex and Citizenship*, Durham, NC: Duke University Press.
Blackman, L. (2012) *Immaterial Bodies: Affect, Embodiment, Mediation*, London: Sage.
Blackman, L. & C. Venn (2010) "Affect", *Body & Society*, 16(7), pp. 7–28.
Born, G. (2005) "On Musical Mediation: Technology, Ontology and Creativity", *Twentieth Century Music*, 2(1), pp. 7–36.
———. (2010a) "Listening, Mediation, Event: Anthropological and Sociological Perspectives", *Journal of the Royal Musical Association*, 134(1), pp. 79–89.
———. (2010b) "The Social and the Aesthetic: For a Post-Bourdieuian Theory of Cultural Production", *Cultural Sociology*, 4(2), pp. 1–38.
———. (2011) "Music and the Materialisation of Identities", *Journal of Material Culture*, 16(4), pp. 376–388.
Brennan, T. (2004) *The Transmission of Affect*, Ithaca, NY: Cornell University Press.
Bull, M. (2000) *Sounding Out the City: Personal Stereos and the Management of Everyday Life*, New York, NY: Berg.
———. (2007) *Sound Moves: iPod Culture and Urban Experience*, London: Routledge.
Clarke, E. (2005) *Ways of Listening: An Ecological Approach to the Perception of Musical Meaning*, Oxford: Oxford University Press.
Clarke, D. & E. Clarke (eds.) (2011) *Music and Consciousness: Philosophical, Psychological and Cultural Perspectives*, Oxford: Oxford University Press.

Clough, P. (ed.) (2007) *The Affective Turn: Theorizing the Social*, Durham, NC: Duke University Press.

Cook, N. (2013) *Beyond the Score: Music as Performance*, Oxford: Oxford University Press.

Cusick, S. (2008) "Musicology, Torture, Repair", *Radical Musicology*, 3, retrieved September 2016: www.radical-musicology.org.uk.

Deleuze, G. & F. Guattari (2004) *A Thousand Plateaus: Capitalism and Schizophrenia*, London: Continuum.

Dell'Antonio, A. (ed.) (2004) *Beyond Structural Listening: Postmodern Modes of Hearing*, Berkeley, CA: University of California Press.

DeNora, T. (2000) *Music in Everyday Life*, Cambridge: Cambridge University Press.

Dyer, R. (1979) "In Defence of Disco", *Gay Left*, 8, pp. 20–23.

Frith, S. (1996) *Performing Rites: On the Value of Popular Music*, Cambridge, MA: Harvard University Press.

Gibson, J. J. (1966) *The Senses Considered as Perceptual Systems*, Oxford: Houghton Mifflin.

Gilbert, J. (2004) "Signifying Nothing: 'Culture', 'Discourse', and the Sociality of Affect", *Culture Machine*, 6, retrieved: www.culturemachine.net/index.php/cm/rt/printerFriendly/8/7.

———. (2013) "The Pedagogy of the Body: Affect and Collective Individuation in the Classroom and on the Dancefloor", *Educational Philosophy and Theory*, 45(6), pp. 681–692.

Gilbert, J. & E. Pearson (1999) *Discographies: Dance Music, Culture, and the Politics of Sound*, London: Routledge.

Goodman, S. (2010) *Sonic Warfare: Sound, Affect, and the Ecology of Fear*, Cambridge, MA: MIT Press.

Gregg, M. & G. Seigworth (eds.) (2010) *The Affect Theory Reader*, Durham, NC: Duke University Press.

Grossberg, L. (1984) "Another Boring Day in Paradise: Rock and Roll and the Empowerment of Everyday Life", *Popular Music*, 4, pp. 225–258.

———. (2010) "Affect's Future: Rediscovering the Virtual in the Actual", in M. Gregg & G. Seigworth (eds.) *The Affect Theory Reader*, Durham, NC: Duke University Press, pp. 309–338.

Hemmings, C. (2005) "Invoking Affect: Cultural Theory and the Ontological Turn", *Cultural Studies*, 19, pp. 548–567.

Henriques, J. (2010) "The Vibrations of Affect and their Propagation on a Night Out on Kingston's Dancehall Scene", *Body & Society*, 16(1), pp. 57–89.

Herbert, R. (2011) *Everyday Music Listening: Absorption, Dissociation and Trancing*, Aldershot: Ashgate.

Hirschkind, C. (2006) *The Ethical Soundscape: Cassette Sermons and Islamic Counterpublics*, New York, NY: Columbia University Press.

Jarman, F. (2013) "Relax, Feel Good, Chill Out: the Affective Distribution of Classical Music", in M. Thompson & I. Biddle (eds.) *Sound, Music, Affect: Theorizing Sonic Experience*, New York, NY: Bloomsbury, pp. 183–204.

Jasen, P. C. (2016) *Low End Theory: Bass, Bodies and the Materiality of Sonic Experience*, New York, NY: Bloomsbury.

Kassabian, A. (2013a) "Music for Sleeping", in M. Thompson & I. Biddle (eds.) *Sound, Music, Affect: Theorizing Sonic Experience*, New York, NY: Bloomsbury, pp. 165–182.

———. (2013b) *Ubiquitous Listening: Affect, Attention, and Distributed Subjectivity*, Berkeley, CA: University of California Press.

Kim-Cohen, S. (2009) *In the Blink of an Ear: Toward a Non-Cochlear Sonic Art*, London: Continuum.

Kivy, P. (1989) *Sound Sentiment: An Essay on the Musical Emotions*, Philadelphia, PA: Temple University Press.

Lawrence, T. (2003) *Love Saves the Day: A History of American Dance Music Culture, 1970–1979*, Durham, NC: Duke University Press.

Lefebvre, H. (2003) *The Urban Revolution*, Minneapolis, MN: University of Minnesota Press.

Leys, R. (2011) "The Turn to Affect: A Critique", *Critical Inquiry*, 37, pp. 434–472.

Massumi, B. (2002) *Parables for the Virtual: Movement, Affect, Sensation*, Durham, NC: Duke University Press.

Mazzarella, W. (2009) "Affect: What is it good for?" in S. Dube (ed.) *Enchantments of Modernity: Empire, Nation, Globalization*, London: Routledge.

Meyer, L. (1956) *Emotion and Meaning in Music*, Chicago, IL: University of Chicago Press.

Overell, R. T. (2012) *Brutal Belonging: Affective Intensities in, and between, Australia's and Japan's Grindcore Scenes*, PhD Thesis, Arts—School of Culture and Communication and the Asia Institute, The University of Melbourne.

Sedgwick, E. K. (2002) *Touching Feeling: Affect, Pedagogy, Performativity*, Durham, NC: Duke University Press.

Stengers, I. (2005) "Deleuze and Guattari's Last Enigmatic Message", *Angelaki*, 10(2), pp. 151–167.

———. (2011) "Wondering About Materialism", in L. Bryant, N. Srnicek & G. Harman (eds.), *The Speculative Turn: Continental Materialism and Realism*, Melbourne: Re.press, pp. 368–380.

Stokes, M. (2010) *The Republic of Love: Cultural Intimacy in Turkish Popular Music*, Chicago, IL: University of Chicago Press.

Subotnik, R. R. (1988) "Toward a Deconstruction of Structural Listening", in E. Narmour & R. Solie (eds.), *Explorations in Music, the Arts and Ideas: Essays in Honour of Leonard B. Meyer*, Hillsdale, NY: Pendragon Press.

Thompson, M. & I. Biddle (eds.) (2013) *Sound, Music, Affect: Theorizing Sonic Experience*, New York, NY: Bloomsbury.

Voegelin, S. (2010) *Listening to Noise and Silence: Towards a Philosophy of Sound Art*, London: Continuum.

Williams, R. (1977) "Structures of Feeling", in *Marxism and Literature*, New York, NY: Oxford University Press, pp. 128–135.

PART II

Introduction:
sonic conflicts, concepts and culture

Dostoevsky's novel, *The House of the Dead* is based upon his experiences in a labour camp after having a death sentenced imposed upon him for sedition commuted to hard labour. Dostoevsky who had been a young lieutenant in the Russian Army was tried by a military tribunal who found

> the defendant Dostoevsky guilty of reading aloud a copy of the criminal letter of the litterateur Belinsky…at gatherings first at the defendant Durov's, then at the defen-dant' Petrashevsky's…Dostoevsky was at the defendant Speshnev's during the reading of the seditious work of Lieutenant Grigoryev entitled "A Soldier's Conversation" … for failure to report the dissemination of the litterateur Belinsky's letter … Lieutenant Engineer Dostoevsky … is to be stripped of his rank and all rights attendant upon his estate and to be executed by firing squad.
>
> *(Dostoevsky 1982: xiv)*

Dostoevsky was sentenced to death for being present whilst a letter was read aloud in a pri-vate home, a letter he had not written and had not read out himself. At the time Dostoevsky belonged to a group which was interested in socialist ideas and met to discuss such things during the tyrannical reign of Emperor Nicholas. In the Russia of that time Emperor Nicholas held power over who and what could be said and employed large numbers of people to infiltrate and eavesdrop on those who may have spoken "out of turn". The history of eavesdropping is a complex one often involving those in power listening to those who are subordinate to them. Listening can also be involuntary as in Agnes Humbert's account of hearing the sounds of tor-ture whilst she was imprisoned in Paris in World War Two for being a suspected member of the French Resistance:

> Yesterday I heard the screams of a man being tortured. When the screams died down, they were followed by deep, throaty laughter. All day I have been haunted by these two sounds: screams and laughter. I don't know which was the more terrible. The laughter, I think
>
> *(Humbert 2008 p. 97)*

Eavesdropping had become more sophisticated than in 19th-century Russia, now States and indeed commercial companies have a rich panoply of technological listening devices through which to hear subject populations with or without their knowledge. Who is permitted to speak, who is silenced and the complex structures as to how these words and silences are interpreted and what might be the consequences are investigated in this section. The role that sound plays in the often contradictory manner in how we experience a sense of the social which itself is the result of power differentials, interests, ideologies, social and cultural differences forms the core of this section.

Paradoxically, silence itself can lead to listening (a theme taken up centrally in the work of Schafer). The experience of "silence" when considered socially has multiple meanings, as articulated by Richard Cullen Rath in this section. Socially, silence may just mean the absence of loud noise or the sounds of nature, as for example, when we visit the countryside or perhaps a desert. Yet nature itself can of course be loud. The sounds of the hundreds of crows that nest in the oak trees around my house break the otherwise quietude of the environment as against the largely silent vistas of mountain ranges or deserts. The experience of silence, Rath points out, is itself socially and culturally mediated. It can be imposed by others, teachers, family heads, slave owners and rulers. Subsequent chapters point to the historical silencing of women, people of colour and those with a variety of perceived "impairments". History is full of the silence of the dispossessed. As documents from which historical data of the sounds and social life of city spaces and cultures testify is so far as they are invariably written by the literate and powerful of the time.

If silence is socially and culturally constructed much the same can be said for noise. Noise for many is understood as unwanted sound – from the humming of the refrigerator that so annoyed Murray Schafer to the noise of ski-riders enjoying themselves to the detriment of others on beaches around the world. Many complain about people speaking loudly on their mobile phones in restaurants, trains and museums, they complain about the throbbing sounds of their neighbours wrap around sound emanating from their televisions audible in the living rooms of neighbours. Noise is often associated with modernity itself – the noise of industry and as such is often perceived as a double-edged sword in so far as noise is simultaneously perceived of as progressive but also polluting. Those, for example, who visiting music clubs might enjoy the intensity of sound whilst for others it represents a health hazard.

Bijsterveld's chapter takes us through waves of dissent and protest about noise in the 20th century and charts the changing attitudes towards noise and indeed the city.

She focuses upon the early class nature of attitudes towards noise from Dickens onwards where the production of noise was perceived to be the domain of the working class and poor. She points to the class based origin of such views together with the design of city spaces themselves whereby the middle and upper classes largely created the categories of acceptable and unacceptable noise. These views were then frequently backed up by scientists and health practitioners who pointed to the health benefits of quietude. For example, troops injured in battle during World War One were often thought to require a quiet convalescence before going back to battle to endure the loudest noises produced by "civilization" to date. Throughout the 20th century Bijsterveld charts the complaint about the sound of others, the sounds of industrial machines, of transport noise, especially that of aircraft.

Bijsterveld points to the figure of Murray Schafer who acknowledged that capitalism was largely behind "noise" introducing a political and economic element to what was his largely anti-noise, anti-urban outlook. In Britain today we have local movements against the extension of a third runway at Heathrow Airport and Bijsterveld accurately portrays these movements as often single issue movements, as "not in our back yard movements". The Heathrow scheme, for example, affects some of the wealthier parts of London thus giving the campaigners a potentially "louder" voice in opposition. Bijsterveld notes that there are changing attitudes to urban living that increasingly embraces the sensory environment as against those earlier attitudes that viewed cities as places of sensory overload as against the sounds of the countryside.

Goodman's piece focusses upon the ways in which propagandist messages are disseminated and listened to. These messages represent a political and cultural subset of the general transmission and reception of mediated messages. From the sounding of the church bell in Alain Corbin's wonderful account of bells in the 19th century to the dominant role of radio in propagating ideological messages from the UK, USA, Russia and Germany throughout the 20th century, the use of technology has demarcated and redrawn the boundaries as to who lies within and without of these messages. Some of those who listened to the resonating bells of community (Corbin and Schafer) might well have been alienated from those very sounds. The imagined community of listeners to forms of State propaganda were often riven with potential alternative values and material, cultural and political interests. Goodman weaves his way primarily through the listening spaces of propagandist messages on the radio in which the spaces of habitation, the street, the café, the home, and the workplace become transformed through these messages. Whilst the development of techniques of persuasion have become an art-form in the 20th and 21st centuries, Goodman points to the concurrent need for hearers to be trained as "attentive listeners". Plato first analysed, in his critique of Greek democracy, the power of political rhetoric – of promising people the earth in order to encourage them to vote – and this remains potent today in the multi-media, multi-sensorial world in which we live.

The desire to re-evaluate within sound studies how we listen to race is the focus of Alex W. Corey's chapter. He focuses upon how we hear race and sound and, concurrently, how power dynamics become embodied in culturally unreflective acts of listening itself. In doing so he argues for the use of the ear as a "critical tool". Corey explores the rich history of writings on race, drawing upon the writings of Ralph Ellison and others. In doing so he points to the ways in which historical modes of sonic categorizations filter through and produce notions of race. This exploration of sound and racial difference has now become a rich course of research in the academy as evidenced by our earlier discussion of the work of Stoever. Furthermore, Cory investigates the relationship between modes of speech, visualization and sonic presence articulated through the rise of media from the phonograph onwards which has produced a "sonic archaeology of the visual" whereby notions of hearing and seeing "race" became increasingly blurred and overlapping. Cory contemplates how sensory organisation itself is deeply value laden as is especially apparent in both issues of race and gender.

Thompson in her survey of gendered sound equally points out that sound studies has given insufficient attention to gender and sound together with race. She points to the work of Clary within music to highlight how Clary discussed gender as existing in the very structure, theory and culture of music. This issue parallels the discussion of race and listening made by Stoever and discussed in the introduction of this volume. Thompson, through a range of examples, articulates the ways in which the gendered voice is created, modified technologically and received. In doing so she exposes the cultural, ideological and essentialized norms that often underpin the false binary of masculine and feminine voices in culture. Importantly she discusses the multiple ways in which these gendered voices are constituted by drawing upon examples of transgendered voices, feminine voices, masculine voices and racialized voices.

Amanda Cachia in her chapter approaches the issue of sensory loss and impairment. These issues have become increasingly recognised within sound studies. The work of Hull and others have brought to life the rich and varied ways in which sensory experience is reorganised by those who may not hear or indeed see. Amanda Cachia's chapter imaginatively focusses upon the work of artist Darrin Martin who is hearing impaired in order to work through the role of sound, space and experience in his work.

The demand for a specifically sonic re-addressing of the experiences of war has gained in volume recently beginning with Suzanne Cusick's analysis of the role of music in torture techniques in America and elsewhere, followed by more philosophically inspired works on sound and war (Goodman 2010), historical accounts (Birdsall 2012; Klimczyk and Swierzowska 2015) and accounts that situate soldiers use of sound and music in the recent wars in Iraq (Gilman 2016; Pieslak 2009; Daughtry 2015). Jonathan Pieslak's chapter focusses upon the role of sound and music in the promotion of the culture of the Islamic State through its media channels. Pieslak describes the development of the Islamic State and its use of sound, and continues with a discussion as to how Islamic terrorism might be combatted. States and other more localised groups have at various times used music as a form of indoctrination and socialisation as well as a form of torture in its own right. Pieslak's chapter is a timely reminder as to the ongoing need to investigate the continued propagandist use of music both at home and abroad.

References

Birdsall, C., 2012, *Nazi Soundscapes: Sound, Technology and Urban Space*, 1933–1945, Amsterdam: Amsterdam University Press.

Dostoevsky, F., 1982, *The House of the Dead*, New York, NY: Limited Editions Club.

Daughtry, J. M., 2015, *Listening to War. Sound, Music, Trauma, and Survival in Wartime Iraq*, Oxford: Oxford University Press.

Gilman, L., 2016, *My Music, My War*, Middletown, CT: Wesleyan University Press.

Goodman, S., 2010, *Sonic Warfare: Sound, Affect, and the Ecology of Fear*, Cambridge, MA: MIT Press.

Humbert, A., 2008, *Resistance: Memoirs of Occupied France*, London: Bloomsbury Press.

Klimczyk, W. and Swierzowska, A., 2015, *Music and Genocide*, Bern: Peter Lang.

Pieslak, J., 2009, *Sound Targets: American Soldiers and Music in the Iraq War*, Bloomington, IN: Indiana University Press.

7

SILENCE AND NOISE

Richard Cullen Rath

John Cage made this observation after visiting an anechoic chamber at Harvard University: "Try as we may to make a silence, we cannot" (Cage, 1961: 8). Inside, where he would find silence if ever he could anywhere, he heard his nervous system and the circulation of his blood for the first time. The experience of sensory deprivation is so disturbingly loud inside that the Central Intelligence Agency of the United States uses it as a method of torture (Benjamin, n.d.). Sound, it seems, is an unavoidable part of life. Cage's experience in the anechoic chamber was one of the inspirations for his famous composition *4'33"*. In it, Cage sets the listener the task of hearing the music in the constructed silence, which turns out to be the noise of coughs and the rustling of programs. Silence, it seems, is what we make of it. Coming at the subject digitally, Raven Chacon, a composer and member of the artist collective Postcommodity, recorded silence at some of the quietest places in North America (Window Rock, Arizona, the Sandia Mountains, New Mexico, and Canyon de Chelly, Arizona). When edited to maximum volume, each has its own noise signature that can be clearly heard as different from the others (Chacon, 1999). Beneath silence, it seems, lies noise in its infinite variety.

Noise can be defined in many ways: as the non-signal component of information, as that which is outside of sound, as dissonant but valued music, as an integral component of timbre, as any unwanted, distracting thing, or sound that has not or is incapable of taking on meaning – yet. It seems to have an intrinsic tendency toward unresolved failure because as soon as it becomes valued or meaningful in itself, it ceases to be noise (Hegarty, 2007: 147, 181, 191–192). Intriguingly, noise can be soothing, and by blocking out more identifiable sounds, it can create the conditions for approaching something like silence, as when urban sleepers put on wave machines to block out traffic noise. And in perhaps the greatest irony, noise can be set against itself as in the case of noise-canceling headphones, to create something approaching silence. Noise is an integral part of many musics, and a powerful metaphor that can be deployed both positively and negatively. What all of these have in common is that they are socially, culturally, and historically defined. One person's noise can be another person's music or silence.

I am thus presently essaying an impossible task. Silence does not seem to actually exist in any empirical sense, and noise is merely what an assemblage of soundways situated in a particular place and time determines it to be (Hegarty, 2007: 5; on soundways, see Rath, 2000: 100–102, 2003: 2). Silence and noise exist in a curious orthogonal relationship with each other. At first they might seem like opposites, in an inverse relation where silence is attained by removing noise and vice versa. This makes common sense, but in Cage's and Chacon's work, when the silence occurs what emerges when we attend to it closely enough is noise.

Not exactly opposites then, silence and noise are more like "frenemies": where the one is sought, the other is nearby, waiting to undermine. Beneath silence, noise. Beneath noise, the specter of the silence. Alternately, noise is transformed through attention to it into the realm of sound or music, *à la* Cage in *Silence* and at a more structural level, in Jacques Attali's *Noise*, where "music is inscribed between noise and silence, in the space of the social codification it reveals" (Attali, 1985: 19). For our purposes we can expand this hypothesis beyond music to all sound. Attali considers noise to be "violence: it disturbs. To make noise is to interrupt a transmission, to disconnect, to kill." Attali's notion of downright murderous noise perhaps reflects more of the violence inherent to Western practices of sovereignty, capitalism, and social order than to any universal characteristic that may be attributed to it. Indeed, a moment later, he observes that noise "does not exist in itself, but only in relation to the system within which it is inscribed" (Attali, 1985: 26). Paul Hegarty goes a little further, arguing that noise is a negativity that only exists in relation to what it is not (Hegarty, 2007: 5). Although Attali and Hegarty reject it, scientists and scholars of communication have particular ideas about the objective nature of noise, so it makes sense to see if these ideas can be socially situated rather than to presume them out of existence.

Hillel Schwartz splits the long history of noise into three overlapping historical shifts. The first emerged in sixteenth-century Europe with the interiorization of noise that coincided with the beginnings of the middle- and upper-class valuation of an increasingly private domestic sphere, along with the rise of silent reading. The second shift emerged from nineteenth-century urban life, where noise came to be experienced as an inescapable, intrinsic part of life. This all-pervasiveness allowed it to escape the purely sonic realm and become a metaphor for the bustling twenty-four-hour cacophony of the nineteenth-century city. The third shift, which we are still in the midst of, witnessed the generative engagement of noise with modernity. The nineteenth-century babble blossomed into the twentieth-century's discourses and technologies of not only banishing or limiting, but of generating and using noise (Schwartz, 2011).

At first, noise seems to be mostly unwanted but has nonetheless found welcome in the hands of digital signal processing (DSP) engineers. The modern "objective" notions of noise they employ can trace their origin to Claude Shannon and Warren Weaver's *The Mathematical Theory of Communication*, which divided the world into sender, signal (namely that which was being communicated), channel, noise (that which hampered or competed with the signal, obscuring it and preventing it from being communicated clearly), and receiver (Shannon and Weaver, 1949). Here noise served as interference, as unwanted interfering sound in a sonic communication circuit. It was something to be reduced if not removed so that the good stuff, the signal, could get through. This is evidenced in magnetic recording by noise reduction schemes like Dolby and dbx. The shift to the digital moved away from this negative formulation of noise as something to get rid of or minimize.

With the emergence of DSP from the 1990s onward – though as Jonathan Sterne has shown, (Sterne, 2012: 3) with much deeper roots – noise began to be reformulated as part of the total information in communication. In DSP – and to a certain extent in music – noise is any unpitched sound. Melodic instruments produce these pitches and their multiples (called harmonics) along with some residual noise (like the breathiness of flutes or the reediness of the saxophone) or non-harmonic resonances (as in the dissonances of bells). While melodic instruments all have differing levels of harmonics and noise that shape their timbre and make them identifiable, drums, cymbals, and percussion – the non-pitched instruments – have no clear fundamental pitch in many cases and are defined almost solely by their noise. The voice combines a set pitch and its harmonics (which linguists call formants) with the rattling of the vocal chords, all shaped by the tongue, teeth, and the inside of the mouth. Musicians have known about this character of noise shaping timbre perhaps forever, but DSP formalized and successfully quantified its use. The point here is that noise is fundamental to the timbre of almost all sounds.

A crucial DSP example of how noise came to be revalued in the digital era is the breaking apart of any sound using what is known as a Fourier transform. Fourier had shown in 1807 that any complex waveform, like sound waves, could be broken into an infinite number of sine waves at different frequencies that were allowed to fluctuate by volume through time. The mathematical function for doing this is called the Fourier transform. It is reversible through its inverse transform, in which the component sine waves are combined to reconstruct a sound.

The Fourier transform helps us understand the odd nature of the relationship between noise and silence. Given an infinite number of sine waves, any sound could be reproduced exactly. In practice, however, an infinite number of sine waves is impossible, so the computation is simplified by giving a set number of "bands" – the sine waves, each at a different pitch – combined with a small amount of broadband noise. In this way, the noise in the reconstruction serves as a sort of glue that holds together the sound. This quality of smoothing out is also part of the way digital audio gets produced in practice through the introduction of small amounts of noise to the ones and zeros, a process called dithering, which smooths digital signals in the same way as for the Fourier transform. In fact, one sound engineering trick is to add a small amount of digitally simulated analog tape noise back into the mix to make it sound less digital. Much of the nostalgic fervor for vinyl revolves around its hiss, rumbles, and scratches. Noise, it seems, adds warmth and atmosphere to digital sounds that are so clean and noise-free as to seem brittle and cold. This kind of noise has as much to do with the medium as it does with the content (Hainge, 2013). While it is easy to think of noise as the opposite of silence, the idea that there is a floor of noise that only emerges as silence is approached seems to be at the base of any empirical approach to thinking about the subject. Objectively then, silence simply does not exist, at least as long as life is going on.

If we turn to the subjective realm, noise has a longer historical arc than its treatment in DSP. The early modern European notion of noise was as loud, unwanted, and often dangerous sound. For example, Puritan Bostonian Samuel Sewall wrote that "the Noise of Yale-College came to me gradually," starting as a rumbling noise and resolving finally into "Thunder-Claps" that came as "an extraordinary and unexpected Alarm" when the college was founded in 1722 (Letter of October 15, 1722, Samuel Sewall to Gov. Gurdon Saltonstall of Connecticut, in 1886: 2:143–144). Over the course of nineteenth-century American history and literature, the "machine in the garden" – exemplified by the steam locomotive plowing noisily through rural quietude – served as a touchstone for the downside of industrial progress (Marx, 1964). As Mark Smith points out, what was the horrible noise of northern factories to southern planters was the hum of industry to the northern capitalist (Smith, 2001).

The subjective meaning and value of noise shifted in the twentieth century, and it is here that the relationship of noise and silence becomes most interesting. Luigi Russolo's *The Art of Noises* began the process of revaluing noise, calling for a futurist music that moved beyond traditional instrumentation to include what he called *intonarumori*, mechanical noisemakers modeled on the sounds of the modern world (Kahn, 1999; Russolo, 1967). Cage, as discussed at the outset, sought to expand the notion of music to include all the sounds of the world, calling music into being from what would usually be considered background noise, not unlike Marcel Du Champ's concepts of the "ready-made," an everyday object that becomes art by dint of it being viewed as such (Kahn, 1999: 178–179; Voegelin, 2010: 80).

Voegelin experiences noise as that which cannot be shut out; it takes over the body (Voegelin, 2010: 44). This conflates ideas of noise and loudness though. While they overlap, noise can sometimes be tuned out. A softer noise can be disturbing and attention-grabbing in context, like a slow irregular drip from a faucet when one is trying to sleep or get silence, but even there, the sound of the faucet does not become apparent until it is *relatively* loud. It is only in the expectation of quiet or silence that the drip can even be heard without selectively attending to it. Unambiguously loud sounds like cyclones or the concerts of the Japanese noise musician Merzbow forcefully grab the attention and cannot be ignored, but here it is the loudness as much if not more than the noisiness at play, a difference overlooked by Voegelin (2010: 47–60). Take for example the British colonist William Strachey, who was caught in a hurricane off Bermuda in 1609. He heard it as a constant din that "worketh upon the whole frame of the body, and most loathsomely affecteth all the powers thereof. And the manner of the sickness it lays upon the body, being so unsufferable, gives not the mind any free and quiet time to use her judgment and empire" (Strachey, 1964: 4, 5). *Loud* noise grabs us and our attention forcefully; it breaks down the ability to form coherent meanings and collapses the distinction between subject and object (Derrida, 1973; Voegelin, 2010: 20).

Nick Smith uses noise artist Masonna to offer then to withdraw the hope of noise as an emancipatory force. Noise is regarded – naively, in his opinion – as freeing us in its incoherence and unclassifiability, in its failure to become meaningful without ceasing to be noise. Although it may seem that way, he counters, capitalism can absorb even the noisiest music because art in the age of global capitalism is the creation of a commodity with no functional or use value, and noise fits right into this – as have a long line of other supposedly disruptive artistic practices (Smith, 2005).

Silence too has many everyday meanings that are produced subjectively rather than objectively. It also has a long history, though not one so carefully charted as noise's. An individual or community can be silent, find silence, fear silence, or be silenced in myriad ways without any kind of objective silence existing. Its meanings multiply once time and place are considered. Silence, it seems, has no inherent moral valence. It can be good or bad, productive or destructive, godly or murderous, created, imposed, or sought out. Sometimes the same silence can be valued differently by different historical actors. In short, silence is a moving target.

When placed in time, silence plays a tremendously important role. Sounds obtain much of their meaning from the punctuated silences interspersed within and between them. Rhythms are as much about absence as the presence of sound, whether in polyrhythmic drum patterns, a Miles Davis solo, a paragraph (for spaces, commas, semicolons, colons, periods, parentheses, and dashes are nothing if not silences). In speech the perceived silences allow us to form words and syllables even when phonetically there are none. Davis, a master in the contrapuntal use of sound and silence, remarked that "I always listen to what I can leave out" (Baraka, 1985: 45; Mowitt, 2002; Prochnik, 2011: 11–12; Rosenthal, 1992: 49). Cage observed that "of all the aspects of sound including frequency, amplitude, and timbre, duration, alone, was also a characteristic of silence" (1961: 19). This is a much more specific and useful set of information about time than vast generalizations about circular or linear time that are often used to frame the subject.

The study of temporal shifts and cultural differences in the use of punctuated silences can tell us much for instance about the differing uses of sound in African American history and its significance for the history of the Americas and the world. At the micro level, for example, one can find meaning in the sounds and silences of Sea Island boatmen rowing white masters while singing rowing songs. In some ways, this was the stereotypical scene of putatively happy enslaved workmen under the guise – and gaze – of white paternalism. Masters and mistresses knew that the tempo of the rowing determined the speed of the work and could demand the rowers to speed up. Here, the silences and sounds that made up the rhythms become important. Through the use of polymeter, found in many of the rowing songs, the rowers could speed up the song yet slow down the rowing by switching from one meter to another, changing the meaning of the silences, the gaps, the rhythms, on the fly. This remains speculative, for in order to be effective it needed to be kept off the horizon of white understanding, and thus is not easily found in the historical record left by planters. The circumstantial evidence, namely the polymeter, can be found in the songs themselves, even when written down long after slavery times (Epstein, 1977; Kemble, 1961; Parrish, 1992).

Longer historical silences tell much as well. Winthrop Jordan reconstructed the planned slave uprising that took shape in Adams County Mississippi in 1861 at least in part by listening to his sources as well as just looking at them. He was able to listen through a thirteen-decade long silence that white Southerners had imposed on the historical record to tease out some of how African Americans and planters viewed and heard each other (Jordan, 1993). In an essay on time and slave revolts, Walter Johnson notes that the planning of slave uprisings needed to take place "off the grid" and in the "interstices of weeks, days, and even hours": that is, in the punctuated silences of the rhythms of everyday life (Johnson, 2002). It is probably not coincidental that Mark Smith, one of the historians who makes the most of historical silence, wrote his first book about time on the slave plantation (Smith, 1997). While much has been written on Black and White conceptions of time on the plantation, and on the musicology of African American music, a focus on the soundscapes – including the silences – of African American life opens up these seemingly disparate subjects as being integrally connected and ripe for further research.

Smith has carefully documented the meanings of slave silences to planters in the antebellum U.S. South, who feared the silence of their supposed property as much as any sounds they might make (Smith, 2001: 68). If the enslaved could be heard, by this logic, their whereabouts and activities could be known. Silence meant the loss of predictability, a key to the control of other human beings. While much has been made of the powerful nature of the sounds of slavery, and to good effect (Rath, 1993, 2000; White and White, 2005), the silences could be a potent tactic for the enslaved as well. Lest we think of silence as capable only of calling unpredictability into being, anthropologist Keith Basso has found – in a foundational essay for those studying silences – that for Western Apaches, keeping silent is often "a *response* to uncertainty and unpredictability in social relations," a pattern he found held among other nearby nations as well (Basso, 1970). Thus, refusing to engage in speech can communicate as much as speech itself and has different meanings in different cultures and contexts.

Silences can take on accusatory meanings. For AIDS activists in the 1980s and beyond, silence rather than Attali's noise was murderous. In the famous formula of Silence=Death, silence in conversation and public media about AIDS because of homophobia was slowing research, with the result of lives lost, tantamount to murder by neglect. Interestingly, this seemingly dramatic claim is the one closest to what we could objectively arrive at for a definition of silence above.

From a different angle, but still contrary to Attali's conception of murderous noise, several recent books have taken up silence from the premises that today's world is too noisy and that silence is something to be sought outside oneself. In this decidedly middle-class preoccupation, the noise of everyday – particularly urban – life is deafening and quite literally killing us all. Hearing loss and heart attacks serve as the bogeys in this story, announcing loudly the perils of the loss of silence in urban spaces from New York to Kolkata. Hearing loss is undoubtedly a part of life as well as an occupational hazard, but the heart attack figures are stridently and uncritically quoted as authoritative from offhand remarks and dubious research (Chakrabarty et al., 1997; Chowdhury et al., 2012: 114; Picker, 2003; Thompson, 2002: 116–168; West Bengal Pollution Control Board, n.d.: 4–7).

Often the narrative follows some sort of quest, with the more nuanced authors discovering along the way silence's residence within. This prescriptive quest for silence is rooted in bourgeois privilege for the most part, and would no doubt dissipate in the back of a cab stuck in traffic if the knight-errant were late for a meeting. Logically, it would seem that if these authors wanted silence so badly they would embrace the onset of hearing loss rather than decrying it! These oftentimes querulous accounts attribute the noise to modern life and assume quite mistakenly that in some golden past, the world was quieter and silence was available (Foy, 2010; LeClaire, 2010; Prochnik, 2011; Sardello, 2008).

In addition, silencing as an activity is often construed as erasure, as in the silencing of the experience of Africans in the Americas through the selection of what counts as an archive (Trouillot, 1995). Tillie Olsen called such imposed silences, especially in the experiences of women, "unnatural silences." These included censorship, abandoned media, purposeful deletions, and repression – sometimes direct (such as a publisher's decision that a work is not marketable) and others indirect (by filling a housewife's or working-class person's days to the brim with other work for example) (Olsen, 1978). As Tara Rodgers notes, invoking poet Adrienne Rich,

> Feminists have often located empowerment within acts of breaking silences, by foregrounding aspects of identity. As Adrienne Rich said, "The impulse to create begins – often terribly and fearfully – in a tunnel of silence. Every real poem is the breaking of an existing silence, and the first question we might ask any poem is, What kind of voice is breaking silence, and what kind of silence is being broken?"
> *(Rich, 2001: 150; Rodgers, 2010: 10–11)*

Rodgers posits a sort of "noise gate" – an audio device that silences sounds below a threshold volume as being in effect in sound studies, effectively silencing the voices of women in the literature on experimental music. The complement to these imposed silencings was a natural silence, such as writer's block, or a period of inactivity Olsen likened to a field lying fallow. While Olsen's aim was literature, it is easy to shift the focus from the visual to the audible realm in applying her categories.

Other silences were prescriptively performed rather than imposed, a sometimes fine distinction. Seventeenth-century maxim writer François de La Rochefoucauld categorized personal silence into the silence of eloquence, the silence of mockery, and the silence of respect, while his younger peer, Morvan de Bellegarde, "listed no fewer than eight varieties; prudent, artful, complaisant, mocking, witty, stupid, approving and contemptuous" according to Peter Burke (1993: 129). The people in the higher positions in the hierarchical societies that defined European social structures from antiquity onward – even into the present – relied on the silence of inferiors to keep society running smoothly. Renaissance and early modern silence was a sign of deference and respect, a way of listening upwards. The foremost practitioners of silence were monastics and the clergy, listening upward to the supernatural. The practice of silencing women in Western culture has a long history, but it was also a prescription that women were supposed to aspire to as much as a forced imposition. In formulating his etiquette rules, Aristotle quoted Sophocles's use of an even older Greek proverb, "silence gives grace to woman." This custom continued through the early modern period and on into the twentieth century, with some vestiges no doubt remaining today. Similar prescriptions were applied to children and other dependents and presumed social inferiors. Those at the front of the Western pecking order had reason for silence as well, such as in not showing their hand in matters relating to other communities and social groups: silences that Spanish writer Baltasar Gracian regarded as "the dissimulation of princes and the discretion of the wise" (Burke, 1993: 125–141).

Many religious practices equated – and still equate – silence with the ability to tune sounds out to achieve an inner stillness. Silence can also be a decision, a silencing of oneself that is prerequisite for listening. Such silence creates an opening for communication with the spiritual world in many belief systems. Hesychasm, the practice of withdrawing from the senses to achieve an inner quietude, has a long history in Christian mysticism (Burke, 1993: 127–128). Quakers, as the Society of Friends are called, have long held meetings where the people sit in silence until someone is inspired to speak by an "inner light" (Bauman, 1983). Trappist monks take a vow of silence, and in Hinduism, *Mauna* is the inner silence of the sage. The achievement of it is central to Yogic meditation practices. One of the Buddha's most famous sermons consisted of him wordlessly holding up a flower. One follower simply smiled. The follower, according to the Buddha, had received everything in that silent moment. This inner silence is the punchline of the wiser varieties of books on the pursuit of silence in modern life as well.

Perhaps the relation between noise, sound, and silence is best captured by Voegelin's explanation of silence as "not the absence of sound but the beginning of listening" (Voegelin, 2010: 83). Noise, then, is the unsculpted marble waiting to be then formed through our listening into the experience of our own idiosyncratic but culturally and historically shaped soundscapes. The two are inextricably entwined with how we hear our worlds.

References

Attali J (1985) *Noise: The Political Economy of Music.* Theory and History of Literature. Minneapolis, MN: U. Minn. Press.

Baraka A (1985) Interview with Miles Davis. *New York Times Magazine*, 15th June.

Basso KH (1970) "To Give up on Words": Silence in Western Apache Culture. *Southwestern Journal of Anthropology* 26(3): 213–230.

Bauman R (1983) *Let Your Words Be Few: Symbolism of Speaking and Silence among Seventeenth-Century Quakers.* Cambridge: Cambridge University Press.

Benjamin M (n.d.) The CIA's favorite form of torture. Available from: www.salon.com/2007/06/07/sensory_deprivation/ (accessed 9 July 2013).

Burke P (1993) *The Art of Conversation.* Ithaca, NY: Cornell University Press.

Cage J (1961) *Silence: Lectures and Writings.* Middletown, CT: Wesleyan University Press.

Chacon R (1999) *Field Recording (1999).* Available from: www.dropbox.com/sh/zzttmcnkginq984/AACwx06ONZms4vQL4jiAettRa.

Chakrabarty D, Santra SC, Mukherjee A, et al. (1997) Status of road traffic noise in Calcutta metropolis, India. *The Journal of the Acoustical Society of America* 101(2): 943–949.

Chowdhury AK, Debsarkar A and Chakrabarty S (2012) Analysis of day time traffic noise level: A case study of Kolkata, India. *International Journal of Environmental Sciences and Research* 12(2): 114–118.

Derrida J (1973) The Voice That Keeps Silence. In: *Speech and Phenomena: And Other Essays on Husserl's Theory of Signs*, Northwestern University studies in phenomenology & existential philosophy, Evanston, IL: Northwestern University Press, pp. 70–86.

Epstein D (1977) *Sinful Tunes and Spirituals: Black Folk Music to the Civil War.* Urbana and Chicago, IL: University of Illinois Press.

Foy GM (2010) *Zero Decibels: The Quest for Absolute Silence.* 1st ptg. New York, NY: Scribner.

Hainge G (2013) *Noise Matters: Towards an Ontology of Noise.* New York, NY: Bloomsbury Academic.

Hegarty P (2007) *Noise/Music: A History.* New York, NY: Continuum.

Johnson W (2002) Time and Revolution in African America. In: Bender T (ed.), *Rethinking American History in a Global Age*, Berkeley, CA: University of California Press, pp. 148–167.

Jordan WD (1993) *Tumult and Silence at Second Creek: An Inquiry into a Civil War Slave Conspiracy.* Baton Rouge, LA: Louisiana State University Press.

Kahn D (1999) *Noise, Water, Meat: A History of Sound in the Arts.* Cambridge, MA; London: MIT Press.

Kemble F (1961) *Journal of a Residence on a Georgian Plantation in 1838–1839.* New York, NY: Knopf.

LeClaire AD (2010) *Listening Below the Noise: The Transformative Power of Silence.* Harper Perennial.

Marx L (1964) *The Machine in the Garden: Technology and the Pastoral Ideal in America.* New York, NY: Oxford University Press.

Mowitt J (2002) *Percussion: Drumming, Beating, Striking.* Durham, NC: Duke University Press.

Olsen T (1978) *Silences.* New York, NY: Delacorte Press/Seymour Lawrence.

Parrish L (1992) *Slave Songs of the Georgia Sea Islands*. Athens, GA: University of Georgia Press.

Picker JM (2003) *Victorian Soundscapes*. New York, NY: Oxford University Press.

Prochnik G (2011) *In Pursuit of Silence: Listening for Meaning in a World of Noise*. Reprint. Anchor.

Rath RC (1993) African Music in Seventeenth-Century Jamaica: Cultural Transit and Transition. *William and Mary Quarterly* 50(3): 700–726.

Rath RC (2000) Drums and Power: Ways of Creolizing Music in Coastal South Carolina and Georgia, 1730–1790. In: Reinhardt S and Buisseret D (eds), *Creolization in the Americas: Cultural Adaptations to the New World*, Arlington, TX: Texas A&M Press, pp. 99–130.

Rath RC (2003) *How Early America Sounded*. Ithaca, NY: Cornell University Press.

Rich A (2001) *Arts of the Possible: Essays and Conversations*. New York, NY: W.W. Norton.

Rodgers T (2010) *Pink noises: Women on Electronic Music and Sound*. Durham, NC: Duke University Press.

Rosenthal D (1992) *Hard Bop: Jazz and Black Music, 1955–1965*. New York, NY: Oxford University Press.

Russolo LF (1967) *The Art of Noise (Futurist Manifesto, 1913)*. Great Bear Pamphlets, New York, NY: Something Else Press. Available from: www.ubu.com/historical/gb/russolo_noise.pdf.

Sardello R (2008) *Silence: The Mystery of Wholeness*. North Atlantic Books.

Schwartz H (2011) *Making Noise: From Babel to the Big Bang and Beyond*. Brooklyn, NY: Zone Books.

Sewall S (1886) *Letter-Book of Samuel Sewall*. Collections of the Massachusetts Historical Society, Boston.

Shannon CE and Weaver W (1949) *The Mathematical Theory of Communication*. Urbana, IL: University of Illinois Press.

Smith MM (1997) *Mastered by the Clock: Time, Slavery, and Freedom in the American South*. Fred W. Morrison series in Southern studies. Chapel Hill, NC: University of North Carolina Press.

Smith MM (2001) *Listening to Nineteenth-Century America*. Chapel Hill, NC: University of North Carolina Press.

Smith N (2005) The splinter in your ear: Noise as the semblance of critique. *Culture, Theory and Critique* 46(1): 43–59.

Sterne J (2012) *Mp3: The Meaning of a Format*. Durham, NC: Duke University Press.

Strachey W (1964) A True Reportory of the Wreck and Redemption of Sir Thomas Gates, Knight, upon and from the Islands of Bermudas. In: Wright LB (ed.), *A Voyage to Virginia in 1609*, Charlottesville, VA: University Press of Virginia, pp. 1–102.

Thompson EA (2002) *The Soundscape of Modernity: Architectural Acoustics and the Culture of Listening in America, 1900–1933*. Cambridge, MA: MIT Press.

Trouillot M-R (1995) *Silencing the Past: Power and the Production of History*. Boston, MA: Beacon Press.

Voegelin S (2010) *Listening to Noise and Silence: Towards a Philosophy of Sound Art*. New York, NT: Continuum.

West Bengal Pollution Control Board (n.d.) Brief report on Status of Road Traffic Noise Levels During Summer 2006 and Winter 2005 in Kolkata Metropolis. Available from: www.wbpcb.gov.in/html/downloads/NoisePollutionReport0506.pdf.

White S and White GJ (2005) *The Sounds of Slavery: Discovering African American History through Songs, Sermons, and Speech*. Boston, MA: Beacon Press.

8

SOUND WAVES OF PROTEST: NOISE ABATEMENT MOVEMENTS

Karin Bijsterveld

Searching for a paradise of sound

In 2006, Waikiki apartment resident Gary Holt and a few companions decided to revive an organization that had been established in 1970 but dissolved in the late 1980s: *Citizens against Noise of Hawaii*. Their island, they claimed, was close to paradise, if only its dazzling noise pollution—by motorcycles, boom boxes, car alarms, and bars—could be reduced (Vorsino 2006). The organization itself was not exactly an island though. It was one out of dozens of new citizens' initiatives against noise established in the 1990s and after, in the industrialized world and beyond. Today, many of these have websites with links to fellow activist centers.

Were these organizations any different from the flurry of noise abatement groups established in the late 1950s through 1970s? Or from the anti-noise societies that originated in the decades before World War II? Does it make sense to distinguish between waves of citizens' noise abatement movements, similar to the three feminist waves or, closer to the aims of the noise fighters, the recurrent upswing of environmentalism (Krarløkke and Sørensen 2006, Dunlap and Mertig 1991)? In terms of timing, noise abatement activism definitively followed a wave pattern: an initial concentration of actions in the early twentieth century and the interwar years, a second during the economic boom of the late 1950s–1970s, and a third in what might be called the "re-roaring" millennium turn. But what about the citizens' definitions of the problem of noise, their views on causes and solutions, their identification of those responsible for or fit to tackle noise, and their styles and strategies of campaigning?

I will answer these questions for the first two time periods—1900s–1930s and late 1950s–1970s—by drawing on publications about the history of noise abatement in the twentieth century, and for the more recent years by analyzing the websites of citizens' initiatives against noise. For the early stages, I will focus on the West, most notably the United States, United Kingdom, Germany, and the Netherlands—the four countries I studied in *Mechanical Sound: Technology, Culture and Public Problems of Noise in the Twentieth Century* (Bijsterveld 2008). For the 1990s and beyond, however, I will, very modestly, broaden my geographical scope, and include an example from India. This has inspired me to take one additional issue into account: the noise abatement movements' representations of the city. These conceptualizations of the urban, I will show, left their mark on the noise abatement campaigns and may account for some of the differences in today's noise abatement rhetoric between activists in industrialized and industrializing countries.

Against unnecessary noise: the first wave in noise abatement (1900s–1930s)

An important early representative of anti-noise citizen's activism, Julia Barnett Rice, had a medical background, was married to a successful business man, and lived alongside the Hudson River in New York. Her engagement with noise started from concern about the din produced by the intense use of steam whistles by riverboat staff at night. Although this likely affected her own life, her public concerns referred to assumptions about the negative effects of noise on the recovery of patients in the hospitals near the river. This made her establish the Society for the Suppression of Unnecessary Noise in New York in 1906 (Thompson 2002: 121).

Historian Emily Thompson situates this initiative in the context of social reform in public health and urban planning, as well as the rise of a new efficiency ideal in industrial labor and aesthetics. Engineers, indeed, started seeing noise as a sign of sub-optimally working machines in the early twentieth century (Bijsterveld et al. 2014: 29). In these years, Thompson explains, the focus was thus not on noise as such, but on noise that was considered unnecessary and preventable. It was the elite, however, defining *which* sounds were needless. These were not the sounds supposed to contribute to economic growth, but the sounds assumed to undermine the vulnerable lives of patients and, as Rice later added, school children. This approach to noise enabled her to secure assistance from business men in addition to doctors, clergymen, and university leaders. Rice made her Society's views public through *The Forum*, a magazine owned by her husband, and succeeded getting legislation accepted that banned needless whistle blowing in ports and harbors in 1907. Moreover, in the first half of the 1910s, many American cities established quiet zones around hospitals and schools (Thompson 2002: 121, 126).

In Europe, the German philosopher Theodor Lessing and the British surgeon Dan McKenzie published their own pamphlets against noise, and Lessing founded the German Association for the Protection from Noise (*Deutscher Lärmschutzverband*) in 1908 (Bijsterveld 2008: 101). They had similar concerns about unnecessary noise as the New York Society, but talked about a wider range of sources, varying from carpet beating and church bells to gramophones, telephones, automobiles, trams, and trains. In both Germany and the United Kingdom, these concerns were phrased in terms of an increasing nervousness, or neurasthenia, among the urban population resulting from overstimulation of the senses. Yet despite this backdrop of cultural pessimism, and apart from establishing lists of hotels that could function as silent refuges, the noise activists took most of the material organization of city life for granted. In contrast, its population, and most notably the lower classes, had to learn to behave in less rowdy ways—as they were considered to be less sensitive to noise than the refined upper classes (Bijsterveld 2008).

Behind these claims were anxieties about how noise might undermine the mental strength of those supposed to act as the intellectual leaders of their nations. Such preoccupations were not new. In the 1860s, mathematician Charles Babbage had teamed up with public intellectuals like historian Thomas Carlyle and writer Charles Dickens to combat the sounds of barrel organ players and other music makers on the streets of London. As John Picker has explained, their campaigns expressed the elite's fear and contempt of the many non-natives populating the trade of street musicians. But their concerns also resulted from the rise of a new class of professional writers—journalists, essayists, novelists—who had to find mental concentration amidst urban din (Picker 2003). The effect of their campaigns as well as later actions against shouters and vendors, in London, New York and elsewhere, was clearing the street from anything but traffic (Thompson 2002: 124).

While these people focused on man-made sounds, their twentieth-century successors increasingly focused on machine-produced sound, notably traffic noise. This was most evident in a campaign that was not a citizen's initiative, although it triggered a wide citizens' response during and after the event: the 1929 campaign by the New York Noise Abatement Commission, chaired by the New York City Health Commissioner Dr. Shirley Wynne. This commission organized a newspaper questionnaire, answered by thousands of citizens, that showed how the noise of traffic and transport—trucks, automobile horns, elevated trains—were among the top of complaints, followed by radios, automobile brakes, garbage collection, street cars, and turnstiles. The commission also sponsored public radio lectures, and collaborated with scientists from commercial labs and other organizations to measure street noise with subjective and objective noise meters that had just been developed in the telephone industry (Thompson 2002: 157–168, Bijsterveld 2008: 104–110). Measuring noise did not immediately help the commission's cause, but it did generate an optimistic tone in the public debate. A 1930 New York City law requiring a permit for using a loudspeaker outdoors was one of its results (Thompson 2002: 151). Still, the commission believed that urban life could only become quieter if the general public would act in less noisy ways (Bijsterveld 2008: 110–117).

In the 1920s and 1930s, noise abatement organizations popped up in cities all over Europe. Metropolitan examples were the *La société pour la suppression du bruit* in Paris, and the Anti-Noise League in London. But Oxford also had a noise abatement committee, and in the Netherlands, a provincial capital like Groningen had a noise abatement committee just as well as Amsterdam (Bijsterveld 2008: 110–112, Bijsterveld 2013: 11–12). Engineers and physicists were among their spokespersons, fostering solutions in terms of noise insulation and the creation of silent artefacts such as the toilets and typewriters exhibited during the Noise Abatement Exhibition in the London Science Museum in 1935. Historian James G. Mansell, however, has recently stressed that in the United Kingdom medical experts like Lord Thomas J. Horder dominated the interwar noise abatement discourse. They revived the late nineteenth and early twentieth-century neurasthenia discourse in their noise abatement writings. While psychologists and psychiatrists had developed serious doubts about the usefulness of this diagnostic label by 1930, physicians kept stressing the prevalence of nervous breakdowns among men of letters, often attributing this to noise. In fact, they believed that the Great War had made modern man even more sensitive to sound than he had already been before (Mansell 2014).

The urban "silence" campaigns themselves predominantly focused on reducing traffic noise, and notably the needless use of the car horn. In the Netherlands, an intriguing discourse coalition between motorist organizations and noise abatement organizations fostered the slogan "Orderly Traffic promotes Silence," intending to have pedestrians, bicyclists and motorcyclists behave more predictably so that motorists would have to use their horns less frequently. Moreover, the second half of the 1930s brought the first legislation banning the use of the car horn at night and installing maximum emitted sound levels for horns and cars in, for instance, the Netherlands and Germany. The result was, again, a street cleared from those who might block the smooth transition of cars and trucks. This was the tragic effect of actions that definitely reduced the hooting, but also gave the floor to an increasingly dense layer of motorized traffic (Bijsterveld 2008: 124–133).

Emily Thompson has noted that the New York Noise Abatement Commission (NAC) was dissolved in 1932, and that the city's anti-noise activism probably suffered from the Great Depression and shifts in the metropolitan political landscape (Thompson 2002: 166). Lilian Radovac has recently extended the time span studied. She shows that the Noise Abatement Council, established in 1934 to translate the NAC's recommendations into regulations, had indeed little success. In 1935, however, a new and larger organization, the League for Less Noise (LLN) took the Noise Abatement Council on board as one of its institutional members, and organized a conference on noise that very same year. Among the speakers were experts from the sciences, but also noise abatement activists from Europe, who seem to have been important sources of inspiration. Together with the New York mayor and his police, the LLN campaigned in a style very similar to that of the Europeans. Its 1935 "Noiseless Nights" focused on civilizing the behavior of the urban population, including actions against honking at night or the rough handling of garbage cans (Radovac 2012: 293). In 1936, the LLN managed to get a code against the excessive use of automobile horns accepted that was modelled after a Paris ordinance, as well as a more comprehensive anti-noise code (Radovac 2012: 298, 294).

Anyone zooming in on the campaigns in different countries of the West will find, no doubt, subtle distinctions in aims and strategies.[1] The foci also changed over time. Protecting children and the sick from noise gave way, for instance, for protecting the health and productivity of the urban population at large, even though elite concerns kept predominating. When zooming out, however, it becomes clear that the pre-war noise abatement movements in the US and Europe shared a focus on educating and civilizing the masses, installing—notably local—regulations against "unnecessary" noise, and seeking assistance from science and technology to map the sources of noise and isolate their homes and appliances from unwanted sound. Noise was seen as an expression of chaos, and a well-ordered city had to enable a fact of life: that many lived and worked densely together, and could not easily escape from the city itself.

Restructuring society: the second wave in noise abatement (late 1950s–1970s)

In Europe, the postwar years were rather tranquil in terms of noise abatement activism, but life itself was full of sound. Roads and bridges had to be rebuilt, the shortage of housing to be remedied and public buildings re-established. The sounds of brick hammering, pile driving and concrete mixing contributed significantly to the postwar soundscapes of Europe's inner cities. In this context of reconstruction, loud sound had positive connotations, and noise abatement did not appear to have top priority. The London-based Noise Abatement League, for instance, was dissolved in 1951 due to a lack of funds. And although the Netherlands officially had a Permanent Noise Abatement Committee (*Permanent Anti-Lawaai-Comité*) as of 1947, its members did not meet up anymore after the mid-1950s. It took until 1968 before the Dutch Congress for Public Health (NCOG) organized a conference on noise that raised quite some press attention. In the wake of this event, the congress' president, a medical expert, initiated the Dutch Foundation for Noise Abatement, or *Nederlandse Stichting Geluidhinder*, in 1970 (Bijsterveld 2008: 197, 273–274).[2]

Other examples of postwar noise abatement organizations were the French Anti-Noise League (*Ligue Française contre le Bruit*, 1958), the British Noise Abatement Society (1959), the Norwegian Association against Noise (*Norsk Forening mot Støy*, 1963), the Austrian Noise Abatement Society (*Österreichische Arbeitsring für Lärmbekämpfung*, which had started as a section of the *Österreichische Arbeitsgemeinschaft für Volksgesundheit*, in 1958), and the, somewhat older German Working Group for Noise Abatement (*Deutscher Arbeitsring für Lärmbekämpfung*, 1952). Several of these initiatives combined their efforts in the International Association Against Noise (*Association Internationale Contre le Bruit*) in 1959.

These foundations, leagues, and associations against noise did not only differ from the ones established prior to World War II in their national rather than local orientation, but also in their framing of noise as a common, generalized issue of public health, and, from the late 1960s onward, as a problem of environmental pollution. Some of their spokespersons still talked about preventable noise, suggesting that not all noise was preventable. But even if it was not, it had to be diminished and tackled in an all-embracing approach. Many of them successfully lobbied for national noise abatement legislation, often framework-laws established in the 1970s and intended to tackle several sources of noise under one heading (Bijsterveld 2008). At the same time, the noise abatement initiatives fostered research and expertise, intended to raise public awareness, and provided services to individuals such as legal advice and companions on noise measurement techniques, insulation materials, or silent restaurants, not unlike the earlier organizations. But whereas the pre-war movement had by and large accepted the status quo of industrial society and crowded cities, the postwar movement more critically assessed societal and urban life itself.

An example is its stance on airports. The arrival of jets at Heathrow prompted some members of the British Noise Abatement Society (NAS) to ring the doorbell of the Minister of Aviation on a Saturday morning in 1960, claiming that "the noise prevented them from sleeping and made life 'unbearable'." Whereas the Minister responded that such noise was unavoidable unless he would close down the airport, NAS president and business man John Connell later suggested to invoke the silent "power of thought" to solve the problem (both cited in Bijsterveld 2008: 198). In Germany, protests against aircraft noise grew way more grim, however. In 1964, the "environmental vicar" Kurt Oeser criticized plans for extending Frankfurt am Main's airport with the argument that people's quality of life should not suffer from economic growth. He established a local committee against aircraft noise, from which sprang the Federal Society against Aircraft Noise (*Bundesvereinigung gegen Fluglärm*) in 1967, providing a roof for the German aircraft noise abatement groups to follow (Brink 2013: 438). Despite a hunger strike, a slum village, huge petitions, and demonstrations in the early 1980s, Frankfurt's "Runway West" opened in 1984. Three years later, a series of Sunday walks to the airport culminated in a clash between the police and militant demonstrators, which tragically and exceptionally took the lives of two policemen (Gerth 2008, Behr 2012). In terms of sound levels, technical jet engine noise control as well as the rise of regulations limiting night flights and establishing maximum noise emission and immision levels brought some relief, in Germany and beyond. With air traffic exploding, however, and perhaps a reduced tolerance for noise due to the perception of new technologies as risks—as health scientist Mark Brink has claimed with reference to Ulrich Beck's work—citizens kept expressing concerns (Brink 2013: 441). Today, nearly each airport has its citizens' watchdog.

Yet one particular source of aircraft noise has been banned quite successfully. As David Suisman (2015) has shown, actions against the sonic boom resulted in an early, yet nearly forgotten victory of the environmentalist movement. Remarkably, the 1970s Coalition Against the Super Sonic Transport (SST) program of the US government was as unlikely as the one against honking in the 1930s. The Coalition included the Citizens League Against the Sonic Boom (CLASB, 1967) and Friends of the Earth (FOE, 1969), organizations pointing at the health, material, and environmental damage caused by SST. But it also managed to involve a group of highly influential economists critical of SST's economic prospects, and, ultimately, senators and congressmen of both democrat and republican denomination worrying about, for one, STT's return on investment. Once again, groups of people with disparate aims successfully united to silence at least one source of unwanted sound.

Whereas many of the associations established during the first wave of noise abatement did not survive the two World Wars, most of the organizations established in the late 1950s and 1960s have survived until today, often with help of federal and state subsidies. Their initiators still had elite backgrounds, but now hired staff to answer the telephone calls of concerned citizens day after day. This enhanced the organizations' professionalism. In style of campaigning, the noise abatement organizations showed several differences. The British NAS president John Connell, for instance, once deplored "the dispassionate attitude" of scientists, whereas one of the initiators of the Dutch NSG warned against expressing too much emotion.[3] And while the NAS had many a business man among its advisors, the DAL most dominantly drew its leaders from medical science and engineering.[4] In their rising professionalism, however, these noise-fighting organizations resembled each other.

This was also true for the second wave's conception of the city. It wasn't staged solely as a prison capturing its residents in work and services anymore. In contrast, it was increasingly seen as a place to flee from—with the countryside and wildlife as the new ideals. The ideas of the founding father of soundscape studies, the Canadian composer and environmentalist Raymond Murray Schafer, are a case in point. For him and his World Soundscape Project (WSP), noise was the keynote of industrial society. Redressing noise was impossible without questioning the principle behind it: capitalism. Rather than foregrounding the negative, however, Schafer wanted to document and preserve the sounds of nature and rural life, and to use sound design and composition to improve the urban soundscape (Schafer 1994 [1977]). This aspect returned in the playful tunes of the noise awareness initiatives popping up in the 1990s.

Play back: a third wave in noise abatement (1990s–now)?

An important offspring of Schafer's work is the World Forum of Acoustic Ecology (WFAE), established in Vancouver in 1993. This Forum and its sections in other countries have collaborated with the World Listening Project (Chicago, 2008), *La Semaine du Son* (Paris, 2004), and the Deep Listening Institute (Kingston NY, around 1996) in organizing the World Listening Day as of 2010. With this day on July 18, Schafer's birthday, the organizers intend to celebrate listening practices and create an awareness of the quality of acoustic environments through education, "sound walks, concerts, radio broadcasts, and internet streams" (Leonardson 2015: 117). In these events, sound artists, recordists, and composers have key roles. Many of them also contribute to the wealth of city-based and partially preservationist initiatives displaying the sounds of specific cities through sound maps (Ouzounian 2014).

It is good to note, however, that the World Listening Project (WLP) has no connections with the International Listening Association (Minnesota, 1979). This association's annual International Listening Awareness Month focuses on listening as the "super hero" of proper communication rather than acoustic awareness.[5] And as of 1996, there has been an International Noise Awareness Day, usually organized in April by the Center for Hearing and Communication (CLC). In contrast, the WLP *has* links with bioacoustics experts like Bernie Krause (Leonardson 2015: 118). With his much-downloaded TED talk, Krause has been able to point out how noise endangers animal life on earth in the tradition of Rachel Carlson's *Silent Spring*.

Although acoustic awareness is considered to be a precondition for noise abatement by the WFAE and its companion organizations, anti-noise activism as such is not their key issue. This distinguishes them from the many post-1990s anti-noise groups that have their roots in Not in My Back Yard (NIMBY) activism. In fact, such and other noise abatement initiatives are so widespread across the globe now that it is hard to represent them in an accurate way. To get the picture nonetheless, I started checking out websites of national noise abatement societies that had survived from the 1960s and 1970s, as well as international web-based resources concerning noise abatement expertise, for links to citizens' initiatives against noise—so basically following the snowball method in a virtual world.

Among contemporary noise abatement groups are many organizations focusing on single noise issues such as leaf blowers, airboats, car alarms, boom cars, piped music, farm cannons, and, as said, airports and aircraft, including helicopters. Many of these initiatives express a "glocal" identity: while focusing their own actions on particular locations, they are well aware of noise abatement as a world-wide endeavor. They often call for civilized behavior, reminiscent of the first wave of noise abatement. And like the second wave organizations, they are service-oriented, but often with lower levels of professionalism and not as media-savvy as the longstanding multi-issue noise abatement organizations. These second wave institutions do not only focus on new issues, such as raising awareness of wind turbine noise, but also seem to have taken elements of the "Schaferist" approach on board by making their actions more positive in tone, for instance through granting prizes.[6]

Some of the larger organizations, such as *Noise Free America* (NFA)—established in 2001 at the campus of UCLA—include naming and shaming in their strategies. NFA's monthly Noisy Dozen for "major noise polluters" is an example.[7] Moreover, some of the NIMBY clubs can produce harshly phrased accusations, in which the health card is played out loud.[8] But that is as "violent" as it gets today, at least at the collective level. This may be related to changing conceptions of the city. Since the 1990s, the city is increasingly the place to be, embraced as an exciting and lively environment offering work and entertainment.[9] Attacking noise too aggressively would be attacking a way of life now widely celebrated. Alternatively, the soundscape awareness approach seems increasingly attractive to those in favor of acoustic environmentalism. It allows for an urban life style combined with a positive and creative take on heightening people's awareness of how the sonic environment co-constitutes the city.

So, whereas the first activists approached the city as an "inescapable place," and many of their postwar successors defined it as a "place to flee from," the city is now "the place to be." I have noted an exception to this trend, however. This concerns noise abatement actions in the industrializing world, such as the Indian campaign Do Not Honk. "In India," so campaigners claim, "unnecessary vehicular honking is the main reason for noise pollution. ... Drivers show no respect to the law that prohibits the use of horns at traffic signals and other silent zones such as areas near hospitals."[10] Listening to these arguments is like listening to the first wave of campaigns once again, as living in cities is not a free choice for all.

Conclusions

We can safely speak about different waves of noise abatement activism. But whereas the identity of the noise abatement societies of the first decades of the twentieth century is clearly discernable from the ones established between the late 1950s and 1970s, the third wave is, as yet, less easy to capture. To be sure, the 1990s through 2010s produced many a new initiative, so in terms of the number of newly established noise abatement societies, the millennium turn certainly produced a new wave. Understanding a recent movement is also more difficult for a historian than characterizing a more distant past. Yet even when taking this into account, the identity of the third wave noise abatement groups seems less consistent than that of the first and second noise abatement waves.

The first wave of noise abatement movements was constituted by elites geared towards unnecessary noise that expressed a chaos from which no one could flee, but that could be tamed to create an orderly city. The second wave consisted of organizations run by the professional middle classes, relying increasingly although not exclusively on ideals of structural and environmental reform, often based on what the sciences had to offer. The third wave displays playful actions linked to artistic performances. Aggressive actions seem to be absent, or merely the work of individuals rather than organizations, and many of the local groups express themselves in terms of first and second wave rhetoric rather than something new. They list sources of noise, plea for civilized behavior, and refer to best practices. Creating noise awareness is also among the aims of organizations identifying themselves as representatives of the soundscapes movement. Their celebration of urban sound today appears to go hand in hand with a revaluation of the city as a place to live a happy life. Where cities are populated by poor majorities, however, noise abatement discourses may return to a plea for reducing unnecessary noise—in a city from which no escape is foreseen.

Notes

1 In *Mechanical Sound* (2008), in fact, I distinguished between the noise abatement societies established in the first years of the twentieth century and those set up in the 1930s. I bring these under one heading now. This is not only because I cover a wider time frame in this article than in *Mechanical Sound* (which ended in the mid-1970s), but also because I think the pre-World War II organizations had a concern with health and civilization in common, see also Mansell (2014).

2 Archives *Nederlandse Stichting Geluidshinder* (NSG), Delft, File Establishment NSG, "Oprichtingsakte," March 24, 1970.

3 Archives NAS, Brighton, [Connell, J.] (1962), "Hon. Secretary's Report," *Quiet Please*, 1(3), pp. 9–10, at p. 9; Archives NSG, File Establishment NSG, NCOG Meeting April 24, 1969, p. 2.

4 Archives NAS, Anonymous (1960), "The Noise Abatement Society," *Quiet Please* 1(1), pp. 4–5; Archives DAL, Düsseldorf, Klosterkötter, W. (1972), "20 Jahre Deutscher Arbeitsring für Lärmbekämfung," *Kampf dem Lärm*, 19(6), pp. 141–143, Springer, P. (1992), "40 Jahre gegen den Lärm: Aus der Geschichte des DAL," *Lärm-Report*, 3, no page numbering.

5 www.speaktolead.com/2013/03/listening-awareness-workshop.html (Retrieved November 20, 2015).

6 See, for instance, the NAS glossy E-zine *SoundScape* and its NAS prize (http://noiseabatementsociety.com) (Retrieved November 26, 2015).

7 www.noisefree.org/ (Retrieved December 3, 2015).

8 See, for instance, Victims of Airboat Noise Unived (VAN), at www.noairboatnoise.com/, and Ban the Cannons, at http://bancannons.tripod.com/matsqui.html (Retrieved January 28, 2016).

9 www.oecd.org/gov/regional-policy/urbandevelopment.htm and www.pbl.nl/infographic/de-stad-in-trek (Retrieved December 17, 2015).

10 http://earthsaviours.in/node/18 (Retrieved November 26, 2015). See also "Govindpuri Sound," by Tom Rice, www.bbc.co.uk/programmes/p02hm1rx (Retrieved January 28, 2016).

References

Behr, S. (2012) "Flughafen Frankfurt Startbahn West: Todesschüsse an der Startbahn," November 1, www.fr-online.de/flughafen-frankfurt/flughafen-frankfurt-startbahn-west-todesschuesse-an-der-startbahn,2641734,20768630.html (retrieved December 14, 2015).

Bijsterveld, K. (2008) *Mechanical Sound: Technology, Culture, and Public Problems of Noise in the Twentieth Century*, Cambridge, MA: The MIT Press.

Bijsterveld, K. (ed.) (2013) *Soundscapes of the Urban Past: Staged Sound as Mediated Cultural Heritage*, Bielefeld: Transcript Verlag.

Bijsterveld, K., Cleophas, E., Krebs, S., and Mom, G. (2014) *Sound and Safe: A History of Listening Behind the Wheel*, Oxford: Oxford University Press.

Brink, M. (2013) "Düsentrieb und Überschall: Der Himmel als Kloake und die Entstehung des Bürgerprotests gegen Fluglärm," in G. Paul and R. Schock (eds.) *Sound des Jahrhunderts: Geräusche, Töne, Stimmen 1889 bis heute*, Bonn: Bundeszentrale für Politische Bildung, pp. 436–441.

Dunlap, R.E. and Mertig, A.G. (1991) "The Evolution of the U.S. Environmental Movement from 1970 to 1990: An Overview," *Society and Natural Resources*, 4(3), pp. 209–218.

Gerth, S. (2008) "Startbahn West: Die Wucht des Widerstandes," April 12, www.spiegel.de/einestages/startbahn-west-a-946846.html (retrieved December 14, 2015).

Kr,øløkke, C. and Sørensen, A.S. (2006) "Three Waves of Feminism: From Suffragettes to Grrls," in C. Krøløkke and A.S. Sørensen, *Gender Communication Theory & Analyses: From Silence to Performance*, Thousand Oaks, CA: Sage, pp. 1–23.

Leonardson, E. (2015) "Sound and Listening: Beyond the Wall of Broadcast Sound," *Journal of Radio and Audio Media*, 22(1), pp. 115–121.

Mansell, J.G. (2014) "Neurasthenia, Civilization, and the Sounds of Modern Life: Narratives of Nervous Illness in the Interwar Campaign against Noise," in D. Morat (ed.) *Sounds of Modern History: Auditory Cultures in 19th- and 20th-Century Europe*, New York/Oxford: Berghahn, pp. 278–302.

Ouzounian, G. (2014) "Acoustic Mapping: Notes from the Interface," in M. Gandy and B.J. Nilsen (eds.) *The Acoustic City*, Berlin: Jovis, pp. 164–173.

Picker, J.M. (2003) *Victorian Soundscapes*, Oxford: Oxford University Press.

Radovac, L. (2012) "The "War on Noise": Sound and Space in La Guardia's New York," in K. Keeling and J. Kun (eds.) *Sound Clash: Listening to American Studies*, Baltimore, MD: Johns Hopkins University Press, pp. 289–316.

Schafer, R.M. (1994) *The Soundscape: Our Sonic Environment and the Tuning of the World,* Rochester, Vermont: Destiny Books (Originally published in 1977 as *The Tuning of the World*, New York, NY: Knopf).

Suisman, D. (2015) "The Environmental Movement's Lost Victory: The Fight Against Sonic Booms," *The Public Historian*, 37(4), pp. 111–131.

Thompson, E. (2002) *The Soundscape of Modernity: Architectural Acoustics 1900–1933*, Cambridge, MA: MIT Press.

Vorsino, M. (2006) "Anti-noise warriors regroup," *The Honolulu Advertiser*, August 21, 2006, http://the.honoluluadvertiser.com/article/2006/Aug/21/ln/FP608210326.html (retrieved August 14, 2015).

9

PROPAGANDA AND SOUND

David Goodman

This article is about propaganda that is heard rather than seen. It canvasses some work done on sound propaganda before the 20th century, but focusses on the decades after the development of radio broadcasting in the late 1920s, the period of greatest concern about sound propaganda. Harold Laswell emphasised in an influential 1934 encyclopaedia entry that propaganda could take "spoken, written, pictorial or musical form" (Lasswell, 1934: 521). While that had always been the case, and there has always been belief about the importance of aural persuasion, in the era of mass media the *different* trajectories, capacities and receptions of visual and aural propaganda became subjects for more frequent reflection. Concern about the social and political consequences of vulnerability to sound propaganda arguably peaked in the mid-20th century, when "totalitarian" regimes were offering practical demonstrations of what monopoly, or attempted monopoly, of aural propaganda could achieve.

Most definitions of propaganda begin with the origins of the word when the Roman Catholic Church founded the Congregation of the Propaganda in 1622, a committee of cardinals responsible for foreign missions. But since the 19th century, the word propaganda has also and more commonly been used to describe deliberate propagation of information to change opinion on an issue, particularly through the use of mass media. Armed with this concept, historians have then retrospectively discerned and named propaganda activities in earlier centuries. Most definitions of propaganda describe not just attempts to change beliefs and attitudes, sometimes through the evocation of emotion or the use of false or misleading information, but more specifically attempts to create carefully planned and sustained opinion change. The *Oxford English Dictionary* defines propaganda as "the systematic dissemination of information, esp. in a biased or misleading way, in order to promote a political cause or point of view." Some modern definitions of propaganda describe it as quintessentially a state activity, but propaganda has also very often been used for other purposes, including those of religion and commerce.

How systematic and calibrated could a campaign of aural persuasion be? The more emphasis was placed on planned campaigns of aural propaganda, the more concern was generated about the possibly weakest link in this chain of communication – the listener. What if listeners tuned out, failed to concentrate or understand? Repetition became one hallmark of systematic intent, aiming to reinforce messages and maximize chances of reaching most of the population. Attempts to manipulate by suggestion were another hallmark of planned and systematic aural propaganda – important enough that American psychologists Hadley Cantril and Gordon

Allport in 1935 defined radio propaganda as "the systematic attempt to develop through the use of suggestion certain of the listener's attitudes and beliefs in such a way that some special interest is favored" (Cantril and Allport, 1935: 48).

The belief that sound propaganda is more effective than visual propaganda has a long history. Visual propaganda has often been reliant on written content, which limited its reception. In non-literate societies, music, poetry, and oral stories spread ideas and could change or reinforce attitudes. Journalist Will Irwin argued in 1936 that consequently hearing still had communicative and affective advantages over the relatively recent invention of reading: "all these ages, that faculty of hearing has been gathering about itself an emotional aura" (Irwin, 1936: 247–248). Adolph Hitler no doubt agreed – he told an interviewer that "the sound is in my opinion much more suggestive than the image" (quoted in Schönherr, 1998: 329).

Proponents of the view that sound propaganda may be more potent than visual point out that visual and especially print media were often in the modern era consumed alone and in isolation – silent, solitary reading spread with the rise of book ownership from the early 18th century; although social media today are interactive, much of the consumption of their texts and images is also solitary and silent (Jajdelska, 2007: 192). Sound has in contrast historically more often been heard in a collectivity of some kind – in a church, at a political rally, in conversation. Lacey, recovering a tradition of public listening, recalls early hopes that radio might become "the natural instrument of collectivist politics and experience" (Lacey, 2013a: 101). Informal familial, group, communal, and public listening to radio were all more common in times and places when receivers were scarce. Strikingly, both those who sought to immunize the population against aural propaganda and those who sought to maximize its effectiveness turned to the same social form: collective listening (Goodman 2016a and 2016b). Organized group listening, in both liberal democratic and totalitarian regimes, became a favored means of monitoring the reception of broadcasts to ensure desired outcomes – civilly expressed diversity of views on the one hand, enthusiastic conformity on the other.

Can there be sound propaganda without words? The bells of Christian churches or the Muslim call to prayer have at various times been regarded as aural propaganda for their faiths. Wordless music can in specific circumstances function as propaganda. The opening of Beethoven's 5th symphony was used in World War II as V for victory (the three short and one long notes sounding out the Morse code for V). Jazz's black origins and mixed race practice gave it propaganda potential. Jazz featured in propaganda broadcasts by both sides during World War II. The US used jazz as an instrument of propaganda for the "free world"; from the mid-1950s the State Department sent top jazz musicians such as Louis Armstrong, Duke Ellington, Dizzy Gillespie, and Benny Goodman to eastern Europe, Africa, Asia, and the Middle East as part of a "self-conscious campaign against worldwide criticism of U.S. racism." In this case there was also something about jazz's improvisational form that could be said to embody "a unique American freedom transcending race" (von Eschen, 2004: 4, 20).

More commonly, however, the label propaganda is reserved for sound or music with some verbal content. Music historians have effectively made the case for thinking of early modern religious music as a form of propaganda. Oettinger describes the role of *Music as Propaganda in the German Reformation*, arguing that in this period it was ultimately impossible to separate sacred songs from those dealing with church politics, which was "the driving force behind hymn composition in the 16th century, and it is difficult to draw the line between political songs that are religious and religious songs that are also political." The hymns of the early Reformation, she argues, were overtly propagandistic – although as regions became increasingly confessionalised "there was less need for musical attacks on other believers" (Oettinger, 2001: 2, 9). Luther believed that music was "an important instrument to 'incite people to do good, and to teach them'" (quoted in Loewe, 2013: 70). He set hymns to popular tunes, believing, Pettegree summarizes, that in order "to communicate the word effectively there had to be an assimilation of sacred music to the tunes people actually knew" (Pettegree, 2005: 44). Loewe also observes that "singing the Reformation message to popular tunes was a powerful and effective means of disseminating Luther's views" (Loewe, 2013: 73). In Protestant schools in the early Reformation period, educators were "often musicians who had been recruited according to Luther's own stated preference for musically able candidates" (Loewe, 2013: 81). Fisher demonstrates that, in Bavaria, music was also an important part of the propaganda for the Counter-Reformation (Fisher, 2014). In the 18th century, the Wesley brothers created Methodist hymns that adapted well-known tunes; several historians of Methodism have observed that the hymns were the most effective form of Methodist propaganda.

The Christian hymn functioned as propaganda in the missionary context, in both Catholic and Protestant traditions. Juan de Zumárragam, the first Franciscan bishop of Mexico City from 1528–1548, was keenly aware of the propaganda power of music. In a letter in April, 1540, he wrote that "Indians are great lovers of music, and the religious who hear their confessions tell us that they are converted more by music than by preaching, and we can see they come from distant regions to hear it" (quoted in Harrison, 2013: 33). In the 17th century too, music was "a seminal part of evangelistic endeavors" for Catholic missionaries in Asia (Irving, 2009: 41). Missionary hymns could however also be turned into anti-colonial counter propaganda. In Kenya in the early 1950s for example, the Mau Mau movement created subversive rewritings of Christian hymns set to well-known hymn tunes, songs one scholar has described as "the most powerful propaganda weapons of the whole Mau Mau movement" (Leakey, 2004: 75).

Other examples could be adumbrated. Some scholars identify folk song, protest, and political songs as propaganda. The case is probably stronger for national anthems, adopted by most European nations in the 19th century (Bohlman, 2004: 155). Sound studies scholars have also speculated about the existence of national soundscapes, elements of which have propaganda potential (Kun, 2014). A strong case has thus been made by many scholars for considering these various explicitly or implicitly polemical musical forms, as propaganda.

Sound propaganda in the broadcasting era

The advent of broadcasting from the later 1920s – and in particular commercial broadcasting – greatly increased attention to the question of propaganda and sound. Commercial advertising on radio in many nations, but especially in the US, provided an incentive and the funds to research mechanisms and techniques of aural persuasion and propaganda that might have more general application. Edward Bernays, who saw earlier than most the parallels between commercial, political, and religious propaganda, wrote in 1928 that "modern propaganda is a consistent, enduring effort to create or shape events to influence the relations of the public to an enterprise, idea or group" (Bernays, 1928: 52). Cantril and Allport acknowledged the parallels but also contrasted the generally "subtle, indirect, concealed" nature of political, economic, and religious propaganda with the usually "frank and revealed" nature of commercial propaganda (Cantril and Allport, 1935: 60).

After the advent of broadcasting, the advertising industry needed to know more about the relative efficacy of visual and aural advertising. At first there was concern that sound advertising might work less well than print advertising. Sound after all made only a transient impression on the listener; if missed or heard imperfectly, the message was gone. Advertisers consoled themselves by comparing a radio advertisement to a billboard, perhaps only glimpsed in passing, and yet known to be an effective mode of advertising (Meyers, 2013: 73–74). Before long, however, with the aid of psychological and sociological research, there was new enthusiasm for heard propaganda and its effectiveness, and radio advertising flourished. Frank Elliott noted that studies of recall before 1932 generally found visual stimulus to be more effective, but after that date more studies found that auditory was superior. It was possible, he speculated, that "the enormous increase of auditory stimulus from radio sets for 78,000,000 Americans listening three to five hours per day, from public address systems everywhere, and from sound films claiming 88,000,000 attendances weekly is developing auditory habits" (Elliott, 1937: 86). Radio, American advertising expert Herman Hettinger asserted, possessed "all the emotional appeal and persuasiveness of the voice," giving it a "power which cold print cannot equal" (Hettinger, 1935: 3). John J. Karol of CBS reported in 1936 that recent research had established "the superiority of the auditory mode of presenting advertising copy as measured in terms of immediate and delayed recall and recognition" (Karol, 1936: 150). One study in 1949 posited enthusiastically that, because of radio advertising's embeddedness in entertainment programming, "radio appeals are developed against a background of emotional excitement, and radio success may be largely due to the fact a considerable portion of the listeners 'do what they are told'" (Cassady and Williams, 1949: 77).

While such claims were no doubt welcomed by advertisers, it was not surprising that with such belief in the efficacy of broadcast propaganda, concern about the political and social consequences of this new persuasive capacity grew significantly in the 1930s. A chorus of commentators now worried that radio might create conformity, homogenize, and standardize opinion (Goodman, 2011: 84–90). Charles Siepmann, who had worked at the BBC for twelve years and then relocated to the United States, argued in 1942 that radio "exerts over many listeners an almost hypnotic influence, so that for them the borderline between fact and fancy becomes obscured" (Siepmann, 1942: 7). Educator Clyde Miller affirmed conventional wisdom when he wrote in 1941 that "of all the channels through which propaganda flows, radio is the most effective in preventing or in accelerating social change." Miller, who was closely associated with the Institute for Propaganda Analysis in New York, was one of many contemporaries who regarded Hitler as a "genius" at broadcast propaganda (Miller, 1941: 69). The political consequences of such belief in the high efficacy of aural propaganda were little short of terrifying. Slightly more optimistically, the proliferation of aural propagandas might – other critics speculated – cancel each other out, creating mere confusion rather than conformity. Educator Keith Tyler wrote in 1939 that the combination of political propaganda and advertising on the air had created a "chaotic warfare of propagandas and counter-propagandas" amidst which "the listener is apt to find himself totally bewildered" (Tyler, 1939: 348). Research on sound and commercial advertising propaganda diminished somewhat in the television era, as radio's share of the advertising dollar fell.

As noted above, effective transmission of propaganda requires attentive hearers as well as a carefully crafted message. The attentiveness of listeners can be monitored in face-to-face settings, but with the invention of technological means of listening at a distance, listener attentiveness became a matter of some anxiety. Those concerned to protect populations from aural propaganda worried about the many distracted listeners to always-on radios – archetypically the busy housewife at home catching snatches of broadcasts in between chores and caring for children, but actually including a wide range of radio listeners who kept their radios playing as they engaged in other tasks and sociable activities. The specific fear was that the distracted listener was far more likely than the attentive one to become a propaganda victim (Goodman, 2010). Cantril and Allport also warned that children were especially vulnerable to propaganda, citing concerns about children and advertising (Cantril and Allport, 1935: 63).

Propaganda works better if there is a monopoly of message provision. Broadcasting is by its nature generally open and public. Unless something intervenes, listeners have a choice of stations. Distribution of sound propaganda through wired as opposed to wireless transmission was one way to limit listener choice. Wired radio had the obvious advantage of being centrally controlled, with no possibility of picking up outside stations by accident or design and it was thus perfectly suited as a propaganda outlet. In 1952 US Senator Henry M. Jackson called wired radio an "Orwellian device" – "no one has yet figured out a counter to this move," he lamented, "which, if carried to its extreme, might take a whole nation off the international air" (Cong. Rec., 1952: A538–539). Wired radio was also in some circumstances cheaper – Lovell argues that it was in the Soviet Union in the later 1920s "the only realistic way of turning radio into a 'mass' phenomenon" (Lovell, 2015: 34). From 1925, a wired radio network was put in place in Soviet cities, beginning with Moscow (Lovell, 2015: 33). By the beginning of World War II, 80% of the seven million listening devices in the Soviet Union were wired rather than wireless (Lovell, 2015: 36). The *New York Times* reported in 2001 on the survival of the wired radio network into the post-Soviet era: "By law, wired radio reaches virtually every building in every city, village and farm in Russia, not to mention much of the former Soviet Union" (Wines, 2001: 4). Postwar Poland had a wired radio system based on the Soviet model, as "an instrument of Communist Party propaganda and agitation on a local level" (Sorensen and Meyer, 1955: 343). Communist China developed an extensive wired radio network, reaching up to 90% of the agricultural cooperatives in some areas.

Wired radio could be used in private homes, but often had a significant public role. Loudspeakers in workplaces and public places enabled direct and uninterfered-with transmission of propaganda messages to the population. An American sociologist studying propaganda reported in 1932 that he had to change rooms in his Leningrad hotel because the first room faced the open square "where a loud speaker functioned from six in the morning until eleven at night. Occasionally a song or dialogue was transmitted. For the most part it was a continuous flow of oratory" (Woolston, 1932: 36). An Indian visitor in 1959 described the soundscape created in China by the "ubiquitous wired radio loudspeaker": "The radio blares away at you in the bus, in the train, in the trolley, in sleepers and dining cars, on street corners, in villages, towns and cities – just about everywhere," playing "news of the nation's progress, industrial output, how to make a smelter, how to defeat the American 'imperialists,' how to be a good Communist, how to be neat, how to denounce the rightists and a thousand other things, interspersed with Chinese opera and marching songs" (Chandrasekhar, 1959: 9). North Korea has had a wired radio network since the 1940s, also connected to loudspeakers in public places. A.N. Lankov recalls: "When I think about my life in North Korea in the 1980s, I still vividly remember this ever-present background sound – the unremitting military marches, occasionally interrupted by news broadcasts" (Lankov, 2007: 53). In Vietnam, wired radio (used mainly for propaganda) has played an important role – a nationwide network of 900,000 loudspeakers survives from the years of early revolutionary struggle (Mares, 2013: 239).

It was Germany's National Socialist regime however that most emblematically embraced and deployed sound propaganda as a tool of governing. Mention of Nazi leaders Hitler and Goebbels became almost self-evident proof of the terrible power of sound propaganda in the wrong hands (Zimmerman, 2006: 433). Kris and Speier's perceptive 1944 study observed that the Nazis had a "preference for the spoken rather than the written word"; radio was their preferred medium for propaganda (Kris and Speier, 1944: 12). Minister of Propaganda Joseph Goebbels described radio as "the most important and far-reaching instrument for leading the people" (Kris and Speier, 1944: 51; Bressler, 2009: 197–210).

To achieve the desired effects, the messages had to be heard by most of the population. The famous *Volksempfänger* radio receiver was produced for the home – cheap to purchase but with poor reception range to limit listening to German stations (tuning in foreign stations was illegal)

– and the *Deutsche Arbeitsfrontempfänger* was installed in factories and other workplaces, where a siren could bring work to a halt in order to allow workers to listen to special broadcasts (Lacey, 1996: 102–103; Bressler, 2009: 197–210). Group listening was favored, so that not only could "experts plan what is said and how it is said … but they can even, to some extent, supervise listening. As a rule, everyone reads for himself, but listening can be done collectively" (Kris and Speier, 1944: 51–52). With this reach into the population and attempted supervision of reception, and the highly centralized regime of broadcasting in the Nazi era, a powerful instrument of sound propaganda had been forged. Lacey concludes that "only radio offered the possibility of affecting the nation as a whole, proclaiming a unified message from a totalitarian regime" (Lacey, 2013a: 110).

Nazi propaganda broadcasts made much use of repetition. Kris and Speier observed that the Nazis preferred repetition to amplification because they believed that "repetition can make words all powerful over the mind, can make man a set of reactions to stimuli" (Kris and Speier, 1944: 23). Goebbels understood that coining and then repeating "distinctive phrases or slogans" enhanced radio propaganda (Doob, 1950: 435–436). He advocated repetition in propaganda, however only up to the point at which the material "has completely convinced the public." Beyond that, repetition diminished the message (a point familiar to students of advertising communication, and one that was still being repeated and researched decades later) (Doob, 1950: 435). Consequently wartime Nazi radio turned increasingly to light entertainment so as not to exhaust listener interest in the political and propaganda themes of its broadcasts (Kallis, 2005: 35). Radio propaganda in general was often repetitive – as Siepmann pointed out in 1942: "we in America, familiar with the increasing profits won from advertising on the radio, are not likely to be in too great a hurry to discount the effectiveness of repetitive suggestion" (Siepmann, 1942: 6). In an ordinary half hour of American radio, Allport and Cantril had reported, the sponsor's name was mentioned between 10 and 25 times (Cantril and Allport, 1935: 63).

Recent scholarship has revised the simple belief that Goebbels was the propaganda genius with total control over a totalitarian publicity machine. As Kallis summarizes, historians now see multiple propagandas emanating from the National Socialist regime, "that cumulatively (through their joint effect but often through their profound contradictions) made up what we may schematically call NS propaganda." Radio, however, of all the available media, held the greatest potential for centralization and uniformity (Kallis, 2005: 8, 31–32). Historians also are more likely now to balance their assessment of the efficacy of Nazi propaganda in the early years with its inability after 1941 to effectively reset expectations or counter news of setbacks and defeats. After 1941, Kallis argues, "the official regime propaganda discourse became discordant with the perceptions of the vast majority of the German civilian population" (Kallis, 2005: 10). This happened in part because of Nazi radio's habit of refuting stories propagated by enemy media. Zimmerman argues that this in the end sapped effectiveness and led to "the creation of media realms that were remote from the world in which most of the population lived" (Zimmerman, 2006: 433).

Internationally, World War II was the heyday of radio propaganda. Charles Siepmann wrote that "radio is an instrument of modern war" (Siepmann, 1942: 3). It became this because, as John B. Whitton explained in 1941, "the miracle of radio has made it much easier than before to spread propaganda in enemy territory. The methods formerly used, such as dropping leaflets from airplanes or free balloons, were very limited in range and influence" (Whitton, 1941: 588). Particularly in crowded and border-filled Europe, radio could in this historically novel way enable voices to be heard in enemy territory, opening up new possibilities for attack abroad and new dangers for morale at home. The personalizing of propaganda messages, and themes of seduction and intrigue, became the specialty of such legendary World War II women propaganda broadcasters as Tokyo Rose and Axis Sally. American-born Iva Toguri, broadcasting from Tokyo as "Orphan Ann," was most likely the "Tokyo Rose" of World War II notoriety. As Ann Pfau has shown, much of what circulated at the time as rumor and as memory ever since – Tokyo Rose's uncanny knowledge of Allied troop movements; her insinuations about the sexual infidelity of wives and girlfriends back home – did not actually happen. Troops imagined hearing things, or heard rumors that they attributed in memory to these almost mythical propaganda broadcasters (Pfau: 2008: Ch. 5; Pfau and Hochfelder, 2009). Christine Ehrick, in a chapter on Urugayan feminist Paulina Luisi and Argentinian populist Evita Duarte (de Peron), has argued evocatively that the female radio propagandists' combination of "the culturally disturbing qualities of (especially acousmatic) female speech with the uncanny intimacy of radio and the technique of modern propaganda" constituted a "key moment in twentieth-century sonic history" (Ehrick, 2015: 103).

Radio propaganda and the battle of international shortwave services remained important after World War II. During the Cold War, Radio Free Europe, Radio Liberty, and Voice of America attempted to reach audiences inside Communist bloc nations, using music as well as speech propaganda. Broadcast hate propaganda is widely credited with sparking the 1994 genocide in Rwanda, as Radio Rwanda urged the killing of Tutsi (Des Forges, 2007: 42–44). Radio advertising continued to be important and after decades of decline in the television era, radio's market share of advertising began to rise again in the 1990s.

American communications research after World War II however severely qualified belief in the potency of radio propaganda. The "limited effects" theory, associated with communications scholars such as Paul Lazarsfeld and Robert K. Merton, rested upon a rejection of what they (inaccurately) characterized as an earlier belief in a "magic bullet" or "hypodermic needle" theory of propaganda (Goodman, 2011: 93–100; Sproule, 1989). The "limited effects" hypothesis led to scholarly skepticism about the persuasive effects of mass media alone and unaided. In their classic essay on "Mass Communication, Popular Taste and Organized Social Action," Lazarsfeld and Merton argued that "the social role played by the very existence of the mass media has been commonly overestimated." But their argument was that "local discussions" could reinforce the content of mass propaganda – they evoked something much more present and participatory than simply listening to the radio, but offered an argument about the significant effects of aural stimulus on attitudes nonetheless (Lazarsfeld and Merton, 1948: 98).

Conclusion

"Limited effects" set the tone for postwar consideration of sound propaganda. Arguably radio propaganda diminished in importance in the television era. Nevertheless, political practice today in many nations places enormous emphasis on being "on message" and on the repetition of the key "talking points" of the day. The attachment to aural repetition and insistence on proactively framing the topics of the day are familiar strategies to students of radio propaganda – even as these tactics encounter difficulties in the more critical, interactive, and dialogic forms of contemporary media.

The most obvious thing to say about sound and propaganda in the internet age is that sound has become less central to communication. Radio survives, even thrives, and takes new digital forms – internet radio, podcasting, and so on. Talk radio retains very large audiences and arguably shapes even as it mirrors political attitudes and opinions. The proliferation of niche broadcasts, the possibility of individualizing one's listening, work however against mass-scale influence and hence against high specific anxiety about sound propaganda (Lacey, 2013b). More broadly we live in a retextualising age. The ubiquitous mobile phone is rarely used for speaking or listening

– much more often it is a device for reading and looking at pictures and for sending text. The dominant concerns about media influence today do not concern sound but images and text. We can now therefore look back on the golden age of radio propaganda and of panic about it as a particularly intense moment in the long history of sound and propaganda.

References

98 *Cong. Rec.* A3 (1952).

Bernays, Edward. (1928) *Propaganda*, New York, NY: Horace Liverright.

Bohlman, Philip Vilas. (2004) *The Music of European Nationalism: Cultural Identity and Modern History*, Santa Barbara, CA: ABC Clio.

Bressler, Eva Susanne. (2009) *Von der Experimentierbühne zum Propagandainstrument: die Geschichte der Funkausstellung von 1924 bis 1939*, Köln, Böhlau.

Cantril, Hadley and Gordon Allport. (1935) *The Psychology of Radio*, New York, NY: Harper & Bros.

Cassady, Ralph Jr. and Robert M. Williams. (1949) "Radio as an Advertising Medium," *Harvard Business Review* 27 (1), pp. 62–78.

Chandrasekhar, Sripati. (1959) "Red China Works Around the Clock," *New York Times*, Feb. 18, p. 9.

Des Forges, Alison. (2007) "Call to Genocide: Radio in Rwanda, 1994," in Allan Thompson (ed.), *The Media and the Rwanda Genocide*, London: Pluto Press, 2007, pp. 41–54.

Doob, Leonard. (1950) "Goebbels' Principles of Propaganda," *Public Opinion Quarterly* 14 (3), pp. 419–442.

Ehrick, Christine. (2015) *Radio and the Gendered Soundscape: Women and Broadcasting in Argentina and Uruguay, 1930–1950*, New York, NY: Cambridge University Press.

Elliott, Frank R. (1937) "Eye vs. Ear in Molding Public Opinion," *Public Opinion Quarterly* 1 (3), pp. 83–86.

Fisher, Alexander J. (2014) *Music, Piety, and Propaganda: The Soundscape of Counter-Reformation Bavaria*, New York, NY: Oxford University Press.

Goodman, David. (2010) "Distracted Listening: On Not Making Sound Choices in the 1930s," in David Suisman and Susan Strasser (eds.), *Sound in the Age of Mechanical Reproduction*, Philadelphia, PA: University of Pennsylvania Press, pp. 15–46.

Goodman, David. (2011) *Radio's Civic Ambition: American Broadcasting and Democracy in the 1930s*, New York, NY: Oxford University Press.

Goodman, David. (2016a) "A Transnational history of radio listening groups I: The United Kingdom and United States," *Historical Journal of Film, Radio and Television* 36 (3), pp. 436–465.

Goodman, David. (2016b) "A Transnational history of radio listening groups II: Canada, Australia and the world," *Historical Journal of Film, Radio and Television* 36 (4), pp. 627–648.

Harrison, Frank. (2013) "The Musical Impact of Exploration and Cultural Encounter," in Michael L. Mark, (ed.) *Music Education: Source Readings from Ancient Greece to Today*, New York, NY: Routledge, 2013, pp. 33–35.

Hettinger, Herman S. (1935) "Broadcasting in the United States," *Annals of the American Academy of Political and Social Science*, 177 (1), pp. 1–14.

Irving, David R.M. (2009) "The Dissemination and Use of European Music Books in Early Modern Asia," *Early Music History*, 28, pp. 39–59.

Irwin, Will. (1936) *Propaganda and the News: Or, What Makes You Think So?*, New York, NY: Whittlesey House.

Jajdelska, Elspeth. (2007) *Silent Reading and the Birth of the Narrator*, Toronto: University of Toronto Press.

Kallis, Aristotle. (2005) *Nazi Propaganda and the Second World War*, Basingstoke: Palgrave Macmillan.

Karol, John J. (1936) "Notes on Further Psychological Research in Radio," *Journal of Marketing*, 1 (2), pp. 150–153.

Kris, Ernst and Hans Speier. (1944) *German Radio Propaganda: Report on Home Broadcasts During the War*, New York, NY: Oxford University Press.

Kun, Josh. (2014) "Sound," in Bruce Burgett and Glenn Hendler (eds.) *Keywords for American Cultural Studies*, New York, NY: New York University Press. [http://hdl.handle.net/2333.1/51c5b1pt]

Lacey, Kate. (1996) *Feminine Frequencies: Gender, German Radio, and the Public Sphere, 1923-1945*, Ann Arbor, MI: University of Michigan Press.

Lacey, Kate. (2013a) *Listening Publics: The Politics and Experience of Listening in the Media Age*, Cambridge: Polity.

Lacey, Kate. (2013b) "Listening in the Digital Age," in Jason Loviglio and Michele Hilmes (eds.) *Radio's New Wave: Global Sound in the Digital Era*, New York, NY: Routledge, pp. 9–23.

Lankov, A.N. (2007) *North of the DMZ: Essays on Daily Life in North Korea*, Jefferson, NC: McFarland & Company.

Lasswell, Harold. (1934) "Propaganda," in Edwin R.A. Seligman (ed.), *Encyclopaedia of the Social Sciences*, London: Macmillan, p. 521.

Lazarsfeld, Paul F. and Robert K. Merton. (1948) "Mass Communication, Popular Taste and Organized Social Action," in Lyman Bryson (ed.), *The Communication of Ideas*, New York, NY: Harper and Bros.

Leakey, L.S.B. (2004 [1954]) *Defeating Mau Mau*, London: Routledge.

Loewe, J. Andreas. (2013) "Why Do Lutherans Sing?: Lutherans, Music and the Gospel in the First Century of the Reformation," *Church History*, 82 (1), pp. 69–89.

Lovell, Stephen. (2015) *Russia in the Microphone Age: A History of Soviet Radio, 1919–1970*, Oxford: Oxford University Press.

Mares, Peter. (2013) "Vietnam: Propaganda is not a Dirty Word," in Louise Williams and Roland, Rich (eds.), *Losing Control: Freedom of the Press in Asia*, Canberra: ANU E Press.

Meyers, Cynthia B. (2013) *A Word from Our Sponsors: Admen, Advertising, and the Golden Age of Radio*, New York, NY: Fordham University Press.

Miller, Clyde R. (1941) "Radio and Propaganda," *Annals of the American Academy of Political and Social Science*, 213, pp. 69–74.

Oettinger, Rebecca Wagner. (2001) *Music as Propaganda in the German Reformation*, Aldershot: Ashgate.

Pettegree, Andrew. (2005) *Reformation and the Culture of Persuasion*, Cambridge: Cambridge University Press.

Pfau, Ann and David Hochfelder. (2009) "'Her Voice a Bullet': Imaginary Propaganda and Legendary Broadcasters of World War Two," in Susan Strasser and David Suisman (eds.), *Sound in the Age of Mechanical Reproduction*, Philadelphia, PA: University of Pennsylvania Press, pp. 47–68.

Pfau, Ann Elizabeth. (2008) *Miss Yourlovin: GIs, Gender and Domesticity during World War II*, New York, NY: Columbia University Press.

Schönherr, Ulrich (1998) "Topophony of Fascism: On Marcel Beyer's *The Karnau Tapes*," *Germanic Review*, 73 (4), pp. 328–348.

Siepmann, Charles. (1942) *Radio in Wartime*, New York, NY: Oxford University Press.

Sorensen, Robert C. and Leszek L. Meyer. (1955) "Local Uses of Wired Radio in Communist-Ruled Poland," *Journalism and Mass Communication Quarterly*, 32 (3), pp. 343–348.

Sproule, J. Michael. (1989) "Progressive Propaganda Critics and the Magic Bullet Myth," *Critical Studies in Mass Communication*, 6 (3), pp. 225–246.

Tyler, I. Keith. (1939) "Developing Critical Listening," *Phi Delta Kappan*, 21 (7), pp. 348–351.

von Eschen, Penny. (2004) *Satchmo Blows Up the World: Jazz Ambassadors Play the Cold War*, Cambridge, MA: Harvard University Press.

Whitton, John B. (1941) "War by Radio," *Foreign Affairs*, 19 (3), pp. 584–596.

Wines, Michael. (2001) "Wired Radio Offers Fraying Link to Russia's Past," *New York Times*, Oct. 18, 2001, p. 4.

Woolston, Howard. (1932) "Propaganda in Soviet Russia," *American Journal of Sociology*, 38 (1), pp. 32–40.

Zimmerman, Clemens. (2006) "From Propaganda to Modernization: Media Policy and Media Audiences Under National Socialism," *German History*, 24 (3), pp. 431–454.

10

SOUNDING OUT RACIAL DIFFERENCE

Alex W. Corey

One afternoon in late 1930s New York City, Ralph Ellison stumbled into the kind of acoustic scene that perks up the ears of sound and race scholars. Ellison recounts that he was circulating a petition in the African American neighborhood of San Juan Hill when he strode down a dark basement hallway and heard "male Afro-American voices, raised in violent argument" behind a closed door (Ellison 1978: 45). The tenement building's physical form governed what Ellison could see and hear—the door a visual barrier occluding the speaking bodies from sight, the hallway an acoustic chamber resonating with the sound of disembodied voices. "Sounding out the lay of the land," Ellison approached the door and played the part of aural sleuth, noting that "the language was profane, the style of speech a southern idiomatic vernacular such as was spoken by formally uneducated Afro-American workingmen" (Ellison 1978: 45). Vocabulary and syntax were not all that conveyed a sense of who these men were; the sonic qualities of the voices—volume, cadence, timbre, and vocal pitch—conjured a precise image of the men in Ellison's mind, as did the location. Ellison paused to assess the situation while his ear gathered more information.

It was not the fact of the raised voices that gave him pause: as a self-proclaimed "slum dweller," he knew that "voices in slums are often raised in anger, but that the *rhetoric* of anger, being in itself cathartic, is not necessarily a prelude to violence" (Ellison 1978: 45). Rather, it was the topic of their argument that provoked further reflection, for these "foulmouthed black workingmen were locked in verbal combat over which of two celebrated Metropolitan Opera divas was the superior soprano" (Ellison 1978: 45). The vernacular culture of urban black workingmen, here, mingles with the lofty culture of opera, a world that prizes literacy not only in the Eurocentric operatic tradition but also in the polite rituals of spectatorship and concert listening. In this heated exchange, Ellison heard how music and sound could traverse boundaries that legal structures and cultural conventions sought to enforce, "for the angry voices behind the door were proclaiming an intimate familiarity with a subject of which, by all the logic of their linguistically projected social status, they should have been oblivious" (Ellison 1978: 45). Forced to reconsider his acceptance of a rigid divide between vernacular and canonical, between the spoken and the composed, Ellison decided to enter the room—to solve the acoustic mystery that had drawn him in.

The image of Ellison "sounding out the lay of the land" might well parallel the state of scholarship on sound and race today. Even as the scope and political thrust of contemporary scholarship often diverges from Ellison's dedication to American melting-pot ideals, Ellison's written reflection on his encounter gestures toward some of the key methods and concerns that scholars of race and sound have developed since the 1980s. Using his ear as a critical tool, Ellison situated himself in his immediate surroundings and reconfigured his understanding of the relationships among social class, race, geography, gender, and aesthetic taste. Furthermore, Ellison draws explicitly on his vernacular knowledge to challenge the scientific racism and institutionally reinforced presumptions of black people's pathological propensity for violence: his experiences as a black man in the rural South and the urban North had taught him that the sounds of anger did not necessarily imply a physical threat. And even if legal structures like Jim Crow sought to draw firm lines between black and white bodies, Ellison heard how sonic cultures could traverse the more permeable boundaries between the lofty aesthetics of Western opera and the vernacular cadence of black, urban speech.

This analogy between Ellison and contemporary scholars is admittedly heuristic, but it draws attention to two overlapping strains of thought that weave through the contemporary research on the intersections of sound, blackness, and racial difference. First, as Ellison did, current scholarship is refining our understanding of the extent to which historical modes of categorizing sound filter through, and indeed produce, conceptions of race. Racial difference is heard, sensed, and not only seen conceptions of racial difference generally draw on cultural assumptions that situate whiteness as a position of decorum and order whereas racialized others are unruly, noisy, and excessive and subject to excessive policing in all senses of the word (Smith 2001 and 2008; Wagner 2009). Musical culture plays an especially important role in studies about the way that sound polices racial boundaries. Some scholarship stresses the extent to which the commercial interests of the music industry drive the historical racialization of musical genres and performance styles (Radano 2003; Miller 2010; Kheshti 2015; Nunn 2015; Hamilton 2016). Other research prioritizes the extent to which music deemed "other" challenged the commercial structures by transforming sound into a resistant social force with an often liberatory potential (Jones/Baraka 1963; Baker 1984; Gilroy 1993; Davis 1998; Kun 2005; Monson 2007; Redmond 2013).

Second, *phonography*, or the writing of sound from the printed page to phonographic disks, has become an increasingly crucial concept in studies of race and sound. Fred Moten's 2003 *In the Break: The Aesthetics of the Black Radical Tradition* and Alexander Weheliye's 2005 *Phonographies: Grooves in Sonic Afro-Modernity* have oriented this line of thought. Building on rich traditions of black feminist thought, African diasporan intellectual history, and continental philosophy, Weheliye and Moten develop theoretical foundations for studying the ways that racial discourse exists in the breaks and resonances between the sonic and the visual. Their research has strongly influenced recent scholarship that refuses to position hearing as modernity's second sense which simply reinforces senses of race based in the visual; instead, the sounding practices of black modern life enact forms of resistance that operate on the lower frequencies, just out of eyeshot (Stoever-Ackerman 2010; Stoever 2016; Stadler 2010a and 2010c; Crawley 2016). Throughout, contemporary research also calls attention to the illuminating power of social knowledge cultivated outside the walls of traditional educational institutions—in studies of Spanish-speaking and chican@ U.S radio (Casillas 2014; Sorensen 2016), Chicana and Cuban music (Vargas 2012; Vazquez 2013), African American music and culture (Monson 1996; Ramsey 2003; Harris-Lacewell 2004; Fischlin, Heble, and Lipsitz 2013), and a broader anthropology of sound (Samuels et al. 2010). The essay that follows traces these intellectual threads through field-defining texts and cutting-edge scholarship that promises to shape the field's ongoing development.

Sound and the color line

Even though "modern discussions of 'race' and racial identity are hostage to the eye" (Smith 2008: 8), sound has long been a critical touchstone in studies of modern race relations. W. E. B. Du Bois, for instance, heard African American spirituals as claims to belonging within a nation that strove to exclude African Americans from the body politic [1903]. Du Bois writes:

> And so by fateful chance the Negro folk-song—the rhythmic cry of the slave—stands today not simply as the sole American music, but as the most beautiful expression of human experience born this side the seas. It has been neglected, it has been, and is, half despised, and above all it has been persistently mistaken and misunderstood; but notwithstanding, it still remains as the spiritual heritage of the nation and the greatest gift of the Negro people.
>
> *([Du Bois 1903] 2007: 168)*

Here, Du Bois employs a sonic logic to demonstrate the permeability of the color line, a dilemma that he elsewhere develops primarily through visual metaphors (see also Stoever 2016). African Americans occupy a double position for Du Bois, for they reside both inside and outside of the United States as a nation; and "it is a peculiar sensation, this double-consciousness, this sense of always looking at one's self through the eyes of others, of measuring one's soul by the tape of a world that looks on in amused contempt and pity" (1903: 8). But if African Americans must cultivate a doubleness of vision that provides access to the nation's racial truths, America itself has a singular musical heritage that sounds forth when black voices rise up in song. J. Rosamond Johnson (1908) would go on to make a similar case, explaining "why they call American music ragtime," and his brother James Weldon Johnson's narrator in *The Autobiography of An Ex-Colored Man* (2015) would repeat the claim that black music—ragtime, in particular—stood for America abroad. This music sounded doubly, as both a symbol of black racial solidarity and a token of racial difference, as symbol of U.S. national coherence and threat to U.S. regimes of white supremacy (Radano 2003: 278–286; Weheliye 2005: 73–105).

The relationship between sound and racial difference has remained a preoccupation for contemporary scholars, many of whom build on Du Bois's identification of a potent resistant force within the "soundscapes"—to borrow a term from R. Murray Schafer—of black and brown lives. Jennifer Lynn Stoever-Ackerman (2010; Stoever 2016), for instance, has coined the term "the sonic color line" to show how racialized soundscapes from the antebellum enslaver's plantation to New York's San Juan Hill in the 1950s made sound into a medium that both delineated racial boundaries and provided avenues for resisting white political dominance. Where Stoever traverses a variety of sonic genres in service of her argument and employs methodologies from literary close-reading to historical ethnography, Shana Redmond (2013) brings a musicological sensibility to her work on the consolidating force of music within black social movements. Bracketing the commercial interests of the music publishing industry and the recording industry, which were largely controlled by white executives, Redmond listens for the insurgent affirmation of blackness that pulses through songs from the Johnson Brothers' "Lift Ev'ry Voice and Sing" to Nina Simone's iconic "To Be Young, Gifted, and Black." Redmond finds crucial continuities between sounds embedded in historical locales as distant as 1920s Harlem and 1970s–1980s South Africa. And Ashon Crawley's 2016 *Blackpentecostal Breath: The Aesthetics of Possibility* draws out a theology of blackness that he calls "otherwise"—never quite new, but an already existing alternative—in collective breath, the breath of Eric Garner's digitally reproduced final words, "I can't breathe," the breath of the Hammond B-3 organ channeled through a Leslie speaker's rotating components, the breath of black worship (2016). These scholars are especially indebted to earlier field-defining work that acknowledged the commercial pressures on black and brown musicians while emphasizing the power of music to express a liberatory potential that exceeded market strictures (Jones 1963; Baker 1984 and 1987; Gilroy 1993; Griffin 1995; Lipsitz 1997; Davis 1998; Kun 2005; and Brooks 2006).

Whereas Stoever, Redmond, and Crawley amplify a collective resistance within black and brown sonic cultures that market interests cannot circumscribe, other scholars prioritize the extent to which music as a commodity has shaped our understandings of racial difference in the first place. Within the music industry and the broader popular imagination, divisions between white and black music were largely products of record companies and sheet music publishers driving a wedge between genres rather than empirical differences in the music's sound. Miller (2010), for instance, argues that early twentieth-century distinctions between race records and hillbilly music inaugurated an increasingly stark division between music associated with whiteness and music associated with blackness. Hamilton (2016) traces how the distorted sound of a Stratocaster guitar could so convincingly conjure an image of whiteness by the end of the 1960s, when this style of playing emerged through the playing of black guitarists from Chuck Berry to Jimi Hendrix. Nunn (2015) examines what it means for music and text to be *Sounding the Color Line*—that is, both reflecting socially significant racial distinctions and permeating the boundaries between racial categories—while constructing sonic visions of the U.S. South. This work is especially indebted, both explicitly or implicitly, to earlier research that explores how the sounds that circulate within musical culture mediate understandings of racial difference and cultural exchange (Lott 1993; Radano and Bohlman 2000; Meintjes 2003; Radano 2003).

Phonography and racialized modernity

Blackness in body and in sound has long been commodified in the United States, and the scholarship of Stoever, Crawley, and Redmond, among many others, extends Fred Moten's (2003) provocative claim that "the history of blackness is testament to the fact that objects can and do resist." Moten's groundbreaking *In the Break: The Aesthetics of the Black Radical Tradition* reconfigures the received split between speech and writing, between sounding presence and visual silence, as he gathers photography, staged and ephemeral performance, print culture, and sound recording together as disparate but conjoined forms of *phonography*. Sound and sight interanimate each other, producing not an accumulation of the senses but a kind of aesthetic and political urgency that only happens where they intersect. His reading of the famous photograph of fourteen-year-old Emmett Till's broken body, who was lynched by white men 1955 for purportedly whistling at a white woman, is especially incisive for its access to the sonic qualities of such a seemingly silent object:

> You lean into it but you can't; the aesthetic and philosophical arrangements of the photograph—some organizations of and for light—anticipate a looking that cannot be sustained as unalloyed looking but must be accompanied by listening and this, even though what is listened to—echo of a whistle or a phrase, moaning, mourning, desperate testimony and flight—is also unbearable. These are the complex musics of the photograph. This is the sound before the photograph:
>
> Scream inside and out, out from outside, of the image. Bye, baby. Whistling. Lord, take my soul. Redoubled and reanimating, the passion of a seeing that is involuntary and uncontrollable, a seeing that redoubles itself as sound, a passion that is the

redoubling of Emmett Till's passion, of whatever passion would redeem, crucifixion, lynching, middle passion, passage.

(Moten 2003: 200–201)

Here, Moten performs a kind of sonic archaeology of the visual, demonstrating how hearing and seeing bleed into each other but never collapse into identical sensory formations. The photograph's palpable silence provokes the sensory reception of its overwhelming loudness. Blackness—both as a philosophical concept and a racial category—is loud but invisible, spectacular yet silent.

No clear account of sound as a racializing phenomenon can exist without accounting, as well, for listening as a racialized act. Focusing on acts of forced listening, for instance, can call attention to the ways that sound can become a tool for political suppression that falls along racial and ethnic lines (Cheng 2016; Goodman 2009). Gustavus Stadler (2015) reminds us of racialized, everyday acts of listening in his sweeping critique of the broader field of sound studies. There is no such thing as the "sound itself" of a police siren divorced from its social context, Stadler argues, and whether a bystander hears it as a promise of help or a threat to safety depends on histories of generations of racial and gendered discrimination in policing as well as personal experience with the police. His point is especially poignant given the ongoing crisis—which is sadly nothing new—of police brutality and the escalation of deadly force against black and brown people. Stadler, addressing the recent publication of a number of reference texts such as *Keywords in Sound*, *The Sound Studies Reader*, and the *Oxford Handbook of Sound Studies*, finds more of a "liberal politics of representation or 'inclusion'" than a sustained engagement with questions of social difference (Stadler 2015). He points readers in the direction of volumes such as Josh Kun and Kara Keeling's edited special issue of *American Quarterly* from 2011 ("Sound Clash: Listening to American Studies," now a book) and his own 2010 edited special issue *Social Text* (*The Politics of Recorded Sound*), both of which are strongly recommended reading for scholars orienting themselves in the field. Like *Sounding Out!*, an American Studies sound studies blog edited by Jennifer Stoever and Dolores Inés Casillas that publishes research addressing issues of sound and social difference, these special journal issues model a range of methodologies for engaging sound and race in intersectional relation to other forms of social difference such as gender, sexuality, disability, class, and nationality.

Stadler's critique contributes to a broader genealogy of thought arguing that blackness and racial difference are constitutive of, rather than ancillary to, modernity. We have known at least since Paul Gilroy's 1993 *The Black Atlantic: Modernity and Double Consciousness* that modernity itself is a racialized concept, that black music and sonic practices have played an integral role in the development of modernity because black people have been central players on a global scale. The pulsing rhythms and dense textures of black music from the spirituals to the blues, from Jamaican sound system culture to New York City's 1980s hip hop scene, tell a story about modernity that centers on, rather than relegates to the margins, the routes, and roots of a transatlantic black culture. On the whole, *The Black Atlantic* constructs an alternative to what David Michael Levin (1993: 101) diagnoses as "the hegemony of vision" within modernity at the same time that it dismantles one of the tacit assumptions of most prior theories of modernity, which Levin's edited collection reproduced—that white, Eurocentric experience is the primary site for discussing modernity's twin ideals of rationality and the liberal subject. For Gilroy, the "counterculture of modernity" emerges because black people live "both inside and outside modernity," and the music of the African diaspora sounds a "cultural sense of the inability of mere words to convey certain truths."

Alexander Weheliye (2005: 4) revises Gilroy's foundational claims for blackness in modernity by situating black "technosonic" cultures, especially those that use reproduction technology like the phonograph, printed writing, and visual media squarely within modernity at the same time that these cultures are relegated to a location outside of modernity. Weheliye suggests that the racist presumptions of black people as "primitive"—historical attempts to exclude black people from modern subjectivity—willfully ignore the extent to which black people have adopted fundamentally modern technologies such as the music video, the feature film, the phonograph, the cassette tape, and Western musical notation and adapted them to suit their own expressive purposes. Refusing to reproduce a version of white-centric modernity, Weheliye argues that black sonic practices from drumming and dialect-writing to the mix tape and beyond are not a "counterculture of modernity" responding to a dominant modernity, as Gilroy would have it; rather, they are enactments of a modernity of their own—perhaps what Crawley might call an "otherwise" modernity, one that flourishes in its own right and answers to no white person. There is a structural antagonism between blackness as it circulates in phonographic forms and modernity's inadequate eye, which always privileges whiteness and light and always shields itself from the blackness it opposes. The sounds of blackness make modernity look as it does and, at the same time, these sounds undo modernity's ability to look.

At stake is the dismantling of a binary division between writing and speech, between sounding presence and written silence, that has structured the study of modern cultures writ large. Weheliye is one of many scholars whose work reconsiders the decades-old distinction between oral and literate cultures, which tended to break along social lines—oral/aural culture tended to associate most directly with minoritized ethnic and socioeconomic groups, whereas the literate represented civilization, the high culture of Europe, the sophistication of whiteness. In the 1980s, scholars of African American culture began a systematic revision to the hard distinction between oral culture and literary production, as scholars showed how African American literature and culture consistently infused the literary with the oral, bringing embodied voice to bear on the printed word as a visual artifact (Baker 1984 and 1987; Gates 1988; Jones 1991; Griffin 1995). This scholarship provides a compelling account of the way that African American cultural production has consistently challenged the hierarchy of literacies within modernity. However, not everyone accepts the divide between literate and oral cultures at face value. Richard Cullen Rath (2003), for instance, addresses the conditions of possibility for such a mode of categorizing culture; Rath challenges what he calls the "literacy hypothesis," or the presumption that oral cultures are pre-modern states of nature that progress to visual-based, literate modernity. Rath writes:

> This literacy hypothesis hinges on the assumption of an older, ear-based way of life. Without that, there is no shift in perception, and without that, no literate/oral divide. Yet orality is not established empirically in these theories; it is established by inference. It is what literacy is not, and serves as a foil. The evidence for the transformation of ear-based oral culture to visual print culture is thus circular. Orality is itself the product of literate minds. So-called oral cultures would have no need for the term.
>
> *(Rath 2003: 3)*

I take Rath's point to be this: dividing modern cultures schematically along oral/literate lines flattens distinctions between so-called oral cultures and, furthermore, threatens to reinforce the literate/oral hierarchy that anthropologists and historians often seek to dismantle. Rath's intervention seems to land most forcefully within disciplines that prize empiricism and accept the literate/oral divide as fundamental to modernity. After all, anthropologists, ethnographers, and African Americanists have long known that as Rath (2003: 174) stated "Native American and

African American soundways were much more complex than a simple attribution of 'orality' would allow" (Levine 1977; Feld 1982; Basso 1985; Jones 1999; Harris-Lacewell 2004; Levin 2006; Fulton 2006).

But the force of Rath's provocative question remains: what would modernity sound like, and what would racial difference entail, if we were to imagine a fundamentally different cultural schema than the age-old distinction between the primitive ear and the modern eye, with the entrenched racial connotations embedded in that sensory split? To address the interpenetrations between sound and racial discourse is not simply an attempt to strap a discrete, racialized aural appendage onto an already stable formation of ocularcentric (white) modernity. After all, sound does not simply filter through the ear, adding a single dimension to our understandings of race or modernity. Rather, as Nina Sun Eidsheim (2015) argues, sound is a multisensory phenomenon, a "vibrational practice" that physically affects us and literally moves our flesh toward the incorporation of different modes of knowing ourselves and others. Perhaps it is this potential for transformation, for knowing modernity anew and otherwise, that the study of sound and race promises.

References

Baker Jr., H. (1984) *Blues, Ideology, and Afro-American Literature: A Vernacular Theory*, Chicago, IL: University of Chicago Press.

———— (1987) *Modernism and the Harlem Renaissance*, Chicago, IL: University of Chicago Press.

Basso, E. (1985) *A Musical View of the Universe: Kalapalo Myth and Ritual Performance*, Philadelphia, PA: University of Pennsylvania Press.

Brooks, D. (2006) *Bodies In Dissent: Spectacular Performances of Race and Freedom, 1850–1910*, Durham: Duke University Press.

Casillas, D.I. (2014) *Sounds of Belonging: U.S. Spanish-Language Radio and Public Advocacy*, New York, NY: New York University Press.

Cheng, W. (2016) *Just Vibrations: The Purpose of Sounding Good*, Ann Arbor, MI: University of Michigan Press.

Crawley, A. (2016) *Blackpentecostal Breath: The Aesthetics of Possibility*, New York, NY: Fordham University Press.

Davis, A. (1998) *Blues Legacies and Black Feminisms: Gertrude "Ma" Rainey, Bessie Smith, and Billie Holiday*, New York, NY: Vintage.

Du Bois, W. E. B. ([1903] 2007) *The Souls of Black Folk*, Ed. B.H. Edwards. New York, NY: Oxford University Press.

Eidsheim, N.S. (2015) *Sensing Sound: Singing and Listening as Vibrational Practice*, Durham, NC. Duke University Press.

Ellison, R. (1978) "The Little Man at Chehaw Station," *The American Scholar* 47.1 25–48.

Feld, S. (1982) *Sound and Sentiment: Birds, Weeping, Poetics, and Song in Kaluli Expression*, Philadelphia, PA: University of Pennsylvania Press.

Fischlin, D., Heble, A., and Lipsitz, G. (2013) *The Fierce Urgency of Now: Improvisation, Rights, and the Ethics of Cocreation*, Durham and London: Duke University Press.

Fulton, D.S. (2006) *Speaking Power: Black Feminist Orality in Women's Narratives of Slavery*, Albany, NY: State University of New York Press.

Gates Jr., H.L. (1988) *The Signifying Monkey: A Theory of Afro-American Literary Criticism*, New York, NY: Oxford University Press.

Gilroy, P. (1993) *The Black Atlantic: Modernity and Double Consciousness*, Cambridge, MA: Harvard University Press.

Goodman, S. (2009) *Sonic Warfare: Sound, Affect, and the Ecology of Fear*, Cambridge, MA: MIT Press.

Griffin, F.J. (1995) *"Who Set You Flowin'?": The African American Migration Narrative*, New York, NY: Oxford University Press.

Hamilton, J. (2016) *Just Around Midnight: Rock and Roll and the Racial Imagination*, Cambridge, MA: Harvard University Press.

Harris-Lacewell, M. (2004) *Barbershops, Bibles, and BET: Everyday Talk and Black Political Thought*, Princeton, NJ: Princeton University Press.

Johnson, J.W. ([1912] 2015) *The Autobiography of an Ex-Colored Man*, Ed. J. Goldsby. New York and London: W.W. Norton & Company, 1–110.

Johnson, J.R. (1908) "Why They Call American Music Ragtime," *The New York Age*. 24 December 1908. New York State Digital Library, 11.

Jones, L. (1963) *Blues People: Negro Music in White America*, New York, NY: Morrow.

Jones, G. (1991) *Liberating Voices: Oral Tradition in African American Literature*, Cambridge, MA: Harvard University Press.

Jones, G. (1999) *Strange Talk: The Politics of Dialect Literature in Gilded Age America*, Berkeley and Los Angeles, CA: University of California Press.

Keeling, K. and Kun, J., eds. ([2011] 2012) *Sound Clash: Listening to American Studies*, Baltimore, MD: Johns Hopkins University Press.

Kheshti, R. (2015) *Modernity's Ear: Listening to Race and Gender in World Music*, New York, NY: New York University Press.

Kun, J. (2005) *Audiotopia: Music, Race, and America*, Berkeley, CA: University of California Press.

Levin, D. (1993) *Modernity and the Hegemony of Vision*, Berkeley, CA: University of California Press.

Levin, T. (2006) *Where Rivers and Mountains Sing: Sound, Music, and Nomadism in Tuva and Beyond*, Bloomington, IN: Indiana University Press.

Levine, L. (1977) *Black Culture and Black Consciousness: Afro-American Folk Thought From Slavery to Freedom*, New York, NY: Oxford University Press.

Lipsitz, G. (1997) *Dangerous Crossroads: Popular Music, Postmodernism, and the Poetics of Place*, London and New York: Verso.

Lott, E. (1993) *Love and Theft: Blackface Minstrelsy and the American Working Class*, New York, NY: Oxford University Press.

Meintjes, L. (2003) *Sound of Africa! Making Music Zulu in a South African Studio*, Durham, NC: Duke University Press.

Miller, K.H. (2010) *Segregating Sound: Inventing Folk and Pop Music in the Age of Jim Crow*, Durham, NC: Duke University Press.

Monson, I. (2007) *Freedom Sounds: Civil Rights Call Out to Jazz and Africa*, New York and London: Oxford University Press.

———. (1996) *Saying Something: Jazz Improvisation and Interaction*, Chicago, IL: University of Chicago Press.

Moten, F. (2003) *In The Break: The Aesthetics of the Black Radical Tradition*, Durham, NC: Duke University Press.

Nunn, E. (2015) *Sounding the Color Line: Music and Race in the Southern Imagination*, Athens: University of Georgia Press.

Radano, R. (2003) *Lying Up a Nation: Race and Black Music*, Chicago, IL: University of Chicago Press.

Radano, R. and Bohlman, P., eds. (2000) *Music and The Racial Imagination*, Chicago, IL: University of Chicago Press.

Ramsey, G. (2003) *Race Music: Black Cultures from Bebop to Hip-Hop*, Berkeley, Los Angeles, and London: University of California Press.

Rath, R.C. (2003) *How Early America Sounded*, Ithaca, NY: Cornell University Press.

Redmond, S. (2013) *Anthem: Social Movements and the Sound of Solidarity in the African American Diaspora*, New York, NY: New York University Press.

Samuels, D., Meintjes, L., Ochoa, A.M. and Porcello, T. (2010) "Soundscapes: Toward a Sounded Anthropology," *Annual Review of Anthropology* 39: 329–45.

Smith, M. (2008) *How Race is Made: Slavery, Segregation, and the Senses*, Chapel Hill, NC: University of North Carolina Press.

———. (2001) *Listening to Nineteenth-Century America*, Chapel Hill, NC: University of North Carolina Press.

Sorensen, L. (2016) "Region and Ethnicity on the Air," *MELUS* 41.2: 7–26.

Stadler, G. (2015) "On Whiteness and Sound Studies," *Sounding Out* (https://soundstudiesblog.com/2015/07/06/on-whiteness-and-sound-studies/).

———. (2010a) "Introduction: Breaking Sound Barriers," *Social Text 102*: 1–12.

———. (2010c) "Never Heard Such a Thing: Lynching and Phonographic Modernity," *Social Text 102* (28.1): 87–105.

Stoever-Ackerman, J. (2010) "Splicing the Color Line: Tony Schwartz Remixes Postwar Nueva York." *Social Text 102* (28.1): 59–85.

Stoever, J.L. (2016) *The Sonic Color Line: Race and the Cultural Politics of Listening*, New York, NY: New York University Press.

Vargas, D. (2012) *Dissonant Divas in Chicana Music: The Limits of La Onda*, Minneapolis, MN: University of Minnesota Press.

Vazquez, A. (2013) *Listening In Detail: Performances of Cuban Music*, Durham, NC: Duke University Press.

Wagner, B. (2009) *Disturbing the Peace: Black Culture and the Police Power After Slavery*, Cambridge, MA: Harvard University Press.

Weheliye, A. (2005) *Phonographies: Grooves in Sonic Afro-Modernity*, Durham, NC: Duke University Press.

11

GENDERED SOUND

Marie Thompson

The instructive voice of the GPS system, or 'sat-nav', has become an audible presence in many people's everyday lives. These navigation devices offer a range of 'male' and 'female' automated voices with different accents, which the user can select according to their own personal preferences. Some devices enable the user to employ a famous voice to issue directions, such as that of Marge Simpson, Mr T or the Dalek from Doctor Who.

Despite the variety of male, female and ambiguously gendered voices available (what is the gender of a Dalek?), sat-navs are often associated in the popular imagination with what is understood as a 'neutral' (that is white, middle class) feminine voice. Indeed, automated voices have often been feminized, partly through their association with 'assistance' – there is, for example, the female-voiced computer of Spike Jonze's 2013 film *Her*; the secretarial voices of smartphone personal assistants such as Cortana and the US version of Siri; and the ubiquitous feminine voices in public spaces that remind listeners to keep their personal belongs with them at all times.

If gender is something that pertains to bodily difference and body-world relations, then it might seem problematic to describe the disembodied, automated voice, such as that of the sat-nav, as 'masculine' or 'feminine'. Yet while gender is a complex material-discursive site, in the field of robotics, the sound of gender is neatly charted in relation to wavelengths. A.O. Roberts describes how gendered speech synthesis is 'actively policed around 100–150 HZ (male) and 200–250 HZ (female)' (Roberts, 2015). In doing so, the field of speech synthesis reproduces the highly problematic cultural tendency to attempt to to 'fix' gender in relation to particular 'biological' and 'physical' characteristics. In conforming to popular imaginations of what gender sounds like, and by understanding gendered vocal expression through ridged dualisms of quantifiable difference, robotics and speech synthesis 'hold up an acoustic mirror to the dominant cultures from which they materialize' (Roberts, 2015).

With the automated voices of sat-nav, the entangled relationship of sound and gender comes to the fore. Sound is gendered insofar as gender is integral to the epistemic, practical and technological apparatus through which it is produced, accessed, experienced and understood (Martin, 1991; Rodgers, 2010a, 2010b; James, 2010; Ingleton, 2016). To talk of 'gendered sound', however, seems to imply that the former (gender) is something that happens to the latter (sound). But this relationship is not simply one of mediation. Sound does not reflect pre-existing gendered modes of being, nor is sound a passive medium through which notions of gender are transmitted. Rather, as I repeatedly assert, gender is constituted 'with, through and alongside' the sonic.

Sound is one of a number of materialities and mediums with which gender is made and remade, produced and reproduced. The relationship between sound and gender is thus multidirectional and co-productive. From this perspective, the automated voice of speech synthesis doesn't just hold up a reflective 'acoustic mirror' but actively (re)produces notions of what gender sounds like.

To describe sound as 'reflecting' gender also risks attributing a stability or rigidity to the latter. Yet on both a 'micro-' and 'macropolitical' scale, gender can be considered dynamic, fluid and mutable. Indeed, although Eurocentric society is primarily organised in relation to two genders, this binary obscures a multitude of masculinities, femininities, a-gender, transgender and genderqueer modes of being, which are co-constituted with other socio-economic categories of embodied difference: for example, race, class, disability, ethnicity, sexuality, age. Gender, then, is not a fixed category that precedes embodied experience; rather it is continually produced and reproduced with the body's 'repeated yet constantly evolving interaction with our social and material worlds' (James, 2010: 24).

I have asserted that sound and gender cannot be cleanly separated insofar as they are produced with, through and alongside one another. Nonetheless, to temporarily assume such a separation is possible in order to draw sound and gender into comparison with one another reveals a number of important similarities. While it is sometimes useful for the purpose of analytical enquiry to treat them as distinct categories, neither sound nor gender exist or are experienced in 'pure' form. As Jonathan Sterne states: 'Sound is always defined by the shifting borders that it shares with a vast world of not-sound phenomena... sound in itself is always shaped by and through its exteriors, even as it acts on and within them' (Sterne, 2003: 343). Just as gender is, in its actuality, is inseparable from, amongst other things, race, class, sexuality, disability, ethnicity, sound, too, in actuality, is inextricably entangled with a variety of 'extra-sonic' processes, relations and norms – from environmental and physical factors such as movement, humidity and atmospheric pressure, to 'social' practices, epistemologies and institutions such as Capitalism, militarism, medical understandings of the human body, architecture and urban planning (Sterne, 2003).

More generally, sound and gender exist amidst the relations between bodies, environments, epistemologies and ideological apparatus. They both occupy the connecting line between the physical and the physiological, the material and the discursive, 'nature' and 'culture' (James, 2010). This connecting line does not mark a straightforward, causal relation, though it has often been presented as such: just as essentialist accounts have understood particular bodies or bodily features as 'causing' particular gendered modes of being, particular sounds or sonic properties have sometimes been understood to 'cause' particular types of social behaviour and psychological effects. And just as sound has been subject to naturalisation, the 'non-naturalness' of gender has often been obscured by these essentialist accounts.

The remainder of this chapter introduces three examples which are used to further interrogate the production of sound and gender 'with, through and alongside' one another. 'Gendered-sound discourses' points to the inextricable relationship of gendered and sonic discourses. 'Gendered-sound production/reception' returns to an aforementioned method of sound-making which many debates on sound and gender have focused: the voice. Here I pay particular attention to the gendered-sound aesthetics and politics of transfeminine voices and the potential disjuncture that arises between gendered voices as they are produced and gendered voices as they are heard through normative expectations of the body-gender-voice relation. The third section, 'Gendered-sound policing', examines how the policing of auditory culture – understood both figuratively and literally in relation to the recent alleged ban on bashment music in Croydon nightclubs – is bound up with longstanding pejorative imaginations of 'disorderly' black masculinity.

Gendered-sound discourses

In the introduction to her once controversial and now canonical *Feminine Endings: Music, Gender and Sexuality*, first published in 1991, Susan McClary asserts that *contra* claims of objectivity, neutrality and social autonomy, music and musicology are inextricably bound up with notions of gender. One of the ways in which this entanglement is expressed is through music's rhetorical formations. McClary highlights how the metaphors of 'traditional' (that is Eurocentric, classical) music theory expose the gendering of musical practice and discourse. The classification of cadence-types according to gender, for example, explicitly reproduces dominant social formations of masculinity and femininity. McClary cites the 1970 edition of the *Harvard Dictionary of Music* which asserts that the a 'masculine' cadence 'must be considered the normal one', occurring if the final chord of a phrase or section occurs on the strong beat, where the 'feminine' cadence 'is postponed to fall on a weak beat' and 'is preferred in more romantic styles' (Apel quoted in McClary, 2002: 9). As McClary notes, in this short dictionary description, its author, Wili Apel, 'has managed to engage some of the most prominent of Western beliefs concerning sexual difference':

> This standard definition makes it clear that the designations 'masculine' and 'feminine' are far from arbitrary. The two [cadences] are differentiated on the basis of relative strength, with the binary opposition of masculine/feminine mapped onto strong/weak. Moreover, this particular definition betrays other important mappings: if the masculine version is ('must be considered') normal, then the implication is that the feminine is abnormal.
>
> *(McClary, 2002: 10)*

Given the explicitly gendered language of McClary's illustrative example, it might be tempting for contemporary readers to dismiss her as stating the obvious. Yet at the time of writing (and indeed sometimes today) music theory was often treated as an abstract and ahistorical system, which was organised around 'naturalised' rules. McClary's work, by contrast, begins from the perspective that the 'structures graphed by theorists and the beauty celebrated by aestheticians are often stained with such things as violence, misogyny and racism' (McClary, 2002: 4).

Where feminist and gender criticism have become reasonably well-established within the field of musicology, partly due to the wide influence of McClary's work, it is has been less prevalent within the broader, trans-disciplinary field of 'sound studies'. Yet sound's discourses (which includes but extends beyond music) are also produced with, through and alongside gendered metaphors, practices and standpoints. Just as McClary showed how the seemingly 'abstract' realm of music theory is in fact 'muddied' by gendered values, scholars such as Tara Rodgers and Holly Ingleton have shown how the historical consideration of seemingly and 'objective', 'neutral' and 'measureable' sonic parameters such as pitch, timbre and amplitude reveals their entanglement with, amongst other things, philosophical and scientific epistemologies of sexual difference. Many of these parameters are largely indebted to the work of nineteenth-century German physicist and physician Hermann von Helmholtz, which has become the normative sonic epistemology that defines the norms and 'laws' of scientific acoustics (Rodgers, 2010b; Ingleton, 2016). Yet general models are by no means neutral models. Helmholtz's acoustics is underlined by, amongst other things, a preference for neoclassical aesthetics, expressed in his prioritisation of purity, simplicity, order and control. Many of these underlying aesthetic priorities are evident in Helmholtz's figure of the sine wave – a singular, simple, neutral, 'pure' and 'clean' tone that is without 'body' and 'colour'. The sine wave has been treated as an acoustic ideal and standard against which all timbral variations are compared (Rodgers, 2010a; see also Schafer, 1994; Kahn, 2001; Evens 2005). And as the benchmark against which 'deviations' are measured, the sine wave is structurally analogous to the white masculine subject (recall the universalising 'normality' of the masculine cadence). Just as 'bodied' and 'coloured' tones are acoustic deviations from the purity of the idealized sine tone, white masculinity has historically been installed as an idealized benchmark against which radicalized and gendered 'deviations' are compared. Moreover, the qualities attributed to the sine tone are also qualities that have historically been attributed to white masculinity and, by extension, 'virtuous' femininity; where those qualities that are antithetical to the 'pure', 'clean' sine wave – for example, 'colour', 'body', chaos, disorder, unruliness, noisiness, dissonance, excess – have constituted racialized 'others' and/or deviant femininities. I shall discuss this further in the final section of this chapter.

More generally, the sonic and the feminine have been frequently articulated in relation to one another. Indeed, it is significant that Helmholtz's sonic parameters helped bring ('feminine') sound into ('masculinist') order; they enable 'unruly', 'immersive' soundwaves to 'analysed', 'controlled' and 'mastered' (Rodgers, 2010b). The rhetorical feminization of sound and its perception can be highlighted in relation to what Jonathan Sterne has labelled 'the audiovisual litany'. The audiovisual litany is a recurring discursive tendency and dominant ideological formation that opposes sound and hearing with vision. Predicated on the sensory registers a universal and ahistorical human subject; the audiovisual litany tends to appear as a list of binary oppositions. One of the key oppositions around which the audiovisal litany is organised is the distinction between sound's 'immersion' and vision's 'distance': 'hearing immerses its subject, vision offers a perspective… hearing involves physical contact with the outside world, vision requires distance from it; hearing places us inside an event, seeing gives us perspective on the event' (Sterne, 2003: 15).

To differentiate the sonic from the visual in terms of immersion is highly problematic: for example, light, upon which vision relies, might too be understood as an immersive phenomenon. Nonetheless, the audiovisual litany remains prevalent in sound's discourses (Schrimshaw, 2015). Moreover, the audiovisual litany's central binarism of sonic immersion/visual distance is also indebted to gendered terminology and imaginations. Indeed, this onto-epistemological distinction has frequently appeared in feminist discourse. The distance, directionality and objectivity of vision associates it with dominant Eurocentric imaginations of masculinity, while the connection of phallocentrism and ocularcentrism is a common tenet of post-1968 French feminist philosophy (Jay, 1994: 526; Irigaray, 1993). Likewise, descriptions of sound as an immersive and surrounding medium resonate with numerous notions of femininity; in particular, the notion of the 'maternal-feminine'. For French feminist philosopher, Luce Irigaray, the maternal-feminine is 'an *envelope*, a *container*, the starting point from which man limits his things' (Irigaray, 1993: 11). Given this connection, it is no accident that many of sound's origin's myths begin with pregnancy and the womb. R. Murray Schafer, for instance, makes apparent the intimate relation between the maternal-feminine, immersion and soundwaves in his discussion of 'first soundscapes'. Schafer asserts that the first sound heard 'was the caress of the waters… The Greek myths tell how man arose from the sea.' According to Schafer, watery beginnings are invoked in antenatal experience: 'the ocean of our ancestors is reproduced in the watery womb of our mother and chemically related to it. Ocean and Mother' (Schafer, 1994: 15). Through such metaphoric figurations, the sonic is feminized and feminine is rendered sonic.

Gendered-sound production/reception

In the discourse on gendered sound, the voice has been positioned as central; prioritised as the primary sonic medium through which gender is produced, transmitted and received. Anne

Carson, in her essay on the gender of sound, describes how feminine voices have been historically denigrated by comparison to their masculine counterparts: 'High vocal pitch goes together with talkativeness to characterize a person who is deviant from or deficient in the masculine ideal of self-control' (Carson, 1992: 119). Carson's observations resonate with those of Rosalind Gill, writing in the context of 1990s UK independent radio, who shows how 'women's feminine voices have been deemed as unsuitable for radio by virtue of being "too shrill", "too high", "too dusky" and "grating"' (Gill, 2000).

As these accounts suggest, the gendering of the voice is often defined in relation to vocal pitch. Moreover, as was highlighted apropos of the automated voice, the relationship between voice, vocal frequency, sex and/or gender has often been presented as an unproblematic biological 'fact'. Some have sought to nuance this correlation by using the now-common distinction drawn between sex-as-biology and gender-as-social to differentiate between 'innate' and 'learned' vocal properties (Stuart-Smith, 2007; Zimman, 2015). However, the sex/gender binary has also been critiqued. Judith Butler, for example, has famously argued that 'sex' as well as 'gender' is socially constructed, insofar as the ways in which biological sex is understood is inextricable from cultural notions of gender – what 'counts' as biological sex is entangled with socio-cultural categories and ideas of gender (Butler, 1993; 2011). Likewise, as Lal Zimman argues in his research into transmasculine voices, although biological sex is often construed as 'fixed' by comparison to the 'fluidity' of gender, the 'biological' body and, by extension, 'biological' sex are in fact malleable – they can be changed through, for example, hormone therapy and other forms of medication, food consumption and exercise. Consequently, 'As we consider the ways gendered embodiment interacts with the voice, it's important to keep in mind that sex is not static, not purely natural, and that it does not necessarily cause gender differences even where correlations exist' (Zimman, 2015: 199). Butler and Zimman's work suggests that the relationship between biology, body, sociality, gender and the voice is far from straightforward. As a result, it becomes questionable as to how it might be possible to distinguish the voice's 'natural' traits from the 'nurtured', the innate from the learned.

The complexity of the relation between body, gender and the voice can take on a particular significance in relation to transgender modes of being. 'Transgender' is an umbrella term that refers to a heterogeneous spectrum of gender manifestations that 'call attention to the fact that "gender" as it is lived, experienced, performed and encountered, is more complex and varied than can be accounted for by the dominant binary of sex/gender ideology of Eurocentric modernity' (Stryker, 2006: 3). Though its meanings may vary in the contexts of medical and psychological discourse, political activism and institutional policy, 'transgender' is typically used to refer to those whose gender in some way differs to that assigned at birth. Some transgender people's gender expressions align with dominant binaries and expectations of body-gender relations (for example being 'masculine men' or 'feminine women'), where others may align with neither or numerous gender categories. Consequently, there is not one but multiple transgender configurations of body-gender-voice relation. However, dominant cultural understandings and expectations of the body-gender-voice relation, insofar as they are largely predicated on Eurocentric modernity's sex/gender binary and assume a neat alignment between these categories, often fail to account for transgender modes of being. Indeed, by perpetuating expectations of what men and women 'naturally' sound like, dominant understandings of the body-gender-voice relation also perpetuate problematic gendered distinctions of 'authenticity' and 'artificiality'. Julia Serano has highlighted that the voice's use in media representations of transgender women's lives – alongside other gendered technologies – lends support to the idea that they are 'fake' or 'artificial' women. Serano notes that the majority of depictions of trans women – whether fictional or real – assume that all trans women want to achieve a stereotypically feminine appearance and gender role. Consequently, these depictions tend to centre on processes of 'feminization', in which trans women are captured '*in the act* of putting on lipstick, dresses and high heels, thereby giving the impression that trans woman's femaleness is an artificial mask or costume' (Serano, 2007: 41). Serano highlights how the road-trip film *Transamerica* exemplifies this phenomenon. The opening scenes of the film depict its protagonist, Bree Osborne, practicing along with the instructional voice-training video, *Finding your Female Voice*, as well as changing into a pink dress suit, padding her bra and putting on stockings, makeup and other cosmetics. In the first dialogue of the film, which follows this opening scene, Bree discusses with a psychiatrist her hormone replacement therapy and discloses other cosmetic procedures that she has undergone. As Serano argues, this opening presentation of cosmetic, medical and sonic feminization 'are clearly designed to establish that Bree's female identity is artificial and imitative, and to reduce her transition to a mere pursuit of feminine finery' (Serano, 2007: 42).

Serano's remarks regarding the perceived 'artificiality' of trans women are in some ways echoed by 'E' in her reflections on the voice and gender. E is a vocalist and musician active in numerous bands and musical projects in the UK. The relation between E's gender and voice is unproblematic: E is a woman and so her voice is a woman's voice. However, there is a disjuncture between dominant social expectations of what a woman's voice is and what, in light of transgender experiences and manifestations of womanhood, a woman's voice might be. This disjuncture requires E to spend 'much of my time on metaphorical tip-toes… I worry that I have to conceal and conform for my own safety and peace of mind… the idea of being seen as something that I'm not feels close to violent to me' (interview with author, 2016). The potential disjuncture between the gendered-voice as it is produced (that is a woman's voice) and the gendered-voice heard and interpreted in relation to social norms of the feminine-female voice is a fraught and threatening space, which can result in misgendering. As a result, E's voice varies in different contexts. However, this variation is not necessarily conscious or intentional:

> Essentially I feel that I have a 'good' voice and a 'regular' voice and there are variations, graduated based on levels of trust… [with people I'm really comfortable with] I trust that dropping my pitch and being lazier with my speech won't invalidate my gender in their eyes…The thing is, the good voice is unsustainable… I can't even work out how it feels in my throat, it's involuntary and a safety issue. I feel I have almost no control over my voice really.'
>
> *(Interview with author, 2016)*

E's remarks highlight the role of the voice in negotiating the complex web of gendered power relations that many trans women are faced with. On the one hand, transfeminine voices can require a reconsideration of what women sound like and what constitutes a 'female voice'. As E states, 'the world needs to get used to more diversity in what it considers a woman's voice (or body for that matter)' (interview with author, 2016). On the other hand, becoming 'hypervisible' (and/or 'hyperaudible') as transgender in certain social contexts can be risky in terms of personal safety, and so there can be a need to conform to normative expectations of the body-gender-voice relation. Yet, in both 'failing' to match up with normative expectations of what 'women' sound like, and in trying to conform to them, trans women risk being labelled as 'fake'. As E explains:

> Trans women are seen as fake, synthetic, cosmetic, performative. With regard to the voice, trans women feel a lot of anxiety about the point in their transition where they will begin to work on it, and how people will react to hearing a different, new voice

from a person they know. It seems put on, unreal and therefore ridiculous. Personally I have come to a point where I know there are several voices inside me, and I choose between them to an extent, and yeah, that makes me feel fake sometimes for sure.

(Interview with author, 2016)

In being heard as 'fake', trans women and transfeminine voices resonate with longstanding Eurocentric tropes that construe femininity and feminine voices as artificial. In this regard, they can be understood not as 'unfeminine' but as '*hyper*feminine'. As Serano notes, femininity has been pejoratively construed by both misogynistic narratives and some strands of feminist scholarship as 'artifice', 'merely performance' and 'false consciousness', particularly by comparison to the 'sincerity' of masculinity (Serano, 2007). This can be exemplified by liberal feminist Naomi Wolf's recent call for young women to 'give up' their 'annoying' and 'destructive' (feminine) vocal habits such as vocal fry, breathiness, soft-spokenness and 'uptalk', which are heard as deferent, hesitant and uncertain. Instead, Wolf calls for young women to reclaim their 'strong female voice' which is heard as 'authoritative' and 'serious' (Wolf, 2015). The 'hyperfeminine' transfeminine voice can thus be thought of as amplifying cultural anxieties around 'fake' femininity. In short, there is nothing more feminine than being heard as inauthentic.

Policing gendered sound

As the previous discussion of the transfeminine voice suggests, the boundaries of the audible are carefully policed: the distinction between what is permitted and unpermitted, wanted signal and unwanted noise, what sounds 'right' and wrong' within a particular social space is a political question that is bound up with, amongst other things, notions of gender. This policing of auditory culture occurs in relation to numerous registers. It may be part of our 'self-management', or it may occur in relation to more formal, institutional channels, such as when we are instructed to switch our phones to silent in particular spaces, like a train carriage or cinema. Sound might be quite literally policed in relation to noise abatement legislation and public order acts.

In March 2016, a bar in Croydon accused the borough's police of banning bashment music in relation to concerns about 'safety', prompting widespread criticism and allegations of racial profiling. Bashment may refer to any kind of Jamaican music or musical gathering but it is also sometimes used to refer to a particular style of upbeat dancehall music. It was reported in *The Guardian* that Roy Seda, the owner of Croydon's Dice Bar, was allegedly approached several times in 2015 by police offers urging him to stop playing bashment, as it was deemed 'unacceptable' by the borough: Seda was said to have received an email from Sgt Michael Emery, a licensing officer in Croydon, which makes reference to 'what the borough finds unacceptable forms of music' (Grierson, 2016). Seda also claims that police had asserted that bashment was 'linked to crime and disorder' (Davies, 2016). It was reported that officers first raised concerns about bashment with the venue when the licensing officer PC Darren Rhodes advised the owner to remove the term bashment from a flyer for the club, along with other advertised musical genres such as R&B, Garage, House and hip-hop. According to Seda, he was 'advised to remove the word "bashment" because the words chart and commercial music is considered safer' (BBC, 2016). In response to the allegations, the Metropolitan police issued a statement claiming that they had not requested a ban on any type of music at Dice Bar but that Seda as licensee had volunteered not to host bashment music events in order 'to tackle "crime and disorder" issues in his venue and *make it safer* [sic.]' (BBC, 2016).

Though the Metropolitan police's statement denies a formal ban on music, it nonetheless maintains a connection between bashment, and, by extension, black clubbers and crime and disorder. Indeed, the alleged 'bashment ban' is one of a number of high profile cases in which the Metropolitan police have been accused of racially profiling 'Urban' music audiences, spaces and nightlife under the guise of 'safety'. This includes the perceived disproportionate restrictions placed on grime events through the use of '696' – the Met police's 'Promotion Risk Assessment Form – 696'. The original form asked promoters for the ethnic 'make-up' of their target audience and details of the music that the event would be playing (Bramwell, 2015: 65). Clubgoers, promoters and artists have suggested that the 696 form is used as a means of shutting down grime nights with little justification beyond 'intelligence about an incident' (Hancox, 2009).

This policing of black musical practices and spaces points to a racialized politics of listening. Blackness is often produced by the ear of the state as disruptive, aggressive and threatening; and thus its sonic manifestations require monitoring, securitisation and abatement. In this regard, the policing of bashment and grime forms part of a long urban history in which 'blackness' and 'noisiness' are heard together. Scholars such as Jennifer Stoever and Emily Thompson, for example, have highlighted how in a US context, social and racial 'others' have been disproportionately targeted by dominant culture's campaigns against noise and abatement legislation. From the perspective of white, dominant culture, blackness has been imagined as both a source of noise and immune to noise (Stoever, 2015; Thompson, 2004).

This racialized politics of listening is also gendered, insofar as it is frequently produced with, through and alongside pejorative stereotypes of black masculinity. This is not to deny the active participation of women in bashment and grime nights as both performers and clubgoers. However, dominant cultural imaginations of black masculinity have often defined it in relation to criminality, deviancy and aggression, many of which are reproduced when black musical spaces, audiences and nightlife are conflated with criminality and disorder. The production of black masculinity as violent criminality is bound to histories of colonialism, slavery and white supremacy (Davis, 1981; Fanon, 1986). Writing in 1952 about the psychopathology of colonialism Frantz Fanon argues: 'In the collective unconsciousness, black = ugliness, sin, darkness, immorality. In other words, he is negro who is immoral. If I order my life like that of a moral man, I simply am not a Negro' (Fanon, 1986: 149). More recently, apropos of US hip-hop, Tricia Rose has highlighted the tension between, on the one hand, an exceptionalism that presents the purported violence and aggression of black masculinity as at odds with a mainstream culture, and, on the other, mainstream cultural endorsements of violent masculinity:

> Throughout the twentieth century especially, violence was wedded to mainstream visions of manhood… The pro-violence, celebratory air associated with military action and action heroes and the fascination with mobsters… hunting, and the regulated violence that fuels boxing, football and hockey have saturated American culture. In every case, these expressions of American values celebrate the male who is able and willing to challenge others to battle and be prepared to act violently.
>
> *(Rose, 2008: 107)*

The conflation of black masculinity and violent criminality is produced with, through and alongside the policing of the urban soundscapes. Hearing bashment and other black musical genres as 'causing' or 'encouraging' criminality and disorder rearticulates and reaffirms long-standing cultural imaginations of black male deviancy. It also exemplifies the ways in which the distinctions upon which the policing of auditory culture relies – between wanted and desirable sound (for example the 'safety' of chart and commercial music) and unwanted and threatening noise (for example the 'aggression' of bashment and grime) – are tied to gendered, classed and racialized social relations.

Conclusion

The relation between gender and sound is one of entanglement. Gender is sonic, inasmuch as sound is a medium through which it is produced, expressed and interpreted; where sound is gendered, inasmuch as its technological and discursive apparatus are bound up with histories and philosophies of sexual difference. This chapter has introduced three examples, which have been used to highlight the ways in which sound and gender are produced with, through and alongside one another. However, there are many other approaches that can be used to exemplify this relation. For example, historiographical work can reveal how certain forms of gendered and racialized labour are overshadowed in histories of sonic culture that are organised around the figure of the 'pioneering' white male inventor (for example Rodgers, 2010a); or how sound technologies and gendered social practices develop through and alongside one another (for example Martin, 1991).

Gender, then, is not simply an addition that muddies the 'purity' of physical waves. Indeed, just as it is questionable as to whether it is possible to talk of the 'purely' biological in isolation from the social with regard to gender, it is questionable whether it is possible to talk of 'purely' physical sound in isolation from its socio-historical epistemologies. Gender is not something that happens *to* sound – a 'social' or 'cultural' add-on to a 'natural' or 'physical' phenomenon; rather, gender and sound, both of which oscillate between the 'natural' and the 'cultural', the 'material' and the 'discursive', the 'physical' and the 'social', occur *with* one another.

References

BBC, 'Club owner says police told him to ban Jamaican Music', *BBC Newsbeat*, 14 March 2016. Available at: www.bbc.co.uk/newsbeat/article/35801841/club-owner-says-police-told-him-to-ban-jamaican-music [accessed 01/08/16].

Bramwell, Richard, *UK Hip-hop, Grime and the City: the Aesthetics and Ethics of London's Rap Scenes* (New York, Routledge, 2015).

Butler, Judith, *Bodies that Matter: On the Discursive Limits of Sex* (New York: Routledge, 1993).

Butler, Judith, *Gender Trouble: Feminism and the Subversion of identity* (New York: Routledge, 2011).

Carson, Anne, 'The gender of sound', in *Glass, Irony and God* (New York: New Directions Books, 1992), pp. 119–142.

Davies, Gareth, 'Exclusive: police in Croydon accused of racial profiling after ban on "unacceptable" Jamaican music', *Croydon Advertiser*, 11 March 2016. Available at: www.croydonadvertiser.co.uk/exclusive-police-croydon-accused-racial-profiling/story-28898260-detail/story.html [accessed 01/08/16].

Davis, Angela, *Women, Race and Class* (New York, Vintage Books, 1981).

Evens, Aden, *Sound Ideas: Music, Machines, and Experience* (Minneapolis: University of Minnesota Press, 2005).

Fanon, Frantz, *Black Skins, White Masks*, trans. Charles Lam Markmann (London: Pluto Press, 1986).

Gill, Rosalind, 'Justifying injustice: broadcasters' accounts of inequality in radio', in Caroline Mitchell (ed.) *Women and Radio: Airing Differences* (London: Routledge, 2000) pp. 137–151.

Grierson, Jamie, 'Croydon bar accuses police of banning Jamaican bashment music', *The Guardian*, 11 March 2016. Available at: www.theguardian.com/uk-news/2016/mar/11/croydon-bar-accuses-police-banning-jamaican-bashment-music [accessed 01/08/16].

Hancox, Dan, 'Public enemy no 696', *The Guardian*, 21 January 2009. Available at: www.theguardian.com/culture/2009/jan/21/police-form-696-garage-music [accessed 01/08/16].

Ingleton, Holly, 'Recalibrating the fundamentals of discipline and desire through the automatic music tent', *Contemporary Music Review*, 35: 1 (2016), 71–84.

Irigaray, Luce, *An Ethics of Sexual Difference*, trans. Carolyn Burke and Gillian C. Gill (Ithaca: Cornell University Press, 1993).

James, Robin, *The Conjectural Body: Gender, Race and the Philosophy of Music* (Lanham: Lexington Books, 2010).

Jay, Martin, *Downcast Eyes: The Denigration of Vision in Twentieth-Century French Thought* (California: University of California Press, 1994).

Kahn, Douglas, *Noise Water Meat: A History of Sound in the Arts* (Cambridge, MA: MIT Press, 2001).

Martin, Michèle, *'Hello, Central?' Gender, Technology and Culture in the Formation of Telephone Systems* (Montreal and Kingston: McGill-Queens University Press, 1991).

McClary, Susan, *Feminine Endings: Music, Gender and Sexuality* (Minnesota: University of Minnestoa Press, 2002).

Roberts, AO, 'Echo and the chorus of female machines', *Sounding Out* 2 March 2015. Available at: https://soundstudiesblog.com/2015/03/02/echo-and-the-chorus-of-female-machines/ [accessed 01/08/16].

Rodgers, Tara, *Pink Noises: Women on Electronic Music and Sound* (Durham: Duke University Press, 2010a).

Rodgers, Tara, *Synthesizing Sound: Metaphor in Audio-Technical Discourse and Synthesis History*. Unpublished doctoral dissertation (McGill University, 2010b).

Rose, Tricia, *The Hip-Hop Wars: What We Talk About When We Talk About Hip-Hop and Why It Matters* (New York: Perseus Books Group, 2008).

Schafer, R. Murray, *The Soundscape: Our Sonic Environment and the Tuning of the World* (Vermont: Destiny Books, 1994).

Schrimshaw, Will, 'Exit immersion', *Sound Studies* Vol.1/1 (2015) pp. 155–170.

Serano, Julia, *Whipping Girl: A Transsexual Woman on Sexism and the Scapegoating of Femininity* (Berkeley: Seal Press, 2007).

Sterne, Jonathan, *The Audible Past: Cultural Origins of Sound Reproduction* (Durham: Duke University Press, 2003).

Stuart-Smith, Jane 'Empirical evidence for gendered speech production: /s/ in Glaswegian', in Jennifer Cole and José Ignacio Hualde (eds.), *Laboratory Phonology 9*. (New York: Mouton de Gruyter, 2007), pp. 65–86.

Stoever, Jennifer, 'Just be quiet pu-leeze': *The New York Amsterdam News* Fights the Post-war 'Campaign against Noise' *Radical History Review*, Vol. 2015/121 (2015), pp. 145–168.

Stryker, Susan, '(De)Subjugated knowledges: an introduction to transgender studies', in Susan Stryker and Stephen Whittle (eds.) *The Transgender Studies Reader* (New York: Routledge, 2006), pp. 1–17.

Thompson, Emily, *The Soundscape of Modernity: Architectural Acoustics and the Culture of Listening in America, 1900–1933* (Cambridge, MA: MIT Press, 2004).

Wolf, Naomi 'Young women, give up the vocal fry and reclaim your strong female voice', *The Guardian*, Friday 24 July, 2015.

Zimman, Lal, 'Transmasculinity and the voice: gender assignment, identity and presentation', in Tommaso M. Millani (ed.) *Language and Masculinities: Performances, Intersections, Dislocations* (London: Routledge, 2015), pp. 197–219.

12

MAPPING HEARING IMPAIRMENT: SOUND/TRACKS IN THE CORNER SPACE

Amanda Cachia

Introduction

Deaf culture and Deaf community builds the basis for Deaf activism, which aims to fight against deaf oppression. This oppression is enacted by a hearing culture that typically misunderstands the experience of the deaf or hearing-impaired person (such as the myth of a silent deaf world), and where a deaf or hearing-impaired person experiences discrimination in their everyday life, such as the failure of a hearing person in learning how to communicate with a deaf person, in hiring a deaf person for a job, or even in the lack of comprehension towards American Sign Language (ASL). ASL is oftentimes stigmatized, and not even considered to be a "legitimate" language that has its own set of variations, dialects, and phonologies. One of the goals of this chapter is to disrupt the mainstream preconceived and stereotypical ideas of the deaf and hearing-impaired experience, which typically assumes that they live a life of mostly silence, where they retain little to no concept of sound. This disruption of stereotypes is achieved through the work of the hearing-impaired artist, Darrin Martin. Sound is a medium in which Martin feels creatively comfortable: sound is not just a medium that he experiences on a daily basis, but he also carves out a relationship with the medium through his practice. Through his multi-sensorial encounters with sound, he produces new knowledge.

More specifically, this chapter will explore how the corner space is defined from Martin's perspective as a hearing-impaired man. What are the sonic and algorithmic contours of this space as experienced through his ears? Martin is based in San Francisco, and makes video, sculpture, paintings, works on paper, sound installation and photography. Martin is interested in trying to connect the visual with the verbal and the sonic, and how those things are approached, through his use of various technologies, becomes generatively complicated by the artist's own negotiated ability with sound. Martin identifies as hearing impaired and he tries to wear the best amplification devices his insurance can muster, and so he wears a Bone Anchor Hearing Aid – BAHA for short. The BAHA is an amplifier that is attached to a screw embedded into his skull. The BAHA takes advantage of the idea that vibrations travel through matter by using the resonance of his skull to send sound vibrations to his healthy inner ear on the opposite side of his head. Martin works extensively with sound through video work. This essay will analyze some of Martin's video work in some detail, particularly work that focuses on his deployment of the sonic within the projecting space of the corner, in order to establish how he multi-sensorially connects the visual with the verbal and the sonic.

I suggest that Martin's powerful multimedia constellation of architectural and tactical gestures within the corner space intersects with notions of sound, acoustics, hearing and access that might follow French philosopher Jacques Rancière's model of "dissensus.'" Rancière's aesthetic rupture, or "dissensus," is "a conflict between sensory presentation and a way of making sense of it, or between several sensory regimes and/or 'bodies'" (Rancière 2010). For example, perhaps it is the eardrum that is aggravated, when it hears a noise or a sound that is several decibels too loud, moving that particularized subjective body outside of its comfort zone. This space of "dissensus" might be considered Martin's typical embodied compass, given the disjunction between sound, location, and repetitive feedback that the artist negotiates on a daily basis. Like the politics of disabled bodies and their atypical forms in space, Rancière says that

> politics breaks with the sensory self-evidence of the "natural" order that destines specific groups and individuals to occupy positions of rule or of being ruled, assigning them to public or private lives, pinning them down to a certain time and space, to specific "bodies," that is to specific ways of being, seeing and saying.
>
> *(2010)*

This so-called natural logic pins bodies to certain designations and to a correct order of the world, but politics – crip politics – invents "new ways of making sense of the sensible" so that there are new configurations between the visible and the invisible, the audible and the inaudible, "new distributions of space and time – in short, new bodily capacities" (Rancière 2010). Crip politics in aesthetics creates a "dissensual" commonsense. It is here that Martin offers us a window into a new sensorial experience in the built environment through alternative perspectives and perceptions.

In this essay, I also argue that Martin's work extends the notion of "deaf gain." Originally coined by the deaf British performance artist, Aaron Williamson, the idea of "deaf gain" is to consider what is actually gained by the state of deafness, instead of focusing on what is ostensibly lost. The state of deafness itself is defined by a sense of loss through the framework of normalcy, where ableist society sees hearing as a prized possession. For example, deaf artist Christine Sun Kim acknowledges the power of hearing through the language she applies to the audist world, such as the notion of hearing as "currency," given the social value that hearing has, and "ghost," given that sound is a commodity that she cannot audibly grasp – it remains invisible to her, so to speak, or transparent. Here, she cleverly translates the typically ocular qualities of the ghost form into a striking audible mode, given it is the audist world that remains elusive to her, rather than the visual one. This major paradigm shift of definitions of deafness from loss to gain first thrust forward into deaf and disability studies rhetoric by Williamson and now supported by others, such as the authors of the large volume *Deaf Gain: Raising the Stakes for Human Diversity*, Dirkson, Bauman and Murray, offers a powerful conceptual position in which the work of Martin shall gravitate (Bauman 2014). Martin's actions and objects, as expressed through sound, vision, and matter, offer articulate illustrations of this empowered and empowering neologism in Deaf Studies, disability studies and mainstream contemporary art histories in general.

d/Deaf Identity & d/Deaf Politics

Martin's hearing loss came later in his life. He first started having hearing issues in his late 20s, where he lost the hearing in his right ear and acquired severe tinnitus after his operation went wrong when he was 31. He also teaches, and he was/is always trying to hear that quiet person in the room. When his hearing loss started happening, he developed a curiosity for American Sign Language, but he didn't ever pursue learning it. He has some deaf friends, but he doesn't really sign with them. Martin characterizes his relationship to sound as a nostalgic one. He said sometimes, through video taping, he can turn up the volume and hear certain sounds that he couldn't hear while he was shooting. For example, in the opening scene from the video "Monograph in Stereo" which was shot in a field of high tension wires near his mother's house, he discovered train sounds in post-production. The train is three miles away, and he used to hear it from his mother's house growing up. The sound of the train whistle at a distance becomes nostalgic for him because he now only has access to it through a mediated device. Despite Martin's challenging relationship with sound, the artist says that he doesn't particularly feel comfortable speaking about Deaf politics:

> I have a feeling of inadequacy with the Deaf community not knowing ASL. Though I have had thoughtful and meaningful exchanges with people who are very deaf mostly through writing, interpreters, and their own abilities to read lips, I have to admit I am still very much in the process of sorting this all out. I am aware of some of the intricacies of Deaf politics, but I am hearing impaired and get by in the hearing world. I don't exactly feel comfortable in a fully hearing world either. I often don't know the location of sound and can become easily confused when my hearing aid settings are not right. However, I have trained many of my friends and acquaintances well.
>
> *(Martin 2014)*

An important aspect to the politics of deaf identification is the term "Deaf culture," which uses a capital 'D' as a means to formally capture the set of learned behaviors of deaf people, who have their own language (sign language, of which there are many all over the world), values, rules, and traditions. Story-telling was an important means of information-gathering in Deaf culture, particularly in older times when access to broadcast media and public communication was curtailed for deaf people owing to Oralism. It is important to share Martin's story, and how he identifies with deafness or hearing impairedness, and even to the stigmatized word "disability." I do this not only in following the footsteps of disability studies, which values the disclosure of the lived experience of disability in order to find commonalities, strengthen identity and build voice within a community, but also in the tradition of Deaf culture, where people always like to learn information about each other so as to build connections. I also share Martin's story about relationships to deafness and hearing impairedness because this is the nature of his work itself, and how he is affected by deafness and/or hearing in different ways. I share these stories not as a means to over-emphasize Martin's background that might seem separate to, or irrelevant in relation to the work itself, but rather as a means to provide an important context and connection to the work discussed in this paper. Thus, I share Martin's background in a bid to connect his personal and professional politics with a wider deaf/Deaf cultural movement.

Synaesthetic corner frequencies

For the first example of Martin's corner-focused work, his single-channel seventeen-minute video, *Monograph in Stereo*, 2004–2005, employs documentary strategies and synaesthetics to convey a narrative regarding his struggle with his hearing loss. The work was made just four years after Martin's hearing began to be affected. He has used his own experience of hearing loss from a damaged eardrum (and the surgery which attempts to improve his hearing) as a jumping-off point for this artistic exploration. The work also stems from research upon the

Figure 12.1 Darrin Martin, *Monograph in Stereo*, 2005, "Untitled (alphabetical letter of 26) overall installation" (image courtesy of Amanda Cachia) and two details of "Untitled (e of 26)" and "Untitled (x of 26)" (images courtesy the artist).

interdependency of the senses with an emphasis on the balance ascertained from binaural hearing and stereoscopic vision and the imbalance caused by their uneven degradation. In the video, images move amongst poetic reverberations of landscapes, interiors, and audiological exam rooms. The complex sound-score mixes tones from a hearing test, electronic music, ordinary sounds such as birdsong, and computer-generated voice reading texts about hearing and perception. The film is divided into several short sections with titles such as *Diagnostic* and *Corner Frequencies*. Martin succeeds in evoking the altered state caused by an abnormality in one's perception, but he also succeeds in using his unusual experiences as a catalyst for creating his own visual/sound compositions (Martin 2014). The artist says that he was also interested in bringing language into the mix, where he could think metaphorically about how fragments of sound build meaning, but that can also simultaneously be broken down to open up an experience that slips between definitions in similar ways that music or poetry may have the power to do.

What is especially provocative about the video is the repetitious nature of the artist's core signifier, the floating corner device, or leitmotif. Random poorly handcrafted corner structures made of wood or veneer flash across each frame of the video, lit up in bright colors. The colors characterize the synaesthetic aspect to the work, given that it is within the physical, architectural space of the corner in a room where the artist finds an advantageous hearing position, as it offers an enclave of sorts, where sound can be trapped. Given the benefit corners provide in terms of acoustic access, we might imagine that the colors that fill out the corner structures in Martin's video symbolize a sound. As the color flashes, so the sound transmits, filters, or vibrates. This movement of color might then be a metaphor for the positive receiving of sound through the artist's BAHA. Given that sound inhabits a transitory, ephemeral, and temporal quality, according to media scholar Douglas Khan, this may also explain why Martin's corners float over seemingly unconnected backgrounds filled with random rural fields, domestic interiors, floating cows, and an occasional pair of male naked legs (Martin 2014). In Gaston Bachelard's seminal text, *The Poetics of Space*, the French philosopher devotes a chapter on the mythology and trope of corners. He claims that the corner is a "negation of the Universe" and that it is a "half-box, part walls, part door" (Bachelard 1994). It is naturally intersectional, atypical, and composed of many seemingly disparate elements. The corner also inhabits stereotypical spatial deviancy for bad behavior, yet it is also one of comfort and safety, where one can hide. Martin plays with all of these ideas in this work.

Sounds continue to pass through all manner of landscape and place in this video, although these particular places and bodies also point to both the locations from the artist's childhood, growing up in a rural area, in addition to his identity as a gay man. Martin's hearing world is one that often incorporates gaps and distortion. Martin, too, has attempted to visually create this experience through the video, where a distorted image illustrates the interrupted access his body has with sound. For example, as we watch Martin's captioned video (where both dialogue and sound are described in great detail by the artist), one frame shows the artist in a medical room undertaking a diagnostic hearing test with a doctor, followed by a quick succession of frames that present the floating corers, cows littering a grassy landscape and pairs of legs. This very disruption of any logical and continuous visual narrative then resembles the acoustic disturbance that is part of Martin's daily reality. We see the artist raising his hand during the exam, to indicate to his doctor that he can hear a particular pitch or tone, and Martin has manipulated the image so as to blur the image with static. As Davidson says, "this visual static interrupts easy viewing and replicates the sensory shorting of neural transmission" (Davidson 2015).

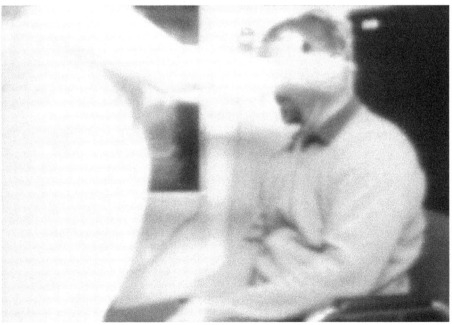

Figure 12.2 (top) Darrin Martin, *Monograph in Stereo*, production still, 2005; (bottom) Darrin Martin, *Monograph in Stereo*, video still, 2005 (image courtesy of the artist).

In addition to employing these synaesthetic strategies, the artist also gives us a clue as to how texture and the tactile world offer alternative modes of sensorial communication. For instance, some of the more abstract frames of *Monograph in Stereo* show odd landscapes made of the kind of bumpy foam rubber often used for soundproofing. While the rubber is meant to block out noise within an environment where sound is not desired by a hearing majority, the material of the rubber is actually quite appealing to the artist, not only for how pleasurable it might feel under the surface of one's fingertips, but also for how it can also transmit information that he is unable to decipher through the BAHA. The use of the material as a landscape is also provocatively suggestive of the artist's own world of sound inside the landscape of his head, which can be an equivalent to the interior of his head as literally soundproofed, thus his full spectrum of hearing is blocked off. Through Martin's unique soundproofed BAHA room, we are provided with an opportunity to explore consciousness and perception through the power of imbalance and disruption.

The architecture of the corner has historically operated as a powerful space for activating various ideas for many artists, but I'd like to especially briefly consider how the corner has been used in three different modes that resonate with Martin's work: first, for its formal physical properties, through the work of Russian constructivist sculpture, especially those that inhabit corner spaces such as the *Corner Relief* series by Vladimir Tatlin, followed by, later on in art history, the minimalist work of Robert Morris. Second, I'd like to consider how the corner has been used as a channel and a metaphor in which to reflect and activate other related social justice ideas, through the work of Adrian Piper and Chitra Ganesh. Third, the corner has been used as a space for playful and performative experimentation through the early video work of Bruce Nauman.

Martin has acknowledged the importance of the formal properties of the work of Russian Constructivists on his own work, especially that of Vladimir Tatlin. Tatlin's canonical *Corner Counter-Relief* (1914) was made, like Martin's corner make-shift structures, using fragments of found, used materials cut into recognizable shapes but re-shaped according to the compositions crafted by the artist's hand. Tatlin strategically used the corner in order to take advantage of the illusion of depth it could offer his painting, so that painting could, in essence, become sculpture, where the frame of the painting was extended out, stretched, and pinned using taut strings into various equally distanced points in the wall (Baier 2012). The corner acted as a type of edge or hinge of orientation, guiding the beginning and the ending of one medium and surface into another. By offering a transformation of two-dimensionality into three-dimensionality, Tatlin was activating a very early sense of the theatricality or performativity of sculpture that artist Robert Morris was interested in.

Morris himself created a corner sculpture, *Untitled (Corner Piece)*, 1964, where a piece of triangular-shaped painted plywood rested on a floor, covering over the bottom portion of a corner wall. By covering over the corner space, Morris was drawing attention to the angularity of the structure – how the angle took up space, or as art historian Annette Michelson describes, how the angle obtruded upon and redefined the corner space (Michelson 2013). This sense of performativity, of objects taking up space in the corner, is powerful and applicable to Martin's work, where the corner acts as a space of corporeal tension with multi-sensorial properties, ranging from the visual, sonic, and tactile.

Adrian Piper used the corner to literally and poetically display one of her videos, *Cornered* (1998), which was screened on a television, and framed by an overturned table, which contributed to the cornering gesture of being locked or hemmed in, and three chairs for watching and listening as part of a larger installation she created at the New Museum in New York in 2000. In the video, a viewer will encounter an image of Piper staring back at them from behind a desk,

Figure 12.3   (top) Martyn Chalk, reconstruction of Vladimir Tatlin's *Complex Corner Relief*, 1915, iron, aluminium, zinc, oil pigment, priming paint, wire and fastening components, 78.8 × 152.4 × 76.2 cm (courtesy of Annely Juda Fine Art, London).

(above) Adrian Piper, *Cornered*, 1988. Table, chairs, monitor, framed birth certificates of Adrian Piper's father, Daniel R. Piper, lighting. Dimensions variable. Collection of the Museum of Contemporary Art, Chicago. © Adrian Piper Research Archive Foundation Berlin.

also positioned into a corner, and she offers a monologue on how her body has been marked as black, cornering her identity into a very limited space (Bowles 2006). A review of the exhibition in the *New York Times* by Ken Johnson surmises that we might all experience this cornering sensation ourselves in our daily lives, where we are stigmatized owing to aspects of our bodies that draw unwanted attention (Johnson 2000). Piper invokes the physical dimensions of the corner as a mode of metaphorical limitation for her personal identity, which she claims here is shrouded in racist ideologies that she cannot escape (Johnson 2000). Her cornering of her blackness is a tight-fitting trap, much as the corner remains a challenging auditory physical space for Martin's eardrum and more symbolically for his identity as a crip, queer man.

Chitra Ganesh creates a large-scale 3D collage and drawing murals where she likes to portray bodies maimed, dismembered, and disabled, where the atypical body becomes a site of transgression as it continues to exceed its limits framed within the normative boundaries of the ocular and vision (Gopinath 2009). Often Ganesh will paint her murals onto walls that are composed of corners, and the artist will utilize these spaces so that her forms become unruly lines of sex and myth within her queer, feminist, disabled re-visioning project. For example, in *A Magician and Her Muse* (2011), a blue outline of a nude woman with a heavily-tattooed arm lays on her side against a bright florescent-painted pink and green background, looking upwards, as a long red, umbilical-like cord pours out of her mouth and spins and circles into the space, around the corner, and up past other figures and objects placed within the mural. The artist's corner-mural collapses any strict notion of "straight composition" by ensuring that her queer composition not only includes two sides, but she also centers the corner. Our gaze is forced to adjust to the rupture that the corner creates to the flow of what would traditionally be a flat wall or canvas surface. The flesh of the nude female figure on the right-hand wall of the mural is being pierced by five sharp daggers, emphasizing how queer, disabled bodies carry a history of wounding, marking, and scarring through violent acts inflicted upon them.

Figure 12.4 Chitra Ganesh, *A Magician and Her Muse*, 2011, mural (image courtesy the artist).

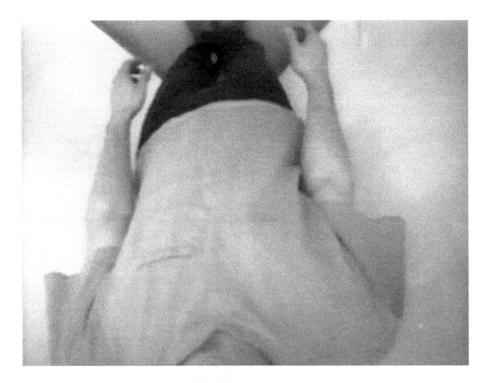

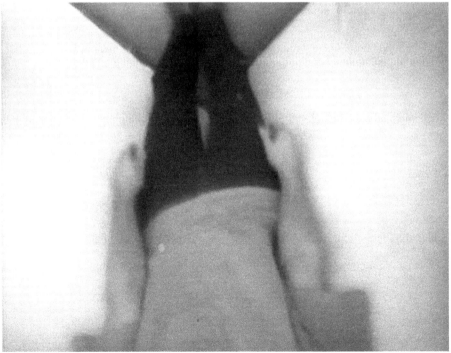

Figure 12.5 Bruce Nauman, *Bouncing in the Corner, No.2*, 1969, 0:59, video stills

Courtesy Electronic Arts Intermix (EAI), New York.

© 2016 Bruce Nauman / Artists Rights Society (ARS), New York

Bruce Nauman's *Bouncing in the Corner, No. 2* (1969) was part of the artist's larger performative series of experiments on his own body captured on video in the 1960s and 1970s. Interestingly, art historian Amelia Jones talks of how Nauman's body acted as a type of hinge during these corporeal experiments, where his body acts as a flexible, indeed elastic, connector between "things, people, or concepts" (Jones 2010). This hinging concept recalls Tatlin's use of the corner as a type of hinge or bridge, connecting the dimensions of painting into sculpture and back. Rather than any material object, here it is Nauman's body that acts as the three-dimensional, theatrical hinge, as his slight frame repetitively bounces, and ricochets back and forth, in and out of the corner in his video. Nauman's visceral habitation of the corner offers a fleshier and evocative illustration of Martin's own auditory occupation and obsession with the corner space – where Nauman literally gets into the corner and messes around with the space in all multi-sensory manner of speaking: Martin gestures at it through his own repetitive representation of its symbolic form in his many video and photographic compositions. Martin's bouncing, theatrical corner also suggests frustrations and challenges given its consistent

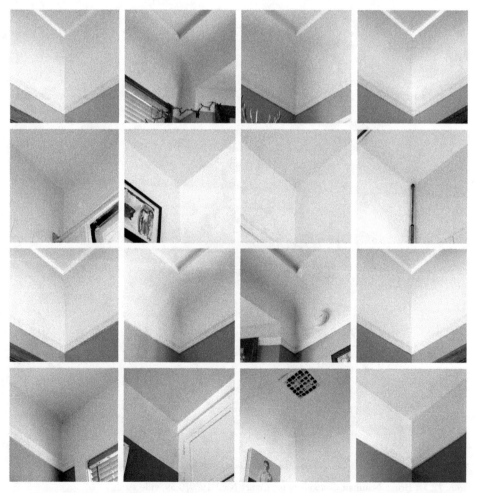

Figure 12.6 Darrin Martin, *Home Coordinates*, 2015, 19 x 19" square photograph each (overall size 88" square) (image courtesy of the artist).

Figure 12.7 (top) Darrin Martin, *Semblance*, 2015 and (above) *Disembody Electric*, 2015 (image courtesy of the artist).

interrupted offering of the flow of auditory information as part of his daily life as a person with a hearing impairment, and also as a person who identifies as disabled and queer. The conflation of the corner's physical, conceptual and acoustic possibilities, demonstrated amongst all these examples, points to how Martin's work importantly contributes to its evolving discourse in contemporary art.

In several of Martin's other works, such as *Semblance* (2015), *Disembody Electric* (2015), and *Home Coordinates* (2015), the artist continues to employ the architectural device of the corner to guide his compositions, but also to experiment with its metaphorical qualities. In the video, *Semblance*, we see the artist's bust spinning in a corner space. The spinning motion actually emulates Martin's ideal acoustic space, where he literally has one ear on each side – from corner to corner, so that he can hear evenly, given that corners typically present hearing challenges for him. The idea of moving in and out of this space physically might emulate the direction and flow of his actual hearing, which is never stable or fixed. *Disembody Electric* conveys this idea further, although the spinning movement in this video is also accompanied by changing electronic frequencies, which affect the horizontal and vertical positioning of the image. In this video, we see the ghostly bust form of a man's body spinning around and around against a floating black background. As the man's body spins, the form and shape of his head, chest, and forearms is occasionally zapped into misrecognition as though it has encountered lightning. The sounds of experimental, electronic beats accompany the zapping actions as if causing the man to spasm. The artist created the exaggerated and dramatic manipulations of the man's form by sending a 3D scan of the image through a wobbulator. He then tweaked the stability of the image by manipulating electronic frequencies through oscillators. An S-curve on Martin's bust emulates the form of dancing. *Home Coordinates* is a series of sixteen square photographs, 20" each. They are presented in a four by four grid and map the upper corners of each of the main living spaces of Martin's apartment (this includes the living room, bathroom, bedroom, and kitchen). Here, Martin is interested in how the four corners begin to unfold as they are butted up against one another, slowly creating an optical illusion through the language of geometric art. Importantly, the act of repetition, doubling, quadrupling, and unfolding through these corners also emulates how sound and acoustics dynamically reverberates and echoes through Martin's own eardrum, and also within rooms themselves.[1]

Conclusion

Through his concentrated deployment of the projecting corner, Martin metaphorically alludes to the nature of communication itself, which is in constant flux, is always out of synch, and is full of gaps, holes, and misinterpretations and misunderstandings. This is part of Martin's daily engagement with sound. Martin demonstrates both Rancière's idea of "dissensus" and Williamson's concept of "deaf gain" simultaneously, suggesting that through a re-organization of the sensorium and especially the capacities of the eardrum, one will understand and experience space in new and profound ways. The vibrations, waves, and curves of Martin's acoustic world contribute to a definitive deaf sonic politics of the corner space that questions and broadens our ideas about how our corpus might begin to engage with private and public architectures of the body and the built environment, differently. More specifically, he offers us a palette of refreshing acoustic algorithms that dislocate and yet shape both the limits and alternative capacities of the eardrum and how that revised eardrum can define or be defined by the possibilities of the corner space. Martin's work ultimately offers a new model of creative access, aesthetics, and the sensorium, which broadens the availability of art to more diverse, hearing-impaired, and deaf audiences.

Note

1 Reverb is particular to the size of the space one is in during the act of hearing (which is why many sound editing tools spatialize their reverb filters from everything to closets to concert halls to outer space).

Further reading

M. Davidson, *Concerto for the Left Hand: Disability and the Defamiliar Body* (Ann Arbor: The University of Michigan Press, 2011), contains a chapter entitled "Hearing Things: The Scandal of Speech in Deaf Performance" which provides another perspective on radical deaf performance. M. Friedner and S. Helmreich, *The Senses and Society* 7.1 (2012): 72–86, provides an excellent overview of the intersection between deaf studies and sound studies in the essay, "Sound Studies Meets Deaf Studies." S. Kim-Cohen, *In the Blink of an Ear: Toward a Non-Cochlear Sonic Art* (London and New York: Bloomsbury, 2009) contains reassessment of sound art from World War II to the present. C. Padden and T. Humphries, *Deaf in America: Voices from a Culture* (Cambridge, MA and London, England: Harvard University Press, 1988), a classic text on d/Deaf culture, community, and activism in the United States.

References

Bachelard, G. (1994) "Corners" in M. Jolas (trans. from French) J. Stilgoe (Foreword) *The Poetics of Space*, Boston: Beacon Press, pp. 136–147.

Baier, S. (2012) "Professional Painting: Tatlin's Counter-Reliefs" in *Tatlin: New Art for a New World*. Edited by the Museum Tinguely, Basel, Germany: Hatje Cantz, to accompany exhibition of the same name, June 6–October 14, 2012, pp. 58–67.

Bauman, H. (2014) "DeafSpace: An Architecture toward a More Livable and Sustainable World" in H. Dirksen, L. Bauman and Joseph J. Murray (eds.) *Deaf Gain: Raising the Stakes For Human Diversity*, Minneapolis, London: University of Minnesota Press, pp. 375–401.

Bowles, John P. (2006) "Adrian Piper as African American Artist," *American Art*, Vol. 20, No. 3, pp. 108–117.

Davidson, M. (2015) "Living Deaf Hearing" in *LOUD silence* exhibition catalogue, curated by Amanda Cachia, gallery@Calit2, San Diego: University of California, pp. 38–41.

Gopinath, G. (2009) "Chitra Ganesh's Queer Re-Visions" in *GLQ*, Vol. 15, No. 3, pp. 469–480.

Johnson, K. (2000) "Adrian Piper" Art in Review in *New York Times*, November 17, www.nytimes.com/2000/11/17/arts/art-in-review-adrian-piper.html, accessed January 5, 2016.

Jones, A. (2010) "Space, body and the self in the work of Bruce Nauman" in A. Dezeuze (ed.) *The 'Do-It-Yourself' Artwork: Participation from Fluxus to New Media*, Manchester, England: Manchester University Press, pp. 145–164.

Martin, D. (2014) Email exchange with Amanda Cachia, July 30.

Michelson, A. (2013) "Robert Morris-An Aesthetics of Transgression" in J. Bryan-Wilson (ed.) *Robert Morris, October Files 15*, Cambridge, MA, London: The MIT Press, pp. 7–49.

Rancière, J. (2010) "The Paradoxes of Political Art" in *Dissensus: On Politics and Aesthetics*, London and New York: Continuum, pp. 134–151.

13

THE SONIC WORLD OF THE ISLAMIC STATE

Jonathan Pieslak

I am presently part of a team researching the mobilizing influence of media—print, music, and video—in the context of terrorism, with a specific focus on Salafi jihadism. Our project brings together scholars from a variety of fields, including political science, communications, musicology, among others, and we are funded by a grant from the U.S. Department of Defense's Minerva Initiative (Principal Investigator: Anthony Lemieux, Georgia State University). My involvement with this research group comes as an extension of my recent book on radicalism and music in which I examine the musical cultures of al-Qa'ida, the American racist skinheads, Christian-affiliated radicals, and eco-animal right militancy (Pieslak 2015).

I arrived at this topic from my previous scholarship on music and the Iraq War (Pieslak 2009). As I researched music's role in U.S. military recruiting and as an inspiration for combat among American soldiers and Marines, I decided to examine, as best I could, what the other side of the conflict was doing: was music a pivotal part of the cultural life of Sunni militants in Iraq? From what I could tell at that time, indeed, it was. And in late 2006, I began following the propaganda of the newly formed Islamic State of Iraq (ISI); the entity that would become the most notoriously violent terrorist group of the 21st century.

This article explores the sonic world of the Islamic State (IS), *al-Dawlat al-Islamiyya*, providing an overview of their sonic production; it proceeds in three parts. First, I introduce my background studying the IS and the cultural dimensions of terrorism and political violence in general. Second, I describe the cultural production of the IS, outlining the group's media history, organizational structure, and output as of April 2016. Finally, I offer some concluding ideas on why cultural production is so important within the jihadi world and suggest avenues for developing practical strategies and policy implications.

Background and the study of culture in terrorism and political violence

My orientation and objectives for this research can be outlined as follows: (1) I pursue research to the best that circumstances allow, trying to understand how human beings employ cultural elements (namely, music) to cultivate and reinforce hateful attitudes towards one another, which often leads to violence in its varied forms; (2) I try to avoid discussions about the validity or justification of the beliefs that motivate radical groups; (3) I employ interpretative frameworks that allow me to reach practical and ethical policy recommendations based on weakening the appeal and activity of the ideologies that provide the foundation for radicalism; (4) I emphasize the benefits of collaboration, maintaining that no single scholar possesses all of the knowledge necessary to fully understand the varied dimensions of jihadi cultural production (Hegghammer 2015). I am especially grateful to my colleagues who have contributed to the refinement of my understanding of jihadi culture, and I will cite and acknowledge them throughout this article. I also wish to thank my three research assistants, who will remain anonymous for privacy purposes, but I am grateful for their translations and in helping me reach a more nuanced understanding of the cultural background on this topic.

Regarding culture, I believe that the cultural dimensions of terrorism and political violence have been downplayed, particularly in post-9/11 research. These disciplines have prioritized what we might call "the hard stuff": ideology, financial and armament resourcing, attacks, training, leadership, and military or tactical expertise. "Softer" elements, like the cultural lives of radical groups, have occupied a fairly peripheral position. Nonetheless, my starting point is the idea that terrorism and political violence cannot be actuated without the ability to convince another person that it is in their best interest to risk their lives and kill other human beings. The so-called "hard elements" that have traditionally been the focus of study in the field matter very little if no one is there to fight. While it is unlikely that any set of solutions will eradicate terrorism and political violence entirely, addressing the root causes for involvement holds considerable promise for weakening the appeal of such groups.

To be clear, I am not dismissing or minimizing the hard stuff, nor am I suggesting an opposing relationship between the two. When Elton Simpson and Nadi Hoofi opened fire on the "First Annual Muhammad Art Exhibit and Contest" in Garland, Texas on May 3, 2015, the investigation rightly focused on these assailants' backgrounds, radicalization, ideological motivations, and planning and execution of the attack. But I might add to this, asking: what inspires a man to go on what was, for all intents and purposes, a suicide mission in the name of a group that he never had any personal interaction with, outside of social media on the Internet? Why did Simpson, only fifteen minutes before the attack, tweet *bay'a* (fealty or allegiance) to the Caliph of the IS, Abo Bakr al-Baghdadi. His tweet read: "The bro with me and myself have given bay'ah to Amirul Mu'mineen. May Allah accept us as mujahideen." ("Amirul Mu'mineen" often translates as "Commander of the Faithful," a phrase which, in this instance, refers to the IS's declared Caliph, Abo Bakr al-Baghdadi.) But just an hour earlier, he also tweeted: "The knives have been sharpened, soon we will come to your streets with death and slaughter! #Qariban Qariba." The tweet is a rather loose translation of lyrics to an Islamic State "song" entitled, "Qariban, Qariba" ("Soon, soon"), which he directs us to in the hashtag. This track provided the soundtrack to the video of the immolation of Jordanian pilot, Muath Safi Youssef al-Kasasbeh, and is frequently used as a soundtrack to the most violent scenes in IS video messaging. If such lyrics were so important that he tweeted them only an hour before embarking on a violent attack that he knew would result in his death, then I think that questions about the role of culture are important to ask—in addition to those about more tactical issues.

My conclusions thus far support the idea that, to paraphrase the well-known counter-terrorism consultant and forensic psychiatrist Marc Sageman, it may be just as much about what a terrorist feels as what they think (Sageman 2008: 157–58). The cultural dimensions of terrorism can be a vitally important part of what motivates people to act violently towards one another, perhaps more so than the professed ideology any violent activist espouses. The German scholar Thomas Bauer echoes Sageman's idea when he proposes that terrorists are not defined by ideas as much as they are by passion (Bauer 2011: 125). If how a terrorist feels and their passion could run similarly to, or even outweigh, their ideological commitment, then the study of culture—and particularly music—has a great deal to contribute to this conversation. Ideology, as reasoned argument in and of itself, may not be the primary motivation behind involvement and action; most IS fighters are not ideologues or intellectuals, and new recruits go through rigorous training in religious law (*shari'ah*). If the appeal of the IS's practice of Islam were the primary catalyst for recruitment, such religious training classes would have no need to be compulsory training.

To close this first section of the article, I would like to suggest that there are many ways to study jihadi cultural production, but my goals towards this endeavor are modest, following the prompt of political theorist and jihadi culture expert Thomas Hegghammer who suggests that the burgeoning field of jihadi culture research should have two immediate goals: (1) to document and describe the cultural production of jihadis, and (2) to examine why jihadis spend so much time and effort creating cultural forms (Hegghammer 2016). I will try to do this in the two parts that now follow.

The sonic world of the Islamic State

The IS is a complex group with a complex history. They have changed their name—at least twice; they seem to have rewritten their historical records, now contending that the establishment of the Caliphate dates back to October 2006 (not June 29, 2014); even their historical status as an al-Qa'ida break-away faction is uncertain (al-Tamimi 2015). In short, this group has a complicated history and ideology that remain the source of considerable disagreement. Even so, I will provide a short introduction to the group to provide a degree of context. While I am reluctant to oversimplify the history and ideology of the IS, it is nonetheless important that the group's sonic world be given some kind of framing, however incomplete. Readers familiar with the group may want to skip ahead a few paragraphs.

The "Islamic State" is a Sunni militant movement emerging from the Iraq War that was first considered to be al-Qa'ida's faction in Iraq (AQI). They changed their name in October 2006 to "The Islamic State of Iraq" (ISI), and then to "The Islamic State of Iraq and al-Sham" ("Sham" is the Arabic word for greater Syria) or "The Islamic State of Iraq and the Levant," in April 2013. Now, they call themselves "The Islamic State" ("*al-Dawlat al-Islamiyya*"), based on their declaration of the Caliphate on June 29, 2014. The group is further known by an Arabic acronym "da'esh", and many governments in the region prefer this label so as not to elevate the group to a nation status. Following Cole Bunzel's report (Bunzel 2015) on the history and ideology of the IS, the group's history can be organized as follows:

1. Zarqawi Prelude (2002–06): the rise of Sunni jihadism in Iraq.
2. ISI (2006–13): a largely failed attempt at state formation, coinciding with a decline in interest from local Sunni jihadis.
3. ISIS (2013–14): the group's re-assertion and territorial expansion into Syria.
4. IS (2014–present): declaration of the Caliphate.

Generally speaking, the group espouses a form of Salafi jihadism, with certain origins in the Muslim Brotherhood's practice of jihadism, namely taking control of the state and fighting Western imperialism in the region, which they view as being the cause of a decline in Islam from public life. The IS tends towards a more dogmatic literalism in their interpretation of Salafi ideology than groups like al-Qa'ida, and their media output underscores, among other points, the following (Bunzel 2015):

1. They are the practitioners of the "true" Islam and Muslims must dissociate from anyone not following their brand of Salafi jihadism.

2. Failure to do #1 amounts to apostasy (hence their liberal application of *takfir* [apostacy or heresy]).
3. Shi'i Muslims are deserving of death.
4. Other groups, like the Muslim Brotherhood and Hamas, are traitors to Islam.
5. They must restore the Caliphate.

An extreme anti-Shi'ite worldview and the desire to restore the Caliphate are probably the most important ideas resounding in their messaging and literature.

Given its history, it seems logical to ask how the IS emerged from the Iraq War? By the late 2000s, they were reduced to an almost entirely clandestine operation and openly mocked on jihadi Internet forums as "a paper state". Bunzel (2015) points to some pivotal factors leading to the IS's resurgence:

1. New leadership. It matters who is in charge, and the first al-Baghdadi and his successor Abo Hamza al-Muhajir were poor public speakers and generally uninspiring. Abo Bakr al-Baghdadi is a much more eloquent speaker (he uses a high/classical-style Arabic reminiscent of bin Laden) and has a much greater personality appeal.
2. Sunni disenfranchisement. Sunnis became increasingly resentful towards the new partisan Shia leadership, and the ISI leadership would exploit this resentment in their appeals to recruit.
3. Syrian civil war. The Syrian civil war was, and still is, being fought along sectarian lines, which allowed the group to increase its ranks through Sunni grievance, and make major territorial gains.

However, like the example I cited earlier of the investigation of the Garland, Texas shootings, I would caution that this is only part of the picture. Adding to these "hard element" points is the fact that the IS has launched the most sophisticated media campaign of any jihadi group in history. Their output is unprecedented in volume and quality, with a far more cinematized conceptualization of what their propaganda should do: dramatic scenes of fighters and battles, HD quality and highly colorized video, special graphics and effects, and, of course, music. Earlier generation jihadi culture was nothing like this. Al-Qa'ida often turned to dry, lecture-format videos, and relied more on personal contact in mosques or other settings for recruitment.

The *Washington Post* ran an excellent article (Miller and Mekhenet 2015) on the IS's media machine in November 2015 in which they interviewed seven IS defectors. All but one said that the principal influences kindling their fervor towards jihad and guiding their decisions to travel to Syria were the videos they saw online, or encounters on social media. Of the videos, one of the defectors said, "Some were like Van Damme movies. You see these men fighting and you want to be one of those brave heroes." One might question if it was the attraction of the IS's practice of Islam (that is the reasoned argument of their ideology) that catalyzed his recruitment, or if the emotional satisfaction of having a "hero" identity and idea of defending the "just" cause of his perceived in-group was the pivotal factor. Crucial to eliciting these kinds of emotionally driven responses is the musical soundtracks that accompany such videos. Finally to the music…

Or, technically, not. For the IS, there is a distinct difference between what they "sound out" and "music." Without opening the Pandora's box of what is or is not music in the context of conservative practices of Islam, I will simply say that there are widely varied interpretations of what constitutes acceptable, unfavored, or forbidden musical practices. Although the IS opposes "music" in all of its forms, there is a distinct genre of allowable sacred cantillation, *anashid*, that complicates the issue. *Anashid* is the plural of *nashid*, the etymology of which derives from *inshad*, a "raising of the voice" usually associated with public recitation of poetry in pre-Islamic times. The term *anashid* is often translated as "Islamic songs" or "Islamic recitation/cantillation", but the genre's origin is more the domain of poetry than music. And I want to be clear that the cultural understanding of *anashid* is, first and foremost, a religious poetic genre than anything related to music (Shiloah 1995; and Matusky and Beng 2004). For the IS, the soundtracks to their videos are populated by sacred recitation, not music, and the sonic world of jihadi culture in general is overrun with jihad-themed *anashid*, also called *anashid jihadiyya* (Pieslak 2015).

So what does the IS's sonic world sound like? The answer is that it has changed considerably over time. From what I have been able to ascertain, there are three primary eras of IS cultural production that seem to correspond with their state-building project. First, there are Zarqawi-era videos characterized as simple documentations of ultra violence, particularly decapitations. These followed a fairly simple formula: most often, a group of jihadis stands behind the victim, there is a reading of offenses, a confession, the pronounement of judgment, optional last words, execution, and a statement of demands. The executioner is typically dressed in a black, military-style uniform, with a mask covering his face. The event was documented on video with no musical soundtrack, little staging, and minimal editing, and then released to the Internet.

On August 15, 2006, the group changed its name to "The Islamic State of Iraq," and established a media foundation, al-Furqan, just over three months later. By the way, a dedicated media foundation is not a new idea to jihadi groups, al-Qa'ida has had its own media production wing, as-Sahab, since 2001. With a centralized production group overseeing official releases, the videos changed. I like to generally characterize this era of IS media as the era of "Go Pro" terrorism.

"Go Pro" Terrorism, 2006–14, notable events

2006, August 15:	Declaration of the ISI (Islamic State of Iraq).
2006, November 21:	First video release from al-Furqan.
2013, April 8:	Declaration of ISIS/ISIL.
2013, August 20:	Establishment of al-Ajnad.
2014, February 3:	al-Qa'ida officially cuts ties with ISIS.
2014, May 31:	Establishment of al-Hayat.

The reason I describe this era as "Go Pro" terrorism (besides the "Be a Hero" slogan) is that many of the videos capture IED attacks against coalition forces taken by fighters hiding in locations and filming the attack; these are short action videos and most often a jihad-themed *nashid* was overdubbed. The IS mostly used *anashid* produced by *munshideen* (reciters or "singers") who were not affiliated with the group and who wrote texts on general jihadi themes, a favorite was the Saudi *munshid*, Abo Ali.

Important during this era was the division of al-Furqan into specific branches. On August 20, 2013, al-Ajnad media was announced and this specific branch of al-Furqan was responsible for producing Arabic-language *anashid* and Surah recitation (Koranic chapter recitation). Videos were still under the domain of al-Furqan but another branch of video production, al-I'tisam Media, was established. It is interesting that this division of propaganda labor and output seems to align with some of the IS's strongest military buildups, attacks, and most significant territorial expansions.

From the that best I can determine, it was around the time of al-Ajnad's founding that the IS began producing group-specific *anashid*. The IS now has member *munshideen* who write *anashid* specifically taylored for the group, explicitly honoring the IS or its declared Caliph (Abu Bakr al-Baghdadi [aka Caliph Ibrahim]). Examples here include: Maher Mesh'al (aka Abo Hajar al-Hadrami [in the IS], and Abo Zubair al-Jazrawi [in Saudi Arabia before joining the IS]) or the *munshid* going by the name "Abo Yassir". Then, on May 31, 2014, al-Hayat was established. This branch of media is responsible for their entire media production in non-Arabic languages, including videos, literature, and *anashid*. Al-Hayat initially demonstrated a preference for *nashid* videos over straight audio releases, with closed captioning in English (not Arabic) for a number of them. However, it is interesting that while 8 out of the first 9 al-Hayat *nashid* releases were *nashid* videos with English subtitles, only 2 of the last 11 have been *nashid* videos.

The third era of IS media production does not differ significantly from what I outlined in the previous one; it is still organized the same way. The main difference is that the IS changed its video strategy corresponding to the declaration of the Caliphate on June 29, 2014. It would be challenging to understate how significant this was. No group—not the Muslim Brotherhood, not AQ, not (really) the Taliban, no one—had truly dared declare itself the Caliphate and issued the mandate of *hijra* (migration) to the established land of "true" Islam. Now a polity, their videos became more about projecting the image of an actual state and governance. Although the violence continued, everything was cast through the lens of the IS's control over lands and people as a legitimate political authority and a law-enforcing state. No longer were they filming drive-by shootings or sneaking around in bushes to film IED attacks. States do not do these things and no longer does the IS (at least not in their own video messaging).

Musically speaking, the breakdown of their production looks like this:

> Total musical/recitation releases: 182 (from the founding of al-Ajnad to April 2016)
>   *Anashid*: 139
>   Surah Recitation: 43
>   *Anashid*:119 in Arabic (mostly released through al-Ajnad)
>   20 in non-Arabic languages (released through al-Hayat)
>   al-Hayat has produced *anashid* in: Kurdish-Sorani (1), Uyghur (1), English (1), Indonesian (1), Russian (1), Unknown (1), German (2), Turkish (2), Chinese (2), Bengali (2), and French (4).

Their *anashid* are an inextricable part of their video messaging as well. As a generalization, the videos tend to present two contradictory portrayals of life in the IS; one is that of a peaceful utopia where citizens enjoy the abundance and prosperity that comes through living under "pure" Islamic law. The other is that of a land ruled by apocalyptic ultra violence and locked in a perpetual condition of war. To examine the *anashid* in these videos, I reviewed a sample set of approximately 35 Arabic-language IS videos, from May 19, 2015 to March 21, 2016. There were 112 instances of *anashid* used as soundtracks. I was able to identify 93 (or 83%). Of those 93, 41 different *anashid* were used. Only 7 *anashid* appeared four times or more; 13 *anashid* appeared three times or more. The 7 most popular, arranged in descending order of popularity, were:

English Title	Arabic Transliteration	Date Released
We will proceed to the excellencies	Sawfa Namdi Lilma'aliyy	August 30, 2015
Our shari'a	Shari'atuna	June 29, 2015
How great is the encampment of heroes	Lillahi Daru Mu'askaru Al-'btaali	2015
Attack Them	Ughzu Alayhim	2015
We have intended	Qad 'azamna	November 14, 2014
Come on, Indulge	Hayya Inghamis	November 29, 2015
We drove towards them	'ilaihim Rakebna	June 18, 2015

In terms of the song texts, there are any number of recurring themes, but some of the most common are those that encourage emigration, venerate martyrdom and fighters, glorify the IS, its leaders, and the re-establishment/rising up of the Caliphate (under "pure" Islamic law), threaten enemies, and call for jihad as the righteous defense of Islam. Below is an example of the unofficial "anthem" of the Islamic State, "Ummati, Qad Laha Fajarun" ("My Ummah, Dawn has appeared").

"Ummati, Qad Laha Fajarun"
"My Ummah, Dawn has Appeared"
My Ummah, Dawn has appeared (seen from afar), so await the clear victory,
The Islamic State has arisen by the blood of the righteous (truthful),
The Islamic State has arisen by the Jihad of the pious (God-fearing),

They sacrificed their souls in the name of truth (righteousness) with constancy and conviction,
To establish in it [the Islamic State] the religion: the law [Shari'ah] of the Lord of the Worlds.

My Ummah, await glad tidings, and do not despair for victory is near,
The Islamic State has arisen, and the dreaded might has appeared (begun),
It has risen to create glory, and the era of darkness has ended,
By loyal men who do not fear warfare,
They have created an everlasting glory that does not perish or disappear.
My Ummah, Allah is our Lord and Protector, so grant your blood,
Victory shall not be reclaimed except by the blood of the martyrs,

Those men, who spent their lives seeking their Lord, [are] in the abode of the Prophets,

They offered their souls to Allah and for the religion [Islam] with self-sacrifice,
They are people of sacrifice and giving; they are people of generosity and honor.
My Ummah, await glad tidings; the sun of resilience (steadfastness) has risen,
We have marched in masses to the hills of ancient glory,
So that we may bring back the light, faith, and the glorious might,

By men who have forsaken the material life, and attained eternal life in the hereafter,

And they have revived the Ummah of glory and the assured victory.

Why cultural forms?

Returning to Hegghammer's goals for contemporary jihadi culture research, I have documented and described some of the cultural production of the IS, so to conclude, I will briefly address his second goal: why jihadis spend so much time and effort creating cultural forms.

The kinds of cultural forms—especially music and videos with musical soundtracks—that we see operating so prominently in the IS are vital to the group's recruitment, member retention, and motivation for fighter action. Why do they spend so much time and effort? Because the group cannot function without it. On paper and in theory, I suppose they can. Culture is not a utility maximizing activity, but only from a rather closed "hard elements" perspective. Culture might be dismissed because one actually needs finances, arms, training, etc. to launch a terrorist campaign; one does not *need* music. But we may want to rethink this assumption.

Violent activists are often robbed of their humanity because they tend to do inhuman things. Their actions may be described as inhuman, but they are still human beings—many of whom became involved with radical ideology, not because of ideological appeal or a pre-standing ideological commitment, but because of very human impulses and processes: social identity formation, finding meaning in one's life, enculturation, emotional responses, social bonding, and others. My book on radicalism offers any number of examples to support this claim.

Why does this matter? If, as I am suggesting, individuals participate in radicalism for a variety of reasons, but not necessarily first and foremost because of the conviction of reasoned argument, then any attempt to make practical and ethical policy recommendations should place less emphasis on pure ideological analysis and rhetoric, and more on the foundational elements of culture. There should be less of a religious or ideological counternarrative (like the U.S. State Department's "Think Again, Turn Away" campaign or U.S. President Barak Obama's foray into Islamic theology, declaring that the IS is not "Islamic") and more of a culturally conceived one. If young men find validation by participating in jihad in ways that involve, not rational cognitive appeal, but social influence and bonding, feelings of heroism, defense of a just cause, identity formation, duty to religion and the protection of those in danger, and others, then we need to contemplate how to satisfy those very human impulses in non-violent ways.

Hegghammer (2016) puts it very well: "If emotion is more important, local authorities may want to spend less time on improving economic situations of youth at risk for radicalization, and more on offering 'substitution activities' that provide emotional rewards similar to those obtained in the jihadi underground." And music is at the heart of many of these "emotional rewards." The anthropology of music, the study of music in social movements, and any number of interpretative lenses on the socio-cultural dimensions of music illuminate music's pivotal role in how we bond, identify ourselves, express emotion, and how we can be influenced emotionally. I am optimistic that this scholarship can contribute to how we understand IS culture; for now, though, we are still in the phases of collecting the data and getting a general idea of what their culture sounds like and how it functions.

Even so, it seems to me that those involved in propogating jihadi culture understand the importance of the sonic world. Turning to a page from AQ propagandist, Anwar al-Awlaqi, perhaps the most important AQ propagandist ever, *anashid* are singled out as a particularly useful way to mobilize jihad. In *44 Ways to Support Jihad* (2009), he wrote:

> Muslims need to be inspired to practice Jihad. In the time of the "Prophet" (Muhammad) he had poets who would use their poetry to inspire the Muslims and demoralize the disbelievers. Today nasheed can play that role. A good nasheed can spread so widely it can reach to an audience that you could not reach through a lecture or a book. Nasheeds are especially inspiring to the youth, who are the foundation of Jihad in every age and time. Nasheeds are an important element in creating a "Jihad culture." It is worth mentioning that al-Awlaki's photograph was the image that Elton Simpson chose for his Twitter profile, and the name of his account, "Shariah is Light", suggests a connection to the popular IS *nashid*, "The Sharia of our Lord is a light."

Consider that within the IS, those involved with the production of media, mostly foreigners, are elevated in status within the group. One of the defectors interviewed by The *Washington Post* (Miller and Mekhenet 2015) said, "The media people are more important than the soldiers. Their monthly income is higher. They have better cars. They have the power to encourage those inside to fight and the power to bring more recruits to the Islamic State." In fact, the media often control day-to-day operations. Battles scenes, public executions, *hudud* crime punishment are highly scripted, with multiple takes, and fighters reading from cue cards. Yes, they run practice takes and choreograph beheadings, with the final lethal blow coming only when the media operative, not the executioner, gives the ok. This is a radically different way of portraying execution from the Zarqawi era, in particular because these grotesque proceedings are accompanied by a musical soundtrack, often attempting to cast the entire spectacle, through a *nashid* and its lyrics, as a religiously sanctioned act.

If we want to understand why the IS's media production is so effective, we need only look in the mirror. In my 2009 book, *Sound Targets: American Soldiers and Music in the Iraq War*, I suggested that similar appeals to honorable duty, defense of a righteous cause, heroism, and country ("state") were underlying messages in the propaganda of U.S. military recruiting. The music that reinforced these messages was critical to getting the target audience, 17–25 year-old males, to respond emotionally. I noted, though, that the same kinds of messaging was sounding through the *anashid* selected by the ISI to accompany their videos (those of the "Go Pro" terrorism era). Counternarratives and strategies to combat the effectiveness of radicalizing propaganda should consider that the foundation of a young man's involvement with a terrorist group (or an established military) seems to have more to do with how they feel about an idea or how an idea makes them feel, than what they think about it in an intellectual sense. For instance, rather than focus on how "Islamic" the IS is or is not, it would be better to avoid theological debates altogether, which invariably come across as condescending and polluted when they come from Western, non-Muslims. As an alternative, one might point out that Salafi jihadi groups, like AQ, have killed eight Muslims for every non-Muslim, and the IS's ratio is far higher. In short, joining the IS means that one is going to primarily kill other Muslims. Promotion of this kind of statistic appeals to a young Muslim man's sense of duty and obligation to Islam more so than discussions on the varied interpretations of religious doctrine.

The solutions to terrorism and political violence do not lie at the end of a rifle. Particularly in relation to Salafi jihadism, military action alone has not solved the problem; it has addressed symptoms not causes and provided the fuel for grievance that lies at the heart of jihadi propaganda campaigns. Ultimately, I am not sure that there is a single solution or that the issues of terrorism and political violence can be completely eradicated from any society. Rather, a more successful effort to diminish the impact of terrorism and political violence may ultimately rest in disrupting someone's ability to convince another human being that it is in their best interest to risk their lives and kill other human beings. And their reasons for taking up arms seem to have a greater degree of complexity than pure ideological commitment.

References

al-Awlaqi, A. "44 Ways to Support Jihad," www.kavkazcenter.com/eng/content/2009/02/16/10561.shtml, accessed November 13, 2013 (originally published February 16, 2009).

al-Tamimi, A. J. (2015) "2006-Announcement of the Caliphate?," www.aymennjawad.org/2015/12/2006-announcement-of-the-caliphate, accessed April 4, 2016.

Bauer, T. (2011) "Die Poesies des Terrorismus," in Meayer A. (ed), *Siebenjahrbuch Deutsche Oper Berlin MMIV–MMXI*, Berlin: Nicolaische Verlagsbuchhandlung.

Bunzel, C. (2015) "From Paper State to Caliphate: The Ideology of the Islamic State," *The Brookings Project on U.S. Relations with the Islamic World*, 19.

Hegghammer, T. (2015) "Why Terrorists Weep: The Socio-Cultural Practices of Jihadi Militants," Paul Wilkinson Memorial Lecture, University of St. Andrews, St. Andrews, Scotland, UK.

_____ (2016, forthcoming) "Introduction," in Hegghammer T. (ed) *Jihadi Culture*, New York, NY: Cambridge University Press.

Matusky P. and Beng, T.S. (2004) *The Music of Malaysia: The Classical, Folk, and Syncretic Traditions*, Burlington, VT: Ashgate.

Miller G. and Mekhenet S. (2015) "Inside the Surreal World of the Islamic State's Propaganda Machine," The *Washington Post*.

Pieslak, J. (2009) *Sound Targets: Music and American Soldiers in the Iraq War* Bloomington, IN: Indiana University Press.

_____ (2015) *Radicalism and Music: An Introduction to the Music Cultures of al-Qa'ida, Racist Skinheads, Christian-Affiliated Radicals, and Eco-animal Rights Militants*, Middletown, CT: Wesleyan University Press.

Sageman, M. (2008) *Leaderless Jihad*, Philadelphia, PA: University of Pennsylvania Press.

Shiloah, A. (1995) *Music in the World of Islam: A Socio-Cultural Study*, Detroit, MI: Wayne State University Press.

PART III

Introduction: sonic spaces and places

A few years ago we held a one-day seminar at Sussex to discuss the nature of sonic bridges – metaphorical bridges, not physical. The seminar was to be held on a Saturday, however, after organising the event we realised that the expected time of winding up the seminar coincided with the end of the local football match. Brighton and Hove Albion, who were then in the English 1st division, had just built a wonderful new stadium adjacent to the university with a crowd capacity of 26,000. The football fans attending the match would all be leaving together at 4.45 and would be funnelled onto the local railway platform – the same platform from which our guests would be using in order to return to their homes. We decided to end the seminar early and as we left in the dusk of a winter's afternoon we heard a tremendous, joyous roar emanating from the stadium, escaping from the open roof across the university and further across the South Downs. Having been a keen football supporter for years I surmised that this second-half roar sounded as if Brighton had just scored the first goal as the joyous roar appeared to be tinged with an element of relief. On returning home I discovered that Brighton had indeed won the match one nil.

My fellow guests had not interpreted the sounds thus, indeed they started to walk more quickly, afraid that they might be caught up in the vast football crowd. The beauty of the unified sounds of delight were subordinated to their desire to escape as soon as possible unhindered. Experiencing sound in space, like other experiences, is multi-sensory – the chill of the wind mingling with sounds of our steps on concrete. The understanding of the multifaceted manner in which sound is created and received in social space has taken a central position within sound studies – yet whatever the soundscape, our apprehension of it differs according to design, interest and personal narrative.

Soundscapes differ according to time of day and seasons. The university campus itself is set in the beauty of the South Downs surrounded by trees with a surfeit of wild birds whose sounds differ with the time of year. The campus is also straddled by a main road – whose sound reaches some but not all of the campus. The football sounds themselves are intermittent – and for some define the rhythm of the year – for others it might well be the university term with its influx of thousands of students who make their way onto the campus that defines the sonic rhythms of place. Returning to my academic colleagues we all heard the sounds of the football crowd, unencumbered in a shared social space – with literally "open ears" – we shared the space with one another, all hearing more or less the same sounds but interpreting them differently according to purpose and interest. All experience is mediated through values, histories and interests. We are not even tied necessarily to spaces in the here and now, as Bachelard suggested that, "inhabited space transcends geometrical space" (Bachelard 1994: 47). Equally, whilst our experience of place and space is frequently mediated by a range of sonic technologies in multiple ways, the recognition that place, in its cultural specificity, is also of singular importance has been more the domain of the work of social scientists – who by necessity study specific practices in specific places, as Bollnow notes: "every location in experienced space has its significance for human beings" (Bollnow 2011: 19). Yet, the very relationship of place to space is famously reversed in the philosophical work of Heidegger when he states that "place has been split into spaces" thereby signifying the singular importance of place. Within this valorization of place, space was also no longer limited to physical space, as the work of Bachelard and others gave increasing prominence to a whole variety of spaces: mythical space, divine space and cognitive space (Casey 1998).

These issues are illustrated in an interview that I carried out in the years following 9/11. In this interview Frank, who lived in upstate New York, described walking around New York wearing what was, then, a fashionable Apple iPod, but instead of listening to music he was listening to the then newly released New York Port Authority's tapes of 9/11. These tapes were transcripts of hundreds of telephone conversations between the trapped inhabitants of the Twin Towers and the police and other emergency services. These tapes are scratchy and partial in nature – fragmented and unclear yet possessing an eerie sense of presence and immediacy. Frank described his own efforts to make sense of what had happened in New York that day through his act of listening and described feeling a sense of being connected to those events through his act of private listening. For Frank the streets of New York were transformed through the auditory presence of the 9/11 tapes – re-imagined and re-lived. The experience he describes is one of getting close to the event, not necessarily aesthetically but cognitively. How different my interviewee's sense of place, belonging and connection to the account of the French historian Alain Corbin in his analysis of the role of the village bell in constructing a sense of connectivity in early 19th-century French village life. Traditionally, for Corbin, connectivity meant some form of inclusivity, often defined geographically in terms of the fixed locale of the village. The sounds of a pealing bell drawing in the lost ship in the fog of night or the lost soul in the mists of the forest create an enduring image of the inclusivity of sound drawing the subject to safety.

Urban dwellers now increasingly move to sound and are simultaneously moved by sound (DeNora 2000). The movement of people through cities has increasingly been a technologically mediated experience; from the sounds of the Muzac corporation in the 1930s to the sounds of radios, the use of Walkmans, Ghetto-blasters, iPods and smartphones. The mediated sonic experience of the city has a rich history. The sonic uniquely permits users to reconfigure their relationship to urban space. Sound both democratizes and privatizes the urban soundscape. The origins of the privatizing auditory impulse are embedded in the cultural training and expectations of urban subjects through the use of a wide range of communication technologies – from the telephone to the automobile (Douglas 2004; Flichy 1995; Sachs 1992).

Thus what constitutes a soundscape for either individuals or collectivities of people is subject to interrogation. The notion of "soundscape" is pivotal, indeed central to sound studies and tends to be used more than any other concept within sound studies. Schafer defines it as "any acoustic field of study. We may speak of a musical composition as a soundscape, or a radio program as a soundscape or an acoustic environment as a soundscape" (Schafer 1994: 7). This section begins with John Picker tracing the historical lineage and meaning of the term pre- and post-Schafer and points to the rich variety of uses of the term together with its ambiguities and limitations. These limitations are integral to the normative nature of Schafer's project in which a non-urban aesthetic remains dominant. Picker demonstrated that for an analysis of soundscapes we need to move from a singularly understood phenomenon to one with a plurality of meanings, empirically, conceptually and culturally. Picker charts the historical derivation and use of this term whilst pointing to different trajectories that we might take in order to understand, analyse and describe our sonic environments. In its historical pre-Schaferian manifestation Picker discusses how soundscape often referred to the landscape, thereby merging the visual with the auditory. He also points to Schafer's use of soundscape as a "literary soundscape". Picker points to the role of the aesthetic in judgements concerning the nature of a "soundscape" pointing in effect to Schafer's rejection of urban soundscapes as consisting of sounds out of place. This brings Picker to the conclusion, as other entries do in this volume, that our understanding and appreciation of "soundscapes" is deeply value laden, historical and cultural.

Tim Edensor addresses the cultural and historical understanding of sonic place and space through the notion of "rhythms", drawing upon Henri Lefebvre's "rhythmanalysis". Places, he argues, have their own distinct rhythms; dynamic and diverse. The sounds of a medieval city differ from contemporary London, New York and indeed Brighton. Edensor charts these diverse and sometimes unifying sonic rhythms of place from the localised sounds of football stadiums to the sounds of singing in local public houses. Rhythms, he argues, became increasingly industrialised as we commute to work and back in automobiles, trains and on foot. The rhythm and swell of movement accompanied by the radio, MP3 players and mobile phones become embodied in bodily rhythms. The individual within the structural – an embodiment of the multiple and contradictory sonic rhythms of urban experience.

Just as cities can be characterized by a profusion of sounds, central to sound studies is a concentration on the reduction of "noise" and a focus on quietude and "silence". Since John Cage's observation of the sounds of his own body in an anechoic chamber where all sounds are excluded and in light of the development of noise abatement societies and legislation, the issues of silence and the diminution of "noise" frequently take centre stage. Bennett Hogg's chapter on "Silence" focusses upon a phenomenologically inspired account of how we attend to what might be considered the silence of landscapes. In doing so he rejects the notion that space exists independently of human beings, arguing that to discuss silence or sounds is to engage in a culturally informed discussion. If we do so, then we discover that silence is not an absolute but rather a "perceptual phenomenon". Through a range of examples Hogg demonstrates that silence is a factor existing within a more generalised ecosystem. In doing so he introduces the reader to the notion of "trans-modal silence", by which he means that silence is a factor in a more general ecosystem system that includes not just sound but our other senses as well.

Just as Hogg describes a phenomenology of silence, so Kytö investigates the sonic relationship between notions of public and private from a cultural and historical perspective, demonstrating the cultural specificity and variability of these concepts as used, understood or ignored. These technological and cultural transformations have, as Kytö argues, changed the ways in which social spaces have been both conceptualized and experienced. Kytö engages in debates concerning the erosion of privacy enacted through a range of technologies that survey everyday behaviour and responses that appear to diminish or eliminate the very distinctions between private and public spheres of experience. In doing so she discusses the nature of an "eavesdropping" culture in which asymmetrical power relationships listen in to the "private" ever more pervasively. Those who embrace such intrusiveness through forms of celebrity culture and the like, to those who attempt to circumvent such intrusiveness is a live cultural debate. The potential intrusion of sound into every space is largely a phenomenon of industrial society – bemoaned by Schafer and celebrated by fans of Musak – but beyond this the ability of telephones, radios and televisions to penetrate and inhabit a wide variety of spaces in traditionally Fordist modes had now extended to more individualistic modes with the arrival of smartphones. Kytö investigates the role that new technologies play in affording both privacy and publicity and discusses the nature of access to sonic databases in order to ask what are we permitted to hear and who is allowed to participate in the sonic 'public sphere'.

Integral to the role of sonic technologies and the habitation of spaces mediated by those technologies is the generation and reception of music. Chow approaches sonic space through the lens of diaspora and ethnicity, and through case studies investigates the power dynamics in the production and reception of music that produce forms of diasporic identities across space and place. In doing so he discusses both the private appropriation of cultural spaces together with the publicly re-enacted forms of sonic diaspora through events such as the Notting Hill Carnival in the UK.

References

Bachelard, G., 1994, *The Poetics of Space*, Boston, MA: Beacon Press.

Bollnow, O.F., 2011, *Human Space*, London: Hyphen Press.

Casey, E., 1998, *The Fate of Place: A Philosophical Enquiry*, Berkeley, CA: University of California Press.

Flichy, P., 1995, *Dynamics of Modern Communication: The Shaping and Impact of New Communication Technologies*, Basingstoke: Sage Press.

DeNora, T., 2000, *Music in Everyday Life*. Cambridge: Cambridge University Press.

Douglas, S., 2004, *Listening: Radio and the American Imagination*, Minneapolis, MN: University of Minnesota Press.

Sachs, W., 1992, *For Love of the Automobile: Looking Back into the History of Our Desires*, Berkeley, CA: University of California Press.

Schafer, R.M., 1994, *The Soundscape: Our Sonic Environment and the Tuning of the World*, Rochester, VT: Destiny Books.

14

SOUNDSCAPE(S): THE TURNING OF THE WORD

John M. Picker

The use of "soundscape" is so prevalent at this point in writings on sound and music, literature, art, history, media, identity, the environment, engineering, commerce, and travel—Jonathan
Sterne calls it "the most enduring spatial figure in sound studies"—that it seems odd to pause
to reflect on it (Sterne 2012: 91). Newbies to the field (you know who you are) likely have
come across "soundscape" and perhaps even adopted it in their work, thinking its meaning was
self-evident and stable and its connotations unremarkable. The purpose of this chapter is not
entirely to disabuse anyone of these notions, since it is inevitable, as well as democratic, that
niche vocabulary migrates from its local origins to more common parlance, and the progression
of "soundscape" certainly follows that path. Rather, I intend to show that there is a longer history of soundscape than we might realize and to recount some of the ways soundscape has both
evolved and stirred debate. For it is a term that, surprisingly to casual and even seasoned students
of sound, has a habit of finding its way into new contexts and provoking strong responses. After
reading this chapter, should you draw upon some version or variation of "soundscape" in your
own writing or conversation about sonic matters, you should be able to do so better informed
of its origins, development, and implications, and better prepared to engage with them if you
so choose.

To begin with what might seem like an obvious starting point, the *Oxford English Dictionary*
offers two definitions of "soundscape": a) "a musical composition consisting of a texture of
sounds," and b) "the sounds which form an auditory environment." The OED entry includes a
handful of examples in print from 1968 through 1977, including *Time* magazine on Debussy's
soundscapes and the Victoria (BC) *Daily Colonist* on the World Soundscape Project. I'll discuss
the problems with this skimpy entry soon enough, but for now, to this basic framework we
could add Canadian composer, writer, and music educator R. Murray Schafer's definition in
his influential *The Tuning of the World* (about which more later as well): "The soundscape is any
acoustic field of study. We may speak of a musical composition as a soundscape, or a radio program as a soundscape or an acoustic environment as a soundscape" (Schafer 1994: 7). In Schafer's
rendering, "soundscape" comes to refer to "a total social concept to describe the field of sounds
in a particular place, or an entire culture" (Sterne 2012: 91). Such a definition requires not only
sound within space but also a listener in a position to hear it. As Steven Connor puts it, "a soundscape is a sound plus a certain kind of relation" (2014: 18).

That is adequate as far as it goes. But before turning to these more established connotations, or even the dictionary definitions, let's first take the word on its face. To many of us, "soundscape" initially comes across as a modern adaptation to the acoustic arena of the familiar term of pictorial art "landscape." Indeed, the earliest published use I have found of it, which predates the examples in the OED by over 60 years, suggests an origin as a term of art, a variation on "seascape," but for related topography. A 1907 article from *Harper's Weekly* concerns the political prospects of the now-forgotten playwright Augustus Thomas in a potential run for mayor of "New Rochelle, where he has long lived in a neighborhood which he dominates" (Anon. 1907: 724). We get this description of his intellectual milieu:

> When THOMAS had a literary bent he had also a theological spasm, and he surrounded himself with congenial comrades at his "Home of the Innocent," at New Rochelle. ROBERT INGERSOLL was his religious instructor; DE WOLF HOPPER furnished the literary entertainment at his Sunday symposiums by reciting "Casey at the Bat"; KEMBLE drew the pictures on the dinner cards; EDWARD SIMMONS [the American impressionist] painted the Soundscape over the mantel, and imbued the atmosphere with anti-Concordian philosophy; the young BARRYMORES lent the attractions of the stage that was to be; JOHN FOX sang the negro melodies; and REMINGTON furnished his usual eulogy upon the "man on horseback."
>
> *("Personal and Pertinent": 724)*

The setting of New Rochelle, on the Long Island Sound, suggests that the use of "Soundscape" here is meant to characterize a painting of a *geographic*, not an acoustic, sound. This is "soundscape" not as appropriation of "landscape" (that is, a sonic landscape) but as *visual homonym*. This is a sense that has been so eclipsed—*drowned out* would be the apt audible and fluid idiom—by post-war usage that this meaning, and the first few appearances I identify in this chapter, are entirely absent in the entry in the OED. To the OED entry we thus could add a third, obsolete meaning: *a painting or view of a geographic sound*. The word in its infancy, it appears, has less to do with the auditory realm, and more to do with the natural and cultural environment of late Gilded Age leisure and luxury.

The next appearance of "soundscape" that I have been able to trace occurs within a similar bourgeois and geographic context, as a neologism for the kind of sensory experience now easily accessible to the ultimate consumer, the automobile owner. This example surfaces in a 1911 article in the *Club Journal* of the American Automobile Association, on touring the Long Island Sound by car (curious that these two early occurrences reveal the New York region as the entry-point of "soundscape" into the lexicon):

> In the village of Westchester you cross a bridge and swing into Fort Schuyler Road. The scenery down this little peninsula is really very charming, with the water of the Sound on both sides. There is something about a great body of water that never fails to fill a scene with life and beauty. The coast may be, and generally is, flat and monotonous, but the restless beat and unwearying energy of the sea, or its little brother, the Sound, always attracts one. You get plenty of these "Soundscapes," especially as you draw near to the attenuated point of the peninsula, where the road takes up most of the available land.
>
> *(Anon. 1911: 514)*

The ostensible reference here is to the Sound as a visual phenomenon, but the significance of the *sound* of the Sound emerges here as well ("restless beat and unwearying energy"). Indeed, this may be the first use of the word that implies what would later become more explicit: soundscape's negotiated relationship among space (especially spaces of the natural environment), mechanization, and a listening subject. The "Soundscapes" encountered on this tour reveal themselves via the symbol of modern space-conquering technology, the car, with the author's predictable obliviousness to the effects of autoroutes and traffic ("where the road takes up most of the available land") on the natural "life and beauty" he (or perhaps she) apparently values. At this early date, the position and impact of the consuming subject is secondary to the restless pursuit of those ultimate modern amenities, the spectacular view and its corollary, the perfect site for high-fidelity audition.

The same consumerist impulse provides the context for my final early instance of "soundscape," again in the sense absent from the OED and yet worth noting for the way it transfers the term to the Northwest coast of the US, not far from Vancouver where it will be resuscitated some decades later by Schafer and his colleagues. Natural space, consumption, and modern convenience coalesce once more, in a real estate listing from the 1944 *Seattle Times*:

UNRIVALED SOUNDSCAPE
    5 Years old—One of those smart, squatty, rambling homes of hollow tile construction literally filled with big oblong plate glass windows, unobstructibly sweeping the main channel of Puget Sound for miles and miles. ("Real Estate": 20)

This is the language of advertising, with a riff on "landscape" to arrive at marketing terminology selling a slice of Puget Sound. "Just 20 minutes to city center, just five years old and just the finest value you will find for $12,500. We've seen none better," the realtors add ("Real Estate": 20). The listing reveals how "soundscape," in this long-lost geographic sense, functions still not yet as primarily or self-evidently an auditory event, but increasingly within a capitalist economy as a consumable, spatial, experiential good: a house with a perfect view.

I have suggested ways that formative appearances of the word, though forgotten, pivot on soundscape's homonymic effect even as they hint at some of its later, more familiar uses. It's time to turn to those now. Beginning in the late '50s, propelled by the rise of the stereo era, which features new techniques to engineer and experience recorded and broadcast sound (Sterne 2013, 2015), "soundscape" returns, emanating post-war hipness on both sides of the Atlantic in discussions of radio drama and musical compositions and performances. A 1958 review of a BBC radio broadcast of Kleist's *Prince of Homburg* praises the producer's "soundscape of the field of Fehrbellin," which "presented a tremendous panorama to the mind's eye," while Hugh Kenner (who, like Schafer, was a student of Marshall McLuhan at the University of Toronto) invokes it in his 1961 discussion of Beckett's radio play *All That Fall*: "Yet even Mrs. Rooney is an illusion; all living is an illusion; the very animals whose ways have not changed since Arcady are merely so many baas and bleats, manifestly generated by the sound effects department. (Beckett has said that he would have preferred the approximations of human imitators to the BBC's painstaking illusion.) Pulsating in acoustic space, the soundscape asserts a provisional reality, at every instant richly springing forth and dying" (Walker 1958: 475; Kenner 1961: 171). This is soundscape as acoustic engineering for a radio audience, or what Neal Verma has called "audiopositioning" (Sterne 2015: 70).

The term continued to be used in conjunction with the visual arts and the ways that painterly techniques could represent the sonic, both figuratively and with respect to the spaces of the natural environment. The abstract expressionist and longtime director of the Cleveland Institute of Art Joseph McCullough, who had studied at Yale with Josef Albers, began painting one or more series of "sound-filled landscapes" titled *Soundscape* as early as 1955–56 (*Soundscape #340* dates from 1958 [Welchans 2012: 5]). This is the first post-war reference to soundscape I have been able to locate; the use is meant to capture the abstract synesthetic representation of sonic experience. McCullough would become known for these works in the '60s, and exhibited at the beginning of the decade a *Soundscape* which, with his companion piece *Bells*, "conjure[d] the auditory and sensory suggestion of tinkling metal tones" (Anon. 1964: 6; Metzler: 17-E). Soundscape also came to be applied in a figurative painterly sense to music. In an essay on Duke Ellington, the English critic Burnett James considered European influences on jazz, and Ellington in particular, with reference to French painting. For James, there were two strands of musical impressionism: one that captured the play of light on an object, embodied in the music of Debussy, and the other, more relevant to Ellington, an "impressionism of mood" best represented by Delius, whose "introduction to *Appalachia* is an extraordinarily evocative natural soundscape" (James 1961).

James's use of the term captures a transition toward the first of the two definitions provided by the OED (once again, in a reference earlier than any cited there): "a musical composition consisting of a texture of sounds." This sense of the term develops over the '60s, not only with respect to the ways that concert music begins to be characterized—so the eminent music critic Paul Hume, reviewing a 1964 performance of Mahler's Sixth by the Boston Symphony Orchestra, could note "the great, often strident brass fanfares that punctuate the farflung soundscape"—but also the ways that contemporary music comes to be conceived (Hume 1964: C9). The 1960s saw the emergence of what the composer Hildegard Westerkamp coined "soundscape composition," a form of musical creation that "employed environmental sound recordings but broke with the European acousmatic school" represented by Pierre Schaeffer's *Musique concrète*: "Soundscape composition, while theorized as a musical style, put constraints on the manipulation of sound sources. Practitioners maintained that the link between source and recording be transparent; the location recorded had to remain recognizable to the listener" (Akiyama 2010: 54). Such projects, undertaken by Westerkamp and others associated with Vancouver's World Soundscape Project, fixed "environmental sound with the intention of denoting a particular place and time" (Akiyama 2010: 55).

I have discussed one, or really two, senses of "soundscape" that have taken us into the 1960s. This leaves the second OED definition, "the sounds which form an auditory environment," the meaning that Schafer focused on and that has become so predominant in general use. Although it's a common presumption that Schafer coined the word, it predated his first use of it, as we've seen, by sixty years. Nor did he arrive at this second sense entirely on his own. Schafer was anticipated in his broad reconception of soundscape as an environmental term by at least two others: Buckminster Fuller and Michael Southworth (Sterne 2013, 2015). Fuller, the developer of the geodesic dome, advocate of the meme of "Spaceship Earth," and prophetic huckster (W. Patrick McCray calls him, as if to echo Disney's imagineers, a "visioneer" [McCray 2016]) drew upon "soundscape" in an environmental sense in his 1964 keynote speech (published in 1966) for the National Conference on the Uses of Educational Media in the Teaching of Music. Fuller begins with a discussion of the theory of the "Epigenetic Landscape," in which "life alters the landscape, then landscape alters the life" and "entropy and evolution are inherent." From here he moves to the correlation between music and the pace of life: "When, in due course, man invented words and music he altered the soundscape and the soundscape altered man. The epigenetic evolution interacting progressively between humanity and his soundscape has been profound" (Fuller 1966: 52).

For Sterne, this is "the earliest [use] ... that casts *soundscape* as a total concept ... meant to denote the entire sonic field of humankind as it exists in dynamic relationship with nature" (Sterne 2013: 186). Schafer may or may not have heard or read this lecture, but as an innovative music educator he would have been interested in its subject matter and certainly was a fan of Fuller, bringing him to Simon Fraser University in the late '60s to deliver a three-hour lecture (Schafer 2012: 96).

A more developed precursor to Schafer's notion of soundscape is that of the architect and urban planner Southworth, whose influence Schafer has acknowledged. Southworth's 1967 MIT Master's thesis, "The Sonic Environment of Cities," was a pioneering analysis of the potential for reformation of the urban soundscape, with a focus on a field study of central Boston. Southworth's thesis is remarkable for the ways it lays out in nascent forms several of the concerns, concepts, and approaches that Schafer and his colleagues would develop, even including the equivalent of a sound map or sound walk. Both in his thesis and the 1969 article based on it, Southworth frequently uses "soundscape," without comment, as synonymous with "sonic environment." Southworth apparently had the idea to adapt his supervisor's term "cityscape" to a new urbanist approach that would consider the ways that city sound could better serve its inhabitants (Sterne 2015: 70). Southworth's goals "to reduce and control noise" and "to increase the informativeness of the soundscape" likely struck a chord with Schafer, who cites the article and reprints the sound map from it in *The Tuning of the World* and admits in his autobiography that he may well have borrowed the term from Southworth: "This is entirely possible; I read the article" (Southworth 1969: 69–70; Schafer 2012: 120).

Schafer's "soundscape" had some precedent, then, in the work of related scholars and public figures, but it was his role to begin to flesh out a theory and practice of acoustic design via the term, for which he became its greatest publicist. As Schafer put it, "it was the research I was beginning to develop that defined the term and brought it to international attention" (Schafer 2012: 120). It's important to recognize that Schafer's conception of soundscape emerges out of his work as a music educator in the '60s. "Soundscape" is a term whose function is pedagogical, as instruction to experience the world differently. Schafer's earliest uses appear in publications like *Ear Cleaning* (1967) and *The New Soundscape* (1969), pamphlets that were intended to assist teachers looking to revitalize what he perceived as basic music pedagogy that had stagnated in the face of more vibrant countercultural trends epitomized by John Cage. Cage's influence was profound, both on Schafer and his conception of soundscape. Early in *The New Soundscape*, Schafer asks his students to define music. Facing the difficulty of doing so, he writes:

> I did not like to think that the question of defining the subject to which we are devoting our lives was totally impossible. I did not think John Cage would think so either, and so I wrote him and asked him for his definition of music. His reply: *Music is sounds, sounds around us whether we're in or out of concert halls—see Thoreau.*
>
> *(Schafer 1986: 94)*

Schafer's Cagean thinking brought avant-garde concepts and practices into the classroom and shaped his own thinking about soundscape. Furthermore, the effects of Cage's (and behind it, Thoreau's) koan-like writing—epitomized by Cage's single-sentence reply in this passage—are equally felt in Schafer's style.

"The whole world is an airport," Schafer quips in epigrammatic, Cagean mode, and this points to a central context for his soundscape efforts (Schafer 1986: 156). They are of a piece with the growing environmental concerns and fears of the social movements of the '60s. Schafer would recall,

> I was beginning to research a new subject which I called the *soundscape*. The sounds of the environment were changing rapidly and it seemed that no one was documenting

the changes. Where were the museums for disappearing sounds? What was the effect of new sounds on human behavior and health? So many questions could be asked for which there were no answers in 1970.

(Schafer 2012: 119–120)

The archiving impulse mentioned here links back at least to the beginnings of ethnographic recording, one of the earliest uses to which sound recording technology was put in the late nineteenth century, but another motivation is even older, dating back in pre-industrial form to the eighteenth century if not even earlier. This was the need to find ways to manage unwanted, primarily urban sound, the problem that, in the wake of post-war environmentalism and massive over-industrialization had by 1970 come to be called *noise pollution*. Schafer the composer presents his sense of soundscape as a form of empowerment against a decomposed or degenerated acoustic environment. Schafer's response to undesirable sound is to encourage cultivating what he believes is desirable sound, which is to say, acoustic design:

It would seem that the world soundscape has reached an apex of vulgarity in our time, and many experts have predicted universal deafness as the ultimate consequence unless the problem can be brought quickly under control … The final question will be: is the soundscape of the world an indeterminate composition over which we have no control, or are *we* its composers and performers, responsible for giving it form and beauty?

(Schafer 1994: 3, 5)

With such language as "vulgarity," "form," and "beauty," it becomes clear that *The Tuning of the World* is a treatise on not merely the problem of noise, but also, more fundamentally, "*aesthetic* control of the acoustic environment" (Adams 1983: 44; my emphasis). Schafer's terminology reflects this aesthetic impulse, adapting words from visual regimes, sound reproduction media, and psychology into memorable, if problematic, neologisms in order to delineate and deconstruct the sonic environment. Among these, from "landscape" he analogizes (though does not coin) *soundscape* ("we can isolate an acoustic environment as a field of study just as we can study the characteristics of a given landscape" [1994: 7]); from "eyewitness," he derives *earwitness* as the individual who can testify to a sound that they have heard; "landmark" yields *soundmark*; "clairvoyance" leads to *clairaudience*, or clear hearing; he characterizes environments as *hi-fi*, in which natural and community sounds can be heard clearly, and *lo-fi*, in which industrialization has led to noise and lack of clarity; and he introduces *schizophonia*, a "nervous" word meant to convey not only acousmatic, mechanically-reproduced sound separated from its source but also the "aberrational effect of this twentieth-century development" (Schafer 1994: 273).

That word choice of "aberrational" is a reminder that aesthetic judgments and invocations are everywhere in Schafer's concept of soundscape. This includes his points of reference, which are not typical in a book about noise pollution, let alone acoustics. Schafer's biography understandably emphasizes his work as a composer, which has obvious bearing on his project of conceiving the sounds of the environment as a composition, but less frequently noted is his significant background in literary studies, including a monograph on E.T.A. Hoffmann and music, and a formative edition of the complete music criticism of Ezra Pound. Schafer's soundscape is as much a product of literary engagement as it is of environmental or musical encounters. *The Tuning of the World* opens with an epigraph from Whitman and makes reference to a who's who of canonical and quasi-canonical writers, not only Pound and Hoffmann but also Remarque, Faulkner, Thoreau, Cooper, Maugham, Mann, Paton, Hugo, Heine, Tolstoy, Woolf, Dickens, Twain, and Wharton. The World Soundscape Project Schafer established in the early '70s included among its investigations "a glossary of all unusual sounds encountered in world literature" (Schafer 2012: 120). A contemporaneous unpublished letter Schafer sent with a copy of *The Tuning of the World* to the literary critic (and fellow *enfant terrible*) George Steiner reads in part:

> I am hoping that the TUNING might serve to move your mind towards a consideration of what I regard as a fertile theme for research: the soundscape in literature. I have charged at it in the opening chapters of the book, probably in too generalized a manner and quite without the equipment of the literary critic. I am fully aware that the quotes from literature which we have in our cross-indexed card file ignore the social and psychological contexts in which the acoustic descriptions occurred. Also, our card file is by no means as exhaustive or detailed as we would like. But the theme of soundscape studies is quite a bit broader than "sounds in literature" and I hope at least that I've been able to announce it without too many stupidities.
>
> *(Letter to Steiner, 12 June 1977)*

"I have no specific plans to do what I am about to suggest," Schafer adds before proposing that Steiner edit or write "a collection of essays (perhaps by different authors) dealing with aspects of the literary soundscape." A response from Steiner appears not to have been forthcoming. Indeed, it would take years for more than a very few literary scholars, Western-focused or otherwise, to recognize the relevance of Schafer's work to their own and explore and establish the significance of the ways that fiction, poetry, and drama render and recreate soundscapes of different eras and communities (for a notable recent example, see Jordan 2016).[1]

The wide range of reference, not only to Western texts but Eastern ones as well, can help partly to explain the book's broader appeal and the consequent popularization of the notion of soundscape, but a further dimension that tends to be overlooked is the book's publication history. *The Tuning of the World* began as a trade book (Knopf) reviewed in the likes of the *New York Times*, was paperbacked in 1980 with an academic publisher (the University of Pennsylvania Press) and a subtitle to clarify the aesthetic objective (*Toward a Theory of Soundscape Design*), and republished over a decade later with Destiny Books, an imprint of Inner Traditions, a press specializing in New Age mysticism, the occult, and self-help, again with a revised title, *The Soundscape: Our Sonic Environment and the Tuning of the World*, where it remains in print. Steven Connor suggests that the retitling of the book indicates the widespread success of "soundscape" as an operative term by the early '90s: giving the book this title "means that the book itself was now itself conceivable as a kind of soundscape—that is, a certain gathering-together or taking-to-be of the whole field of modern sound that may itself count as a kind of soundscape" (Connor 2014: 17). More than this, the continual shifts in publisher and title indicate the elusive nature of the soundscape concept, especially as it migrated from Schafer's text into the wider world.

As if to push back against its omnipresence as well as its slipperiness, some prominent scholars and sound artists have expressed their dissatisfaction with soundscape and proposed other terms as supplements or replacements. Steven Feld speaks for many when he objects to the ways that Schafer's soundscape betrays a visualist bias in its approach and terminology; Feld prefers "acoustemology," in part because it "refuses to sonically analogize or appropriate 'landscape,' with all its physical distance from agency and perception" (Feld 2015: 15). Acknowledging the earliest mentions of the word as a visual homonym, as I did at the outset of this chapter, grant the charge of visualist bias a different dimension, though no less weight. Tim Ingold claims that soundscape "has outlived its usefulness" and should be abandoned, since "the environment that we experience, know and move around in is not sliced up along the lines of the sensory pathways by which we enter into it" (Ingold 2007: 10). For Ingold and others, soundscape does not do justice to the experience of being in the world:"our metaphors for describing auditory space should be derived not from landscape studies but from meteorology" (Ingold 2007: 12). Stefan Helmreich concurs:"The soundscape is shadowed by an acoustemology of space as given and listener as both apart from the world and immersed in it" (Helmreich 2010: 10). In place of Schafer's and soundscape's *immersion*, Helmreich offers "transduction" and "transductive ethnography" as more useful concepts for approaches such as his own, one attentive to underwater sound.

For certain scholars, Schafer's soundscape is a product of "a somewhat romantic materialist environmentalism" and as such is premised on the "assumption that sound is only a matter of the vibrations of the source, leaving undertheorized the social, ideological, or political positionalities of listeners" (Samuels et al., 2010: 331, 335). The absence of awareness of the listener's politics and space is echoed in Jonathan Sterne's critique, which sees the "essence" of soundscape as "a stable audioposition, one from which the entire world is available to be heard." For Sterne, Schafer's soundscape is "a historical artifact of hi-fi culture," and as such it "hides the work of shaping perspective" that it shares with the multichannel audio technologies of the post-war era (Sterne 2015: 79, 80). Sterne suggests that the soundscape obscures its own subjectivity. What is more, it has deluded us all: "What if we used the soundscape concept to build a metaphorical 'world record collection' to behold, while wearing our metaphorical smoking jackets in our mental living rooms, with 'world pictures' hung prominently on the walls, and we didn't even know it?" (Sterne 2015: 81).

Schafer's soundscape has found its way into the thinking of social geographers, though here too not always comfortably. Pioneering Finnish geographer J. G. Granö anticipated the sound-scape concept by several decades (without using the term) in his *Pure Geography* (1929). He developed a system of "proximics," in which he delineated "auditory phenomena" as part of the "medium," or surround, within the "proximity," the part of the environment perceivable by the senses. Granö even divided proximities between "natural" ones (waves, wind, birdsound) and "artificial" ones (voices, traffic, industry): Schafer's hi-fi and lo-fi soundscape *avant* both *la lettre* and the language of multichannel audio. More contemporary geographers have found in the Schaferian soundscape a valuable correlation with Granö's ideas and advocated for greater awareness of sound or more attention to improving sonic environments in geographic study (Smith 1994; Porteous 1990). However, arguing for the value of "auditory geography," Paul Rodaway claims that "there is a tension" in Schafer's use of soundscape between the soundscape as an aesthetic object and as an auditory experience, "a process of engagement" (Rodaway 1994: 86). Soundscape, for Rodaway, is "deceptively attractive" because it implies a static object and detached listener in a privileged position, while "auditory experience is far more dynamic and the sentient participates within the sonic environment" (Rodaway 1994: 86). Rodaway suggests that soundscape and Schafer's related terms are useful, but only to a point: "its metaphorical basis reminds us of the limitations of language" and "the complex relationships between the different senses" (Rodaway 1994: 89).

Among historians, some have downplayed Schafer's work even as they reconstruct past sound-scapes, while others who use Schafer's term make implicit nods to the kinds of problems Sterne and Rodaway identify. Alain Corbin writes alongside but without citing Schafer in his pioneer-ing history of what he calls the nineteenth-century French "paysage sonore" (even though this phrase has been widely recognized as the French for "soundscape," the English translation of Corbin's book elides this phrase in the subtitle, and elsewhere in the text renders it as "audi-tory landscape"), in particular its "sonorités campanaires" [campanarian sonorities] (Corbin 1994, 1998; Schafer 2010). Following Corbin while reintegrating Schafer, Emily Thompson defines soundscape "as an auditory or aural landscape," but she goes on to redirect the term away from Schafer's anti-noise aesthetic to the rise of a modern constructed sonic environment that, at the level of signals, is manipulated by architectural acousticians: "The physical aspects of a soundscape consist not only of the sounds themselves, the waves of acoustical energy permeating the atmosphere in which people live, but also the material objects that create, and sometimes destroy these sounds. … A soundscape, like a landscape, ultimately has more to do with civilization than with nature, and as such, it is constantly under construction and always undergoing change" (Thompson 2002: 1–2). The title of my own book of literary and cultural history, *Victorian Soundscapes* (2003), nods to Schafer even as it offers subtle revision. My title, and my approach in the book, deviate from Schafer's *The Soundscape* and its echoes in other singular "Soundscape" titles to capture the ways in which sonic environments in an era defined by urbanization, industrialization, and the birth of modern sound media are in their essence subjective, value-laden, and contested—multiple sensory experiences instead of a singular one. I analyze Victorian writers' experience and expectations of sound with the understanding that it is largely written records, with all their partiality, that constitute "Victorian soundscapes." Other recent titles that explore sites of historical fissure and ideological conflict, such as Karin Bijsterveld's *Soundscapes of the Urban Past* (2013) and Carolyn Birdsall's *Nazi Soundscapes* (2012), follow suit, recognizing the value of plural "soundscapes" in the vocabulary of apprehension (in both senses) of past experiences.

At present, we find "soundscape," and soundscapes, everywhere: not only analyzed by academics but also deliberated in international bodies, reconstituted into artistic works and museum exhibits, even bought and sold as meditation and sleep-inducing digital downloads. In 2014, in response to the concern that the use of the term had become "idiosyncratic and ambiguous," the International Standards Organization formalized the definition of soundscape for the purposes of measuring, reporting, planning, and management (ISO 12913-1: v). Their definition emphasizes human perception: the ISO differentiates between the "acoustic environment," which is "sound at the receiver from all sound sources as modified by the environment," and the soundscape, which is the "acoustic environment as perceived or experienced and/or understood by a person or people, in context" (ISO 12913-1: 2; see Figure 14.1).

The ISO efforts are an attempt to render soundscape practical and useful as an applied tool in soundscape ecology and other areas where the preservation and management of sound is paramount (Truax 1978). It is perhaps less of a stretch than it might initially seem to link their notion of soundscape to that of Mark Hagood (2011), who emphasizes the relationship between listeners, media, and power when he characterizes the work of noise-cancelling headphones

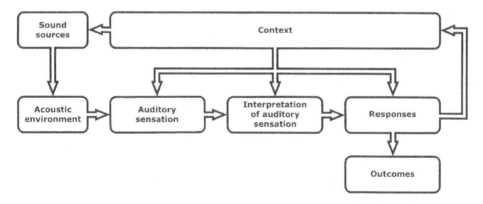

Figure 14.1 "Elements in the perceptual construct of soundscape." ©ISO. This material is reproduced from ISO 12913-1:2014 with permission of the American National Standards Institute (ANSI) on behalf of the International Organization for Standardization. All rights reserved.

worn by white business travelers as *soundscaping*. For Hagood, "soundscape" becomes a neoliberal verb, a way of enacting socioeconomic distinction within mobile personal space. With the ISO's and Hagood's meanings, we have come full circle from the first uses of "soundscape" over a hundred years ago. Each points to the ways that "soundscape" continues to be associated with the central position of the listener in the marking, and marketing, of space.

The arc I have traced in this chapter, from a singular soundscape to a plurality of soundscapes, reflects not just the spread of the word across disciplines and borders but also the multiplicity of meanings and perspectives the term has come to encompass. If this has induced excessive policing of discourse in some (Kelman 2010), others remain more at ease with the free movement of language to express the subjectivity of experience; for those in the latter camp (Bijsterveld 2013), there is the subtle recognition that "soundscapes" provides. As with any idea, no single writer, discipline, philosophy, or organization owns soundscape. Indeed, following Sterne, we might be inclined to think the concept has tended to own *us*. While aspiring students of sound should not feel compelled to adopt it, neither should they feel obliged to accept earlier definitions if they do. As I have shown, some of the most interesting work in the field has adapted the century-old term in the process of drawing attention to new perspectives on auditory history and culture.

Note

1   I thank Murray Schafer for providing a copy of his letter to George Steiner. I also wish to acknowledge the broader influence on my thinking of Jonathan Sterne's two recent overlapping essays on the history of soundscape, which I recommend to anyone with further interest in the subject.

References

Acoustics—Soundscape—Part 1: Definition and Conceptual Framework, ISO 12913–1:2014(E).

Adams, S. (1983) *R. Murray Schafer*, Toronto: University of Toronto Press.

Akiyama, M. (2010) "Transparent Listening: Soundscape Composition's Object of Study," *RACAR: Revue d'art canadienne/Canadian Art Review* 35.1, pp. 54–62.

[Anon.] (1907) "Personal and Pertinent," *Harper's Weekly* 51 (18 May), p. 724.

[Anon.] (1911) "A Day-End Trip Through Colonial Manors," *The Club Journal* 3, pp. 514–15.

[Anon.] (1964) "The Fabulous Fifty," *Cleveland Plain Dealer* (28 April), pp. 5–6.

Bijsterveld, K. (2013) *Soundscapes of the Urban Past: Staged Sound as Mediated Cultural Heritage*, Bielefeld: Transcript.

Birdsall, C. (2012) *Nazi Soundscapes: Sound, Technology, and Urban Space in Germany, 1933–1945*, Amsterdam: Amsterdam University Press.

Connor, S. (2014) "Rustications: Animals in the Urban Mix," in M. Gundy and Nilsen B. J., eds., *The Acoustic City*, Berlin: Jovis, pp. 16–22.

Corbin, A. (1994) *Les cloches de la terre: Paysage sonore et culture sensible dans les campagnes au XIXᵉ siècle*, Paris: Albin Michel.

———. (1998) *Village Bells: Sound and Meaning in the 19th-Century French Countryside*, Thom, M., trans. Basingstoke: Papermac.

Feld, S. (2015) "Acoustemology," in Novak, D. and Sakakeeny, M., eds., *Keywords in Sound*, Durham: Duke University Press, pp. 12–21.

Fuller, B. (1966) "The Music of the New Life," *Music Educators Journal* 52.6, pp. 52–60, 62, 64, 66–68.

Granö, J. G. (1997) *Pure Geography*, Granö, O. and Paasi, A., eds. Hicks, M., trans. Baltimore: Johns Hopkins University Press.

Hagood, M. (2011) "Quiet Comfort: Noise, Otherness, and the Mobile Production of Personal Space," *American Quarterly* 63, pp. 573–89.

Helmreich, S. (2010) "Listening Against Soundscapes," *Anthropology News* 51.9: 10.

Hume, P. (1964) "Boston Symphony Presents Concert of True Sophistication," *Washington Post, Times Herald* (2 December), p. C9.

Ingold, T. (2007) "Against Soundscape," in Carlyle, E., ed., *Autumn Leaves:Sound and the Environment in Artistic Practice*, Paris: Double Entendre, pp. 10–13.

James, B. (1961) *Essays on Jazz*, London: Sidgwick and Jackson.

Jordan, J. O. (2016) "Dickens and Soundscape: *The Old Curiosity Shop*," *E-rea: Revue électronique d'études sur le monde anglophone* 13.2. Online: http://erea.revues.org/4943

Kelman, A. (2010) "Rethinking the Soundscape: A Critical Genealogy of a Key Term in Sound Studies," *Senses and Society* 5, pp. 212–34.

Kenner, H. (1961) *Samuel Beckett: A Critical Study*, New York: Grove Press.

McCray, W. P. (2016) "Life as a Verb: Applying Buckminster Fuller to the 21st Century," *Los Angeles Review of Books* (21 June). Online: https://lareviewofbooks.org/article/life-verb-applying-buckminster-fuller-21st-century/

Picker, J. M. (2003) *Victorian Soundscapes*, Oxford: Oxford University Press.

Porteous, J. D. (1990) *Landscapes of the Mind: Worlds of Sense and Metaphor*, Toronto: University of Toronto Press.

"Real Estate." (1944) *Seattle Times* (12 September), p. 20.

Rodaway, P. (1994) *Sensuous Geographies: Body, Sense, and Place*, Abingdon: Routledge.

Samuels, D. W., Meintjes, L., Ochoa, A. M., and Porcello, T. (2010) "Soundscapes: Toward a Sounded Anthropology," *Annual Review of Anthropology* 39, pp. 329–45.

Schafer, R. M. (1986) *The Thinking Ear: Complete Writings on Music Education*, Toronto: Arcana.

———. (1994) *The Soundscape: Our Sonic Environment and the Tuning of the World,* Rochester, VT: Destiny Books. Originally published as (1977) *The Tuning of the World,* New York: Knopf; in paperback as (1980) *The Tuning of the World: Toward a Theory of Soundscape Design*, Philadelphia: University of Pennsylvania Press.

———. (2010) *Le Paysage Sonore: Le Monde Comme Musique,* Gleize, S., trans. Paris: Wildproject. Originally published as (1979) *Le Paysage Sonore,* Paris: J.-C. Lattès.

———. (2012) *My Life on Earth and Elsewhere*, Erin, Ont.: Porcupine's Quill.

Smith, S. J. (1994) "Soundscape," *Area* 26, pp. 232–40.

Southworth, M. F. (1967) *The Sonic Environment of Cities*, Thesis, M. City Planning, MIT. Stephen M. Carr, Supervisor.

Southworth, M. F. (1969) "The Sonic Environment of Cities," *Environment and Behavior* 1, pp. 49–70.

Sterne, J., ed. (2012) *The Sound Studies Reader*, New York: Routledge.

———. (2013) "Soundscape, Landscape, Escape," in Bijsterveld, K., ed., *Soundscapes of the Urban Past: Staged Sound as Mediated Cultural Heritage*, Bielefeld: transcript, pp. 181–93.

———. (2015) "The Stereophonic Spaces of Soundscape," in Théberge, P., Devine, K., and Everrett, T., *Living Stereo: Histories and Cultures of Multichannel Sound*, New York: Bloomsbury Academic, pp. 65–83.

Thompson, E. (2002) *The Soundscape of Modernity: Architectural Acoustics and the Culture of Listening in America, 1900–1933*, Cambridge: MIT Press.

Truax, B., ed. (1978) *Handbook for Acoustic Ecology*, Vancouver: ARC Publications.

Walker, R. (1958) "Princes in Darkness," *The Listener* 59 (13 March), pp. 474–75.

Welchans, R. and Sackerlotzky, R., eds. (2012) *Joseph McCullough: Remembrances*, Cleveland: Artists Archives of the Western Reserve.

15

THE SONIC RHYTHMS OF PLACE

Tim Edensor

Walter Ruttmann's 1927 film, *Berlin, Symphony of a Great City*, set to a musical score, is an impressionistic portrayal of the passage of one day in the life in a large metropolis. Organized into five acts, the movie portrays the dynamic rhythms of the city: the dawn and start of the working day, the crescendo of the multiple rhythms of rush hours, the busy mobilities of passengers, pedestrians and vehicles, lunch-time, the rhythms of factory work and financial transactions, and the vigorous rhythms of nocturnal urban pleasures. What is striking about the film is that there are no recorded sounds, yet the musical score renders explicit the diverse, dynamic, sonic polyrhythms that occur throughout the day.

Henry Lefebvre underlines how places are dynamic settings, possessing no essence but ceaselessly (re)constituted out of the elements that flow from, to and across them. In his work on rhythmanalysis, Lefebvre considers that these vital qualities can be partly characterized by the multiple rhythms that produce this ongoing spatial fluidity. While these movements, pulses, and flows produce numerous ephemeral, contingent, and unpredictable moments, they also constitute a 'polyrhythmic ensemble' (Crang, 2001) that reproduces regular patterns and consistencies, what Amin and Thrift call the 'repetitions and regularities that become the tracks to negotiate urban life' (2002: 17). Accordingly, one way in which we may discern the particularity of place is by identifying the multiple rhythms that range from those that are 'slow or fast, syncopated or continuous, interfering or distinct' (Lefebvre, 2004, 69), in addition to their combinations in '*bundles, bouquets, garlands* of rhythms' (ibid, 20). Lefebvre thus insists that repetitive movements and actions, phases of growth and decline, and distinctively linear and cyclical rhythms, provide a backdrop to everyday life that is simultaneously usually stable but ever-changing: 'everywhere where there is interaction between a place, a time, and an expenditure of energy, there is *rhythm*' (2004: 15).

Crucially, rhythms signify diverse temporal scales: those that resonate with epochal and geological time, life-cycles, annual and seasonal events, weekly routines and daily procedures, as well as those enmeshed in the human body (Edensor, 2010). The differently scaled rhythms of place are also produced by multiple agencies that include the non-human effects of weather, light, tidal patterns, and the daily, seasonal, and annual rhythms of animals and plants, growth, and decay. As far as social rhythms are concerned, regular cultural practices and institutionalised processes instantiate legal, conventional, and traditional pulses on place that include rhythms of trading and commerce, work and leisure, traffic and transport, and ritual and commemoration.

These are consolidated and supplemented by the co-ordinated routines of individuals who rhythmically align their daily and weekly practices with each other and in accordance with or at variance to these organized conventions and rules. The habits of individuals are thus sometimes disrupted or clash with collective rhythms but are more usually accommodated within them. Accordingly, this imbrication in the personal and collective rhythms of place as well as the non-human rhythms that flow across it produces a sense of belonging sedimented not only in habituated ways of culturally practising space and bestowing it with meaning, but in the embodied sensing of familiar space.

Inhabitants thus become unreflexively attuned to the sensations of place, habituated to scenes, textures, smells, sounds, and a host of affordances that are experienced repetitively and regularly. These sensory experiences, rarely subject to conscious thought, are enmeshed in the homes, neighbourhoods, travels, routes and events that are embedded in the quotidian spaces and banal 'place ballets' (Seamon, 1979) which undergird ways of doing, feeling and sensing. As Lucy Lippard comments, 'If one has been raised in a place, its textures and sensations, its smells and sounds, are recalled as they felt to child's, adolescent's, adult's body' (1997: 34). Interaction with space is thus never solely subject to symbolic signification but also to an embodied knowledge partly constituted by a sensual understanding deepened by time and embedded in memory (Noble, 2004). This sensory situatedness is thus shaped by familiarity with the smells, sights, textures, temperatures and sounds of place, characteristics that may usually be unnoticed but might come to mind when we are in unfamiliar settings in which their absence is replaced by other strange sensations.

It is in this context that Lefebvre's insistence on the centrality of bodily rhythms can inform an exploration of the sensory rhythms of place. He insists that 'to grasp a rhythm it is necessary to have been grasped by it' (2004: 27), and here he foregrounds the 'respirations, pulses, circulations, assimilations' (2004: 5) of the body, further arguing that the regulated 'rational' rhythms of industrial and bureaucratic life are constantly in contact with 'what is least rational in human being: the lived, the carnal, the body' (ibid: 9). It is through our senses and the effects of stimuli on the body that we can identify the sensory rhythms of place. This is not merely an auditory relationship, for 'the porosity of our bodies means we also *feel* sound waves' (Duffy et al., 2011: 18). And importantly, neither is it solely a cognitive matter, for as Duffy et al. claim, 'the body's capacity to sense rhythm opens up the in-betweenness of sensing and making sense' (ibid: 19). Brandon Labelle labels this alignment with the rhythms of place a form of 'auditory scaffolding' through which bodies become accommodated to place (Labelle, 2008).

Accordingly, this chapter explores how sonic beats are central constituents in soundscape of place, how, as Lefebvre (2004: 87) contends, a rhythmanalyst is 'capable of listening to a house, street, a town as one listens to a symphony, an opera'. In so doing, besides being aware of our own bodily rhythms, we might become attuned to the rhythms made by humans and non-human agencies. First then, we can pay attention to how, according to Tom Mels (2004: 3), humans are 'rhythm-makers as much as place-makers', and part of this aptitude involves the production and performance of multiple auditory rhythms. Consider that throughout history and geography how the incantations of shamans, the ubiquity of drums, the chants of monks, and the auditory effects of dancing bodies have been part of nearly every society's cultural modes of expression (Hendy, 2014). The advent of the enlightenment and ever-more advancing technology has generated soundscapes increasingly typified by the mechanical rhythms of industrial production, motorized transport, and electronic media. Such sonic rhythms invariably intersect with the collective and individual rhythms of routines and scheduling. Second, rhythms are also incessantly produced by non-human forces, ranging from the patterns of weather that, for instance, herald the heavy beat of monsoon rains and the bursts of tropical thunder, to the noises made by creatures, such as the recurrent cries of birds, the pulsing beat of crickets, and the croaking repetitions of frogs.

I will thus focus upon how these auditory rhythmic elements characterize daily and annual place-temporalities, and how they signify the distinctive parts of cities. I will also examine how sonic rhythms change according to social and cultural processes, certain sounds appearing and others emerging, and perhaps becoming more varied and contested as work schedules, leisure pursuits and cultural events become more flexible, transcending the more regular sonic rhythms of yesteryear.

The rhythmic marking of the time and space of place

Shifting sonic rhythms mark place-temporality (Wunderlich, 2010) in numerous ways, grounding a sense of the predictable practices and cyclical events that unfold over time to (re)produce place. In considering the effects that register the phases of the passing day we might identify the throb of morning rush hour traffic, the hubbub of schoolchildren making their way to school, the mid-morning quiescence that settles for a while, streets suddenly animated by the sounds and movements of those seeking lunch, the evening clatter of cutlery in the suburbs on a summer evening, the excitable nocturnal clamour of theatre, and club-goers in city centres and the boozy exclamations at pub closing times.

Most obviously, daily temporal passage is inscribed by the bells that mark out the metronomic passing of quarter-hours, half-hours, and hours. The renowned chimes of Big Ben in the clock tower of the Palace of Westminster extend across London as well as the nation in recorded sound that heralds radio and television news bulletins. In Edinburgh, the custom of firing a cannon on the battlements of the city's castle to proclaim the arrival of 1pm, formerly installed to relate the time to ships in the Firth of Forth, continues to echo across the city each day. These sonic rhythms of the everyday are also evocatively conjured in musical endeavours to capture the mood of place at distinctive times. The Indian classical music tradition of performing morning, twilight, and midnight ragas resonates with the tone of the time by expressing distinctive rhythms and melodies. In a different musical register, the late night / early morning sounds of the post-clubbing atmospheres of South London are evoked on Burial's 2007 cd, the melancholic *Untrue*, with snatches of music, conversation, vehicles and other sounds that occur well after dark, supplementing low key beats.

The rhythmic sounds of place also extend beyond the diurnal to mark distinctive occasions within the annual cycle of events. In the UK, consider the summer bank holiday, where noisy crowds move into streets, cars clog up the roads of esteemed rural settings, and children's voices resound through the back gardens of residential districts. Less festive commemorations, including those performed during important national(ist) ceremonies, might include the sober incantations of religious or political figures, the reverberating drumbeats, bugles and drums of marching soldiers, and the precise sounds of horses' hooves.

More celebratory auditory rhythms are generated at the proliferating numbers of festivals that are colonizing the summer months of many European locations, part of the intensified 'eventification' through which local commercial and political interests seek to attract ever-larger numbers of tourists, shoppers, investors and new inhabitants (Jakob, 2012). Large and small music festivals and art-oriented events offer a series of rhythms through which participants' bodies may align. This highlights how bodily capacities to sense rhythm are conjoined as audiences or those participating in a festive procession or ritual, clap, walk, and sing in unison, forming a temporary collective body that together reinforce the pulses and cadences of the event (Duffy et al., 2011). Music may significantly intensify such collective participation in and experience of rhythm. For instance, in discussing the resonances afforded by popular music at festivals, Jackson discusses how '(T)he deeply sensual quality of the bass, its material succulence, penetrates the flesh like an alternative heartbeat that initiates a new physicality' (Jackson, 2004: 29). He further highlights how 'intoxication, the crowds and the music all work together to create new physical and emotional rhythms that underpin an alternative experience of self-in-world' (ibid: 30). The powerful rhythms produced at such events may disorient and repel those unused to them, perhaps those who prefer more sedate forms of entertainment and social engagement. However, enthusiastic participants are key co-producers of these rhythms, prepared to contribute and ready through prior anticipation to engage in the pulsing rituals that combine to produce potent atmospheres (Edensor, 2012). For example, both the highly organized rhythms of running, race management, broadcasting and policing, and the more festive rhythms of drummers and bystanders coalesce during sporting mega-events such as the Berlin Marathon (Edensor and Larsen, 2017). More broadly, like football fans who chant and clap rhythmically in order to encourage their team's performance on the field, rhythmic co-production facilitates a sense of absorption in the occasion. However, as Duffy et al. (2011) point out, a failure to co-ordinate and synchronize the order of events can generate a sense of arrhythmia and the consequent dissatisfaction and detachment of festival-goers.

Indeed, particular sounds can puncture the usual unfolding of predictable rhythms. The insistent, blaring pulse of emergency vehicles, felt in the body and exciting attention, produce speculation about what it is that has caused the urgency conveyed by the sound. Less dramatically, during summer afternoons, the melodic chimes of ice-cream vans grab the attention of children, and during the build-up to elections, vehicles crisscross urban space to broadcast their slogans.

An utterly transformed soundscape can be produced by responses to unexpected and sudden events that break the usual rhythms of place, such as a storm or heavy snowfall. The thick snow that fell in Manchester at midday after many years of absence was greeted by a sudden outpouring of people to walk and play, the air resounding with shouts and muffled footsteps. The customary roar of cars was silenced as they were suddenly coerced into a crawl by the treacherous conditions. In a different context, when Manchester City won the Premier League title league in May 2012, the noise that typically drifts away following the match as fans leave the stadium was spread to many areas of the city, as jubilant fans celebrated long into the night, drinking in large congregations outside bars and pubs.

This latter example highlights how the rhythms of sound are distributed across designated areas, with the stadium a temporary venue for rhythmic chanting and clapping on match days (Edensor, 2015). Places are composed of clusters of rhythmic hubbub and quiescence. It is expected that the din of noisy revellers may echo into the night in central entertainment districts but not in residential areas. The vivid sense of moving away from major thoroughfares to become surrounded by the quieter rhythms of the city's side streets and back alleys is a commonplace urban experience. Likewise, besides offering visual and tactile relief from urban clamour, parks are intended to foster a less harsh soundscape, with birdsong and the swaying of trees masking the urban racket beyond. The rhythms of lawnmowers, the clink of crown green bowls and the quack of ducks is accompanied by the laughter of children, and the creaking of roundabouts and swings in playgrounds. The quieter auditory rhythms of British suburbia perhaps commence with the clink and rattle of early morning milk and postal deliveries, followed by the hum of cars as commuting drivers leave their homes for work and children are driven to school. The day then settles into a quieter configuration of low noise until the accumulating sounds that herald the return from school and work, before a settling into hushed evenings.

Certain areas of the city seem to compress the articulation of different rhythms, most notably train and bus stations. For instance, at Piccadilly station in Manchester, the sounds of trains sliding into and away from platforms, intermittent loudspeaker announcements and the surging footsteps of disembarking and embarking passengers are supplemented by the slower murmurs produced by those waiting for tickets, the gleeful cries of reacquaintance and the ceaseless, even mechanical swish of the escalators. In a different vein, signature jingles aid orientation on many of Tokyo's subway stations, contributing sonic identities to places and adding to the rhythmic structure of journeys.

Besides the diverse rhythms of particular urban spaces in any city, different cities are sites for extremely diverse and contrasting sonic rhythms. At variance to the rather regulated rhythms of many western cities is the soundscape of the Indian bazaar (Edensor, 2000). Here, sounds that would likely be minimised or banished in European and North American urban settings are free to combine, startling those unused to such sonic irruptions and rhythms, perhaps producing something akin to what Simmel describes as neurasthenia in his account of the sensory overload experienced by inhabitants of the early modern city. Since many animals are allowed to roam free, the utterances of cows, monkeys, and goats carry across space, along with human chatter and the cries of street-traders, religious orators, and political speakers. Diverse forms of traffic – bicycles, rickshaws and motorbikes, bullock carts, buses, lorries, and cars – collectively compose a shifting mechanized pulse. In addition, chiming temple temples and the *adhans* emitted from mosques must compete with loud Bollywood tunes that often dominate sonic experience.

The changing sonic rhythms of place

In addition to revealing the distinctive temporal phases and spaces of place, sonic rhythms also evoke the historical transformations of place. For instance, Alain Corbin (1998) shows how in 19th-century France, the recurrent chiming of the church bells constituted the most regular sonic human intervention in daily life, signifying regular periods of worship and festivity, as well as momentous occasions, warnings, and calls to congregate. Church bells continue to mark Sunday service in Christian settings but do not stand out from the soundscape of place as distinctively as they once did, having to compete with a host of contemporary rhythmic sounds that would have been absent. Similarly, the qualities of the muezzin's frequent calls to prayer in Islamic places, drifting across space five times daily, has changed in many cases with the use of amplified electronic recordings.

For those cities that emerged through industrial production, the sounds of manufacture (together with smells, sights and air quality) generated by cotton, iron, coal, shipbuilding, chemical and engineering production forged distinctive rhythms that marked the daily timetable of place. The relentless pulsating of cotton looms, rotation of pit winding gear, and clang of riveters, as well as numerous mechanical sounds and the shouts of workers escaped from these sites of production to resonate more widely. In many industrial locations, factory sirens would announce the commencement or cessation of shifts, as captured in Arseny Avraamov's remarkable *Symphony Of Factory Sirens*, staged in Baku in 1922. Similarly, in coastal settings the rhythms produced by the pulsing beams of light emanating from lighthouses were complemented by the regular boom of the foghorn, warning ships of maritime perils in foggy conditions. In an era of GPS and satellite technology, lighthouses have largely been decommissioned and consigned to heritage status, curtailing the luminous and sonic pulsations that formerly constituted powerful components of the rhythms of place. To commemorate the demise of the working life of Souter Lighthouse in South Shields, a Foghorn requiem, devised by Lise Autogena and Joshua Portway and composed by Orlando Gough, featured the lighthouse's foghorn and those of 50 ships that gathered in the adjacent North Sea, together with a local brass band (Autogena and Portway, 2018).

Industrial sonic rhythms are now largely absent not only due to the absence of production but also because of the intensification of the regulation of sound. Noise abatement policies have minimised many of the most disruptive auditory rhythms though conflicts over the continuous noise of traffic and aircraft persist. These tendencies to quieten the city have culminated in the redistribution of sonic rhythms so that quieter, though no less insistent sounds predominate. Some attribute this slow transformation to the dominance of commercial and bureaucratic forces that colonise everyday time and space, with Kanngieser contending that. 'changing soundscapes of eviction and construction evidence changing distributions of power and governance' (Kanngieser, 2015: 81).

In exemplifying this, Jean Paul Thibaud (2014: 2–4) suggests that increasingly, 'explicit strategies to sensibilize inhabited space' transform the media through which we experience the world, the sounds, odours, lights, colours, temperature and air quality that shape the conditions under which we apprehend place. As he asserts, 'urban design no longer just focuses on objects but also what is between the objects'. Thus designers attempt to produce affective tonalities, exemplified in such qualities as a 'soothing sonority', 'lively square' or 'heavy odour'. This appears to resonate with Trevor Boddy's (1992: 123–124) earlier depiction of what he terms the 'analogous city' in which a 'new urban prosthetics' incorporates 'incessant whirring', 'mechanical breezes', 'vaguely reassuring icons', 'trickling fountains' and 'low murmurings' that filter out 'troubling smells and winds'. Besides the rhythms instantiated by the muzak played in lifts, enclavic holiday resorts and shopping malls, and the saturation of festive songs to underscore the advent of the Christmas season in commercial spaces, the car has also increasingly become a sensorially controlled environment with the accelerated advancement of 'auditory cocooning' (Bijsterveld, 2010).

In contemporary cities and elsewhere, a familiar, rhythmic soundtrack to life is the constant background hum of vehicular traffic, frequently complemented by airplane and train noise, but intensified at particular periods of the day. Nevertheless, so prevalent are these sounds of mobile rhythms that they are rarely noticed. Yet this mechanical throb is of recent origin, and has certainly become more prevalent with the growing number of vehicles on roads. At the edges of my street in Manchester lies a remnant of the road that existed a hundred or so years ago, surfaced with cobbles. Ideally suited to gain purchase for the numerous horse and carts that plied their trade along Victorian and early 20th-century thoroughfares, cobbled surfaces would have afforded a wholly different, distinctive mundane sonic rhythm constituted by cartwheels clattering along and the clip clop of horses' hooves, a soundscape utterly eclipsed by the ubiquity of mechanised vehicles. Indeed, the increasing use of streets as single-purpose channels of movement organized to offer seamless passage for vehicles (Sennett, 1994) has reduced the rhythmic sonic diversity that once persisted. Along central urban streets of the 1920s and 1930s in British working-class streets, a medley of traders, entertainers and musicians, children playing – including the incantations of girls' skipping games (Labelle, 2008) – would have contributed to a richly rhythmic urban sound.

Staying within my neighbourhood, older folk insist that the dawn chorus of today is a pale echo of the melodious clamour of yesteryear. While a few blackbirds and robins produce isolated calls in the early morning, many of the other birds that would have accompanied them, so the elderly neighbours claim, are no longer present. Instead, the most frequent non-human auditory rhythms are provided by the harsh call of the magpie, the chatter of grey squirrels, and the meowing of the local cats that have proliferated in recent years, perhaps acting to reduce the avian diversity of the past.

Yet certain auditory rhythms, like smells, have the potency to bring to memory sharp impressions of yesteryear. For example, the short-lived 1970s craze for *clackers*, two hard plastic balls attached to a string that could be manoeuvred to swing up and down rapidly to collide, produced a piercing, rhythmic clacking sound that resonated across British school playgrounds, before they were banned on the grounds of safety (the balls could cause fractures to wrists and hands), is now occasionally heard following the production of safer versions of the toy. More evidently, particular musical rhythms can also recall certain historical periods that capture an atmosphere of a particular event or period of time. The first time I went to Los Angeles in 1972, the ubiquitous *Joker*, by the Steve Miller Band, seemed to be playing everywhere, adding to the alterity and unfamiliar ambience I sensed during a first encounter with this most singular of American cities. Similarly, on my first visit to the Notting Hill Carnival, the calypso rhythms of Explainer's *Lorraine*, seemingly the theme song of that year's celebrations, repeatedly cajoled dancers and bystanders into movement. Such sonic rhythmic experiences are inextricably linked with memories of place and event.

Contestation and the mutability of sonic rhythms

The increasing prevalence of commercial and bureaucratic sonic rhythms underlines the capacity of some to impose and install rhythms of all sorts on place. Thus the regular auditory rhythms of place inevitably signify the power of certain people to normalize the sensory qualities of place, to distribute the auditorily sensible (Rancière, 2006) and instantiate forms of common sense and sensing. Yet though many of the commonplace sonic rhythms of place are installed by political, commercial, and institutional powers, things are always liable to break down, with blackouts, traffic gridlock, and strikes causing arrhythmic sounds. Moreover, dissonant actors may produce their own sounds that contest the ordinary, regulated urban soundscape, as, for instance, with the cacophonous, harsh beats of the 'pots and pans' protestors in recent urban demonstrations (Hendy, 2014).

A further effect of the power to install rhythms on space is through what Lefebvre terms 'dressage', the disciplining of the body through repetitive rhythms so as to produce a certain automatism. The rhythmic march of disciplinary military drills, supplemented by brass bands, in ceremonial parades testify to this somatic regulation. However, other similarly embodied pursuits, equally solicited through repetitive entrainment, may articulate more pleasurable sounds. Shannon Hensley shows how through prolonged practice in dancing rumba, Cubans absorb rhythm into their bodies. Also consider the rhythmic slaps and shouts of cheerleaders, or the clapping and chanting of football fans as they make their way to the match. Other groups adopt auditory tactics to assert their own sonic identities on space, as, for instance, Labelle (2008) details in his account of the heavy, mega-bassbeats favoured by Mexican-American youths to imprint their presence on the streets of Los Angeles, saturating space with rhythmic intensities. We might also refer to the use of i-pods and other personal stereo devices through which listeners may move to their own beat as they travel across place, providing private rhythms that set the pace for daily actions and often bypass dominant auditory rhythms (Bull, 2000; 2005).

In a different context, Bandak explains that the city is often 'a place of dense cohabitation ... in which different attempts at making it a place of continuous belonging are constantly at play', exemplifying his argument with a discussion of how Christians claim space in predominantly Muslim Damascus through sonic repetitions and reiterations in religious ceremonies and parades (2014: s259).

In this chapter, I have endeavoured to show how a combination of sonic rhythms gives a distinctive texture to place, contributing to the affective intensities and sensory orientations of belonging. This recognition also highlights how our bodies cannot be conceived as detached from place but are folded into spatial being and knowledge (Duffy et al., 2011) into a relationship with place. Extended inhabitation and enduring familiarity means that they may often be overlooked and only noticed when they change or lamented when they disappear. Yet though these auditory rhythms may collectively solicit a stable, reliable sense of belonging for a spell, they are liable to dissipate or abruptly terminate, like our own bodies and so many other elements within a vital, volatile world. For in focusing upon a range of location, I have undercut any suggestion that there are normative rhythmic soundscapes and emphasised that they are shaped by particular historical, social, and cultural contexts, which they, in turn, articulate.

References

Avraamov, A. (1922) Symphony Of Factory Sirens, www.youtube.com/watch?v=Kq_7w9RHvpQ

Amin, A. and Thrift, N. (2002) *Cities: Reimagining the Urban*, Cambridge: Polity.

Autogena, L. and Portway, J. (2018) 'Foghorn Requiem', in V. Strang, T. Edensor and J. Puckering (eds) *From the Lighthouse: Interdisciplinary Reflections on Light*, London: Routledge.

Bandak, A. (2014) 'Of refrains and rhythms in contemporary Damascus: urban space and Christian-Muslim coexistence', *Current Anthropology*, 55 (supplement 10): s248–261.

Bijsterveld, K. (2010) Aucoustic cocooning: how the car became a place to unwind', *The Senses and Society*, 5(2): 189–211.

Boddy, T (1992) 'Underground and overhead: Building the analogous city', in Sorkin, M (ed) *Variations on a Theme Park*, New York: Hill and Wang.

Bull, M. (2000) *Sounding out the City*, Oxford: Berg.

Bull, M. (2005) 'No dead air! The ipod and the culture of mobile listening', *Leisure Studies*, 24(4): 343–355.

Corbin, A. (1998) *Village Bells: The Culture of the Senses in the Nineteenth-Century French Countryside*, New York: Columbia University Press.

Crang, M. (2001) 'Rhythms of the city: temporalised space and motion', in J. May and N. Thrift (eds) *Timespace: Geographies of Temporality*, London: Routledge.

Duffy, M., Waitt, G., Gorman-Murray, A. and Gibson, C. (2011) 'Bodily rhythms: corporeal capacities to engage with festival spaces', *Emotion, Space and Society*, 4(1): 17–24.

Edensor, T. (2000) 'Moving through the city', in D. Bell and A. Haddour (eds) *City Visions*, London: Prentice Hall.

Edensor, T. (ed) (2010) *Geographies of Rhythm: Nature, Place, Mobilities and Bodies*, Farnham: Ashgate.

Edensor, T. (2012) 'Illuminated atmospheres: anticipating and reproducing the flow of affective experience in Blackpool', *Environment and Planning D: Society and Space*, 30:1103–1122.

Edensor, T. (2015) 'Producing atmospheres at the match: fan cultures, commercialisation and mood management', *Emotion, Space and Society*, 15: 82–89.

Edensor, T. and Larsen, J. (2017) 'Rhythmanalysing marathon running: "'A drama of rhythms'"', *Environment and Planning: Economy and Space*, 50(3): 730–746.

Hendy, D. (2014) *Noise: A Human History of Sound and Listening*, London: Profile.

Jackson, P. (2004) *Inside Clubbing: Sensual Experiments in the Art of Being Human*, Oxford: Berg.

Jakob, I. (2012) 'The eventification of place: Urban development and experience consumption in Berlin and New York City', *European Urban and Regional Studies*, 20(4): 447–459.

Kanngieser, A. (2015) 'Geopolitics and the anthropocene: five propositions for sound', *GeoHumanities*, 1(1): 80–85.

Labelle, B. (2008) 'Pump up the bass: Rhythm, cars and auditory scaffolding', *The Senses and Society*, 3(2): 187–204.

Lefebvre, H. (2004) *Rhythmanalysis: Space, Time and Everyday Life*, trans. S. Elden and G. Moore, London: Continuum.

Lippard, L. (1997) *The Lure of the Local: Senses of Place in a Multicentered Society*, New York: The New Press.

Mels, T. (2004) 'Lineages of a geography of rhythms', in T. Mels (ed) *Reanimating Places: A Geography of Rhythms*, Aldershot: Ashgate.

Noble, G. (2004) 'Accumulating being', *International Journal of Cultural Studies*, 7(2): 233–256.

Rancière, J. (2006) *The Politics of Aesthetics: The Distribution of the Sensible*, London: Continuum.

Seamon, D. (1979) *A Geography of the Lifeworld*, London: Croom Helm.

Sennett, R. (1994) *Flesh and Stone*, London: Faber.

Thibaud, J.-P. (2014) 'The backstage of urban ambiances: When atmospheres pervade everyday experience', *Emotion, Space and Society*, 15: 39–46

Wunderlich, F. (2010) 'The aesthetics of place-temporality in everyday urban space: the case of Fitzroy Square', in T. Edensor, (ed) *Geographies of Rhythm: Nature, Place, Mobilities and Bodies*, Farnham: Ashgate.

16

GEOGRAPHIES OF SILENCE

Bennett Hogg

Space and place, silence, and sound

Since at least the time of the ancient Greeks, philosophers have tried to grasp how the particular and the general relate to one another in the fields of human perception and experience. There is a strong tradition that space exists as it were *a priori*, a three-dimensional emptiness that is subsequently filled with "places". In a similar way, silence is understood as a background absence within which sounds can occur. In the following discussions I aim to first of all draw upon three different phenomenologically informed accounts of space and place in order to challenge the notion that space precedes place, and in so doing put in place a way of thinking about human experience more generally that is strongly phenomenological in orientation. I then will confront the phenomenologically problematic separation of seeing and hearing, arguing that our experience is profoundly transmodal, and that in our experience of place, seeing and hearing work together to generate a sense of place, to the extent that silence, rather than being an absolute quality analogous to conventional understandings of space, is something that can be perceived and even generated by looking. In this I shall draw on a range of different cultural materials, including literature and music, as well as my own experiences framed in terms of phenomenological enquiry.

In *Human Space* [1963], Bollnow notes that time has been philosophised more than space, a bias that comes down to the inescapably anthropocentric nature of knowledge: "Compared to time, which concerns the innermost centre of humanity, space seemed philosophically less rewarding, because it seemed to belong only to the outer environment of mankind" (Bollnow, 2011, p. 16). Bollnow is at pains to deconstruct this familiar Cartesian position, taking a phenomenological stance with respect to space, writing that we would be

> expressing ourselves carelessly if we say that life takes place 'in space'. Human beings are not present in space as an object ... is present in a box, and they are not related to space as though in the first place there could be anything like a subject without space. Rather, life consists originally in this relationship with space and can therefore not be separated from it even in thought ... space is [not] simply there, independent of the human being.
>
> *(Bollnow, 2011, pp. 23–24)*

His distinction between "mathematical" and "experiential" space are both included in this relationship, but the latter names what we might call the phenomenological understanding of space, the former an understanding of space as an abstraction, leading to the notion of space as an empty, homogenous quality (Bollnow, 2011, pp. 15–25). A similarly positivist understanding of time as an empty and homogenous quality in which events simply accumulate is of course critiqued by Benjamin in his late *Theses on the Philosophy of History* (Benjamin, 1999 [1940], pp. 252–255).

In a more recent phenomenological account of space, Casey makes related observations where space is traditionally understood as an abstract quality, and place as something like Bollnow's "experienced" space. For Casey, as for phenomenology in general, perception is "the crux in matters of place". This is an understanding of place as a series of interconnected, specific, and experiential qualities, marked with meanings that may be mnemic, culturally shared, imagined, or individual. Traditional metaphysics sets up a powerful (and still-influential) paradigm that place must emerge *from and within* space, where the latter stands for an absolute, transcendent substantiality which precedes any instance of place. Place, in this view, is a secondary, subjective quality superimposed upon space understood as abstract and objective. This, however, is far from being consistent with a phenomenological view; as phenomenologists we have, in short, "no choice but to begin with experience" (Casey, 1997, p. 16). This being the case, how can space pre-exist experience in any useful way? Does space, as an abstract quality, not emerge as secondary to the concrete experience of place? Space, then, is an abstracting *from experience*, rather than a transcendent, pre-existent, abstract quality. In Casey's view place is general and space is a particular construction subsequent to place (Casey, 1997, pp. 16–17).

A third phenomenologically informed perspective helps to round this out. Ingold, as an anthropologist, questions the traditional, Enlightenment ideology that form arises as an abstract, mental idea that is then imposed onto inert, otherwise formless matter. This is emblematised in the "ancient inclination in Western thought" to think of cultural embodiment as "a movement of *inscription*, whereby some pre-existing pattern, template or programme … is 'realised' in a substantive medium" (Ingold, 2000, p. 193). However, Ingold asserts that

> the forms of artefacts are not given in advance but are rather generated in and through the practical movement of one or more skilled agents in their active, sensuous engagement with the material … [artefacts] emerge … within the relational contexts of the mutual involvement of people and their environments.
>
> *(Ingold, 2000, p. 88)*

The notion of space as an abstract, pre-existent tabula rasa of inert substance waiting to be formed by imagined or reasoned design into "place" is then clearly not something a phenomenologically informed exploration could sustain. In one of the foundational texts of a phenomenological geography Tilley writes: "Space has no substantial essence in itself, but only has a relational significance, created through relations between people and places" (Tilley, p. 11). Space as a general and undifferentiated substrate that place is made *out of* – that which is left behind when you take place away, in a sense – cannot be accounted for in the work of either of the authors mentioned so far.

There is a metaphysical congruency between space and silence, insofar as both have traditionally been framed as Ur-conditions prior to the construction of place upon space, or the imposition of sound over silence. R. Murray Schafer, for example, writes of silence as "the great and beautiful backdrop over which our actions are sketched and without which they would be incomprehensible" (Schafer, 1994, p. 258). The hyperbole of this statement aside (actions as *incomprehensible* without silence?), it marks out an almost ubiquitous conceptualisation of silence as background, as a primal state over which information is "sketched", what is left behind when the sound stops. Space and silence seem like pre-ordained conditions, whereas place and sound seem like things *done*, figures against a ground, forms inscribed into inert substance. What if we reverse this logic, though, as Casey and Ingold have done with human relations to space/place?

If, as I have already implied, silence is *not* an absolute, general, and undifferentiated substance but a perceptual phenomenon, including silence within the continuum of the field of sound – rather than as its antithesis – is unproblematic. As we increase the frequency of an oscillator beyond about 18KHz, for example, a sonograph will show us that there are still sound waves, but we can no longer perceive them. The same situation pertains with amplitude, and the threshold of perceptual silence here is affected by the energy of the signal, the distance of the listener from the signal, and the physical state of medium through which the signal passes. The sound of a struck bell may seem to have died out until we place our ear closer, and even when "silent" sound can still be detected technologically.

Silence, then, marks the threshold of perception within the continuum of sound rather than its radical and absolute absence. In Ferneyhough's *Second String Quartet* Fitch differentiates between "literal and 'functional' silence" where "the latter [permits] certain *glissando* sounds to filter through" (Fitch, 2014, p. 300). Unstable with respect to pitch, and played using bowing techniques such as *sul ponticello* and *col legno trattato* that destablise the instruments' familiar timbres, these *glissandi* seem like musical sounds that are already "eroded", and on their way to silence. The poetic conceit that we are hearing them *through* silence, as it were, only serves to deepen the idea that silence is a phenomenon within the field of sound, not the antithesis of sound. This last point is crucial for my argument – it is not simply the case that we need to have sound in order to *differentiate* and thus bring into being silence. Silence, as I conceive it here, is both less absolute and more mutable than "literal" silence as, indeed, are the boundaries of such a literal silence as I have proposed above.

That silence is integral to music is, of course, nothing new. Cage identifies Satie and Webern as having had the insight that duration is the only parameter able to account for all of music because only duration can encompass silence; silence has no pitch, timbre, articulation, or dynamic (Cage, 1987, p. 63). This has tended to support notions that musical silence tends very strongly towards the temporal end of the space-time continuum. Indeed, silences in music very often determine rhythm, pacing, articulation, and so forth, predominantly temporal aspects of music. There is a danger, though, that the striking veracity of Cage's insight forecloses alternative possibilities for silence: silence, contra Cage, *may* in fact include dynamics and timbre, if we shift the approach from an absolute to a relational one, and from one that sees sound and silence as mutual opposites towards one that understands them as contingencies within a continuum.

In the late 1940s, Schaeffer demonstrated, with his experiment of the *cloche coupée* (the "cut bell") that the perceived timbre of a sound cannot be accounted for only with respect to the "vertical" organisation of its constituent harmonic partials, but is also determined by the way in which the sound is initiated. If one makes a recording of a bell, and then removes the initial attack, the resulting sound is more or less unrecognisable as a bell; a recording of a piano note treated this way sounds more like a flute than a piano. Perhaps the most significant development of Schaeffer's discovery has been in the evolving ideas of Smalley, for whom spectromorphology, as a means for organising sound into music, brings into dynamic relations the physical and the temporal aspects of sounds (Smalley, 1986). Taking this a step further, I would argue that silences have timbre, not in the physical, spectral sense, but insofar as their effect is determined, like the timbre of physical sound, as much by how they are initiated and ended as by their "substance".

Can we separate a silence from its initiation? Isn't it true that *qualities* of silence are as deter-mined – and here I speak phenomenologically – by how they are arrived at? Two silences of exactly the same duration and sound pressure levels will "sound" different if one is the result of a sudden extinction of a sound wave, the other arrived at after a slow fading of the sound. Not only will the subjective experience of their duration be affected by how these silences are initiated, but the emotional and associative factors of the silences will be quite dramatically different – a sudden silence may sound aggressive, or stunned, whereas a silence arrived at after a fading of the sound could be melancholic, valedictory, or even just musically "right". Just as every sound has a starting transient that is part of its characteristic spectromorphology, so too do silences. If sound is an ecosystem rather than a string of dissociated and discrete events, every sound leaves behind *its own silence* when it ends; to philosophise an ontology of silences, they are *plural* qualities rather than portions of an absolute quantity, and they arise with and are part of the world of sounds. Ontologically, they are presences rather than absences.

In his famous experiment in search of silence in the anechoic chamber, Cage can hear his blood and nervous system sounding, and he arrives from this experience at the impossibility of silence. Voegelin, though, finds the embodied experience of silence leads her to the tantalizing suggestion that silence opens up a form of dialogue. Alone, indoors, in a snow-covered land-scape, she finds that her listening is "a generative process not of noises external to me, but from inside, from the body, where my subjectivity is at the centre of the sound production, audible to myself". For Voegelin, this experience suggests that "Silence is not the absence of sound but the beginning of listening", and she draws a strong distinction between her experience and Cage's account of the anechoic chamber. Rather than a sonic "vacuum" that "denies external sounds a path to the ear and the sound of blood pumping through the body and the tingling of the nervous system starts to be audible … the external sounds are so small … that they come to play with my body, close up and intimate" (Voegelin, 2010, p. 83). This stimulates a kind of close, attentive listening through which the inside of the body re-emerges as a sound source, evoking something like an improvisation between internal bodily sounds and tiny sounds in the external world, driven by a particular sense of silence.

Silence is also clearly a spatial as well as a temporal phenomenon, both metaphorically and literally. Voegelin's silence is already geographical, situating insides and outsides, engaging with climatic conditions, architecture, and subjective, embodied consciousness. The dialogue she points towards is reminiscent of musical improvising, and it is suggestive too that we often talk about "making space" or "placing" sounds in improvised – but also in composed – music. To make space, musically, we often fall silent, or are instructed by the notation to fall silent. In pol-yphonic music these spaces we make are located rather than absolute, relative spaces, emplaced silences, within a texture that may in fact be constantly sounding. If I am singing the bass part in a madrigal, a rest in the notation of the bass part "causes" a silent place in the music to emerge, a place that is metaphorical in the temporal dimension, but concrete in the spatial dimension; there is a silence, momentarily, in the physical place where I am standing that is surrounded by sound, and which is maintained until I start singing again. We tend to talk about there being a silence here or there, rather than now or then. I have heard conductors, for example, say "there is a silence here in the tenor line", here rather than a silence "now", partially because of nota-tion (the conductor might point to a place in her score), but also because the silence *is* here, not *now*; there is still sound in the "now" but not in the "here", the space, real (where the tenors are standing) or virtual (the space in the music), where the silence is located. The other voices continue to sound around the silence left by the tenor. That silence is spatial in a more complex sense than that elucidated by Cage, follows from this.

Spatial silence(s)

Ann Rosén and Sten-Olof Hellström's *Rumslige Tystnader/Spatial Silence* (2005) is an interactive sound installation that developed from research at KTH, Stockholm between 2001 and 2003.[1] The project began from speculation into the practical application of the phenomenon whereby silence can be theoretically generated by wave cancellation, the generation of inversions of soundwaves present in a particular place which then cancel out those soundwaves and produce temporary zones of silence. The complexity of sound waves, and their almost constant mutability, means that actually achieving this under everyday conditions is currently an impossibility, but Hellström and Rosén developed a free-standing installation in which small pockets of "silence" could be discovered by the inquisitive and patient listener.

Ten loudspeakers are attached to a scaffolding cube. In another part of the room a large bass speaker emits a constant, low-frequency drone. A microphone in the room monitors this sound and, via a Max/MSP patch, informs the generation of a sound wave designed to cancel out the drone, emitted by the scaffolding speakers. However, room acoustics and reflection means that a mathematically "perfect" cancellation is not possible, but small "pockets" of silence are formed inside the cube of loudspeakers at points where complete phase cancellation occurs. The listener must move around inside of the cube searching for these "spatial silences". A sudden drop in the amplitude of the drone indicates the proximity of one of these spots, and the listener can find themselves drawn into a place no more than 30 or 40 centimetres wide where for a moment the constant drone disappears.

These silent places, as I imagine them, are reminiscent of the silent places I have mentioned above in connection with polyphonic music. There is a distinction, though, in the way in which Hellström and Rosén's silences are experienced by the listener. It is unremarkable to be in a room filled with sound, and for that sound to stop momentarily. It is a very different experience when one's own movement and intention uncovers silence and can then move in and out of the silence more or less at will. The knowledge that the sound continues *outside* of the pocket of silence, as it were, is confirmed by a slight movement of the head that proves its continuity exterior to the silent space within the installation.

In his autobiographical writing published posthumously as *Outline* in 1949, the British painter Paul Nash exemplifies the ways in which movement in a landscape can go hand in hand with the experience of spatial silence. Walking home as a child, he writes how crossing a stile into woodland after open fields is an entry into a silent and listening world.

> Whereas in the open fields [the path] seemed to run unhindered at top speed … it now appeared to falter and creep along in the twilight of the wood. … I, too, was influenced by the atmosphere of the wood. Here I trod more circumspectly, glancing from side to side. It was very quiet and still. Outside, the fields and sky, on a fine day, might be shouting at the tops of their voices, but in the wood everything seemed to be listening. (Nash, 1949, p. 40)

Earlier in his childhood he recalls being taken to Kensington Gardens by his nurse, where after an everyday life in which everything was circumscribed and controlled "[w]ith a shout and a sudden turn of speed you had broken through the invisible barrier … [Kensington] Gardens were my first taste of the country. Here I became aware of trees, felt the grass for the first time, saw an expanse of water, *listened to a new kind of silence*" (Nash, 1949, p. 34, emphasis added). Nash's writing makes it clear – "a new kind of silence" – that silence is a relational quality, coloured by the transition from one place to another, by the embodied experience of crossing thresholds, and by changes to his personal, subjective disposition consequent on this movement out of which the experience of "silence" emerges. In the case of Walser's short story, *The Walk*, the silence of a woodland sets off hyperbolic imaginings in which silence is "inhaled … and whose virtues I drank and quaffed with due ceremony", suggesting that "all kinds of inaudible voices echo and sound" along with "music out of the primeval world" (Walser, 2013, pp. 71–72). I suggest that this is not *just* poetic expression (though that is part of it) but that the reports of such experiences of silence point towards its transmodality.

Transmodal silence

I have been gradually steering away, throughout this chapter, from the notion that silence is a straightforward absence of sound waves towards a phenomenologically informed position in which silence is a factor within the ecosystem of our worldly experience, a geographical factor which, along with multiple others, serves as the material from which we have life worlds and selves, selves with which we experience our worlds. Having already outlined ways in which movement and intentionality are, under certain conditions, indispensable to silence, I would now like to focus explicitly on the transmodal aspects of our geographical experience of silence.

Though the technologies that most of us live with on a daily basis have played a major role in separating vision and hearing (radio, recordings, personal stereos, etc.) it is important to resist ideologies that seek to consolidate and reify such separations.[2] Taking the interconnectedness of seeing, hearing, and the other senses into account leads me to the inescapable conclusion that just as our experience of sound is transmodal, so is our experience of silence. Tanizaki, for example, illustrates this in his classic *In Praise of Shadows* where he discusses the sense of presence created by something as simple as a tastefully positioned alcove in a traditional Japanese house. A simple, empty space draws light in such a way that shadows form in the emptiness.

> There is nothing more. And yet, when we gaze into the darkness that gathers behind the cross beam, around the flower vase, beneath the shelves, though we know perfectly well it is mere shadow, we are overcome with the feeling that in this small corner of the atmosphere there reigns complete and utter silence; that here in the darkness immutable tranquillity holds sway. The "mysterious Orient" of which Westerners speak probably refers to the uncanny silence of these dark places.
>
> *(Tanizaki, 2001, pp. 32–33)*

Without the careful design of the house to draw shadows into such an alcove – and through this to evoke silence and tranquillity – the alcove would be "a mere void". That it is *not* a void is because shadows and silence fill it with presence, mediating but also engendering one another.

The absence of shadow, or indeed any other visual references, in the disorientation of a white-out blizzard in the Cairngorm Mountains, makes "[s]cale and distance impossible to discern" for Robert Macfarlane. He does not mention sound in describing this experience, but the transmodal dimension to any instance of vision extends here into the near negation of proprioception through the elision of normal vision: in the blizzard "[s]pace is depthless. Even gravity's hold feels loosened: slope and fall lines can only be inferred by the tilt of blood in the skull. It felt, for that astonishing hour up on Ben a' Bhuird, as if we were all flying in white space" (Macfarlane, 2016, p. 67). If effects of vision can seem to negate the effects of gravity, and to fill alcoves with a tangible presence of silence via seeing shadows, it would seem that they offer productive places from which to investigate silence and space.

Silence – or near silence – is experienced transmodally in W. G. Sebald's *Vertigo*. Lying awake in the early evening by the shores of Lake Garda the massive presence of the mountains diminishes the loud sounds of the bars in the town over the lake to "a mere dull pulsation, … a negligible disturbance measured against the huge bulk of the mountain that towered so high and steep above the quivering lights of the town" (Sebald, 2002 [1990], p. 92). Though this is not a silence, as such, the mediating effect of the visible – almost tangible – presence of the mountain is able to transmodally dwarf the otherwise insistent, loud music of the lakefront. More acutely, emerging from a long winter walk in a forest back near the author's home in Bavaria, "as the whitish-grey snow fell, its silence completely extinguishing what little pallid colour there was in those wet deserted fields" (Sebald, 2002 [1990], p. 178), verges on the synaesthetic; it is the *silence* of the snow that bleaches out the colour from the landscape.

The wooded valley of the River Wansbeck runs along fields near to where I live in Morpeth, Northumberland. Walking there on a windy day in November the fields to my right had recently been ploughed, and lay a dull greyish-brown under overcast, blustery skies. On my left, as I walked, the steep valley, filled with almost leafless trees, surged and roared in the wind coming from the North East, off the sea some six miles away. I stood still for a moment, and closed my eyes to surrender to what I knew would be the immersive sound of the seething woodlands, and for a few moments I felt the immersive, multidirectional power of the loud, broad band of noise. When I opened my eyes, though, I experienced something of a jolt; though the wind continued to roar on my left side, to my right the open, barren fields were silent, and I was suddenly aware that I could *see* their silence, not in any hallucinogenic or synaesthetic sense, but simply that rejoining sight to listening revealed to me the silence of the fields in contrast to the roar of the woods.

Descending the valley sides, I made my way to the wide path that runs alongside the edge of the river itself, a long, straight tunnel through closely packed and overhanging trees that in Summer obscures the sky above almost totally. To my right was the sound of the river water rushing towards me and onwards behind me over shallow rapids. Above, and around, the wind continued its attack on the trees, and again, I closed my eyes, experienced the immersive, omnidirectional surge of noise and then, on opening them again, *saw* the tunnel of silence in front of me, looked into the open space between the trees for sounds, and found none. Closing my eyes again I managed to maintain – or I imagined that I maintained – the sense of the silence in front of me, but turning once or twice around was again immersed in sound, only to find the tangible silence stretching out before me when I opened my eyes again, and looked once more down the path. I have since tried this with friends while out walking, and once it is pointed out to them, they too have experienced some personal version of this phenomenon.

Grimshaw, who among other things has worked extensively with virtual reality gaming environments, and who is thus strongly engaged with the issues around the interactions of seeing and hearing, notes that "sound is the means not to locate objects in a world but rather to locate ourselves in relation to other objects" (Grimshaw, 2015, p. 96).

> We … place (rather than find) sounds somewhere within the system of which the mind is comprised. … This locating of sound is learned and develops through early childhood into an automatic act of placement and it explains the close and cross-modal relationship to vision as we, while babies, cast around, looking for the source of a sound wave, beginning to learn the associations between movement, size, and material and sound waves.
>
> *(Grimshaw, 2015, p. 96)*

He cites the McGurk Effect, in which identical phonemes are heard differently when they are lipsynched to film of speakers, pronouncing related but different sounds. As examples of this "cross-modal effect of multi-modal stimuli ... being perceived as one event ... the ability to locate sounds other than where their sound wave sources are" (Grimshaw, 2015, p. 92) he also cites the way voices in the cinema or on television appear to originate from the mouths of the actors, even though no such sound source is actually located there. The ability, then, developed since infancy for vision to mediate and even to over-ride hearing is reasonably unproblematic to accept, and so the idea that silence is something one can *see* and, on the basis of that, can locate within an otherwise full sound world is similarly uncontroversial. Saying that, though, does not really mitigate the sense of shock and of wonder I felt on experiencing it in actuality for the first time.

Though several authors have made an excellent case for reclaiming sound, and sonic experience, for philosophy (Voegelin, 2010; Idhe, 2007 [1976]; Attali, 1985; Schafer, 1994 [1977]) the value of this work is best appreciated as a dramatic expansion of thinking about how we inhabit our worlds, rather than as "revenge" against the undeniable dominance of the visual in modern, Western cultures. As Ingold puts it separating out the sonic from the visual may have "served a useful rhetorical purpose in drawing attention to a sensory register that had been neglected relative to sight", but such an approach has now "outlived its usefulness" (Ingold, 2007, p. 10).

Taken as self-contained projects, perhaps, the work of the authors just mentioned may have sought to tip the balance between sound and image, but none of them make consistent claims for their separation. Idhe, for example, as one of the first commentators to make the case for taking sound (and voice) seriously on their own philosophical terms, notes how "[s]ilence seems revealed at first through a visual category" (the box of paperclips he can see on his desk is "mute") (Idhe, 2007 [1976], p. 50). Though "[s]ilence is the horizon of sound, yet the mute object is silently *present*" just as Tanizaki's shadowed alcove is filled with a silence that is experienced as a presence (Idhe, 2007 [1976], p. 50). The muteness of objects disappears as they move. A fly buzzes past Idhe as he stares at the box of paperclips, prompting him to remark that "'[v]isualistically' sound 'overlaps' with moving beings" (Idhe, p. 50). The silences I experienced walking beside the Wansbeck were indeed silences of immobility against swathes of noise generated by trees and water in motion, but they were also *visually generated* silences, suggesting that the "visualistic", as Idhe calls it, is not limited to motion that generates sound. Silence is also "visualistic", as his own remarks about the mute object whose silence appears to originate in the visual testify. Ultimately Idhe's call for a recalibration between the visual and the sonic is one in which their inter-determination is re-emphasised, rather than that one dominant phenomenon replaces another.

Idhe's point about the sonic overlapping visualistically with movement puts another personal experience of spatial silence into a useful context. In July 2014, I was involved in a project with Deniz Peters, of the Kunst Universität, Graz, and Sabine Vogel, a flautist with whom I have worked for several years as part of Landscape Quartet. I suffer quite badly from arthritis in my knees, and having once climbed the rough forest track to Schweizeben, the area of high Alpine pastures at the top of Weitenthal near to Brück-an-der-Mur in eastern Austria, I was reluctant to do so again and so while Sabine and Deniz took "the scenic route" I walked the Macadamised forest road alone. The route was actually no less scenic than the one the others were walking, but it was considerably more even under foot.

The weather was hot, and bright sunshine accompanied the first hour or so up the track. As it is in the mountains, though, the weather began to quickly turn, and following the smooth arrival of a heavy bank of low-lying grey cloud, the wind dropped to nothing, and, as happens when storms are in the vicinity, the birds fell quickly silent. The track up to Schweizeben is broad, and so at many points the expanse of open space that Weitenthal contains fills one's vision. As the wind, the trees, and the birds all fell silent I found myself the only moving object in an expanse of woodland, trailing along beside myself the crunch of my boots on the Macadam. In the stifling humidity, and muffled silence, I had the experience that I was walking inside of a narrow tunnel created by the sound of my own footsteps. There was literally not another sound to be heard, and the experience, despite the openness of the spaces around me, was actually claustrophobic.

And then suddenly it began to rain, huge, languid drops of rain plopping to the earth and spluttering through leaves, and in an instant the claustrophobia lifted, and the space of Weitenthal opened up again, finding a congruence between the visual and the sonic that had been suspended as I walked through the sonic tunnel of my own making. A similar, though not identical, experience happened to me in a large stand of Scots Pine inside of Thrunton Woods, Northumberland. Draughts of high breezes could be heard threading their way through the surrounding mixed woodland, approaching, veering off in other directions, but often swishing through the pines and setting up an almost oppressive high-frequency whispering above my head. At such points the intensity of the sound blocked out all other sounds, and the effect was, as on the way to Schweizeben, almost claustrophobic. But as the breeze above passed on, and the sound subsided, the bleating of the sheep I could see in fields almost a mile away, a lone car speeding along the distant A697, and the barking of a dog, invisible, on the other side of the hill were suddenly audible, accompanied by a tangible sensation of space physically opening up again, just as the sound of rain had opened up the space of Weitenthal. Silences mediate a phenomenological geography, then, by mediation of the visual sense as well as the aural, affording an experience of geographical space and place that defies straightforward ascription to one or the other senses.

The mutability of geographic silence

Edward Thomas, poet and nature writer, died in April 1917 near Arras in northern France. His connection with landscape, and with the spatial experience of landscape through walking, is amply testified to in his published poetry and prose, as well as in Macfarlane's *The Old Ways* in which Thomas figures prominently (Macfarlane, 2012). After his death a collection of writings were issued in 1928 entitled *The Last Sheaf*, and in this collection is a short autobiographic description called "Insomnia". In the early hours of the morning Thomas wakes up, unable to sleep again, as a robin begins to sing alone outside in the garden. "Beyond him the wind made a moan in the little fir-copse as of a forest in a space magically enclosed and silent, and in the intervals of his song silence fell about him like a cloak which the wind could not penetrate" (Thomas, 2011, pp. 28–29). This is not a literal silence, though, as Thomas notes a little later. That the moaning of the wind in the fir trees continues *during* the "silence" of the robin's singing is underlined as daylight begins to arrive, and "the song in the enclosed hush, and the sound of the trees beyond it, remained the same" (Thomas, 2011, p. 29). The image this evokes is of another kind of geographic, transmodal silence. The "hush" surrounding the robin seems almost like a bubble of silence within the moaning soundscape of the wind through the trees. When the bird breaks off from singing, this "hush" closes in around it like a cloak, so we can imagine that when the bird sings, the cloak of silence is pushed away again and this opening and closing of the silence takes on an almost respiring, plastic quality, an expanding and contracting envelope of "silence" situated *inside of* the continual drone of the wind, but which the wind "could not penetrate". The "cloak" acts as a garment against the force of the wind, but also against its sound in a tight concatenation of metaphors. Voegelin also invokes the image of a cloak of silence, a "transparent cloak that bares what it covers is silence as the call to listen to the world and to myself, as things in the world" (Voegelin, 2010, p. 93). Cloak here is not *only* a metaphor but seems to have an agency of its own, something that as it covers, renders bare that which is covered. The mutable, breathing cloak of silence that surrounds Thomas's robin singing before the dawn seems the perfect exemplification of this idea.

Silence, then, considered as an element of geographic space/place marks not only places where sound is absent, but places where sound can be *seen* to be absent. I have tried to show not only the transmodal aspects of silence when experienced in different ways, and in different emplacements, but also how cultural materials such as literature and music can inform and condition the experience of silence. In exploring the situatedness of silence, I have also tried to outline ways that we might think past some of the received wisdom concerning silence *per se*, that it is without timbre or dynamic, for example, as Cage proposed, and that it is an exclusively sonic phenomenon. Drawing on personal experiences of silence in landscapes, and on accounts of others' experiences, I hope to have opened up some space within which to consider, from different perspectives, both silence and place as lived elements within a wider, geographical phenomenology.

Notes

1 see http://cid.nada.kth.se/tystljud/engindex.html
2 Perhaps the most vigorous and persuasive arguments for resisting such separations of the sense come from Ingold, see Ingold, 2000, pp. 243–287 and Ingold, 2007.

References

Attali, J. (1985 [1977]). *Noise: The Political Economy of Music*. Minneapolis, MN and London: University of Minnesota Press.

Benjamin, W. (1999 [1940]). "Theses on the Philosophy of History", in *Illuminations*, ed. Hannah Arendt. London: Pimlico, pp. 245–255.

Bollnow, O. F. (2011 [1963]). *Human Space*. Trans. Christine Shuttleworth. Joseph Kohlmaier (ed.). London: Hyphen Press.

Cage, J. (1987 [1968]). "Forerunners of Modern Music", in Cage, J. *Silence*. London: Marion Boyars.

Casey, E. S. (1997). "How to get from space to place in a fairly short stretch of time: Phenomenological prolegomena". In Steven Feld and Keith H. Basso (eds.), *Senses of Place*, pp. 13–52. Santa Fe, NM: School of American Research Press.

Fitch, L. (2014). "Brian Ferneyhough's String Quartets", in *Zero to Four. Modernism and the String Quartet II: Contemporary Music Review*, 33/3, pp. 290–317.

Grimshaw, M. (2015). "A brief argument for, and summary of, the concept of sonic virtuality". *Danish Musicology Online; Special Edition 'Sound and Music Production'*. www.danishmusicologyonline.dk/arkiv/arkiv_dmo/dmo_saernummer_2015/dmo_saernummer_2015_lyd_musikproduktion_05.pdf -accessed 16:21GMT 23.12.2016

Idhe, D. (2007 [1976]). *Listening and Voice: Phenomenologies of Sound* (2nd edition). Albany, NY: SUNY Press.

Ingold, T. (2007). Against Soundscape, in *Autumn Leaves: Sound and the Environment in Artistic Practice* (pp. 10–13), A. Carlyle (ed.). Paris: Double Entendre.

Ingold, T. (2000). *The Perception of the Environment: Essays on Livelihood, Dwelling and Skill*. London and New York: Routledge.

Macfarlane, R. (2012). *The Old Ways: A Journey on Foot*. London: Hamish Hamilton.

Macfarlane, R. (2016). *Landmarks*. London: Penguin Books.

Nash, P. (1949). *Outline: An Autobiography and Other Writings*. London: Faber and Faber Ltd.

Schafer, R. M. (1994 [1977]). *The Soundscape: Our Sonic Environment and the Tuning of the World*. Rochester, VT: Destiny Books.

Sebald, W. G. (2002 [1990]). *Vertigo*. London: Vintage Books.

Smalley, D. (1986). Spectromorphology and Structuring Processes. In Simon Emmerson (Ed.), *The Language of Electroacoustic Music* (pp. 61–93). Basingstoke and London: The Macmillan Press Ltd.

Tanizaki, J. (2001 [1933–4]). *In Praise of Shadows*. Trans. Thomas J. Harper and Edward G. Seidensticker. London: Vintage Books.

Thomas, E. (2011). *Selected Poems*. Matthew Hollis (ed.). London: Faber and Faber.

Voegelin, S. (2010). *Listening to Noise and Silence: Towards a Philosophy of Sound Art*. New York and London: Continuum.

Walser, R. (2013 [1917]). "The Walk". In Walser, R. *The Walk*. Trans. Christopher Middleton. London: Serpent's Tail.

17

SOUND TRANSFORMATIONS IN SPACE

Meri Kytö

During the past few years, voice command devices or "intelligent personal assistants" as they are also called, have been brought to market. These are software that can be used with voice interaction like Microsoft's Cortana, Amazon's Echo and Apple's Siri. They "listen" to commands, answer questions and perform tasks by accessing online resources. Having a voice, they seem somewhat reminiscent of sentient computers familiar from science fiction films like the serene HAL-9000 from Stanley Kubrick's *2001: A Space Odyssey*. Although the devices are not sentient (yet), their users have puzzled feelings concerning the style and the aim of communication one has with a machine, and also because it feeds information into the guts of a multinational company. A *Guardian* journalist finds himself sympathizing with the Echo software, activating it with its name (the key word is "Alexa"):

> It was not that [the Echo] seemed human, exactly, [–] but that it – she – seemed to merit respect. Yes, partly out of anthropomorphism. And partly out of privacy concerns. Don't mess with someone who knows your secrets. The device, after all, was uploading personal data to Amazon's servers. How much remains unclear.
>
> *(The Guardian 2015, November 21)*

The concern over sonic data privacy, storing indexed personal data, surveillance and developments in automated voice and sound recognition is one of the many current topics in discussions of privacy and technological advancements. The ubiquitous use of mobile devices and online connectivity form a specific type of spatial relationship with technology, what geographers Rob Kitchin and Martin Dodge call code/space (Kitchin & Dodge 2011). With this kind of spatial formation becoming more common, privacy is perceived to be under threat and gradually disappearing, causing deterioration of social order ending up in Orwellian future. In this argument, privacy is understood as a synonym for data protection.

Although questions of data privacy are important and current, a broader perspective on the issue of public and private *space* reveals that there are far more ways to approach these concepts than guarding one's personal information. Especially when approaching the matter through auditory culture – as sounding out and listening in – the complexity of cultural formations begins to show. This chapter explores the elusive relationships of public and private spaces through sound and listening. The aim is to introduce and ponder various aspects of the public–private phenomena, especially in relation to sound and space.

Conceptual approaches

Conceptualizing public and private space takes some effort as the concepts are often used in implicit ways. The rather loose and somewhat normative or idealistic use of the words has meant that they have gathered qualities as floating signifiers. As concepts that cause immense social and material repercussions, this is rather unfortunate.

The relationship between public and private is often presented as a dichotomy in the vernacular. They can refer to many types of polarizations depending on the context they are used in. These polarizations include official/unofficial, political/apolitical, general/specific, explicit/implicit, state owned/owned by private sector, national/local, written/orally communicated, common/personal etc. In his thorough book on privacy Daniel Solove, who specializes in data security and privacy law, claims quite laconically that no one can articulate what privacy means (Solove 2009: 1). Solove categorizes the Western definitions of privacy into five themes: right to be left alone; limited access to the self; secrecy and control over personal information; protecting personhood; and right to intimacy (Solove 2009: 12–38). The need for dichotomic spatial taxonomies often springs from the normative need to interpret laws and regulations, from the vertical relationship between the state and the citizen. Some of these categories can be understood as spatial formations, and not only metaphors of space. The so-called "spatial turn" (Soja 2000), a theoretical discussion originating from cultural geography in the 1980s, has influenced the ways space and place have been conceptualized. In arguing that spatiality is fundamentally constructive of social life and this needs to be taken seriously if one is to make sense of society is an argument easily understood in relation to soundscapes and the lived sonic environment.

In different fields of research the conceptualization emphasizes different views on the relationship and supposed essence of public and private space. A common discourse in understanding the public, especially in studies that draw from communication research, is to place it in relation with normative models of democracy, that is how democracy should work. This becomes apparent in the vocabulary used (for example "participation", "voice", "listening to the people"). The emphasis on normative democracy is based on the theory of the "public sphere" (*Öffentlichkeit*) by Jürgen Habermas (1962), who developed the model of communication as a function in structuring civil society. The oral history of mediated communication and media representations is also portrayed in a spatialized term used by Marshall McLuhan and Edmund Carpenter when they talk about "acoustic space" (McLuhan & Carpenter 1966: 65–70).

Besides the normative point of departure there is the bottom-up methodology in tackling public and private space and how it is sensed. The descriptive approach takes on empirical methods in asking how technology reforms the sense of public and private space, who or what regulates what can be heard in certain spaces, what are the uses and functions of public and private sonic space etc. Despite the conceptual insolvabilities, the frame of categorical opposition serves endless potential for the researcher interested in auditory culture. As analytical tools, they present themselves as ideal types but everyday sonic environments are more often in a dynamic relationship: something in-between or in a state of becoming. Because of these dynamics, it is more relevant to analyze what kind of public is being constructed against what kind of private than to define what privacy or publicness in themselves are (Peteri 2006: 58). Following along the same lines is anthropologist Christena Nippert-Eng, who emphasizes that for a researcher it is more interesting to listen to what level of publicness or privacy people want to keep things and information in (Nippert-Eng 2010:4). Political theorist Hanna Pitkin concludes that because there are so many ways to understand the relationship of public and private, it is crucial to sort out who gets to define what is going on in these relationships (Pitkin 1981: 238–239).

The use of power over sonic spatial privacy in urban space is a subject of interest especially in the context of sonic surveillance and neural networks capable of sound source identification. Also negotiations of sonic territoriality and noise are an ongoing debate, where intentional sound sources like loudspeaker systems on the street (for example Kreutzfeldt 2010) are discussed in a different tone than sound sources that are understood as a by-product or otherwise inevitable to the public infrastructure. Sound does not have to be electrically mediated to be part of the noise debate: the history of busking shows that the problem of social differences has been a key factor of irritation in the commercialized urban environment (Kytö & Hytönen-Ng 2015).

The history of mediated sounds and sound technology is scattered with dystopic thoughts concerning the development of personified design. Radio was seen as passivating its audience who were not able to speak up and be heard (Lacey 2013: 144). Overtly personified (media) content could lead to people not encountering each other, not involving themselves in discussions of common issues, dissolving of the sense of community and thus of societal structure. People might not feel connected to the democratic community they should be part of (Couldry & Turow 2014; see also Mouffe 2000: 74, 97). Media history scholar Kate Lacey writes in her meticulous book *Listening Publics: The Politics and Experience of Listening in the Media Age* that politics itself is made possible only by the listening attention of another: listening constitutes "a kind of attention to others (and otherness) and, importantly, being attended to that is the perquisite both of citizenship (as distinct from community) and of communicative action" (Lacey 2013: 165). In her argument public space is equally or even more about listening than speaking up or finding a voice. A public is then contingent on there being people willing to actively take up listening to others, who are not part of a pre-given collective identity (Lacey 2013: 172, see also Warner 2002: 58).

Nippert-Eng (2010: 324) emphasizes the importance of that: "like the work on gender the work on privacy is dynamic and done in response to a specific interactional context". Musicologist Georgina Born (2015) elaborates:

> interpreted adjectivally, in the active sense of the publicizing (or public-making) and privatizing propensities of music and sound – they register processes that are at once social, material and spatial. Moreover, abandoning the merely dualistic conception of the terms makes it possible to highlight the relational nature of their articulation, their mutual constitution and multiplicity.

Privacy and publicness can thus be something *done* in relation to others. Public and private spaces are to be understood as changing spatial relations in which social practices, values and belongings are shared and contested in.

A sense of place and the everyday

Space can be understood as embedded spaces in a spatial taxonomy where the public space contains the smaller more private spaces, from the impersonal and institutional public space to the communal space of social relations and onwards to the intimacy of the home and finally to the personal space of ones body (Madanipour 2003). If approached through listening, the experience of space is an articulation of overlapping categorizations or combinations of interrelations, in the veins of "semi-public" – like shopping malls and public lavatories – or "quasi-private" – like open-plan offices and women's prayer area in mosques – or "publicly pri-vate" (see Schwartz 2011: 336–337) – the telephone booth (Picker 2016) and the confessional. Understanding and knowing place acoustemologically – that the experience of place potentially could always be grounded in an acoustic dimension (Feld 2005: 185) – helps in understanding the phenomenological aspects of spatial experience.

To understand the multiplicity of doing public or private, it should be pondered from several intersectional, cultural and contextual angles. Privacy of the individual – which in itself is his-torically a relevantly new idea – is usually connected to Western culture (Warner 2002: 26–31) where it is taken as a privilege and of positive value. The favorable associations of either privacy or publicness are usually linked to a legitimation of a bourgeois view of life, "the ultimate gener-alized privilege, however abstract in practice, of seclusion and protection from others (in public); of lack of accountability to 'them', and of related gains in closeness and comfort of these general kinds" (Williams 1976: 243).

As an example of positive connotations, in Finland the talk of privacy is very commonplace and effortless. It might be surprising or even confusing to a Finn to think that speaking out loud about one's need for privacy can in other situations be understood as rude and a sign of distrust of your friends and family. It is considered normal within Finnish society to seek exclusion and to abandon most forms of social interaction when leaving to spend the summer in a secluded forest cottage, and this is not considered as a radical parting message to one's community or a sign of mental problems (Kivimäki 2012: 68).

One should remember that being or becoming westernized does not explain the need for privacy (Miller 2001: 15; see also McDougall 2002). On the other hand, it is noteworthy that privacy can signify privacy of groups (families or minorities) more so than privacy of individ-uals. Ethnographer Lydia Sciama, who has studied Mediterranean cultures in the context of privacy, urges us to observe methods of communication: How are things communicated, what is communicated and to whom? What is done in separation from others? (Sciama 1993: 96). Listening closely to these ways of doing, interpretation of the line between public and private sense of space can be achieved. It is also important to identify which groups value and do privacy actively.

The bourgeois division to public and private is part of the historical narrative of moderni-zation. To distance oneself from the metanarrative of modernization and repositioning oneself in relation to the culture at hand and the language it uses is what sociologist Nilüfer Göle calls for. In her book *Modern mahrem* (*The forbidden modern*, 1997) she refers to intimacy, home, secrecy, women's space, the space that is forbidden for outsiders and the family of the man to see. By using the word "mahrem" Göle points to the difficulty of describing private space in the Western / modern sense of the word. It becomes more than a question of translation, seen as an analytical category to understanding intimacy, sexual segregation and morals in Muslim communities. If she had used the word "private" instead of the Turkish word "mahrem" it would have possibly ignored the special qualities and features of the Muslim home (Göle 2011: 20).

Social anthropologist Yael Navaro-Yashin questions this metanarrative by noting that west-ernization in itself is a category of historical analysis, one that is still seen in postorientalist stud-ies and their references to the "modern". If talking about westernization of a culture, one has to accept the notion of the historical differences of the East and West. This is the way to reveal categories that are used in arguments about "cultural origins" (Navaro-Yashin 2002: 10).

Spaces are reproduced in everyday life. Many researchers have been interested in the every-day because it is often boring, banal and taken for granted. The critical view, originating from Henri Lefebvre (1991) and Michel de Certeau (1980), emphasizes that the seemingly normal habits can conceal structures that can in return (if unnoticed) lead to inequality between people.

Leaning on the thoughts of Lefebvre one could say that the production of sonic space – our ways of structuring it as something done or understood – is part of constructing meaning in the everyday. Spaces may seem trouble-free, even "natural", but they still enable us to certain kinds of social relationships and crop other kinds out. Everyday practices form up most of the ways we use sonic media and sound in general. The repetitious, common and non-dynamic way of structuring doing is what the everyday consists of: consuming, leisuring, routining and using tacit acoustic knowledge. These situations can be conceptualized as practices that valuate and categorize, are part of identity work or sense of belonging. Regardless of current the ubiquity of sonic media (see Kassabian 2013) and the possible homogenization of sonic space the everyday media is always concrete, experienced in contextualized time and space.

Secrecy, domesticated soundscape and regulating the acoustic horizon

A key method to achieving privacy is through secrecy. Secrecy may cover positive or negative pieces of information; it might mean indifferent or dangerous, happy, sad, small or larger things. Secrecy is the means by which we try to assure that things really are as private as we wish them to be. The selective processes of secrecy and disclosure are essential in the endeavor to privacy (Nippert-Eng 2010: 2, 17, 24–25). Secrecy is closely connected to the feeling of control over the soundscape. Privacy is called for when there is a need to deny, restrict access to acoustic space or to shut out individuals or groups, excluding disturbing factors and making sure one is not under surveillance. Musicologist Ola Stockfeld writes in his article, "Cars, Buildings and Soundscapes" (1994), that time he spends driving a car may be the only chance for recurring self-reflection, an option for a peaceful moment of attentive radio or music listening: in the car you can be who you want, and be at peace (Stockfeld 1994: 31). Similar spaces for escaping social pressure for concentration and sonic tranquility can be found in library reading rooms, working compartments in trains and by using personal stereos in a crowded bus (see Bull 2013). For some parents of small children the only place for a peaceful moment in a restricted acoustic space is the home bathroom.

These kinds of sonic seclusion techniques are an illuminating example of how different sonic spaces are embedded and the ways sound transforms space. When using a personal stereo with headphones the private space can continue at a click of an icon when going out of the front door. Paradoxically the public space then becomes sonically private, and only when one returns home the personal stereo is switched off and the listening can "open up" to the environment (Thibaud 2003: 324).

Controlling spatial acoustic information is controlling the acoustic horizon (see Truax 2001: 67). Sometimes this is accomplished by the formation of a masking effect (like fountains and ventilator hum), but sometimes, acoustic communication can also be regulated by spatial elements like windows and doors. In Northern Italy it is customary to regulate the acoustic horizons of homes by opening and closing window shutters. As important acts of achieving sonic privacy, the shutters also visually communicate the connection the inhabitants have with the street and community outside: in the evenings the closed shutters cut off the domestic space from the street. During the day, the open shutters indicate the resident is up and awake, doing chores and duties according to local work ethics (Vikman 2007: 128–129). Architect Olivier Balaÿ has noted that in 19th-century France, city houses were built with broad thresholds or even smaller in-between rooms between bigger rooms with sitting areas for socializing. These smaller rooms had double doors in both ends and the doors could be kept closed, slightly ajar, or open depending on the need for privacy that the masters of the house desired from their house servants (Balaÿ 2003: 244–246).

Domestication of acoustic space means the practices and choices involved in the interpretation and shaping of the acoustic environment that aim to create a pleasant, anticipated, familiar, safe or homely soundscape. The acoustic spaces or urban homes in particular are porous and in continuous flow, consisting of the city as public acoustic space and the private lives of neighbors carried by sound leaking into the interior of homes. This spatial conflict, together with related cultural codes and values, causes city dwellers to adopt a variety of approaches to both sound and management strategies concerning listening.

Domestication of technology is a theme of research that intersects many strands on the construction of private and public space, looking into the use and construction of technological systems in their historical and societal context and seeing gadgets as socially produced artifacts (MacKenzie & Wajcman 1999). Domestication of audio technology is audible in the ways we regulate the acoustic horizon of our private space: how we monitor the volume of our TV sets at home, use headphones with our laptops in the library or belt out choruses together with the car radio.

Digitization affects sonic spaces not only in "adding up" the availability and mobility of audio, but also in "shutting down". The transformation of various acoustic spaces can be partly explained by changes in the technological and material environment producing what is commonly called the self-service society. Advances in digitalization have changed various soundscapes (shops, libraries, banks, schools, offices) that formerly required interaction with another person in public. For example the ambiance of university exams, which have moved from large auditoriums to solitary computer rooms and were previously written in hand on paper but now on the screen with a keyboard, is an example demonstrating the subtle but effective influences on the everyday lived environment (Uimonen, Kytö & Ruohonen 2017). Regulating one's acoustic horizon when running banking, shopping or other errands is much simpler sonic regulation-wise when sitting next to one's own laptop than standing in a line with other clients in a public space. The presence of others, if perceived as pervasive, also affects the topics people are willing to talk about during mobile phone conversations. A study showed that students from Finland, Germany, Korea and the United States differ in what topics they avoid discussing on mobile phones, for example: grades, sexual activity, interpersonal relationships, money or medical conditions (Worthington et al. 2012: 52).

Philosopher Julie Inness sees intimacy in the core of privacy, saying that privacy "is the state of possessing control over a realm of intimate decisions, which includes decisions about intimate access, intimate information, and intimate actions" (Inness 1996: 140). Sonic intimacy and corporeal resonance of sound are aspects of sonic space that are being studied more and more. Intimate information and sonic privacy in general are methodologically and ethically challenging topics. What, then, is the relationship between listening to a private soundscape and eavesdropping? The Swedish word for eavesdropping is "tjuvlyssna", "to thieve listen", underlining acts of criminality, stealing information, as well as the Finnish word "salakuunnella", secret listening. Intentionality is crucial in eavesdropping as intentionality reveals the immorality of the act. When writing about listening, adapting and plagiarism in music history, philosopher Peter Szendy writes that merely listening to something may be considered theft, which is later courteously disguised as transcription or adaptation (Szendy 2008). This extreme interpretation, however, does not add to the understanding of social situations concerning violation or stretching the rules of cultural privacy.

In addition to the avoidance of conducting research in secret, people should also be given the freedom to decide for themselves what kind of information they provide to others in everyday life. Researchers in this respect must be alert and open-minded, and not assume too much. Sometimes the things that the researcher considers beyond the line of privacy are issues that the participants want to share and make known. When considering domestic sonic space, not everything that occurs in the home is felt necessary to be concealed. Anthropologist Daniel Miller encourages us to forget the fear of intrusiveness in a situation where the researcher is present in the home environment. According to him, we must empathically understand the diverse ways in which important and intimate relationships with the domestic space are constructed (Miller 2001: 1, 15). What remains is the discursive relationship between the private and public soundscape. Public space gets its meaning in relation to private space and this means different things in different cultures and in different situations. Sometimes there is no need to enter the private space to listen to where the line between appropriate and inappropriate is drawn.

References

Balaÿ, O. (2003) *L'espace sonore de la ville au XIXe siècle*, Bernin: A la croisée.

Born, G. (ed.) (2015) *Music, Sound and Space: Transformations of Public and Private Experience*, Cambridge & New York: Cambridge University Press.

Bull, M. (2013) "Remaking the urban: the audiovisual aesthetics of iPod use," in C. Gorbman, J. Richardson, J. & C. Vernallis (eds.) *The Oxford Handbook for New Audiovisual Aesthetics*, New York & Oxford: Oxford University Press.

Carpenter, E. & Marshall McLuhan (1966) "Acoustic Space," in E. Carpenter & M. McLuhan (eds.) *Explorations in Communication*, Boston, Beacon Press, pp. 65–70.

De Certeau, M. (1980) *L'invention de quotidien*, Paris: Folio essais.

Couldry, N. & Turow, J. (2014) *"Advertising*, Big Data, and the Clearance of the Public Realm: Marketers' New Approaches to the Content Subsidy," *International Journal of Communication*, 8 (2014), pp. 1710–1726.

Feld, S. (2005) "Places sensed, senses placed: toward a sensuous epistemology of environments," in Howes, D. (ed.) *Empire of the Senses: The Sensual Culture Reader*, Oxford: Berg, pp. 179–191.

Göle, N. (2011 [1991]) *Modern mahrem: Medeniyet ve örtünme*, Istanbul: Metis.

Habermas, Jürgen (1990/1962) *Strukturwandel der öffentlichkeit: Untersuchungen zu einer kategorie der bürgerlichen gesellschaft*, Berlin: Suhrkamp.

Inness, J.C. (1996) *Privacy, Intimacy, and Isolation*, Oxford: Oxford University Press.

Kassabian, A. (2013) *Ubiquitous Listening. Affect, Attention, and Distributed Subjectivity*, Berkeley: University of California Press.

Kitchin, R. & Dodge, M. (2011) *Code/space: Software and Everyday Life*, Cambridge, MA: MIT Press.

Kivimäki, S. (2012) "Aito Suomi-kuva. Lektio," *Kulttuurintutkimus* 29(3): 67–69.

Kreutzfeldt, J. (2010) "Acoustic territoriality and the politics of urban noise," *Soundscape the Journal for Acoustic Ecology*, 10(1), pp. 14–17.

Kytö. M. & Hytönen-Ng, E. (2015) "Busking and negotiations of urban acoustic space in South Bank, London," in M. Bull & L. Back (eds.) *The Auditory Culture Reader, 2nd edition*, London: Bloomsbury.

Lacey, K. (2013) *Listening Publics: The Politics and Experience of Listening in the Media Age*, Cambridge & Oxford: Polity.

Lefebvre, H. (1991) *The Production of Space*, Oxford: Blackwell.

MacKenzie, D. & Wajcman, J. (eds.) (1999) *The Social Shaping of Technology*, Maidenhead: Open University Press.

Madanipour, A. (2003) *Public and Private Spaces of the City*, London: Routledge.

McDougall, B. (2002) "Particulars and Universals," in B. McDougall & A. Hansson (eds.) *Chinese Concepts or Privacy*, Leiden, Boston & Köln: Brill.

Miller, D. (2001) "Behind closed doors," in D. Miller (ed.) *Home Possessions: Material Culture Behind Closed Doors*, London: Berg, pp. 1–19.

Mouffe, C. (2000) *The Democratic Paradox*, London: Verso.

Navaro-Yashin, Y. (2002) *Faces of the State. Secularism and Public Life in Turkey*, Princeton & Oxford: Princeton University Press.

Nippert-Eng, C. (2010) *Islands of Privacy: Disclosure and Concealment in Everyday Life*, Chicago: University of Chicago Press.

Peteri, V. (2006) *Mediaksi kotiin. Tutkimus medioiden kotouttamisesta*, Tampere: Tampere University Press.

Picker, J. M. (2016) "The telephone booth: Fixed mobility and the evolution of sonic space," in M. Bull & L. Back (eds.) *The Auditory Culture Reader*, 2nd Edition, London: Bloomsbury.

Pitkin, H. (1981) "Justice: On relating private and public," *Political Theory*, 9(3), pp. 327–352.

Schwartz, H. (2011) *Making Noise: From Babel to the Big Bang and Beyond*, New York: Zone Books.

Sciama, L. (1993) "The problem of privacy in Mediterranean anthropology," in S. Ardener (ed.) *Women and Space: Ground Rules and Social Maps*, Oxford: Berg, 88–112.

Soja, E. (2000) *Postmetropolis. Critical Studies of Cities and Regions*, Oxford: Blackwell.

Solove, D. (2009) *Understanding Privacy*, Cambridge, Mass. & London: Harvard University Press.

Stockfeld, O. (1994) "Cars, buildings and soundscapes," in H. Jarviluoma (ed.) *Soundscapes. Essays on Vroom and Moo*. Tampere. Tampere University Press.

Szendy, P. (2008) *Listen – A History of Our Ears*, New York: Fordham University Press.

The Guardian (2015) "Goodbye privacy, hello 'Alexa': Amazon Echo, the home robot who hears it all," November 21, 2015.

Thibaud, J.-P. (2003) "The sonic composition of the city," in M. Bull & L. Back (eds.) *The Auditory Culture Reader*, Oxford & New York: Berg, pp. 329–355.

Truax, B. (2001) *Acoustic Communication, 2nd edition*, Westport, CT: Ablex.

Uimonen, H., Kytö, M. & Ruohonen, K. (2017) *Muuttuvat suomalaiset äänimaisemat*, Tampere: Tampere University Press.

Vikman, N. (2007) *Eletty ääniympäristö. Pohjoisitalialaisen Cembran kylän kuulokulmat muutoksessa*, Tampere: Tampereen University Press.

Warner, M. (2002) *Publics and Counterpublics*, New York: Zone Books.

Williams, R. (1976) *Keywords: A Vocabulary of Culture and Society*, London: Harper Collins.

Worthington, D., Fitch-Hauser, M., Välikoski, T., Imhof, M. & Kim, S. (2012) "Listening and privacy management in mobile phone conversations: cross-cultural comparison of Finnish, German, Korean and United States students," *Empedocles: European Journal for the Philosophy of Communication*, 3(1), pp. 43–60.

18

DIASPORA AS METHOD, MUSIC AS HOPE

Yiu Fai Chow

In November 2013, something unusual happened during the television show *Holland's Got Talent*. To begin with, a person with a Chinese background participated in a talent show dominated by white, and to a lesser extent, black bodies. After Wang Xiao, a Chinese research student in the Netherlands, finished his performance, he was greeted with a laughing articulation of "surplise" by a jury member Gordon, a white Dutch singer.[1] The articulation, a stereotyping reference to the presumed Chinese difficulty to pronounce the "r" sound, was followed by more racist remarks, including the most cited "Which number are you singing? Number 39 with rice?".[2]

While Gordon tries to defend himself against national and international critique by qualifying his remarks as "jokes", the incident lays bare not only the everyday racism in Dutch society (Essed and Hoving 2015), but also one key understanding in sound studies that this chapter seeks to tease out: sound in its configuration with our social experience, community, our relational experience, and power (Bull and Back 2003: 4). In other words, inasmuch as our ears are supposed to stay open, hence indiscriminate and democratic to the outside world (unlike other senses, for instance, our eyes), hearing, and by extension the voice or sound that wants to be heard, is always already a matter of "positionality" (Sterne 2012: 4). In his position in the Dutch racial majority, Gordon does not hear Wang sing – his ears are tuned to the sound the Chinese are wont to make, presumably: the funny mispronunciations and the take-away utterances. As a member of the Chinese diaspora, like it or not, Wang needs to try very hard not to be relegated to the place where he is supposed to be (the catering business), and to claim his position to sing, to be heard. The Chinese diaspora is particularly disadvantaged in this case as they are generally not known for their musical talents. Think of black diaspora, their assumed musical DNA and heritage, and thus their radically different and vantage position in the world of music. More succinctly put, our ears accommodate, but our hearing discriminates.

This chapter is about the diaspora and the politics of being heard, or, to paraphrase Stuart Hall, the war of auditory positions (Hall 1996). And my focus will be on the Chinese case of popular music. To state the obvious as a caveat, diasporic auditory culture is not and should not be confined to popular music, or music, for that matter. However, given my own research experience and the bulk of scholarship on diasporic (popular) music, rather than other forms of sound, I have chosen to orientate the chapter this way. I will first attempt an outline of the field and highlight its major trajectories: sense of belonging, hostland, music production, and the location of the periphery. I will then use a case originated from the Chinese diaspora in the Netherlands not only as their explication; more importantly, I aim to posit some of the possible trajectories to take diasporic music studies further. I plead for hope, for (imagined) homeland, for more than music and for gender. The case I have been following is a Dutch-Chinese girl, 15 when we first met, in Amsterdam, almost 26 by the time I penned this chapter, a professional singer moving from her Dutch hometown to Shanghai, by way of Hong Kong, then based in Taipei. I will end the chapter by questioning the field of diasporic studies with technological developments, with the intersectional perspective, and finally the limits of the field itself.

Triangulating music with time and place

Originally referring to the dispersal of Jewish people from Palestine around 70 C.E. and subsequently to that of other populations (Vertovec 1997), diaspora, as I argue elsewhere, is always already "embedded in metaphors of scattering and displacement" and diasporic experience "conceptualized as living between homeland and hostland, and valorized from such metaphors to an archetype of identity negotiation, community construction and potential resistance" (Chow 2011: 787). The complex interplay and identification between "where you are from" and "where you are at" underwrites the two key terms in diasporic inquiries: roots and routes (Gilroy 1993; Clifford 1997). For all its hybridity and difference, diaspora subverts the kind of boundary formulation, particularly the nationalistic, that is fixating and assimilating, tilting towards "the recognition of a necessary heterogeneity and diversity" (Hall 1990: 235) Particularly influential and relevant for our purposes here is Paul Gilroy's seminal book on the African diaspora where music, in this case black music and its aesthetics as well as circulation, is inserted to triangulate with place and time, to understand the dynamics and politics between there and here, between then and now (Gilroy 1987).

The coupling of diaspora and music continues. In an overview article on diaspora and music, Thomas Solomon tracks the increasing attention music scholars have given to the concept of diaspora since 1990s, to the extent that diaspora is "firmly established as a paradigm for music research" (Solomon 2015: 202). Solomon's article is in turn a confirmation and continuation of what Georgina Born and David Hesmondhalgh observe fifteen years earlier. Against a backdrop of ethnomusicology and its preference for "traditional musics" as object of study, the authors note that "it is diasporic music that has moved to the centre of attention" (Born and Hesmondhalgh 2000: 25). This paradigm shift is a challenging move. In her introduction to a special issue on musical performances in the diaspora, Tina K. Ramnarine flags up the key words of diaspora – "difference", "otherness", "hybridity", and so forth – that challenge ethnomusicology's "cherished presumptions about music mapped onto geographies and societies" (2007: 2–3). It punctures what Mark Slobin identifies in his overview article as the persistent and homogenizing model, or myth, of one society having one music (Slobin 2003), and its concomitant racial and cultural power structure as illustrated in the Gordon controversy mentioned earlier. In that sense, diasporic music is always already vocal, literally and metaphorically. The messiness, the complexity and the specificity of diasporic music-making are to find its political voice to question certain reified thinking on place and identity, that they are neat and tidy categories.[3]

Explaining the appeal of music to diasporic populations, and thus the emergence of diasporic music as a field of practices and inquiries, Solomon spotlights two reasons. On the one hand, music is fluid, extra-territorial, and "travels far and wide", readily accessible and usable to the diaspora. On the other, music invites people to "pleasurable embodied experience and to communal sociability", both of which resonate with those who oscillate and negotiate their sense of being between the homeland and the hostland (Solomon 2015: 205–6). These two reasons correspond in turn to two major trajectories in the study of sound, namely the scientific and the technological, as well as the human and the experiential (Chow and Steintrager 2011). Focusing on the latter, Vic Seidler recalls his growing up experience with language and music in a migrant family, and foregrounds the importance of the study of diasporic sounds in the fundamental connection "between 'being listened to' and the notion that you are 'being seen' as a person in your own right" (2003: 401).

Doing diasporic music study

In the following, I will explicate four major trajectories of doing diasporic music study. Needless to say, the list is more indicative than exhaustive, more crisscrossing than parallel.

Belonging

Let's start with Seidler's autobiographical account, which is illustrative. It opens with a series of intimate memories of his Jewish mother (who had to flee Vienna from the Nazis) and himself (who grew up in the postwar Jewish refugee community *and* in north-west London), juxtaposing them with migratory experiences of some people the author knows. For Seidler music is what enables "outsiders" to "make ourselves at home" in the hostland (Seidler 2003: 403) – a kind of "social glue", to borrow a metaphor (Vertovec 2004); but some other diasporic members, he notes, have no such urge to feel a sense of belonging to the hostland. The vexing issue of belonging, of identity, home, and community, as weaved in the fabric of diasporic experience and memory, informs the first trajectory of doing diasporic music study. Which, in turn, flows out from the abovementioned embodied experience and communal sociality that Solomon singles out.

Similarly, Angela Moran, in her book-length treatise on Irish music outside Ireland, structures her investigation around sites for Irish musical performance in Birmingham including churches, public houses, and concert halls (2012). Taking cues from Pierre Nora's definition of such sites as "where memory crystallizes and secretes itself" (cited in Moran 2012: 8), Moran follows the Irish musical sound to these sites of music-making, probing, in the meantime, into the diasporic gamut of experience, memory, identity, and community, imbricating to the central issue of where one belongs.

Hostland

How this issue of belonging is to be answered, how disaporic identities and communities are configured by their sounds, as Seidler's account testifies, needs to be "specified historically and culturally" (2003: 403). But then the concern, put more elaborately, is not only *how* but also how one finds his place, his home, his very being in *where* he is at. Moving from the *how* to *where* diasporic music studies are situated, Seidler's account also testifies to the primacy of the hostland; in his case, Britain, or London. Seidler is deliberating his and his fellow migrants' experience in the context of Britian and London. Solomon, in his overview article theorizing diaspora and music, cites a series of studies, all of which take the hostland as their site of inquiry, including Turkish hip-hop in Berlin (Solomon 2009), *raï* music in Paris (Marranci 2003), and Portugese music in Malaysia (Sarkissian 2002) – just like Moran's study of Irish music in Birmingham.

This is what I would call the paradox of diasporic music studies. While the notion of diaspora privileges an (imagined) homeland, inquiries surrounding its music are mostly situated in the hostland. It follows that such inquiries usually resonate with concerns of cultural diversity, living with difference, identity politics loosely grouped under discussions of multiculturalism – in the hostland. Ramnarine, for instance, casts her study of Carnival performances at the Victoria and Albert Museum largely in conceptions of the multicultural society of London: "how do we understand musical life in a multicultural society" (2007: 7).[4] Indeed, the title of Gilroy's book *There Ain't No Black in the Union Jack* (1987) – black diaspora in a postcolonial era and the multicultural society of the United Kingdom – has probably set the framing for many diasporic music studies to come.

Production

If the above two trajectories correspond with sound's human and experiential dimensions in the multicultural society of the hostland, what follows stems more immediately from the other tradition of sound studies: the technicality, the making of music. In the words of Chow and Steintrager, "technical skills, instruments, and experiments, often rendered measurable and quantifiable, become the means of charting the sonic as mediated by machines and technologies" (2011: 4). Such a way of charting the sonic is particularly taken by ethnomusicologists. As suggested by Solomon, the "long-standing interest of ethnomusicologists in the practices of music-makers" has left their mark on diasporic studies of music, namely an accent on music production, not consumption (2015: 212). The special issue edited by Ramnarine is typical.

In its introductory article, Ramnarine, by confining the "musical performance" in the title of the issue into "music-making", has clearly articulated that the research concern is not so much on diasporic music, but more specifically on diasporic music-making. Contributions to the issue delve into the kind of diasporic music-making, which, she argues, can be understood as "in the ordinariness of creative production, as musicians working as individual agents in their everyday environments, making musical choices that suit them and the audiences" (Ramnarine 2007: 7). Another common object of diasporic music study, *bhangra*, demonstrates similar concern with the practices of music-makers and making. Laura Leante, for instance, investigates the musical processes through which the original *bhangra* from the villages of Punjab has mutated to its current form in Britain (Leante 2004). She does so largely by way of street processions, disco performances, musical and lyrical texts, styles and subgenres, as well as instruments, to illustrate how British *bhangra* has become a means for migrants to construct their diasporic identity in their new home.

Periphery

Amidst various practices of music-makers and making, particular genres and their associated diasporas enjoy particular theoretical and empirical attention. *Bhangra* is one of them. Leante's study ensconces itself in a series of studies, tracing back to, for instance, Gerd Baumann's (1990) and Gayatri Gopinath's (1995) studies, both on *bhangra* in Britain. Similarly, *raï* music, presumably originated from Algeria which travels to the West, is well researched by, among others, Joan Gross, David McMurray, and Ted Swedenburg in the French context (2001), and Gabriele Marranci as a "global" sound (2003). The research popularity of *bhangra* and *raï* is in turn an index of their popularity among substantial populations of South Indian diasporic populations in Europe and North America as well as Algerian and Arabic migrant communities in Europe.

Such postcolonial embedding also applies to the investigation of Africa diaspora and music. Gilroy, terming the African diaspora as Black Atlantic, also the main title of his influential book, reflects on contemporary musical forms of the African diaspora and how they function to (re) claim a pre-colonial past and to challenge notions of national culture (1993). Refracting the industrial importance of black music – and the global dominance of the Anglo-American scene where it thrives – is the prominent interface between black diaspora and academic inquiries on music. See for instance the edited volume exploring the African diaspora through the musical perspective by Monson (2003).

Thus has become one major trajectory in diasporic music studies, that is, tracking and investigating the roots and routes both music and diaspora take, to borrow Solomon's terminology, from the "periphery" to "the West", between "developing countries and the big cities of 'the West'" (Solomon 2015: 212–13). Such periphery-West configuration, in turn, often conflates with that of the colonized-colonizer, as shown in the studies surrounding Black Atlantic and British *bhangra*. There are of course exceptions, notably the Irish and the Jewish diaspora, for instance the works cited earlier by Moran and Seidler. Furthermore, there are isolated studies, for instance, on Korean diaspora in Russia, Uzbekistan, and Kazakhstan (Um 2000) and on the Chinese diaspora in the Netherlands (Chow 2011). While the former study is exceptional in its delinking from the postcolonial and the West, the latter, similarly not postcolonially grounded, follows a diasporic subject away from the West. And this is the case I will use for the rest of this chapter to posit some supplements I find necessary to enrich existing diasporic music study.

From Diana Zhu to Wang Shi'an

I met Diana Zhu in 2006, when she was 15. It was the final of a singing contest for Chinese diasporas in Europe, held in Amsterdam, the winner of which would go to Hong Kong to join the global event, competing with winners from North America to South Africa. Born in 1990 of parents who migrated from Shanghai, Diana grew up in a small town in the Netherlands. She dreamt of a music career when she was a child. In particular, she wanted to become a singer in China. Diana did not win the global Chinese singing contest but she got a contract with Warner Music Kong Kong. In 2009, Diana moved to Shanghai to prepare herself for launching her music, and her contract was transferred to Warner Music Taiwan. In 2011, Diana moved again to Taipei. Subsequently, in 2013, under an artist name of Wang Shi'an, or Diana Wang, she released her debut album, which earned her some music awards in Taiwan.[5] In 2014, she released a series of singles. In between, Diana participated in a number of reality and talent shows as well as television drama series.[6] In 2015 she left Warner. In 2016, under Taipei-based label Cros Music, Diana started releasing songs in English; the first single was titled "Home".

The following discussion is based on fieldwork done for my published article (Chow 2011) and subsequent data collection stretching from 2011 to now, including additional rounds of interviews with Diana and her music producers in late 2011 as well as casual, private exchanges between Diana and me throughout the years.[7] In contradistinction with most diasporic studies, musically or not, I have chosen to focus on one individual; I call this "follow the person", inspired by Scott Lash and Celia Lury's "follow the object" (2007: 16), premising on the urge to "go beyond (media) representation and the foregrounding of movement, dynamic constitution between agents in cultural production" (Chow 2011: 796). From here, I want to use Diana and all her interplay with practices of music-making for the present purposes, namely to show in relief what else, and more, can be done in diasporic music study. Simply put, what I intend to do now, inspired by Kuan-hsing Chen's "Asia as method", is to use Asian diaspora as method, to mobilize "critical studies of experience in Asia … to pose a different set of questions" (2010: 14–15).

Hope

Diana's eyes shone whenever she recalled her childhood memories in Shanghai. She told me the sound, the people, the hustle and bustle of this big city, always in contrast with the quiet in the Dutch town she grew up with. After her very first visit to Shanghai, Diana did something she later attributed to as one decisive act, one life-shaping moment in her life. "Back in the Netherlands," she told me, "I did a drawing for my class. I drew a girl holding a microphone, singing. I was six, or perhaps five. And then I told them that was Asia, I liked Asia. And my dad and mom came from China, and I was Chinese. I wanted to go back. To sing, I like singing" (cited in Chow 2011: 784).

And she did go back, first Shanghai then Taipei. While Diana's articulation of her dream is drenched in memories of her experience in Shanghai as a child, mingled with longings for the "roots" of her parents, it is not only about the roots, the past, or memories – it is also about the future, about imagination, about hope. While issues of belonging, of identity, home, and community, as discussed earlier, dominate diasporic music studies, Diana's case speaks for a desideratum: hope, her own hope, projected to and potentially configuring individual diasporic life. Obviously this is not to disparage theoretical and empirical concerns with who one is and where one belongs; Diana's hope to make a music career in China, however, foregrounds the need to understand a (imagined) homeland not only as somewhere to go back to, as a potential sense of belonging, but also as something to look forward to, as a real drive of longing.

Homeland/centre

Indeed, while I commenced my following of Diana in Amsterdam, her hope led her and me all the way to the other side of the world: first Shanghai and then Taipei. Reverting to the terminology mentioned earlier, this study is about the periphery in the West and then "back" to the periphery. The usage of the word "back" is of course problematic as Diana was not born there and the kind of music she grew up with, loved, and received training in, namely gospel music, was not particularly Chinese either. Even more problematic is the qualification of China as the "periphery", as we are experiencing the Rise of China as a major player in global politics and economics, albeit lesser in cultural terms. In that sense, the case of Diana represents another departure from dominant diasporic music studies, in that it is not confined to the paradigm of periphery-to/in-the West and its primary concern is not on the hostland but the (imagined) homeland.

It should be added that Diana's anchoring her musical hope on China, not on the Netherlands, is also related to her predicament as a diasporic member, namely that the Dutch-Chinese population does not invoke the kind of musical talents readily embodied by, say, the black diaspora, and is generally ostracized from the Dutch world of popular music. See the Gordon controversy I cited at the beginning of this chapter. Diana's hope does point to her and her fellow Chinese' "symbolic marginalization" in the Netherlands (Chow 2011). At the same time, her decision to pursue her career in China, an emerging global power offering greater opportunities for diasporic Chinese such as Diana, inserts her to the state-capital nexus writ large in the popular music industries. She was told by Warner to go on a diet, to perfect her command of "standard" Chinese, and to change her beloved black musical genres to more mainstream Chinese pop; in short, Diana was stripped of her possibility to perform a different Chinese-speaking woman singer, of her subversive potentials to dominant versions of Chineseness (Chow 2011). It was not coincidental that the first single she released after Warner, in 2016, was titled "Home", a pop rock number sung entirely in English and, in her own words, "based on R&B".[8] The study of Diana indicates a realignment of concerns from multiculturalism in the hostland to nationalism in the homeland.

Music?

So far I have been discussing the music released by Diana, as it was music that guided her from the Netherlands to China – or at least the Chinese market, as her subsequent base of Taipei remains the major supplier of Chinese-language popular music and and pop stars. However, she has done far more than making music. In 2011, I interviewed Diana again after the publication of my study. It took place in Taipei and she told me almost right away her participation in a reality-cum-talent show in China the year before. In a secluded resort outside Beijing, she spent six months with 15 other young female contestants learning, in her view, two important things: how to face the camera, and how to be obedient. Subsequently, Diana was also assigned to a variety of "jobs", such as presenting pop charts, interviewing veteran singer-celebrities, and also joining a dance competition. To date, she has acted in three online or television drama series.

"You can't simply be a singer," according to Terry Leung, of Warner Taiwan in charge of Diana's first release. In an interview with me during the same period when I met Diana again, he mentioned the changes in the market, not only in Taiwan but also in Asia as a whole, where a singer "has to do TV dramas or films as well" to enhance exposure and profile, eventually to bring economic returns through, for instance, product endorsement when the sale of music itself cannot sustain. That Diana joined the reality-cum-talent show was the idea of the big boss, with the same marketing logic, Terry said. What Diana has been doing and what Terry has explained pose a stark contrast with one emphasis of diasporic music study: on music-making. Quite apart from the inquiries on musical style, genre, instrument, and other aspects of production, the case of Diana underwrites the need of diasporic music study to take into account specificities of local practices of cultural production, in this case the Chinese, where music-making can hardly be investigated on its own; rather, as argued by some scholars on media studies, it should be situated in a cross-media context and the convergence culture (Jenkins 2008).

Gender

That studies of music cannot be of music alone is particularly gendered. During my interviews with Diana and her music producers, her body was always an issue. More accurately, her body was perceived as not fulfilling the idealized version of Asian femininity: too fat. When I first saw Diana, in Amsterdam, she, at 1.64 metres, weighed 60–70 kg, she told me. When I met her the second time, in Shanghai, she weighed 48 kg. Her father told me later that the target Warner set for Diana was 43. Reducing weight was the "most important request" Warner imposed on her if she was to make a music career in China (Chow 2011: 800). When I met Diana in Taipei, she finished half of her fruit tea and told me how she took in her food and drinks in terms of "portions". During the worst period of her dieting, Diana fainted a couple of times, generally frail.

That the career of a female singer is not to be anchored, at least not only, on her vocal ability, but also, or even more fundamentally, on her bodily appeal is especially blatant if compared to how a male colleague is treated. In my study, I compared Diana to Khalil Fong, who, with similar diasporic and musical backgrounds and under the same label at that point, was debuted totally faceless, without embodiment, so that all attention could be diverted to his voice, his musical upbringing, and talents (Chow 2011: 801). Such radically different treatments call for gender sensitivity in studies of diaspora, music included. While feminist scholars have long been cautioning against the conflation of youth cultures with boy cultures (McRobbie 1981), popular music studies as well as diasporic music studies continue to tilt towards the male experience. As an exception underlining the rule, Moran flags up "gender" as an analytic category in her study of diasporic Irish music, as "women are typically overlooked" (Moran 2012: 13). In the words of Connell and Gibson, "[p]opular music remains an industry permeated by gendered norms and expectations at all levels" (2003: 8). Inquiries in diaspora and music have to sensitize themselves to gendered dimensions so as not to flatten diasporic experience into the male kind.

Coda

To end this chapter, I want to paraphrase Ramnarine's formulation as the lynchpin of doing diasporic music studies. While she refers to ethnomusicologists' ways to negotiate "the contradictions between asserting the historical specificities of diaspora and avoiding the rigidities of diasporic essentialisms" (Ramnarine 2007: 1), I posit the need to be specific – historically, locally, gendered, and so on – precisely to show the diversity of diasporic experience within diaspora. I venture to open up some paths that I consider promising for further exploration. I will sketch three.

First, in connection with technological developments. How do diasporas use new technologies such as mobile sonic devices and social networks for their musical production, circulation and consumption? How do these technologies reconfigure diasporic experience, identity and community, in their hostland and/or homeland? Take Michael Bull's ethnographic study of iPod uses as example, where he demonstrates how such devices are mobilized to privatize and aestheticize urban space (Bull 2013). If such investigation is reframed to a diasporic context, what would the "sonic bubbles" of diasporic members do? How different and how similar to "general" users?

Second, from the perspective of intersectionality. As explicated by Leslie McCall, "[i]nterest in intersectionality arose out of a critique of gender-based and race-based research for failing to account for lived experience at neglected points of intersection" (McCall 2005: 1780). In other words, researchers should alert themselves to the intersections of the diasporic (racial/ethnic) not only with gender, as discussed earlier, but also with other demographic categories or identity markers, such as age, class, and so forth. Age is particularly noteworthy given the bias of popular music industries and studies for young consumers. What objects of study would emerge if one looks beyond young diasporic members' connection with music? I am at once reminded of the sonic preferences of some older Dutch-Chinese people I know: Chinese opera and Buddhist music (and chanting), both uncharted territories under studies of diasporic music, or sound, for that matter.

Finally, the limits of the field itself. Quoting Franz Kafka's short story "The Silence of the Sirens", Chow and Steintrager recuperate "a still more fatal weapon than their song, namely their silence" (cited in Chow and Steintrager 2011: 3). Given the limited space left here, it would be impossible to elaborate and engage with their thinking on the Sirens and their resisters, on female silence and male hearing. I would allow myself only to raise the possibility of diasporic silence as an object of inquiry – say, when a diasporic member or community is not allowed, encouraged, or willing to speak its "mother tongue", or listen to music made thereof?[9] From here, the last question to ask is: how far can we talk of "diaspora"? In her essay provocatively titled "Against Diaspora", Shu-mei Shih takes issue with the study of "Chinese diaspora" (2010). According to Shih, there are at least two problems: on the one hand, it is "complicit with China's nationalist calling to 'overseas Chinese' who are supposed to long to return to the homeland"; on the other, it "unwittingly correlates with and reinforces the Western and other non-Western … racialized constructions of Chineseness as perpetually foreign" (Shih 2010: 32).

While Shih proposes the "sinophone" as an alternative for the Chinese diaspora, the thorny task for "diasporic" studies of music and sound is, I believe, to remain vigilant, informed indeed by the keywords of specificity and diversity, as to decide or balance the emphasis on the former or latter of any hyphenated identity marker.

Notes

1 Chinese names used in this chapter are written in the Chinese way, that is, family name first, except when they are commonly known as otherwise. All the translations from Chinese to English are done by the author.
2 To view the fragment concerned, go to: www.youtube.com/watch?v=3wzEPgpSRm4. For a commentary regarding the controversy and the response by Chinese and Asian diaspora, see Kartosen (2016).
3 Academically, when music is put in tandem with cartography and biography, the study of diasporic sound can be understood as a significant way "to redress the rather neglected place of geography in any analysis of popular music" (Connell and Gibson 2003: 4). Discussing from the discipline of geography whose concern is usually visible, Susan J. Smith argues alternately for the urgency to insert cultures of sound and music in study of place (1997).
4 There are at least two dominant versions or ideal models of multicultural society, fusion and diversity, or more vernacularly, the melting pot and the salad bowl, both of which, as Ramnarine points out, are grounded in difference (2007: 6). Diasporic music studies tend to configure their politics towards the latter.
5 It is a common practice in the Chinese-language pop music world for artists not to use their real names. Usually, record labels will consult fortune-tellers to coin an artist name, as in the case of Diana. As Diana is used to being called by her friends, including myself, as Diana, I will continue using this for the rest of the chapter.
6 The title song of Diana's debut album has attracted more than three million YouTube viewings when I am writing this, 14 August 2016 (www.youtube.com/watch?v=ZuvLtTAsbGc). Arguably her greatest solo hit, "Love Exists", released as the ending theme song of a television drama series she acted in and only as a single, has attracted more than 23 million YouTube viewings (www.youtube.com/watch?v=Qu1ZTCEw6wg). In July 2018 Diana moved to Hong Kong and started releasing music under the indie label set up by Khalid Fong.
7 For a reflection on the research project on Diana and me as a researcher, as someone working in the music industries, and as a fellow diasporic member, see Chow 2011. I was born and grew up in Hong Kong, relocated to the Netherlands in 1992. In 2011 I moved "back" to Hong Kong where I currently am based.
8 See: www.youtube.com/watch?v=mrEee4bhc7Y.
9 Singapore, with its privileging of mandarin Chinese as state-sanctioned mother tongue for the Chinese diaspora to the extent of not allowing Cantonese-speaking pop music to be played in public, is a case at point.

References

Baumann, G. (1990). "The Re-Invention of Bhangra: Social Change and Aesthetic Shifts in a Punjabi Music in Britain", *The World of Music*, 32(2): 81–95.
Born, G. and Hesmondhalgh, D. (2000). "Introduction: On Difference, Representation, and Appropriation in Music", in Born, G. and Hesmondhalgh, D. (eds.) *Western Music and Its Others: Difference, Representation, and Appropriation in Music*, Berkeley, CA: University of California Press.
Bull, M. (2013). "IPod Use: An Urban Aesthetics of Sonic Ubiquity", *Continuum: Journal of Media & Cultural Studies*, 27(4): 495–504.
Bull, M. and Back, L. (2003). "Introduction: Into Sound", in Bull, M. and Back, L. (eds.) *The Auditory Culture Reader*, Oxford and New York: Berg.
Chen, K.H. (2010). *Asia as Method: Toward Deimperialization*, Durham and London: Duke University Press.
Chow, R. and Steintrager, J.A. (2011). "In Pursuit of the Object of Sound: An Introduction", *Difference*, 22(2/3): 1–9.
Chow, Y.F. (2011). "Hope Against Hope: Diana Zhu and the Transnational Politics of Chinese Pop Music", *Cultural Studies*, 25(6): 783–808.

Clifford, J. (1997). *Routes: Travel and Translation in the Late Twentieth Century*, Cambridge, MA: Harvard University Press.

Connell, J. and Gibson, C. (2003). *Sound Tracks: Popular Music, Identity and Place*, London: Routledge.

Essed, P. and Hoving, I. (eds.) (2015). *Dutch Racism*, Amsterdam and New York: Rodopi.

Gilroy, P. (1987). *There Ain't No Black in the Union Jack: The Cultural Politics of Race and Nation*, London and New York: Routledge.

Gilroy, P. (1993). *The Black Atlantic: Modernity and Double Consciousness*, London: Verso.

Gopinath, G. (1995). "Bombay, U.K., Yuba City: Bhangra Music and the Engendering of Diaspora", *Diaspora*, 4(3): 303–321.

Gross, J., McMurray, D. and Swedenburg, T. (2001). "Arab Noise and Ramadan Nights: Rai, Rap, and Franco-Maghrebi Identities", in Lavie, S. and Swedenburg, T. (eds.) *Displacement, Diaspora, and Geographies of Identity*, Durham, NC: Duke University Press.

Hall, S. (1990). "Cultural Identity and Diaspora", in Rutherford, J. (ed.) *Identity: Community, Culture, Difference*, London: Lawrence & Wishart.

Hall, S. (1996). "New Ethnicities", in Morley, D. and Chen, K.H. (eds.) *Stuart Hall: Critical Dialogues in Cultural Studies*, New York, NY: Routledge.

Jenkins, H. (2008). *Convergence Culture: Where Old and New Culture Collide*, New York, NY: New York University Press.

Kartosen, R.A. (2016). *Young Asian Dutch Constructing Asianness: Understanding the Role of Asian Popular Culture*, PhD Thesis, University of Amsterdam.

Lash, S. & Lury, C. (2007). *Global Culture Industry: The Mediation of Things*, Cambridge: Polity Press.

Leante, L. (2004). "Shaping Diasporic Sounds: Identity as Meaning in Bhangra", *The World of Music*, 46(1): 109–132.

Marranci, G. (2003). "Pop-Raï: From a 'Local' Tradition to Globalization", in Plastino, G. (ed.) *Mediterranean Mosaic: Popular Music and Global Sounds*, London: Routledge.

McRobbie, A. (1981). "Settling Accounts with Subcultures: A Feminist Critique", in Bennett, T. (ed.) *Culture, Ideology and Social Process*, London: Batsford Academic and Educational Ltd. in association with the Open University.

McCall, L. 2005. "The Complexity of Intersectionality", *Signs: Journal of Women in Culture and Society*, 30(3):1771–1800.

Monson, I. (ed.) (2003). *The African Diaspora: A Musical Perspective*, London: Routledge.

Moran, A. (2012). *Irish Music Abroad: Diasporic Sounds in Birmingham*, Newcastle upon Tyne: Cambridge Scholars Publishing.

Ramnarine, T.K. (2007). "Musical Performance in the Diaspora: Introduction", *Ethnomusicology Forum*, 16(1): 1–17.

Sarkissian, M. (2002). "Playing Portuguese: Constructing Identity in Malaysia's Portuguese Community", *Diaspora*, 11(2): 215–232.

Seidler, V. (2003). "Diasporic Sound: Dis/Located Sounds", in Bull, M. and Back, L. (eds.) *The Auditory Culture Reader*, Oxford and New York: Berg.

Shih, S.M. (2010). "Against Diaspora: The Sinophone As Places Of Cultural Production", in Tsu, J. and Wang, D. (eds.) *Global Chinese Literature*, Leiden: Brill.

Slobin, M. (2003). "The Destiny of 'Diaspora' in Ethnomusicology", in Clayton, M., Herbert, T. and Middleton, R. (eds.) *The Cultural Study of Music: A Critical Introduction*, London: Routledge.

Smith, S. (1997). "Beyond Geography's Visible Worlds: A Cultural Politics of Music", *Progress in Human Geography*, 21: 502–529.

Solomon, T. (2009). "Berlin-Frankfurt-Istanbul: Turkish Hip-Hop in Motion", *European Journal of Cultural Studies*, 12(3): 305–327.

Solomon, T. (2015). "Theorizing Diaspora and Music", *Urban People / Lidé Města*, 2: 201–219.

Sterne, J. (2012). "Sonic Imaginations", in Sterne, J. (ed.) *The Sound Studies Reader*, New York, NY: Routledge.

Um, H.K. (2000). "Listening Patterns and Identity of the Korean Diaspora in the Former USSR", *British Journal of Ethnomusicology*, 9(2): 121–142.

Vertovec, S. (1997). "Three Meanings of 'Diaspora', Exemplified among South Asian Religions", *Diaspora*, 6(3): 277–330.

Vertovec, S. (2004). "Cheap Calls: The Social Glue of Migrant Transnationalism", *Global Networks*, 4(2): 219–224.

PART IV

Introduction: sonic skills: finding, recording and researching

The kinds of skills that scholars of sound employ in listening to, finding and in the recording of data have methodological and theoretical implications. In this section I discuss the need for a methodological eclecticism within the field of sound studies – by which I mean an open-mindedness that refuses to be drawn into methodological specialisms that might be associated with any traditional or indeed innovative subject area. The types of questions that sound scholars have been asking themselves involve what, if any, are the distinctive characteristics of studying the sonic, as against any other sensory mode? In order to ask these questions, issues of periodicity become important due to the absence of recorded sounds before the age of mechanical reproduction. What challenges does this periodicity then pose for historical research? In parallel to this is the contemporary question as to how we might research the sonic in an age of sonic databases and archives deriving from the late 19th century when sound recordings began to the present day?

A central question researchers address is what, if any, are the special characteristics of sound and how might these "characteristics" be translated into sonic methodologies. If the distinctiveness of sound tends to lie in its temporal and spatial nature, then historically sound tends to be defined by their specificity and immediacy – this siren that I hear in the street outside – and by their transitoriness – the person shouting in the street outside my office who has now walked away. The history of sonic experience has until the age of mechanical reproduction been one of the irretrievable disappearances of sounds. We can, for example, view a Michelangelo sculpture in Florence but we cannot hear the voice of Michelangelo – although we can read his diaries.

There are, of course, differing arguments as to how we should study sound from sociologists, anthropologists and historians, as distinct from those that consider themselves mainstream "sound studies" researchers or sound artists. In the main, the object of research and the questions that the researcher wishes to ask and explore determine the methods that they will choose. Beyond that, what counts as "data" to be used is partially a function of the disciplinary adherence of the researcher. The tension between what might be called traditional methods of research, undertaken by cultural historians such as Alain Corbin's study of village bells that relied largely upon French parish documents and those of contemporary sound studies scholars who wish to use methodologies more related to the "sounds themselves", is articulated by Gallagher and Prior:

"We identify two broad methodological strands: sonic ethnographies, which rely on both conventionally written and more-than-textual representations of sonic qualities; and soundscape studies, which encompass a wide range of methods, including field recording, sound mapping and sound walks" (Gallagher and Prior 2014: 272).

Gallagher and Prior highlight what has become a pressing issue in sound studies – to what extent should our methods intrinsically involve sound as sound rather than the translation of the sonic into another medium, the medium with which you are reading this introduction at present – script? It should be noted that the contributors to this volume use a wide range of methodologies that are orientated to their research areas and questions. This is precisely the point of sound studies to embrace a wide range of methodologies rather than to hypostasize any one method or subset of methods. Jennifer Lynn Stoever's recent work on the sonic colour line represents how scholars might employ a range of methodologies without essentializing any one method:

> "The fields methodological freedom (within sound studies) greatly enabled my scholarship in African American literature, music, and history…I meet sound where, when, and in what form I find it, not as an object of study, but as a method enabling an understanding of race as an aural experience with far reaching historical and material resonance" (Stoever 2016: 18).

Stoever's interrogation of the cultural politics of listening in the US draws upon a wide range of written and sonic material in order to make her case for the sonic colour line. She argues that literary texts themselves "not only produce and represent their own sounds but also represent and record the processes of sound's social production" (Stoever 2016: 24). The written is essentially the sonic – a point that Maya Jasonoff has recently made in her study of the cultural significance of Joseph Conrad, "all writing is an act of translation. It turns something you see or sense into something you say" (Jasonoff 2017: 161).

Each sensory mode poses methodological issues based upon the specificity of the sense to be investigated. Whilst we might agree with Brandon La Belle's description of sound as, "intrinsically and unignorably relational: it emanates, propagates, vibrates, and agitates; it leaves the body and enters others; it binds and unbinds, harmonizes and traumatizes; it sends the body moving, the mind dreaming, the air oscillating" (LaBelle 2010: 468). Yet the cultural, historical and political context within which any sound is made and received is crucial as we have noted in section one of this volume. Sounds do not speak for themselves. Sounds "have meanings that can only be fully understood within their particular cultural context" (Howes and Claassen 2014:2). So, for example, one of the challenges that might face a curator of a sound-based exhibition in a museum is one of contextualization:

> we need to stress the preeminent importance of contextualizing the sounds that museum visitors hear. Rather than simply feeding sounds to ears, we need to help visitors understand the context in which those sounds were produced, and how their reproduction can tell us not only about the nature of the past, but also us about our own intellectual preferences and prejudices. (Smith in Morat 2014: 20)

The development of sonic recording technologies has transformed our sonic data bases and brought about new opportunities and challenges. The 20th century saw a dramatic change in the sonic environment through a range of acoustic technologies such as telephones, microphones, loudspeakers, phonographs, radios, tape recorders, compact discs, cellular phones, MP3 players, digital voice mail and talking computers. With the advent of recording technologies such as the phonograph in the late 19th century up until the advent of digital technologies in the 21st century, sounds can increasingly be captured for research purposes. The ability to fix, transpose and transport sound arose with the phonograph in the late 19th century with its ability to document sound events. Erika Brady (1999) estimated that fourteen thousand cylinder recordings of North American Native Americans were made by ethnologists between 1890 and 1935 – these cylinders are now deposited in a wide range of museums and university departments and symbolize the growing cultural value attached to collecting sonic history. What could be better than archiving the dying sounds of a culture for future reference and clearer understanding of lost sonic worlds? This desire to record had, she argues, positivist motivations – the recordings as such were interpreted as being objectively true – an accurate representation of that which was being recorded. Brady argues that these cylinders were seen, ironically, given the present methodological concerns mentioned above, as mechanical tools enabling the researcher to transcribe sonic material into written text. It is for this reason, she argues, that many researchers failed to mention how indeed their material was gathered – the process of recording was frequently not mentioned by ethnographers of the time. Early critics of the use of the phonograph by ethnographers mentioned the transformation and impoverishment of the ethnographic encounter in which the ethnographer relied upon the recoding machine to do all of the work. Importantly, in its "fetishizing" of the sonic as representing what we would now refer to as a "false objectivity", the recording was blind to all forms of nonverbal contextualization embedded in and acting beyond the recorded sound – the physicality of the culture in its ritualistic and material form. Hidden from view was the asymmetrical power relations embodied in the use of the ethnographic encounter between the researcher and the Native American. This example demonstrates the way in which theoretical concerns are bound to methodological ones and to the dangers of extracting the sonic from an understanding of embodiment more generally and the cultural specificities within which the sonic practices are enacted and understood.

Carolyn Birdsall's chapter deals with the finding of, storing of, and evaluation of sound, both historically and in contemporary society. She traces the rich and complex history of the "search" for sounds and the role that sound studies has played in this exploration. In doing so, her analysis is divided into three parts: the various ways in which sounds past and present are uncovered, retraced and constructed, the ways in which sound is stored, ordered and classified and lastly issues around sound such as writing. In doing so she discusses the rich history of sonic research and the ways in which the technologies of the 20th century have shaped sounds empirically, politically and aesthetically. She points to the recent development towards discussing ecologies of the media (relations between media) as against focussing upon individual mediums – such as radio, for example. Yet the storing and cataloguing of sounds poses problems of access and reuse. Birdsall discusses the significance of where material is stored and the selection of material to be stored or discarded that are as much economic, cultural, political and organizational. These choices then inform what is to be considered "official" history and memory. To the extent to which those sounds being stored and catalogued are "western" sounds that tends to produce a Eurocentrism with sound studies despite the pioneering work of anthropologists like Steven Feld. Birdsall concludes by advising critical reflection amongst those researching sound – critical reflection in relation to their own blind spots and assumptions concerning the nature, meaning and use of the sounds retrieved and stored.

Mattern also investigates how we might explore the sonic spaces of the past and present, but approaches the issue from the perspective of sonic archaeology which she argues discloses the materiality of sonic spaces and opens up alternative sonic vistas for us to understand. We live, she argues, within a largely unseen sonic landscape – of infrastructures that underpin much of our daily activity. From the sound installations on Brooklyn Bridge set up to understand and listen to the micro-rhythms/and stress of different building materials; to the listening to the internal mechanisms of machines from the computers at Bletchley Park; to the sounds of the Philips PASCAL computer; to the forensic architecture of drones; to listening to the architecture of ancient sites from the ancient Agora in Greece; to the "Oracular Chamber" of Hal Saflieni Hypogeum, the ancient cemetery in Malta. Through the use of a range of technologies Mattern argues that we are able to re-discover the sonic nature of design and culture of the past and the present which is the domain of both sonic artists and sonic archaeologists.

Blake Durham follows Mattern by asking how we save sounds in the digital age? In doing so he addresses three interlocking modes of online curation: individualized reflexive consumption (see Nataraj in this volume for examples of this), collaborative projects and online algorithmic cultures. Durham argues that the development of new and innovative "curated experiences" are often based on lifestyle experiences (such as Instagram). Just as we have citizen journalists he argues that we now have citizen online curators. This has produced the development of what he refers to as a "participatory self" whereby the subject broadcasts themselves through sites such as "Rate your Music". In addition to this, new forms of collaborative curation exist whereby curation is de-individualized through the development of aggregated collections of music. Here consumers/listeners are asked to categorize music in a variety of forms, the results of which feed back into personalised sequences of consuming. Durham argues that these commercial and structural directives to consumers, whereby they themselves enact and reconstruct patterns of consumption constitute forms of "free labour" for large corporations. These corporations enact editorial interventions of their own choosing and the flows of information gained are non-reciprocal.

Voegelin, like Mattern, discusses the hidden potential for sonic technologies to make audible that which we can't see. She does this through a close analysis of the work of several sound artists (Radique, Gupta and Pamela Z) whereby through the disembodiment of sound, the body itself is reconfigured. Voegelin traces the cultural, aesthetic and political possibilities of such a technologized sound art. In doing so she discusses the radical potential role that technologies play in sound art, not as a function that permits the sound artist to do something, but rather as "a complex occurrence that produces its own aesthetic".

Tom Rice returns us to the more traditional subject of ethnographies of sound and tackles the rich history of anthropological ethnographies in order to discuss the "sensory turn" in ethnographic research. Drawing upon the work of Steven Feld and his study of the Kaluli, he demonstrates the increasing attentiveness to sound amongst anthropologists, arguing that ethnography was always a listening methodology and not merely an observational and scriptural form of research. Rice points to the strength of ethnography as a method that lies precisely in its local sensitivity (a point made by Howes in Section 1 of this volume) and its immersion in the culture to be studied. Anthropologists, he argues, are increasingly attentive to a general engagement with the senses.

Rice continues by discussing his own ethnographic studies of hospital wards in Edinburgh and London in order to demonstrate the ways in which the soundscape is read differently by various participants (patients, nurses and doctors) before discussing Chandola's work on the slums of Govindpuri in India and Michael Gallagher's work on a Scottish primary school, drawing out the sonic class divides in Chandola's work and the role of sound in controlling and disciplining in the work of Gallagher. Rice argues that if we analyse sonically based fieldwork then we should recognise a changing balance between text and sound in cultural representation – that text itself will be insufficient as a representation of the sensory world.

The soundwalk is perhaps the most notable method associated with sound studies. Frauke Behrendt takes us through the varied and complex nature of the soundwalk by discussing its historical derivation in the work of Westerkamp, Cardiff and others and by tracing the varied nature of contemporary soundwalks as representing a diverse set of aims; "educational", "urban" and "artistic" – indeed as practice itself. She usefully points to future directions and applicability of soundwalks in terms of virtual reality, locative games and augmented reality, thus bringing the soundwalk firmly into the contemporary digital world.

In the concluding chapter of this section Paul Nataraj demonstrates a space wherein sound art, technology and cultural memory meet in his work on vinyl, materiality and memory. Nataraj demonstrates the complex intervening of theoretical assumptions about music, its materiality and the ways in which it is enacted through personal narrative. He does so by discussing vinyl as a palimpsest – just as when we listen to the gruesome tapes of Jonestown from the 1970s – which are overdubbed – so we can hear, according to Nataraj, the layers of individual experience and memory embedded into vinyl – which Nataraj has constructed as a socio political artwork. In doing so he demonstrates how sound as sound is inflected with personal narrative, cultural specificity and the industrial matter (the vinyl and the recording practices) underpinning the experiences upon which these are based.

References

Brady, A., 1999, *A Spiral Way: How the Phonograph Changed Ethnography*. Jackson: Mississippi University Press.

Gallagher, M. and Prior, J., 2014, "Sonic geographies: Exploring phonograph methods", *Human Geography*, 38(2):267–84.

Howes, D. and Classen, C., 2014, *Ways of Sensing: Understanding the Senses in Society*. London: Routledge.

Jasonoff, M., 2017, *The Dawn Watch: Joseph Conrad in a Global World*. London: Collins.

LaBelle, B., 2010, *Acoustic Territories: Sound Culture and Everyday Life*. New York: Continuum Press.

Morat, D., 2014, *Sounds of Modern History: Auditory Cultures in 19th and 20th Century Europe*. New York: Berghahn.

Stoever, J.L., 2016, *The Sonic Color Line: Race and the Cultural Politics of Listening*. New York: New York University Press.

19

TECHNOLOGIES OF SOUND ART

Techno-cultural occurrences

Salomé Voegelin

Technology changed the way sound art could be done in a gallery. If you wanted continuous sound you either had to do it kinetically, with a machine of some kind, or you would have a tape loop that ran round the gallery. But now you just have the digital thing, and you run a loop. Sound art with loudspeakers seems to be what people use mostly, loudspeakers and playback technology, and the loop is usually tailored – maybe in a lot of cases it is at most ten minutes, not four hours. You can enter it and leave it. It does not develop into anything else.

(Eastley, in Gardner and Voegelin eds, 2016, pp 161–162)

This is a quote by Max Eastley speaking at a colloquium about the relationship between sound art and music staged at the London College of Communication, UAL, in 2012. His take on the impact of technology on the development of gallery-based sound art serves as an interesting starting point for an essay debating the technologies of sound art inside and outside the gallery.

Eastley is a musician and sound artist who most famously produces Kinetic sculptures and Aeolian harps, and works with both human intervention and energies of the natural environment. The context of his practice, his interest in the forces of electricity, wind, water and ice for the production of sound works, as well as his engagement with ecological issues bring an ideological angle to the discussion of technology and particularly to the discussion of technologies of sound art. They curtail partisan observations on the mechanics and application of technology, and focus the debate on issues of authenticity, translation, opportunity and availability. His quote brings scrutiny and care into what could easily become a simple history of technological development and use.

Following his reservations, this chapter proposes to consider technology in relation to sound art not as a tool or in terms of a historical chronology, but as a complex 'occurrence' that produces its own aesthetic, historical and ideological processes and interactions of which the resulting work, its exhibition and consumption, necessarily and unavoidably speak.

To engage in this language of technology I will first consider the notion of instrumentality versus operationality, and seek to confer this differentiation through the practices of Éliane Radique and Shilpa Gupta. Their work enables me to understand technology, its development and status within sound art, not simply as an acceleration of existing and dominant aesthetic and ideological applications, but as unexpected operations that sidestep and defy instrumentality.

Technologies of sound produce, compose, organise and playback invisible material. They make audible and thinkable what we cannot see, but they can also cut what seemed to logically belong together away from its source, to make it available as an autonomous possibility that disturbs through the potential for dis-placement, and causes anxiety as well as joy through the subsequent practice of re-placement: inventing new associations whose links are relevant not only in relation to an individual re-presentation but as a consciousness, as an intuition that things do not belong together as fixedly and normatively as we might have thought they did.

Sound art as a genre is defined by the technological and conceptual possibility of this dis-placement. It is enabled contextually, in relation to influence and genre, by the split away from a purely musical and visual arts practice; and it is enabled materially as well as conceptually by the plural possibilities autonomous sound affords the artist.

The concept of the technological autonomy of sound is central to sound art's identity and potential. Its practice is at once inspired and facilitated by the separation between sound and source, and an expression of this separation.

Even if, as in Eastley's case, the work is based on a relationship between force, human or natural, and sound, which reinstates or emphasises rather than severs the connection, the key remains that the separation is conceptually and actually possible and thus the auditory imagination as creative impulse includes this possibility.

Eastley's technologies are relational and causal but not deterministic. His play with causality opens the space of influence to new possibilities. However, his works retain an analogue integrity in the sense that the relationship between what causes the sound and what the sound is remains intact.

By contrast when I saw Pan Sonic in concert for the first time in what must have been 1997, I witnessed the complete dis-placement not only of the sound itself but also of the body. Instrumentality had not been abandoned but became machinised and dramatised in the light of open laptops. The virtuosity of these performers, each seated at their laptop, neatly in one row, ceased to be measurable by their body movement and its creation of a perfect sound. Both body and movement had morphed into the sound playing 'in front of them', playing in front of me, staring at the back of open laptop lids that reflected back to me only my own audition.

The technological dis-placement of sound corresponds with the technological dis-placement of the body of the performer and of the listener.

The body too has a sound that can be cut from its physical identity, from its substantial objectivity, to float as ephemeral subjectivity and become autonomous material for artistic production. In this chapter I strive to hear this ephemeral subjectivity in the work of performer, composer and media artist Pamela Z, to get to understand the possibilities of the sounding body in relation to the possibilities of technology, not as disembodiment or absence, but as mobile invisibility and pluralisation.

The technologies of sound are techno-cultural occurrences: from the radio, the phonograph, the reel to reel machine, to the first clunky Sony Walkman (with radio incidentally) and MP3 player, they expand and freeze space and elaborate a different relationship between space, time and things; they create a different sense of material and of self through the presentation of invisible processes and possibilities. But it is not only playback but also the occurrences of production that trigger a different sense of the world, of material and of self: the possibilities of the cut up, synthesis, manipulation, editing and composing challenge and question how things belong together and where they belong.

By considering the technologies of sound art as complex occurrences, I hope this chapter can contribute to a meditation on technology as a material process and as an ideological act that has its own agency and identity, whose possibilities enable and define artistic practice. Following on from this, in conclusion, I want to distinguish the dis-placement that defines and enables sound art from the seemingly unavoidable and necessary rupture with the historical continuum that Jacques Attali identifies it with, and venture with Kodwo Eshun into a techno-future, a place outside chronology, from which sound art comes as an autonomous practice that has its own tone.

Instrumentality versus operationality

'The tools for making electronic music are not innocent: true sound "mediums", they are an interface to ghosts of technoscientific projects past' (Rodgers, 2010, p. 6.) These ghosts are the ideologies and socio-political interests of those projects and while the sound of a current use of those interfaces within the context of sound art might only hold a lingering radiation of the technoscientific purposes that drove those projects, it is enough to keep them within the belief systems that gave rise to them, and within the political and philosophical sense that organises their conception.

Tara Rodgers points to the link between audio and military technology in the United States, a connection that can be assumed to hold globally. I would like to add to her technoscientific past a musical and instrumental past that crucially radiates and informs a current sonic practice also. Between military purpose and musical tradition the technologies of sound art are at once enabled by and exist in the shadow of aesthetic and ideological powers whose contamination into the work are part of its condition and are often the concern of its production also. 'Machine Music doesn't call itself science because it controls technology, but because music is the artform most thoroughly undermined and recombined and reconfigured by technics. Scientists set processes in motion which swallow them up' (Eshun in Cox and Warner eds, 2007, p. 159).

Sound art shares machines and institutions with military and scientific research, and it shares software and instrument design with musical practices. The technology of sound art can both recombinate and be recombinated, to use Eshun's term, by science and music. These connections affect not only the listener but also the sound artist. They carry with them a transcendental techno philosophy of functionality and truth, and a musicological focus on instrumentality and virtuosity. Thus they promote the idea that a correct use of an instrument or tool presents an ideal application of its potential, be that in relation to a scientific enquiry or in terms of a musical expectation, that at once brings forth its hidden ability and leads us to its proper truth. However this correct and proper truth is not music's truth or sound's truth and neither it is science's truth, but is the truth of the tool itself as the truth of the ghost of science past, whose interpreter, the instrumentalist and the lab-scientist, has been swallowed by the invisible nominalism of its function.

Thus important for the radical use and critical understanding of technologies of sound art is whether we are working with its occurrence, or have already been swallowed up by technics: whether, in other words, we are using technology within its possibilities or have inadvertently been subsumed into its normative and normativising ideology.

Martin Heidegger's notion of the Zeug, the tool, is still relevant in this regard because it presents the ambiguity between what is inherent and what can still be found and done. For Heidegger the tool is situated between the thing, das Ding, which is the form and fabric as it is given to the senses in their basic being, and the work, das Werk (Kunstwerk), which is the world that is created from the form and fabric of the thing, to show its truth as an aesthetic truth and beauty. At this in-between place the tool performs another thing: 'Das Zeughafte des Zeuges besteht in seiner Dienstlichkeit', 'the toolness of the tool exists in its facility' (Heidegger, 2008, p. 26). It is the purpose of the thing, as fabric and form that is there before our use of it and that at once drives us towards its use and is revealed and confirmed in this utilisation.[1] In relation to sound art, the logic of these functional relationships articulate scientific perfection and musical virtuosity misconstrued as a scientific and aesthetic truth respectively. The performer must play the work in its best realisation, a realisation that in its potential exists always already in the instrument and the notation, but that is confirmed by the perfection of his play, which in turn confirms the status of the performance and of the work within the canon of best works.

Within this ideology, sound technology has been employed for the purpose of perfecting the sound and eradicating human error. For Glenn Gould the aesthetic truth of music in the recording era is not the concert situation and the vagaries of the life take, but the editorialised work of the record. In his quest for perfection he famously embraced postperformance technological interventions and the cut and splice that enabled him to make the recording with 'the overwhelming sense of power which editorial control makes available' (Gould in Page, 1987, p. 339).

For Gould the technological dis-placement of the cut does not herald a divorce from musical prescription, but enables acceleration towards its perfection. The recording apparatus presents the ultimate tool to realise virtuosity and instrumental precision, which, in turn, leads him to predict that 'the habit of concert going and concert giving, both as a social institution and as a chief symbol of musical mercantilism, will be dormant in the twenty-first century' (Ibid., p. 332). His technology-enhanced instrumentality is not an occurrence but an application of control. It does not dis-place the piano but extends and amplifies its ideology.

However, besides this instrumentality, the notion of technology as a means to an end, Heidegger also recognises the human condition and activity involved in technology, and takes account of the influence of the unknown of the thing: 'Jenes Ungewohnte hat jedoch einst als ein Befremdendes den Menschen angefallen und hat das Denken zum Erstaunen gebracht' ('This unknown has once assailed humanity with its strangeness and has caused thinking to become astonishment') (Heidegger, 2008, p. 16).

The glimpse of the strange opens a small gap from which to prise open the transcendental framework and move between the tool and its function; to abandon instrumentality, truth and the correct use of technology, to subvert and re-recombinate the means *and* the end, and bring the fallacy of the body as a 'thing' back into the mix.

Using the transcendental drive against itself to understand the given not as an ideal but as a human condition, technology can bring us to this alien that will engender astonishment and a new thinking. Transcendental logic of concealment and discovery divorced from expectations and logic can find all sorts of possibilities. The cut, the dis-placement, enabled by the technologies of the reel to reel and latterly digital technology, which I suggested is pivotal to the conceptualisation of sound art, at once works on the material and on the ideology of sound: moving towards autonomy from a visual referent and away from historical and philosophical reference and domination to exist beyond the spectre of music and the ghosts of military science in the production of different technological possibilities that do not function effectively, but operate purposelessly.

The cut, digital or analogue, is technology as occurrence. Its process is not that of instrumentality and the virtuosity of performance, but the purposeless operation of materiality finding its own contingent and subjective idealities. Thus the understanding of technology not as a tool but as a radical occurrence of sound art moves technology from instrumentality into operation: the doing of technology as work, as effort rather than as aim, where we are not swallowed by the invisible nominalism of its function and ideology, but practice its possibilities with our own.

This use of technology as occurrence is most apparent in the practice of Éliane Radique, a French electroacoustic composer who had initially studied under the tutelage of Pierre Schaeffer and Pierre Henry, and had subsequently been assistant to Henry, but because her practice did not follow their orthodoxies of electroacoustic composition, 'because I was working the way I was working, which was absolutely an injury towards the basic principle of musique concrète (…) I had to do my way alone' (Radique in Rodgers, 2010, p. 59).

Instead of pursuing the compositional approach of concrete music, Radique produces durational, very slowly evolving sonic works from the sustained tones of an ARP 2500 analogue synthesiser. Her piece, *Transamorem Transmortem* from 1973, first performed in 1974, for example, seems inexhaustible, and does not impose itself as a work but as another slice of the soundscape, entering and thickening its pace almost unnoticed. It moves invisibly through unhurried, almost imperceptibly modulating high frequencies, trembling on a steady hum. It does not produce the space of a Werk, an artwork or composition, but an extension of things, reminding us of the sonic possibilities of all things and of ourselves, in an inadvertent everyday existence rather than within a purposeful aesthetic.

> Before the greatest achievement Before the greatest detachment. At the limit of the frontier space of the unconscious – tuned waves – 'consonant things vibrate together'. Where does the change happen? In the inner field of perception or the exterior reality of moving things in the course of becoming. 'And time is no longer an obstacle, but the means by which the possible is achieved'.[2]
>
> *(Radique, 1973)*

This text from the liner notes of the 2011 release of the composition reflects on her understanding of time and space and things, and of how they come together in consonant vibrations 'by which the possible is achieved'.

Nothing about the work feels like she is using the synthesiser as an instrument. There is no disparity between the sound and her body to suggest a sense of technical application, and there is no gap in the material for ideas of perfection or virtuosity to enter into the duration of her work. The causality of the sound is not that of instrumentation but of itself as it operates in the world: as it vibrates and exists with other things and other bodies, that of the composer and that of the listener. By expanding synthesised sounds, sounds of a technological birth, that come from nowhere, she produces an invisible limitlessness that distracts the nominal sense of where things come from, how they belong together and how they find meaning. Her drones eschew reference and exist instead through the transient associations of their durational existence. In this way she rejects the technology as a means of production towards an end, and composes it as material instead; and she dis-places the access to the meaning of the work into its temporality, to focus on the invisible mobility of sound as it exists rather than what it produces.

Interesting in this regard is a short anecdote picked up by Rodgers in her interview of Radique in 2006 regarding the keyboard, the control device, of the ARP 2500. 'Of course I didn't use the keyboard, I left it in New York when I moved the synthesizer to France. I didn't want to take the keyboard, (…) So by leaving it in New York I was sure that I would just work with the potentiometers' (Ibid., pp. 56–57).

Leaving the keyboard behind implies a deliberate dissociation from the designed functionality and normative use of the synths. It is a strategic move that averts the dominant, technoscientific persuasion of the tool and renders it a thing, whose thinging is free from the ideologies of a nominal instrumentality. Another way to subvert and re-recombinate the means and the end of artistic practice is evident in Shilpa Gupta's installation, *I keep falling at you*, from 2010, which consists of a 'dark cloud of microphones like angry bees',[3] that hang from the ceiling of the gallery, over 1,000 of them. These microphones have been rewired to configure them as loudspeakers. The reversed wiring diverts the functional flow between sound capture and its reproduction, and instead of receiving sound allows the microphones to sound their own voice, demanding its own context. Directions are reversed and nominal positions and relationships are put into question. The mute recorder has become the playback device and attained agency to exact revenge and finally say what was on its mind all along. The text spoken through the 'wrong' end of these 1,000s of hanging microphones repeatedly chants:

> I keep falling at you
> But I keep falling at you (chorus, repeat)
> Your garden is growing on me
> I will take it away with me
> To a land which you can mark no more
> Where distances don't grow anymore
> I keep falling at you
> But I keep falling at you (chorus repeat).[4]

Through the reversal of output and input, the chant amplifies the critique of colonial dominance and ideology hinted at in the text. The work corrupts the technoscientific orthodoxies of microphony and amplification and thereby interrupts the political orthodoxies of power and dominance. The technology is the occurrence of the material and of the concept, it does not function but operates on the nominal to make it speak another way.

In this sense Gupta's work does not only cut the cord of source and sound, it also cuts into the infrastructure of sonic production. Her work literally cuts the microphone cord and reverses the feed of technology to subvert and pervert its nominal articulation and dominance and to operate less purposefully on the textures of a normative world.

Bodies of technology

The fact that humans are sounding too, a thing that things, means that the technologically enabled separation of sound from its source, the dis-placement and the subsequent possibilities of re-placement or even unplacement of that sound; the defiance of an attributal or descriptive and interpretative role and perfect instrumentality, applies to the human body and to identity also. The body as thing thinging can be dis-placed by the technologies of sound. This however produces not a disembodiment, as it is so often termed particularly in relation to the radio. The body is not absent but pluralised: as sonic thing it is the body of its mobile and invisible possibilities. The recorded voice has thus not lost its substance but performs it; free from the constraints of a visual identity it moves as a formless form. All that is lost is visual certainty and definition.

In this way, the notion of operationality as effort is radical in relation to the body and in terms of prescribed parameters of identity as well as in relation to notions of sociality and communication: the body dis-placed by the technologies of sound can separate itself from what it is supposed to do, how it is supposed to function and affirm itself in its socio-political context. It can question the identity of the visual body, expand it and open a space for possibilities. It can deny the invisible nominalism that defines its visual appearance and reject the dominant expectations that limit its reception, to be a formless form, not swallowed by technological ideologies but coinciding with their operation.

Pamela Z's 'You' from *A Delay is Better* (2013) cuts the voice and cuts the cord to a dominant articulation and science. The word 'You' repeats and proliferates, building a rhythm and making a song that is not musical and correct but sings a techno-body-truth that is not realised by technology but practices the coincidence of the body and the machine.

Her works' knowledge is not that of the history of technology, or of music and arts' genealogy, but of its production. The voice and technology meet in the experience of expansion and inexhaustibility, where the language of the voice and the language of technology produce a different articulation that expresses their coincidence rather than their causality. Her voice speaks the language of technology in a pluralising form; formless and ephemeral. This language of technology is unable to swallow her body in its ideology but pluralises it into the possibilities of the language of her voice. To be as voice an expanded plurality and invisible techno-thing that does not deny but transforms the body into its possibilities, which are retained, at least as radiation, even once the machine that enabled its expansion is switched off.

The thread between voice and technology is not causal; it presents neither a necessity nor an ideal. The techno-voice expands the physical and the conceptual capacity of the body, as much as it expands the material and conceptual capacity of technology. They are as occurrence not this or that but are simultaneous with each other, and point towards a simultaneity with other things and other sounds. Technology as occurrence does not produce a thing but expands the capacity of things: of material, of bodies and of thought, to be themselves and to be with other things; expanding what things are, how they belong together and where they belong.

Pamela Z's voice is not ideal, it does not respond to the expectations of harmony or perfect pitch, but 'sings' a technological space that is the possible space of her articulation. Expansive and plural, it has entered the elastic reality of sound where as a mobile and invisible body it exists outside the necessity of its bio-cultural definition and instrumentality, and generates itself in the coincidence of a technological occurrence as sound and in sound.

The array of technologies involved in her practice is considerable. However, the material and conceptual cut that dis-places sound art from the expectation of hearing the right sound, the right material, the right articulation, means that in the context of sound art this technology is not limited to its own perfection and purpose, but operates on the possibilities of itself and of the voice, and dis-places technological and musical criteria of value and validity beyond existing comparisons in more contingent threads. The microphone, the amplifier, the feedback pedals, cords and sockets, BodySynth™, VST plugins, et al.,[5] enable the plural materialisations of her body and 'operate' on its texture and spatiality. This technological operation is not only the means of her work but is its occurrence that is also its end, as an inexhaustible end of plural means that articulates as the coincidence of both languages: technological and vocal.

Sound art's techno-futures

The works of Radique, Gupta and Pamela Z each demonstrate the possibilities of technology as an occurrence that is operational rather than functional, a thing rather than a tool, and that is the expansion and re-recombination of bodies, voices and technologies vibrating together. All three artists work with the technological dis-placement of sound from its source, to move into possibilities, taking the absence of a defining referent as a means to generate formless forms of drones, microphones and bodies.

These dis-placements could be read within Jacques Attali's notion of the rupture of the historical continuum, which happens out of necessity when an existing organisation is being pushed to an extreme, 'to the point where it creates the *internal* condition of its own rupture…', and results in a new harmony, in a new mode of sonic production (Attali, 2002, p. 35).

However, within such necessity the resulting rupture is tied historically and chronologically to the dominant of which it presents but a different organisation: the normal and expected consequence of historical change that reconfigures and replaces the dominant from its own ground.

Instead, I prefer to see the dis-placement outside this chronology and the inevitable debt it implies to the past, which thus always already determines the limitations and values of the future, dragging the dominant ideology as a ghost of technoscientific and instrumentomusical projects past into its work. In this way we could read it within Kodwo Eshun's Futurerhythmmachine, and avoid with him a '[r]earview hearing' (Eshun, 1998, p. 78), and instead expect a present sound to arrive from the future, in a sonic futurism that 'doesn't locate you in tradition; instead it dislocates you from origins' (ibid., p. 1).

It is not this or that, the past or the present, convention or its rupture, a thinking which ties the future into a dialectics of change. Instead the present comes from an unknown place born not from a visual source and history but from its own invisible occurrence whose operationality does something within the things of the present that consequently owe their form and function not to the past, to what we know, but are measured on the formless purposelessness of the alien that rendered thought astonishment.

This is one way to understand and discuss the technologies of sound art which avoids their practice and discourse being swallowed up by their dominant uses within music, their instrumentality and concurrent notions of virtuosity, a right sound and aesthetic truth; or by the demands of a scientific truth, and its focus on discovery and application.

Sound art, to go back to Eastley, has been enabled by technology, digital and analogue. However, sound art is also challenging and reframing technological processes by taking them into its practice, making them an occurrence of its own operation, a material rather than a tool, that does not harmonise and confirm, or recombinate the dominant, but that dis-places its ideology. Technologies of sound art dis-place sound from the dominant tone of music and science: the monochord that comes from the past and determines the future as a homogenous rearview hearing which confirms and stabilises the past and lacks a present articulation.[6] This dis-placement, the working outside the realms of instrumental and scientific truth, in the subversive and radical sphere of purposeless operation and science fiction, makes the invisible nominalism visible and ultimately challenges its legitimacy through different and pluralised notions of sound, listening, art and technology.

Notes

1 The term Zeug in German literally means stuff rather than tool, which is colloquially known as Werkzeug, 'stuff used for work'. This linguistic detail causes me to consider that the tool of the Zeug is not other than the stuff, the stone, metal, wood, etc., at least initially, but is its Wertschätzung, its evaluation in relation to its potential utilisation and thus it is apparent as a tool only to insiders, to those familiar and in agreement with the criteria of evaluation: what something should be used for and what needs to be done. For those not within this partisan community, it remains just stuff.

2 Éliane Radique from the liner notes of *Transamorem Transmortem* IMPREC337 CD, available online http://importantrecords.com/imprec/imprec337 (accessed 25.03.18).

3 Peter Weibel 2013 quoted at www.tirochedeleon.com/item/305036 (accessed 01.22. 2016).

4 Shilpa Gupta, *I keep falling at you* (2010), spoken text element of work, reprinted with permission from the artist, available at http://shilpagupta.com/pages/2010/10ikeepfalling.htm (accessed 25.03.18). Printed with permission of the artist.

5 In an interview with Cathy Lane, published in *Playing with Words*, Pamela Z lists in detail all the technology she works with, she does not elaborate but makes a point of a comprehensive inventory.

6 Frances Dyson, in her book *The Tone of our Times* (MIT, 2014), discusses ways to think about the world by what its tone rather than its sound reveals about the ecology of our political systems and subjectivities. Working through religious rituals and the act of acclamation to parliamentary systems and philosophical language, and on to the tenor of the voice and its media-political reality, she suggests the tone reveals the dominant ideologies of the present to be based on the interest of the monochord: the historical unit of the tonal system, that required that irrational ratios and the possibility of the incommensurable were 'to be concealed at all costs' (p. 23). Following her I believe we can discern

not only the tone of the political economy of our time but that the technological economy too has a tone, which equally sounds the suppression of the apparently irrational to maintain its principle. Sound arts' subversion of technological functions and instrumentality retunes this tone, to sound plural incommensurabilities that reveal and dis-place the ideologies of a technological monochord.

References

Attali, J. *Noise the Political Economy of Music*, translated by Brian Massumi, London: University of Minnesota Press, 2002 [orig. 1977].

Cox, C. and Daniel Warner (eds.), *Audio Culture, Readings in Modern Music*, New York, NY: Continuum, 2007.

Dyson, F. *The Tone of Our Times, Sound, Sense, Economy and Ecology*, London: MIT Press, 2014.

Eshun, K. *More Brilliant Than the Sun: Adventures in Sonic Fiction*, London: Quartet Books, 1998.

Gardner, T. and Salomé Voegelin (eds.), *Colloquium: Sound Art – Music*, London: Zero Books, 2016.

Gould, G. 'The Prospects of Recording' in the *Glenn Gould Reader*, Tim Page ed., London: Faber and Faber, 1987.

Heidegger, M. *Der Ursprung des Kunstwerkes*, Stuttgart: Reclam, 2008 [orig. 1950].

Lane, C. (ed.) *Playing with Words*, London: CRiSAP, RGAP, 2008.

Radique, E. *Transamorem Transmortem* liner notes, IMPREC337 CD, Groveland, MA: Important Records, 2013 http://importantrecords.com/imprec/imprec337 (accessed 25 March 2018).

Rodgers, T. *Pink Noises, Women on Electronic Music and Sound*, Durham, NC: Duke University Press, 2010.

20

FOUND IN TRANSLATION: RECORDING, STORING AND WRITING OF SOUNDS

Carolyn Birdsall

This chapter deals with a notion that is prevalent in sound studies, namely, of sound as "lost." It involves the suggestion that sound is underappreciated or even repressed, and needs to be "found," and thus recovered, reconstructed and re-evaluated in scholarly analysis. This discourse implies that sound is a phenomenon that is ephemeral, lacking or incomplete, as a state of affairs that prompts a search for its traces, inscriptions or other means to reveal sonic and auditory phenomena. By implication, the possibility of being found heralds sound as rich, fascinating and compelling. This narrative is sometimes connected to essentialist definitions of sound (and hearing) pitted in opposition to image (and seeing). These oppositions, which Jonathan Sterne (2003: 15) dubs the "audio-visual litany," tend to reinforce universalist and crude simplifications of sound in terms of temporality, immersion, interiority and affect.

The persistence of the lost and found narrative attached to sound should be contrasted to the establishment of sound studies as a recognized and recognizable field (or interdiscipline), in the wake of a "sonic turn" during the course of the 1990s and early 2000s. In a survey of scholarship in sound (culture) studies, Michele Hilmes (2005) noted that the idea of sound as an emerging or burgeoning area of enquiry had already been evident for over a century. This argument acts as a cautionary reminder to scholars not to reproduce polemics that exaggerate sound as ignored, repressed or lost (Smith 2004). While sound scholarship can be found in a variety of disciplinary contexts, and is not restricted to a particular method or approach, during recent years the field has undergone various forms of institutionalization, as evidenced by graduate study programs, faculty hires and numerous dedicated scholarly organizations, networks and platforms. Another mark of how sound – and its study – has found institutional approval and academic interest is not only via special issues and single-authored monographs; the growth of publisher interest is also suggested by an abundance of readers, handbooks, keyword collections and research companions, which includes the present publication (cf. Bull and Back 2003; Sterne 2012; Pinch and Bijsterveld 2011; Novak and Sakakeeny 2015; Papenburg and Schulze 2016).

With this background in mind, the following chapter will cover various attempts to "find" sound, not only as the result of formal method, but also in the myriad of ways in which sounds – past and present – are uncovered, retraced or reconstructed. The first section will deal more generally with sound recording and playback, and how sound has been understood as discoverable within multiple media modalities and formats. It will therefore examine the predominant means by which sound has been represented or rendered through acts of translation.

The second part reflects on the storage of sound, but also related processes of ordering and classifying sound, forms of canonization and institutional frameworks and infrastructures that allow for some sounds – over others – to be preserved and made accessible. The final part raises questions about sound as writing: not only in terms of its inscription or notation, but also how specific professional and applied contexts produce particular languages and epistemologies of sound. As such, all three sections will allow for observations as to how sound has been variously conceived through a series of discursive, institutional and aesthetic-technological frameworks.

Recording, representation, (re)mediation

Within sound studies, there has been a substantial scholarly attention to the mechanical invention and functioning, as well as the promotion, dissemination and adoption of sound recording and playback devices. In the history of technology, Thomas Edison's announcement of his phonograph invention has led to the year 1877 being enshrined as the "birth" of sound recording. More recent scholarship has challenged this narrative's focus on a single year and inventor, emphasizing instead the co-existence of other devices in the same period. Leon Scott's phonautograph, for instance, has been investigated as a device that also created recordings of sounds – as visual traces – but did not facilitate their playback.

The commercial presentation of sound recording and playback envisaged a range of possible applications for Edison's "Talking Machine," ranging from educational instruction and the dictation of audio letters to the collection of family "albums" and the voices of famous figures (Edison 1878). Such applications draw attention to the way in which new technologies like the phonograph were framed or made legible according to existing cultural practices of writing and copying in the late nineteenth century (Sterne 2003; Schwartz 2014). The subsequent, mass dissemination of sound recording and playback devices has been outlined, for instance, as bound up with notions of liveness, authenticity and fidelity (Thompson 1995). The social construction of the home phonograph around 1900, furthermore, drew on the existing gender-typing of consumption and domestic music performance, a process in which the phonograph served as "a translation device between the private and public spheres" (Gitelman 2004: 71).

In the public realm, a common articulation about phonography was that it captured segments of time, but also allowed for manipulations of time (through speed, delays) and subsequent redistribution of sounds across space (Levin 1990). The act of recording, moreover, was framed in terms of inscribing a wide range of sonorities; while Friedrich Kittler has noted this prevalent discourse of "all sounds," his account of phonographic inscription refers to an opposition between sounds and unsounds (Kittler 1999). The phonograph not only recorded sounds, but the device also produced its own forms of interference that could be heard in playback. The presence of noise was, of course, a major issue for those engaging with transmission technologies of sound telegraphy, telephony and, later, radio broadcasting. For both transmission and inscription technologies, then, the noise (or feedback) produced by the technological device has been cited as influential for medium-specific sound conventions and aesthetics (Campbell 2006).

On the whole, sound recording – whether by means of phonographic inscription, tape or other formats – has been understood as a studio art (Schmidt Horning 2013). In addition to commercial, studio-based recording, this ability to manipulate parameters (such as speed and volume) has also figured strongly in artistic responses to phonography. Notable examples of twentieth-century production examined in sound studies scholarship include avant-garde art and music composition; experiments with playback, loudspeakers and loudness; and new styles of vocal presentation and cultural expression (see, for instance, Moholy-Nagy 1926; Kahn 1992; Weheliye 2005; Kelly 2009; Devine 2013). In a similar vein, advancements in recording techniques (for example multi-track stereo, Dolby Noise reduction) and formats (for example LP, CD, mp3) have provided new tools for shaping sound in recording and post-production (Katz 2010; Frith and Zagorski-Thomas 2012).

A conventional historical timeline, therefore, would probably cite a historical shift from mechanical recording to electrically powered recording devices, and subsequent improvements in recording techniques, sound quality and standardization (for example recording and playback speed). This narrative is sometimes used to imply that sound recording – particularly in the later shift from analogue to digital recording – has continued to gain an ever-improving quality of fidelity and realism (Mowitt 1987; Evens 2005). A useful argument, in this context, can be gleaned from James Lastra's argument to discontinue using the term *sound reproduction* – due to its assumption of an exact copy – in favor of *sound representation* (2000: 123–153). This emphasis paves the way for a longer historical view of competing discourses of realism, as well as efforts to achieve sound fidelity via particular techniques of representation (see also Wurtzler 2007: 229–250).

In the study of media technologies, there has been a shift away from examining any one particular medium to a concern with constellations or ecologies of media (Thorburn and Jenkins 2003). Tom Levin (2010), for instance, has urged for scholars to develop longer genealogies of sound inscription as occurring across multiple devices prior to Edison's 1877 invention; his media archaeological view on the long history of recording includes examples of voice capture dating back to China in the seventeenth century. An interest in the connections between media, as facilitating cross-media aesthetics has also been fueled by the work of David Bolter and Richard Grusin (2000). Their concept of "remediation" offers a means to consider how television and digital platforms re-use content – such as feature films, music, broadcast recordings – produced by other media. In this vein, some scholars have taken phonographic recording as a site for considering intermedial phenomena – for example, styles of media performance in popular, spoken-word LPs – that have tended to be ignored in related disciplines like media, theatre and popular music studies (Smith 2011).

The remediation concept, therefore, provides a means – also in sound studies – to consider partial connections between media. Much attention has been devoted to intermedial aesthetics produced in the context of the 1920s to 1940s, as prompted by both commercial interests and aesthetic experimentation between sound recording, radio, cinema and early television (Wurtzler 2007; Forman 2012; Birdsall 2014). Meanwhile, other scholars have reinvestigated the early period of "silent" cinema from the vantage of sound recording to challenge a film historiography that neglects the place of the phonograph (Feaster and Smith 2009; Altman 2007). Another effort is to consider how recorded sound has historically interacted with print media, whether in the form of synesthetic interplay with the visual arts, in exchange with the newspaper and illustrated magazines, in audiobook remediations of print literature, or inscriptions of sound in Braille books (Currid 2006; Rubery 2011).

Lastly, the formation of modern recording media and sound aesthetics has been explored in terms of sounds produced via the materiality of urban built environments, indoor spaces and technological infrastructures (Thompson 20043; Blesser and Salter 2009; Mattern 2013). More generally, such work raises questions about the traces left by recorded sound in various arenas of culture and media representation, and its potential to play a role in popular memory (Kenney 2003); it is to these more specific themes for lost and found sound – concerning storage, preservation and accessibility – that the next section will turn.

Storage, preservation, access

In recent years, there has been a growing scholarly attention to formal and informal processes by which recorded sounds have (or have not) been actively stored, preserved and made accessible. Where the previous section discusses processes of capturing and representing sound, in various formats and forms, this section is more interested in selection, canonization and possibilities for access and re-use.

One of the key means by which the storage and distribution of recorded sound has been historically communicated to others is through lists, catalogues and discographies. In the commercial, recorded music industry, which emerged in the last decades of the 1800s, both major and smaller record companies released catalogues listing their phonograph and gramophone recordings (Day 2001; Gronow and Saunio 1998; Symes 2004). Another means for ordering these recordings – at the time of and since their release – is via matrix numbers and factory codes, which provide additional information about their production context to collectors and archivists. In professional practice, library and archive catalogues have been a predominant tool to keep track of their collections, but also classify them according to author, title, year, genre and other categories.

Apart from private and research-based collections, there are only a few early examples of entire institutions devoted to the collection of sound recordings. One of the more well-known forerunners is the establishment of the Phonothèque nationale in Paris in 1938, which formed part of the Bibliothèque National and established a national legal deposit (Hoffmann 2004: 416–417). In the case of the United States, the Library of Congress (LoC) has played an important role in collecting commercial and culturally significant sound recordings from the 1920s onwards, as well as the later commissions granted to figures like John and Alan Lomax to record a variety of singers and oral storytellers for the LoC's Archive of Folk-Song (now American Folklife Center).

Some institutions have tended to focus only on recordings from their own national or regional recording industries; other institutions – like the British Institute of Recorded Sound (BIRS), formally constituted by Patrick Saul in 1948 – have proclaimed to have an interest in collecting all recorded sound. Despite such claims, institutions like BIRS maintained a strong preference for musical repertoire, preferring to collect classical music and opera recordings, including radio broadcasts (Saul 1956), while resisting and sometimes refusing to acquire popular music genres such as Jazz, Pop and Rock.

While there were prior discussions about the organization of sound recordings, the formal development of a professional discourse can be identified with the establishment of the International Association of Music Librarians (IAML) in 1949, under the auspices of UNESCO in Geneva. Within the framework of IAML, subcommittees were formed to address common issues of international standards for classification and preservation methods, but also addressing different types of collections, from sheet music and musical instrument to radio sound archives and music recordings. In the case of radio archiving, national broadcasters in Europe had already pioneered collections of live and pre-recorded programs from the late 1920s onwards, but it was only in the post-war era that most of these archives were subject to active institutional policies and preservation strategies (Birdsall 2016). A more specific organization devoted to the archiving of sound recordings emerged from the IAML subcommittees in 1969, with the formation of the International Association of Sound Archivists (IASA). In the US context, a group of librarians and private collectors officially formed the Association for Recorded Sound Collections as a joint endeavor in 1966 (Hoffmann 2004: 1020–1021).

In recent years, there has been a renewed awareness of the role of archivists in determining what comes into archives, priorities for preservation and restoration as well as selecting, deleting and discarding parts of collections (Cook 2011). In response, commentators have called for a renewed awareness of the ways in which archivists participate in processes of selection, particularly in foregrounding significant recordings, which often reveals a conservative bias towards the voices of famous people and recognized historical events. Such recordings are often presented as valuable and desirable recordings for interested stakeholders in the present, as presented to radio and filmmakers, museums, researchers and for educational purposes. While there is a longer history of audio-visual media as teaching aids in the classroom, the selection and presentation of sounds for research and educational purposes was further encouraged by institutions dedicated to multimedia and documentation resources between the 1950s and 1970s, such as the National Audio-Visual Aids Library (in the UK), Institut für Film und Bild in Wissenschaft und Unterricht (in West Germany) and Stichting Film en Wetenschap (in the Netherlands).

Processes of canonization can be attributed to the re-use of sound recordings in radio, television, film and digital media production. In some contexts like North America, re-use of recordings in the first decades of broadcasting were variously promoted or prevented due to commercial interests or copyright regulations (Kompare 2004). Both in broadcasting and film, it is not only selections or full-length recordings that have been re-used, but also shorter clips or sound bites, with the sounds used for station idents or studio logos (opening credits) operating as identifiable brands. Idents and jingles tended to be stored on disc or tape, and held in station sound libraries, but as forms of commercial advertising have rarely been treated as valuable objects of scholarly study (Taylor 2012; Seay 2016).

The storage and preservation of recorded sound is thus connected to the value attached to it, and the status of a recording as a stand-alone archival record or part of a particular collection (with well-documented provenance). The archival status of a record can also vary depending on whether it is held in a national or research archive, a corporate archive or in a private collection. This status may also depend on the type of recording (voice, music, sound effects), whether it is a master or copy, and the carrier it is held on (disc recording, tape, digital format). All of these factors can play an influential role in determining the extent to which (digital) preservation is considered necessary or urgent, with format obsolescence one of the most frequently articulated challenges for audio preservation (for example The British Library's 2015 funding campaign "Save our Sounds"). The proliferation of digitized recordings and online access to media collections – through YouTube, the Internet Archive and other platforms – has prompted discussions of increased democratization and challenges to the "gatekeeping" function of archivists (Noordegraaf 2010). At the same time, online curation has come to play an increasingly significance role in sound archival outreach and educational efforts, such as the recent Europeana Sounds portal (Franzen 2016).

In the current archival landscape, there has been an increased circulation of – and interest in – recordings that have not necessarily passed through formal archives, from bootleg and amateur recordings through to various forms of user generated content (UGC). In this context, the proliferation of remix techniques, along with what has been dubbed "retromania" (Reynolds 2011), has fueled an interest in compiling and recycling of archive and found footage materials (Baron 2014). These processes of circulation have also led to experiments with "viral" sounds (Cooper and Piard 2015) and investigations as to the "spreadability" of recorded sound in contemporary media culture (Jenkins, Ford and Green 2013). In other areas, committed groups and fans of musical subcultures have taken preservation and access matters into their own hands by forming DIY archive initiatives (Brandellero et al. 2013).

One interesting aspect to the recovery of "lost" sounds is the affirmation of users on the basis of shared memory. The online initiative by former student Brendan Chilcutt, entitled the Museum of Endangered Sounds, has generated a lot of buzz, since it not only includes the highly designed signature sounds of consumer electronics and gaming devices, but also sounds that were by-products of technical processes, such as dial-up Internet. The appeal to shared memory and memorialization has also served as a motivating force for NPR's "Lost & Found Sound" program, with a special series devoted to the sonic traces of 9/11 in 2001 drawing on first-person accounts, voice-mail messages and personal archives (www.sonicmemorial.org). The recovery and reorganization of ephemeral sounds has also prompted a raft of sound and soundscape mapping projects, in which the locatedness of past and present sounds are geo-tagged onto maps of particular cities, if not whole countries (Ouzounian 2014). In other cases, the unearthing of lost sound has generated an interest in forgotten media practices that are rarely held by archives and circulate in private collections and Internet sites eBay; one such form is creation of acoustic letters, for which the scholar Tom Levin has established the online Phono-Post resource (www. phono-post.org).

In general, scholars have noted a conservative impulse motivating some past archival initiatives, which may also lead to present-day preservation initiatives to operate under a default mode by which audio recordings of famous politicians, intellectuals, artists and the cultural elite are given priority (Müske 2010). Given the relationship between recorded sound, official history and memory processes, critical perspectives on how recorded sound is stored, preserved and made accessible are needed. The biases and absences in the archival record require scholars of recorded sound to remain attentive to absences of archives and the frequent denials on the basis of race, ethnicity, class, gender, sexuality, disability and mental health. These exclusions have been challenged in numerous and repeated efforts to generate oral history archives with audio recordings documenting personal experience and testimony, along with the preservation of community radio recordings, such those held by the Pacifica Radio Archive (Birdsall, Parry & Tkaczyk 2015). While problematic audio collections require further interrogation of implicit power relations, attempts at "close listening" to these archival recordings in the present often face incommensurable challenges to interpretation (Hoffmann 2015). The following section will pick up on such questions of interpretation and knowledge production, with particular attention to how specific professional and applied context produce particular understandings of and practices with sounds, both wanted and unwanted.

Writing, language, epistemology

One of the more common observations articulated in sound studies literature is that academic publication culture – primarily based on written language – poses significant challenges to the task of accounting for the acoustic properties and dimensions of sound. While the written word is posited as a translation or even a flattening of sound (Schafer 1994 [1977], Bull and Back 2003), the English language, for instance, has been deemed as highly biased towards visualist thinking, further hampering the project of developing sound vocabularies (Jay 1993). In film and media studies much robust work has been done not only to redress visual(ist) theory by formulating tools of sound theory, with challenges to established notions of purely visual or sound media (Mitchell 2005) and efforts to account for audiovisuality in media culture (Chion 1994; Richardson, Gorbman and Vernallis 2013). Such research, moreover, has placed an emphasis on audience reception, with a particular attention to the role of sensory engagement and embodied perception of audiences/users (Bull 2000). The implicit purpose of sound studies to dislodge the primacy of vision may, in fact, come at the expense of other modalities of perception, with Deaf Studies acting as a corrective by acknowledging more diversity in the experience of sound, language and music, often via tactile and visual processes of communication and perception (Friedner and Helmreich 2012).

An important intervention in sound studies research has been the attention to the significance of science and medicine in the co-formation of modern listening practices and understandings of sound in the nineteenth century and earlier. Jonathan Sterne's work has occupied a prominent place in these discussions, given his attention to a broader set of developments that produced modern sound culture. In particular, Sterne observes the rise of "techniques of audition" – framed in terms of reason and scientific rationality – as the basis of professional knowledge in modern medicine and sound telegraphy (2003: 31–177). Listening – via the stethoscope or telegraph – served as a "symbol of modernity, sophistication, skill, and engagement" (2003: 137), prefiguring the creation and use of sound reproduction technologies in the second half of the nineteenth century. In Emily Thompson's study of the emergence of modern architectural acoustics in the decades after 1900 (2003), the desire to rationalize and control sound in performance spaces is contextualized against the backdrop of noise abatement campaigns in urban environments.

In recent decades, historians of science and technology have also worked to challenge the assumption that science and medicine have, for centuries, relied on vision, display and the image in the production of scientific knowledge (Jones and Galison 1998; Wise 2006). In this vein, the turn to the embodied dimensions to scientific research has allowed for an increased understanding of the contribution of nonvisual senses and conditions of "epistemic cultures" (Knorr-Cetina 1991). One of the key developments recognized by researchers is the role of sound in laboratory-based research from the early nineteenth century onwards, particularly in the emergence of interdisciplinary research on acoustics and hearing, which involved disciplines such as physics, phonetics, ethnology and musicology (Kursell 2008: 3). Subsequent research has elaborated on this historical development from the mid-eighteenth century onwards, specifying cross-pollinations between music and science in the development of new research conditions (for example soundproof rooms), methods (for example sonification), instruments (for example tuning forks, oscillators) and instrumentation (Hui, Kursell and Jackson 2013).

Such work has paved the way for a broader understanding of sound in science and in specific research cultures in laboratory settings (Mody 2005). In the introduction to the *Oxford Handbook of Sound Studies* (2011), co-editors Trevor Pinch and Karin Bijsterveld stress that the individual contributions provide a broader scope of how "sonic skills" are not only figured in the lab, but also in the field, the clinic, the design studio, in domestic and online environments. Pinch and Bijsterveld's discussion of listening skills and knowledge production lays out a tripartite focus, namely on how professionals have acquired these skills and used their ears in their work; how these forms of listening were operative in knowledge production and instrument development; and the ongoing contestation of listening skills as a valid "way of knowing" (2011: 11–12). Against the background of ongoing debates about the relationship between visual and sonic skills, Sterne and Akiyama (2011) have criticized ongoing assumptions of sensorial separation, noting the contingencies by which techniques of sonification and auditory display prepare data for particular senses. They argue that "the articulations between particular senses and kinds of sense data are incredibly weak … [suggesting] that sound scholarship must be ever more vigilant about that shifting border between the sonic and nonsonic" (Sterne and Akiyama 2011: 547). Recent debates in the history of science have also sought to thoroughly deconstruct visual representation, and have urged scholars to account for the temporal processes of interaction and knowledge formation in scientific practice (Coopmans et al. 2014).

Of particular interest for sound studies is the particular languages used to describe and make sense of sounds. In the crossover between sociology of technology and sound studies, scholars have been attentive to the ways in which practitioners and enthusiasts of sound have developed their own, specific means of verbalizing particular sounds. In the case of professional discourse, scholars have paid particular attention to the recording studio as a site for the development of "hands-on techniques" and "tacit" knowledge amongst sound engineers, particularly as this field established formal training schools from the 1980s onwards (Porcello 2004; Schmidt Horning 2013). The formation of sonic skills in a particular area of practice can often draw on existing expert language and techniques, as has been observed in the competing principles articulated by radio engineers and telephone engineers working in the new field of synchronized sound film in the late 1920s and 1930s (Lastra 2000). Amateur groupings, such as "sound hunters" in the 1950s and 1960s, also developed popular knowledge of sound in developing their own aesthetic preferences and descriptive categories for the sounds they wished to record (Bijsterveld 2004). Marc Perlman (2004) has studied a particular strand of audiophilia – with its roots in post-war home electronics consumption – in which a group of primarily middle-aged men have idealized "hi fi" audio, creating particular uses, values and ways of talking about sound. Nonetheless, the privileging of masculinist sound cultures in recent historiography has been critiqued by Tara Rodgers (2015), whose research on early synthesizers has stressed the significance of uncovering alternative narratives of sound production practices.

We can also trace a number of research fields in which phonographic sound recording in the late nineteenth century was not only an epistemic tool, but was also constitutive to the foundation of knowledge in a field. In ethnography and ethnomusicology, phonography was understood as providing a data source, in similar terms to other indexical media like photography, while also complementing researchers' linguistic and music notation (Brady 1999; Ames 2003). Access to such collections, however, is often limited by the fragility of many recording formats and playback devices, and the degradation of recordings, whether held on disc, tape or digital formats. Much of the knowledge of such recordings has been communicated through paper documentation, which require scholars to become aware of the production of these recordings in tandem with bureaucratic and clerical work cultures, and thus mediated via particular genres and forms of "paper knowledge" (Gitelman 2014).

Given that many Western research fields were or became colonial disciplines, it is also essential to problematize such research in the context of imperial control and frontier expansion, with implicit hierarchies and forms of mishearing or misinformation underpinning knowledge production (Ochoa Gautier 2014; Lange 2015). In a similar vein, anthropologist Steven Feld has argued against a predominance of Western epistemologies of sound, with his own fieldwork with Kaluli communities in Papua New Guinea revealing a society grounded in "acoustemology" or a sound-based epistemology (Feld and Brenneis 2004). More generally, Feld has been critical of Eurocentrism in sound studies, and its predominant emphasis on media genres and sound technology, arguing instead for "more 'sound agency studies,' more 'sound actant studies.' I want more 'sound plural ontology studies,' or 'sound relationality studies.' Or 'sound companion species studies'" (Feld and Panopoulos 2015). In another critique of sound studies, Gus Stadler (2015) has argued that the chapters selected for readers and handbooks seem to claim a lack of bias. Stadler argues that this is evident in the general use of terms like "the listener," "the ear" and "the voice" that mask an implicit reproduction of whiteness, and has the potential to "guarantee the coherence and legibility of a field in formation" (2015: n.p.).

Such comments serve as an important caution to sound scholars to reflect on one's own blindspots and assumptions, and to push the boundaries of the normative tendencies within the field. Working in a similar vein to Feld, some recent scholarship has sought to take questions of agency, relationality, sonic materialism and plural ontologies as a point of departure (Born 2005; Chow and Steintrager 2011; Cox 2011). By way of a broad response, this chapter has called for the importance of acknowledging the persistent discourse in which sound has been presented in some contexts as the academy's repressed other or as an intellectual savior to established disciplines. Its departure point was therefore the persistent notion of sounds as lost cultural phenomena. In response, the three sections have outlined key aspects – namely, the recording, storage and writing of sounds – that reveal sounds and how they are conditioned by discursive, institutional and aesthetic-technological frameworks. To this end, it has insisted on the means by which sounds have been remediated, reconstructed and re-used, and thus found in translation.

References

Altman, R. (2007) *Silent Film Sound*. New York, NY: Columbia University Press.

Ames, E. (2003) "The Sound of Evolution," *Modernism/Modernity* 10(2), pp. 297–325.

Baron, J. (2014) *The Archive Effect: Found Footage and the Audiovisual Experience of History*. New York, NY: Routledge.

Bijsterveld, K. (2004) "'What do I do with my Tape Recorder...?': Sound Hunting and the Sounds of Everyday Dutch Life in the 1950s and 1960s," *Historical Journal of Film, Radio and Television* 24(4), pp. 613–34.

Birdsall, C. (2014) "Sound Aesthetics and the Global Imagination in German Media Culture around 1930," in D. Morat (ed.) *Sounds of Modern History: Auditory Cultures in 19th- and 20th-Century Europe*, London: Berghahn, pp. 256–77.

Birdsall, C. (2016) "Sound in Media Studies: Archiving and the Construction of Sonic Heritage," in J. G. Papenburg & H. Schulze (eds.) *Sound as Popular Culture: A Research Companion*, Cambridge, MA: MIT Press, pp. 133–48.

Birdsall, C., Parry, M. & Tkaczyk, V. (2015) "Listening to the Mind: Tracing the Auditory History of Mental Illness in Archives and Exhibitions," *The Public Historian* 37(4), pp. 47–72.

Blesser, B. & Salter, L-R. (2009) *Spaces Speak, Are You Listening?: Experiencing Aural Architecture*, Cambridge, MA: MIT Press.

Bolter, J. D. & Grusin, R. A. (2000) *Remediation: Understanding New Media*, Cambridge, MA: MIT Press.

Born, G. (2005) "On Musical Mediation: Ontology, Technology and Creativity," *Twentieth-Century Music* 2(1), pp. 7–36.

Brady, E. (1999) *A Spiral Way: How the Phonograph Changed Ethnography*, Jackson, MS: University Press of Mississippi.

Brandellero, A., et. al (eds.) (2013) "Special Issue: Popular Music as Cultural Heritage," *International Journal of Heritage Studies* 20(3). pp. 224–40.

Bull, M. (2000) *Sounding Out the City: Personal Stereos and the Management of Everyday Life*, Oxford: Berg.

Bull, M. & Back, L. (eds.) (2003) *The Auditory Culture Reader*, Oxford: Berg.

Campbell, T. C. (2006) *Wireless Writing in the Age of Marconi*, Minneapolis, MN: University of Minnesota Press.

Chion, M. (1994) *Audio-Vision: Sound on Screen*, New York, NY: Columbia University Press.

Chow, R. & Steintrager, J. A. (2011) "In Pursuit of the Object of Sound: An Introduction," *differences* 22(2–3), pp. 1–9.

Cook, T. (2011) "'We Are What We Keep; We Keep What We Are': Archival Appraisal Past, Present and Future," *Journal of the Society of Archivists* 32(2), pp. 173–89.

Cooper, P. & Piard, M. (2015) "Can Audio Go Viral? NPR Launches Audio Experiment on Facebook," accessed 1 June 2016 at www.npr.org/sections/thisisnpr/2015/12/17/459372755/can-audio-go-viral-npr-launches-audio-experiment-on-facebook.

Coopmans, C. et al. (eds.) (2014) *Representation in Scientific Practice Revisited*, Cambridge, MA: MIT Press.

Cox, C. (2011) "Beyond Representation and Signification: Toward a Sonic Materialism," *Journal of Visual Culture* 10(2), pp. 145–61.

Currid, B. (2006) *A National Acoustics: Music and Mass Publicity in Weimar and Nazi Germany*, Minneapolis, MN: University of Minnesota Press.

Day, T. (2001) *A Century of Recorded Music: Listening to Music History*, New Haven, CT: Yale University Press.

Devine, K. (2013) "Imperfect Sound Forever: Loudness Wars, Listening Formations and the History of Sound Reproduction," *Popular Music* 32(2), pp. 159–76.

Edison, T. A. (1878) "The Phonograph and Its Future," *The North American Review* 126(262), pp. 527–36.

Evens, A. (2005) *Sound Ideas: Music, Machines, and Experience*, Minneapolis, MN: University of Minnesota Press.

Feaster, P. & Smith, J. (2009) "Reconfiguring the History of Early Cinema Through the Phonograph, 1877–1908," *Film History: An International Journal* 21(4), pp. 311–25.

Feld, S. & Brenneis, D. (2004) "Doing Anthropology in Sound," *American Ethnologist* 31(4), pp. 461–74.

Feld, S. & Panopoulos, P. (2015) "Athens Conversation," accessed 1 June 2016 at www.stevenfeld.net/interviews.

Forman, M. (2012) *One Night on TV is Worth Weeks at the Paramount: Popular Music on Early Television*, Durham, NC: Duke University Press.

Franzen, R. (2016) "European Sounds: An Interface into European Sound Archives," *Sound Studies: An Interdisciplinary Journal 2(1), pp.* 1–4.

Friedner, M. & Helmreich, S. (2012) "Sound Studies Meets Deaf Studies," *The Senses and Society* 7(1), pp. 72–86.

Frith, S. & Zagorski-Thomas, S. (eds.) (2012) *The Art of Record Production: An Introductory Reader for a New Academic Field*, Aldershot: Ashgate.

Gitelman, L. (2004) "How Users Define New Media: A History of the Amusement Phonograph," in D. Thorburn & H. Jenkins (eds.) *Rethinking Media Change: The Aesthetics of Transition*, Cambridge, MA: MIT Press, pp. 61–79.

Gitelman, L. (2014) *Paper Knowledge: Toward a Media History of Documents*, Durham, NC: Duke University Press.

Gronow, P. & Saunio, I. (1998) *International History of the Recording Industry*, London and New York: Cassell.

Hilmes, M. (2005) "Is There a Field Called Sound Culture Studies? And Does it Matter?" *American Quarterly*, 57(1), pp. 249–59.

Hoffmann, A. (2015) "Introduction: Listening to Sound Archives," *Social Dynamics* 41(1), pp. 73–83.

Hoffmann, F. (ed.) (2004) *Encyclopedia of Recorded Sound*, vol. 1.: A-L., New York and Oxon: Routledge.

Hui, A., Kursell, J. & Jackson, M. W. (2013) "Music, Sound and the Laboratory from 1750–1980," *Osiris* 28, pp. 1–11.

Jay, M. (1993) *Downcast Eyes: The Denigration of Vision in Twentieth-Century French Thought*, Berkeley, CA: University of California Press.

Jenkins, H., Ford, S. & Green, J. (2013) *Spreadable Media: Creating Value and Meaning in a Networked Culture*, New York: New York University Press.

Jones, C. & Galison, P. (eds.) (1998) *Picturing Science, Producing Art*, London: Routledge.

Kahn, D. (1992) "Introduction: Histories of Sound Once Removed," in D. Kahn & G. Whitehead (eds.) *Wireless Imagination: Sound, Radio, and the Avant-Garde*, Cambridge, MA: MIT Press, pp. 1–29.

Katz, M. (2010) *Capturing Sound: How Technology Has Changed Music*, Berkeley, CA: University of California Press.

Kelly, C. (2009) *Cracked Media: The Sound of Malfunction*, Cambridge, MA: MIT Press.

Kenney, W. H. (2003) *Recorded Music in American Life: The Phonograph and Popular Memory, 1890–1945*, New York, NY: Oxford University Press.

Kittler, F. A. (1999) *Gramophone, Film, Typewriter*, trans. G. Winthrop-Young & M. Wutz, Stanford, CA: Stanford University Press.

Knorr-Cetina, K. D. (1991) "Epistemic Cultures: Forms of Reason in Science," *History of Political Economy* 23(1), pp. 105–22.

Kompare, D. (2004) *Rerun Nation: How Repeats Invented American Television*, New York: Routledge.

Kursell, J. (ed.) (2008) *Sound of Science / Schall im Labor: 1800–1930*, Berlin: Max Planck Institute for the History of Science.

Lange, B. (2015) "Poste restante, and Messages in Bottles: Sound Recordings of Indian Prisoners in the First World War," *Social Dynamics* 41(1), pp. 84–100.

Lastra, J. (2000) *Sound Technology and the American Cinema: Perception, Representation, Modernity*, New York, NY: Columbia University Press.

Levin, T. Y. (1990) "For the Record: Adorno on Music in the Age of its Technological Reproducibility," *October* 55, pp. 23–47.

Levin, T. Y. (2010) "Before the Beep: A Short History of Voice Mail," in N. Neumark, R. Gibson & T. van Leeuwen (eds.) *Voice: Vocal Aesthetics in Digital Arts and Media*, Cambridge, MA: MIT Press, pp. 17–32.

Mattern, S. (2013) "Ear to the Wire: Listening to Historic Urban Infrastructures" *Amodern* 2, at http://amodern.net/article/ear-to-the-wire.

Mitchell, W. J. T. (2005) "There are No Visual Media," *Journal of Visual Culture* 4(2), pp. 257–66.

Mody, C. M. (2005) "The Sounds of Science: Listening to Laboratory Practice," *Science, Technology & Human Values* 30(2), pp. 175–98.

Moholy-Nagy, L. (1926) "Musico-Mechanico, Mechanico-Optico," *Anbruch* 8, p. 401.

Mowitt, J. (1987) "The Sound of Music in the Era of its Electronic Reproducibility," in R. Leppert & S. McClary (eds.) *Music and Society: The Politics of Composition, Performance and Reception*, Cambridge: Cambridge University Press, pp. 173–97.

Müske, J. (2010) "Constructing Sonic Heritage: The Accumulation of Knowledge in the Context of Sound Archives," *Journal of Ethnology and Folkloristics* 4(1), pp. 37–47.

Noordegraaf, J. (2010) "Who Knows Television? Online Access and the Gatekeepers of Knowledge," *Critical Studies in Television* 5(2), pp. 1–19.

Novak, D. & Sakakeeny, M. (eds.) (2015) *Keywords in Sound*, Durham, NC & London: Duke University Press.

Ochoa Gautier, A. M. (2014) *Aurality: Listening and Knowledge in Nineteenth-Century Colombia*, Durham, NC: Duke University Press.

Ouzounian, G. (2014) "Acoustic Mapping: Notes from the Interface," in M. Gandy & B. Nilsen (eds.) *The Acoustic City*, Berlin: Jovis, pp. 164–73.

Papenburg, J. G., & H. Schulze (eds.) (2016) *Sound as Popular Culture: A Research Companion*, Cambridge, MA: MIT Press.

Perlman, M. (2004) "Golden Ears and Meter Readers: The Contest for Epistemic Authority in Audiophilia," *Social Studies of Science* 34(5), pp. 783–807.

Pinch, T. & Bijsterveld, K. (2011) "Introduction: New Keys to the World of Sound," in T. Pinch & K. Bijsterveld (eds.) *The Oxford Handbook of Sound Studies*, Oxford: Oxford University Press, pp. 3–39.

Pinch, T. & K. Bijsterveld, (eds.) (2011) *The Oxford Handbook of Sound Studies*. Oxford: Oxford University Press.

Porcello, T. (2004) "Speaking of Sound: Language and the Professionalization of Sound-Recording Engineers," *Social Studies of Science* 34(5), pp. 733–58.

Reynolds, S. (2011) *Retromania: Pop Culture's Addiction to Its Own Past*, Basingstoke: Palgrave Macmillan.

Richardson, J., Gorbman, C. & Vernallis, C. (eds.) (2013) *The Oxford Handbook of New Audiovisual Aesthetics*, Oxford and New York: Oxford University Press.

Rodgers, T. (2015) "Tinkering with Cultural Memory: Gender and the Politics of Synthesizer Historiography," *Feminist Media Histories* 1(4), pp. 5–30.

Rubery, M. (ed.) (2011) *Audiobooks, Literature, and Sound Studies*, New York and London: Routledge.

Saul, P. (1956) "The British Institute of Recorded Sound," *Fortes Artis Musicae* 3(2), pp. 170–73.

Schafer, R. M. (1994 [1977]) *The Soundscape: Our Sonic Environment and the Tuning of the World*, Rochester, VT: Destiny Books.

Schmidt Horning, S. (2013) *Chasing Sound: Technology, Culture and the Art of Studio Recording from Edison to the LP*, Baltimore, MD: Johns Hopkins University Press.

Schwartz, H. (2014) *The Culture of the Copy: Striking Likenesses, Unreasonable Facsimiles*, revised and updated edition, Brooklyn, NY: Zone Books.

Seay, T. (2016) "Sonic Signatures in Record Production," in J. G. Papenburg & H. Schulze (eds.) *Sound as Popular Culture: A Research Companion*, Cambridge, MA: MIT Press, pp. 347–53.

Smith, B. (2004) "Listening to the Wild Blue Yonder: The Challenges of Acoustic Ecology," in V. Erlmann (ed.) *Hearing Cultures: Essays on Sound, Listening and Modernity*, London: Berg, pp. 21–41.

Smith, J. (2011) *Spoken Word: Postwar American Phonograph Cultures*, Berkeley, CA: University of California Press.

Stadler, G. (2015) "On Whiteness and Sound Studies," *Sounding Out!*, accessed 1 June 2016 at https://soundstudiesblog.com/2015/07/06/on-whiteness-and-sound-studies/.

Sterne, J. (2003) *The Audible Past: Cultural Origins of Sound Reproduction*, Durham, NC: Duke University Press.

Sterne, J. (ed.) (2012) *The Sound Studies Reader*, New York, NY: Routledge.

Sterne, J. & M. Akiyama (2011) "The Recording that Never Wanted to be Heard and Other Stories of Sonification," in T. Pinch & K. Bijsterveld (eds.) *The Oxford Handbook of Sound Studies*, Oxford: Oxford University Press, pp. 544–60.

Symes, C. (2004) *Setting the Record Straight: A Material History of Classical Recording*, Middletown, CA: Wesleyan University Press.

Taylor, T. D. (2012) *The Sounds of Capitalism: Advertising, Music, and the Conquest of Culture*, Chicago, IL: University of Chicago Press.

Thompson, E. (1995) "Machines, Music, and the Quest for Fidelity: Marketing the Edison Phonograph in America, 1877–1925," *The Musical Quarterly* 79(1), pp. 131–71.

Thompson, E. (2004) *The Soundscape of Modernity: Architectural Acoustics and the Culture of Listening in America, 1900–1933*, Cambridge, MA: MIT Press.

Thorburn, D. & Jenkins, H. (eds.) (2003) *Rethinking Media Change: The Aesthetics of Transition*, Cambridge, MA: MIT Press.

Weheliye, A. G. (2005) *Phonographies: Grooves in Sonic Afro-Modernity*, Durham, NC: Duke University Press.

Wise, M. N. (2006) "Making Visible," *Isis* 97(1), pp. 75–82.

Wurtzler, S. J. (2007) *Electric Sounds: Technological Change and the Rise of Corporate Mass Media*, New York, NY: Columbia University Press.

21

SONIC ARCHAEOLOGIES

Shannon Mattern

Materiality has been among the most widely resounding conceptual refrains in media and cultural studies over the past two decades. While our digital lives and media landscapes ostensibly became more virtual, placeless, and weightless, we – media and cultural scholars, artists, and designers – turned our attention to our gadgets' guts; to the chemistry, physics, and even geology behind their construction, operation, and disposal; and to the heavy infrastructures undergirding our supposedly ethereal existences. Media archaeology, in particular, by emphasizing the materiality of media – the stuff, the institutions, the infrastructures, the labor practices, the code, the algorithms – has given rise to new, non-teleological modes of historiography that aim to trace media's peripheral routes and forgotten paths (see Huhtamo and Parikka 2011; Parikka 2012). Caleb Kelly (2009), Mara Mills (2011), Jentery Sayers (2013), Jacob Smith (2015), Jonathan Sterne (2003), and Siegfried Zielinski (2006) have re-sounded such historical audio artifacts as musical automata and songbirds, hearing tubes, stethoscopes, phonautographs, shellac discs, magnetic recording devices, hearing aids, and audio-cassette tapes.

Recognizing the myriad forces and entangled temporalities shaping the historical terrain from which such devices emerged, media archaeologists have come to question the "old"/"new" media divide – to recognize that "old" media were once "new," too – and to regard material engagement with their research subjects as a vital means of critical investigation, or what Wolfgang Ernst calls "epistemological reverse engineering" (Ernst 2011: 239; see also Marvin 1988). Archaeological research thus takes place not only in libraries and archives, but also in labs and studios, where screwdrivers and emulators, magnifying glasses and contact microphones, soldering irons and audio-editing software serve as integral research tools.

In this chapter we'll examine several such sonic-archaeological media researchers, designers, and artists who listen to media – to their internal machinery, their code, their pipes – in order to give voice to their mechanisms of operation. But we'll also examine another terrain of sonic-archaeological investigation: the field site, the archaeological dig. Taking media archaeology *literally*, we'll examine how archaeologists of the trowel-wielding variety have long adopted media technologies, including audio recorders and editing software, to better understand how archaeological sites might have functioned as sonic spaces.[1] We'll explore how archaeoacoustics – which melds techniques and sensibilities from archaeology, audio production, and sensory history – allows us to hear echoes from sites of the distant past.

Listening as diagnostic, epistemic, and historical method

Sound serves as a useful diagnostic tool. We can often hear malfunctions – a clanging pipe, a stuttering hard-drive, an irregular heartbeat, a coughing engine – we might not be able to detect or diagnose otherwise. In February 2016 Loughborough University posted a PhD "studentship" focused on "listening to infrastructure" in order to "provide early warning of deterioration and facilitate targeted maintenance and renewal" of the UK's "aging geotechnical assets": its rail lines, petroleum and potable water pipelines, offshore wind turbines, bridges, earth-retaining structures, and foundations. Researchers would listen for Acoustic Emissions, stress waves generated when such structures move and deform. This applied research extends a tradition among sound artists who have sonified various infrastructural elements, particularly bridges. In 1983, for the 100th anniversary of the Brooklyn Bridge, which at the time had a steel grid roadway (it has since been paved over), Bill Fontana (1983) mounted eight microphones under the bridge and broadcast the sounds to the plaza of the World Trade Center, via speakers embedded within the façade of One World Trade Center. More recently, sound artist and filmmaker Kevin T. Allen (2012), one of my own former thesis students, produced a haunting small-gauge film mixing the sounds of three of New York's major bridges – the Brooklyn, Manhattan, and Williamsburg – which he collected via contact microphones that pick up vibrations. Such works make sensible the micro-rhythms and macro-scale physical stresses that our infrastructures withstand and amplify the distinct mechanics of their different materials and construction techniques.

Other artists have proposed that there's much to be learned by listening to technical and media infrastructures: WiFi networks, cell phone connections, GPS, and other systems dependent on electromagnetic waves (see Mattern 2011). In 2004 German composer/sound artist Christina Kubisch began hosting her "Electrical Walks," in which participants use specially designed headphones that translate electromagnetic signals within the environment into sounds, thus disclosing the myriad waves and particles that not only make possible their ATM transactions and signal their surveillance by ubiquitous CCTV, but that also perpetually envelop and penetrate their bodies.[2] Her work resonates with growing public concerns about the potential health effects of ubiquitous and invasive electromagnetic signals – ever present in the universe, but now harnessed and targeted by devices we regularly carry in our pockets or near our brains. On a similar wavelength, Shintaro Miyazaki (2013) and Martin Howse also use logarithmic detectors, amplifiers, and wave-filter circuits to transform electromagnetism into sound, and thereby reveal the "rhythms, signals, fluctuations, oscillations and other effects of hidden agencies within the invisible networks of the 'technical unconscious.'" Howse (2014) frames such experiments as "forensic" epistemological investigations, which question what we can know, through transduction, about a seemingly imperceptible wireless world.

Myriad artists have used sound to index media's rhythms – both their mechanical movements and signal-processing operations. Consider, for instance, the audible physical rhythm of a Vandercook press or a 3D printer, a 16mm film projector or a high-speed book scanner. Sound artist and scholar Matt Parker (2015a, 2015b), as part of his "Imitation Archive" project, recorded the groans, hums, and crunches of historic calculating and computing machines at The National Museum of Computing at Bletchley Park, UK. Parker then mixed his 116 individual recordings into ten compositions, which are intended to give voice to the successive "movements" of computing history: "the 'always on' durational nature of many of the machines," "the clunking masses of early relay-based machines," the "whirring monoliths of the 1980's mainframe era," and "the high frequency whir of modern day server units." We learn about the evolving processes of computation by listening to the internal mechanisms of these machines. Howse and Miyazaki's Detektors project (2010–12) applied similar methods to contemporary electronic devices, including mobile phones, cameras, and hard drives, and artist-scholar Jamie Allen has examined the epistemologies given voice in lie detectors and the Church of Scientology's E-meter (Allen n.d.; Detektors n.d.; Institute of Experimental Design and Media Cultures 2016). These skills of diagnostic and forensic listening are of critical importance to archivists – particularly audio-visual archivists – because their work to preserve cultural heritage typically requires preserving archival media's recording and playback devices, too.

Even the seemingly abstract algorithms driving media-machines' operations are rhythmic and lend themselves to listening. Howse and Miyazaki's method of "algorhythmics," they claim, allows us to "hear that our digital culture is not immaterial, but consists of lively, rhythmical, performative, tactile and physical … machinic assemblages" (Detektors; see also Parikka 2012: 151–2). Miyazaki's and Michael Chinen's AlgorhythmicSorting program, for instance, sonifies the "rhythmic and pattern generating behavior" of different sorting algorithms: bubble sort, merge sort, heap sort, and so forth (Studio Algorhythmics n.d.; see also Ernst 2013). Yet algorithmic sonification isn't merely a clever means of making computational processes intelligible to non-specialists. Listening has long been an essential skill in computer engineering and programming. As Miyazaki (2012) reports, some early mainframes like the UNIVAC I and the Philips PASCAL computer featured an auditory interface, which transformed signals into sound via a speaker. Louis D. Wilson, one of the chief engineers for the BINAC, recounts that, in testing the computer, he and his colleagues discovered that they could recognize the machine's patterns via static on the lab's radio. Other early computer engineers noted that their machines and programs had a "characteristic sound."

The modes of listening, or what Jonathan Sterne would call "audile techniques," of these seasoned engineers were shaped by their professional training and their historical and cultural contexts. Engineering – and *listening* – during and after the War, amidst computing's incunabula, were quite different practices than they are today. While there is much debate within sensory history about the epistemology of historical "reenactment," Wolfgang Ernst, who practices an engineering-oriented version of media archaeology, proposes that "reenact[ing] the sound-generating setting" can shed light on "auditory perception in the past" (2013: 175).[3] In creating his archive at Bletchley Park, Parker (2015c) sought to reflect the architectures and environments within which the computers operated; after all, these contexts were integral to the way Alan Turing and his colleagues would have listened and responded to their machines. While Parker had no presumptions of "re-creating" the acoustics of the labs in which these machines operated, he did acknowledge their architectural "habitats" through sonic allusion, by weaving the rooms' signature acoustics (that is, their impulse responses) into his compositions.

The site of sounding and listening is also of critical importance to the work of Lawrence Abu Hamdan and Susan Schuppli, both of whom employ variations on sonic archaeology in their "Forensic Architecture" research. In his Earshot project, Hamdan (n.d.) worked with Defense for Children International, a human rights organization, to conduct an "audio-ballistic analysis" of a May 2014 incident in the occupied West Bank. Hamdan's forensic methods – which involved creating spectrograms of gunshots and 3-D models of the urban crime scene – provided critical evidence in establishing that Israeli soldiers shot and killed two teenagers with live ammunition, rather than rubber bullets, as they claimed. His modeling techniques have attracted attention from international media and governments. Schuppli, meanwhile, has investigated the sonic nuisance of drone surveillance in northern Pakistan. Not only are the drones' round-the-clock, high-frequency buzz and occasional deafening missile-strikes the source of much "psychological grief" – from anxiety and depression to post-traumatic stress disorder – but, as Schuppli (2014) proposes, their sonic effects might also be sufficiently harmful to constitute a violation of humanitarian law (see also Bishop 2011; Goodman 2010). Schuppli's, Hamdan's, and Parker's archaeological work requires attention to the particular acoustic properties of their research sites. They must attend not only to the sound, but also to its resonance chamber; to both the signal and all the ambient noise through which it must pass.

Listening to ancient places

Archaeologists and acousticians working in the field of *archaeoacoustics* have applied similar sensibilities in examining the sonic architectures of ancient sites, from Stonehenge to Peruvian temples to American petroglyph sites (see, for instance, Blesser & Salter 2007; Sample 2012; Watson & Keating 1999). Archaeologists have a long history of employing a wide repertoire of media techniques and technologies – field notes, drawings, maps, photographs, films, satellite imagery and GIS, material artifacts, etc. – for "making manifest the past (or, crucially … allow[ing] the past to manifest itself)" (Olsen, Shanks, Webmoor & Witmore 2012: 93). Archaeacousticians, or sonic archaeologists, also make use of such tools as omnidirectional or "bouquet" microphone and speaker arrays, binaural mics, amplifiers, field recorders, and sophisticated modeling software. They measure their research sites' impulse responses, standing waves, and reverberation times, and conduct on-site sonic tests by playing instruments and singing as their ancient subjects might have done.[4] Of course there's much conjecture involved in piecing together ancient multisensory experiences and ancient builders' intentionality, and the speculative nature of such archaeoacoustics research has generated debate (see Drake 2012; Scarre & Lawson 2006).[5] Archaeoacousticians certainly don't intend to "re-enact" ancient sounding or listening experiences, as Ernst proposes, or to be able to approximate "auditory perception in the past." Still, opening the ears during archaeological investigation allows for a recognition that human experience is, and always has been, multisensory, and that ancient spaces have long functioned, either by accident or by intention, as resonance chambers and transmission media for sonic activity – for public address, interpersonal communication, ritual or musical performance, and so on.

Mathematician and archaeologist Iegor Reznikoff (2012), who has studied Paleolithic art in caves throughout Europe, has identified a correlation between a site's resonance and its concentration of markings; he suggests that densely decorated sites were likely the location of rituals using instruments and chant.[6] At Chichen Itza, the Mayans built a pyramid along the narrow end of their Great Ball Court, which was surrounded by vertical stone walls. "By adding reflections and resonances," researchers have discovered, the Ball Court could "augment the perceived mass and size of the leader's voice, raising his stature and perceived power" (Blesser & Salter 2007: 85–6; see also Lubman 2006). And in a network of tunnels beneath the city of Chavín, Peru, archaeologists found a set of marine-shell trumpets, *pututus*, corroborating their theory that, somewhere between 1500 and 400 BCE, the tunnels functioned as a series of resonance and sound transmission tubes. "Tones in the same frequency range as both human voices and the shell trumpets produced consistent resonances in the alcoves" (Smith 2011). Archaeologists have also examined sound-amplifying wall niches, including one curved, carved projection known as the "Oracular Chamber," in the Hal Saflieni Hypogeum, an underground cemetery used in Malta from 4000 to 2500 BCE (Stroud 2014). They've surmised that it was no accident that, somewhere between the eighth and sixth century BCE, the Elamites situated their Kūl-e Farah open sanctuary near the opening of a gorge in present-day southwestern Iran; the site was geologically predisposed to function as a "giant sound box" (Henkelman & Khaksar 2014). And informed by Vedic Hinduism, which places great importance on acoustics – particularly speech and music – archaeologists have been exploring the sonic properties of stone in ancient Indian architecture.

The ancient Greeks' appreciation of acoustics was also informed by spiritual and metaphysical beliefs: they made use of oracular sites, where the gods could speak to mortals; their Archeron

Necromacy employed acoustic effects befitting the "gates to Hades"; and Pythagoras's "harmony of the spheres" proposed the existence of a harmonious natural order (see Blesser & Salter 2007: 77–89). "Given their strong interest in all forms of aural activities, including music, oration, rhetoric, and religion," Barry Blesser and Linda-Ruth Salter write, "the ancient Greeks were likely to have been aware of how these activities were influenced by spatial acoustics" (Blesser & Salter 2007: 94). The diversity of activities in the open *agora*, for instance, invited walking and casual conversation, and generated a cacophony of all citizens' voices (those voices, of course, rarely included women's, slaves', or many foreigners'). In the amphitheater, meanwhile, the stepped seats of rough-hewn limestone acted – whether by design or by accident – as an acoustic filter, suppressing low-frequency background noise and isolating the higher-frequency performer's voices (Ball 2007). The theaters' location, often among rolling hills, also provided favorable acoustic conditions.

While renowned for its theatrical innovations, ancient Greece is also the quintessential example – among archaeologists, classicists, philosophers, rhetoricians, political scientists, architectural historians, etc. – of a civilization founded upon a particular structural form of rational communication: the linking of meeting places, debate, and democracy. Architectural historian Anthony Vidler (2005) argues that Plato's ideal city – of which we find six versions throughout his oeuvre – is primarily "a city of discourse," which "exists first and foremost for the dialogues themselves." Aristotle, too, prescribed a city that would contain no more people than could hear a herald's voice.[7]

Classicist Christopher Lyle Johnstone, noting in 1997 that "physical setting [had] been virtually ignored" in rhetorical scholarship, draws on archaeological research to explore how the architecture of Athens' *agora*, where most civic functions were carried out until the early sixth century, and the architecture of its civic buildings – including the law courts, stoa, and various auditoria – shaped both an orator's delivery and his audience's engagement, and even limited the size of the audience (juries usually numbered at least 200, and more typically close to 500) (Johnstone 1997: 99; see also Johnstone 2001). He, like those archaeologists practicing archaeoacoustics, acknowledges the speculative and conjectural nature of his work. Yet he proposes that the stoa – long, narrow structures with walls (typically made of stone) along both short ends and one long side, and an open colonnade along the other long end – had a "pronounced reverberation effect," which had the potential to distort speakers' voices (2001: 137–8). Experienced speakers, however, "might have selected [their] cadences so as to take advantage of the building's acoustical properties"; if they found the structure's acoustic "sweet spot," the rhetorical effect could be "mesmerizing and engrossing" (Johnstone 1997: 103; Johnstone 2001: 138). Meanwhile, in the *Bouleutêrion*, the square or rectangular council house, tiered seating, high ceilings, and internal columns allowed speakers and auditors to see one another, cultivating a sense of intimacy, and permitted some degree of acoustic subtlety; "thus could a speaker employ an ordinary speaking voice in addressing a fairly large audience, and thus could he make the sorts of asides and sotto voce comments that would be ineffective in a less intimate setting" (Johnstone 1997: 106; see also Sennett 1994: 56–7).

In the fifth century BCE, the political assembly moved to the Pnyx Hill. A short walk from the agora, it was also far removed from the agora's mobility and cacophony. The Pnyx's formal design "emphasized the seriousness of attending to words," Richard Sennett argues; it "made political use of … sitting, spectator bodies" (Sennett 1994: 60, 66). Yet its physical setting also had affective power; the scenery cultivated pathos and ethos. From this site,

> one could look toward the Acropolis and see the Nike Temple nestled neatly inside the larger Parthenon behind it, as though the arrangement of these two temples was

deliberately designed for the speaker (from among an all-male assembly) with this orientation in mind: winged victory nested within the temple of the city's patron goddess, declaring hegemony held by her citizens…. The ancients understood the importance of the view offered by the assembly place. (Fredal 2006: 4)

The broader topography was also part of the scene. Blesser and Salter argue that the rolling hills and mild climate of many ancient Greek cities – the fact that the *demos* could meet out-of-doors, or in open buildings, and appreciate the surrounding scenery – "contributed to the success not only of the amphitheaters but also of Greek democracy, which might not have flourished without the frequent, publicly shared experiences" that these meeting places made possible (Blesser & Salter 2007: 95).

For the Romans, too, cities were predicated on rhetoric: "Never in my opinion," Quintilian (ca. 95C.E.) writes, "would the founders of cities have induced their unsettled multitudes to form communities had they not moved them by the magic of their eloquence" (see also McEwen 1993). The Roman architect Vitruvius tells of ancient builders who sought to cultivate acoustics that maximized the "clearness and sweetness" of orators' voices (1914: 139). One of their techniques – inspired by the principles of harmonics, and inventive though ineffectual – involved placing bronze vessels beneath the seats of an auditorium, which would supposedly resonate with and amplify the voice.

In 1872 archaeologists found in the Roman Forum a marble relief representing an emperor, either Trajan or Hadrian, standing on the Forum's Rostra Augusti (speaker's platform), delivering a public address or adlocutio (an address to the army). In Julio-Claudian times, the emperor often delivered speeches from across the forum, on a platform at the Temple of Divus Iulius, while his heir occupied the Rostra Augusti. Inspired by such finds, architectural historian Diane Favro and classicist Christopher Johanson are creating digital models of the Forum to understand how the space accommodated funeral processions, multisensorial affairs choreographed to appeal to multiple audiences. With further research, they're attempting to model and understand, in part, how the Forum functioned *acoustically* as a space for speech and pageantry: "How did accompanying sounds reinforce the activities? …Where did spectators stand? …What route to the forum was taken by participants?" (Favro & Johanson 2010: 15). They want to understand how the material urban landscape functioned as an "infrastructure" for the sights and sounds of these public events – how various architectures "dictated the choreography" and "created a formal tableau" that assigned status to particular sensory experiences (Favro & Johanson 2010: 31).[8] Johanson again articulated the challenges of modeling the sounds of ancient sites: With so many variables – the dimensions and materials of the buildings surrounding the plazas, each of which is a "tightly controlled sonic environment," and the myriad waterworks throughout Roman cities – it's hard to piece together a recreation of what they would've sounded like, how they functioned as infrastructures for mediation.[9]

Archaeoacousticians and sonically minded architectural and urban historians have also examined the sonic properties of 17th-century New England meeting houses and 19th-century public auditoria and mechanics halls; the booming commercial streets of early-modern London; and the battlefields of the Civil War and the underground bunkers of 20th-century warfare; the pealing bells that defined village boundaries and structured village life from the 7th through the 19th century throughout Western Europe and in colonial Latin America; the *muezzins* that have broadcast the call to prayer in cities across the Islamic world for over a millennium; and the carefully considered acoustics of Byzantine churches and 16th-century mosques.[10] These sounding spaces, in containing, transmitting and reverberating the sound waves projected into them, function as media themselves. Archaeoacousticians, like their media-archaeologist counterparts, have to understand architectures' and cities' materials and mechanisms of acoustic operation. We might thus regard archaeoacoustics as a symphonic-scale version of sonically attuned media archaeology – one in which ancient media, including voices and musical instruments, resound within ancient architectural instruments.

Notes

1 For more on the *literal* archaeology of media archaeology, see Mattern 2013a and Mattern 2015.
2 See also Mattern 2013b for more on multisensory means of experiencing and comprehending infrastructure.
3 See also Smith 2007 for a discussion of reenactment's methodological and epistemological concerns.
4 See Kolar 2013 for more on archaeoacoustic methods.
5 Sensory history has addressed similar epistemological and methodological concerns; see Smith 2007.
6 Much of this final section of the chapter is drawn from Mattern 2013a and the "Speaking Stones: Voicing the City" chapter in my *Code and Clay, Data and Dirt: Five Thousand Years of Urban Media*, published by University of Minnesota Press in 2017.
7 "For who can be the general of such a vast multitude, or who the herald, unless he have the voice of a Stentor?" Aristotle 1998: 1326b5-7.
8 Favro identifies several other studies examining how rituals and processions shaped the form of ancient Rome, focusing in particular on "the close connections among events, meaning, and the physical locale." A continuing blind spot, or silence, in such work, Favro argues, is the perspective of non-elite participants (Favro 1999: 369).
9 Christopher Johanson, interview with the author, February 26, 2013. For more on modeling sensory history, see the work of Richard Beacham at Kings College London, who aims to model ancient theaters; and the work of the LCSE-MSI Visualization Laboratory at the University of Minnesota (in collaboration with Christopher Johnstone, whom we encountered earlier), which aims to model the acoustics of ancient Greek theaters and auditoriums particularly "how variables of architecture design affected the sound, sight lines, and behaviors of speakers and listeners" ("Ancient Greek Rhetoric" n.d.; Beacham, n.d.).
10 Most of these cases are addressed in the "Speaking Stones: Voicing the City" chapter in my *Code and Clay, Data and Dirt: Five Thousand Years of Urban Media*.

References

Allen, J. (n.d.) "The Lie Machine," *Jamie Allen*, accessed December 22, 2016, at www.jamieallen.com/the-lie-machine/.

Allen, J. (n.d.) "Recomposing the E-Meter," *Jamie Allen*, accessed December 22, 2016, at www.jamieallen.com/recomposing-the-e-meter/.

Allen, K. T. (2012) "Bridge," Filmography, accessed December 22, 2016, at www.phonoscopy.com/works.html#filmography.

"Ancient Greek Rhetoric in Immersive Virtual Reality" (n.d.) Minnesota Supercomputing Institute, accessed December 22, 2016, at www.msi.umn.edu/content/ancient-greek-rhetoric-immersive-virtual-reality.

Aristotle. (1998) "Politics," in J. Barnes (ed.) *Complete Works of Aristotle*, Revised Oxford Translation, New York, NY: Princeton University Press.

Ball, P. (2007) "Why the Greeks Could Hear Plays from the Back Row," *Nature*, March, accessed December 22, 2016, at www.nature.com/news/2007/070319/full/news070319-16.html.

Beacham, R. (n.d.) "THEATRON – Theatre History in Europe: Architectural and Textual Resources Online," *Didaskalia* 6(2), accessed December 22, 2016, at www.didaskalia.net/issues/vol6no2/beacham.htm.

Bishop, R. (2011) "Project 'Transparent Earth' and the Autoscopy of Aerial Targeting: The Visual Geopolics of the Underground," *Theory, Culture & Society*, 28(7–8), pp. 270–86.

Blesser B. & Salter, L-R. (2007) *Spaces Speak, Are You Listening?: Experiencing Aural Architecture*, Cambridge, MA: MIT Press, pp. 67–97.

"Detektors" (n.d.) Shintaro Myazaki, accessed December 22, 2016, at http://shintaro-miyazaki.com/?work=detektors.

Drake, N. (2012) "Archaeoacoustics: Tantalizing, but Fantastical," *Science News*, February 17, accessed December 22, 2016, at www.sciencenews.org/view/generic/id/338543/description/Archaeoacoustics_Tantalizing_but_fantastical.

Ernst, W. (2011) "Media Archaeography – Method & Machine Versus History & Narrative of Media," in E. Huhtamo and J. Parikka (eds) *Media Archaeology: Approaches, Applications, and Implication*, Berkeley, CA: University of California Press, pp. 239–55.

Ernst, W. (2013) "Toward a Media Archaeology of Sonic Articulations," in J. Parikka (ed.) *Digital Memory and the Archive*, Minneapolis, MN: University of Minnesota Press, pp. 172–83.

Favro, D. (1999) "Meaning and Experience: Urban History from Antiquity to the Early Modern Period," *Journal of the Society of Architectural Historians* 58(3), pp. 364–73.

Favro, D. & Johanson, C. (2010) "Death in Motion: Funeral Processions in the Roman Forum," *Journal of the Society of Architectural Historians* 69(1), pp. 12–37.

Fontana, B. "The Brooklyn Bridge Sound Sculpture at One World Trade Center, New York, 1983," *Resoundings*, accessed December 22, 2016, at http://resoundings.org/Pages/Oscillating.html.

Fredal, J. (2006) *Rhetorical Action in Ancient Athens: Persuasive Artistry from Solon to Demosthenes*, Carbondale, IL: Southern Illinois University Press.

Goodman, S. (2010) *Sonic Warfare: Sound, Affect, and the Ecology of Fear*, Cambridge, MA: MIT Press.

Hamdan, L. A. (n.d.) "Earshot," accessed December 22, 2016, at http://lawrenceabuhamdan.com/new-page-1/.

Henkelman, W. F. M. & Khaksar, S. (2014) "Elam's Dormant Sound: Landscape, Music and the Divine in Ancient Iran," in L. C. Einix (ed.) *Archaeoacoustics: The Archaeology of Sound*, Proceedings of the Archaeoacoustics Conference, Malta, 2014, Myakka City, FLOTS Foundation, pp. 211–31.

Howse, M. (2014) "Sonic Archaeology," Harvestworks Workshop, April 5–6, accessed December 22, 2016, at www.harvestworks.org/apr-56-sonic-archaeology-workshop/.

Huhtamo, E. & Jussi Parikka (eds) (2011) *Media Archaeology: Approaches, Applications, and Implication*, Berkeley, CA: University of California Press.

Institute of Experimental Design and Media Cultures. (2016) "U.S. Media Archaeology Lab Hosts Apocryphal Technologies, March, accessed December 22, 2016, at www.ixdm.ch/u-s-media-archeology-lab-hosts-apocryphal-technologies/.

Johnstone, C. L. (1997) "Greek Oratorical Settings and the Problem of the Pnyx," in C. Johnstone (ed.) *Theory, Text, Context: Issues in Greek Rhetoric and Oratory*, Albany, NY: State University of New York Press, pp. 97–128.

Johnstone, C. L. (2001) "Communicating in Classical Contexts: The Centrality of Delivery," *Quarterly Journal of Speech* 87(2), pp. 121–43.

Kelly, C. (2009) *Cracked Media: The Sound of Malfunction*, Cambridge, MA: MIT Press.

Kolar, M. (2013) "Tuned to the Senses: An Archaeoacoustic Perspective on Ancient Chavín," *The Appendix*, July 22, accessed December 22, 2016, at http://theappendix.net/issues/2013/7/tuned-to-the-senses-an-archaeoacoustic-perspective-on-ancient-chavin.

Kubisch, C. (2004) "Electrical Walks: Electromagnetic Investigations in the City," accessed December 22, 2016, at www.christinakubisch.de/en/works/electrical_walks.

Loughborough University, "Listening to Infrastructure: Acoustic Emission Sensing of Geotechnical Infrastructure to Improve Resilience," accessed February 5, 2016, at www.lboro.ac.uk/study/finance/research/studentships/studentships/listening-to-infrastructure-acoustic-emission-sensing-.html.

Lubman, D. (2006) "Acoustics of the Great Ball Court at Chichen Itza, Mexico," *Journal of the Acoustical Society of America* 120, accessed December 22, 2016, at http://asa.scitation.org/doi/abs/10.1121/1.4777330.

Marvin, C. (1988) *When Old Technologies Were New: Thinking About Electric Communication in the Late Nineteenth Century*, New York, NY: Oxford University Press.

Mattern S. (2011) "SoundMatter," "No Thing Unto Itself: Object-Oriented Politics," CUNY Graduate Center, October 20, accessed December 22, 2016, at www.veralistcenter.org/engage/event/241/no-thing-unto-itself-objectoriented-politics/.

Mattern, S. (2013a) "Ear to the Wire: Listening to Historic Urban Infrastructures," *Amodern* 2, accessed December 22, 2016, at http://amodern.net/article/ear-to-the-wire/.

Mattern, S. (2013b) "Infrastructural Tourism," *Places Journal*, accessed December 22, 2016, at https://placesjournal.org/article/infrastructural-tourism/.

Mattern, S. (2015) *Deep Mapping the Media City*, Minneapolis: University of Minnesota Press.

McEwen, I. K. (1993) "Hadrian's Rhetoric I: The Parthenon," *RES: Anthropology and Aesthetics* 24, pp. 55–66.

Mills, M. (2011) "Hearing Aids and the History of Electronics Miniaturization," *IEEE Annals of the History of Computing*, 33(2), pp. 24–45. Reprinted in J. Sterne, (ed.) (2012) *The Sound Studies Reader*, New York, NY: Routledge.

Miyazaki, S. (2012) "Algorhythmics: Understanding Micro-Temporality in Computational Cultures,"

Computational Culture, accessed December 22, 2016, at http://computationalculture.net/article/algorhythmics-understanding-micro-temporality-in-computational-cultures.

Miyazaki, S. (2013) "Urban Sounds Unheard-of: A Media Archaeology of Ubiquitous Infospheres," *Continuum: Journal of Media & Cultural Studies*, 27(4), pp. 514–22.

Olsen, B., Shanks, M., Webmoor, T., & Witmore, C. (2012) *Archaeology: The Discipline of Things*, Berkeley, CA: University of California Press.

Parikka, P. (2012) *What Is Media Archaeology?* Malden, MA: Polity.

Parker, M. (2015a) "The Imitation Archive," *Earth Kept Warm*, accessed December 22, 2016, at www.earthkeptwarm.com/the-imitation-archive/.

Parker, M. (2015b) "The Imitation Archive Part 1: Recording the Sounds of the World's First Computers," *British Library Sound and Vision Blog*, May 15, accessed December 22, 2016, at http://britishlibrary.typepad.co.uk/sound-and-vision/2015/05/the-imitation-archive-part-1-recording-the-sounds-of-bletchley-parks-historic-computers-.html.

Parker, M. (2015c) "The Imitation Archive Part 2: Making Music from the Sounds of the World's First Computers," *British Library Sound and Vision Blog*, May 26, accessed December 22, 2016, at http://britishlibrary.typepad.co.uk/sound-and-vision/2015/05/the-imitation-archive-part-2-.html.

Quintilian, *Institutio Oratoria* (ca. 95CE), 2.16.9, accessed December 22, 2016, at http://perseus.uchicago.edu/perseus-cgi/citequery3.pl?dbname=LatinAugust2012&getid=1&query=Quint.%202.16.15.

Reznikoff, I. (2012) "On the Sound Related to Painted Caves and Rocks," in J. Ikäheimo, A. Salmi & T. Äikäs (eds.) *Sounds Like Theory* XII, Nordic Theoretical Archaeology Group Meeting, Oulu, April 25–28, Monographs of the Archaeological Society of Finland 2, pp. 101–109, at www.sarks.fi/masf/masf_2/SLT_07_Reznikoff.pdf.

Sample, I. (2012) "Stonehenge was Based on a 'Magical' Auditory Illusion, Says Scientist," *The Guardian*, February 16, accessed December 22, 2016, at www.guardian.co.uk/science/2012/feb/16/stonehenge-based-magical-auditory-illusion?newsfeed=true.

Sayers, J. (2013) "Making the Perfect Record," *American Literature*, 85(4), pp. 817–18.

Scarre C. & Graeme Lawson, G. (eds.) (2006) *Archaeoacoustics*, Cambridge, UK: McDonald Institute for Archaeological Research.

Schuppli, S. (2014) "Uneasy Listening," in Forensic Architecture (ed.) *Forensis: The Architecture of Public Truth*, Berlin: Sternberg Press, pp. 381–92.

Sennett, R. (1994) *Flesh and Stone: The Body and the City in Western Civilization*, New York, NY: W. W. Norton.

Smith, J. (2011) "Listening to the Gods of Ancient Peru," *Archaeology Magazine* 64(4), accessed December 22, 2016, at http://archive.archaeology.org/1107/trenches/chavin_de_huantar_caves_acoustics.html.

Smith, J. (2015) *Eco-Sonic Media*, Berkeley, CA: University of California Press.

Smith, M. M. (2007) "Producing Sense, Consuming Sense, Making Sense: Perils and Prospects for Sensory History," *Journal of Social History* 40(4), pp. 841–858.

Sterne, J. (2003) *The Audible Past: Cultural Origins of Sound Reproduction*, Durham, NC: Duke University Press.

Stroud, K. (2014) "Hal Saflieni Hypogeum – Acoustic Myths and Science," in L. C. Einix (ed.) *Archaeoacoustics: The Archaeology of Sound*, Proceedings of the Archaeoacoustics Conference, Malta, Myakka City, 2014, FLOTS Foundation, pp. 37–43.

Studio Algorhythmics. (n.d.) "Algorhythms of Sorting," accessed December 22, 2016, at http://algorhythmics.ixdm.ch/?p=152.

Vidler, A. (2005) *"How to Invent Utopia: The Fortunes and Misfortunes of Plato's Polis,"* Mellon Lecture, Canadian Centre for Architecture, Montreal, Canada, May 17.

Vitruvius. (1914) *The Ten Books on Architecture*, Cambridge, MA: Harvard University Press.

Watson A. & Keating, D. (1999) "Architecture and Sound: An Acoustic Analysis of Megalithic Monuments in Prehistoric Britain," *Antiquity* 73(280), pp. 325–36.

Zielinski, S. (2006) *Deep Time of the Media: Toward an Archaeology of Hearing and Seeing by Technical Means*, Cambridge, MA: MIT Press.

Portions of this chapter are modified, with permission, from "Ear to the Wire: Listening to Historic Urban Infrastructures," *Amodern* 2, (2013), and my *Code and Clay, Data and Dirt: Five Thousand Years of Urban Media*, published by University of Minnesota Press in 2017.

22

CURATING ONLINE SOUNDS

Blake Durham

This chapter addresses some of the key debates and issues raised in relation to curatorial functions of digital sound cultures, with particular attention to curation on licensed music streaming services. It addresses three overlapping but distinct orders of curation: first, curation as individualized practices of recombinatory and reflexive consumption; second, curation as collaborative, archival, and educational projects carried out by distributed regimes of value; third, curation as the primary output of algorithmic cultures online, wherein cultural technologies are engaged in the automation of classification and presentation. The examples provided in this chapter demonstrate that each of these curatorial practices is mutually mediating, with each order of curation—individualistic, collaborative, and algorithmic—intersecting, informing, and shaping the other (Born 2011). Much in the same way that it is impossible to speak about the online curation of sound without considering the technical infrastructure that engenders digital socialities, we must also address the mutating forms of curatorial labor that are appropriated and instrumentalized in the production of automated curation. A rigorous analysis to the sociotechnical systems of curation online must address the agencies at work within these assemblages, parsing whose tastes and values are being performed, and to whose benefit these curatorial acts serve.

Curation as it relates to the soundscapes of the internet is often hazily defined, but it generally refers to processes by which cultural objects are selected, classified, hierarchized, sorted, and displayed online. It seems indisputable that much of participation in social media networks is characterized by the interaction with or creation of 'curated' experiences: individuals are constantly engaged in curatorial functions, including searching, filtering, sorting, remixing, adding, saving, sharing, and so forth, which are each usefully understood as a form of selection and presentation. The impetus to curate personal collections of digital media is now ubiquitous across social media platforms, from the lifestyle-oriented 'visual discovery' site Pinterest, to the personal image collections of Instagram: music is perhaps most emblematic of this movement, with approaches to curation representing the chief point of product differentiation for competing digital music services.

The term 'curate' has been problematically adopted in digital marketing industries, particularly in reference to the user-generated content of Web 2.0, in which often-banal engagements with digital consumption are construed as active curatorial production. Notably, visual arts curator Hans Ulrich Obrist has argued against this appropriation of the metaphorical utility of curation, noting how it ignores the historical realities of museums, collections, and their caretakers. Chief among Obrist's criticisms of online curation is that it ignores the professional status of curators: the preservation and organization of museum artifacts as a profession is significantly dissimilar to the creation of playlists or the sharing of hyperlinks. Here, Obrist attempts to distinguish between *expertise* and mere *interest*, relying on problematic notions of competencies and credentials that are prone to the reification of institutional hierarchies. Historically, curatorial labor was performed by figures both formally and informally recognized as cultural intermediaries: not only museum curators, but also radio DJs, record store clerks, librarians, journalists, critics, and so forth. However, the primary objection that can be raised against Obrist's attempt to reclaim the institutionalized status of curation is that it fails to recognize user-generated content as a form of free labor. As will be addressed further in regards to algorithmic curation, data collected from the individualistic modes of curation generate significant value for shareholders in digital cultural industries: as such, it is important to address new and evolving consumption and collection practices in terms of the work extracted from participants.

The genealogy of online sonic curation can be readily connected to the Renaissance aristocratic collection displays known as 'cabinets of curiosities', considered to be significant precursors to modern museums (Impey and MacGregor 1985). Cabinets of curiosities, most often a room within a household containing numerous miscellaneous artifacts, were used to display objects carefully selected to demonstrate the collector's knowledge of in a variety of subjects. In a manner that prefigures anthropological work on the materialities of consumer culture (Miller 1987), cabinets of curiosities were assembled in service of Enlightenment identity formation: the skulls, relics, art objects, and other oddities, along with their meticulous arrangement, signaled a complex assemblage of social position, wealth, intellectual achievement, and aesthetic taste. The curation of sound online via playlists and other recombinatory formats functions in much the same way, reconfiguring personal consumption practices into virtual cabinets of the self: through the creation, maintenance and circulation of these lists, participants come to understand curation in terms of both personal collection practices as well as public performances of aural literacies.

Individualized curation

Individualized curation is here understood as practices of collection and arrangement in which the primary motivation for curation is the affordance of particular modes of personal consumption. The unprecedented volume of content uploaded to digital repositories necessarily entails user participation in categorizing and sorting objects, in order to combat the problem of choice overload: digital curation and ownership is as much concerned with exclusion as it is acquisition, carving individualized tastes and experiences out from generalized libraries. Tom McCourt (2005) argues that it is the very 'immateriality' of digital music that animates this desire to curate, collect, and recontextualize, with curation serving to reify ownership. This can take the form of assembling a personal collection of music, constructing themed playlists to suit personal moods, building context-specific playlists that are designed for function in particular spaces or activities, or genre-oriented lists of artists, labels, and releases. Anja Nylund Hagen (2015), in her study of Spotify and WiMP users, demonstrates the rich heterogeneity of curatorial approaches to streaming libraries, along with differing understandings of the nature of musical collections within a subscription service.

The creation of playlists is the dominant organizational form for music on Spotify, both for private consumption and for public circulation: while individualized playlists are the primary means for users to manage their streamed library, these are (often unknowingly) publicly accessible, effectively instrumentalizing the labor of its users. Personal collections are reabsorbed into the streaming service's networks of cognitive capital, in the form of curatorial knowledge circulated through public playlists. Therefore, curation is central to the crowdsourcing of individualization, amounting to free labor that Tiziana Terranova argues is found in 'the expansion of the cultural industries [into] process[es] of economic experimentation with the creation of monetary value out of knowledge/culture/affect' (Terranova 2000: 38). Inasmuch as the problem of choice overload is central to the rise of user curation in digital cultures, music's unique affordances for identity formation and distinction are equally indicted in the structures of online participation. This is epitomized by YouTube and its long-running slogan, 'Broadcast Yourself', wherein the participatory self can equally take the form of contributing content to the site or curating a collection of videos that collectively represent personal creative identities. Playlist creation and the curation of musical materials also function as technologies of the self, where acts of musical consumption are intimately connected to the elaboration of identity and the regulation of mood. Tia DeNora's work (1999, 2000) on everyday practices of consumption demonstrates the diverse affective qualities of sound—its engendering of excitement, tranquility, catharsis, and so forth—and how these characteristics are reflexively understood by individuals. Likewise, personal collections of music online are often used to publicly articulate and negotiate identity. The site Rate Your Music (RYM), originally designed as a collaborative online database for rating and ranking musical releases, also hosts a vibrant, animated online sociality, one in which prestige and symbolic capital are negotiated through the cataloguing of personal collections. By assigning each release personally possessed a rating between 1 and 5 stars, participants are not only engaging in critical evaluation, but are also broadcasting and curating their musical identity, with RYM profiles standing in as curated representation of individual collections: Rate Your Music's sociality is equally bound up in its dual emphases on 'rating' and 'your music', wherein the performance of musical ownership and critical judgment are the primary medium for the expression of social relations.

Collaborative curation

Many forms of online curation are not so intimately connected to individual pursuits of symbolic capital, instead systemically designing curatorial functions into practices to highlight and categorize content, what we might usefully term 'deindividualized' curation. The work of individuals here is aggregated into browsable collections, offering a distributed yet collaborative environment for curation to take place. Social media content aggregators such as Reddit depend on the cumulative efforts of its userbase to make high-quality content more visible over less relevant content through a 'voting' system, though the technical specificities of the sorting systems of user-generated sites evidence the complex sociotechnical arrangements at stake: the solicitation and aggregation of evaluative judgments is often contentious and prone to undemocratic consensus-building, emically referred to as internet 'hiveminds'.

Not all such sound cultures online are assembled solely around music: indeed, YouTube plays host to innumerable channels dedicated to audio-centric video, such as field recordings, foley, 'binaural beats', and the burgeoning subculture of auditory sensualists organized around so-called Autonomous Sensory Meridian Response (ASMR) audio. Likewise, the collaborative sonic archive freesound.org hosts over 300,000 audio files and millions of registered users, with each contribution holding Creative Commons licenses permitting creative adaptation and circulation of the sounds. Freesound is perhaps the premiere example of folk taxonomies of sound online, with curatorial participation taking the form of creative deployments of metadata tags: common strategies for classifying and curating sound include functionalist (for example, 'sleep'), formalist (for example, '110bpm'), contextual (for example, 'civil defense'), and technical (for example, 'moog-minitaur') criteria.

An invitation-only, highly governed music file-sharing site, here pseudonymised as Jekyll, offers an apposite case study for examining the conflicts and tensions performed by curatorial regimes online. The tagging system on Jekyll is deployed in a manner that evokes the hybridity of genre: by not restricting user categorization of music to single genres, the classification practices of curators are a mode of creative judgment, based on the combination of salient tags. For instance, a release by the New Zealand musical comedy duo Flights of the Concords was collaboratively tagged 'alternative, comedy, electronic, folk, hip-hop, new.zealand, 2000s'. Here, the genre tagging system notes secondary generic characteristics that speak to particular musical elements rather than conventional genre limitations, which would place the group solely within 'comedy'. Similarly, artists frequently cited as performing across genres, such as Radiohead (a particularly popular group on Jekyll), have as many as 11 tags on a single release. Conversely, many releases are accepted with only single genre indicators: 'hip-hop' is particularly often encountered as a standalone tag, indicating genre-specific divergences in approaches to classification and contribution.

Jekyll's administrative decision to redefine the 'hardcore' tag, and the collaborative editing project that followed, offers insight into the governmental dynamics of collaborative curation. Jekyll moderators announced that the official tag 'hardcore' was no longer permitted and all new releases were to conform to 'hardcore.dance' or 'hardcore.punk', despite neither subgenre being commonly referred to with either modifier. All qualified Jekyll members were asked to assist in reviewing and correcting the existing torrents, choosing whether the appropriate tag for the upload was 'hardcore.dance', 'hardcore.punk', or removing the hardcore designation completely, as users had adopted the 'hardcore' tag to indicate aurally 'intense' releases, which staff decided should be discontinued. Several types of criteria were provided to assist in distinguishing between hardcore punk and dance, beginning with accompanying tags: for instance, releases with 'hardcore' and 'gabba' tags were likely to be marked 'hardcore.dance', while 'hardcore' and 'alternative' almost always fit within 'hardcore.punk'. Approximately 20,000 and 30,000 torrents were affected, and at least 3,000 releases required further individual examination: participants were asked to investigate either by researching the release itself—for instance, looking up the record label and the genres with which it was associated, as well as the artist's classification on music databases Discogs or Allmusic—or determining its generic relations by aesthetic judgment. This could involve critical listening, looking for instrumentation and vocal stylings unique to the convention of the respective genres, or even considering the album art, as generic conventions applied to the graphic design, typography, and art direction of most hardcore releases.

This example of collaborative editing projects exemplifies why metadata is of interest: much in the way playlists and other curated assemblages bear witness to the dynamics of listener labor online, the paratextual data supporting and informing listening experiences is also the product of collaborative curatorial labor (Straw 2009). Jeremy Morris (2012) explores how ID3 tags and the Compact Disc Database (CDDB)—two keystones of sonic metadata—both originated as hobbyist programming projects, which were collaboratively worked upon and then eventually absorbed into the corporate infrastructures of the cultural industries. Technologies of curation are prone to these appropriations, as the arrangements which make content more useful for collectors—making sounds more easily sorted, located, and understood—also benefit the cultural intermediaries who attempt to extract profit from the usage of these works. Nonetheless, collaborative curatorial projects continue to proliferate: the open source music encyclopedia Musicbrainz hosts one of the most comprehensive databases of music metadata and paratexts, all gathered from the participatory contributions of over 250,000 volunteer editors.

These case studies of the participatory processes of circulation offers insight into a key component of online curation: the manner in which networks of musical circulation are constructed by the extraction of labor from participants, while simultaneously, these systems enact processes towards 'configuring the user', shaping not only personal consumptive and curatorial practices, but also notions of taste, quality, and aesthetic judgment (Woolgar 1990). The policing of official and unofficial tags in Jekyll can be understood as a technology of governance over both musical objects and individual subjects, requiring the aesthetic judgments of users to conform to predefined standards of musical identity and classification. The 'hardcore' tag splitting project perhaps best encapsulates the dynamics of collaborative online curation. Circulation's dependency on the collective musical knowledge of its participants—the necessity of assembling a rationally ordered musical index in order to function properly— is here evidenced within the elicitation of member participation in determining *which* 'hardcore' each of the thousands of releases belonged to, while also rejecting the expressive potential of 'hardcore' as a descriptive modifier of other musics. This propensity towards the formalization of informal practices of exchange online is instructive in recognizing how curation is equally instrumentalized by both licensed and extralegal systems of circulation.

Algorithmic curation

Lastly, automated technical systems for classifying, recommending, and programming sound objects, here broadly characterized as algorithmic curation, must be assessed in comparison with individualized and collaborative approaches. Automated music recommendation systems, emerging from decades of research in the field of Music Information Retrieval, seek to identify musical similitude through the accumulation and analysis of salient information, such as user activity data, acoustic characteristics, metadata tags, and critical reviews. The most widespread technique for automated curation, collaborative filtering, is a schema based on a relational model of aesthetic taste: if a statistically significant number of consumers who 'like' Object A also like Object B, these items will be understood as related, and future consumers of the former will be recommended the latter. While earlier iterations of recommendation systems were easily critiqued as reductive and often counterproductive—collaborative filtering techniques are prone to highlight the most common and well-known similar artists and works, which is antithetical to the objective of discovery—algorithmic curation has expanded in scale and scope. Recommendation systems are now involved in the production of automated 'curated' experiences: from online radio to context-aware playlist generation, digital circulation is widely marked by the influence of algorithmic decision-making.

Humanistic anxieties of the deterministic potentials of algorithmic cultures are commonplace: Tarleton Gillespie (2014) describes a tension between 'editorial' and 'algorithmic' logics, with hierarchies of expert knowledge and institutional backing on the editorial side, and putatively rational systems of automation based on the analysis of datasets on the other. Proponents of both editorial and algorithmic logics suggest that their respective approach to digital curation proffers the best response to the challenges engendered by the vastness of online content archives present, the so-called 'choice overload' problem (Burkart 2013). Apple Music and Tidal have both publicly aligned their approach to curation with editorial logics, with Apple Music's homepage offering a preferential endorsement of (personalized) musical expertise: 'With so much great music to hear, it's nice to have someone in the know helping you find exactly the right tracks. Our experts handpick songs, artists and albums based on what you listen to and like.' Spotify has been widely described as an algorithmically oriented service, with features such as the automated personalized playlist generator Discover Weekly attracting particular attention, it also bears clear evidence of editorial interventions at work. This can be most clearly witnessed in the company's featured playlists, curated by an editorial team and categorized by mood, moment, or genre.

However, this tension between the editorial and algorithmic should not be construed as immutable: all algorithmic recommendation systems involve editorial interventions, and quantitative audience response data has shaped the editorial decisions of terrestrial radio programming for decades. Furthermore, imagining these approaches as discrete entities problematically ignores the immanently sociotechnical nature of algorithmic production. Nick Seaver argues against accepting this technological formalism, saying, 'we can see the variety of people, epistemologies, and methods that constitute "data science." We can see the countless choices involved in cobbling big data together, moments of ambivalence and constraint […]' (Seaver 2015: 43). The finding that technical objects are generated by humans, refracting sociocultural norms, ideologies and practices, is not unique: studies of technical cultures have long demonstrated the contingency and socially constituted arrangements of these systems. In the case of music curation online, the divide between editorial and algorithmic approaches is similarly muddied by a consideration of the specificities of what these techniques entail: at Spotify, the Browse editorial team relies on complex data sets and analytics of aggregate listening sessions to assist in choosing new musical works, using algorithmic functions to inform rather than generate playlists—Spotify Creative Director Richard Frankel summarized the editorial team's reliance on analytics at CES2016 as 'Data Drives Direction'. Likewise, the extent to which these algorithmic systems can be said to function without human intervention is too often overstated, requiring frequent technical maintenance, attention, and realignment. For Pandora's Music Genome Project, one of the pioneering algorithmic music recommendation systems, musicologists analyze each work atomistically, with music scored with respect to 450 possible 'genes' (that is, formal and sonic characteristics): Pandora's recommendation system is perhaps the most 'editorialized' mode of algorithmic curation online. Persons and algorithms thus mutually mediate the other, reciprocally engaged in the work of curation.

A final consideration in the analysis of algorithmic curation is the issue of non-reciprocal data flows: that is, the manner in which data from users' everyday listening practices is systematically and involuntarily extracted and instrumentalized. These dual processes of surveillance and appropriation are akin to what Mark Andrejevic (2002) has called 'the work of being watched'. In digital market research, value is captured from watching consumer behavior, reshaping individuals listening practices and affective musical experiences into a form of (unconscious) free labor. In the case of licensed streaming services, these databases of user behavior are used to shape the output of automated curation features. For example, Spotify's most widely used algorithmic curation function, Discover Weekly, generates appropriate playlist sequences for individualized playlists by recombining sequencing data from the billions of user-generated playlists on the service: songs that often appear sequentially on user curated playlists will regularly be paired together on algorithmically curated Discover Weekly playlists. Likewise, the Fresh Finds series, which purports to identify 'up and coming' new music, crawls music blogs to identify emerging artists, locates the users on Spotify who are listening to these artists, and then marks these users as trendsetter. The newly released music these trendsetters discover is compiled by Spotify staff into playlists and released each week. These examples reflect broader realities about algorithmic curation and recommendation, namely that the exchange relations of digital repositories of sound and its participants extend beyond the financial exchange of subscription fees and advertising revenue.

Conclusion

It is now apparent that the supposed emancipatory potential of 'convergence culture' have not yet come to pass for the sound cultures of the internet: one must be careful to not overlook cultural intermediaries and the continued importance of editorial functions in circulation

(Jenkins 2006). Here, it is instructive to consider Aditi Deo's (Deo 2015) study of the informal digital music economies of Indian 'download vendors', who acquire large quantities of music from online 'cyberlocker' sites (and fellow vendors), and transfer bulk collections onto memory cards for customers who do not otherwise have internet access. She writes, 'These collections, on the one hand, normalized unexpected musical juxtapositions [...] [and] often excluded certain canonical elements of popular Indian music' (Deo 2015: 11). Their curatorial interventions 'also introduced reorganization of music in creative genres based on customer requests: sad songs, songs of betrayal, "beechwale" or the "middle" songs—that is, Hindi film songs from the decade of 1990s, etc.' Concerns about the overreach of algorithmic curation or the pervasive individualization of the internet are held in sharp contrast to the richly social selections of download vendor circulation, as well as the previous example of Jekyll, wherein the hierarchical dynamics of this unique social formation mediate the curatorial output of its collaborative projects. Further evidence for the continued importance of editorial intermediaries can be found in the widespread movement by cultural institutions associated with the curation of sound to adapt their collection for the internet: museum archives of field recordings are increasingly digitized and presented in novel ways to engage new audiences and bring to light the social and political situations of these artifacts. Ethnomusicologist and curator Noel Lobley writes, 'future sound curation is likely to be most effective when music heritage is embedded in locally meaningful events, collaboratively designed to immerse people in recorded heritage' (Lobley 2015: 247). Likewise, scholarship on digital cultures of curation should foreground the immanent socialities of curation, illuminating the webs of social relations enacted through the collection, arrangement, and recommendation of sound objects.

Related topics

References and Further Reading

Andrejevic, Mark. "The Work of Being Watched: Interactive Media and the Exploitation of Self-Disclosure." *Critical Studies in Media Communication* 19.2 (2002): 230–248.
Born, Georgina. "Music and the Materialization of Identities." *Journal of Material Culture* 16.4 (2011): 376–388.
Burkart, P. "Music in the Cloud and the Digital Sublime." *Popular Music and Society* 37.4 (2013): 393–407.
DeNora, Tia. "Music as a Technology of the Self." *Poetics* 27.1 (1999): 31–56.
DeNora, Tia. *Music in Everyday Life.* Cambridge: Cambridge University Press, 2000.
Deo, Aditi. "Digital Modes of Music Circulation in India: From Vernacular Music Archiving to Extralegal Music Vending." Presented at Indian Institute of Science Education and Research, Pune, May 2015: http://musdig.music.ox.ac.uk/wp-content/uploads/2013/07/AD_India_Website_Report-300615.pdf
Gillespie, Tarleton. "The Relevance of Algorithms," in Gillespie, Tarleton, Pablo J. Boczkowski and Kirsten A. Foot (eds.), *Media Technologies: Essays on Communication, Materiality, and Society.* MIT Press. 2014: 167–194.
Hagen, Anja Nylund. "The Playlist Experience: Personal Playlists in Music Streaming Services." *Popular Music and Society* ahead-of-print (2015): 1–21.
Impey, O. R., and MacGregor, A. The Origins of Museums: The Cabinet of Curiosities in Sixteenth and Seventeenth-Century Europe. Oxford: Clarendon Press. 1985.
Jenkins, H. *Convergence Cultures: Where Old and New Media Collide.* New York: New York University Press, 2006.

Lobley, Noel. "Curating Sound for Future Communities." *The Palgrave Handbook of Contemporary Heritage Research*. Basingstoke, UK: Palgrave Macmillan (2015): 234–247.

McCourt, Tom. "Collecting Music in the Digital Realm." *Popular Music and Society* 28.2 (2005): 249–252.

Miller, Daniel. *Material Culture and Mass Consumption*. Oxford: Basil Blackwell Ltd, 1987.

Morris, Jeremy W. "Making Music Behave: Metadata and the Digital Music Commodity." *New Media & Society* 14.5 (2012): 850–866.

Seaver, Nick. "Bastard Algebra." In *Data, Now Bigger & Better!*, eds. Bill Maurer and Tom Boellstorff. Chicago: Prickly Paradigm Press, 2015.

Straw, W. "Cultural Memory and Listening Preservation." *Convergence: The International Journal of Research into New Media Technology* 15.3 (2009): 259-262.

Terranova, Tiziana. "Free Labor: Producing culture for the digital economy." *Social Text* 18.2 (2000): 33–58.

Woolgar, Steve. "Configuring the User: The Case of Usability Trials." *The Sociological Review* 38.1 (1990): 58–99.

23

ETHNOGRAPHIES OF SOUND

Tom Rice

It is only comparatively recently that it has become possible to write about 'ethnographies of sound'. Historically, sound has generally been somewhat overlooked in ethnographic work. There is, however, a developing consciousness among ethnographic researchers of the importance of attending to sound and an increasing awareness that listening is integral to their work. In addition, there has been growing recognition of the value of ethnographic research in approaching the study of sound worlds, and researchers in this area are acknowledging the benefits of using sound recordings and compositions as well as or instead of written text in the presentation of ethnographic material. More and more, ethnographic work is being produced 'in' as well as 'on' or 'about' sound.

What is meant by 'ethnographies of sound'? Few researchers use 'ethnography of sound' or 'sound ethnography' to describe their work. 'Ethnography' and 'sound' are both also difficult terms to define in their own right, let alone in conjunction. Perhaps we can say that 'ethnographies of sound' set out to describe and reflect upon the sound world of a particular group of people who may share a space or who are linked through a set of shared practices. Researchers often gain direct experience of the sound world under study as part of their research process, adopting a position of participant observer or listener in relation to it. 'Ethnographies of sound' point to ways in which social, cultural, environmental, technological and historical context guides the creation, reception and interpretation of sound in a particular setting. They show sensitivity to local sonic forms and their interplay with sociality.

Ultimately it is perhaps not especially productive to try to create a definition of 'ethnographies of sound' and to list works that appear to conform to the definition, so in this chapter I take a different approach. After giving a perspective on the intellectual conditions under which sound has emerged as a concern in ethnography within the discipline of anthropology, I give four examples of sound-focused ethnographic studies, including my own. I describe the kinds of activities in which the researchers in question have engaged and explain some of the perspectives they have generated. I try to illustrate how an ethnographic approach can be helpful and valuable as a means of engaging with sound. Finally, I consider ethnographies *in* sound, and argue that they represent an important development in ethnographic work.

Sound in ethnography, from background to foreground

In traditional anthropological ethnographies, sounds are frequently mentioned as details or are used in evoking the atmosphere of a fieldwork site (for a good example see Mead 1928: 14). But while sounds may be notable presences in the research setting, they rarely form a focus of the research itself. This lack of direct and careful attention to sound might be attributed to a visualist bias at the heart of the ethnographic enterprise. As Clifford writes, traditionally, ethnography has involved techniques of observation and participant observation that appear to emphasise the importance of 'looking at... or, somewhat closer, "reading" a given reality' (Clifford 1986: 11). At the same time, ethnographic outputs have tended to take the form of written texts (and, to a lesser extent, photographs and films) that demand primarily visual attention. In more recent years, however, some researchers have called for recognition that attending to sound is in fact an integral aspect of ethnographic research. For instance, Cohen and Rapport point out that:

> Geertz's famous answer to the question, 'What does the anthropologist do? He writes', is a curiously thin description of what actually happens. Before they write, they do all those things which we gloss in the cliché of participant observation. Above all, they listen... (1995: 12).

Forsey, too, argues that 'listening is at least as significant as observation to ethnographers. Ethnography is arguably more aural than ocular, the ethnographer more participant listener than observer' (Forsey 2010: 561). He points to the centrality of the interview and 'engaged listening' in ethnographic research and asserts that '[m]uch of what passes for ethnography... is based upon what we hear rather than what we see' (Forsey 2010: 566). Gallagher and Prior write that 'listening is a routine part of ethnography and interviews' (2014: 268). On this basis it could be argued that virtually all ethnographies are 'ethnographies of sound' at some level.

The move to correct or revise the notion that ethnography is an inherently visualist enterprise is part of a wider move in contemporary Western academia towards engagement with the senses. In anthropology, what is now known as the 'sensory turn' developed in the 1980s and 1990s out of an earlier wave of anthropological interest in embodiment (Howes 1991a: 3–4; Pink 2009: 11). A fundamental premise of 'sensorial anthropology' is that sensory perception is a cultural as well as a physical act (Howes 1991b: 167). That is, the senses are not only mechanistic receptors of information but are also mediators of social value. The value accorded to types of sensory experience varies historically and cross-culturally. The emergence of the anthropology of the senses represents an effort within the discipline to galvanise study of the non-visual senses in particular. It also calls for greater reflexivity and creativity in the use of the senses in ethnographic representation. Ethnographic engagement with sound, and appreciation of its role in the research process, can be understood as part of the turn towards what Stoller (1997) calls a 'sensuous scholarship'.

Some examples of 'ethnographies of sound'

Sound may have been largely overlooked in classic anthropological ethnography, but in the related field of ethnomusicology, where fieldwork has often involved the researcher residing with a community for a lengthy period, documenting, analysing and participating in local musical practices, ethnographic work is arguably inherently sound-focused. Here, though, instrumental and/or vocal performances have tended to be of primary interest, and little attention has been given to the wider sonic space within which musical activity unfolds. There have, however, been important exceptions. For instance, in his book *The Forest People* (a work of both anthropological and ethnomusicological interest) Turnbull (1961) describes the lives of the Mbuti pygmies of the Ituri rainforest. He is sensitive to what, following Schafer (1977), we might call the local 'soundscape' or 'acoustic ecology', and suggests that understanding the sonic environment is necessary in order to gain a full comprehension of the indigenous musical practices he observes. His focus is the *molimo*, a complex notion, simultaneously a musical instrument (somewhat like a trumpet), a set of songs, a festival and a healing ritual. Turnbull describes how *molimo* playing and singing takes place within and in response to a rainforest setting animated and enriched by the sonic presences of animals and insects. Turnbull is sensitive to these sounds and the particular aural sensibilities the pygmies bring to them. But if Turnbull's ethnography is an ethnography of sound he does not explicitly describe it as such. He is not directly concerned with the intellectual implications of producing ethnography with a sonic focus and does not, for instance, explicitly discuss the centrality of listening to his methodology. *The Forest People* was, however, a strong influence on the anthropologist and ethnomusicologist Steven Feld, who was perhaps the first to consciously propose and deliberately construct what might be regarded as an academic ethnography of sound.

Feld's work on the Kaluli, a small group living in the densely rainforested area of Bosavi, Papua New Guinea, is seminal and has influenced many researchers who have subsequently produced works that might be regarded as 'ethnographies of sound' (Feld [1982] 1990). I touch on Feld's work below and explain some of his influence on my own research. I also use two examples, one from urban studies and another from social geography, to illustrate that ethnographic work on sound has been carried out in disciplines beyond anthropology. Indeed, ethnographic approaches to sound and auditory culture have been used in a wide variety of fields, including radio, radio art and sound art, media and communication studies, science and technology studies, sociology, musicology and social psychology.

An ethnography of rainforest sound

Feld first visited the Kaluli in 1976, when he began to conduct ethnographic fieldwork in the traditional anthropological mode, living for a year in one of their villages and learning their language. He returned to work with the Kaluli on several occasions up until 2000, studying their sophisticated understanding and appreciation of their sound-rich rainforest environment. Feld found that listening and sonic knowledge were of great value to the Kaluli in practical tasks such as navigation and hunting because vision was of limited use as a distance sense in the rainforest. At the same time, forest sounds had been woven in complex ways into Kaluli traditions of cosmology, poetry and song.

Willis suggests that ethnography involves seven methods of analysis: participant observation, observation, 'just being around', group discussions, recorded discussions, informal interviews and use of existing sources (1974: 12–14). Feld appears to have used all of these techniques in his efforts to develop an understanding of the significance of sound in Kaluli life. But it is particularly noticeable that an ethnographic approach gave Feld a means of 'being with people in sound' and created opportunities for sounds to act as elicitation devices (Feld and Brenneis 2004: 465). For instance, he describes an occasion when he was sitting with an interlocutor outside a hut, listening to the sounds of birds in the surrounding rainforest. Feld was keen to learn from the man which bird was producing the calls that could be heard. His interlocutor's insistence that the sounds were not simply the calls of birds but 'voices in the forest' was part of Feld's realisation of the importance of local ethno-ornithology in Kaluli systems of sonic interpretation (Feld [1982] 1990: 45).

Another interesting feature of Feld's methodology is that he positions himself as an apprentice in learning to hear like a Kaluli. For instance, he describes how, when making recordings of bird sounds in the forest, children helped him to direct his microphone to the right point in the forest canopy, allowing him to develop his appreciation not only of their skill at tracking sonic sources but also their particular grasp of the spatiality of rainforest sound (Feld 2015: 17–18). He describes, too, how he would play multiple tracks of his forest soundscape recordings to his research participants, allowing them to twiddle the knobs of the cassette player, creating 'an ethnoaesthetic negotiation' through which he was able to begin to understand how the Kaluli hear 'the dimensionality of forest sound, how they would balance a mix of birds, water, cicadas, voices and so forth' (Feld & Brenneis 2004: 467).

An ethnographic approach, then, allowed Feld to recognise the importance of sound 'to making sense, to knowing, to experiential truth' in Kaluli lifeworlds and he describes his work as 'an ethnographic study of sound as a cultural system' among the Kaluli (Feld 1996: 97, [1982] 1990: 3). In one of his analyses, Feld combines the terms 'acoustic' and 'epistemology' to produce the neologism 'acoustemology', which he uses to describe the set of hearing, listening and sounding practices that he observed to have become consolidated as Kaluli culture (1996: 97). In particular, Feld asserts the importance of a sonic epistemology of emplacement in understanding the way in which the Kaluli relate to their environment, challenging an intellectual tradition that assumes vision to be the primary sensory mode in which people across cultures engage with place and landscape.

An ethnography of hospital sound

Feld's work has been a strong influence on my own research on sound in the hospital context. This unfolded through two projects, one conducted at the Edinburgh Royal Infirmary in Scotland and the other at the Cardiothoracic Unit of St Thomas's Hospital in London. Having established that, like rainforests, hospital wards could be spaces of real sonic intensity, I was interested to see if sonic epistemologies equivalent to those Feld had identified in the non-Western, deep rural and technologically comparatively unsophisticated setting of Bosavi could be uncovered in the Western, urban and technologically intensive environment of a modern hospital.

I first became interested in hospital sound in 1999 whilst volunteering at *Red Dot Radio*, the Edinburgh Royal Infirmary's hospital radio station. My job at the station was to visit patients on the wards in order to collect song and music requests. Talking to patients it became apparent that one of the reasons they listened to the hospital radio was to escape temporarily from the sounds of the wards. This was before the time of personal MP3 players and smartphones. Privatised listening and the use of mediated sound to manage an external sonic environment was not ubiquitous and many of the patients I spoke to were elderly and did not use the tape-based personal stereos which were available. Patients described how the ward soundscape was characterised by the bodily sounds of other sick patients, by the talk and movement of nurses as they administered care, and by tones of medical technologies. Ward sounds disrupted patients' sleep and woke them early, creating annoyance and agitation.

I lived within a few miles of my fieldwork site and visited the wards between 6 and 10 pm every day for three months. This sustained contact allowed me to build relationships with long-term patients over several weeks. Pink suggests that sensory ethnographers should 'seek routes through which to develop experienced-based, empathetic understandings of what others might be experiencing and knowing' (Pink 2009: 65). I found that immersion in the ward environment did enable me to acquire an empathetic understanding of patient experiences of hospital sounds. Like Feld, through 'being with people in sound' and practising situated listening I was able to have in-depth conversations with patients about the soundscape. It became apparent that ward sound was important to patients' lives in other ways beyond its perception as 'noise'.

Sounds could carry valuable information, indicating that meals were about to be served or that medicine would soon be dispensed. Sounds could also have a powerful bearing on patients' wider experiences of illness and hospitalisation. For instance, several people described how sounds such as the footsteps of nurses or the tones produced by monitoring machines reminded them of their being under continual surveillance in hospital and served to compound feelings of disempowerment and medical objectification that they already associated with hospitalisation. Sounds were closely bound up in patients' constitution of themselves as 'patient selves' (Rice 2003: 4, 2013: 35).

Situated listening also allowed me to appreciate that patients held just one set of sonic perspectives on hospital life. Nurses, too, used listening on the wards both to monitor the patients in their care and to make decisions about where and how to direct their attention. At the same time, doctors whom I observed using stethoscopes on the cardiology wards of Royal Infirmary were clearly directing their sense of hearing towards discovering and identifying anatomical and physiological changes in patients' bodies. This realisation of the co-existence of multiple layers of sonic knowledge and experience in the hospital setting led to the second ethnographic project at the Cardiothoracic Unit at St Thomas' Hospital in London in 2004. Over the course of a year I conducted participant observation in the hospital. I was given access to the wards to interview patients and nurses and was also allowed to sit in on doctors' consultations and accompany them on ward rounds. In addition, I was able to attend tuition sessions attended by medical students, and focused in particular on the classes in which the students were taught to listen to patients' bodies using the stethoscope. Through close ethnographic attention I was able to appreciate the variety of ways in which auditory capacities acquire direction and focus, and sounds become endowed with particular meanings and associations within the cultural environment that the hospital represents.

As had been the case in my initial study, situated listening was crucial to extending my appreciation of patient engagement with hospital sound. It was also important for grasping the ways in which nursing staff were responsive to ward sounds: how a degree of noise could be conceived of as an indicator of activity and sociability, but that above a certain threshold it became a sign of disorder and loss of control. Like Feld's work with the Kaluli, my participation in classes where students learned to use the stethoscope constituted an apprenticeship in listening, though in this case in a formal educational setting. An 'ears on' approach was essential to enabling me to understand how auditory knowledge was applied, reproduced and transmitted in the medical setting, and allowed me to grasp thoroughly the embodied nature of important medical skills (Lachmund 1999: 440). I could appreciate firsthand the challenges that teaching doctors faced when attempting to communicate sensory knowledge and was able to witness, for instance, the difficulties involved in establishing consensus on the character and significance of sounds as diagnostic signs. This ethnographic perspective gave me insight into how sensory minutiae could both underpin and undermine the production of medical knowledge.

An ethnography of slum settlement sound

Tripta Chandola is an urban researcher based in Delhi. She has conducted ethnographic research in a settlement in the south of the city known locally as the 'slums of Govindpuri', examining the soundscape of the area and the listening practices of its residents. Also influenced by Feld, Chandola explores the 'ways in which sound is central to making sense' within an economically deprived and socially marginalized community in a major metropolis (Feld 1996: 97). Chandola explains how the particular architecture and construction of the slum, as well as its extreme population density, create an acoustically intense environment. The scarcity of certain resources is also audible. Water, for instance, is somewhat sporadically piped into the slum and the thud of both full and empty jerry cans is an almost constant accompaniment as residents move through the lanes to and from sites where the collection of water is possible (Chandola 2013: 7).

Chandola's ethnographic approach allows her to appreciate the local politics of sound in Govindpuri and the ways that sound often articulates social difference (for instance, along the lines of gender, caste and religion) in non-visible ways. She describes, for instance, how the expectation for women to be quiet and subdued in relation to men is performed and lived out in daily social interactions, but also witnesses loud verbal disputes and confrontations between women that often erupt and reverberate through the lanes of the slum during the day when many men are away at work. She explains how accents and musical styles associated with different areas of India index the tendency for communities of migrants from the same regions to occupy particular lanes of the settlement, and how particular caste groups can also be sonically identified though aspects of habitus such as accent, speech volume and style of expression. Religious tensions are also discernible in the soundscape. The diffusion of the Islamic call to prayer over the settlement has triggered complaints from some Hindu residents, while members of the Muslim community sometimes complain at what they see as the disrespectful noisiness of some of their Hindu neighbours.

Importantly, Chandola does not consider the settlement residents' understanding of their sonic environment to represent a particular skill or body of knowledge as is the case in Feld's work on the Kaluli and my own on the listening practices of hospital doctors, nurses and patients. She also does not see her fieldwork as an apprenticeship in learning to listen as her informants do. Chandola argues that as a middle-class outsider she cannot claim to truthfully inhabit the slum dwellers' sonic perspective. Instead she seeks to cultivate an understanding of how her informants' 'listenings' (the ways in which they listen, the things they are obliged to listen to, and the interpretations they bring to what they hear) are expressive of their low status and relative powerlessness both in relation to their middle-class neighbours and within wider Indian political discourse (Chandola 2012: 393–397, 2013: 4).

A long-term resident of Dehli herself, at the time of writing Chandola lives just a few miles from the slum settlement. Her extensive local knowledge has allowed her to gain an understanding of how the politics of sound in Govindpuri fits into wider political currents in the city. The slum residents are frequently described as being 'noisy' by their middle-class neighbours (Chandola 2012: 399). This description, Chandola argues, constitutes part of a broader effort on the part of middle-class residents to emphasize the physical, social and moral degeneracy of slum dwellers and to legitimise efforts to have them relocated. The framing of the slums dwellers as 'a problem' can in turn be linked both to wider government efforts to empower the middle classes and to collaborative efforts between the government and urban planners to remove slums in order to bring about the rapid development of Delhi into a 'world-class, clean, and green city' (Chandola 2014: 213). Chandola's ethnography of sound, then, allows her to show how the lived sonic realities of Govindpuri residents are enmeshed within wider social and political developments.

An ethnography of primary school sound

Michael Gallagher is a social geographer. One of his projects involved his undertaking ethnographic fieldwork in a suburban primary school in Scotland. While he initially intended to study how space was produced by teachers and pupils in the school, he describes being 'struck by the importance attached to quietness within the school culture' during his fieldwork period, so that sound became a focus of his research (Gallagher 2011: 51). Gallagher spent all of his research time working with just one class in order to develop a rapport with participants and to produce a detailed and in-depth account of the everyday dynamics of classroom life.

Gallagher does not appear to direct questions to the children and teachers with whom he is working or invite them to articulate or reflect on the ways in which sound becomes significant in the classroom. At the same time, although he was evidently a participant in some classroom activities, he adopts the position of a somewhat detached listener/observer. The fact that he produces rich ethnographic data on the sonic culture of the classroom independently of interview techniques is interesting because it demonstrates that sensory practice often occurs independently of verbalisation and below the level of conscious attention, but is nonetheless discernible to the fieldworker through its performance or enactment.

Taking a Foucaultian perspective, Gallagher explores how sound is used both as a subject and object of control in the primary school. He remarks that teachers seek to regulate noise levels by looking and listening out for children who are making noise, but he also points to the use of, for instance, spoken warnings and bells as signals for children to be quiet. He details occasions when surveillance is ineffective or incomplete and children get away with making noise. At other times they become participants in their own subjection, monitoring both their own noise and that of others in the classroom. Gallagher shows that 'the exercise of power through discipline and surveillance, whilst commonly thought of as taking place primarily through vision, may also rely heavily on sound and hearing' (Gallagher 2011: 47). He proposes 'panauralism' as a development of 'panopticism', illustrating how ethnographic work on sound can lead to an acoustic interrogation of key concepts within social theory, not necessarily discrediting them but augmenting their possibilities and potentials by considering them in what one might call a sonic light (Gallagher 2010: 268).

Ethnography 'in' sound

The vast majority of outputs produced by ethnographers including those mentioned above are 'texted endeavours' (Gershon 2013). However, as Brady's (1999) research on the use of the phonograph in anthropological work makes clear, sound recording has a long history in ethnographic research and sound recording devices have long been part of the ethnographer's toolkit. Responses to the emergence of the phonograph and views as to its suitability for ethnographic fieldwork were initially mixed, but most fieldworkers seized upon the technique as a valuable research aid. Brady details how, between 1890 and 1935, numerous American ethnographers applied it to what they saw as the urgent project of documenting the language and aesthetic expressions of cultures they perceived to be in danger of undergoing radical change or of succumbing altogether to the forces of the new world. Phonography promised a way to 'save the lore' (Brady 1999: 52). It was an efficient means of producing what were widely regarded as accurate and objective records of disappearing verbal and musical forms such as traditional folktales, epics, ballads and proverbs.

As sound recording technology evolved, ethnographers incorporated new devices into their data gathering processes. By 1933 early acetate recorders were appearing on the market and by 1945 tape recorders, which were lighter, easier to use, and which offered superior sound quality and recording capacity were widely adopted in ethnographic field research. Advances in analogue and later in digital audio technology also greatly enhanced the capacity of ethnographers to both record and edit sound. But though sound recording is thoroughly integrated into ethnographic work at the level of process, academic convention still emphasises text as the definitive ethnographic product. Sound recordings have obvious advantages over text when it comes to capturing the presence, complexity and experiential immediacy of sound. They can have great descriptive and illustrative power and can express sonic details and qualities that are difficult to convey in a written ethnography. Some academic publishers (particularly in the field of ethnomusicology) have produced ethnographic books with accompanying records, and in more recent years, CDs or links to sound files that are available online. But as Feld points out, even where it is provided, audio rarely receives the same attention as the written text it is designed to accompany (Feld and Brenneis 2004: 470–71). Sound has, at most, played a supporting role in relation to written material in academic ethnography.

Despite cultural barriers to the recognition of sound works as legitimate academic products, ethnographers have experimented and continue to experiment with using sound in representing 'the sonorous, enculturated worlds inhabited by people' (Samuels et al. 2010: 330). Editing techniques allow sonic forms to be isolated and brought together in informative, expressive and thought-provoking ways, enabling the creation of 'sonic ethnographies' or ethnographic work that is 'in' as well as 'on' or 'about' sound. As part of his research among the Kaluli, for example, Feld produced a radio programme entitled *Voices in the Forest*. Tape recordings were layered on a multi-track recorder to construct a sonic portrait of daily life in a Kaluli village, with sounds from across a 24-hour period being condensed into a 25-minute programme. The forest soundscape at different phases of the day was interwoven with the sounds of corresponding village activities: waking, working, relaxing. These activities are accompanied at various points by sounds of conversation, laughter, crying, calls, whistling and songs. Feld seeks to give an 'impression of the sound world as lived, condensing and intensifying the relationship of people to the time and space in the forest' (Feld and Brenneis 2004: 465).

In 2014 I teamed up with Tripta Chandola, whose research is described above, to make a radio documentary for the BBC World service called *Govindpuri Sound* (Rice and Chandola 2014). This was very much an attempt to present some of the major themes of Tripta's research *in* sound. The programme involved a two-week recording trip, with about 80 hours of material ultimately being edited into a 53-minute programme. *Govindpuri Sound* combines ambient sound recording, interview and narration in order to document the character of the sonic environment of the slum settlement. Like *Voices in the Forest*, it is narratively constructed to condense a day into a shorter time frame, beginning with the domestic sounds from houses in one alleyway of the slum as it comes to life in the early morning and ending in the same alleyway as it quietens down in the late evening. The documentary touches on some of the distinctive 'soundmarks' of the slum and explains how daily activities such as collecting water are acoustically distinctive (Schafer 1977: 274). It also contextualises the slum soundscape through comparison with other Delhi sounds and sonic environments: the honking of car horns on nearby roads (which constitute a kind of auditory horizon for the slum residents), the controlled ambience of a carriage on the new metro system with its near-constant safety and security announcements, the quiet of a neighbouring middle-class area. While the programme at times adopts a (Western) outsider's auditory perspective on slum life (emphasing difference and unfamiliarity), *Govindpuri Sound* as a whole is produced through 'extensive ethnographic knowledge and consultation with local people about the sounds recorded' (Samuels et al. 2010: 336). The programme attempts to represent both the settlement sounds and residents' ways of listening to them.

Anthropologist Rupert Cox and sound artist Angus Carlyle have used sound installation and audio in accompaniment with text and video in their collaborative ethnographic project *Air Pressure*, about two Japanese farming families whose land is almost entirely engulfed by Narita International airport. The farmers continue to work their land despite the intense noise and efforts by the authorities to relocate them. Cox and Carlyle record the soundscape of the farm: subtle, gentle sounds of birds, insects and other wildlife, as well as those of everyday working practices (some of which are traditional and possess a distinctively human cadence) are juxtaposed with the mechanical roar of jets as they pass sometimes just tens of metres overhead. As Gallagher and Prior point out: 'had the researchers taken a more traditional ethnographic approach using written field notes, the peculiar sonic geography of the site could not have been conveyed with such visceral, affective intensity' (2014: 271).

The balance between text and sound in cultural representation, then, appears to be shifting. There is a growing sense among ethnographers working on sonic culture that '…we should no longer accept "silent" publications on sound' and a corresponding movement towards producing work in which listening and recording are central to the ethnographic process and in which audio composition (often contextualised by text and images) is a key ethnographic product (Peek 1994: 488). Such work demands listening from its audience as a primary mode of engagement. In future, then, ethnographic representations will require listeners as well as, and even instead of, readers and viewers.

References

Brady, Erika. 1999. *A Spiral Way: How the Phonograph Changed Ethnography*. Jackson: University Press of Mississippi.

Chandola, Tripta. 2012. 'Listening into Others: Moralising the Soundscapes in Delhi'. *International Development Planning Review* 34(4): 391–408.

Chandola, Tripta. 2013. 'Listening in to Water Routes: Soundscapes as Cultural Systems'. *International Journal of Cultural Studies* 16(1): 55–69. DOI: 10.1177/1367877912441436

Chandola, Tripta. 2014. 'I Wail therefore I am'. In Matthew Gandy and Benny. J. Nilsen (eds.) *The Acoustic City*, pp. 212–217. Jovis Verlag.

Clifford, James. 1986. 'Introduction: partial truths'. In James Clifford and George. E. Marcus (eds.) *Writing Culture: The Poetics and Politics of Ethnography*, pp. 1–26. Berkeley, Los Angeles and London: University of California Press.

Cohen, Anthony. P. and Nigel Rapport. 1995. 'Introduction'. In Anthony P. Cohen and Nigel Rapport (eds.). *Questions of Consciousness*, pp. 1–20. London: Routledge.

Feld, Steven. [1982] 1990. *Sound and Sentiment: Birds, Weeping, Poetics, and Song in Kaluli Expression*. Philadelphia: University of Pennsylvania Press.

Feld, Steven. 1996. 'Waterfalls of Song: an acoustemology of place resounding in Bosavi, Papua New Guinea'. In Steven Feld and Keith H. Basso (eds.) *Senses of Place*, pp. 91–135. Santa Fe: School of American Research Press.

Feld, Steven and Don Brenneis. 2004. 'Doing Anthropology in Sound'. *American Ethnologist* 31(4): 461–74.

Feld, Steven. 2015. 'Acoustemology'. In David Novak and Matt Sakakeeny (eds.) *Keywords in Sound* pp. 12–21. Durham and London: Duke University Press.

Forsey, Martin. G. 2010. 'Ethnography as participant listening'. *Ethnography* 11(4): 558–572.

Gallagher, Michael. 2010. 'Are Schools Panoptic?' *Surveillance and Society* 7(3/4): 262–272.

Gallagher, Michael. 2011. 'Sound, Space and Power in a Primary School'. *Social and Cultural Geography* 12(1): 47–61.

Gallagher, Michael. and Jonathan Prior. 2014. 'Sonic Geographies: exploring phonological methods'. *Progress in Human Geography* 38(2): 267–284.

Gershon, Walter. 2013. 'Resounding Science: a sonic ethnography of an urban fifth grade classroom'. *Journal of Sonic Studies* 4(1): http://journal.sonicstudies.org/vol04/nr01/a08

Howes, David. 1991a. 'Introduction: "to summon all the senses"'. In David Howews (ed.) *The Varieties of Sensory Experience: A Sourcebook in the Anthropology of the Senses*, pp. 3–21. Toronto: University of Toronto Press.

Howes, David. 1991b. 'Sensorial Investigations'. In David Howes (ed.) *The Varieties of Sensory Experience: A Sourcebook in the Anthropology of the Senses*, pp. 167–191. Toronto: University of Toronto Press.

Lachmund, Jens. 1999. 'Making Sense of Sound: auscultation and lung sound codification in nineteenth-century French and German Medicine'. *Science, Technology, and Human Values* 24(4): 419–50.

Mead, Margaret. 1928. *Coming of Age in Samoa*. New York: Harper Collins.

Peek, Philip. 1994. 'The Sounds of Silence: cross-world communication and the auditory arts in African societies'. *American Ethnologist* 21(3): 474–94.

Pink, Sarah. 2009. *Doing Sensory Ethnography*. London: Sage.

Rice, Tom. 2003. 'Soundselves: An Acoustemology of Sound and Self in the Edinburgh Royal Infirmary'. *Anthropology Today* 19(4): 4–9.

Rice, Tom. 2013. *Hearing and the Hospital: Sound, Listening, Knowledge and Experience*. Canon Pyon: Sean Kingston Press.

Rice, Tom and Tripta Chandola. 2014. *Govindpuri Sound*. BBC World Service documentary. www.bbc.co.uk/programmes/p02hm1rx

Samuels, David. W., Louise Meintjes, Ana M. Ochoa and Thomas Porcello. 2010. 'Soundscapes: toward a sounded anthropology'. *Annual Review of Anthropology* 39: 329–45.

Schafer, Murray R. 1977. *The Tuning of the World*. New York: Knopf.

Stoller, Paul. 1997. *Sensuous Scholarship*. Philadelphia: University of Pennsylvania Press.

Turnbull, Colin. 1961. *The Forest People*. London: The Reprint Society.

Willis, Paul E. 1974. *'Symbolism and Practice: a theory for the social meaning of pop music'*. Stencilled Occasional Paper. Birmingham: Centre for Contemporary Cultural Studies, University of Birmingham.

24

SOUNDWALKING

Frauke Behrendt

Introduction

Soundwalks offer an intriguing combination of simplicity and complexity. By focussing on the simple act of walking and listening, soundwalks create the potential for opening our ears, bodies and minds to the sounds within us, around us and the soundscape of the world. Soundwalks are a mobile listening experience and provide a shift in attention that can change how we attend to the world. On many soundwalks I participated in or on those I guided myself, I experienced how this simple practice can have a profound impact on those who soundwalk.

Westerkamp's seminal text on soundwalking (first published in 1974, revised in 2001) defines soundwalks as "any excursion whose main purpose is listening to the environment" (Westerkamp 2001). In a later article, she reflects on soundwalking in the context of our media-saturated lives:

> This simple activity of walking, listening and soundmaking, invariably has the effect of not only re-grounding people in their community but also inspiring them about it, about creating a more balanced life between the global attraction of the computer and the local contact and touch with live human beings and reality.
>
> *(Westerkamp 2011: 12)*

Westerkamp's practice comprises soundwalks with audio recording but also unmediated soundwalks "an exploration of our ear/environment relationship, unmediated by microphones, headphones and recording equipment". The relationship between walking, listening, soundscape, and media is at the heart of debates and practices around soundwalks.

With Schafer and Truax, Westerkamp was part of the 1960s-founded World Soundscape Project. The project and its key figures are widely credited and cited as the "inventors" of soundwalks, as part of their considerations of soundscapes and acoustic ecology. McCartney gives a good overview of soundwalking in the tradition and context of acoustic ecology (McCartney 2004). Schafer and Truax's well-used online handbook defines soundwalks as "a form of active participation in the soundscape" with the purpose of "encourag[ing] the participant to listen discriminatively, and moreover, to make critical judgments about the sounds heard and their contribution to the balance or imbalance of the sonic environment" (Schafer and Truax, n.d.). For Truax, soundwalks are "the most direct aural involvement possible with a soundscape" and "a good practice to open one's ears" (Truax 2012: 196). Schafer differentiates between soundwalks and listening walks: "A listening walk" features "concentration on listening" while a "soundwalk is an exploration of the soundscape of an area using a score [a map] as a guide" (Schafer 1994: 212–213), that is, a pre-planned, or composed activity.

Westerkamp, Schafer, Truax, and other colleagues at the World Soundscape Project audio often recorded their soundwalks. Truax argues for soundwalks without mobile recording technologies: "Soundwalking is best done with the only intent being listening, without the distraction of operating a recorder." However, this practice is then followed up with soundwalks that feature mobile recording technologies – "[a]fter various soundwalks have been completed, the listener can make a more informed choice about recording, along with what is the best way to represent the soundscape through recording", and then post-production – "[l]ater in the studio, the question as to what is a reasonable representation of the soundscape can be judged based on that experience" (Truax 2012: 196).

McCartney's (2014) research is key for the intersection of soundwalking and sound recording, as well as for considerations of artistic approaches to soundwalking and working with soundwalk material in the artistic and musical context (for example installations). McCartney's definition is: "[a] soundwalk is an exploration of a location through walking, in which listening becomes the primary mode of attention" (McCartney 2012).

Walking is a key element of soundwalks. Chapman (2013) draws out connections between mobility studies and soundscape studies, with the former focussing on movement more generally, and the latter specifically on walking, and specifically soundwalks. Both mobility studies and soundwalks use movement as conceptual tool. Soundwalking "stipulates a consistent re-localisation of our listening perspective as paramount to coming to terms with the sonic character of an environment" (Chapman 2013). Listening in relation to other modes of mobility than walking is an area that has attracted far less attention than walking, but there is some artistic and research engagement with other forms of mobility such as cycling (McCartney 2004) and driving. Listening is of course not restricted to walking, and this mode can be replaced or supplemented with other forms of human mobility, such as wheeling or cycling. These mobile listening activities are then sometimes called sound rides. The focus on walking raises issues around accessibility and diversity (McCartney 2014), as our acoustic environment is experienced through a range of mobilities, and their associated politics of mobilities.

Almost all research published on soundwalks is from Western researchers, artists and institutions, which is reflected in the approach in terms of the cultural, social, political, and economic context. Most publications on soundwalking are from Canada, France, the UK, and Germany. This chapter only considers publications in English. In the mid-to-late 2000s, publications considering soundwalks started to appear in a range of fields, largely with a view to developing or using it as a qualitative research method, often in conjunction with other methods or tools. Alongside publications in the area of soundscape research where soundwalking was traditionally discussed (for example *Journal of Soundscape Ecology*), these include cultural geography (Butler 2006), urban planning (Adams et al. 2008), social science (Hall, Lashua, and Coffey 2008), and feminist theory (Mohr 2007). The early 2010s, with the emergence of a more robust field of sound studies and associated journals, saw considerations of recording and listening in relation to soundwalking (Reyes 2012) and also publications with a more media and/or computing approach (Paquette and McCartney 2012; Altavilla and Tanaka 2012). In addition to this well-known Western tradition of soundwalking, there are other histories and practices of soundwalking that emerged in other locations and at other times (see McCartney 2014).

A media-inclusive definition of soundwalking

Soundwalks combine a specific form of human mobility – walking – with a specific way of sensory attention – listening, and do so in a variety of ways and with a range of purposes, while often featuring elements of talking, silence, and media. This definition proposed here is wide, including mobile listening practices where walkers wear headphones to listen to or engage with sound from media devices in addition to listening to their soundscape. Soundwalking can be understood as research and practice that is not about sound but in sound, as well as not about walking but in walking. Soundwalking is a spatio-temporal, embodied, situated, multi-sensory and mobile practice. Soundwalks are used across a wide range of academic disciplines as well as artistic/creative practices, including as method, tool, and methodology. The concept and history of soundwalks is closely related to the soundscape concept, the history of acoustic ecology and considerations of listening. Over time, soundwalks have been considered and used by an increasing range of research and practice fields, including sound art, media studies, sound studies, urban planning, social science.

While the key components of a soundwalk are listening to sounds and being mobile by walking, there is great variety when it comes to the detail of these components such as the location, length, and route of the walk, as well as the sounds focussed on, the group size of the listeners, the ration of walking and being stationary, the use of media for recording or playing back sound, the amount of talking, and of course the aim of the soundwalk.

As this chapter will show, there is a range of elements that feature in soundwalks in various combinations, often describing a range of options. On the one hand, soundwalks often feature silent elements, if not the entire walk is conducted in silence. On the other hand, reflective discussion is often a key part of soundwalks, in between silent elements or at the end of a silent walk. Interestingly, discussions around social and class aspects of "noise" and "silence" (Bijsterveld 2008) are not always considered in discussion around soundwalking. There is a distinction between soundwalking as an expert practice – for examples as research method or as artistic practice – and a more democratic understanding of soundwalking as something everyone can do, a more participatory, non-expert approach. Soundwalks can be understood as individual practice or as group experience. Audio recording can be a key aspect of soundwalks or not feature at all. A soundwalk can be an end in itself or a means for something else. It can be artistic and creative or used as a research method to measure experience. Soundwalks can take place in busy urban environments or in remote landscapes. Those on a soundwalk could wear headphones (listening to their own audio recordings or to other audio) or not. They could add sounds to the soundscape in real-time through talking or with instruments, or aim to minimise their own sounds. Soundwalks can have a pre-described route or an improvised one. They can be one-off events or repeated activities, at the same time of the day/week/year or with variation.

This chapter considers the educational and pedagogical aspects of soundwalks, soundwalks as method for urban planning as well as the artistic and qualitative aspects of soundwalks, followed by a conclusion.

Educational soundwalks

The educational and pedagogic aspects of soundwalks are present in all practices and discussion around it. In addition, there are specific considerations of the various pedagogical purposes of soundwalks. Tinkle considers soundwalking to be part of sound pedagogy (Tinkle 2015), Dietze (2000) discusses projects with school students, and Butler (2007) provides an early consideration of the use of locative audio for teaching. Reyes (2012) discusses the use of soundwalks with sound recording as educational practice, where students walk with headphones and microphones and listen to the sound recorded by a microphone in real-time. The EARS 2 (2016) project provides very useful and accessible instructions and teaching material for soundwalking, aimed at a secondary school teachers and students as audience, but with wider use for all those considering to use soundwalks in their teaching.

Urban planning and soundwalks

Semidor wrote one of the first detailed accounts on using soundwalking for architecture and urban planning, is widely cited, and has remained active in this area, for example through the COST Action TD0804 Soundscapes of European Cities and Landscapes. Semidor's (2006) method is an autoethnographic approach to soundwalking where the researcher is the soundwalker that also records the walk with (binaural) field audio recordings, photographs, and fieldnotes (Semidor 2006). Many studies have been influenced by her method for soundwalking in the context of architecture and urban design.

Soundwalks can be used for "evaluating urban soundscapes" (Jeon, Hong, and Lee 2013). Jeon, Hong and Lee provide a good overview of soundwalks in the context of other methods for evaluating soundscapes. They propose the method "individual soundwalk" where individual experts walk in a specified area with a start and end point (but no prescribed route); they are equipped with an annotated map indicating "major soundscape elements", select their own stopping points for evaluating their soundscape with a questionnaire, and spend one hour for their walk (Jeon, Hong, and Lee 2013). Their paper concludes that "the individual soundwalk procedure has advantages for measuring diverse subjective responses and for obtaining the perceived elements of the urban soundscape" (Jeon, Hong, and Lee 2013).

Augoyard's "Qualitative listening in motion" method uses walking, environmental recordings, and interviews along a route chosen by the interviewee: "The interviewee picks up sounds with the microphone on the extension arm and comments to the interviewer on what he or she is listening to and recording" (Uimonen 2011: 258).

Soundwalking is an important aspect of "demonstrating the importance of individual experience in assessing the soundscapes of urban environments" to move beyond noise abatement and towards a more complex understanding of urban soundscapes and associated design and policies (Adams et al. 2006: 2385). Building on this, the research team on the Positive Sound-scapes Project developed soundwalking as a sociological method and as a tool that could be used in urban planning and associated disciplines (M.D. Adams et al. 2008). This research team reports detailed results of their mixed-method approach including "structured soundwalks" and explain how soundwalks can be used at various stages of the research process (M.D. Adams, Davies, and Bruce 2009). They also produced a report for a UK government agency (DEFRA) that lists soundwalks as one of the methods for soundscape assessments (Payne, Davies, and Adams 2009) and this report also includes an extensive literature review. Adams et al. give an overview of using the soundwalk as methodology for researchers and participants: "Some have employed it as a means through which the researcher immerses themselves into the urban soundscape while others have used it as a way of engaging others into the practice of listening to and describing the city" (Adams et al. 2008: 2).

Adams and his colleagues use soundwalking as evaluative method and understand this as "active form of participation in the soundscape, the essential purpose of which is to encourage participants to listen discriminately and to make critical judgments about the sounds heard and their contribution to the balance or imbalance of the sonic environment" (Adams et al. 2008: 4). Their own method involves walking a specific route (featuring a range of urban features) in silence, with stops in each of the "typical" locations (such as a square) where a semi-structured interview are used to discuss questions about the locations and their sounds (Adams et al. 2008: 5). This is used in conjunction with pre- and post-soundwalk questions. The researchers argue this method makes it "possible for the researchers and the participants to have a shared sensory experience of the urban environments under investigation, thus enabling a deeper and more meaningful semi-structured interview to take place" (Adams et al. 2008: 6). The combination of walking and focussed listening "was significant in enabling a more far-reaching exploration of the responses made about spatiality and the relationship between the built environment, the urban infrastructure, the design of the city, and its soundscapes" (Adams et al. 2008: 6).

Several methods work with soundwalking methods that include talking while walking and listening where "participants were allowed to communicate with each other thus interacting with and adding to the soundscape", facilitating a real-time soundscape evaluation "rather than reflecting upon a memory of it in a post-walk interview" (Payne, Davies, and Adams 2009: 41). Thibaud and colleagues developed a recording-based soundwalking method called "Commented City Walks" that aims to "gain access to the in situ sensory experience of passers-by" (Thibaud 2013). Participants walk and listen while also describing their experience orally in real-time (recorded). This concept (and detailed research protocol) is based on three key aspects: studying perception in-situ, working with the close link between perception and motion, as well as using the sensory perception in-situ as trigger for verbalization.

Soundwalks as qualitative and artistic method

In addition to the context of urban planning, soundwalking is also used as qualitative research method in various ways. Hall et al. (2008) give a good overview of a range of approaches that use sound and walking and are relevant for social science research. These are discussed as alternatives to qualitative interviews, with a focus on walking-talking approaches such as the go-along or the mobile interview, while their "walking tours" method draws on soundwalks and interviews (Hall, Lashua, and Coffey 2008). Davies et al. (2013) give a detailed account of using soundwalks in conjunction with interviews as research method.

Soundwalks are an important method and methodology for qualitative research across disciplines and "the potential of this medium to create flowing, multi-sensory and embodied ways for social and cultural geographers to research the outside environment" (Butler 2006: 889) is increasingly recognised by researchers. Butler observes that soundwalks are also "useful for presenting site-specific cultural geography to the public in an accessible and inclusive way" (Butler 2006: 889). McCartney suggests that "[s]oundwalks followed by conversations about the walks provide a way for people to think through the cultural, musical, political, sonic and social meanings of everyday sounds in particular places" (2012: 2). O'Keeffe's work provides a detailed account of using a combination of mobile sound methods, including autoethnographic and participant soundwalks (O'Keeffe 2015). Mohr (2007) discusses soundwalks as part of the artistic process from a dance/choreography perspective on the listening body.

Uimonen describes a combination of soundwalks and qualitative interviews and/or post-walk surveys. He proposes the method "recorded listening walk" that "encompasses not only the recording of sounds, but also editing and discussion" (Uimonen 2011: 256). The focus is not on the recording as product but "the act of recording itself: listening to environmental sounds and documenting the thoughts they evoke" (Uimonen 2011: 257). Uimonen discusses the use of media technologies and how they construct electroacoustic communities, for example by combining soundwalks, recordings and the Internet and/or online/GPS mapping technologies. These are often soundscape projects that involve some soundwalking and they tend to be more "inclusive" in terms of understanding a range of media and online technologies as part of them.

Drever (2008) discusses the use of soundwalking for artists and creative ends as well as for social science research. He gives a musical-artistic approach to soundwalks (and towards considering their routes) as "a subtle, transformative, personal, sensitive practice, whilst simultaneously being a highly social analytical sound audit and ritualistic auditory experience" (Drever 2008). He discusses the support – "[t]he group also provides support for one another, helping maintain the discipline of focused listening" – and performance aspects of the group element of soundwalking: "[t]here is of course a strong performance aspect to a group of silent people walking down a street slowly in a crocodile" (Drever 2008). Drever also stresses the importance of the leader in taking away practical and safety concerns (for example around the route) to facilitate listening focus: "The role of the leader here is fundamental, taking on all the daily concerns of timekeeping and navigation, leaving the walkers the erstwhile unprecedented luxury of focusing on listening" (Drever 2008). This is confirmed by McCartney: "[t]he work of the soundwalk leader is crucial in designing structures for activities, suggesting listening strategies, and leading discussions" (McCartney 2012).

Butler combines a sound art and cultural geography perspective to consider soundwalking. He discusses a range of artistic examples, including Cardiff's work and more commercial examples such as soundwalk.com. Butler has a wide understanding of soundwalks and discusses a range of media in relation to and as part of soundwalking, contributing a useful discussion around engagement with the public and memories through soundwalks (Butler 2006).

The artist Janet Cardiff uses the term "audio walk" rather than soundwalk. Other common terms for audio walks are audio trails, sound trails, and some also include audio guides and sound guides. McCartney states that "audio walks share with soundwalks their emphasis on sonic experiences of particular places, but there are some significant differences in concepualization and practice" (McCartney 2014: 228). However, the wide definition of soundwalks proposed in this chapter (see introduction) also includes media-rich forms of soundwalks such as Cardiff's audio walks (see Batista and Lesky 2015; Nedelkopoulou 2011). This means soundwalking includes listening to "added" sounds (also those activated through GPS, for example Rueb's work, see Rueb) and listening to things that are not usually in the range of human auditory perception, such as Kubisch's "Electrical Walks" where the audience listens to the sound of electromagnetic fields of their surroundings (Kubisch 2016).

This wider definition embraces a range of media engagement as part of soundwalking to move beyond the distinction McCartney makes in terms of how people pay attention to their soundscape in relation to media (McCartney 2014: 229). This chapter argues that listening to additional audio (for example via headphones) does not prevent engagement with the current soundscape around the listener, as is often argued. Hearing these "added" sounds can in fact lead to listening to and engagement with the "existing" soundscape (Behrendt 2012).

Butler introduces the term "memoryscapes" for "outdoor trails that use recorded sound and spoken memory played on a personal stereo or mobile media to experience places in new ways" (Butler 2007). This focus on memories of the past in sound and audio walks is shared by Schine who "explores how the production of memory and act of remembering are evoked during the process of memory walks (or soundwalks) as a way of understanding and engaging with the world" (Schine 2016), drawing on interesting research on walking and memory recall. This chapter's wide definition of soundwalks also includes these more narrative and memory/history-related forms of media-rich walks.

Akio Suzuki uses offline media for his series "Oto-date" soundwalks where the artist leaves ear/feet-shaped stencils on the ground around town to mark a listening route for the audience

(Lacey 2016). At the other end of the spectrum in terms of media are soundwalks that are entirely online and do not require "traditional" walking. Ferrington (2002) gives an overview of early online soundwalks and a more recent discussion of online soundmaps (Mechtley, Cook, and Spanias 2013) also considers soundwalks. In addition to these web-based soundwalks, there are also discussions of virtual reality soundwalks (Signorelli 2013, 2014), and discussions of sound in relation to walking in computer games (Collins 2013). In these instances, the walking is not done by the physical body of the participant, but by a virtual body or avatar. This might stretch the definition of the soundwalk in terms of the "walking" but is still part of the broad understanding of the practice proposed in this chapter.

Conclusion

The wide range of soundwalking practices and discussions presented throughout the chapter show how soundwalks are used in a wide range of academic and artistic ways. Pedagogical and educational aspects of soundwalks are at the heart of the practice and help to spread the word about them further. Urban planning is an example of how the practice of soundwalking has been used as a more formal method or tool in the context of planning, design and policy. The qualitative and artistic aspects of soundwalks illustrate the diversity of creative and academic practices around soundwalking.

Soundwalks are also used and discussed in the context of health (Nazemi et al. 2013). The pace of relaxed walking is deemed important in terms of its relation to the heartbeat (McCartney 2014: 213). The slow pace of a soundwalk and the attention to the body and the environment that is fostered by walking and listening also lends itself to understanding soundwalking as a mindful activity with health and wellbeing implications. Here, we return to Westerkamp who observes "[t]o walk in a group without talking is a rare opportunity in this day and age where few of us engage in spiritual worship and meditation" (Westerkamp 2011: 13). The context of health and wellbeing is important for the future research agenda of soundwalking.

This chapter proposed a broad understanding of "soundwalks", both in terms of the "sound" and in terms of the "walking" that could both include media-aspects. This points towards a focus on media for a future "soundwalking" research agenda. This could include further explorations of soundwalking in relation to computer games, virtual reality, locative games, augmented reality etc. The broad understanding of soundwalking proposed in this chapter highlights the intersection of listening, walking and media. The constantly evolving world of media media informs, shapes and changes our practices and experiences of walking, listening and interaction with soundscapes. For soundwalks, it is the interplay between media, walking and listening that opens our ears, bodies and minds to the sounds within us, around us, and the soundscape of the world.

References

Adams, Mags D., Trevor Cox, Gemma Moore, Ben Croxford, Mohamed Refaee, and Steve Sharples. 2006. "Sustainable Soundscapes: Noise Policy and the Urban Experience." *Urban Studies* 43 (13): 2385–98. doi:10.1080/00420980600972504.

Adams, Mags D., William J. Davies, and Neil Spencer Bruce. 2009. "Soundscapes: An Urban Planning Process Map." *Inter.Noise*. http://usir.salford.ac.uk/2465/.

Adams, Mags D., N.S. Bruce, W.J. Davies, R. Cain, P. Jennings, A. Carlyle, P. Cusack, K. Hume, and C. Plack. 2008. "Soundwalking as a Methodology for Understanding Soundscapes." In *Proc. Institute of Acoustics*, 30: 1–7. http://usir.salford.ac.uk/2461/.

Altavilla, Alessandro and Atau Tanaka. 2012. "The Quiet Walk: Sonic Memories and Mobile Cartography." *Proc. of Sound and Music Computing Conference (SMC)*, 157–62.

Batista, Anamarija, and Carina Lesky. 2015. "Sidewalk Stories: Janet Cardiff's Audio-Visual Excursions." *Word & Image* 31 (4): 515–23. doi:10.1080/02666286.2015.1053044.

Behrendt, Frauke. 2012. "GPS Sound Walks, Ecotones and Edge Species.pdf." *Soundscape* 12 (1): 25–28.

Bijsterveld, Karin. 2008. *Mechanical Sound: Technology, Culture, and Public Problems of Noise in the Twentieth Century.* Cambridge, MA: MIT Press.

Butler, Toby. 2006. "A Walk of Art: The Potential of the Sound Walk as Practice in Cultural Geography." *Social & Cultural Geography* 7 (6): 889–908. doi:10.1111/j.1749-8198.2007.00017.x.

———. 2007. "Memoryscape: How Audio Walks Can Deepen Our Sense of Place by Integrating Art, Oral History and Cultural Geography." *Geography Compass* 1 (3):360–72. doi:10.1111/j.1749-8198.2007.00017.x.

Chapman, Owen. 2013. "Sound Moves: Intersections of Popular Music Studies, Mobility Studies and Soundscape Studies." *Wi. Journal of Mobile Media* 8 (1). http://wi.mobilities.ca/sound-moves-intersections-of-popular-music-studies-mobility-studies-and-soundscape-studies/.

Collins, Karen. 2013. *Playing with Sound.* Cambridge, MA: MIT Press.

Davies, William J., Mags D. Adams, Neil S. Bruce, Rebecca Cain, Angus Carlyle, Peter Cusack, Deborah Hall, et al. 2013. "Perception of Soundscapes: An Interdisciplinary Approach." *Applied Acoustics* 74 (2): 224–31. doi:10.1016/j.apacoust.2012.05.010.

Dietze, Lena. 2000. "Learning Is Living: Acoustic Ecology as Pedagogical Ground. A Report on Experience." *The Journal of Acoustic Ecology* 1 (1): 20–22.

Drever, John. 2008. *Silent Soundwalking : An Urban Pedestrian Soundscape Methodology.* Available at: https://research.gold.ac.uk/8655/1/aia-daga13_Drever_soundwalking_paper.pdf.

EARS 2. 2016. "Soundwalks." Accessed May 12. http://ears2.dmu.ac.uk/learning-object/soundwalks/.

Ferrington, Gary. 2002. "Soundwalking the Internet." *The Journal of Acoustic Ecology* 3 (1): 34.

Hall, Tom, Brett Lashua, and Amanda Coffey. 2008. "Sound and the Everyday in Qualitative Research." *Qualitative Inquiry* 14 (6): 1019–40. doi:10.1177/1077800407312054.

Jeon, Jin Yong, Joo Young Hong, and Pyoung Jik Lee. 2013. "Soundwalk Approach to Identify Urban Soundscapes Individually." *The Journal of the Acoustical Society of America* 134 (1): 803–12. doi:10.1121/1.4807801.

Kubisch, Christina. 2016. "Electrical Walks." Accessed July 29. www.christinakubisch.de/en/works/electrical_walks.

Lacey, Jordan. 2016. *Sonic Rupture. A Practice-Led Approach to Urban Soundscape Design.* Bloomsbury Academic.

McCartney, Andra. 2004. "What Is a Sound Ecologist to Do?" *The Journal of Acoustic Ecology* 5 (2): 8–9.

———. 2012. "Meaningful Listening through Soundwalks." In *Proceedings of the Electroacoustic Music Studies Network Conference*, 1–5. Stockholm.

———. 2014. "Soundwalking: Creative Moving Environmental Sound Narratives." In *The Oxford Handbook of Mobile Music Studies. Volume 2*, edited by Sumanth Gopinath and Jason Stanyeck, 212–37. Oxford: Oxford University Press.

Mechtley, Brandon, Perry Cook, and Andreas Spanias. 2013. "Sound Mapping on the Web: Current Solutions and Future Directions." *Proceedings of the Symposium on Acoustic Ecology.*

Mohr, Hope. 2007. "Listening and Moving in the Urban Environment." *Women & Performance: A Journal of Feminist Theory* 17 (2): 185–203. doi:10.1080/07407700701387325.

Nazemi, Mark, Maryam Mobini, Diane Gromala, and Tyler Kinnear. 2013. "Soundscapes : A Prescription for Managing Anxiety in a Clinical Setting." ACM CHI: Paris: France.

Nedelkopoulou, Eirini. 2011. "Walking Out on Our Bodies Participation as Ecstasis in Janet Cardiff's Walks." *Performance Research* 16 (4): 117–23. doi:10.1080/13528165.2011.606058.

O'Keeffe, Linda. 2015. "Thinking Through New Methodologies. Sounding out the City with Teenagers." *Qualitative Sociology Review* 11 (1): 6–32.

Paquette, David, and Andra McCartney. 2012. "Soundwalking and the Bodily Exploration of Places." *Canadian Journal of Communication* 37 (1): 135–45. http://search.ebscohost.com/login.aspx?direct=true&db=ufh&AN=75262594&site=ehost-live.

Payne, Sarah R., William J. Davies, and Mags D. Adams. 2009. *Research into the Practical and Policy Applications of Soundscape Concepts and Techniques in Urban Areas (NANR 200).* Available at: http://usir.salford.ac.uk/27343/1/Payne_et_al_Soundscapes_Defra_2009.pdf.

Reyes, Ian. 2012. "Mediating a Soundwalk: An Exercise in Claireaudience." *International Journal of Listening* 26 (2): 98–101. doi:10.1080/10904018.2012.678096.

Rueb, Teri. "Teri Rueb." www.teriirueb.net/i_index.html.

Schafer, R. Murray. 1994. *The Soundscape: Our Sonic Environment and the Tuning of the World.* Rochester, VT: Destiny Books.

Schafer, R. Murray, and Barry Truax. (n.d.) "Soundscape." www.sfu.ca/sonic-studio/handbook/Soundscape.html.

Schine, Jennifer. 2016. "Movement, Memory & the Senses in Soundscape Studies." *Sensory Studies*. Accessed May 12. www.sensorystudies.org/sensorial-investigations/movement-memory-the-senses-in-soundscape-studies/.

Semidor, Catherine. 2006. "Listening to a City with the Soundwalk Method." *Acta Acustica United with Acustica* 92 (6): 959–64.

Signorelli, Valerio. 2013. "Soundwalking in Virtual Ambiances: Applying Game Engine Technologies in Soundscape Studies." *EAEA-11 Conference 2013*, no. Track 2: 281–88.

———. 2014. "Unfolding the Soundmaps . Suggestions for Representing and Sharing the Sensory Form of Urban Spaces Through Virtual Environments and Web-mapping Technologies." In *Invisible Places, Sounding Cities*. Viseu. Available at: http://invisibleplaces.org/invisibleplaces.html.

Thibaud, Jean-Paul. 2013. "Commented City Walks." *Journal of Mobile Media* 7 (01): Available at: http://wi.mobilities.ca/commented-city-walks/.

Tinkle, Adam. 2015. "Sound Pedagogy: Teaching Listening Since Cage." *Organised Sound* 20 (02): 222–30. doi:10.1017/S1355771815000102.

Truax, Barry. 2012. "Sound, Listening and Place: The Aesthetic Dilemma." *Organised Sound* 17 (January 2012): 193–201. doi:10.1017/S1355771811000380.

Uimonen, Heikki. 2011. "Everyday Sounds Revealed: Acoustic Communication and Environmental Recordings." *Organised Sound* 16 (03): 256–63. doi:10.1017/S1355771811000264.

Westerkamp, Hildegard. 2001. "Soundwalking." *Originally Published in Sound Heritage, Volume III Number 4, Victoria B.C., 1974*. www.sfu.ca/~westerka/writings page/articles pages/soundwalking.html.

———. 2011. "Exploring Balance & Focus in Acoustic Ecology." *The Journal of Acoustic Ecology* 11 (1): 7–13.

25

SURFACE TENSION: MEMORY, SOUND AND VINYL

Paul Nataraj

The mass-produced record was the most potent symbol of the power of the music industry, and some might argue is becoming so once again. Emile Berliner's invention of the disc and his introduction of little 'Nipper', the dog listening attentively to 'His Master's Voice', introduced the music industry proper. The process of manufacture, and importantly Berliner's insistence on the use of these new technologies to record music rather than just the speaking voice, took recording from the hands of the amateurs into the realms of professional expertise (Osbourne, 2012). Since then, as Attali states, 'music has become a strategic consumption, an essential mode of sociality for all those who feel themselves powerless before the monologue of the great institutions' (Attali, 1985: 100). Music in this sense frees us from the monotony of the work place, from the grind of daily life. Whatever the style, according to Attali, it provides some element of resistance, that still sits comfortably, for the most part, within the system that it is allegedly opposed to. Music opens up a space where signification can be negated, and pleasure can ensue. Even though the record is the symbol of sonic fixity, throughout the history of recording, the unique materiality of the record has given rise to creative misuses and subversive practices that have at once revolutionized and disrupted not only the music industry, but also wider cultural creative practices, and as corollary the record buying public, or cultural consumers themselves. In so doing, the use of the record in different contexts has a truly political overtone. Working in the tradition of artists such as Milan Knizak (1996) and Christian Marclay, my own practice-led research project, 'You Sound Like a Broken Record' (YSLABR), has sought to explore the complex relationship between some of the splintered fragments the vinyl records' heterogeneous ontology, opening a productive dialogue between industry, user, artefact, artist, music, and society. I have done this by creating palimpsests, carving ethnographic interviews onto the surface of discs donated to me by their owners. Drawing from this practice, in this chapter I will explore the theoretical underpinnings of instantiating the record and owner as palimpsest.

The main focus will be the story of Sheena and her relationship with David Bowie's 'Station to Station'. I highlight some of the conflicting, reflective, and interweaving narratives and explore their tensions and productivities as they are played out on, in, and through the material, text, and experience of the vinyl record. The personal narrative repositions the record as a complex, vibrant repository and mediator of our sometimes-ignored inner selves. The weight of the records' gravity spins us out in new directions, into a variety of life choices that change the trajectory of our existences. As one of my respondents Tony says when he first heard the Buzzcocks and became 'like a drug addict, hung up the football boots, and after that it was music every single night' (Tony, interview).

Martin Irvine, quoting Bordieu's theory of collective misrecognition, makes the point that, '[w]e are continually socialized into maintaining – under heavy ideological pressure – ways of pre-serving the misrecognition of sources, authors, origins, works, and derivations in order to sustain these social categories as functions in the political economy and the intellectual property legal regime for cultural goods' (Irvine, 2015: 17). Bartmanski and Woodward also describe this process as the industry developing 'master narratives that seem to govern the production and reception of culture' (Bartmanski and Woodward, 2015: 102). So music, despite what many of us like to think, does not float free of its representational bolt-ons, whether they are discursive, social, or visual. But these multiple mediations cause tension. Not only can some musicological writing, as Chan succinctly observes, 'reduce vibrant musics to lifeless corpses fit for autopsy' (Chan, 1998), but these mediations also interfere with the individual experience of listening. These paratexts are not solely reductive however, they can be simultaneously instructive. They allow us to contextualize our listening and in many cases they play an important pedagogic role. However, they can also be problematic because they are often hegemonic in character. They can be compromised by their modes and contexts of their production, historically fixing meaning to music and therefore play-ing a vital role in the maintenance of a certain story of music, whose ontology is not that simple to apprehend. If we want to fully realize the communicative potential of music and to see all the nuances of its effects, to provide us with a 'thickness' of expression that goes beyond that of the market expectation, whilst also valuing the role of these discursive systems to provide the space for opposition thus the production of rogue elements, then the stories of the non-expert, the part-time music fan, the ones who lost interest at some time along the way, are equally important to unpack. As Hesmondhalgh (2013) highlights in his work, music can't always be discussed in terms of exuberance and joyousness, sometimes it is the darker, more troubling aspects of our sociality that it speaks to, those moments where words fail us but something must be expressed. If we want to fully appreciate the complexity of our own musical journeys, to give agency to the value and power of our own subjectivity, one could be persuaded by Barthes' compulsion to kill the author. As Burke notes, 'to impose an author on a text is to impose an archaic monoism on a brave new pluralist world' (Burke, 1998: 24), and in the multifarious life of the record this would be an espe-cially reductive approach.

Barthes writes, '[t]he *explanation* of the work is always sought in the man or woman who produced it, as if it were always in the end, through the more or less transparent allegory of the fiction, the voices of a single person, the *author* "confiding" in us' (Barthes, 1977: 143). In the music industry this is the process of creating the star, producing the saleable image, writing the commodified narrative that at once demystifies and simultaneously mythologizes in a process that potentially freezes form and stifles creativity. Although I don't posit the totalizing effects of the professional critical voice over the discourse of music, its influence cannot be ignored. Musical meaning is not created autonomously by the object of music itself, and as Middleton writes, '[a]ll music existing and newly produced, is unavoidably affected, its meaning becoming more obviously contingent' (Middleton, 1990: 95).

Looking to the 'destination' of the musical text by speaking to those who have developed a personal connection with these objects, new perspectives are highlighted: perspectives that may be able to reposition an individual subjectivity in the hierarchy among industry, listener, music, object and the artist that they have called upon with the stab of a diamond-tipped needle. Each disc represents a series of times, spaces, and experiences woven together through the continued use of the record in new settings and new contexts throughout its life cycle. For me, Bob

Marley's 'Catch a Fire', 1973, first press, in the fold-out Zippo sleeve, is not just an album that I love dearly because of its musical content and its rarity, but it is also the memory of finding the money that I bought it with in a Christmas card given by a kind aunt and uncle. They too have become the story of that record. I remember vividly seeing it on the wall in Astonishing Sounds in Burnley, just after Neil had moved the shop from Northgate in Blackburn, and being filled with hope that I would actually be able to hold it in my hands. The intense feeling of excitement tinged with trepidation at handing over what I thought was a crazy amount of money for a record, whilst at the same time glowing inside that one of these objects would be mine, is something I feel every time I look at the cover, let alone pick the 'thing' up. Being able to buy it was linked to luck, success, competition, but also love. I loved Bob, and this was a way of showing that love; the first press, knowing about it, caring about it, letting other people know I cared about it. Having the object that represented a moment in time where the power was wrested from the hegemony of rock music and placed into the hands and voices of a group of ghetto boys – holding the symbol of that shift. It made me part of it, and it made me feel that I could effect the inequalities of power that I perceived as my 16-year-old self. And now where is it? Locked away in storage, and I'm frustrated that I can't excavate it to relive its sounds as I write this, somehow listening to the mp3 on YouTube won't do. I feel as though I've let it down; how can this be possible, it's just a record after all? But it's the symbolic power it holds of speaking to my personal hopes for the future that is telling. It's not that I've let the record down; I've somehow failed its ideals, and thinking of it reminds me of that. It's bittersweet. I knew of the record because I had read about it in Timothy White's biography of the dreadlocked star. It was through him that I understood the record to be important, its novelty packaging was more than just a gimmick, it represented the fact that Island Records had the faith to back this music, it was an exercise in belief. Tim told me that…

The record, then, has an existence in my memory that is constructed by a series of narratives intertwining to create the object as I know it. All these disparate elements, drawn across space and time come to make up the gestalt of ownership. The relationship is not developed in isolation, and even though one can love a piece of music, a record or an artist in the confines of one's private space, this love is also shared with those around us. These are some of the 'social imaginaries afforded by music' (Born, 2011: 379), and are extremely important in trying to ascertain the subjective value of such objects. My interviewees talk about friends, family, places, spaces, journalists, TV, film, and the wider cultural landscape as wrapped up in their emotional attachment to the object. These disparate elements are very much a part of the complexity, and for some the beauty of the record's significance. 'I just remember loads of people liking that kind of thing, and playing it and getting to know people through stuff like that' (Adam, interview).

These experiences layer and shift over time, they build up on the record's surface like dust, forming a patina through which the music changes its hue. These layers build up and intertwine, creating what Derrida describes as an 'assemblage' of writing that suggests how the text has 'the structure of interlacing, a weaving, or a web, which would allow the different threads and different lines of sense or force to separate again, as well as being ready to bind others together' (Derrida, 1968: 127). By lifting one layer away from another, a personal ecology may be found that unveils the nuances of the object and shows how and where that object came to be its present self, how it accumulated its 'thing' power. The unique materiality of the record affords it multifunctional capacities as sonic storage, art object, and pedagogic prompt, carrier of the subversive and mainstream simultaneously, making the ontological ambiguity at play in the vinyl record troublesome to unpick. Yet there are some familiar voices that reach us through the chains of interrelationships linked by the groove that act like silken threads of signification inscribed into the lives of the listener. Lifting each of the layers that accumulate on the fragile surface of the record can help us to reassess its value as a cultural icon.

Palimpsests appeared in the medieval world as writing was a costly pursuit and consequently was tightly controlled. Parchment was incredibly expensive and so new scripts had to be written on top of old. Vellum sheets were scrubbed clean in order for this new writing to take place, yet this erasure proved to be impermanent. Over the years the original writing began to bleed back through the newly inscribed work as prolonged exposure to the atmosphere generated 'a ghostly trace … in the following centuries as the iron in the remaining ink reacted with the oxygen in the air, producing a reddish-brown oxide' (Dillon, 2005: 245). In this way a spoor of history is intertwined with the present of the text, as Gosta highlights, '…the writing of the past penetrates the writing of the present, and poses an interruption to the presents unfolding in the very presentation of itself' (Gosta, 2011: 708). The power relations of the time, engendered in the mechanizations of writing, could literally be read in the temporally entwined, twisting inscriptions contained on the one page. The restrictive cost of new parchment meant that decisions had to be made as to which texts would be preserved and which would be erased. Daughtry points out that subversive pagan mythology was often rewritten with the word of God. That which was deemed valueless was literally erased. Silencing voices written, as well as spoken, constructed the future in the image of the powerful. However over the course of time, these lost voices reappeared, and in doing so illuminated the political structuring of previous communities through this discursive positioning.

As music constantly struggles to be freed of its past both sonically and sociologically, its past forms, traditions, and conventions continue to resonate in its present. No matter how hard it tries, through its different mutations and paradigms of modern practice, the dream of originality is always a beat away. Therefore in order to properly constitute a history of music one must forgo the idea of completism. Yet thinking about the enmeshments in a 'palimpsestuous' (Dillon, 2005) way can draw some new roads on music's map, even if finding and accounting for every byway is a cartographic impossibility. Eisenberg writes that '[a] record is a world: It is the world scratched by man in a form that may survive him' (Eisenberg, 2005: 210). Thus the record becomes our guide. It can act as a sonic cartographer's notebook forming triangulation points from which to navigate our tangled musical landscapes and to try and find our place amongst the increasing range of actors engaged with maintaining its trunk roads. Thinking about the record as a layer in the ever accreting palimpsest of a personal musical journey allows for us to 'trace multiple histories, and multiple authors' (Daughtry, 2013: 4), and in so doing we approach the object dialectically. Daughtry, quoting Andreas Huyssen speaking about architectural palimpsests, describes being able to 'read these spaces intertextually and recovering "present pasts" from the abyss of cultural amnesia' (Daughtry, 2013: 5). In other words, in a displacement of this idea from the architectural to the cultural material, the vinyl record produces a site that witnesses these intertwining 'present pasts'.

The idea of the palimpsest is especially telling in the case of tracing some of the meandering ontology of the vinyl record because the record itself goes through a physical transformation every time it is played, as David Toop rather dramatically notes: '[t]he needle plough[s] through the spiralled groove, wearing away both itself and the music it transmits. Each performance writes its own slow suicide note' (Toop, 2003: 126–7). The action of the needle reading the groove causes a deterioration of the records' surface, and the degenerative work of time and physical context also plays its tune on the physical nature of the grooves and consequently is telling of its history. It speaks of the objects' uniqueness and personal connection, in a way that gives value to the demotic:

> I mean you look at my copy of it, it's a mess because I battered it to pieces, I mean, I
> can't even clean it no more, and 'Chemistry' which is on the flip side, which not many

people played, which is probably the best track, or the one that I most like, is scratched at the end, but I've kept it because it's the original copy, it's the one I bought originally.

(Alex, interview)

So can the multilayered writing of the palimpsest offer us an analytical tool when thinking about the vinyl record and our relationships to it? The metaphor of the palimpsest can work on various levels here. It is at once the structuring of the text of the record itself through its means of production and its subsequent marketing comprising the paratexts created to support and explain its existence. And it is equally the process of memory formation that has given rise to the complex formation of the text in the mind of the listener. Musical memories are extremely complex beasts, liminal, labile, and multivalent. Constantly in flux and continually unfolding in a nexus of family, friends, places, and spaces internal and external. Caught between the highly personal and the paratexts of the industry, bound in love and loss, technologically constituted but bedded in our corpo-reality; shifting temporally, based in the past and emergent through present experience, produced by 'several people writing together' (Barthes, 1977: 144), these memories become 'palimpsestuous'. The beauty of the palimpsest is a gestalt complexity where each individual participant (I think here of participants also as sounds, writings, videos, and so on, not just people) is nominally sealed beneath the next user, yet the participants' voice is faintly audible through the morass of enmeshed experiential fibers that make up its ever-changing surface. So the palimpsest is fluid, mirroring the constant writing and erasure of sound across our auditory space. As we are subjected to a frag-mented sonic journey dispersed through a myriad of narratives that are constantly inflected by our subjective position in the soundscape, the text of the record is caught in what Barthes describes as 'a tissue of quotations drawn from the innumerable centers of culture' (Barthes, 1977: 146). It could be argued then that Barthes, in killing the author, is actually describing the palimpsestuous nature of the text in his analysis. In constructing the text we are, in Dillon's words, producing an 'involuted phenomenon where otherwise unrelated texts are involved and entangled, intricately interwoven, interrupting and inhabiting each other' (Dillon, 2005: 244). There is something very Barthesian about this for me. In addition if we are to take up Barthes' assertion that 'the text's unity lies not in its origin but in its destination' (Barthes, 1977: 148), as stated previously, then my respondents' framing of the importance of the record to them 'is necessary to overthrow the myth' of the genius musical voice, and resurrect the owners' subjectivity in relation to the vinyl record.

Let me introduce Sheena. In our interview, we discussed her original copy of 'Station to Station' by David Bowie that she 'bought when it came out … in 1976, and I was sixteen'. I'll let her take up the story:

I bought it in Windham, which is a small market town in Norfolk, which is where I was living at the time … I was already a huge Bowie fan, I had all his other albums, the reason this one is so significant is that it made me take, probably a different course in life … It opened my eyes to something I realised I wanted, maybe it was because I was sixteen and trusted him because I was such a big fan, where he was going influenced where I was going … I was just beginning to think I can't stand being in Norfolk much longer … I want to travel and I want to discover the world, when I bought this record, and knew what was happening in the artist's life, it just made me think God, I can't wait to get out there.

(Sheena, interview)

This record allowed Sheena to see Windham differently, it opened up a portal to the imagined 'new world' that was waiting, full of promise, if only the reality of the present would free the young Sheena from its shackles. The record represented escape for her, surrounded by posters of the 'Thin White Duke' in her bedroom, head buried in a copy of the New Musical Express – 'I was an avid reader of the NME, probably unhealthily obsessed by it' – dreaming of following her hero into fresh and exciting worlds. As Eisenberg poetically imagines, '[w]hen a record is lifted over the platter, a transparency or slide is fitted over a segment of space and time. The effect is a double exposure' (Eisenberg, 2005: 206). This speaks directly to the metaphor of our palimpsest. It may be only an imaginary moment, but as Hesmondhalgh explains further, 'music's distinctive language is one of compressed and elliptical reference to our inner lives and our prospects … it is close to dreaming in this respect' (Hesmondhalgh, 2013: 16). Sheena is looking into the Woolworths window in Windham, and seeing herself in Bowie's little clique heading for Hanza studios.

> … he went to Europe, he went to Berlin in fact, and that just chimed with me, because I was doing French and German, I was really interested in Europe, I read that he had come to hate America, and the other thing that is relevant here is that, I'd been to America a few times because I've got a really weird family background, which meant that my Mum married an American airman when I was quite young, had my sister and they went to America. And I had this really strange childhood, where I didn't really know where I belonged, and I went to America a few times, and in rural Norfolk no-one went outside, so I said I'd never been anywhere. It's really interesting in that I didn't count America.
>
> *(Sheena, interview)*

Here we can get a glimpse further into the fabric of the story that makes this record so important for Sheena. The story of her family and her relationship to them is inscribed into its grooves. She says that she 'trusted' Bowie, that she wanted to follow him to Europe, and like him was unable to come to terms with the idea that America had any romance attached to it whatsoever. America had wronged them both. Love was to be found in the futuristic potency, sophistication, and elegant quietude of Europe.

The record spoke to Sheena of the one world being subsumed into another.

> The album before that was 'Young Americans' which was very soul, very black, um, soul music, influence which I also loved, um, the albums after it were, the Berlin trilogy, which were all very electronic, and experimental, and so this was a kind of combination of the two, it's a transitionary record, and it's, you know, very much, very respected for that now but, it's got a lot of soul in it, it's got a lot of melody and emotion, but it's also got some really hard, you know, harsh electronic, um influences as well, and was, it's, it's, it's just, it was a bit of a gear crunch, I think, kind of a record, and that, I just felt that was a gear crunch time in my life and it, sort of resonated with me.
>
> *(Sheena, interview)*

It is interesting when considering the paratexts that surround Sheena's emotional connection with the record that she doesn't speak of lyrics. Instead she speaks of sounds used and the juxtaposition of the new and the conventional. The album itself opens with a phased train recording (echoing the work of Pierre Schaffer's music concrete output), which pans across the stereo field, and is processed to the point of near abstraction. This floats into a wailing electric guitar that maintains its place in the background of the mix just playing noises and tones rather than notes. A slow, open, minimal soul-esque but angular groove enters center stage. Some dissonant organs and synths fill the spaces behind this central drum and bass duo, fulfilling Sheena's assertion that the mix between harsh electronic sounds and soulfulness was the experimental and transitionary aesthetic of this record. The song 'Station to Station' is literally split in two halves, the slower crunchy roller turning on its head to become a pulsating disco stomper in the second half of the journey. We hear Bowie and his band trying to make sense of a number of contingent sonic experiences and personalities. The music takes on new sounds he has been hearing through the medium of recording, sounds he is chasing, indicating what he wants to get to in Berlin, the sounds of bands like Neu, Kraftwerk, and Can. It is evident that Sheena hears into the layers of this record and recognizes her own situation reflected right back at her. The tension of her current situation trying to break free from the constraints of both the past and the future played out through dissonance in the present. New sounds are vying for space with the old, new forms are taking over in the soundscape and the memory of the immanent becoming of the self, that this record sonically represents for her, remains traceable in the palimpsest of experience, over-laid with the passing of time. No matter how many years have passed by, the entanglements are still inscribed and are evidently legible for Sheena in the grooves of this record. She relates the story with great passion, and the detailed description and knowledge she displays are arresting. 'The palimpsest enables something that has disappeared from sight to resurrect; a trace to linger' (Bartolini, 2014: 520). I suppose the question is, would she have had the same reaction to this record without the NME, without the obvious retrospective reading, without the interferences from remembered images from Bowie's film, 'The Man Who Fell To Earth', which provided the cover image for the record. Would it have touched her in the same way without these social-izing accretions onto the text itself? Born describes the musical object as a 'constellation of mediations' (Born, 2011: 377), which I find to be an extremely useful way to describe it, texts and counter texts invisibly linked like silken threads of light reaching and interacting with one another in the black space of the records' surface.

As we can ascertain from just this tiny snippet of Sheena's story, her relationship with this record is very personal and special to her. For example, at the end of the interview, holding the record in her hands for the last time before handing it to me so I could take it away and inscribe it with her story, she said, 'that was the object that made me feel so strongly, that made me make one decision rather than another, it's quite sobering actually, humbling you could say (laughs)…' The power of the 'thing' to evoke such deep feelings and to be able to store influential memories is evident here, but does not tell us the whole story.

Sheena was obviously in love with Bowie: 'I sort of thought of him as a soul mate, and I just trusted him, he just always seemed to reflect where I was, he was always showing me the next thing.' In the way she tells the story it could be read that she trusted him more than she trusted her own family. As with any great story, however, there must always be the 'helper', as defined by Propp, who aids our hero in their success. Sheena's helper during this time was the famous music magazine the New Musical Express:

> When I was growing up, because it was strange you know, the family situation, I was an only child in a quite out of the way place, and music was important to me, you know the New Musical Express was my life-line, that led me into my career, which was working in record shops for many years.

Sheena is extremely knowledgeable not only about Bowie, but the wider musical milieu. She eloquently expresses an evolutionary taxonomy of bands and records that were influenced by or influenced Bowie, and so found their way into her own listenership. She speaks of Bowie's oeuvre not only with passion and enthusiasm, but also with great detail and factual expertise. For example, she elucidates on Bowie's use of the cut-up method when writing lyrics, describing the process as Bowie taking a 'meta-approach'. Yet this understanding is not coming from the record itself, and one can be quite certain that it is not coming from Bowie himself.

So we must then think carefully about the influence of the NME as an important layer in the palimpsestuous whole of Sheena's listening and the formation of her relationship with this record and the music it carries. Although Sheena has engaged deeply with the writings in the NME over the period of her extensive involvement in music, this is not the sole narrative of her experience. It is intertwined with her own story, her personal interaction with the record, and her road drawn on the map of its apprehension. The NME becomes a conduit for Sheena to embrace the detail of her hero's life. The writings become a way of contextualizing his experience, and it provides a hook for her to attach herself to a position inside this music generally, but specifically inside the expression of Bowie's alienated experiences... 'for many years being passionate about music was a big part of my identity, I suppose I wanted people to know.' She obviously loves/d Bowie, and felt a kinship, a closeness, an emotional bond, through the music he was part of creating. She was able to identify herself through these sounds he presented, the songs he fostered. This knowledge and the sharing of this passion required an empirical as well as emotional subjectivity, which could then be shared and allow for what we see now as a rounded and comprehensive understanding of his work and its relation to her as an individual.

The NME provided the basis to consolidate what Hesmondhalgh refers to as music's 'semiotic indefiniteness' that 'gives it a superior power to engage with our emotions' (Hesmondhalgh, 2013: 16). Sheena repeats the canonical information about the work, the process of lyric writing, the places of creation, and the musical expression channeling Bowie's interior tensions. Barthes explains that by 'allotting itself the important task of discovering the Author (or its hypostases: society, history, psyche, liberty) beneath the work: when the Author has been found, the text is 'explained' victory to the critic' (Barthes, 1977: 147). This explanation provides further dialectical enmeshments within the 'palimpsestuous' reading of the vinyl record. Sheena's use of the NME to become closer to the author himself, to better understand the music that she loves, could be read as a reductive process. The temporal elisions that make up the palimpsest articulate a constant becoming, where the text is never stagnant and is constantly in flux, knowing that it is equally past, present, and future subsequently. The constant iterations open the text to the imagination of the listener, allowing us to explore the poetics of music's materiality. Therefore, the totalizing effects of the industrial voice which, some have argued, silences all individuals under its blanket of white noise, in no way accounts for the kind of collusion that we find in stories such as Sheena's. It could be said that these paratexts maintain the status of the author that Barthes so convincingly killed, and in part, the impact on the listeners' imagination is a regressive one – looking for meaning outside of the text does not allow one to fully immerse oneself in the act of listening. Yet through the palimpsest the promise of resurrection is always possible, all the voices remain, and have the potential to be unveiled again to produce new and productive alliances at the point of the text's destination in the future. The point of departure that made the record so very powerful in the first place still exists, it is just muffled under the blanket of time.

There is an apparent togetherness, a link between those who value vinyl records and their corporeality. As we age the record ages with us, a constant reminder of our own fragility. It is often ascribed with human characteristics, as the record is spoken of in terms of its warmth, its flaws, its softness, its ageing patinas, its smell, and so on. The sense of an object's life running in parallel with our own appeals to something within us, beyond just engaging with its functional purpose. Yochim and Biddinger have described a 'persistent alliance between records and anxieties between life and death' (Yochim and Biddinger, 2008), a conception of this little black disc as somehow transcendent.

As I have mapped out above in the case of Sheena's story, the musical journey is one that is traced, yet untraceable, through the continuous intertwining of lived and mediated experiences dissecting the grooves and troughs of daily life. As we take our collections with us on this journey, 'the vinyl record becomes a palimpsest that has a history of layered marks that you can't erase, incidental scratches become a natural part of the piece, not a mistake but integral to its meaning and composition' (Estep, 2001: 39). As do we, the vinyl record loses a few cells everyday, changing its sounding properties, the roughness of life flattening the sound, dulling the sharpness of its comment, fading out the voice over time, weakness taking hold, the volume dropping, and a softness enveloping the communication. The materiality of the record exposes its 'grain'. The dirt sticks. It sticks to us as it sticks to the record, and is destructive for both in its accumulation. New sound worlds open up as each day passes; just as the fleshy voice changes with each cigarette, as each coffee, each conversation, song in the shower, party, and kiss destroys us slowly, so it does with the records we keep to remember these moments by.

There has been a constant adumbration of death throughout the history of recording. Records themselves are the carriers of ghostly voices being spun forth from the illegible grooves. The dead are enlivened through the technology of the phonograph, a library of lost voices captured in vinyl sarcophagi, for example. Kittler described the wax cylinder as 'the corpse that speaks' (Kittler, 1986: 83). Technologies that reproduce sound invoke a liminal netherworld, a space inside an in-between embodied space. Reproduction platforms displace the voice, giving the listener access to a disembodied persona emanating from somewhere beyond the realms of possibility, strangely untraceable and certainly untouchable, an uncanny presence pervading the private space of the listener. The vinyl record when unsheathed from its cardboard sleeve seems to act as a black hole or a portal. Notions of loss and absence are palpable in this acousmatic space, yet the listener holds the power of reanimation. The vinyl voodoo doll stabbed by the needle is resurrected time and again, screaming its invocation from the depths of the groove, but in a macabre paradox we kill the very thing that we also love. 'This gouging scoring action of the needle adds a spectre of pain to the process of playing the record, linking phonography to dentistry, carving inscription onto gravestones, vaccination, the art of tattooing, acupuncture, piercings, heroin, murder' (Toop, 2003: 126).

In these private trysts we commune with our chosen author, we call on them to explain how we feel, how we look, what we think about the world from which we are attempting to escape through their noise. For in that one side of playing time, out to the horizon on their sound wave, we have to 'create a king worthy of killing' (Burke, 1998: 26). But as I have shown above, 'you are free to fill your mind with the music itself, or the music with your mind' (Eisenberg, 2005: 204). So writer after writer, performer after performer, is unable to fully extricate us from ourselves, we are at one with them, singing along, reading the sleeve notes, the articles and interviews and muddying up the signal.

Yet the surface of the record, which 'is kind of taboo … poses a temptation' (Bartmanski and Woodward, 2015: 85). It acts as the mechanized embodiment of the siren song, drawing us into hypnotic spiral and affording us a tactile pleasure. The record is transformative, and has a tradition of being transformed. So I took up my awl and with the trepidation inherent in the act of destruction, began to cut a new narrative, to expose these intersecting voices, and open up the static circle to new boundaries of usage.

References

Attali, J. (1985), *Noise and the Political Economy of Music* (Manchester University Press).
Barthes, R. (1977), *Image, Music, Text* (Fontana Press).

Bartmanski, D. and Woodward, I. (2015), *Vinyl: The Analogue Record in the Digital Age* (Bloomsbury).

Bartolini, N. (2014), Critical Urban Heritage: From Palimpsest to Brecciation, *International Journal of Heritage Studies*, 20(5), 519–533.

Born, G. (2011), Music and the Materialization of Identities, *Journal of Material Culture*, 16(4), 376–388.

Burke, S. (1998), *The Death and Return of the Author: Criticism and Subjectivity in Barthes, Foucault and Derrida* (Edinburgh University Press, 2nd ed.).

Chivers, Yochim E. and Biddinger, E. (2008), It Kind of Gives You That Vintage Feel: Vinyl Records and the Trope of Death, *Media, Culture and Society*, 30(2), 183–195.

Chan, S. (1998), Music(ology) Needs A Context – Re-interpreting Goa Trance, *Perfect Beat*, 3(4), 93–97.

Daughtry, J. (2013), Acoustic Palimpsests and the Politics of Listening. *Music and Politics*, Music and Politics, Vol. VII(1).

Derrida, J. (1968), Differance, in Badminton, N. and Thomas, J. (eds), *The Routledge Critical and Cultural Theory Reader* (Routledge, 2008).

Dillon, S. (2005), Reinscribing De Quincey's Palimpsest: The Significance of the Palimpsest in Contemporary Literary and Cultural Studies, *Textual Practice*, 19(3), 243–263.

Eisenberg, E. (2005), *The Recording Angel: Music, Records and Culture from Aristotle to Zappa*, originally published in 1987 (Yale University Press, 2nd ed.).

Estep, J. (2001), Words and Music, in Criqui J-P, (ed.), Conversation with Jan Estep, *On & By Christian Marclay* (MIT Press, 2014, 39–48).

Gosta, T. (2011), Sir Walter's Palimpsests: Material Imprints and the Trace of the Past, *European Romantic Review*, 22(6), 707–726.

Hesmondhalgh, D. (2013), *Why Music Matters* (Wiley Blackwell).

Irvine, M. (2015), Remix and the Dialogic Engine of Culture: A Model for Generative Combinatoriality, in Navas, E., Gallagher, O., and Burrough, X. (eds), *The Routledge Companion to Remix Studies* (Routledge, 2015, 15–43).

Kittler, F. (1986), *Gramophone, Film, Typewriter* (Stanford University Press).

Knizak, M. (1996), Destroyed Music [online] available at www.milanknizak.com/195-hudba/220-destruovana-hudba/ [accessed 24.5.15].

Middleton, R. (1990), *Studying Popular Music* (Open University Press).

Osbourne, R. (2012), *Vinyl: A History of the Analogue Record* (Ashgate).

Toop, D. (2003), Performative Image, Inscribed, Even: The Fluid Sound Worlds of Christian Marclay, in Criqui, J-P. (ed.), *On & By Christian Marclay* (MIT Press, 2014, 125–133).

PART V

Introduction: technology, culture and sonic experience

Walter Benjamin first coined the phrase "technological sensory training" when he argued that technology had

> subject(ed) the human sensorium to a complex kind of training (and that) during long periods of history, the mode of human sense perception changes with humanities entire mode of existence. The manner in which human sense perception is organised, the medium in which it is accomplished, is determined not only by nature but by historical circumstances as well.
>
> *(Benjamin 1973: 216)*

This reorganization of the senses, of which sound plays a significant role has impacted upon our relationship to others, the world, and ourselves. It has also acted to transform our understanding of distance, intimacy and our sense of place; public, private, and global. More recently it has changed our understanding of what it is to be a consumer and producer of cultural goods. The potential transformative connection between communication technologies, culture, and experience has been central to the work of a number of cultural and media theorists. Paul Virilio (1989) pointed to the role of the media in creating a transformed "logistic of perception" whilst Jonathan Crary equally pointed to a "restructuring of perceptual experience" (Crary 1999). These theorisations of technological mediation within the cultural and sensorial field remained largely visually orientated for many years – even in the work of Benjamin in contrast to other Critical Theorists of the 1930s whose work was multi-sensorial in orientation.

Central to this transformation of experience was the changing experience of a technologized sense of space and place. Martin Heidegger understood the ramifications of this transformation when he stated that:

> The frantic abolition of all distance brings no nearness: for nearness does not consist in shortness of distance. What is least remote from us in point of distance, by virtue of its picture on film or its sound on the radio, can remain far from us. What is incalculably far from us in point of distance can be near to us.
>
> *(Heidegger 1972: 165)*

269

Heidegger, writing in the 1940s, points to the multi-sensory abolition of mediated distance embodied in much media use. Peters subsequently notes the specific auditory nature of this transformation, "the succession from the 'singing wire' (telegraph), through to the microphone, telephone, and phonograph to radio and allied technologies of sound marks perhaps the most radical of all sensory reorganisations in modernity" (Peters 1999: 160). Peters, like Benjamin and Heidegger before him, points to the transformed sensory and cognitive relation between prox-imity, distance, and importantly presence. Biocca and Levy celebrate this sensory transformation in their discussion of virtual reality technologies stating that "we are building transportation sys-tems for the senses … the remarkable promise that we can be in another place or space without moving our bodies into that space" (Biocca and Levy 1995: 23). Observations of this type led Crary to question the relevance of the very relationship between a traditionally held under-standing of what might pass for "materiality" in which the very relationship between subject and object becomes problematized (Crary 2013).

The mediatized environments that most of us inhabit are apparent when we take a walk in any industrial city today, when we sit in a café or take a train we observe people texting whilst walking – their attention focussed on the screen of their phone, their finger touching and scroll-ing through a myriad of applications embedded in their phones, they may be speaking instruc-tions through Siri or some other mobile sonic app to an unknown other or machine. Users of a range of mobile technologies experience space as simultaneously intimate, close, and distant. Data accessed locally and globally enables users to situate themselves in time and space, from discovering precisely where they are standing via the use of GPS systems to finding out what their favourite celebrity in a far distant continent has had to eat that morning. The movement of people through urban space has increasingly become a technologically mediated experience in the 20th and 21st centuries; from the sounds of the Muzac Corporation in the 1930s to the sounds of radios, the use of Walkmans, ghetto-blasters, iPods, and smartphones. The mediated sonic experience of living in a city has a rich history. These practices are entwined in a range of cultural values as articulated by Jonathan Sterne who argued that

> audible technique was rooted in a practice of individuation: listeners could own their acoustic spaces through owning the material component of a technique of producing that auditory space – the "medium" that now stands for a whole set of practices. The space of the auditory field became a form of private property, a space for the individual to inhabit alone.
>
> *(Sterne 2003: 160)*

From this perspective, technologies, values and experience are indissolubly linked.

It is to this linkage that Henriques and Reitvelt point in their traversal of Echo from Greek myth to contemporary recording techniques. The age of mechanical reproduction ushered in the ability to systematically reproduce sounds thereby disembodying them and creating the era of the "copy". The "copy" mimics the original and becomes an "echo" of its original. The ability to recreate, to give a semblance to the "original", poses epistemological issues together with a set of cultural evaluations. Does the copy have the same value as the original – in auction houses across the world the answer is a resounding no. Yet in the music industry there often is no original as performances are spliced together from recording studios and increasingly homes from around the world. Julian Henriques and Hillegonda Reitvelt articulate these issues in their chapter by proceeding from Echo as represented in Greek myth from Ovid onwards. Echo, they argue, enables us to think of sound's role afresh in terms of time and space; about how we might situate ourselves sonically in time and space. The original formulation of Echo in Greek myth also represents power. Echo in Greek myth appears to be the punishment meted out to women whose voice is too provocative – they dissolve into mere echo – disembodied.

Equally, Echo represents a partial history of recorded sound – a technologized sound – as echo and reverberation become keynotes to the recording of and reception of much music from the Jamaican dancehall of the1970s to the recordings of Phil Spector and beyond. The authors take us on a journey of technologically mediated echo that incorporates issues of ownership, originality and mimicry in music – and the concurrent value judgements associated with these ideas.

Thor Magnusson continues with an evaluation of recording and consuming practices through a re-evaluation of the history of media technologies of consumption in their role of transforming the spaces of production and reception. From the development of the telephone which transformed notions of embodiment and the voice whereby the voice became simultaneously disembodied and intimate, to the history of radio and music listening which both hid and exposed the cultural voice of the performer. The history of these transformations, Magnusson points out, have been largely sequential and linear – a performer turns up at a studio, sings and plays into a piece of equipment which records the performance on wax, shellac, magnetic tape and now digitally. The performance is then reproduced and sold. The purchaser traditionally played the music in the home but increasingly anywhere. Collective forms of reception traditionally occurred in specific spaces, club, concert halls, open air music festivals and the like. Magnusson points to the continual transformation through new technologies of what it is to make music, perform music and listen to music in a networked world which has the ability to make all of these practices more malleable – continually subject to change. These practices have become more interactive and non-linear – thus transforming not merely the spaces of production and consumption, but also the time through which these practices are performed by building technological platforms of change. Whilst Magnusson points out that many of these changes have been located in the more avant-garde areas of the cultural spectrum, he looks at the use of sound and music in video games that replicate the increased participation and creation of sound by those who participate and play. Thus the non-linear practices embodied in platforms on the web move into wide areas of popular culture.

The history of sonic inscription and the materialisation of sound from Adorno onwards is the subject of Jacob Smith's chapter. He takes Eisenstein's path-breaking book of 1986 as a template through which to investigate both the history and cultural range of inscription. From the earliest crude recording techniques that favoured certain sounds over others in their reproducibility to the sophisticated role of modern recording studios, music has been filtered through the technologies that record and reproduce sounds. Smith charts the changing nature of recording technologies in relation to the changing nature of music itself, both in terms of its form but also its gendered and racial identity. The cultural affordances created by the ability to record any sound are many and profound. Smith extends his analysis beyond music to discuss sound studies interest in recording the sounds of disappearing nature, indeed he points out the historical contingency of Edison's inventions being used to record music as distinct from its use as a voice recorder and so on. The history of the recorded voice transforms our ability to hear over time and space. It enables the listener to hear the voices of the dead as a form of personal narrative articulated through the music chosen in which listeners may remember or imagine their own defining moments in life. Recorded sounds also become emblematic of a cultural period frozen in time on the grooves of a record which are often associated with the specific locales of the recording studios that produced these sounds – the Detroit of Tamla Motown and so on. The history of recorded sound, as Smith points out, is a history of increasing cultural and geographical mobility both in terms of production and consumption with notions of "world music" and "Americanisation" becoming closely tied up with the social and economic affordances created by sonic inscription. Smith points to the rich heritage of recording and points to the immense scope of future research into its ever-changing landscape.

Alex Russo turns to the investigation of an alternative medium – the radio and its sound. Russo points out that paradoxically much traditional work on the history of radio has stressed the organisational nature of radio whilst neglecting the sounds produced by the radio (in a similar vein it might be argued that until recently – television studies understood the medium through images, whilst the sounds of television were understood as "text"). Russo discusses the various theoretical responses to radio sound as ranging from the celebratory and radical understanding of radio to the more cautious stemming from fears of the power of radio propaganda and of passive modes of consumption. Russo points to the common acceptance of theorists such as Benedict Anderson who operationalised the notion of 'imagined communities' through which much radio theorising has taken place. Russo points out that this very understanding of what mediated communities represent has been contested in terms of what a "public" consists of and what might constitute "counter-publics" of race, class, gender, locality. Russo also points to the power of radio in decoupling our traditional understanding of voice, body, and locality. This decoupling takes on new forms through the use of radio sounds and other technologies that shift time and place in new ways like the mobile phone, tablets, and other new media thus pointing the way to new avenues of sonic research.

Remaining with the medium of the radio, Louis Neibur focusses upon the early years of the British Broadcasting Corporation and the early history of the production of avant-garde sounds within a corporation that was dependent upon audience size – and hence popularity. He charts the development of technologies that enabled a more adventurous approach to sound in radio theatre that enabled radio producers to move away from sonic realism to forms of sonic expressionism more redolent of early Soviet cinema and French musique concrete. These avant-garde sound productions found an institutionalised home in the BBC's Radiophonic Workshop after World War Two. Neibur's chapter points to the central role of the development of "sound effects" in the BBC and in radio more generally that resonate more broadly within debates concerning the relationship between "normal" and "avant-garde" sounds and cultural and institutional assumptions that lie at the heart of radio production.

Cara Wallis returns, in her chapter, to an analysis of the cultural and gendered nature of the telephone. Just as the radio replicates and challenges cultural assumptions concerning cultural tastes, identity, and consumption patterns, so the telephone also represents a cultural mirror to changing social and cultural attitudes towards gender and gender roles in society. Cara Wallis discusses the use of the telephone as an instrument that both confirms notions of the "feminine" voice whilst also at times subverting it. She charts the early use of the telephone as mirroring the gendered, class, and racial divide within America in the 20th century whereby only certain feminine voices were deemed appropriate in telephone exchanges until the 1960s. These voices were largely white and middle class. However, Wallis also argues that the telephone as a means of communication is in continual transformation – from the traditional telephone exchange to the rise of global call centres and of automated voices such as Siri and such like that are used on mobile phones and other devices. She asks what then becomes of the gendered voice within the apps available on these devices? Wallis argues that we must not assume the literalness of the voice as 'gender' is also replicated in the ways in which text messages are sent as users insert their 'voice' into their texts through a range of speech strategies. Thus paradoxically returning voice to text – to the written word.

We conclude this Part with Thomas Artiss's discussion of structures of feeling, a term taken from the work of Raymond Williams. In doing so we return to the themes taken up at the beginning of this Part – the relationship between technologies, values, and experience. Artiss draws upon his own work amongst the Canadian Inuit community and their use of their local radio station together with personal observations of his experience of his local "soundscape" in North London in order to explain the affective power of mediated sound. Artiss discusses affect through the notion of mediated structures of sonic feeling that originally draw upon the work of Schafer and Feld, thus demonstrating their continued relevance within contemporary sound studies together with the work of Williams, De Nora, and others in order to discuss the power of mediated sound through an understanding of "structures of feeling" that relates to how radio listeners in Northern Canada use and request music that connects them to their own personal narrative as well as with the structures of feeling embedded within the wider community, thereby reminding us of the continued connections between technologies, cultures and sonic experience.

References

Benjamin, W., 1973, *Illuminations*, London: Penguin.

Biocca, F. and Levy, M. (eds), 1995, *Communication in the Age of Virtual Reality*, Hillsdale, NJ: Lawrence Erlbaum Associates.

Crary, J., 1999, *Suspension of Perception: Attention, Spectacle and Modern Culture*, Cambridge: Cambridge University Press.

Crary, J., 2013, *24/7, Late Capitalism and the End of Sleep*, London: Verso.

Heidegger, M., 1972, *Poetry, Language, Thought*, London: Joanna Coter Books.

Peters, J. D., 1999, *Speaking to the Air: A History of Communication*, Chicago, IL: University of Chicago Press.

Sterne, J., 2003, *The Audible Past: Cultural Origins of Sound Reproduction*, Durham, NC: Duke University Press.

Virilio, P., 1989, *War and Cinema: The Logistics of Perception*, London: Verso.

26

ECHO

Julian Henriques and Hillegonda Rietveld

Introducing echo

With an echo we hear both the original sound source and its reflection, noticing the delay between one and the other. Echo is therefore a particular type of reverberation, from the Latin verb reverberare, to strike back or reflect. It is defined as a propagation effect in which, according to Augoyard and Torgue (2005: 111), "sound continues after the cessation of its emission". Reverberation occurs when surfaces bounce back or reflect auditory waves. Unlike an echo, though, reverberation is most often perceived as almost simultaneous with the produced sound, a resounding that effectively amplifies through instant diffusion of sound waves. Singing in the shower, for example, we hear our own voice in a louder and seemingly fuller version as it resonates against the hard surfaces of the bathroom. In such enclosed spaces, resonance and reverberation overlap as the harmonics of the original sound are reproduced. By contrast, stepping inside an anechoic chamber is sufficient to recognise the importance of this reflection for our day-to-day hearing; it can be a thoroughly disconcerting experience to be without this resonance of one's voice, as though it never leaves the body.

Reverberation is especially important in that it allows us to locate ourselves in our environment with reflected auditory vibrations of air, water, and other media. Our auditory world extends 360 degrees around us, unlike our visual field. Some animals, such as bats, have refined this sense through their faculty of echolocation. Resonance thereby provides information about the spatial characteristics of where we move and orient ourselves in the world, often in combination with other senses. Even the feeling of a room, a place, or a building – its atmosphere – can be determined by the acoustic properties of its surfaces; as a space can feel cold and forbidding when hard, reflective surfaces dominate, or warm and inviting when filled with soft, absorbent surfaces.

The perceived time lapse between the transmission of an auditory event and its reception due to the distance between the source of the sound and its reflective surface means that echo marks out not only space but, importantly, time. While resonance positions the listener in a distinct space, by contrast echoic delay can produce a sense of dislocation. The sound of an echo is hereby clearly perceived as arriving from elsewhere, "not-from-this-world, of the super-natural" as Locket (2003) puts it. The delayed return of the sound has an "othering" effect, a separation between self and other. This can appear as an ephemeral memory and even as a double, a doppelganger or a sonic shadow. In this way, we can feel alienated from the sounds we produce or that are produced nearby and as a consequence, rather than acting as a sonic shadow an echo may ultimately act as a sound in its own right.

Separated from the original sound event through time, the acousmatic qualities of an echo – as a voice heard but with its source hidden – may be considered as a type of recording process. A sound recording separates the moment a sound is made from the occasion in which it is heard – the delay between one and the other may lead to the recording being fetishised in absence of the performer and the performance (Middleton 2006). In order to address the spatial, temporal, and political aspects of the echo, our discussion concentrates on the role of recording techniques and technologies in re-producing, augmenting, and manipulating these echoic effects. In music production both echo and reverberation are used to play with the potentials of sound recording. We argue therefore that ultimately echo is emancipated from the domain of the sound effect to emerge as a sound source in its own right – by means of both analogue and digital technologies.

Echo's aura

Reverberating sounds, particularly echoes, have played an important role in various cultures. This is evidenced, for example, by cave paintings at acoustically significant places that provide a natural echo (Reznikoff 1995), some of which process and reproduce sounds of animals depicted in rock art (Waller 2006). Another example is the Austrian vocal art of yodelling where the reflective surfaces and distance between mountains are used as a component of the musical performance. Such echoic effects were further harnessed for religious and ritualistic purposes in man-made structures. Reverberation of the voice within acoustically reflective surfaces of large structures, such as temples and cathedrals, can amplify the sense of importance of the speaking person, and thereby lends an impressive aura and power to their message. Till (2010) has, for example, found that the circle of Stonehenge not only has echoic properties, resonating harmonically with specific standing waves as may be expected from a circular structure, but it also has reverberating properties. Stories about the magical qualities of echoic such as sound effects have been passed down the generations, as with the unfortunate nymph Echo in Greek and Roman mythologies.

Etymologically, Echo provides the term in the English language with overtones of resonance, reverberation, and resounding. There are numerous versions of this, but one element seems to remain relatively stable. Echo's predicament is that she can only speak by repeating the words that others have spoken to her, rather than her own words. In one version of the story, she echoes the words of the god Pan, to end up with her body being shredded to pieces and then strewn round the world (Doyle 2005). Another version of the Echo myth can be found in Ovid's *Metamorphoses*, the classic Latin translation of Greek myth (2008). Here the goddess Juno (Hera in Greece) curses Echo for her idle talk that had the effect of distracting Juno from Zeus' extra-marital affairs. Upset by the punishment, Echo hides in a forest, where she encounters a visual version of her alienating situation in the person of Narcissus, who misrecognises his own reflection in a pond as that of another person with whom he falls, obsessively, in love with. When he hears Echo reflect the final parts of his sentences back to him, he mistakenly thinks someone else is speaking. Narcissus nevertheless fails to recognise Echo as a person in her own right, which in turn hurts Echo's passionate feelings and desperate desire to communicate with him. Consumed by grief her body fades away, leaving only the haunting ghostly sound of her echoic voice, as a decentred and invisible being.

Ovid's version of Echo's story is of interest to our argument as notions of power are being played out with respect to who is being heard, who initiates speech and who is aurally (in) significant. In a brief discussion of the blind love story between the image-obsessed Narcissus and the invisible resounding Echo, Derrida (2007) argues that Echo produces her own voice from the fragments of speech she repeats. DeArmitt (2014) further discusses Derrida's various meditations on the subject, emphasising that Narcissus depends on Echo to hear himself. Echo appropriates (eats, cannibalises) Narcissus' speech and that of others to emancipate herself from her marginalised position by making herself heard (Rietveld 2015). Yet, to do this Echo always has to be listening and, like a recording device, apply her memory (see also Albright 2014).

Echo's dub

The creative potential of reverberation and echo was first seized upon in Jamaican recording studios in the early 1970s. The recording engineers on that Caribbean island, perhaps most famously King Tubby, King Jammy and Lee "Scratch" Perry, created the reggae-related musical genre know as dub. The analogue technologies then available – sprung steel reverb plates the size of doors – were often used in conjunction with tape-delay machines such as the Roland Space Echo RE 201, a long recording tape that would record a sound would diminish with every repeat until finally fading to silence; the longer the tape loop, the longer is the delay in its echoic return.

It was by making creative use of reverberation and echo as music production techniques that these Jamaican pioneers had a very significant musical influence that extends up to the present. Along with the Phil Spector in the USA and George Martin in the UK, they established the studio engineer and the producer as a creative force and the sound studio itself as a musical instrument. As Peter Doyle (2005: 5–6) describes, echo and reverb were a feature of the very first popular music recordings: "Echo and reverb made it seem as thought the music was coming from somewhere … with the addition of echo and reverb, 'place' and 'space' had become part of the larger musical equation." Doyle charts an early history of such techniques, up until the use of stereophonic tape recording. "A number of key artists … knowingly made use of spatio-acoustic conditions in order to present uniquely their own 'sense of self'" (ibid: 7). Doyle comments: "The merest touch of echo and reverb could greatly alter the emotive impact of sounds produced, and the affective change often seemed to be out of proportion to the purely sonic changes wrought by these effects" (ibid: 4). It is this emotive power of echo we discuss here.

When multi-track recording became popular during the mid-1960s in Jamaica, echo effects could be manipulated in a more sophisticated manner. The particular Jamaican geographical and historical use of echo reveals some of the most interesting features of echoic phenomena more generally, in several distinct respects. In the first place, the term "dub", meaning to copy, is itself echoic as a studio technique of overdubbing instruments onto a riddim (bass and drum) track. A practice emerged whereby different artists would voice their own lyrics and occasional melodic riffs from keyboards or guitar, over the same riddim track (Marshall and Manuel 2006; Hitchens 2014). Some of these riddims would inspire numerous such "versions" by a variety of different artists, the most popular of which is single riddim compilation albums.[1] The most versioned riddim track is reputedly King Jammy and Wayne Smith's "Under Mi Sling Teng", first released in 1984 with, to date, nearly 400 different versions.[2]

In the second place, if versioning draws attention to the repeating nature of echo, "dub plate specials" emphasise its uniqueness. Dub plates are the one-off acetate pressings (rather than vinyl) that a sound system owner commissioned a popular artist to record a unique version of their hit that incorporates a special mention of that particular sound system. Dub plates are the ammunition the sound system selector (elsewhere known as the DJ) has in his or her arsenal to fire off against their rivals a sound – to win the approbation of the audience. Thus the unique pressing of the dub plate version exploits the "aura" or unique creative power of an original dubbed copy (Eshun 1998: 189). In addition, the echo effect is widely used from the repertoire available in the selector's sound effects (SFX) console.

The third respect in which dub music exploits the actual echoic character of our auditory experience is in the experience of space and time in the dancehall session. Reggae music is associated with the "toasting" technique pioneered in Jamaica by U Roy, later developing into DJing (talking over the recording, jockeying the disk) as the antecedent to rap. This can be called an additive aesthetic that contrasts with subtractive echoic one of dub, where all but a hint of melody and vocals have been removed creating room within the musical soundscape for drum and bass to dominate.[3] This emptying out of the music track, stripping it back to its raw building blocks, opens up an echoic space for the listener to inhabit with a sense of involvement and belonging (Henriques 2011: xx). The sheer physical size of the sound system's phonographic technology with tweeters at the top of the speaker stack (sometimes even hung in the trees) and the (much larger) scoop bass bins at the bottom create a vertical array of frequencies opening up a sonic dimension to space itself (Henriques forthcoming 2020).

Most important, in the dancehall session there are three speaker stacks each pointing directly into the crowd in the middle of the dance floor between them, so the sound is heard directly from the cones of the speakers themselves. This is especially effective with the liminal volumes of sonic dominance (Henriques 2003). Such direct auditory diffusion contrasts with non-phonographic live gigs where the speakers are either side of a stage focusing attention on the performer. It also contrasts with the more familiar experience of surface-reflected echoic listening discussed above. Indeed the lack of echo or reverberation that normally positions and orientates the listener in the sound system session's direct diffusion no doubt inspired the musician to substitute their own echo, dub, and reverberation. In this way they filled the gap in the space of performance with the music's own sonic spatiality, extending the present by elongating the decaying tail of a sound. Such echoes themselves repeat a refrain as in the West African trope of call-and-response, or antiphony, often heard in the dancehall between MC and the audience.

The final respect in which dub music reveals echo's qualities more generally is how echoic gaps in the soundscape operate in a similar manner to how rhythm works musically. This is to continually and simultaneously evoke associations with a just disappeared past and anticipating an as yet unrealised future. So, as well generating a sense of belonging, echo generates a sense of longing. This was also reflected in the Rastafarian ideology embodied in reggae music that sought an escape from the inequities of Babylon to journey to the Promised Land of Zion, or a mythical "Africa". As with Nirvana, the fact that this was a heterotopia (or no-place) made it all the more powerful, as various researchers have commented. In the words of Erik Davis (2010: 246) on dub pioneer Lee "Scratch" Perry, "Good dub sounds like the recording studio itself has begun to hallucinate". Such is the power of echo in the production of an alternatively imagined time-space. As Louis Chude-Sokei (1997: np) states,

> it is through dub that the mixing board becomes an instrument, and sound becomes isolated within the context of music as the focus of production. It is through dub that the fundamental dynamic of human thought – sound, silence and echo – becomes foregrounded through technology. And it is though dub that memory becomes the explicit focus of ritual.

Further to remembering and anticipating, the deconstruction and decay of echo provides an auditory image of the historically enforced discontinuities, disjunctures, and shattered landscapes.

In this political context, Michael Veal (2007: 197) treats "dub's heavy use of reverb as a sonic metaphor for the condition of diaspora", arguing that the echoic fragmentation of conventional narrative song is musical destruction of the Master narrative – and an articulation of an echoic history.

Echo's revenge

While tape-based analogue delay produced a recognisable recorded sound in the 1970s, during the early 1980s the process of digital delay was introduced to the array of effects in recording studios. Early digital recording technology made it possible to record fragments of sound or music and to repeat these while controlling the amount and length of decay more precisely than the tape-delay machines mentioned above. Other uses were soon adopted, as the digital recording of sound could be inserted wherever this was required or needed in a track. If the chorus of a song sounded particularly good, for example, and there was no time to re-record, this fragment could be repeated wherever the chorus was required in the song structure. From remedial work on the recording, it was a small step to consider the digital echo delay as a phenomenon in its own right that mimics but does not diminish in time, and so would not behave as an ephemeral side effect. This was further developed into what we now know as the digital sampler, of which the Fairlight CMI was one of the first to be commercially successful. With such devices echo becomes a sound in its own right, in addition to being either a natural phenomenon, or an analogue diminishing recorded effect, or scattering that breaks up and "others" the original sound source. In the digital domain the spatial dimension is easily manipulated, the ephemeral sonic quality of an echo is continuously available.

Back in the 1970s, New York-based hip-hop and disco DJs started to create music from existing recordings during their live performances. In addition, Fikentscher (2013) shows that programming recordings in a specific sequential re-contextualises them within a narrative order that suits the theme of the event, the venue, the crowd and the style of the DJ. Not only were music recordings selected and played, and sung or spoken over, but DJs also started to use snippets of recordings, to produce a new structure, during the event. In the context of underground disco this was done, for example, by overlaying an *á cappella* vocal over an instrumental track (Lawrence 2003). In hip-hop, DJs started to "cut" and repeat of parts of recordings, often isolating the middle-eight, or rhythmical solo "break" within a song, if only for one or two bars (measures). With two copies of the same record, as well as two turntables and a mixer, the DJ is able to do this live, in response to the dancing crowd. Competitive DJ practices, such as turntablism and controllerism, have further developed such styles of DJing (Katz 2012).

When the digital sampler became financially more accessible during the mid-1980s, its use was quite quickly expanded from an engineering device to a creative composition tool (Porcello 1991). "Samples" (fragments of music recordings) were appropriated, placed in a new structure, repeated as rhythmical devices, and used as hooks to new songs. In house music, electro, and other electronic dance music genres, sampling techniques became as highly tuned as turntable skills. A telling example of this is "The Amen Break", which forms the core of one of the standard break beats in hip-hop productions, based on a particular drum break from just four measures of a 1969 B-side soul recording, "Amen, Brother" by The Winstons (itself a version of Jester Hairston's 1963 composition "Amen"), played by Gregory S. Coleman. There is a delayed snare in the third measure, and in the fourth measure it is omitted, creating suspense (Nuttall 2011). Like the gasp of breath, producing an instant of desire for closure, this is sufficiently present to excite the listener whenever it is played. Electro artist Kurtis Mantronik (Kurtis el Khaleel, as part of Mantronix, 1988) re-constructed this drum rhythm track as part of "King of the Beats", by splicing the break and mixing version of this with samples from other recordings. Mantronix's version became a popular tool for DJs to layer with other musical recordings and copies also found their way into the record bags of rave DJs in the UK, who would speed it up to adjust to the needs of their hardcore rave crowds, thereby producing a genre-defining sound that ultimately led to break beat genres such as jungle and drum and bass (Harrison 2004). The fragmented and displaced echo of a soul track, via electro and rave music, thus became the foundation of a set of new electronic dance genres (Butler 2006).

Echo's voice

On the basis of the echoic character of the analogue and digital recording techniques outlined above we suggest that a new composite syncretic voice is produced from the fragments of existing recordings. This raises an original autonomous voice from multiple, often socially mar-ginalised, alienated, and ephemeral sources. Sampling practices can be considered as hauntings from a past, to be appropriated or remembered. Echoic elements are found and recombined to create a new voice. This can be an empowering procedure, generating a composite identity that, rather than repeating the past, re-sounds it in and for the here and now, to produce a new sense of the future.

As shown above, New York-based rap artists, for instance, developed the cultural technique of using recorded fragments to make rap the characteristic lyrical form of performance heard within hip-hop. Rose (1994) applauds their resolve and creativity under social pressure, arguing that marginalised by lack of opportunity and racism, a sense of strength and pride was pro-duced through rap's use of sampling, fragmentation, and flow as aesthetic forms. Sampling may involve long hours "digging the crates" as it is called, raiding rare records and original sources for the production of new materials. Selections may well be made because the texture is right, or because the borrowed voice suits a particular mood, regardless of the original source or its intention. At other times, homage is paid to a politically significant voice, such as Martin Luther King's, for example as with Grandmaster Flash and The Furious Five's "The King" (1988).

Such sampling practices have produced interesting debates on authorship and authenticity. Where the sample is recognisable, legal clearance has to be obtained and a royalty paid to musi-cian who originally composed it. This raises broader issues of ownership of cultural products, which tends to favour established artists over creative sampling practices (Schumacher 2004). The music publishing and recording industry has tended to deem hip-hop artists' sampling as a type of stealing, rather than an original, creative work in its own right. Such arguments may stand within the legislative context of IP (intellectual property) courts. One critique, however, is that this has the effect of silencing the composite voice born of oral cultural continuum that gave birth to hip-hop as, for example, Rose (1994) argues. The notion of culture as a free common good – and the echoic sound as a voice in its own right, in particular – is evidently at odds with the capitalist notion of the individual ownership of private (intellectual) property (Schloss, 2011).

Who owns the echo then? In this journey from the phenomena and myths of echo, through to analogue and digital production techniques, and on to sampling, this key question remains. Is echo original or a form of mimicry? Is Echo's voice that of a person, or an auditory shadowing device? The relational and reciprocal charcteristics of sound make both possible, simultaneously. As with dub music, echo calls back both from the past and forward to the future. Ultimately, then, there is both mimicry and an original sound is produced. And so, here is Echo, speaking out in her own voice, finding her own creativity, through the selection and reproduction of sonic fragments. Her echoic technique, it could be said, is one that the rest of us now share.

Notes

1 According to David Katz (2003: 166), "At Studio One in 1965, Roland Alphonso blew sax on a song called 'Rinky Dink' using the rhythm (sic) of Lee Perry and the Dynamites' 'Hold Down' with the vocals removed. The first single version album is credited as Rupie Edwards' Yamaha Skank on the My Conversation riddim" (see Toop 1995: 118).

2 Frenkieh Riddim Database 2011, Sleng Teng Riddim (1985): 10, 361–380 http://riddims.frenkieh. com/show/riddims/18/page_10/. See also David Katz, www.theguardian.com/music/2014/feb/20/ wayne-smith-sleng-teng-revolutionised-dancehall-reggae, accessed 20 July 2016.

3 Producer Bill Laswell (1997, 2001) has made a specialty of spatialized ambient remixes of studio multi-tracks of Bob Marley, Miles Davis, and countless others.

References

Text

Augoyard, Jean-Francois and Torgue, Henri (2005) Sonic Experience: A Guide to Everyday Sounds, translated by Andrea McCartney and David Paquette, Montreal: McGill-Queen's University Press.

Albright, Jonathan (2014) Amazon's Echo: Who's Listening? 8th November. https://medium.com/d1g-est/amazons-echo-3624bb654139#.19zbtoser (Accessed 14 January 2017).

Butler, Mark J. (2006) Unlocking the Groove: Rhythm Metier, and Musical Design in Electronic Dance Music. Bloomington, IN: Indiana University Press.

Chude-Sokei, Louis (1997) "Dr. Satan's Echo Chamber": Reggae, Technology and the Diaspora Process, Bob Marley Lecture, Institute of Caribbean Studies, Reggae Studies Unit, University of the West Indies, Mona; reprinted in Chimurenga, 13, March 2008, np.

Davis, Erik (2010) Dub, Scratch and the Black Star: Lee Perry. Nomad Codes: Adventures in Esoterica. Portland, OR: Verse Chorus Press: 236–252.

DeArmitt, Pleshette (2014) The Right to Narcissism: A Case of an Im-possible Self-Love. New York, NY: Fordham University Press.

Doyle, Peter (2005) Echo and Reverb: Fabricating Space in Popular Music Recording, 1900–1960, Middletown, CT: Wesleyan University Press.

Eshun, Kodwo (1998) More Brilliant Than the Sun: Adventures in Sonic Fiction, London: Quartet.

Fikentscher, Kai (2013) "It's Not the Mix, It's the Selection": Music Programming in Contemporary DJ Culture, Attias, Bernardo A., Gavanas, Anna, and Rietveld, Hillegonda C. (Eds) DJ Culture in the Mix: Power, Technology, and Social Change in Electronic Dance Music. London and New York: Bloomsbury Academic: 123–150.

Henriques, Julian (2003) Sonic Dominance and the Reggae Sound System, in The Auditory Culture Reader Bull, Michael and Back, Les (Eds) The Auditory Culture Reader. Oxford: Berg, pp. 451–480.

Henriques, Julian (2011) Sonic Bodies: Reggae Sound Systems, Performance Techniques and Ways of Knowing, London: Continuum

Henriques, Julian (forthcoming 2020) Sonic Media, Durham, NC: Duke University Press.

Hitchens, Ray (2014) Vibe Merchants: The Sound Creators of Jamaican Popular Music. London: Routledge, pp. 133–154.

Katz, David (2003) Solid Foundation; An Oral History of Reggae. London: Bloomsbury.

Katz, Mark (2012) Groove Music: The Art and Culture of the Hip-Hop DJ. Oxford and New York, NY: Oxford University Press.

Lawrence, Tim (2003) Love Saves the Day: A History of American Music Culture, 1970–1979. Durham, NC and London: Duke University Press.

Locket, Alan (2003) Cavernous Resonance: Reverberation, Echo and Elsewhereness. Albient (blog) LiveJournal. http://albient.livejournal.com/1012.html (Accessed 4 June 2016).

Marshall, Wayne and Manuel, Peter (2006) The Rhythm Method: Aesthetics, Practices and Ownership in Jamaican Dancehall. Popular Music, 25 (3): 447–70.

Middleton, Richard (2006) 'Last Night a DJ Saved My Life': Avians, Cyborgs and Siren Bodies in the Era of Phonographic Technology. Radical Musicology, Vol. 1. www.radical-musicology.org.uk/2006/Middleton.htm

Nuttall, Tom (2011) Seven Second of First: How a Short Burst of Drumming Changed the Face of Music. The Economist. 17 December. www.economist.com/node/21541707 (Accessed 9 July 2016).

Ovid (Publius Ovidius Nasso) (2008) Metamorphoses, trans. A.D. Melville. Oxford and New York: Oxford University Press.

Porcello, Thomas (1991) The Ethics of Digital Audio-Sampling: Engineers' Discourse. Popular Music, Vol. 10 / Issue 1 (January), Cambridge University Press: pp. 69–84.

Reznikoff, Iegor (1995) On the Sound Dimension of Prehistoric Painted Caves and Rocks in Taratsi, E (Ed), Musical Signification. Berlin: Mouton de Gruyter: pp. 541–558.

Rietveld, Hillegonda C. (2015) Burial's Echoic Loneliness in Theresa Beyer, Thomas Burkhalter, and Hannes Liechti (Eds) Seismographic Sounds – Visions from a New World. Bern: Norient: pp. 133–135.

Rose, Tricia (1994) Black Noise: Rap Music and Black Culture in Contemporary America. Middletown, CT: Wesleyan University Press.

Schumacher (2004) "This is a Sampling Sport": Digital Sampling, Rap Music and the Law in Cultural Production in Foreman, Murray, and Neal, Mark Anthony (Eds) That's the Joint: The Hip-Hop Studies Reader (1st Edition). New York and London: Routledge: pp. 443–458.

Schloss, Joseph (2011) Sampling Ethics. Foreman, Murray, and Neal, Mark Anthony (Eds) That's the Joint: The Hip-Hop Studies Reader (2nd Edition). New York and London: Routledge: pp. 609–630.

Till, Rupert (2010) Songs of the Stones: An Investigation into the Acoustic Culture of Stonehenge. IASPM Journal 1(2): pp. 1–18. www.iaspmjournal.net/index.php/IASPM_Journal/article/view/308/548 (Accessed 5 June 2016).

Toop, David (1995) Ocean of Sound, London: Serpent's Tale.

Veal, Michael (2007) Dub: Songscapes and Shattered Songs in Jamaican Reggae, Middletown, CT: Wesleyan University Press.

Waller, Steven J. (2006) Intentionality of Rock-art Placement Deduced from Acoustical Measurements and Echo Myths in Scare, C. and Lawson, G. (Eds) Archeoacoustics. Cambridge: McDonald Institute for Archaeological Research: pp. 31–40.

Video

Laswell, Bill (1997) "Dreams of Freedom: Ambient Translations of Bob Marley in Dub". Universal/Island. ASIN: B000005HQ1.

Laswell, Bill (2001) "Panthalassa: The Music Of Miles Davis. 1969-1974". Columbia/Sony. ASIN: B000024XT4.

Derrida, Jacques (2007) "Speech is Blind" – Jaques Derrida on "Echo and Narcissus". Canal utilizatorului hiperf289. www.youtube.com/watch?v=ya46wfeWqJk (Accessed 5 June 2016).

Harrison, Nate (2004) "Can I Get An Amen?" NKH Studio. http://nkhstudio.com/pages/popup_amen.html (Accessed 9 July 2016).

Discography

Grandmaster Flash and the Furious Five (1988) "The King" from On the Strength album, Electra 60769.

Mantronix (1988) "King of the Beats". B-side of "Join Me Please… (Home Boys – Make Some Noise)". Capitol Records (V-15386). US. www.youtube.com/watch?v=z_BxXeqvzvE (Accessed 9 July 2016).

The Winstons (1969) "Amen, Brother". B-side of "Color Him Father". Metromedia Records (MMS-117). US. www.youtube.com/watch?v=p6EDM7HWWQs (Accessed 9 July 2016).

Yamaha Skank, Prod. Ruppee Williams (1974) "Various". Success Records, SRL LP 015.

27

SOUND AND MUSIC IN NETWORKED MEDIA

Thor Magnusson

Introduction

The Internet is an ideal platform for most forms of musicking (Small, 1998): it is now used extensively in the composition, performance, dissemination, and listening of music. The ecology of media musicians operate in today is substantially different from the one where music was written on physical media, released by a relatively small number of major labels, sold in shops, selected for play by radio DJs, and reviewed by established writers in the printed press. We have moved from this hierarchical situation to one where music-sharing websites, video channels, social media, and online artist profiles on the Web provide listeners with greater access to the world's music via both commercial and alternative channels. Our new musical media have three key characteristics that separate it from older formats: they are networked, multimedia, and processor-based. This enables us to write music in the form of code, opening up the potential for interactivity and non-linear music that might include visuals and tactile outputs via the screens, sensors, and motors of our player devices. For this reason, the Internet is not merely a different conduit for distributing and communicating about music: it presents a drastic change in terms of which media properties musicians have at their fingertips for composing, performing, and listening to new music.

The computational nature of processor-based media allows for interactivity, generativity, and greater awareness of space and time. Moreover, the Internet's technical communication protocols provide the condition for revolutionised practices in sharing and listening to sound and music. They allow for streaming audio from servers to clients in the forms of computers or mobile devices, and current peer-to-peer technology is so effective that the music we listen to might not even be streamed from a server, but "picked up" from existing packages already in transit on the net. Live music can now be streamed directly to people's mobile media devices (often referred to as "phones"), equally as video or audio only. Networked musical performance is being explored by musicians in distributed locations across the globe, where real-time collaboration is streamed to listeners in one or more locations. Composers and producers work on new music over the Internet via dedicated software packages, e.g, *Digital Musician* or *OhmStudio*, or online code repositories, such as Github. Listeners communicate, share, and collaborate via diverse online social media. Platforms now exist where listeners can contribute to the creative process of an artist in the studio, and artists are setting up channels for fans to take part in the creative process. Crowdsourced music networks enable musicians to perform in warehouses or people's homes outside the traditional music industry settings (see, for example, Sofar Sounds – www.sofarsounds.com).

There is no shortage of accounts on now the Internet has altered the production, dissemination, and consumption of music (Leonhard 2008; Leurdijk & Nieuwenhuis 2012; Wikström & DeFillippi 2016). Whilst the music industry is still adapting to the transformed media landscape by experimenting with diverse competing business models, research and hacker labs across the globe are developing innovative techniques of musicking that reflect the qualities of our new media. The nature of this new technology is so open, flexible, and fast-changing, that when the music industry arrives at a comfortable business model, new musical practices will have appeared that threaten those very structures, requiring a further move, a chasing, and a reinvention of how to deal with the new developments. The changes discussed here differ from the media-technological evolution of the past, as the current transformations are not simply those of new distribution formats (for example, vinyl, cassette, CD, or MP3), but in what we define as being at the core of musical practice, bringing about a re-assessment of our notions of creator and listener. With the new processor-based and networked media, music itself is continually reinvented through critical experimentation and re-evaluation: a situation is emerging, where, in addition to musical content, style, and social context, musical creativity also involves a critical engagement in the way music is created, disseminated, and listened to.

This chapter responds to this transformation in media practices by asking: what do the unique qualities of the Internet offer sound artists, creative musicians, and researchers? What does it mean when listening devices are not simply readers of linear data, but processors that can calculate, respond to time, location, motion, emotion, activity, and general network/social network data? Composers are now faced with an abundance of new compositional parameters brought about by this new interconnected medium, for example the potential for non-linear and generative algorithms, multimedia content, spatiotemporal awareness, interactivity, and interagency. If former technological developments, such as the transition from mono to stereo playback formats, added important parameters to musical expression, we might argue that the affordances presented by current music technologies might transform music in an unprecedented scale. The musical context discussed in this chapter is, therefore, one where the function of being on networked and processor-based media is integral to the composition, dissemination, and listening of a specific type of new music.

Composing

As mentioned above, in the twentieth century our common sonic media have been reading machines of linear data: sound is represented as magnetic values on tape, transcribed as incised grooves on vinyl, or stored as numbers in digital file formats. The media players – such as the tape machine, the turntable, or the CD or MP3 player – faithfully reproduce this data as amplified electronic currents reaching the loudspeakers. These file formats maintain the linear nature of a much older tradition, that of musical notation. Music stored as instructions for human or machine playback in a linear format is so engrained in our thinking that it can take some effort, both for musicians and the industry, to begin thinking outside this paradigm and discover the new compositional strategies offered by contemporary technology.

In typical accounts on the origins and functionality of common Western musical notation, we find a file format, a standard, where composers write works with a varied degree of control, which defines how much space the interpreter has for creative expression. With musical notation becoming increasingly determining (a word not necessarily to be seen as negative) in the twentieth century – to the degree that it began to stretch the technical capabilities of performers, as in the music of Xenakis, or even be physically impossible to perform, as in the work of Ferneyhough – experimental musicians, often working with musical machines in the form of tape recorders and computers, began to be interested in writing music in non-linear formats. Whilst live musical performance is never identical, and improvisation, or extemporisation, are important elements in any musical culture, it could be said that in Western classical music this element of difference became increasingly subjugated during the Romantic period, and not finding its way back until in mid-20th-century experimental music.

We must acknowledge, however, that on a closer look into the genealogy of musical notation we discover that the musical score is of a much more complex nature than typically portrayed: since its diverse origins in many geographical locations and historical periods, the contemporary musical score has potential for non-linear interpretation, user input, and contextual (or "site-specific") performance. Here, we find precedents in an artistic method often called "generative arts." This production method, and related ontological view of the art work, can be traced back to antiquity, or rather, the idea of creating rules, tools, structures, or machines that reproduce instances from a certain recipe can be found in human cultures of all times. Examples include Chinese wind chimes, Indian textile templates, Islamic tiling, or, say, the algorithmic rules in the *Musikalisches Würfelspiel* often attributed to Mozart.

Since the 1950s, composers have experimented with non-linear, open, generative, algorithmic, stochastic and aleatoric music (the terms are many) via alternative methods of writing, adding syntax or secondary notation, or otherwise augmenting the graphical symbols we have come to think of as musical notation. But what these approaches have in common is to engage the creativity of the performer and delegate parts of the musical composition to the instrumentalist, or even non-trained performers as we find in the example of Cornelius Cardew. Other composers, such as John Cage, embraced the incidental, the aleatoric, or the random as important elements in their music. In the words of Gerhard Eckel, from 1996, who sees the change in technology effectively affording the potential of a "new musical artefact":

> The traditional musical artefact is the score (that is a text) or the tape in the case of electronic music. Typical for the old musical artefact is that it represents music linearly in time, that is that the representation of music is organised along a time line. By new musical artefact I understand a representation of music which describes music in terms of a model, in terms of mechanism capable of generating the music (the meta-composition). Thus, the fundamental difference between old and new artefact is the absence of a linear text, implying the absence of the traditional.
>
> *(Eckel 1996)*

Henri Pousseur's work *Scambi* could illustrate and give context to where we will be heading now: in 1957, Pousseur spent time in Studio di fonologia musicale di Radio Milano and realised a piece of recorded synthesized sounds stored on short pieces of tape that were to be arranged by the performer of the piece. Pousseur wrote a musical score with careful instructions on how to arrange the tape loops according to specific generative rules. Interpreting the work meant arranging the tapes into one piece, a process that made its execution quite difficult and laborious. This example demonstrates how changes in thinking in the 1950s – also expressed in the post-structuralist theories of Barthes, Derrida, Eco, and Foucault – began to lay the foundations of the way we work with sound in an age of networked processor-based computers.

Graphic scores, verbal notation, poetic instructions, and other experimental formats, developed since the 1950s for writing music, are conceptual and technical predecessors to the generative or algorithmic approaches we find in new media. Twentieth-century experimental musicians critically questioned almost every convention of musical practice that had been established over the past centuries: how can music be ruptured in space and time? (Does the performance have to happen at one location? Can it take place in many sessions? Is there a need for the stage? How can sound be spatialised?). How can we rethink the link between the composer and the interpreter? (How might composers delegate their authority? How can the musical piece benefit from the unique experience of each performer?), how can we reconsider the relationship between the work and the audience? (What possibilities open up when music becomes interactive? What is the role of the listener in such music?).

This section has raised some of the questions composers posed when they were able to start thinking about their work in a non-linear way, embracing the novel qualities of the new media. There are no simple answers to the question of how we compose for media players that can sense movement, temperature, brightness, touch; that know the time of the day, the date, geographical location, GPS coordinates of work, home or school; that can parse big data from its user's social networks such as friends' behaviour, distance between people, key locations, and communication patterns; that can sense user patterns, daily routines, bodily activity, and in some cases biological data, such as heartbeat, temperature, food consumption, sleep cycles, etc. All this data can be applied as compositional parameters that define how the music is rendered when played. Like the context specificity of an Indian raga, which is played at specific periods in the year and at specific times in the day, our new music can adapt to how many times it has been listened to, what other music has been played previously, which friends have listened to it, when and where, and in what context. This is a music where rhythm might depend on temperature, the equalisation of the bass might change depending on the time of the day, and the lyrics adapting to the age of the listener, for example! The possibilities are infinite and, as will be further argued in this chapter, it is highly unlikely that any standards for composition, product descriptions, or strategies of evaluating these pieces of music will be established, as this technology will continually evolve, and continue to involve further our personal data, body, and life in general.

Performing

In his 1977 book *Noise: The Political Economy of Music*, Jacques Attali famously argued that music is always ahead of other cultural domains in adopting and adapting to new technologies and business models. Observing the development of music technologies, it is clear that whenever a new technological infrastructure appears at any level of society (with corresponding changes in equipment and production practices), a musician will apply this technology in musical composition or performance. In the context of this chapter on sound and music in networked media, it is relevant to mention that one of the earliest electronic musical instruments was indeed a networked instrument, the *Telharmonium*, which would transmit audio to people's homes via the wired telephone network. Invented by Thaddeus Cahill in 1896, the instrument was live on the wires in 1900–01 in Washington, D.C., but the instrument was later transported to New York, where concerts began in 1906 to subscribed users. The Telharmonium was initially successful, but technical and financial difficulties resulted in the service ending in 1908. As an initial excursion into music technology performance and dissemination, the Telharmonium was an important predecessor for ideas that were to manifest later in the 20th century.

By the late 1970s, technologies for electronic music had evolved so far that various composers began experimenting with composing interactive music. The performer could play his or her instrument, which would be connected to a computer. The computer could be programmed such that it "read" or "listened" to what the performer was doing and responded appropriately according to how the composer had programmed the computer. In this context, Joel Chadabe coined the term "interactive composing" in 1981 "to describe a performance process wherein a performer shares control of the music by interacting with a musical instrument" (Chadabe 1997: 293). Interactive music is a process where the performer reacts to a system, which in turn reacts to the performer. For Laurie Spiegel the potential for interactivity is a positive thing:

> This doesn't imply a dilution of musical quality. On the contrary, it frees us to go further and raises the base-level at which music making begins. It lets us focus more clearly on aesthetic content, on feeling and movement in sound, on the density or direction of experience, on sensuality, structure and shape – so that we can concentrate better on what each of us loves in music that lies beyond the low level of how to make notes, at which music making far too often bogs down.
>
> *(Spiegel 1986)*

For Spiegel, the listener at home would not only perform, but compose as well. Computer software can respond to something the performer does and this response creates a new action with the performer. In such a situation, the listener becomes a composer, a performer, an improviser, or an interactive listener. Indeed, the traditional musical terminology of a composer, performer, and listener – which can be contextualised with Shannon's (1948) information theoretical model of a transmitter, channel, and receiver (with unwanted noise always entering the channel) – proves to be insufficient and outdated in this new context. For this reason, new terms are being introduced, such as "comprovision," "interactor," "prosumer," and more, to reflect the new situation, and how new subjectivities form with changed technological infrastructure and methods. In 2000, Josephine Bosma addresses this new reality of collaborative composing, so elegantly predicted by Attali (1985) in 1977 in a stage he called "composing," by coining the word "musaic" in an essay for the new media festival Futuresonic:

> Musaic is like a tapestry, a mosaic, or an ocean of sound bites and samples ranked and ordered according to individual taste or choice. Musaic is the condition of music and sound once it is channeled [sic] through computer networks like the internet. Music is no longer a finished, static product that can be taken for granted. On the contrary, the listener becomes the producer of her or his own sound environment. The listener is also composer and musician; for want of a better term, a "musicianer".
>
> *(Bosma, 2000)*

This was written in the context of 1990s net art (or net.art – a distinction too complex to delve into here) which, in a modernist tradition of exploring formal qualities of media, focused on the conditions of the net as a platform for creation and communication, as expressed by Tilman Baumgaertel in an article written in 2002:

> Net art addresses its own medium; it deals with the specific conditions the Internet offers. It explores the possibilities that arise from its taking place within this electronic network and is therefore "Net specific." Net art plays with the protocols of the Internet, with its technical peculiarities. It puts known or undiscovered errors within the

system to its own use. It deals creatively with software and with the rules software follows in order to work. It only has any meaning at all within its medium, the Internet.

(Baumgaertel 2002)

In his 2005 article on Net music in the journal *Organised Sound*, Golo Föllmer surveys the field
emerging in the previous decade of distributed online music. Framing the problematics of net
music as those of space, time, and the machine, Föllmer presents a typology that includes categories such as remix lists, soundtoys, hypermusic, instruments, algorithmic installations, networked
performances, and more. This classification served well and gave an accurate picture at the time,
but is less relevant today, as the practical context is now more fluid, heterogeneous, and multi-
mediated than we had a decade ago. With maturing hardware and software technologies – for
example, HTML5 (with its just-in-time compilation, OpenGL rendering, and WebAudio API)
and new virtual reality software development kits – we find that collaborative, distributed, multiuser, and intermedia approaches have enabled the production of work that is less focused on
form or genre, equally involving elements from the arts, music, and performance. Indeed, what
Föllmer points out, somewhat presciently, is the role of the user as a maker, something we find
very strongly in contemporary maker cultures: "The greatest depth of interaction can take place
when the complete musical environment, including sound material, compositional apparatus
and interaction design, is open to be influenced or even constructed by the user, as is the case
with authoring software" (Föllmer 2005: 191). Today, entering shops such as the Rough Trade
record store in Shoreditch, one finds that, in addition to now selling books, coffee, and muffins,
there is a considerable shelf space dedicated for maker technologies, such as the Arduino micro-
chip computer, modular synth-building equipment, and necessary soldering implements.

Much has happened in the field of networked music since Föllmer's text. For Pedro Rebelo, a
practitioner of networked music, the advent of network music marks a shift in the power structure of traditional performance, as the "fragmentary, fleeting and dynamic nature of networked
relationships presents opportunities for conceiving of creative practice in a manner that does
not rely on the centrality of the theatre company or the concert hall" (Rebelo, 2009, 388). As a
result of this interest in networked music, we have seen the Networked Music Festival (http://
networkmusicfestival.org), themed journal issues on networked music (for example, Contemporary Music Review in 2005 and 2009, and Organised Sound in 2005 and 2012), new protocols being applied in all major software packages such as the Open Sound Control (a UDP/IP
and TCP/IP protocol that can send data over networks), and bespoke sound games appearing,
many of whom are created as multiuser spaces for collaboration. In these musical environments
the distinction between playing music and playing a game becomes blurry, as, for example, in
the *Guitar Hero* game, the performance is both about playing and scoring points. We might be
entering a period where the game studies concept of "gameplay" (Salen & Zimmerman 2004)
will be a relevant criterion for musical compositions. The next section will provide a short contextual history – not an exhaustive one, but highlighting some important threads leading to the
situation in which composers and music technologists now find themselves.

Listening

Above we have discussed how new computational telecommunication technologies afford new
ways of composing and performing music. But how do we listen to this music? Where can we
listen to it? What channels are there for listeners to engage with these new works? Questions
such as these exemplify the problems involved in creating a channel, a form, a set of criteria for
understanding this new form of music. Since there are no specific compositional conventions

or technological standards to adhere to, this has inevitably resulted in a rather chaotic picture of where to find and how to engage with such music. This confusing landscape can be illustrated by an excursion through the history of networked and computational music. The following description of experiments, projects, inventions, and artists points to instances that exemplify the potential of the new technologies. If the two sections above have explored the compositional and performative concerns that underpin this approach of thinking about music, the projects below can give an indication of the heterogeneous roles listeners have in these projects.

Networked digital computers provide a new context for musical creativity and it is appropriate to solidly base our tracing back with Elisha Gray's *Musical Telegraph* from 1874, Clément Ader's *Theatrophone* demonstrated in 1881 in Paris at the Exposition of Electricity, and Thaddeus Cahill's *Telharmonium* from 1896, already mentioned above. These technological inventions can be seen as predecessors of distributed music consumption that explored many of the concepts musicians are currently dealing with. Real-time performance over distance, subscription services, electronically generated sounds, and remote, yet live, musicians are all issues that are still being experimented with, and reinvigorated via online media.

In the history of electronic music we find multiple modular (networked/collaborative) approaches for ad-hoc assemblage building, where electric sound generating devices are connected together via diverse means. This was initially done through voltage control (VC) currents, where the output of one device might control some functionality of another device. When synthesizers began to be mass produced and popular amongst musicians of all styles (from baroque to contemporary to popular music), the need for a common protocol became pressing, and in 1983 we saw the birth of the MIDI protocol (Musical Instrument Digital Interface). With MIDI, machines played by one or more performers could be synchronised. However, although MIDI was necessary and solved certain problems of communication between commercial devices, it was seen by many as a reactionary and limited protocol that focused too much on the established Western tonality and musical theory, at the cost of experimental approaches in contemporary music, as well as world musics. Although useful, MIDI eclipsed the development of more experimental work taking place using the digital computer. An example worth mentioning is the League of Automated Composers, a group founded in the late 1970s at Mills College, California. Consisting of John Bischoff, Jim Horton, and Rich Gold, this collective developed a system of networked KIM-1 microcomputers that enabled improvised performances that explored human-machine, as well as human-machine-human interactivity, by means of a computer network. Tim Perkis became a member of the group, which soon after morphed into another ensemble, The Hub, later joined by Chris Brown, Scot Gresham-Lancaster, Mark Trayle, and Phil Stone. The Hub would write software for their personal computers, which would communicate according to custom protocols. Based in the bay area, these composers were instrumental in organising events featuring experimental networked music, represented for example by the 1986 festival "THE NETWORK MUSE – Automatic Music Band Festival" with a primary focus on networked music (Brown & Bischoff 2002).

In the 1980s, performers started looking into the use of satellite technologies for interconnected performances across distant locations. In 1985, Godfried-Willem Raes (Ghent), Charlie Morrow (New York), and Phil Dadson (New Zealand) worked on a performance called *International Solstice Radio Satellite Project*, which was an interactive multicast broadcast supported by the Flemish National Public Radio. Another example, from 1994, is a collaboration between video artist Steina Vasulka, Morton Subotnick, and David Rosenboom, where they explored satellite tele-performance between three locations (Santa Monica, New York, and Santa Fe) in an event they called "TeleConcert." The Vasulkas also worked with artist and theoretician Don Foresta using the MARCEL network for networked high bandwidth artistic performances in the 1990s and 2000s. In 1997, musician Sergi Jordà developed the *Faust Music Online* system for the Catalan theatre and performance group La Fura dels Baus. The software was written for the Windows 95 operating system, and when installed, the user could contribute to a real-time soundtrack used in the performances of the Faust show, as well as listen to and build upon existing works. Jordà mentions that such user collaboration is effectively a musical "exquisite corpse," referencing the famous Surrealist game of illustration. The Faust Music Online software ran online for many years and inspired a generation of computer musicians to think of a musical instrument, and indeed a musical piece, as something that can exist online, be performed by amateurs as well as professional composers, and collaborated on, shared. and stored. Another example is the use of the Internet in sound installations: in 2000, Atau Tanaka and Kasper Toeplitz created a piece called *Global String*, a multi-site network music installation, connected via the Internet. The string was a thick physical wire (12 millimetres in width and 15 metres in length), that could be plucked, but the resonating body of the instrument was the telecommunication network itself, consisting of small TCP/IP packages and the inbuilt latency of the network. The wire connected to other wires elsewhere in the world and the sound from the installation was the collected resonance of the wires, modulated by the latency of the Internet.

An important event for online and networked music is the development of the Open Sound Control (OSC) protocol. This UDP/IP and TCP/IP 32-bit protocol offers a drastic speed increase compared with MIDI, as well as higher numerical resolution. (The 8-bit MIDI protocol would for example only offer 127 note or velocity values, often considered crude by trained performers.) The intention behind the protocol was to establish a communication channel between computers, between different software applications, between software and hardware. The OSC protocol was implemented in diverse experimental software in the early 2000s (see Wright 2005), but has now become a standard in many commercial software packages. Much of the networked musical work today, where control information or code is exchanged, uses this protocol. For example, during the recent Network Music Festivals, performances have been given with performers situated in diverse locations across the globe, as we find with the system used by the group Glitchlich, which uses custom-built networked software that fuses the idea of a musical piece and a networked instrument, or co-located as exemplified by the live coding ensemble Benoit and the Mandelbrots, where the four members of the band sit on stage with connected laptops and live code an audiovisual performance (Magnusson 2014).

With the technological infrastructure opening up avenues for artistic exploration involving the Internet as a medium for composition – not merely dissemination – the possibilities are immense. A good example might be John Eacott's work *Floodtide* (www.floodtide.eu), which uses information from tidal patterns in rivers, or the sea, and translates those in real-time into musical scores that are played by an orchestra in a particular performance location (for example at the Lighthouse by the Thames), and by people at home who can interpret the scores live using their instruments. Similarly, Andrew Hugill's work on the digital opera, the *Imaginary Voyage* series (www.theimaginaryvoyage.com), remediates the traditional opera in an online Web context. Composer Craig Vear has also worked on digital opera, called *A Sentimental Journey*, which was composed for networked laptops and musicians responding to generative visual scores (Vear 2016). There were two audiences for the piece: one "out there" on the Internet, and another "in here" in the same theatre space as the music performance. Reflecting on his piece, Vear says,

> Surprisingly, the general audience experience was one of unification, and as such, the audience (remote and local); the musicians, their music and their voices; the audio material and computer performers; and the idea of the book, memory and imagination existed in another (liminal) space.
>
> *(Sheil & Vear 2012)*

Computer games are, in many ways, an ideal environment for generative and interactive audiovisual media composition. Immersed as 1st or 3rd person avatars in 3D worlds, or operating with signs and animations in 2D worlds, the player can interact with the music, or "play" the music, indeed erasing any conventional distinction between playing a game and playing music. Japanese multimedia artist Toshio Iwai pioneered this field with work such as the *Otocky* game from 1987, via diverse audiovisual music systems, such as SimTunes in 1996, culminating in his *Electroplankton* in 2005. With games such as *Rez* or *Vib Ribbon* in the early 2000s, creators began exploring the role of sound as a functional element in the gameplay, as opposed to mere ornamentation. In Rez, for example, the player flies through a 3D visualisation of a computer network – a visual imagery often attributed to William Gibson's highly visual descriptions of cyberspace in his book *Neuromancer* – attacking viruses and other malevolent objects. The sound track changes dynamically depending upon the player's performance of the game. The gameplay consists of collecting targets that can be locked and then terminated by releasing the "lock-on" button, on a controller that gives haptic feedback to game events. The music is fast and rhythmic, seamlessly representing the events in the game, producing sets of quantised highlight notes and sound effects as part of the play mechanism. Vib Ribbon, on the other hand, enabled the user to load in their own music and the terrain in each level of the game would be generated from the musical events. This was done through a spectral, amplitude, and onset analysis of the music's sonic content. *Audiosurf* is a similar game that takes this idea to the third dimension. A dedicated research into audiovisual gameplay has been conducted by Nullpointer, whose games *AVSeq*, *In Ruins*, and *Permutation Racer* are practical research projects into generative audiovisual artforms (see www.nullpointer.co.uk). Other recent games, such as *Proteus*, *Panoramical*, or *Thumper*, make use of sound as an essential gameplay element and like Vib Ribbon, the sound and music has been composed specifically with the knowledge that the sound track will be constructed through the play. The generative nature of these games have demonstrably set their composers a challenge which they have risen to.

Since its inception, musicians have explored the potential of the Second Life virtual online world for real-time streamed global performances (Gagen & Cook 2016). There are diverse ways this can be done, but a popular mode is to perform as an avatar, streaming the music directly from the studio to an audience spread around the globe (www.youtube.com/watch?v= GnQIWNItxns). This is all happening in a virtual world, at a particular location inside the game. Although cruder in its appearance, a more modern and popular online world is Minecraft, where people can build houses, villages, and cities using blocks of different material types. Certain elements in Minecraft can be used to program, such as Redstone and Command blocks, and people have created complex musical sequencers, as if the user is inside a machine that generates the music. In Minecraft there are Mods that allow for streaming audio, others that offer environmentally sensitive music that changes as you navigate the world. With virtual reality headsets, such as HTC Vive and Oculus Rift, we now find games built in immersive 3D worlds where the user can build modular synths, navigate spaces, and generally be immersed in the music-making process via avatars that might even be motion-tracked people. This offers new channels for musical education, as distance learning might easily take place in these environments. Here, issues of embodiment, latency, distance, spatial arrangement, 1st vs. 3rd person perspectives, etc., become interesting research topics, as we get ready for playing, studying, and generally communicating in the virtual worlds.

The mobile phone app is also an excellent platform for interactive musical works, since, via the phone's sensors and social networks, the composer can retrieve data about users or their friends, but also allow users easily to share their work. Smule is a pioneering company that has created instruments, such as the *Ocarina* (Wang 2014), rap-making software, such as the *Autorap*, and other audio games. *Papa Sangre* took the audio game literally and got rid of all visual elements, so the game is sound-only. Locative media projects making use of geotracking have been created for "sound walk" projects where the listener walks around the city (or other spaces) and mixes the music. Projects such as *No Tours* (www.notours.org) or *UrbanRemix* (http://urban-remix.gatech.edu) enable composers to compose "in space," where the listener will receive different sounds depending on their navigation in a city or natural landscape. The majority of research into the interactive and collaborative platform of the musical app has been done in academic labs or hacklabs around the world, but there are pioneering artists who are picking up on developments, such as Brian Eno – a long-term advocate of generative music – with his *Bloom* app that allows the listener to perform the music, or Björk's *Biophilia* app that opens up the guts of the music and invites the listener onto an explorative journey.

The recent Web Audio API is a standard proposed by key actors in the media computing industry (Google, Mozilla, the BBC, etc.) with the aim of making an audio content platform that is supported by all browsers on all operating systems on all computers. This would solve many of the technical problems that game creators are constantly effaced with. This standard is new, but there is already an academic conference (WAC – Web Audio Conference) and diverse user groups for works created using it. (See for example https://musiclab.chromeexperiments.com.) At IRCAM in Paris, Norbert Schnell leads a project called *CoSiMa* (http://cosima.ircam.fr) which sets out to create a platform that can be used by composers and musicians to compose bespoke pieces of music for interactive co-locative performances (Schnell et al. 2015). In some of their early pieces – for example, *Chloé X Ircam, Terminal, and CollectiveLoops* – they invite people to pick up their mobile devices (phones, tablets, laptops) and log onto a Web page, which becomes people's instrument and notational score at the same time. The audience is then able to perform using the loudspeakers on their device, which at times has resulted in a multichannel audio piece of 1,000 distributed speakers.

Conclusion

By inspecting the diversity of possible approaches when thinking about sound on the Internet, it becomes clear that the myriad of new communication technologies has altered our conception of what a musical product is, how it is disseminated, and what our role as listeners is, thus challenging established business models and cultural critique. The Internet is clearly more than a mere conduit for music, it is a platform for computational systems to interact across space and time; where data can be exchanged, retrieved, and generated, affecting other nodes in the global network of musical apps, systems, and software. The Internet presents tools, methods, ideas, and ideologies that become part of the materials we use in musical composition and performance. With the practically infinite compositional affordances brought by the new media, it is unlikely that we will see an established standard for interactive, generative, networked compositions, but rather witness a mentality of innovation that explores which musical parameters have appeared for new musical thinking. And as we saw in this chapter, this is old news: musicians have always embraced new technology in their work and this will not change. Therefore, it is not simply the technical standards that will be fluid and reject concretisation, but also the social engagement with this new work: how it is marketed, disseminated, listened to, and discussed. Indeed, musicologists reviewing such work might need to have an understanding, if not practical knowledge, in computer programming, since a large part of the work is notated in code.

This chapter also discussed the liveness of notated processor-based music. Music has always been about difference, context, location, time – it has never been possible, even desirable, for a musical piece to be played exactly the same way, except for a very short period – a mere century!

– marked by the advent of sound recording. The signs are that with current developments, music will be moving into more adaptive media environments, with apps, games, and virtual reality becoming prominent musical platforms, both for live and composed music (which includes notated, recorded, and programmed music). As we have explored, one of the issues (not wanting to see it as a "problem") with the way new music is created for processor-based networked media, is that there are no software protocols, no hardware standards, no ideological, or aesthetic views on what an interactive and networked piece of music might be. Although this might be seen as a problem, perhaps in terms of reviewing or marketing, it can also be considered positive and exciting, since this diversity and lack of conventions becomes a condition of much invention and innovation. The chaotic picture is not merely due to heterogeneous aesthetics or lack of unified art forms, but can also be explained by the problems posed by how differently hardware manufacturers support software protocols, the variance between the three main operating systems (Linux, OSX, and Windows), different browser implementations of mark-up languages, non-conformity in security management, myriad of hardware protocols, persistent software updates, and so on.

This piece was written in 2016. After two decades of faulty and nauseating virtual reality headsets, we are now seeing products on the market that will drastically change the way we think about cultural productions and education. For composers, performers, and educators of music, this new addition to the media landscape is as drastic as the advent of the Web in the 1990s, and it is certain that musical practices are about to change in novel ways. When our musical media afford composition and performance that can be visual, spatial, locative, interactive, collaborative, tactile, evolving over time, etc., we enter a period in musical evolution where the distinction of playing music and playing a game becomes complex, where music becomes more than a linear sound-only file format, but becomes multisensory, interactive, and, undeniably, a phenomenon that rejects definitions.

References

Attali, Jacques. 1985. *Noise: The Political Economy of Music*. Minneapolis: University of Minnesota Press.

Baumgaertel, Tilman. 2002. *net.art 2.0. – Neue Materialien zur Netzkunst/New Materials towards Net Art*. Nürnberg: Institut für moderne Kunst, p. 24.

Brown, Chris & Bischoff, John. 2002. *INDIGENOUS TO THE NET: Early Network Music Bands in the San Francisco Bay Area* http://crossfade.walkerart.org/brownbischoff/IndigenoustotheNetPrint.html [accessed November 2016].

Bosma, Josephine. 2000. *Musaic, the Merging of All Sound Spaces* www.josephinebosma.com/web/node/77 [accessed November 2016].

Chadabe, Joel. 1997. *Electric Sound: The Past and Promise of Electronic Music*. New Jersey: Prentice Hall.

Eckel, G. 1996. "Camera Musica: Virtual Architecture as Medium for the Exploration of Music," in *Proceedings of the 1996 International Computer Music Conference*, International Computer Music Association, San Francisco.

Föllmer, G. 2005. "Electronic, aesthetic and social factors in net music," in *Organised Sound*, vol 10(3): 185–192.

Gagen, Justin & Cook, Nicholas. 2016. "Performing Live in Second Life," in (eds.) Whiteley, Sheila & Rambarran, Shara. *The Oxford Handbook of Music and Virtuality*. Oxford: Oxford University Press.

Leurdijk, Andra & Nieuwenhuis, Ottilie. 2012. *Statistical, Ecosystems and Competitiveness Analysis of the Media and Content Industries: The Music Industry*. Luxembourg: Publications Office of the European Union http://ftp.jrc.es/EURdoc/JRC69816.pdf [accessed November 2016].

Leonhard, Gerd. 2008. *Music 2.0* www.futuristgerd.com/2012/01/11/get-the-pdf-of-my-music-20-book-for-just-pay-with-a-tweet-or-facebook-post/ [accessed November 2016].

Magnusson, Thor. 2014. "Herding cats: Observing live coders in the wild," in *Computer Music Journal*, vol 38(1): 8–16.

Rebelo, Pedro. 2009. "Dramaturgy in the network," in *Contemporary Music Review*, vol 28(4–5): 387–393.

Salen, Katie & Zimmerman, Eric. 2004. *Rules of Play: Game Design Fundamentals*. Cambridge, Massachusetts: The MIT Press.

Schnell, Norbert, Robaszkiewicz, Sébastien, Bevilacqua, Frederic, and Schwarz, Diemo. 2015. "Collective Sound Checks – Exploring Intertwined Sonic and Social Affordances of Mobile Web Applications," in *Proceedings of the Ninth International Conference on Tangible, Embedded, and Embodied Interaction*, New York, pp. 685–690.

Shannon, Claude E. 1948. "A mathematical theory of communication," in *Bell System Technical Journal*, vol 27 (3): 379–423.

Sheil, Áine & Vear, Craig. 2012. "Editorial," in *International Journal of Performance Arts and Digital Media*, vol 8(1): 3–9.

Small, Christopher. 1998. *Musicking: The Meanings of Performing and Listening*. Hanover: University Press of New England, p. 8.

Spiegel, Laurie. 1986. *Music MouseTM – An Intelligent Instrument* http://tamw.atari-users.net/Atari_Music_Mouse_Manual.pdf [accessed November 2016].

Vear, Craig. 2016. "Gesamtkomposition and the digital opera: A sentimental journey," in *International Journal of Performance Arts and Digital Media* vol 12(1): 61–81.

Wang, Ge. 2014. "Ocarina: designing the iPhone's magic flute," in *Computer Music Journal*, vol 38(2): 8–21.

Wikström, Patrik & DeFillippi, Robert (eds.) 2016. *Business Innovation and Disruption in the Music Industry*. Cheltenham: Edward Elgar Publishing.

Wright, Matthew. 2005. "Open Sound Control: an enabling technology for musical networking," in *Organised Sound*, vol 10(3): 193–200.

28

ORDINARY AND AVANT-GARDE SOUND IN BRITISH RADIO'S EARLY YEARS

Louis Niebur

Radio had since its inception struggled with both realistic representations of sound and more abstract, experimental sound techniques. This was especially true in the realm of British radio. This chapter will trace the history of British sound techniques in radio from its inception until the mid-1950s, as electronic techniques for sound production began overtaking more traditional methods of sound production.

The robustness of sonic experimentation in British radio (as opposed to other nations) can be partially attributed there to a continual support from the theatrical establishment. Some producers have also seen the strength in experimentation as originating in the monopoly power of the BBC; not having to satisfy advertisers led to greater freedom to push sonic boundaries. Radio pioneer Tyrone Guthrie noted that:

> Radio offered a more promising field than the cinema, because, in Great Britain at all events, it is free from the anxieties of commercial competition. As a result of this the BBC has subordinated the question of Popular Appeal to Principle of Moral Philosophy; but has, none the less, been moderately adventurous and quite encouraging to technical experiment.
>
> *(Guthrie 1931: 7)*

The influence of the theater was very much felt in the first examples of radio drama broadcast by the BBC in the early 1920s, with the majority of productions derived from works that had initially been successful there, what Productions Director R.E. Jeffrey called a "bastard cultivation from the stage" (Jeffrey nd: 12). These early broadcasts tended to be unexceptional, and consisted mostly of traditional thrillers, adaptations of Shakespeare and light comedies, with little conception of the special problems of radio. Sound effects for early productions faced the reality that what worked on the stage didn't necessarily work over primitive microphones. The need for specially written plays that could cater to radio's unique qualities was acknowledged in 1926 by John Reith, the head of the BBC, in a memo to Station Directors, where he stated that "It seems to me that in many of our productions there is too much striving for theater effect and too little attempt at discovering the actual radio effect when the play is received in distant homes" (Briggs 1961: 282). Experimentation had in fact begun a few years earlier, when in October 1924, the BBC dedicated £50 "for experimental purposes in connection with the production of sound effects," and the next month allowed the additional services of an "effects man" (Briggs 1961: 201).

Radio comedy in the 1930s frequently took advantage of the humorous possibilities of sound, instead of simply broadcasting straight performances of music hall routines which had proved successful up to that point. For example, *Bandwaggon*, which debuted in 1938, and starred the duo Arthur Askey and Dickie Murdoch, was notorious for putting characters in situations that would have been impossible to realize in any medium outside of radio, and the luxury of sound effects. In one sketch, Askey is heard to emerge from a theater floor playing the cinema organ. The organ doesn't stop rising, but instead continues on until it breaks through the ceiling, with a resounding crash. Once producers and writers realized the potential of radio for creating a boundary-free environment for their characters to inhabit, the possibilities were limited only by the imagination of the listener and the ingenuity of the sound engineer.

It was a piece of equipment, the Dramatic-control Panel, employed first in 1928, and redesigned in art deco fashion by the modernist architect Wells Coates for the BBC's Broadcasting House, that was to have the greatest impact on early sonic experimentation in radio. The Dramatic-control Panel enabled producers to separate and control different groups of actors and sounds and was ostensibly created to help give producers greater control over certain balance problems apparent when crowd noises were required in combination with smaller groups of actors. Unlike production methods in America and on the Continent, with the Dramatic-control Panel, the crowds and principal actors could be linked to separate microphones in different studios, enabling the producer to adjust individual microphone volume levels. It soon became apparent to a couple of open-minded producers that it could be used more creatively, however, and that in fact the Dramatic-control Panel could allow vast and varied configurations of performers in a seemingly unlimited spectrum of performance spaces and situations. Among the most influential producers who took advantage of this opportunity were Mary Hope Allen, Archie Harding, and Lance Sieveking.

Roger Eckersley, director of programming through the 1930s, described at the time the typical tour he would give to visitors of the complex of studios surrounding the Dramatic-control Panel at Broadcasting House:

> The room is small, but what I believe is called functional – that is a hundred per cent designed and utilized for its own special purpose. In the center of it stands the instrument itself with a steel-framed chair or two drawn up to it. … In brief, the producer sits here, controlling remotely the activities of his cast, his music, his effects.
>
> He has perhaps his leading actors in one studio, his supporting cast in another, his music in another, and his effects in the effects room. Telephone lines connect each studio with the panel, and he is listening on ear-phones. Let us suppose in the course of a play a dance is going on. The hero and heroine are in the ballroom. The butler summons them to say their taxi is waiting.
>
> Dance music is coming from studio A at a steady level – Enter butler, from Studio B, superimposed over the music from Studio A. Sound of door shutting from effects room as they leave the ballroom.
>
> The producer quickly switches off his dance music with a turn of his Studio A knob, and when the front door is opened brings in and up the noise of a taxi ticking outside from effects room. In the meantime the conversation between our hero and heroine is kept up at a constant level from Studio C.

To watch the producer in a complicated piece of work is rather like watching a virtuoso at the organ.

(Eckersley 1946: 110–113)

One can feel the invigorating sense of novelty in Eckersley's description of these production techniques, as well as an effusion of technological wonder. The future of dramatic production Eckersley sees is one of machine-age, factory efficiency, but one that is ultimately musical as well, the role of the producer equated with that of the virtuosic organist.

Sieveking's legendary productions have not survived in recorded form, but in his surviving scripts, and his book, *The Stuff of Radio*, he detailed his production methods, providing a unique insight into the earliest thinking about radio sound as art. His "scores" (as he called his scripts) indicate the dexterity required by the player of the Dramatic-control Panel. In sound, Sieveking anticipated by at least one year some of the types of visual effects explored by Soviet filmmakers, such as cross-fades, montage, and wipes, as recent scholar David Hendy has observed (Hendy 2012). In particular, Sieveking noted a similarity between his ideas and those of Svevolod Podovkin, who had written about the effectiveness of slowing down motion in a film for emphasis, concentrating on specific images. Pudovkin wrote in 1931 that:

When a director shoots a scene he varies the position of the camera, bringing it closer to or pulling it back from the actor depending on whether he wants to draw the audience's attention to the overall pattern of the movement of to the individual's face. In this way he controls the spatial construction of the scene. Why should he not do the same with time as well? Why not give momentary prominence to some detail of the movement by slowing it down on screen and thus letting it be seen particularly vividly and incredibly clearly?

(Pudovkin 2006: 187–188)

Sieveking shifted this emphasis onto the word, sometimes to give added significance to the meaning of these words, and sometimes to focus attention onto the sounds produced by the words themselves.

Intimate Snapshots, originally produced in 1929 was the first radio drama to explore this idea in depth. In this play, Sieveking combined slow-motioned sounds with mechanically altered musical elements to produce a *musique concrète*-like texture. Taking advantage of the intimacy of microphone technology, he has his character speak very close and quiet as he fades up a sloweddown percussive jazz band on top of the voice. The play concludes this way, with the formal shape of the sounds defining the character and the musical nature of the sounds. He notes that "actually, the music was made by playing a piece of contemporary 'hot syncopation' very, very slowly indeed on an electric-pick-up gramophone. When amplified, its hesitating, long-drawnout thuds had an almost terrifying significance" (Sieveking 1934: 35–37).

Sieveking identified several different primary genres of sound effect in use in early radio, of which this demonstrated the *Symbolic, Evocative Effect*, defined by him as "a record of abstract rhythm of a churning and insistent nature, definitely not classifiable under the usual heading of 'music,' used to express confusion in a character's mind." This became one of the principle and earliest uses for *musique concrète* in radio drama in the late 1950s. In its non-electronic form, it will be prominent in the works immediately preceding the first concrete works, such as in Giles Cooper's *Mathry Beacon* from 1956. In this play, Cooper gives the stage direction that, "The sound made by the Deflector is a high, rhythmic humming. While musical in its effect it must not appear to be instrumental in origin" (Cooper 1966: 14). Another, equally important genre was the *Impressionistic Effect*, defined as

> a quick and comic fanfare used to mark the exits and entrances of a character in a dream; or the use of artificial echo or a voice, to indicate that the speaker is dead; or choral shouting of repeated phrases to startle the listener and mark in his mind the crisis in the character's mind.
>
> *(Sieveking 1934: 66)*

This genre, which appears straightforward (albeit ubiquitously) in comic programs like *ITMA* (It's That Man Again), will be amplified and distorted, perfected, many would say, to absurd effect in the *The Goon Show* by the late 1950s. Sieveking presaged all of these later uses, however, in Tyrone Guthrie's dramatization of Aldous Huxley's *Antic Hay*, when he used a recording of the Charleston played at gradually increasing speed by having the turntable manually sped up using a finger on the record, a technique used extensively by later *musique concrète* composers.

Sieveking repeated his "slowing down" technique, which he labeled a "sound time close up" in a 1934 play, *The Wings of the Morning*. To produce it, Sieveking used nine studios; three for the cast, one effects, one gramophone, and four echo rooms. The excerpt starts with a fascinating example of what film sound theorist Michel Chion calls in film "synchresis"; a synchronization between sound and image (Chion 1990). Here, a clock's accelerated ticking symbolically transforms into the running footsteps of our protagonist, representing his panic. This panic is again transformed into a slow-motion sequence where the action returns to the clock. This second scenario is familiar to any viewer of action films, a slowing down of action before the resolution of a countdown. However, here, the sound time close-up transfers us almost to another dimension, where Sieveking uses acoustic perspective to disorient his listeners "as if you were either going under, or coming to from an anaesthetic" (Sieveking 1934: 210):

OGILVIE: (*counting*): Six, seven, eight, nine, ten.

(*The clock begins to tick faster and faster and faster. It gradually becomes* HOLLAND's *running footsteps. Suddenly they stop. There is a pause filled with nameless apprehension. The acoustic changes. You have left* OGILVIE's *rooms and are outside the Headley Museum.*)...

(HOLLAND *is heard running. His footsteps gradually become a clock ticking very fast indeed. It gradually gets slower and slower and slower. From a great distance off, you hear* OGILVIE's *voice counting, counting, backwards.*)

OGILVIE (*growing slower with the clock*): Seventeen, sixteen, fifteen, fourteen, thirteen, twelve, eleven, ten, nine, eight, seven, six, five, four, three, two, one and

SOUND-TIME– now – (*very slow indeed*) how – do – you –

CLOSE-UP feel? Did – you – get – it?

Creating this sense of disorientation was a specialty of Sieveking's, and is most prominent in his two *Kaleidoscopes*, where he would have been responsible for controlling the output of all eight available studios and mixing them live. His virtuosic combinations of forces embody a kind of jazz-age modernity, a *bricolage*, similar in style to contemporary Hollywood's representation of "city life" in such films as *This Modern World*, and *42nd Street*, or Eisenstein's collage technique, a perfect example of what Andreas Huyssen called "an invasion of the very fabric of the art object by technology" (Huyssen 1986: 9). More than representing the rough and tumble of urban life, the intentional use of music, sound effects, and dialog together inextricably combined creates the effect of defamiliarization; by combining jazz with Beethoven, the Wedding March with machine guns, each of these things takes on a new significance, becomes symbolic. Sieveking observed that "what astonishingly illuminating and beautiful results can be made by using odd unlabeled sounds very much in the same way as Swinburne used to evoke beauty by using words as so much sound rather than as so much sense" (Sieveking 1934: 61).

Throughout the 1920s and 1930s, in acknowledging the newness of their art form and its unique qualities, and borrowing heavily from film (the techniques of juxtaposition, fades and swells, superimposition, montage, and distance), the more experimental radio producers began pushing the limits of what audiences accepted, and in the process discovered new ways to tell stories; indeed, new kinds of stories to tell. As Rudolf Arnheim, a German writing about his own country's radio innovators, noted at the time:

> Here there is really something quite individual. With the expressive means of pure sound: acoustic relationship between expression of speech and music, annihilation of softer sounds by louder ones, translation of mood and character into dynamics of sound—by such means spiritual experiences are embodied in a new material taken from it and yet possessing its own laws; but the laws of the sound-world only becomes effective and recognizable when one is aware of this sound-world quite alone, without any recollection of the "missing" corporeal world.
>
> *(Arnheim 1936: 194)*

This ethereal sound-world could be as abstract as the internal thoughts of its protagonist required, and in this next step of storytelling, sound-dramatists were dealing with the same conceptual issues contemporary British composers were facing, and would continue to face a generation later when confronted with the question of musical storytelling without the benefit of tonality. Since radio drama was no longer forced to be primarily concerned with recreating "corporeal" worlds, techniques evolved that made it possible to represent a more abstract world. Despite this, there were those at the BBC, particularly manager Val Gielgud, who objected to this more imaginative use of sound effects. Although Gielgud was hardly an "enemy" of progressive radio, he nevertheless positioned himself firmly against the use of sound effects in all but the most obvious situations. Gielgud believed that sound effect's "significance to the radio play is little greater than that of the thunder sheet or the coconut shell to the stage play" (Gielgud 1957: 90). Radio sound effects in the 1920s and 1930s for radio were mostly of the kind first standardized on the stage, and were essentially literal. Filson Young wrote that:

> They [effects and sounds other than the human voice] have been used most successfully hitherto in connection with narratives and dramatized readings, and in descriptive monologues, as illustrations and images in mental retrospect.... But their use in drama pure and simple has never yet, I think, been successfully related to the more subtle form of art.
>
> *(Young 1933: 145–146)*

Experimental productions by Sieveking and fellow producers thrived on an environment that was conducive to risk-taking. The Research Section, founded in 1928 on encouragement from

Val Goldsmith, the Director General's assistant, consisted of Sieveking, Harding, Allen, and E.J. King-Bull, each of whom was committed to making radio that defied categorization, that moved it as an art further from its stage roots, and closer to something they referred to as "pure radio." Lauded critically as an inspiration for radio stations elsewhere in the world, it facilitated creative production as no other internal organization would, and whose broadcasts inspired Filson Young to write:

> It is obvious that the first direction in which we should look for development in the art of the microphone is in the field of what are called "Productions" – *i.e.* radio-dramatic activities ... we have heard some very queer experiments of this kind; some have contained thrills, and others may have seemed merely eccentric extravagance. The point is that they were experiments, and that they were and are leading somewhere.
>
> *(Young 1933: 5–6)*

During its brief existence, the Research Section faced constant attacks from within the BBC for its apparent mandate to think, rather than to do. Colleagues perceived and resented their being somehow above the everyday pressures of ordinary producers, while at the same time entitled to the use of "public" equipment. The primary problem seems to have been that the Research Section was an experimental studio without a studio, an "untidy" situation, as Gielgud put it. They were also responsible for producing plays that were less popular than more traditional plays. These plays often had little or no plot and required the audience to accept techniques considered radical at the time, with their modernist Joycean stream of consciousness narratives. Although the BBC was not obliged to base all its decisions on audience figures, it was a concern nevertheless that their broadcasts were appealing to an elitist "highbrow" audience. Gielgud himself was not sympathetic to the kind of work they were doing and cynically observed that, "A play labeled 'experimental' might as well have been labeled 'poison'" (Gielgud 1957: 68). A combination of unpopularity within the BBC, low ratings, and a lack of equipment for its exclusive use led to its dissolution upon the retirement of its coordinating head, R.E. Jeffrey, in the early 1930s. The administration told Gielgud in confidence that he had to "take the Research Section under [his] wing, or it must be disbanded" (Gielgud 1965: 67–68). Gielgud's solution, an ingenious one, was to create a completely new department, outside of Drama, and responsible for creating programs that didn't fit into that category; those programs that had arisen because of the kind of innovations brought about by the Research Section. He created an experimental department with a regular stream of commissions, and with all the bureaucratic and administrative backing the higher echelons of the BBC had felt were necessary but absent in the Research Section. This new department, "Features," continued the experimentation started under the Research Section. Defined technically as "a story without a plot," features became integral to the war effort, developing a kind of propaganda that depicted the British Government's perspective without the more overt devices of drama or melodrama. D.G. Bridson's *March of the '45*, first broadcast in 1936, exemplified the continuation of Sieveking's multi-studio methods within the new, more focused Features Section. The outrageous, decadent productions of the 1920s, which seemed to revel in their excess, stand in contrast to the socialist depression-era features of the 1930s, although nothing but the subject matter had changed; inventive and innovative sound design formed the core of these productions.

With the start of World War Two, the continuing innovation that had marked the previous 20 years came to a near standstill, mostly because the addition of the Services Radio Programme consumed a hefty portion of the yearly budget. Austerity was the watchword of the day and experiments like the Research Section's had gone out of fashion during the depression of the

1930s. Add to this the onset of war and such extravagance became impossible. Finally, with the decamping of the Drama and Features Departments out of Broadcasting House in London (for fear of bombing) to Manchester and other points North, producers lost the stability of fully equipped studios, and even reliable broadcasting equipment. Gielgud remembers that during the war, the Dramatic-control Panel, "with all the opportunities for misuse afforded by that fascinating invention – were replaced by non-compensating mixing units working under conditions only to be comprehensively categorized as 'lash-up'" (Gielgud 1957: 84).

This doesn't mean that during the later 1930s and into the war years, radio was exclusively the domain of light music and news. In 1937, the original radio piece found a new home on the "Experimental Hour." This was modeled after the Theatre Workshop at the Columbia Broadcast Service in the United States. The program ended with the war, but because of Features Department's involvement with the war effort, and the development of new mobile recording equipment (though in England, not yet tape recording), dialog, sound, and music could be combined as never before. Other successful Feature's productions included Edward Sackville-West's poetical narrative *The Rescue* with music by Benjamin Britten, which challenged listeners' conceptions of how music, sound effects, spoken word, and music *as sound effect* can interact in a radio broadcast.

The development of the radio drama and feature into unique and successful genres was to have profound effect on the way post-war radio broadcasting took shape. With the split into three distinct "programmes" (or "networks") there was more room in the schedules for the kind of programming considered too high-brow in earlier years. Comedy series adapted many of the sound effects developed for radio drama, first in wartime favorites like *ITMA*, and after the war, *The Goon Show*. But radio drama in the 1950s would also find inspiration from continental studios, particularly France's RTF, and the work of musical pioneers Pierre Schaeffer, André Almuro, and Pierre Henry, who had developed techniques for manipulating sound on tape and disc.

For example, in the mid-1950s the BBC pioneered the use of unusual sound in its own productions of continental avant-garde "Theatre of the Absurd" works, as exemplified by Jean Paul Sartre, Samuel Beckett, Jean Anouilh, and others. This fundamentally different and original drama was united in the representation of "a world deprived of a generally accepted integrating principle, which has become disjointed, purposeless – absurd" (Esslin 1980: 399). With roots in 19th-century nonsense poetry, music hall traditions, and early 20th-century surrealism, these authors' works represent the disjointed senselessness and irrationality of the universe through narrative and structural distortions. Sonically, this off-kilter world was represented though the adoption of *musique concrète* techniques and the use of electronic sounds for the first time in Britain. This led, by the end of the 1950s, to the creation of the BBC's own electronic music studio, the Radiophonic Workshop, primarily for the implementation of these techniques in radio drama.

But in the immediate post-war years the BBC didn't only encourage the development of avant-garde sounds; Ludwig Koch's radio broadcasts, *Music of the Sea*, and *Paris*, from 1951 and 1952 respectively, were billed as "sound pictures without words" in the *Radio Times* and were carefully, logically, and artistically modeled sound sculptures. They used the latest in outside broadcast technology and recording equipment, including high-tech microphones and newly available tape recorders, and attempted to capture as realistically, evocatively, and authentically as possible the subject or theme of the broadcast. Koch's sound pictures were an intermittent but regular feature of the BBC's radio broadcasts of the 1940s and 1950s, and are the epitome of a certain kind of broadcasting conceived of at radio's inception as one of its most valuable assets: the ability to play "live" sounds from often exotic locations. Koch's programs take this idea to a new level of sonic "impressionism" and, with few words of explanation and no hint of plot, present a collection of representative sounds which together illustrate his theme. The musicality of such a technique did not go unnoticed in the press, as this 1951 *Radio Times* article illustrates:

> In his youth, in his native city of Frankfurt, he enjoyed the acquaintance of Clara Schumann and Brahms, and it was here that he made his first recording—at the tender age of eight—with a novel machine that his father brought back as a present from Leipzig Fair. On a wax cylinder Ludwig recorded a bird singing in a cage. The year was 1889, and the recording still exists—the earliest example of recorded bird-song ... Koch hopes that if people sit and listen quietly, as they would sit and look at a painting, his sounds will stimulate the imagination in the same way as a painter's colours.
>
> *(Radio Times 1951)*

However effective and new Koch's sound portraits were as radio, they still were intended to be realistic representations of their subject, so that if their source was obscured in the final broadcast, then the work would have been deemed a failure.

Beginning in the early 1950s, radio audiences began to grow tired of the relentless barrage of "realistic" sound effects in radio drama, and suggested a reduction in the general use of sound effects overall. In his influential guide to the philosophy and production of radio drama, *The Art of Radio*, Donald McWhinnie decried the use of constant "realistic" sound effects for radio, preferring the role that the occasional but well-placed effect can have in furthering a story. He noted that, "in radio, as in poetry we attain definition by concentrated intuitive short cuts, not by a mass of elaboration and detail" (McWhinnie 1959: 51).

The Drama Department script editor observed in 1958 that "we now receive much more essentially radio material than the sort of scripts that are written with no particular medium in mind" (Hardwick 1958: 14–15). Alongside this was a willingness to expand the role of sound effects, letting them act in some respects as music. Following McWhinnie's idea that sound effect can act as storyteller, these new, more abstract sound effects worked in combination with dialog to forge a rich atmospheric texture. Rayner Heppenstall's 1952 feature, *Dear Sensibility*, was one of the first productions to demonstrate this attitude. This work, which was an impressionistic sketch based on Laurence Sterne's autobiographical memoir, *A Sentimental Journey*, concerned itself with the minute details of Sterne's trip through France and Italy. Heppenstall described his method as:

> In fact the "stream of consciousness" or "interior monologue" of Joyce, Dorothy Richardson, Virginia Woolf—a narrative method which quickly exhausted itself in the novel but which, I would claim, is of the very essence of radio, little as it has been copied so far. It is a method which demands self-abnegation from the rest of the cast, whose lines are so many sound effects. A programme of this kind is essentially a concerto for solo voice and sound effects.
>
> *(Heppenstall 1952: 8)*

Here the voices, the dialog itself, have been reduced to their sonic components to act as effect and background to the main speaker.

The Third Programme (1946–1970), the BBC's radio network dedicated to "difficult" and more avant-garde programming was exceedingly confident in its dramatic and poetic broadcasts, and during its first ten years commissioned some of the most important radio plays ever to emerge from that genre, including Dylan Thomas's *Under Milk Wood* and Samuel Beckett's

All That Fall. It is from within this system, and the network that would take most seriously the project of high modernism, that the first serious use of electronic sound in Britain took place as part of an effort to incorporate what had been purely musical ideas into established dramatic movements. With the new network, plays that explored more controversial ideas or less accessible storytelling techniques finally had an outlet. Just as the pressure was growing to remove the gratuitous use of realistic sound effects, there was a strong and growing desire for sound effects that were much less literal than had been the vogue in the past. These sounds would find materiality in the output of the BBC's Radiophonic Workshop (1958–1998), and, along with the rise of television, change the ways radio depicted sounds, both natural and avant-garde.

References

Arnheim, R. (1936) *Radio*, trans. by Margaret Ludwig and Herbert Read, London: Faber and Faber.

Briggs, A. (1961) *The Birth of Broadcasting*, vol. 1 of *The History of Broadcasting in the United Kingdom*, Oxford: Oxford University Press.

Chion, M. (1990) *Audio-Vision: Sound on Screen*, New York: Columbia University Press.

Cooper, G. (1966) *Mathry Beacon, in Giles Cooper: Six Plays for Radio*, Letchworth, Hertfordshire: BBC Books.

Eckersley, R. (1946) *The BBC and All That*, London: S. Low, Marston & Co.

Esslin, M. (1980) *Theatre of the Absurd*, New York: Penguin Books.

Gielgud, V. (1957) *British Radio Drama: 1922–1956*, London: George G. Harrap & Co.

Gielgud, V. (1965) *Years in a Mirror*, London: Bodley Head.

Guthrie, T. (1931) *Squirrel's Cage and Two Other Microphone Plays*, London: Cobden-Sanderson.

Hardwick, M. (1958) "More Radio Writers Than Ever Before and More Scope for Them," *Ariel*, 3:10.

Hendy, D. (2012) "Painting With Sound: The Kaleidoscopic World of Lance Sieveking, a British Radio Modernist," *Twentieth Century British History*, 24(2), 169–200.

Heppenstall, R. (1952) "In the Steps of Laurence Sterne," *Radio Times*, January 18.

Huyssen, A. (1986) *After the Great Divide: Modernism, Mass Culture, Postmodernism*, Bloomington: Indiana University Press.

Jeffrey, R.E. (n.d.) Introduction to *Radio Drama and How To Write It*, by Gordon Lea, London: Allen & Unwin.

McWhinnie, D. (1959) *The Art of Radio*, London: Faber & Faber.

Pudovkin, V. (2006) "Time in Close-Up" in *Vsevolod Pudovkin: Selected Essays*, edited by Richard Taylor. Translated by Richard Taylor and Evgeni Filippov, London: Seagull Books.

Sieveking, L. (1934) *The Stuff of Radio*, London: Cassell and Co.

Young, F. (1933) *Shall I Listen: Studies in the Adventure and Technique of Broadcasting*, London: Constable and Co.

29

REMASTERING THE RECORDING ANGEL

Jacob Smith

When Evan Eisenberg's book, *The Recording Angel*, was published in 1986, it struck reviewers as the first study of its kind. One critic called it "the first full-length book on the implications and effects of recording on music" (Parelels 1987: H24). Another wrote that, given the "enormous impact" of recording technology on "the musical life of our era," it was surprising that so little had been written about it (Fantel 1986: H23). These reactions to Eisenberg's book are surprising given that they occurred more than a century after Thomas Edison invented the phonograph in 1877. As a point of comparison, a book published in 1986 on the implications of Edison's later invention – the motion picture – would not have struck anyone as the first of its kind; in fact, it would have joined a sizable literature on the history and theory of film. It seems that Eisenberg had discovered an intellectual terrain that had long been hidden in plain sight.

I have a special affection for *The Recording Angel* because it was an important resource for me as I studied the history and theory of recorded sound as a graduate student in the early 2000s. At that time, the book still seemed to exist in a class of its own. The study of recorded sound has expanded considerably in the last fifteen years, due in part to the emergence of the field of sound studies. Themes in Eisenberg's book provide a useful point of reference for an overview of the academic study of recorded sound in the era of an incipient sound studies.

The angel's quill and the machine's ear

Eisenberg's title, *The Recording Angel*, refers to a logo for the record company EMI that depicted "a winged cherub sprawled on a record and using a quill to engrave it" (Eisenberg 1988: 63). As with the RCA-Victor logo "His Master's Voice," the recording angel is a rich image to think with, and was discussed in the German media theorist Friedrich Kittler's analysis of the gramophone around the same time that *The Recording Angel* was published. Eisenberg and Kittler's attention to that image is indicative of a scholarly tendency to understand sound recording devices as reading and writing machines.

The poet Rainer Maria Rilke addressed the status of phonographic grooves as a form of inscription in his essay "Primal Sound" (1919), which compares the grooves on wax cylinders to those on the inside of the human skull (see Kittler 1999: 39–41; Gunning 2003). Phonographic inscription also fascinated Theodor Adorno, whose essay "The Form of the Phonograph Record" (1934) approaches the phonograph disc in terms of "the contours of its thingness"

(Adorno 2002: 278). Adorno wrote that the record was a new form of musical writing, a "scriptal spiral" that "survives in time" (Adorno 2002: 280). In a key early work of contemporary sound studies, Lisa Gitelman made a systematic study of the phonograph as part of a genealogy of inscription, dictation, and phonetic shorthand (Gitelman 1999). Patrick Feaster has advanced that project, and points out that the term "phonography" has "almost always been defined contrastively, relative to some other practice of inscription that is perceived as less aurally expressive" (Feaster 2015: 139). Mara Mills expands this area of inquiry into disability studies, revealing the close connection between the development of sound technologies and devices for the deaf and blind communities (Mills 2011; Mills 2015).

The "thingness" of the phonograph has also been discussed in terms of the simulation of the human body. Here, the iconic image is not the recording angel's quill but Alexander Graham Bell's "ear phonautograph," images of which have appeared in several influential sound studies texts. James Lastra reproduces that image in the context of an argument about the simulation of the vocal apparatus and ear in the design of early talking machines (Lastra 2000: 34–5). For Jonathan Sterne, Bell's device is illustrative of the ear as "a mechanism for transducing vibrations"; a "tympanic mechanism" (Sterne 2003: 34). These examples show that scholarship in sound studies has been in dialogue with the social history of technology, film "apparatus theory," and media archaeology, fostering an interest in the cultural history of technological devices.

Eisenberg was interested in technological devices to the extent that they allowed him to discuss recorded music. The close association between recorded sound and music is one explanation for the paucity of scholarship on the more general category of phonography, as compared to medium-specific work on film. To the extent that phonography was considered the domain of music, and as long as musicologists were relatively uninterested in the forms of popular music most associated with sound technology (jazz, rock, disco, hip hop, etc.) the medium would remain underexplored. The focus on music also hindered the investigation of the many other uses to which recorded sound has been put. One review of *The Recording Angel* compared the invention of the phonograph to the invention of musical notation: "In both instances, the aim was the preservation and conveyance of music" (Fantel 1986: H23). In fact, the preservation of music was not the driving force behind the invention of the phonograph, as indicated by the fact that music ranked a poor fifth on Edison's initial list of applications for "the gathering up and retaining of sounds hitherto fugitive." Ahead of music, Edison promised letter-writing, dictation, books, and "Educational Purposes," and only then mentioned music, which was quickly followed by "Family Record; Phonographic books; Musical-Boxes; Toys; Clocks; [and] Advertising" (Edison 1878: 527).

Scholarship in sound studies has expanded the investigation of recorded sound to encompass the variety of phonographic writing indicated by Edison's list, including spoken word recordings, film sound design, radio transcription, dictation, telephone answering machines, field recording, and home recording (see for example Morton 2000; Smith 2011a; Russo 2010; Bijsterveld 2008). Edison helped to inaugurate a long and diverse history of recorded sound industries, and scholars such as Gitelman, Emily Thompson, and David Suisman have outlined the complex evolution of phonograph companies from being purveyors of a technological wonder to a business instrument to an entertainment device (Gitelman 1999; Thompson 1995; Suisman 2009). Numerous scholars have described the ways in which sound has been commodified: note Adorno's concerns about "regressive listening" and musical standardization; Jacques Attali's anxieties about an era of repetitive mass production; Eisenberg's account of "music's backwards metamorphosis, from butterfly to chrysalis" to become a commodity; and Jeremy Wade Morris's recent analysis of the "digital music commodity" (Adorno 2002; Attali 1996; Eisenberg 1988: 24; Morris 2015). The industries built upon recorded sound have continued to proliferate in the digital era, including sound art, podcasting, audiobooks, ringtones, audio branding, and sound design for digital games. One thing is certain: in the era of sound studies, the recording angel's quill is busier than ever.

Icons of phonography

One of Eisenberg's central concerns was the interaction of musical performance and recording technology. In one section of the book, he refers to Louis Armstrong and Enrico Caruso as "icons of phonography." For Eisenberg, an icon of a new art was someone with a personality so powerful that they seem to be present when they aren't, someone "so in command" of their art that they turn a medium's "disadvantages into advantages" (Eisenberg 1988: 146). While historians such as Feaster and Tim Gracyk have demonstrated that Armstrong and Caruso were not the first phonographic celebrities, Eisenberg's investigation of how those "icons" developed modes of performance in tandem with particular assemblages of recording technology has been taken up by subsequent scholars (Feaster and Smith 2009; Gracyk 2013).

Sterne describes how "easily recognizable forms of human speech" such as rhymes and popular quotations were used as testing material for the early phonograph, mobilizing "conventionalized language" to help the machine in "doing its job of reproducing" (Sterne 2003: 247). Feaster develops this theme through the concept of "phonogenic" sonic subjects: "voicings of communicative behavior" intended for "sonic mediation across time and space" (Feaster 2015: 145). Similarly, in his discussion of "phonograph effects" – the "manifestations of sound recording's influence" on musical culture – Mark Katz includes the time limitations enforced by recording formats and the ways in which particular technologies have been more or less "receptive" to certain instruments or performance styles (Katz 2010: 31–41).

As the example of Armstrong and Caruso indicates, vocal performance is a particularly resonant case study for considering phonogenic styles and phonograph effects. During the "acoustic era" of sound recording, sound was funneled through a horn to a flexible diaphragm that transferred vibrations to a stylus that engraved grooves onto a wax disc. No electronic amplification was involved in this process, and so performances had to be quite loud in order to produce a viable recording (Katz 2010: 37–9). Dynamics of the acoustic era favored vocal performers who had developed techniques to address audiences in large spaces, such as opera singers, political orators, variety stage performers, auctioneers, and street performers (Siefert 1995: 430–1). Electric recording with sensitive new microphones allowed for new protocols, such as the male radio "crooners" described by scholars like Alison McCracken (McCracken 2015; Smith 2008). Neepa Majumdar and Amanda Weidman explore the interplay of vocal performance and sound technology with regards to female playback singers and recording artists in the Indian film industry (Majumdar 2001; Weidman 2006; Weidman 2015). Kay Dickinson examines the interplay of gender, voice, and technology with records to recordings of female singers treated with vocoders and digital autotune applications (Dickinson 2001).

McCracken, Majumdar, Weidman, and Dickinson reveal the ways in which cultural notions of gender shaped the interplay of voice and technology, and Lindon Barrett and Alexander Weheliye are among scholars who write about how ideologies of race have become refracted through the recorded voice. An important distinction for both authors is that between a "singing voice" associated with the enactment of blackness and embodiment, and a "signing voice" associated with whiteness and disembodiment (Weheliye 2005; Barrett 2009). Alice Maurice's investigation of the promotion of African American voices in early sound films reveals a dual strategy to emphasize both the "hyperpresence of black bodies in order to deflect attention away from the apparatus" as well as offering those same bodies "to show off the prowess of the apparatus" (Maurice 2002: 33, 45). Scholarship such as this suggests that who or what counts as an "icon" of media performance at any historical moment is dependent upon a set of social assumptions about skill, technique, identity, embodiment, and authenticity.

Just as important as the interaction of performance styles and recording technologies was the new kind of spaces where these interactions took place: recording studios. Scholars have produced histories and ethnographies of the recording studio and placed it within a broader "soundscape of modernity" characterized by the ability to control the depiction of sonic spaces (Horning 2013; Morton 2004; Thompson 2002). Performers were not the only creative presence in the studio, and Eisenberg took a keen interest in the "genealogy of the popular producer" (Eisenberg 1988: 124). *The Recording Angel* is attentive to the evolution of mixing and overdubbing in studio production, such that popular recordings were often "pieced together from bits of actual events… like the composite photograph of a minotaur" (Eisenberg 1988: 109). Likewise, one of Katz's phonograph effects was "manipulability," the ability not to simply capture sounds in the studio, but to manipulate them, and so create sonic performances that "could never have existed" (Katz 2010: 41). Kittler took an interest in "time axis manipulation" and "time axis reversal": the ability of studio producers to speed up, slow down, or reverse sound recordings (Kittler 1999: 34–5).

Eisenberg wrote primarily about classical music, opera, jazz, and rock, but in the decades since the 1980s, the cutting edge of sound production has moved to dub, hip hop, and electronic music. Michael Veal explores the aesthetics of Jamaican dub, a style in which the "pop song was electronically deconstructed and reconfigured by a generation of studio engineers" (Veal 2007: 34). DJ culture popularized the use of the turntable as a musical instrument, and Mark J. Butler explores the live performance of recorded sounds by DJs and laptop artists. Butler describes the various techniques by which performers have interfaced with recorded sounds, as well as performative modes like "passion-of-the-knob moments," which are characterized by the "strange incongruity" that arises when "a musician directs exceptionally intense expressivity toward a small, technical component associated with sound engineering" (Butler 2014: 101).

Another trajectory of recorded sound production involves moving outside of the studio. Inspired by the work of John Cage and the Canadian composer R. Murray Schafer's influential work on soundscapes, a cohort of sound artists and field recordists including Hildegard Westercamp, Bernie Krause, Francesco Lopez, Jana Winderen, Annea Lockwood, and Chris Watson have developed a genre of phonography that relies upon the use of portable sound equipment (Schafer 1994; Lane and Carlyle 2013). For Krause, there is a political and scientific dimension to this type of recording, since field recordings can serve as data sets that track the loss of habitat in our era of eco-crisis. Krause tells the story of recording in a forest before and after the area was opened to logging. To the eye, the site appeared "wild and unchanged," but his recordings revealed the loss of biodiversity. Krause concludes that "wild soundscapes are full of finely detailed information, and while a picture may indeed be worth a thousand words, a natural soundscape is worth a thousand pictures" (Krause 2012: 70–1). The genres of field recording and environmental sound art provide another indication of the historical variability of what might count as an "icon of phonography," and feature a new set of sonic icons such as the song of humpback whales, the creaking of melting glaciers, the buzz of tropical insects, and the sonification of weather data.

The social record

Returning to the EMI logo of the recording angel, we might wonder about the uses to which the angel's etchings will be put. Given that EMI was a large corporation aiming for a mass market, their recordings were most likely destined to create what Kate Lacey calls a "listening public" (Lacey 2013: 7–8). That is, the recording angel logo reminds us that recorded sound circulates. As Katz puts it, "when music becomes a thing it gains an unprecedented freedom to travel" (Katz 2010: 14).

Michael Denning describes how new vernacular musics emerged during the era of electrical recording in the 1920s and traveled through "an archipelago of colonial ports, linked by steamship routes, railway lines, and telegraph cables" (Denning 2015: 38). As Denning demonstrates, the portability of recorded sound can have important social effects, altering musical history, upsetting aesthetic hierarchies, reconfiguring listening publics, and even helping to pave the way for a post-colonial sensibility. Scholarship on recorded sound's portability has often focused on compact cassette technology. Consider Peter Manuel's classic study of cassette culture in India, as well as work on cassette sermons in Islamic culture by Annabelle Sreberny-Mohammadi, Ali Mohammadi, and Charles Hirschkind (Manuel 1993; Sreberny-Mohammadi and Mohammadi 1994; Hirschkind 2009).

The portability of sound creates a certain paradox whereby sonic commodities circulate through public spaces but are often experienced in isolation. Eisenberg was fascinated by such solitary listening, referring to the trope of the "desert island disc" to assert that

> the paradox of music for a desert island is right at the heart of phonography. To take the sounds of a full-fledged culture, sounds made possible by the efforts of thousands of musicians and technicians over the course of centuries, and enjoy them privately in your own good time: that's the freedom records give you.
>
> *(Eisenberg 1988: 44)*

The ethical dimension of solitary listening has been central to scholarship on mobile music listening, from the cassette Walkman to the Apple iPod. Michael Bull writes that iPod users move through space in an "auditory bubble," and asserts that iPods are "tools enabling the urban citizen to move through the chilly spaces of urban culture wrapped in a cocoon of communicative warmth whilst further contributing to the chill which surrounds them" (Bull 2007: 3, 18). David Beer counters by claiming that the users of mobile music remain "an integrated yet distracted part of the aural ecology and informational structures of the city" (Beer 2007: 848; see also Gopinath and Stanyek 2014).

Mobile music is only one social use of recorded sound. Environmental or ambient recordings were part of Eisenberg's study, and he tracks a lineage from Erik Satie's "furniture music" to the Muzak corporation (Eisenberg 1988: 75). Subsequent work on environmental or "ubiquitous" music has been published by Sterne, Timothy Taylor, Tim Anderson, Joseph Lanza, and Anahid Kassabian (Sterne 1997; Taylor 2009; Anderson 2006; Lanza 2003; Kassabian 2013). Eisenberg also writes about the use of recorded music in courtship, referring to the phonograph as the "Cyrano machine" (Eisenberg 1988: 87). Other facets of recorded sound in social life explored by sound studies scholars include wiretapping, mood regulation, sound as a military weapon, as erotica, as accompaniment to exercise, and as a component of product design (DeNora 2000; Smith 2008; Daughtry 2015; Goodman 2010; Gopinath 2013; Beckerman 2014; Bijsterveld 2008).

Eisenberg pays particular attention to record collecting as a social practice. In one chapter, he describes a collector whose home contains stacks of discs on every available surface (Eisenberg 1988: 1, 17). In another chapter, Eisenberg describes his college friend Tomas, who is a passionate collector of opera records and an out gay man (Eisenberg 1988: 41). The case of Tomas's opera fandom indicates how the portability of recorded sound could foster not only listening publics, but listening "counterpublics" (Warner 2002). Wayne Koestenbaum describes the connection between gay culture and opera fandom, and he notes that opera records "changed home's meanings. Home bent to accommodate opera." "The category of 'homosexuality' is only as old as recorded sound," he writes, and "both inventions arose in the late nineteenth century, and concerned the home. Both are discourses of home's shattering" (Koestenbaum 1993: 47). Koestenbaum describes vernacular practices of what Kittler called "time axis manipulation":

> turn Caruso into a woman by speeding him up; turn Galli-Curci into a man by slow-ing her down… A recorded voice is genderless sound waves. Thus a disc's revolutions teach something truly revolutionary: that the pitch of a voice, which we take to be an indicator of gender, can be changed once sound passes into the home listener's magic cabinet.
>
> *(Koestenbaum 1993: 61)*

Eisenberg's chapters on record collectors were ahead of their time in their concern for the reception of media texts, but they also highlight how much has changed in the culture of recorded sound since 1986. In our current moment, collections of sound are found on hard drives and smartphones rather than stacked on the surfaces of one's home (although the sale of vinyl discs has been making a notable comeback). Likewise, iTunes and online services like Spot-ify have mainstreamed "mix tape" and playlist culture. As recorded sounds continue to proliferate they will certainly take on new social functions, and scholars of sound will have to keep their ears open to emerging developments.

The recording angel of history

At one point in his book, Eisenberg suggests that the recording angel logo reveals the record company to be in the business of determining "what each musician's afterlife shall be" (Eisen-berg 1988: 63). The phonograph, after all, is a "durative" form of media; that is, it is a modern communication technology that transforms moment-to-moment human communication into a form that endures over time (Williams 1980: 55). This ability to reanimate communicative events from the past has meant that recorded sounds have been frequently associated with the afterlife, ghosts, and death. "Record listening is a séance where we get to choose our ghosts," Eisenberg writes (Eisenberg 1988: 57).

Early phonograph industry promotion praised the device for its ability to preserve the voices of loved ones and capture the words of "great men" before they died. Sterne writes of the RCA-Victor mascot Nipper as illustrative of "the peculiar Victorian culture of death and dying into which sound recording was inserted," since some have postulated that the dog is seated on a coffin, listening to the voice of a recently deceased master (Sterne 2003: 301–2, see also Brady 1999: 47–8). Such discourses are part of a broader tendency to associate modern media technologies with the supernatural and uncanny, a tendency that Jeffrey Sconce has discussed under the rubric of "haunted media" (Sconce 2000). In the domain of recorded sound, examples include the use of tape recorders to record the voices of the dead, the playing of records back-wards in order to reveal hidden occult messages, and a fascination with the sonic reanimation of the voices of dead celebrities (Sconce 2000; Smith 2011a, 2011b; Stanyek and Piekut 2012).

A related set of questions has to do with recorded sound and memory. William Howland Kenney examines the relationship between recorded music and collective memory in early twentieth-century American cultural life, and finds that "the phonograph's repetitive function acted as a major aid to memory by resounding the patterns of sensibility embedded in commer-cialized musical formulas from the past" (Kenney 1999: xix). Theodore Gracyk refers to research on the human perception of timbre to suggest that our difficulty in retaining specific timbres in memory is the basis for a desire to play the same records again and again (Gracyk 1996: 59–60). The result is that popular recordings tend to saturate the everyday experience of listeners at a given time, such that the specific sounds of a given record, heard years later, can powerfully trigger the memory of a bygone era.

There is an irony here, that the most "contemporary" sounds at a given moment are destined to be the ones that most powerfully index the past. Some critics have identified a crisis with regards to popular sound and collective memory that occurred during the first decades of the twenty-first century. That crisis was given aesthetic expression by a genre of electronic music dubbed "hauntology" and associated with artists such as Philip Jeck, Burial, the Advisory Circle, and the Caretaker. Mark Fisher writes that by the mid-2000s, "it was becoming clear that electronic music could no longer deliver sounds that were 'futuristic'" (Fisher 2012: 16). Fisher holds that hauntological recordings restore "the uncanniness of recording by making the recorded surface audible again," via "the foregrounding of the sound of vinyl crackle," which "unsettles the very distinction between surface and depth, between background and foreground. In sonic hauntology, we *hear* that time is out of joint" (Fisher 2013: 48–9).

With this invocation of the contour of recorded sound's thingness, I would like to conclude by returning to the image of the angel etching onto a disc. The hauntological crackle transforms the cherub-like angle into an uncanny phantom. Moreover, recorded sound in the digital era might be imagined as the angel unbound from the materiality of the disc, with sounds existing everywhere and nowhere in a heavenly and dematerialized "cloud." The hauntological crackle serves as a reminder however, that digital sound technologies still leave a material footprint via data farms and the "high tech trash" of our digital devices (see Smith 2015).

The figure of the recording angel and Eisenberg's pioneering book help us to track a set of recurring tensions across the century-long experience of recorded sound: tensions between material object and dematerialized presence; between acts of embodied performance and studio-enhanced writing; between solitary listening and far-reaching listening publics. *The Recording Angel* is now part of a growing bookshelf on the history and theory of recorded sound, but scholars and practitioners may still find it to be a useful point of reference as they track the new figures, tensions, and historical trajectories that they discover in the widening spiral of phonography.

References

Adorno, Theodor W. *Essays on Music*. Berkeley: University of California Press, 2002.

Anderson, Tim J. *Making Easy Listening*. Minneapolis: University of Minnesota Press, 2006.

Annabelle Sreberny-Mohammadi and Ali Mohammadi. *Small Media, Big Revolution*. Minneapolis: University of Minnesota Press, 1994.

Attali, Jacques. *Noise: The Political Economy of Music*. Minneapolis: University of Minnesota Press, 1996.

Barrett, Lindon. *Blackness and Value*. Cambridge: Cambridge University Press, 2009.

Beckerman, Joel. *The Sonic Boom*. Boston: Mariner Books, 2014.

Beer, David. "Tune Out: Music, Soundscapes, and the Urban Mise-en-scene," in *Information, Communication & Society*, vol. 10, no. 6, December 2007.

Bijsterveld, Karin. *Mechanical Sound*. Cambridge, Mass: MIT Press, 2008.

Brady, Erika. *A Spiral Way*. Jackson: University of Mississippi Press, 1999.

Bull, Michael. *Sound Moves*. London: Routledge, 2007.

Butler, Mark J. *Playing with Something that Runs*. Oxford: Oxford University Press, 2014.

Daughtry, J. Martin. *Listening to War*. Oxford: Oxford University Press, 2015.

Denning, Michael. *Noise Uprising*. London: Verso, 2015.

DeNora, Tia. *Music and Everyday Life*. Cambridge: Cambridge University Press, 2000.

Dickinson, Kay. "Believe?: Vocoders, Digital Women and Camp," in *Popular Music*, vol. 20, no. 2, 2001, pp. 333–347.

Edison, Thomas A. "The Phonograph and Its Future," in *The North American Review*, vol. CXXVI, no. CCLXII, May/June 1878.

Eisenberg, Evan. *The Recording Angel*. New York: Penguin Books, 1988.

Fantel, Hans. "The Phonograph and Its Impact on the Art of Music," *New York Times*, December 21, 1986, p. H23.

Feaster, Patrick. "Phonography," in Novak, David and Sakakeeny, Matt eds. *Keywords in Sound*. Durham: Duke University Press, 2015, pp. 139–150.

Feaster, Patrick and Smith, Jacob. "Reconfiguring the History of Early Cinema Through the Phonograph," in *Film History*, vol. 21, 2009, pp. 311–325.

Fisher, Mark. "What is Hauntology?" in *Film Quarterly*, vol. 66, no. 1, Fall 2012, p. 16.

Fisher, Mark. "The Metaphysics of Crackle: Afrofuturism and Hauntology," in *Dancecult: Journal of Electronic Dance Music Culture*, vol. 5, no. 2, 2013.

Gitelman, Lisa. *Scripts, Grooves, and Writing Machines*. Stanford: Stanford University Press, 1999.

Goodman, Steve. *Sonic Warfare*. Cambridge, Mass: MIT Press, 2010.

Gopinath, Sumanth. *The Ringtone Dialectic*. Cambridge, Mass: MIT Press, 2013.

Gopinath, Sumanth and Stanyek, Jason eds. *Oxford Handbook of Mobile Music Studies, Vols. 1 & 2*. Oxford: Oxford University Press, 2014.

Gracyk, Theodore. *Rhythm and Noise: An Aesthetics of Rock*. Durham: Duke University Press, 1996.

Gracyk, Tim. *Popular American Recording Pioneers, 1895–1925*. Berkeley: University of California Press, 2013.

Gunning, Tom. "Re-newing Old Technologies: Astonishment, Second Nature and the Uncanny in Technology from the Previous Turn-of-the-Century," in Thornburn, David and Jenkins, Henry eds. *Rethinking Media Change: The Aesthetics of Transition*. Cambridge: MIT Press, 2003, pp. 39–60.

Hirschkind, Charles. *The Ethical Soundscape*. New York: Columbia University Press, 2009.

Horning, Schmidt Susan. *Chasing Sound*. Baltimore: Johns Hopkins University Press, 2013.

Kassabian, Anahid. *Ubiquitous Listening*. Berkeley: University of California Press, 2013.

Katz, Mark. *Capturing Sound*. Berkeley: University of California Press, 2010.

Kenney, William Howland. *Recorded Music in American Life*. New York: Oxford University Press, 1999.

Kittler, Friedrich A. *Gramophone, Film, Typewriter*. Stanford: Stanford University Press, 1999.

Koestenbaum, Wayne. *The Queen's Throat*. New York: Da Capo, 1993.

Krause, Bernie. *The Great Animal Orchestra*. London: Profile Books, 2012.

Lacey, Kate. *Listening Publics*. Cambridge: Polity Press, 2013.

Lane, Cathy and Carlyle, Angus eds. *In the Field: The Art of Field Recording*. Devon: Uniformbooks, 2013.

Lanza, Joseph. *Elevator Music*. Ann Arbor: University of Michigan Press, 2003.

Lastra, James. *Sound Technology and the American Cinema*. New York: Columbia University Press, 2000.

Majumdar, Neepa, "The Embodied Voice," in Wojcik, Pamela and Knight, Arthur eds. *Soundtrack Available*. Durham: Duke University Press, 2001, pp. 161–181.

Manuel, Peter. *Cassette Culture*. Chicago: University of Chicago Press, 1993.

Maurice, Alice. "Cinema at its Source: Synchronizing Race and Sound in the Early Talkies," *Camera Obscura*, vol. 17, no. 1, 2002.

McCracken, Allison. *Real Men Don't Sing*. Durham: Duke University Press, 2015.

Mills, Mara. "Do Signals Have Politics? Inscribing Abilities in Cochlear Implants," in Pinch, Trevor and Bijsterveld, Karin eds. *The Oxford Handbook of Sound Studies*. Oxford: Oxford University Press, 2011, pp. 320–346.

Mills, Mara. "Listening to Images: Audio Description, the Translation Overlay, and Image Retrieval," in *The Cine-Files*, vol. 8, Dossier on Film Sound, Spring 2015.

Morris, Jeremy Wade. *Selling Digital Music*. Berkeley: University of California Press, 2015.

Morton, David. *Off the Record*. New Brunswick, NJ: Rutgers University Press, 2000.

Morton, David L. *Sound Recording*. Baltimore: Johns Hopkins University Press, 2004.

Parelels, Jon. "Play It Again, Sam," *New York Times*, April 19, 1987, p. H24.

Russo, Alexander. *Points on the Dial*. Durham: Duke University Press, 2010.

Schafer, R. Murray. *The Soundscape: Our Sonic Environment and the Tuning of the World*. Rochester, Vermont: Destiny Books, 1994.

Sconce, Jeffrey. *Haunted Media*. Durham: Duke University Press, 2000.

Siefert, Marsha. "Aesthetics, Technology, and the Capitalization of Culture: How the Talking Machine Became a Musical Instrument," *Science in Context*, vol. 8, no. 2, 1995.

Smith, Jacob. *Vocal Tracks*. Berkeley: University of California Press, 2008.

Smith, Jacob. *Spoken Word*. Berkeley: University of California Press, 2011a.

Smith, Jacob "Turn Me On, Dead Media: A Backwards Look at the Re-enchantment of an Old Medium," in *Television and New Media*, vol. 12, no. 6, November 2011b, pp. 531–551.

Smith, Jacob. *Eco-Sonic Media*. Berkeley: University of California Press, 2015.

Stanyek, Jason and Piekut, Benjamin. "Deadness: Technologies of the Intermundane," in Sterne, Jonathan, "Sounds like the Mall of America," *Ethnomusicology*, vol. 41, no. 1, Winter 2012, pp. 22–50.

Sterne, Jonathan. *The Audible Past*. Durham: Duke University Press, 2003.

Suisman, David. *Selling Sounds*. Cambridge, Mass: Harvard University Press, 2009.

Taylor, Timothy. *Strange Sounds: Music, Technology and Culture*. New York: Routledge, 2009.

Thompson, Emily. "Machines, Music, and the Quest for Fidelity: Marketing the Edison Phonograph in America, 1877–1925," *The Musical Quarterly*, vol. 79, no. 1, Spring 1995.

Thompson, Emily. *The Soundscape of Modernity*. Cambridge, Mass: MIT Press, 2002.

Veal, Michael. *Dub*. Middletown: Wesleyan University Press, 2007.

Warner, Michael. *Publics and Counterpublics*. New York: Zone Books, 2002.

Weheliye, Alexander G. *Phonographies*. Durham: Duke University Press, 2005.

Weidman, Amanda. *Singing the Classical*. Durham: Duke University Press, 2006.

Weidman, Amanda. "Voice," in Novak, David and Sakakeeny, Matt eds. *Keywords in Sound*. Duke University Press, 2015, pp. 232–241.

Williams, Raymond. *Problems of Materialism and Culture*. London: Verso, 1980, p. 55.

30

RADIO SOUND

Alexander Russo

As befits a set of technologies and practices whose histories span well over 100 years, radio's relationship to sound has taken on many meanings depending on the social, cultural, technological, and historical contexts of its use. Some points of intersection between sound studies and radio studies lie in the following areas: radio sound as technologically mediated communication, radio sound and community and public formation, the aesthetics of radio sound and the radio voice, and radio sound and avant-garde practice. While this entry creates these categorical divisions for the purposes of typology, in practice, these concerns are more often mutually determining than analytically distinct.

A caveat: Radio sound encompasses frequencies that are perceivable by humans and those that are not. Radio sound is an encoding of sound on a radio wave via variations in amplitude AM or frequency FM. AM has a far more limited dynamic range and frequency response than FM. Dynamic range is the extent of loud to soft sounds and frequency response is the high and low range in pitch. Radio signals are optimized around human perceptive limits. For example, while an individual with exceptional hearing might hear sounds from 20hz to 20,000 hz, FM stations typically broadcast from 50hz to 15,000hz. Moreover, there are other sounds that are solely machine hearable, such as subcarrier frequency waves that have uses such as providing track information for visual display on receivers, produce stereophonic effects, or serving as a trigger for Emergency Broadcasting System alerts. While not radio per se, this approach reflects Jonathan Sterne's (2012) call to understand media history as a history of compression, rather than verisimilitude.

Defined at a general level, the technological parameters of radio sound is a sound wave transduced into an electrical signal which are amplified and distributed through space and reassembled into sound by a receiver. The signals themselves are not audible without further mediation via receiving technology. Thus, the 21st-century cellular "telephone" is known as "wireless" as it carries vast amounts of visual data in contradistinction to what wireless was understood to be 100 years ago. Indeed, the parameters of those communicative exchanges one to one or one to many have themselves changed form. Moreover, the meanings of those changes for the culture in which they operated carry with them an additional set of values. Radio sounds are, therefore, as much about social and cultural categories and points of unity and fracture as they are about the possibilities of technologies of transmission and reproduction.

Radio in the context of sound studies understands the broadcasting of acoustic artifacts as sound as such, rather than as a mode of content. For example, radio is most frequently used as a medium for the transmission of music, but rather than focus on the genres or formats that organize the content, we need to understand the sounds themselves. There are certainly some important interventions here, Jonathan Sterne (2003), Emily Thompson (2004), and Steve Wurtzler (2007) explore how radio technologies overlapped with other types of electrical amplification and reproduction, especially in the start of electrical reproduction. For these authors, the techniques of sonic production and reception heralded modes of modernity, via subjectivity, architectural acoustics, and institutions of cultural production. Although these works are not explicitly about radio, they rely on the historical fact that prior to the invention of electrical recording radio had greater sound fidelity than acoustically recorded phonograph records. Likewise, the FM band has greater sonic fidelity than the AM band, and this has affected the kinds of sounds that have been deemed appropriate for each. This distinction is not simply a practical one. In this volume, other sections address sound categories that overlap with radio sound. Radio advertising sounds provides one such example and leads to another caveat that radio sound cannot be understood in isolation from other forms of sound and techniques of reproduction and dissemination. With this in mind, there some conceptual concerns and categories of analysis that have addressed radio sound per se.

Radio sound: foundational approaches

Radio studies has recently begun to pay more attention to the sounds of radio as a cultural phenomenon. The first generations of radio histories tended to emphasize institutional and policy histories in part because of a perceived paucity of archival sound material. Encyclopedic, multivolume histories like Christopher Sterling and John Kittross (2001), Asa Briggs (1961, 1965, 1970, 1979, 1995) and Paddy Scannell and David Cardiff (1991) provide important institutional and technological context but devote less attention to the sounds of the programs themselves. Part of this neglect was due to the limited number of works that considered radio as sound.

Bertolt Brecht (2015) envisioned radio as a potentially democratizing force that allowed for participation by audience members and produced aspects of "epic theater" for radio. Rudolf Arnheim (1936) also saw in radio the potential for a communication not encumbered by vision. Arnheim is remarkable for offering one of the only discussions of the uniquely aural aspects of radio aesthetics. His account of the perceptual and spatial characteristics of sound theorized new modes of experience; ones that possessed a democratizing potential. His contemporaries, Theodor Adorno and Max Horkheimer (1997), were less optimistic and saw radio as a means of standardizing not just culture but thought itself. They reacted with alarm to the use of broadcasting by the Nazi party. This view of radio matched debates in the United States in which radio was viewed with some trepidation by scholars like Hadley Cantril's (1940) study of the "panic" surrounding Orson Welles' *War of the Worlds*. Although subsequent revisits to the incident have challenged the extent of the "panic," Cantril's work reflects anxiety about the seeming ability of radio to summon a credulity among certain segments of the listening populace. Other contemporaries were less troubled and the Paul Lazarsfeld-led radio studies (1940, 1941, 1948) reflect a more functionalist approach, which saw radio as meshing with existing institutions and belief systems.

Radio sound as technologically mediated communication

Radio sounds of intercommunication has its origins in a pre-broadcasting moment (although this too is contested as with the example of Radio Hirmondó, the telephone based wired broadcast network that preceded wireless radio). For early observers, radio sounds took the form of direct person-to-person communication via tones like the Morse Code. Here the sounds of transmission and reception were neither the voice nor intended for widespread reception. Even after the widespread introduction of music and voice broadcasting, short wave radio continued the tradition of coded and otherwise unintelligible transmission, as illustrated by the example of numbers stations run by government spy agencies to communicate with agents around the world. Conceptual radio sound as two-way communication speaks to some of the cultural imaginaries of communing with the dead, as chronicled by Jeffrey Sconce (2000). As Susan Douglas (1989, 2004) argues, ham radio operators offered forms of masculine mastery and exploration, even as the operators themselves were sometimes viewed as suspect. Interconnection also provides the groundwork for radical conceptions of radio such as Brecht's ideas of radio sound as democratic feedback loop. Although, as Sconce notes, these developments did not occur without some amount of anxiety. For Sconce, early radio's ability to connect across space and time was understood to exist even to the afterlife. Later, as a medium of broadcasting, the sounds from the speaker reflected anxieties about the decreasing autonomy of the individual within large networks and institutions. In contrast, the shift from one to many carries with it the symbolic weight of the receptive capabilities (or lack thereof) of the audience. The move to broadcast radio has been animated by its community defining characteristics.

Radio sound communities

Benedict Anderson's (2006) work on "imagined communities" has been widely utilized by radio scholars. While Anderson's work addressed the conjunction of print capitalism, vernacular languages, and national identity, radio's connective capacity and linguistic orientation has been seen as similarly reflective of a potential to facilitate communal identity. A range of authors has explored radio sound's capacity to unite and divide social groups. These related conversations have been anchored by the work of Michele Hilmes (1997) and Susan Douglas (2004). Hilmes looks at the ways in which race, class, and gender provide crucial cultural signifiers that anchored radio's potential to evade the visual signifiers of identity in interwar United States. The conjunction of economics, technology, and language allowed radio to circulate cultural narratives that defined "who we are and who we are not." For Hilmes, radio voices worked to both stabilize and undermine understandings of identity. Only certain types of speech were permitted and this worked to standardize and homogenize language. At the same time, however, radio's lack of visual referents also threatened to undermine the stability of visually determined racial markers and allowed for various types of cultural ventriloquism and cross dressing. Susan Douglas (2004) examines community formation via attention to modes of listening. At certain moments these identities were nationally based, but in other periods the sound-based communities revolved around modes of aural engagement, for example, imaginative listening of baseball games produced via sound effect and narration or intensive listening to high-fidelity psychedelic recordings in the 1960s. Building on these dynamics of broadcast sound and community, Alexander Russo (2010) and Susan Squier (2003) examine the ways in which communities defined at a smaller level than the nation also used aligned specialized content of radio broadcasts with cultural affinities. Russo argues that network radio was not wholly hegemonic. A parallel ecosphere of station representatives, radio transcription producers and distributors, and spot salesmen served to localize and regionalize national content in ways that appealed to geographically defined audiences. Squires' anthology reflects a range of work that focuses on the ways that race, class, and gender were activated by radio-based communities. Similarly, Ari Kelman (2009) and Delores Ines Casillas (2014) examine the complicated positions of, respectively, Yiddish and Spanish-language broadcasts within majority English-speaking United States seeing within them the ability to create sub-altern publics within the larger radio sphere.

Parallel histories of broadcasting and national community in other countries are addressed by authors like Joy Hayes (2000) on Mexican radio and Thomas Hajkowski's (2010) and Simon Potter's (2012) work on the ways that the imperial imagination accompanied British radio broadcasting. This nationalistic orientation informed the types of programs beamed from England but also influenced the ways in which British colonies such as Canada, New Zealand, and Australia modeled their national broadcasting services on that of the BBC – at least to some extent. As Canadian historian Mary Vipond (1992) argues, the commercial models of its Southern neighbor also influenced radio in Canada. In the postwar period, colonial independence movement also tapped into these elements of radio sound. Writing in 1965, Franz Fanon wrote on how the radio both gave listeners access to non-colonial forms of information, anti-colonial programs, and served as an index of their struggles based on the severing of jamming operations arrayed against anti-colonial programs. In another example, Brian Larkin (2008) looks at how the practice of public listening in Nigeria "reorganized the practice of leisure." Within the United States, radio served as a nexus for protest and negotiation over representation in sound-based programs and with their producers, as both Kathy Newman (2004) and Elena Razlogova (2011) have charted. Finally, Michele Hilmes argues that the sound of both British and American radio in the interwar period was based on global circuits between the two countries. Although ostensibly opposed to one another, the public and privately oriented systems defined themselves via the "constant precence of the other."

Radio sound publics

National identity can also have more ominous overtones depending on the form of government. There is a voluminous history of radio sound and propaganda. Kate Lacey (1996) and Carolyn Birdsall (2012) address the complex relationship of the Nazi government with its audiences and the ways it challenged straightforward distinctions between public and private. Steven Lovell's (2015) work on Soviet-era radio in Russia addresses the far different path taken in that country as a result of conflicting dictates of propaganda and popular programming. There are many histories of the Anglo-American radio propaganda as well. Holly Shulman (1990) examines how propaganda was conceptualized by the Voice of America as a means to achieve policy goals of the US government. Gerd Horten (2002) explores the ways that commercial entertainment was integrated into national propaganda apparatus during World War II. Sian Nicholas (1996) and Christina Baade (2011) examine similar dynamics in the UK during the same period although the latter author focuses on on musical broadcasts. Finally, Melissa Dinsman examines (2015) the efforts of literary modernists to craft radio programs that achieve maximum comprehension and propaganda value.

Questions of public and private sound have also engaged radio scholars to a significant degree. While in one sense radio offers public discourse, available to all who choose to listen, it is largely consumed privately, in individual homes and automobiles. This apparent contradiction has inspired a range of approaches and insights. Raymond Williams (2003) sees radio broadcasting as prefiguring television's mobile privatization in its centralizing address to individual homes. Jason Loviglio (2005) has highlighted the affective dimensions of the radio voice and how those connections blurred the boundaries of public and private, creating what Loviglio calls "intimate publics." Other authors like Douglas Craig (2000) and Bruce Lenthall (2008) are more identifiably political in their focus on politicians' use of radio. Finally, addressing the category public interest radio sound, Matthew Ehrlich (2011) examines the evolution of radio documentary in the postwar period, arguing that radio reflected a variety of strains of political thought even as it shifted from a docudrama to documentary mode. Similarly, Heather Hendershot (2011) examines how far-right conservatives ran afoul of public interest regulations in the 1950s and 1960s.

Radio sound and the voice

Another fruitful sonic arena for radio studies has been the voice. The radio voice has particular characteristics, chiefly its lack of corporeality. There are multiple implications of the disembodied electrical voice. For Marshall McLuhan (1994) the electrified radio voice was an "extension of man," a prosthetic that somewhat counterintuitively was a "hot" medium that directly affects the receiver of the message and makes the medium a resonant "tribal drum." For Michele Hilmes (1997) the disembodied voice has "uncanny" characteristics that "threaten to set off a riot of signifiers," particularly around identities like race and gender that are rooted in the body. John Durham Peters (1999) uses the disembodied voice to explore and express the ambiguities of the communication process, which tends to privilege the face to face above the mediated. Edward Miller (2003) argues that, during the 1930s, the newfound possibilities of listening to technologized, unseen voices resulted in "an uproarious connectedness" (Miller 2003: 8) an uncanniness of dread and powerlessness. Allison McCracken (2015) has recently charted the ways in which electrical amplification technologies allowed for the softer voice of crooning an intimacy via microphone technique. Christine Ehrick (2015) explores the ways that gendered hierarchies structured the soundscape of Argentinian and Uruguayan broadcasting during the 1930s and 1940s.

Radio sound aesthetics

Discussions of radio aesthetics engage with sound in both traditional and avant-garde forms. As far as traditional aesthetics, Andrew Crisell (1986) has charted a semiotic approach to radio sound. Following Arnheim, he controversially argued that radio is a "blind" medium. Other authors, like Tim Crook (1999), take issue with that characterization, noting that radio uses words and sound effects to create images within listeners' minds. Historical examinations of the BBC's aesthetic practices appear to be more significant as the United Kingdom has a longer and ongoing record of producing radio drama, as compared to the United States. See Peter Lewis (1981), John Drakakis (1981), Dermont Rattigan (2002), and Louis Niebur (2010) on the history of BBC radio drama. Rattigan and Niebur, in particular, focus on the elements of sonic performance in radio narratives and electronic effects, respectfully. Practices of literary adaption to radio, especially by modernist authors like Ezra Pound and Samuel Beckett, among others, have received special attention via Margaret Fisher (2002), Todd Avery (2006), Timothy Campbell (2006), Kevin Branigan (2008), Debra Cohn et al (2009), Jeff Porter (2016), and Matthew Feldman et al. (2014). The histories of American radio aesthetics have been written by Shawn VanCour (forthcoming) and Neil Verma (2012). VanCour explores the process by which radio producers both modified existing dermatological techniques of the stage and created new radio-specific features that would define the boundaries and practices of radio drama. Verma addresses a later time period, arguing that radio expressed changing models of the imagination, in essence serving as a proxy for cultural understanding of mental processes. Significantly, his model of the spatial positioning of the listener that itself was a proxy for political movements and the hopes and fears of radio's power. Additionally, Michael Socolow (2016) examines the ways that radio broadcasts of the 1936 established techniques of sporting spectacle that would carry over into television.

On the side of avant-garde radio sound, Douglas Khan's collaboration with Gregory Whitehead (1992) produced a collection of essays on radio art that jump-started an extended conversation in the 1990s. Radio served as a venue for sound-based arts to exhibit their work and as a source of institutional and technological support. Artists like Pierre Schaeffer, for one, picked up their craft through their experience as radio sound engineers. In this respect although Douglas Kahn's (1999) monograph focuses on how "practices of inscription," like the return of the repressed, bubble up frequently and repeatedly in radio transmission. Daina Augaitis et al. (1994) provide an essay collection that covers various avant-garde practices. Allen Weiss (1995) sees modernist themes of alienation and the fracturing of the self in the radio body. He sees the work of avant-garde radio artists such as Antonin Artaud and Valère Novarina as prefiguring what cultural critics of the 1980s and 1990s described as postmodernism's schizophrenic subjectivity. Daniel Gilfillan (2009) looks at German radio as a site for aesthetic innovation in the Weimer and Postwar periods and Louis Niebur (2010) examines the history of the BBC's Radiophonic Workshop to mine its influential role in bringing experimental, electronic sounds to British radio drama from the late 1950s through the 1990s.

Listening to radio sound

Although much radio scholarship has focused on the technologies of sound reproduction, the aesthetics and of radio sounds like voice and sound effects as signifiers, and the types of communication enabled, a final category of analysis is the practice of listening. Scholars in this vein utilize different methodologies and approaches, but all engage with questions that stem directly from sound studies. Paddy Scannell's (1991) phenomenological engagement discussion of listening places it within the context of structuring everyday life. Jo Tacchi's (1997) oral histories of radio listening provide a material history of reception. David Goodman (2011) examines anxieties around distracted listening in the 1930s and how radio sought to address anxieties around passive reception via its "civic ambition." Charles Fairchild (2012) critiques contemporary commercial radio aesthetic and argues for a set of aural aesthetics that will facilitate democracy. Additionally, Kate Lacey (2013) puts listening at the center of the public sphere. She argues against an artificial binary that sees the voice and the word as central to the constitution of publics and relegates listening to the sidelines as mere reception. In contrast, she sees listening as an active practice that "bridges both the realm of sensory embodied experience *and* the political realm of debate and deliberation" (Lacey 2013: 8).

In the twenty-first century, the boundaries of radio sound have become porous. The techniques of "reality radio" (Biewen and Dilworth 2010) that have invigorated long-form audio narrative on public broadcasters have proven durable enough to transfer to other modes of distribution via internet-based podcasts. Thus, while certain aural aesthetics are triumphant, other key characteristics, like liveness and transmission, are no longer essential. The convenience of feed-based online distribution makes non-synchronous listening not only possible, but preferable. Smartphones allow for the portable storage of programs that both replicate and extend the aural aesthetics of radio drama and documentary. Like cable and on-demand video producers, radio producers have discovered that being freed from the shackles of the broadcast clock (and its attendant assumptions about listener attention) allows for greater flexibility and creativity in audio forms. The entrance of private equity financing into audio production has allowed for an explosion of high quality programming but also raises issues about the future role of public broadcasting. In recent years, special issues of radio-oriented journals have begun to address these questions of media specificity within the podcast-era. Convergence media have had a similar effect on other media, whose definitions become fuzzier by the minute. Still, the robust histories of broadcast sound as a form of representational technology promise future innovations and cultural import.

References

Adorno, T.W. and Horkheimer, M., (1997). *Dialectic of Enlightenment.* Verso Books.

Anderson, B., 2006. *Imagined Communities: Reflections on the Origin and Spread of Nationalism.* Verso Books.

Arnheim, R. (1936) *Radio.* Faber & Faber.

Augaitis, D., Lander, D., Moser, M.A., Berland, J., Bull, H., Ready, P., Kittler, F., Westerkamp, H., Kahn, D., Migone, C. and Grundmann, H., 1994. *Radio Rethink: Art, Sound and Transmission: Selected Survey of Radio Art in Canada, 1967–1992.* Walter Phillips Gallery.

Avery, T. 2006. *Radio Modernism: Literature, Ethics, and the BBC, 1922–1938.* University of Massachusetts Press.

Baade, C.L., 2011. *Victory Through Harmony: The BBC and Popular Music in World War II.* Oxford University Press.

Biewen, J. and Dilworth, A. eds., 2010. *Reality Radio: Telling True Stories in Sound.* University of North Carolina Press.

Birdsall, C., 2012. *Nazi Soundscapes: Sound, Technology and Urban Space in Germany, 1933–1945.* Amsterdam University Press.

Branigan, K., 2008. *Radio Beckett: Musicality in the Radio Plays of Samuel Beckett.* Peter Lang.

Brecht, B., 2015. *Brecht on Film & Radio.* Bloomsbury Publishing.

Briggs, A., 1961, 1965, 1970, 1979. 1995. *The History of Broadcasting in the United Kingdom. Vols 1–5.* Oxford University Press.

Campbell, T.C., 2006. *Wireless Writing in the Age of Marconi* (Vol. 16). University of Minnesota Press.

Cantril, H., 1940. *The Invasion from Mars: A Study in the Psychology of Panic.* Transaction Publishers.

Casillas, D.I., 2014. *Sounds of Belonging: A Cultural History of Spanish-Language Radio in the United States, 1922–2004.* University of California Press.

Craig, D.B., 2000. *Fireside Politics: Radio and Political Culture in the United States, 1920–1940.* Johns Hopkins University Press.

Crisell, A., 1986. *Understanding Radio.* Methuen.

Crook, T. 1999. *Radio Drama: Theory and Practice.* Psychology Press.

Dinsman, M., 2015. *Modernism at the Microphone: Radio, Propaganda, and Literary Aesthetics During World War II.* Bloomsbury Publishing.

Douglas, S.J., 1989. *Inventing American Broadcasting, 1899–1922.* Johns Hopkins University Press.

Douglas, S.J., 2004. *Listening in: Radio and the American Imagination.* University of Minnesota Press.

Drakakis, J., 1981. *British Radio Drama.* Cambridge University Press.

Ehrick, Christine, 2015, *Radio and the Gendered Soundscape: Women and Broadcasting in Argentina and Uruguay, 1930–1950.* Cambridge University Press.

Ehrlich, Matthew. 2011. *Radio Utopia: Postwar Audio Documentary in the Public Interest.* University of Illinois Press.

Fairchild, C., 2012. *Music, Radio and the Public Sphere: The Aesthetics of Democracy.* Palgrave Macmillan.

Fanon, F., 1965. "This is the Voice of Algeria." *A Dying Colonialism.* New York: Monthly Review, pp. 69–98.

Feldman, M., Mead, H. and Tonning, E. eds., 2014. *Broadcasting in the Modernist Era.* Bloomsbury Publishing.

Fisher, Margaret, 2002. *Ezra Pound's Radio Operas: the BBC Experiments, 1931–1933.* MIT Press.

Gilfillan, D., 2009. *Pieces of Sound: German Experimental Radio.* University of Minnesota Press.

Goodman, D., 2011. *Radios Civic Ambition: American Broadcasting and Democracy in the 1930s.* Oxford University Press.

Hajkowski, T., 2010. *The BBC and National Identity in Britain, 1922–53.* Oxford University Press.

Hayes, J.E., 2000. *Radio Nation: Communication, Popular Culture, and Nationalism in Mexico, 1920–1950.* University of Arizona Press.

Hendershot, Heather. 2011. *What's Fair on the Air: Cold War Right-Wing Broadcasting and the Public Interest.* University of Chicago Press.

Hilmes, M., 1997. *Radio Voices: American Broadcasting, 1922–1952.* University of Minnesota Press.

Horten, G., 2002. *Radio Goes to War: The Cultural Politics of Propaganda during World War II.* University of California Press.

Kahn, D. and Whitehead, G., 1992. *Wireless Imagination Sound, Radio, and the Avant-Garde.* Routledge.

Kahn, D., 1999. *Noise, Water, Meat: A History of Sound in the Arts.* MIT Press.

Kelman, A.Y., 2009. *Station Identification: A Cultural History of Yiddish Radio in the United States.* University of California Press.

Lacey, K., 1996. *Feminine Frequencies: Gender, German Radio, and the Public Sphere, 1923–1945*. University of Michigan Press.

Lacey, K., 2013. *Listening Publics: The Politics and Experience of Listening in the Media Age*. John Wiley & Sons.

Larkin, B., 2008. *Signal and Noise: Media, Infrastructure, and Urban Culture in Nigeria*. Duke University Press.

Lazarsfeld, P.F., 1940. *Radio and the Printed Page*. Duell, Sloan, and Pearce.

Lazarsfeld, P.F. and Stanton, F., 1941. *Radio Research, 1941*. Duell, Sloan, and Pearce.

Lazarsfeld, P.F., 1948. *Radio Listening in America*. Prentice-Hall.

Lenthall, B., 2008. *Radio's America: The Great Depression and the Rise of Modern Mass Culture*. University of Chicago Press.

Lewis, P.E., 1981. *Radio Drama*. Longman Publishing Group. D.

Lovell, S., 2015. *Russia in the Microphone Age: A History of Soviet Radio, 1919–1970*. Oxford University Press.

Loviglio, J., 2005. *Radio's Intimate Public: Network Broadcasting and Mass-Mediated Democracy*. University of Minnesota Press.

McCracken, A., 2015. *Real Men Don't Sing: Crooning in American Culture*. Duke University Press.

McLuhan, M., 1994. *Understanding Media: The Extensions of Man*. MIT Press.

Miller, E.D., 2003. *Emergency Broadcasting and 1930s American Radio*. Temple University Press.

Newman, K.M., 2004. *Radio active: Advertising and consumer activism, 1935–1947*. University of California Press.

Nicholas, S., 1996. *The Echo of War: Home Front Propaganda and the Wartime BBC, 1939–1945*. Palgrave Macmillan.

Niebur, L., 2010. *Special Sound: The Creation and Legacy of the BBC Radiophonic Workshop*. Oxford University Press.

Peters, J.D., 1999. *Speaking into the Air: A History of the Idea of Communication*. University of Chicago Press.

Porter, J. 2016. *Lost Sound: The Forgotten Art of Radio Storytelling*. University of North Carolina Press.

Potter, S.J., 2012. *Broadcasting Empire: the BBC and the British world, 1922–1970*. Oxford University Press.

Rattigan, D., 2002. *Theatre of Sound: Radio and the Dramatic Imagination*. Carysfort Pr.

Razlogova, E., 2011. *The Listener's Voice: Early Radio and the American Public*. University of Pennsylvania Press.

Russo, A., 2010. *Points on the Dial: Golden Age Radio Beyond the Networks*. Duke University Press.

Scannell, P. and Cardiff, D., 1991. *A Social History of British Broadcasting*. Basil Blackwell.

Scannell, P., 1991. *Broadcast Talk* Sage.

Shulman, H.C., 1990. *The Voice of America: Propaganda and Democracy, 1941–1945*. University of Wisconsin Press.

Sconce, J. 2000. *Haunted Media: Electronic Presence from Telegraphy to Television*. Duke University Press.

Socolow, M. 2016. *Six Minutes in Berlin: Broadcast Spectacle and Rowing Gold at the Nazi Olympics*. University of Illinois Press.

Squier, S.M. ed., 2003. *Communities of the Air: Radio Century, Radio Culture*. Duke University Press.

Sterne, J. 2003. *The Audible Past: Cultural Origins of Sound Reproduction*. Duke University Press.

Sterne, J. 2012. *MP3: The meaning of a format*. Duke University Press.

Sterling, C.H. and Kittross, J.M., 2001. *Stay Tuned: A History of American Broadcasting*. Routledge.

Tacchi, J.A., 1997. *Radio Sound as Material Culture in the Home* (Doctoral dissertation, University of London).

Thompson, E.A., 2004. *The Soundscape of Modernity: Architectural Acoustics and the Culture of Listening in America, 1900–1933*. MIT Press.

VanCour, S. (forthcoming) *Making Radio: Early Radio Production and the Rise of Modern Sound Culture*. Oxford University Press..

Verma, N., 2012. *Theater of the Mind: Imagination, Aesthetics, and American Radio Drama*. University of Chicago Press.

Vipond, M., 1992. *Listening In: The First Decade of Canadian Broadcasting, 1922–1932*. McGill-Queen's University Press.

Weiss, A. 1995. *Phantasmic Radio*. Duke University Press.

Williams, R., 2003. *Television: Technology and Cultural Form*. Routledge.

Wurtzler, S.J., 2007. *Electric Sounds: Technological Change and the Rise of Corporate Mass Media.*. Columbia University Press.

31

STRUCTURES OF SONIC FEELING

Tom Artiss

I begin again to ask myself what it could have been, this unremembered state which brought with it no logical proof of its existence, but only the sense that it was a happy, that it was a real state in whose presence other states of consciousness melted and vanished. I decide to attempt to make it reappear ... I find again the same state, illumined by no fresh light ... I do not know yet what it is, but I can feel it mounting slowly; I can measure the resistance, I can hear the echo of great spaces traversed.

(Marcel Proust 2005)

For three hours each weekday afternoon in the northern Canadian Inuit community of Nain, Labrador, the daily broadcast of the local radio station (OKâlaKatiget) can be heard in almost every enclosed space with a functioning electrical socket. Programming includes local news, public service announcements, personal messages, bingo, and music, all contributing as much to local auditory life as yelping husky dogs and shifting sea ice. Drawing from ethnographic research conducted in Nain, this chapter introduces and discusses technologically mediated *structures of sonic feeling*: imprints of hearing experiences that articulate subjective constellations of sound, time, and space.

In the soundscapes created by radio in Nain, structures of sonic feeling are formed in different ways, on multiple levels, and with varied intensities over time. Particular radio announcers, musical selections, news themes, programming formats, broadcasting technology, and community members in the mid-1980s, for example, combined in ways that make the overall sound experience recognizably distinct from the one resulting from a similar combination today. From this, I am concerned, first, with the affective force of mediated sound, and second, with the human interventions into its fields of reception, converted and repurposed by hearing actors from products of sound-making technology into means for the production and circulation of affective subjectivities.

One's noise, another's music

Technologically mediated sounds may predate Alexander Graham Bell, but their theoretical provenance can be located in R. Murray Schafer's acoustic ecology (1994 [1977]). Soundscapes – Schafer's auditory equivalent to landscapes – were, in part, a prescriptive solution to noise pollution. The problem, as he saw it, was not a technologically enhanced cacophony but, rather, our responses to it: noises "are the sounds we have learned to ignore" (Schafer 1994: 4). If the tendency is to block out undesirable sounds, Schafer believed we should be attuned to the whole *mix*, to discriminate between "destructive sounds" and those that ought to be "preserved" (ibid.). Developing a discriminating ear – "clairaudience" or "clear hearing" (ibid.: 10, 11) – is key to a heightened appreciation of all sound experience, both as aesthetic raw materials and as musical compositions (ibid.: 5): "Today all sounds belong to a continuous field of possibilities lying *within the comprehensive dominion of music*. Behold the new orchestra: the sonic universe! ... And the musicians: anyone and anything that sounds!" (ibid.: 5, his emphasis).

Structures of sonic feeling, as a category of analysis, emerges from Schafer's "soundscapes" (co-extensive here with music), but there are at least two ruptures in its genealogy. The first has to do with his interest in soundscapes as a socio-historical analytic. Following Marshall McLuhan (1962) – himself indebted to Harold Innis (1951) – Schafer identifies structural relationships between societies and their sonic production, writing that

> music is an indicator of the age, revealing, for those who know how to read its symptomatic messages, a means of fixing social and even political events ... the general acoustic environment of a society can be read as an indicator of social conditions which produce it and may tell us much about the trending and evolution of that society.
>
> *(ibid.: 7)*

The idea that music reflects society was a significant extension of contemporary scholarship occupied primarily with music itself, presuming a cultural product independent of social, political, and historical forces. But the homology model – music as index – has since been extended by authors identifying ways in which music not only reflects but also inflects its social and historical contexts (Frith 1996; Stokes 1994; Feld 1996; Born and Hesmondhalgh 2000). While acknowledging a debt to Schafer's contributions, Steven Feld identifies a structuralist slant that sonically analogizes landscape, distances agency from perception, replaces occularcentrism with sonocentrism, and isolates sound from human and non-human relations (Feld 2015: 15). His alternative, "acoustemology," is a theorization of sounding and listening that "centralizes situated listening in engagements with place and space-time ... and prioritizes histories of listening and sounding and their reflexive productions of feedback" (ibid.). I will return to subjective, agential interventions in sonic space and place below. For now, three more terms from Schafer's acoustic ecology are relevant: "keynote sounds," "signals," and "soundmarks" (1994: 9).

Keynotes are "the sounds over which a culture is created" (Schafer: 2005). They are ubiquitous, quotidian sounds such as the scratching of a quill pen on paper in early modern times, or the electrical hums of lighting systems and air conditioning today (ibid.) – the sonic backdrops of a society in history. Signals, by contrast, are deliberately prominent and include sounds made by mobile phones and train whistles. Soundmarks, which receive the bulk of Schafer's attention, are "sounds that obtrude over the acoustic horizon ... prominent sounds possessing properties of uniqueness, symbolic power, or other qualities that make them especially conspicuous or respectfully regarded" (ibid.). Highlighting a parallel between soundmarks and landmarks, Schafer proposes thinking about a foghorn in Vancouver in much the same way as we regard a cathedral, castle, or bank tower (ibid.). Unlike keynotes (mundane) and signals (grating), "once a soundmark has been identified, it deserves to be protected, for soundmarks make the community unique" (1994: 10). To extend Schafer's architecture metaphor, if "a bicycle shed is a building; Lincoln Cathedral is a piece of architecture" – as *Buildings of England* author Nikolas

Pevsner once opined (in Sutton 1999: 7) – then ringtones are noise and foghorns are musical instruments. Just as a cathedral rises above its surrounding urban grime and chaos, soundmarks represent sonic cultural value against a backdrop of noise pollution. But what about the mundane sounds of everyday life that *are* registered, significant, and meaningful? Do not subjective responses to sounds vary? Can one person's noise be another's music?

To share an example from my own experience, each Friday, usually around 6:30 a.m., the recycling is collected on my street of Victorian terrace houses in North London. For a lot of people in the area, sounds made by the contents of green plastic recycling boxes as they are emptied into larger plastic wheeled bins – which in turn are emptied into collection trucks – is a familiar one. For me, it starts faintly in the distance at the end of the street and gradually gets louder with each repetition, until the council worker reaches my box, on the sidewalk just below my bedroom window. As the rhythm continues, the volume fades. It takes a team of three workers approximately twenty minutes to collect all the recycling on my street and if I am asleep, the sound usually wakes me up. Having lived here for several years, numerous responses are triggered. If I haven't put the box out the night before, it is panic. In general, though, the sound has become intertwined with a subjective history of people, place, and time; interconnected individual experiences related to, for example, love, death, professional successes/failures, and even important global events – for the latter, a sound that punctuated *this* place when *that* happened.

Notably, the singular designs and materials of both the bins and their contents produce sounds unique to them and their combinations. If the bins were tin, as they might have been twenty or thirty years ago and perhaps still are in other urban centres, the sounds produced would differ in significant ways. The particular layout of terrace houses also contributes to a distinct resonance. My street is unusually wide, like a boulevard, and is broken up at the halfway point by a garden square. While similar sounds may be repeated in other streets and boroughs, variations in materials, design and context can result in subtle differences that may not be perceptible at a cognitive level but might be registered at an affective one. This means that the sounds of recycling collection at another time and place are less likely to produce an equivalent affective response, although occasionally they will. The result – a unique, technology-afforded sonic composition – is an important feature of my cultural-sensorial tapestry. Even if they have no composer, the mundane, contingent character of sounds such as these does not make them less culture-bound.

As Raymond Williams noted in the 1960s and 1970s, while the formal and inscribed aspects of bourgeois cultural production are easy to mistake for culture itself, if culture is limited to symphonies, plays, poetry, novels, etc., a lot of people – especially, for him, the working classes – would be left with no culture at all. Williams saw this as an analytical shortcoming, not an existential one. If established gauges were ruling out culture in large swathes of the population, then the gauges were inadequate, not the groups being considered. Culture, he answered, "is not only a body of intellectual and imaginative work, it is also and essentially a whole way of life" (Williams 1960: 344). Turning the lens away from cultural artifacts of the bourgeoisie, he focused instead on a neglected substrate of "living practices." These "structures of feeling" – also described by him as "characteristic elements of tone" and "social experience in solution" – are elusive because the phenomena they refer to are "at the cusp of semantic availability" (Williams 1977: 132–33). Perhaps it is for this reason that subsequent interpretations and applications vary greatly; the concept's vagueness may even contribute to its appeal. Named but not defined, structures of feeling can do a lot of different work.

As for the recycling on my street, what was initially an undesirable sound that woke me up early most Friday mornings eventually became a distinct, intangible artifact in my living sensory archive. It does not need a place on a value-spectrum to become culturally significant.

Schafer's soundmarks, like landmarks, are those salient, inscribed referents of sonic space that, by their prominence and prestige, overshadow and diminish keynotes and signals. But the everyday noises, ones that do not qualify as soundmarks, can also inform our understanding of soni- cally mediated social space-time. Structures of sonic feeling are not constituted via "important" sounds alone. Their emergence and continuity rely equally on everyday, mundane sounds, even those that might be thought of as sources of noise pollution. They are the sonic extension of Williams' expanded version of culture. But that is not all.

DItY (doing it to yourself) with music

As a shorthand for "tonal" elements of quotidian social experience, structures of feeling became a foundational concept for theorists concerned with ways in which affects are entangled with sense objects and how these intersections inform social understanding, relationality, and agency. Kathleen Stewart's ordinary affects, for example, form clusters around objects, scenes, and tech- nologies. Sensory triggers such as sound, smell, and taste form host structures for the articulation and expression of common emotions and feelings (2007: 1–6). The ways in which affects cling to sense objects is the first of two related themes addressed in the remainder of this chapter.

Daily throughout the year, OKâlaKatiget receives dozens of requests for songs to be played on air. When a request is phoned in – the most common method – a receptionist writes down the details on recycled paper, ruler-torn especially for the purpose into approximately 3 × 5-inch slips. Each request includes the title of the song, the name of the requester, and the name of the person or persons to whom it is dedicated. Requests frequently include the reason why some- thing is being requested (e.g., birthday, wedding anniversary, condolences for a deceased loved one, congratulations for an achievement, etc.), and, occasionally, a personalized message (e.g, "lots of love from Mom," "love you and miss you"). Depending on the time of year, the number of requests can range from a dozen to over fifty per day.

Sharing and connecting are the most evident and frequent reasons to request a song. Expres- sions of friendship and love – both familial and romantic – are common. Much more rare are songs requested to unload or inflict negative sentiments such as anger, jealousy, or resentment. On one occasion *Who Let The Dogs Out* by Baha Men was dedicated to the current lover of the requester's ex-husband. After a hastily called meeting, three radio producers decided not to play it because they thought the intent was spiteful. While examples like this are rare, they indicate the extent to which requested songs are laden with affective potency. More common were songs requested to call up painful past experiences.

For Gordon Obed, a radio producer and DJ at the station, Kris Kristofferson's *Road Warrior's Lament* reminds him of his young grandson, who died in a tragic boating accident. The song was played at his grandson's funeral and has since become an "anthem of lost loved ones" (Obed, 2010). He says that even though hearing it makes him sad, he does not mind playing it on air when requested by others. Sometimes he plays it unprompted. Other times, when he is not working, he calls in to request it himself (ibid.). He does not want to keep reliving the tragedy, and yet he continues to be drawn to a song that reminds him of it.

On one level, the relationship between requester and song is a private one, indexing feel- ings and emotions within the individual subject. Tia DeNora has theorized similar private engagements with music in terms of the creation, care, and maintenance of emotional iden- tities (DeNora 1999: 32). As a "technology of the self," she writes, music serves as "a resource to which people turn in order to regulate themselves as aesthetic agents, as feeling, thinking, and acting beings in their day-to-day lives" (ibid.: 45). In DeNora's terms, Obed requests *Road Warrior's Lament* "for the ongoing work of self-construction, and the emotional, memory, and biographical work that that project entails" (ibid.: 32). "Musical materials," she writes, "provide the terms and templates for elaborating self-identity," for listeners to "literally 'find' themselves in musical structures" (ibid.: 49). Here DeNora is adding a musical perspective to a constructivist line of inquiry in cultural sociology about the subject in late modernity. Erving Goffman's dramaturgical social interaction (1956) and the theorizations of Ulrich Beck and Anthony Giddens advancing reflexive modernity (Beck 1992; Giddens 1990, 1991) are notable precursors. Lash and Urry follow with "aesthetic reflexivity" denoting non-cognitive processes of self-maintenance associated with artistic consumption (Lash and Urry 1994). I propose extending this line a step further to consider processes of emotional self-regulation as *affective* reflexivity.

Marcel Proust famously describes this process in *Swann's Way*, the first volume of *In Search of Lost Time*. The passage in question relates how a morsel of madeleine cake dipped in tea unlocked intense feelings from his childhood in Combray (2005: 51–54). Chance encounters such as these – that take us deep into our emotional repositories and activate long-forgotten or dormant sense-memories – are not uncommon; most have experienced something similar. However, while the accidental, taste-triggered reunion with a sensing and feeling past is the theme for which his lines are most remembered, what follows – his subsequent efforts to recapture "this all-powerful joy" (ibid.: 51) – is equally important. Like a scientist in a lab, he tries to recreate the conditions that preceded the effect, first with tea and cake, and then by returning with his mind to the critical moment. In the end, he manages both to reactivate the sense-experience and to identify the precise, buried memory associated with it.

For Proust, the madeleine became an instrument of affective reflexivity, the means for a purposive engagement with the sense–emotion environment and, by extension, for the mediation of emotional subjectivity. In terms of analysis, from here we can identify different levels of technological mediation where mediating properties shift from the technologies themselves to their products. Sound recording technologies, for example, have made it increasingly possible, easy even, to refashion, rework, reconfigure other people's creative outputs. Cut and paste approaches to music production like the mash-up, collage, and remix are now ubiquitous modes of contemporary expression. In the context of DIY music cultures, and their relationships to space and place, found musical objects are repurposed to make new music objects.

For Thomas Porcello, the recording studio is a site of both creation and documentation, where engineering technologies are used to invent new sounds and replicate natural ones (2005: 273). Working from Feld, he proposes "techoustemology" as a way to describe technological mediation that implicates contemporary thought-, feeling-, and action-responses to acoustic environments (ibid.: 270). One of his aims is to shift the focus from "the examination of the products of sound engineering" to "the processes of engineering as a vital aspect of contemporary cultural life" (ibid.: 269). While structures of sonic feeling are tied to these processes – or "everyday *uses* of technology by social actors" (ibid.) – they differ in one key respect. Whereas Porcello is primarily concerned with the ways in which actors "craft sonic artifacts and environments," structures of sonic feeling looks beyond the processes of creating artifacts and environments to the ways the outcomes of these processes are themselves received, engaged, and utilized – strategically or otherwise – to craft feelingful subjectivities. Returning to Schafer and Feld, then, to techoustemology, we can add the emotional and psychological tactility of sound. "Hearing," as Schafer writes, "is a way of touching at a distance" (1994: 11). By looking at ways in which the soundscapes of media are engaged as technologies of the self, the recording studio of Porcello can be a metaphor for the soundscapes they help create, as sites and means of a different kind of subjective production.

With structures of feeling, Williams presages recent contributions by theorists of affect seeking to understand and interpret a range of extra-cognitive phenomena heretofore largely understudied (Stewart 2007; Blackman 2012, 2008; Gregg and Seigworth et al.; 2010; Berlant 2011, 1998; Massumi 2002, 1995; Brennan 2004; Deleuze and Guattari 1987). Teresa Brennan locates a substrate of emotions independent of the individual experiencing them (2004: 13) and suggests "affects find thoughts that suit them, not the other way around" (ibid.: 7). Similarly, Brian Massumi, interpreting Deleuze, defines affect as a "pre-personal intensity" (Deleuze and Guattari 1987: xvi). In such terms, underneath – or before – the unique personal experiences articulated via the sounds of recycling collection, for example, exist basic, raw, autonomic, even biological affective capacities and potencies common to all. In theory, such a prepersonal plane, independent of individual experience – desires, intentions, agency – is not subject to individual interventions and engagements, strategic or otherwise. I am suggesting, by contrast, that structures of sonic feeling arise from co-presences of and movements between these two ideal states, personal and prepersonal.

This is not a new idea. As early as 1993, Mark Slobin was writing that "music seems to have an odd quality that even passionate activities like gardening or dog-raising lack: the simultaneous projecting and dissolving of the self" (Slobin 1993: 141). And Simon Frith in 1996 writes that "we both express ourselves and suborn ourselves – or lose ourselves – in acts of musical participation" (Frith 1996: 110). Ethnographic examples of musically mediated social interactions also reveal co-presences of or movements between these states. Returning to the Obed example, requesting or playing *Road Warrior's Lament* is an assertion of selfhood, in the form of proprietary feelings (*his* grief), *and* a mainline into a collective plane of "singularity" (Deleuze 2001: 25–34). In a community where few have escaped the tragic loss of a loved one, grief is something almost everyone shares.

Conclusion

This chapter merges and extends several distinct but interconnected theoretical trajectories that overlap in selected ways to offer a category of analysis mirrored in practice, which I am calling structures of sonic feeling. R. Murray Schafer's acoustic ecology establishes capacities for subjective constellations to take shape around audition. But like the bourgeois culture of Raymond Williams's critiques – which might admit cathedrals but reject bicycle sheds – it also presumes a hierarchy. Williams's answer, structures of feeling, recognizes a substrate of experience-based cultural sensibilities distinct from the forms they may take. For him, cathedrals, operas, and foghorns are expressions of culture, not culture itself. Similarly, quotidian sonic experiences such as recycling collection on my street can become extra-linguistic cultural artifacts in our living sensory archives. But again, as with Proust – where the relationship between Combray and a madeleine, between source and trigger, is half the story – structures of sonic feeling are not fully realized until their affective field is reflexively engaged. Whereas Porcello emphasizes ways in which subjectivity is brought to bear on music production via technology, towards a reconfigured musical end, DeNora shows the reverse is also possible: technologically mediated sound used as a means for the reconfiguration of the feeling self. In short, I am proposing that DeNora's technologies of the self can be stretched ever so slightly to cover the affective tactility of mediated sound and how it is engaged to both assert and dissolve the feeling subject.

While technologies that did not exist in Proust's time are clearly not a necessary condition for affective reflexivity, they certainly can enhance it, as David Bowie presciently observes:

> The context and the state of content is going to be so different to anything we can envisage at the moment, where the interplay between the user and the provider is going to be so sympatico, it's going to crush our ideas of what mediums are all about.

It's happening in visual art. The breakthroughs at the early part of the century; people like Duchamp were so prescient with what they were doing and putting down. The idea that the piece of work is not finished until the audience come to it and add their own interpretation and what the piece of art is about is the grey space in the middle. That grey space in the middle is what the 21st century is going to be about.

(David Bowie 1999)

Via the radio station in Nain, *Road Warrior's Lament* and other frequently requested songs fill out and enliven Bowie's "grey space in the middle," creating structures of sonic feeling, activated and reactivated by subsequent song requests. And if we zoom out from the particular relationship between a requested song and its attendant structures of sonic feeling, and consider, for example, the sonic space resulting from a single day's three-hour broadcast, involving a dozen or more requested songs, a constellation of structures of sonic feeling is generated from a patchwork of songs – a collage, a mash-up, a remix of feeling selves. If DIY means doing music yourself, then DItY is doing structures of sonic feeling to your self with music.

References

Beck, U. (1992) *Risk Society*, London: Sage Publications.

Berlant, L. (1998) "Intimacy: A Special Issue," *Critical Inquiry*, 24 (2), 281–88.

_____ (2011) *Cruel Optimism*, Durham, NC: Duke University Press.

Blackman, L. (2008) "Affect, Relationality and the Problem of Personality," *Theory, Culture & Society*, 25 (1), 23–47.

_____ (2012) *Immaterial Bodies: Affect, Embodiment, Mediation*, London: Sage Publications.

Born, G. and D. Hesmondhalgh (2000) "Introduction: On Difference, Representation, and Appropriation in Music," in G. Born and D. Hesmondhalgh (eds) *Western Music and its Others: Difference, Representation, and Appropriation in Music* (1–58), Berkeley, CA: University of California Press.

Bowie, D. (1999) "David Bowie Speaks to Jeremy Paxman on BBC Newsnight," YouTube (www.youtube.com/watch?v=FiK7s_0tGsg), accessed 12.5.16.

Brennan, T. (2004) *The Transmission of Affect*, Ithaca, NY: Cornell University Press.

Deleuze, G. (2001) *Pure Immanence: Essays on a Life*, New York, NY: Urzone.

_____ and F. Guattari (1987) *A Thousand Plateaus: Capitalism and Schizophrenia* (trans. B. Massumi), Minneapolis, MN, and London: University of Minnesota Press.

DeNora, T. (1999) "Music as a Technology of the Self," *Poetics*, 27, 31–56.

Feld, S. (1996) "Waterfalls of Song: An Acoustemology of Place Resounding in Bosavi, Papua New Guinea," in S. Feld and K. Basso (eds) *Senses of Place* (91–135), Santa Fe, NM: School of American Research Press.

_____ (2015) "Acoustemology," in D. Novak and M. Sakakeeny (eds) *Keywords in Sound* (12–21) Durham, NC: Duke University Press.

Frith, S. (1996) "Music and Identity," in S. Hall and P. du Gay (eds) *Questions of Cultural Identity* (108–27), London: Sage Publications.

Giddens, A. (1990) *The Consequences of Modernity*, Stanford, CA: Stanford University Press.

_____ (1991) *Modernity and Self-Identity: Self and Society in the Late Modern Age*, Cambridge: Polity Press.

Goffman, E. (1956) *The Presentation of Self in Everyday Life*, Edinburgh: University of Edinburgh Social Sciences Research Centre.

Gregg, M. and G. J. Seigworth (2010) "An Inventory of Shimmers," in M. Gregg and G. J. Seigworth (eds) *The Affect Theory Reader* (1–28), Durham, NC: Duke University Press.

Innis, H. (1951) *The Bias of Communication*, Toronto, ON: University of Toronto Press.

Lash, S. and J. Urry (1994) *Economies of Signs and Space*, London: Sage Publications.

Massumi, B. (1995) "The Autonomy of Affect," *Cultural Critique*, 31, 83–109.

_____ (2002) *Parables for the Virtual: Movement, Affect, Sensation*, Durham, NC: Duke University Press.

McLuhan, M. (1962) *The Gutenberg Galaxy: The Making of Typographic Man*, Toronto, ON: University of Toronto Press.

Obed, G. (2010) Personal communication, Nain, Labrador.

Porcello, T. (2005) "Afterward," in P. D. Green and T. Porcello, (eds) *Wired for Sound: Engineering and Technologies in Sonic Cultures* (269–282), Middletown, CT: Wesleyan University Press.

Proust, M. (2005) *In Search of Lost Time: Swann's Way*, (trans. C. K. Scott Moncrieff and T. Kilmartin), London: Vintage Books.

Schafer, R. M. (1994 [1977]) *Our Sonic Environment and the Soundscape: The Tuning of the World*, Rochester, VT: Destiny Books.

—— (2005) "The Sounding City," in *Sensuous Explorations of the Urban Landscape*, lecture series hosted by David Howes at the Canadian Centre for Architecture in collaboration with Concordia University, Montreal (url: www.david-howes.com/senses/sensing-the-city-index.htm), accessed 21.5.16.

Slobin, M. (1993) *Subcultural Sounds: Micromusics of the West*, Hanover, NH: University of New England Press.

Stewart, K. (2007) *Ordinary Affects*, Durham, NC: Duke University Press.

Stokes, M. (1994) "Introduction: Ethnicity, Identity and Music," in Martin Stokes (ed) *Ethnicity, Identity and Music: The Musical Construction of Place*, Oxford: Berg Publishers.

Sutton, I. (1999) *Western Architecture*, London: Thames and Hudson.

Williams, R. (1960) *Culture and Society: 1780–1950*, New York, NY: Doubleday.

—— (1977) *Marxism and Literature*, Oxford: Oxford University Press.

32

GENDER AND THE TELEPHONIC VOICE

Cara Wallis

In the 1870s Alexander Graham Bell introduced his "talking box" to the public, and although early uses included piping in news, church services, and music to people's homes, relatively quickly the device became rather stabilized as a form of point-to-point communication. Since those early days, numerous sounds have been associated with landline telephony (buzzers and rings; new phrases and patterns of speech) and have been compounded by mobile telephony (ringtones, ringback tones, message alerts), but in this chapter, I draw inspiration from that early name for the telephone – the talking box – to focus on one particular type of sound: the gendered voice associated with the telephone. The telephone, and by extension, the voice associated with it, is intimately connected to culturally constructed notions of gender, and this has been true since the phone industry encouraged such associations, which early on were extremely limiting for women. At the same time, women's telephone use has been constitutive of modes of individual and collective empowerment that have upset these taken-for-granted norms. Drawing from interdisciplinary scholarship, this chapter presents an overview of the evolution and meaning of this gendered voice, both human and mechanical – from the practiced voices of the early "hello girls" to the female "voice" in mobile communication.

Research on how the telephonic voice has been gendered has been situated within broader historical analyses of the telephone's development undertaken by feminist scholars (Martin 1991; Rakow 1992) or within studies of mobile phone use in an array of contexts, particularly the home and workplace (Dobashi 2005; Poster 2007; Rakow and Navarro 1993; Wajcman, Bittman, and Brown 2008). Much of this work (see in particular Frissen 1995) derives its impetus either directly or indirectly from Lana Rakow's (1992: 1) argument that the telephone is a sight for the negotiation of "gender work," or "social practices that create and sustain individuals as women or men" and "gendered work," or "productive activity assigned to women." Rakow made this assertion based on her study of women's use of the landline telephone in a small community in the United States. In this chapter I utilize her notion of gendered/gender work to synthesize research on the gendering of the telephonic voice in diverse contexts and to show how engagement with telephony has simultaneously reinforced culturally constructed ideas regarding gender while opening up space for resistance against and transformation of such norms, particularly on the part of girls and young women.

In what follows, in order to situate my analysis, I first provide an overview of Rakow's (1992) argument regarding the gendered and gender work of telephony. The chapter then proceeds in two main sections. In the first, I trace the gendering of the telephonic voice in the context of labor and industry, beginning with the early female operators in the US and Canada and continuing to the present in global call centers and smartphone apps. In the second, I focus on how users of telephony have gendered the telephone in ways that have both conformed to and resisted corporate and socio-cultural norms. Of course, mobile phones allow for voice as well as text and visual data. I argue, however, that this gendered voice still prevails in a textual medium. The chapter concludes with a discussion of how social media use follows prior patterns while having the capacity to shake the durability of the gendered telephonic voice.

The telephonic voice and gendered/gender work

In her influential book, *Gender on the Line*, Lana Rakow (1992) provides insight into how the telephone operated as a gendered technology among her participants in a small midwestern community in the United States. Based on six weeks of fieldwork, she found that most women did indeed talk more on the telephone than men in the community; however, contrary to popular constructions of the "chatty" female, the bulk of their talk was anything but "idle" (a word even many of the women used to describe their time on the phone). Instead, Rakow shows how the women used the telephone in the maintenance of family and community life. Discussing the mutually constitutive nature of gender and technology, she argues that differential telephone use by men and women is not merely about culturally constructed notions of gender. Rather,

> the telephone is a site at which the meanings of gender are expressed and practiced. Use of the telephone by women is both gendered work – work delegated to women – and gender work – work that confirms the community's beliefs about what are women's natural tendencies and abilities.
>
> *(Rakow 1992: 33)*

In other words, the reason the voice on the phone was often female was connected less to women's "natural" affinity for talking (or gossip) and instead to women's location in the domestic sphere, where they bore the burden of care work for family. On the other hand, men's minimal use of the telephone was a way for them to affirm culturally constructed notions of masculinity. Men's aversion to using what they deemed a feminized technology meant that women became "operators" of the house via the telephone – scheduling appointments, shopping, checking in on loved ones, etc. – giving the women a degree of power and control even while they maintained traditional gender roles. However, although women could use the telephone for pleasure and to transcend their limited mobility, Rakow (1992) argues that the telephone also helped reinforce the isolation of women from the public realm of power and opportunity. Although Rakow focused on landline telephone use in the mid-1980s, her notion of the gendered/gender work of telephony has had continued salience in studies of both fixed and mobile phone use, as I discuss below.

Inventing the operator

When the first telephone exchanges were created, boys who had been employed in telegraph offices were brought in to operate the switchboards. However, management deemed their behavior unsuitable because they were rude to subscribers and delighted in pulling pranks such as deliberately crossing wires. A solution to such unruly boys was quickly found through hiring young women who, despite taking a job outside the private realm of the domestic home, conformed to Victorian notions of proper femininity: they were white, US-born, and middle- or high-school educated, and they came from the middle class or those who had middle-class aspirations (Frissen 1995; Green 2001; Martin 1991). These young women were also thought to be serious, obedient, and patient, and they could be paid less. Furthermore, Kenneth Lipartito (1994) has argued that because most subscribers were upper-class men, phone companies "were not above exploiting male solicitude for the weaker sex" (Lipartito 1994: 1084). Thus, by the late 1880s the occupation of telephone operator had become gendered work in the United States, Canada, and several parts of Europe (Maddox 1977).

Because operators could be heard, but not seen, their voices became a central focus as telephone companies began constructing the "ideal" operator. As Michele Martin (1991) details in her study of the emergence of the female operator in Canada, this telephonic voice was not necessarily natural but rather was precisely shaped and disciplined in various stages. In the early development of telephony, the operator was supposed to have a pleasant voice, yet the content of her speech was not rigidly regulated, and conversations between operators and subscribers were fairly common. Operators were considered key resources, and they offered information on weather, train schedules, and sports results to subscribers who they most likely knew by name (Fischer 1992).

Once telephony started to develop as an economic enterprise, however, operators in urban areas were discouraged from talking with subscribers outside of a prescribed realm of phrases (their rural counterparts had much more freedom in this regard). In the mid-1880s more regulations were put in place, and a chief operator was installed to listen in on the operators' interactions with customers (Maddox 1977; Martin 1991). By the turn of the 20th century, the decreasing autonomy of the operator was matched by the increasing focus on the quality of the operator's speech. Operators were provided with standardized phrases to use with customers and standardized answers to their questions (Martin 1991). They also had to take enunciation classes and adopt a particular tone considered calming and that conveyed bourgeois norms of courtesy. The Bell Company actively produced the gender work of the operator, for example through such exhortations as, "Get the smile in your voice" (Martin 1991: 95). Summarizing this situation, Martin states (1991),

> For operators, the voice itself, and not the worker as an entire being … was the 'agent' representing the class, moral values, and personal characteristics of the operator....The more mechanized the labor process became, the more impersonal was the contact between subscribers and operators, and the more important the voice.
>
> *(Martin 1991: 92)*

Phone companies staked their success on the operator's voice, and this voice was fetishized and objectified in the same way that visual mediums came to objectify certain female body parts. Just as the women's bodies were invisible, their actual labor was elided in the public sphere. The gender/gendered work they performed was presented as a "labor of love" (Martin 1991: 60).

Although the phone industry constructed an extremely narrow role for operators, women who took these jobs knew they were entering into a profession that offered them a certain degree of respect and independence during a time when social mores relegated most women to the private sphere (Lipartito 1994; Mayer 2014). The work was demanding and stressful, but it also came with benefits not available in other types of employment, including meals, guaranteed breaks, athletic clubs, and other activities (Lipartito 1994; Martin 1991; Mayer 2014). For some women, the job also had the potential to fulfill fantasies of romance. This other meaning of the "labor of love" was certainly prevalent in the popular imagination, as novels and short stories of the era frequently contained a heroine operator who met her wealthy, attractive husband because of her voice (Martin 1991: 95).

Clearly, the benefits and social mobility afforded the operators were mutually constitutive with the social exclusions upon which the idealized image of the operator was constructed. Although a common belief is that young women were hired because phone companies wanted to save money, Venus Green (2001) has argued that if that had been the case, women of color would have been chosen to fill the role. Instead, the "paternalistic racial ideology" of the telephone company managers meant that only white women could be civilized "lady" operators serving white upper- and upper-middle-class clients, and this ideology was perpetuated as telephony spread. It was indeed gendered work, but only some women could do this gender work. Early on, those with "strong ethnic accents" or those who were even assumed to have an accent based on their racial or ethnic background were prohibited from this career (Green 2001; Lipartito 1994).

The "white lady" image began to change in the United States in the late 1960s due to a combination of demographic shifts in urban areas and new federal regulations regarding equal employment opportunities. However, the hiring of substantial numbers of black women operators was not necessarily welcomed by the telephone industry or subscribers. As Green (2001) notes: "By the 1970s, for many subscribers and telephone workers, the operators' reputation had changed from the selfless white heroine to the incompetent, lazy, rude, and undeserving 'hardcore' black woman" (Green 2001: 220). Bell propagated the notion of unqualified workers that they were "forced" to hire and allowed working conditions to substantially decline. Green goes on to describe customers in turn calling operators derogatory racial slurs and complaining that they were rude or did not have clear enunciation. Some also made sexual comments to them, presumably feeling license to do so because they were not "white ladies" but instead black women. Because the operators' telephonic voice did not conform to previously taken-for-granted assumptions, they faced extreme prejudice and harassment, becoming a scapegoat for anxieties generated by larger cultural, economic, and demographic transformations. These women took such jobs because they believed it would be a form of social and financial advancement. However, at the same time that Bell was proclaiming its compliance with civil rights laws, it was moving toward a more automated system, in essence hiring African American women "into an occupation that not only paid low wages but was becoming technologically obsolete" (Green 2001: 227). Maddox (1977) notes a similar situation in Great Britain, when large numbers of immigrants from rural areas were hired by the British Post.

The shifts within the phone industry discussed by Green (2001) provide a foreshadowing of much broader transformations that would affect the voice of the operator as the world economy became more integrated and globalized. The confluence of technological developments, changing modes of economic production, and the desire on the part of industry for "flexible" labor gave rise to the global call center starting in the 1980s and 1990s. In locales ranging from western and eastern Europe, to South Asia, to parts of Africa, and the rural United States, employees in call centers follow a gendered division of labor reminiscent of the earlier US and Canadian phone industries. While males tend to be employed in IT services (with greater remuneration and opportunities for advancement), the majority of those who provide customer service are women (Belt, Richardson, and Webster 2002). Like their predecessors who served domestic customers, these women (and men) are the target of managerial control and discipline, which often focuses explicitly on the voice through scripts, training in a politeness, and exhortations to "smile" on the line (Belt, Richardson, and Webster 2000, 2002; Richardson and Marshall 1996).

In the global economy, call centers have become both a source of revenue for transnational corporations and anxiety for the employees who in turn are targeted by customers who perceive them as "stealing" local jobs or not providing adequate service. Customers have no way of knowing where the person with whom they are speaking is except to concentrate on the voice – the phrasing, pitch, enunciation, pronunciation, etc. The fixation on the voice is so strong that in several global call centers, employees are trained to fake an American accent, even when their native language is English. In India, for example, call center employees, both male and female, are forced not only to adopt an American accent, but also to take on a whole new personality complete with an American name and hobbies (Poster 2007).

Call centers are associated with fixed-line telephony, yet in the age of mobile media and smartphones, the gendered/gender work of the female telephonic voice has found a new form in personal assistant applications such as the iPhone's Siri. Originally available on Apple's App Store, Siri was built into the iPhone beginning with the 4S in 2011. Users can ask Siri for help with everything from finding a restaurant to reciting the lyrics of a pop song. Although Siri will deny having a gender if asked, it is not incidental that the original version of Siri in the United States (and other countries such as Australia) had a female voice (though now users are allowed to choose voices). The voices for Amazon's Echo, Microsoft's Cortana, and other personal assistants are also female. Research into computer human interaction in the US has found that both men and women find female voices to be more pleasant (Griggs 2011). They are also thought to be helpful, particularly if the topic concerns relationships or care work, while male voices are thought to be more authoritative, especially regarding technical topics (Nass 2010). Such findings confirm longstanding, culturally constructed ideas regarding the "proper" tone of women's voices. The telephone industry has constructed and capitalized on such notions, from the voice of the "hello girls," to the global feminization of telephonic service work, to the female voice of Siri and other digital assistants.

Shaping the voice of the subscriber

The gendered and gender work just discussed in relation to telephone operators is no less evident when examining the telephonic voice of subscribers. However, although early on the industry constructed a masculine telephonic voice, women actively shaped what came to be predominant uses of telephony. Moreover, the gendered patterns later associated with the landline (discussed below with a focus on western contexts) have been multiplied but also transformed with the global spread of mobile communication.

When the telephone first began to diffuse, it was only affordable to relatively elite members of society. Despite most subscribers' social standing, however, a "high-class" technology quickly became associated with "low-class" behaviors – shouting, cursing, and mumbling. Thus, in the eyes of the telephone companies, just as the ideal operator had to be shaped and disciplined, so too did the ideal subscriber. Although some training focused on the technical aspects of telephony, such as how to call the operator, the majority focused on telephone etiquette that related directly to the voice – clear enunciation, a pleasant tone, proper volume, and polite language (Fischer 1992; Martin 1991; Rakow 1992). Michele Martin (1991: 134) notes that even the ubiquitous "Hello" was initially seen as rude ("Are you there?" was more appropriate).

Just as phone companies sought to shape the subscriber's voice to align with notions of Victorian propriety, they also had a narrow view of who that subscriber should be: namely white, male, and elite. The telephone was gendered masculine in advertisements that portrayed it as a tool for business that enabled a "Multiplication of Power" and "The Voice of Success" for the "Man for the Moment" (Fischer 1992). When residential service was first advertised, the emphasis was similarly on business, with the businessman's wife portrayed as an efficient household manager thanks to the telephone (though ad copy stressed that women should obtain their husband's consent in obtaining a phone) (Fischer, 1992). By the turn of the century, as housewives were increasingly targeted in ad campaigns, the focus was still on utilitarian uses such as shopping or to reduce labor and drudgery. Only after the 1920s, and particularly after the Depression, was the phone marketed as a way to enrich relationships or alleviate loneliness (Fischer 1992; Frissen 1995; Martin 1991).

Despite the industry's narrow conception of telephony, several scholars have shown that women ignored such strictures and were instrumental in transforming the meaning of the telephone. When women's voices began to occupy the telephone, however, there were numerous complaints and resistance to their "chattiness," "frivolous" uses, and "idle" talk (Fischer 1992; Martin 1991; Marvin 1988). Rural women in particular were stereotyped as gossips and eavesdroppers on party lines, the primary mechanism of early rural telephony. For example, in a letter to a Kansas newspaper in 1911, a man wrote that "when two old windy sisters on a party line once get astraddle of the wire, nothing short of re-enforced lightning will ever shake 'em loose under an hour" (Kline 2000: 45). Such sentiments were common in newspapers and magazines of the time and later in early films.

The gender and gendered work of telephony is revealed both in its early masculine construction as a tool for productive labor and women's use of the phone for undertaking uncompensated reproductive labor. Importantly, Rakow (1992) shows how the women in her study made a distinction between "visiting," which "creates and maintains the relationships upon which families and communities are built," (Rakow 1992: 37) and "gossiping," which is "idle" or "selfish" (41). Researching Australian women's use of the telephone, Ann Moyal (1995) also found that "'kinkeeping' floods the lines" (289). Similarly, Brenda Maddox (1977) cites a 1970 survey of 31 American women (most were married) in which they connect their telephone use largely to domestic duties, even using the phone receiver as an early DIY baby monitor while at a neighbor's house. Studies from Canada, France, and England have also revealed that women were more likely to talk on the phone than men (Claisse and Rowe 1987; Fischer, 1992; Frissen 1995; Smoreda and Licoppe 2000). Thus, Martin (1991) attributes the shift in industry attitudes towards sociability via the telephone to women's practices. Several scholars have also noted how the ability to communicate orally without visual cues allows for a certain type of intimacy that differs from (and can be easier for some than) face-to-face communication, and that women were more likely to appreciate this aspect (Moyal 1995; Rakow 1992).

It was not just grown women who came to be most associated with talking on the telephone and who appreciated the intimacy it afforded. Mary Celeste Kearney (2005) has shown that as the telephone diffused more broadly across the US after World War II, the white, suburban "chatty" girl monopolizing the family phone was a common trope in fiction and non-fiction popular writing. According to Kearney, middle-class teenage girls "challenged the traditional dynamics of private and public spheres by depriviliging the domestic roles and practices associated with members of their sex in favor of non-domestic roles and practices associated with members of their generation" (Kearney 2005: 584). In photo essays in publications like *Life* magazine, girls are described as engaging in "gab fests" and "jabbering into the phone" (Kearney 2005: 584), much to the consternation of parents, especially fathers who wanted to use the phone for business. Rakow (1992: 35) relates how people in the community she researched thought that young women were constantly on the phone. A young woman told her, "Girls *talk* on the telephone, guys say what they have to say and get off. Girls are different. That's the way girls are" (italics in original).

The counterpoint to this audible telephonic voice is, of course, the inaudible voice at the other end of the line and the anxieties it engenders. In the early days of telephony, long before the girls who were the subject of Kearney's (2005) analysis territorialized the phone lines, there was particular fear that daughters would enter into "irregular associations" (Marvin 1988: 79).

Similarly, in the media that Kearney surveyed, parents of teenaged boys did not have a problem with their use of the phone; however, when their teenaged girls called boys there was disapproval (this was true in Rakow's community in the 1980s as well). Girls were seen as violating social norms of proper behavior and evading parents' supervisory role. When parents were present or tried to clandestinely eavesdrop, girls would use their own secret telephonic language to keep their conversations private. Nonetheless, even with the girls' tactic, the phone enabled anxious parents to contain their daughters in the safety of the domestic sphere (Kearney 2005: 1355).

Such gendering of the telephonic voice has been heightened, but also broken down, with the global diffusion of mobile telephony, as evidence from a wide range of geographical locales and among diverse populations suggests. Leopoldina Fortunati (2009) has argued that we should understand the gendered and generational uses of mobile phones in terms of the mobile's linkage to immaterial labor, primarily the domain of women, and which includes communication and emotional labor for "interaction, affects, love, [and] sex" (Fortunati 2009: 31). At the same time, mobile phones have particular affordances, such as text messaging, that have enabled new practices that both affirm and challenge prior notions of the gendered voice on the line. The literature on gender and mobile telephony has become quite vast, but the following discussion focuses on themes that reveal the durability, but also the flexibility, of the gendered telephonic voice: mothering/reproduction; intimacy; and the (dis)empowerment of adolescent girls and young women.

First, however, to speak of the gendered mobile "voice" requires a brief qualification. Questions have arisen as to whether and how much mobile messaging resembles speech or written language, and though a fine-grained analysis is beyond the scope of this chapter, a simple answer is that it appears to resemble aspects of both. Pertinent to this discussion is that text messaging is speech-like in its immediacy, interactivity, and degree (or lack) of formality (Ling, Baron, Lenhart and Campbell 2005). Although a text is ostensibly inaudible, there is nonetheless a textual voice, as evidenced by the extensive ways that users (especially teens and young adults) try to insert their "voice" into their texts through such strategies as omitting final punctuation, avoiding capital letters, adding extra letters (for example, "heyyy"), and inserting emojis so as not to sound short or rude (Ling et al. 2014). Moreover, people speak of being able to "hear" their interlocutor's voice in a text message (Hjorth 2011). In much of the research discussed below, the authors often do not distinguish voice calls versus text messages, and with applications such as Siri, this blurring has only increased.

The mobile phone, like the landline before it, was initially marketed to relatively elite businessmen, who made up the majority of early adopters globally. Despite such intentional marketing, when early survey results of US mobile use were published, headlines played upon the seeming reversal of previous gender stereotypes by announcing, for example, that guys "gabbed" more (Cingular 2003). Upon closer inspection, such surveys revealed that men were using mobile phones for work obligations (or as status symbols), thus maintaining earlier associations with telephony as a male tool for business. Nonetheless, many surmised that the mobile phone was a technology that potentially blurred the previously taken-for-granted association between masculinity and technology. For example, Lemish and Cohen (2007) argued that Israeli men and women characterized the role of the mobile phone in their lives in very gendered language, yet their actual practices did not manifest such large differences.

Despite the possibility of the mobile phone disrupting the gender and gendered work noted earlier, research examining women and care work has found that mobile phone use confirms and exacerbates previous patterns. In one of the earliest studies, Rakow and Navarro (1993) observed that mobile phones enable "remote mothering," meaning that middle- and upper-class women who were early adopters of mobile telephony in the US used their mobile phones to handle domestic responsibilities related to caregiving. Women were working "parallel shifts," with family matters often bleeding into work hours via the mobile phone, while men used the phone as "an extension of the public world" (Rakow and Navarro 1993: 155). Chesley (2005) also found that women experience more "family-work spillover," and Wajcman, Bittman, and Brown (2008) noted that men's mobile voice is often for more instrumental purposes. Indeed, women's use of mobile phones for carrying out domestic caregiving has been observed in a wide range of locales (Dobashi 2005; Lim and Soon 2010). In transnational contexts as well, mothers working abroad use mobile phones for what Madianou and Miller (2013) call "intensive mothering," often much more so than fathers (Parreñas 2005). Summarizing these phenomena, Lim (2014) argues that mobile phones have not alleviated women's burden of "double work."

If remote or intensive mothering has been portrayed as sometimes adding strain to women already juggling work and home, it also gestures to a positive feature of the gender/gendered work associated with mobile telephony; that is, how mobile phones, like the landline before, amplify relational intimacy. For men and women, the mobile phone is a personal technology, often carried on the body and carrying inside intimate details of one's life. However, as Hjorth and Lim (2012) argue, "mobile intimacy," or the *"overlaying of material-geographic and electronic-social"* (italics in the original) has seemed to be inordinately linked to women. This intimacy has been observed between mothers and daughters (Wajcman, Bittman, and Brown 2008; Tacchi, Kitner, and Crawford 2012) and grandmothers and grandchildren (Sawchuk and Crow 2012), and among women and their intimate partners (Hjorth 2011).

Compared to adult women, in the lives of female adolescents and young women the linkage between mobile communication and gendered/gender work is more ambiguous. On the one hand, studies have found that girls emphasize the interactivity of mobile phones, and they are more likely to have longer conversations and send longer text messages than boys (Oksman and Rautiainen 2003; Ling et al. 2014). Moreover, among teens and young adults of diverse ethnic, religious, socio-economic, and geographic backgrounds, the stereotype of the "chatty" female persists (Green and Singleton 2007; Wallis 2013). On the other hand, scholars have observed that girls and young women feel empowered to use mobile phones to break down gender stereotypes (Ellwood-Clayton 2003; Hijazi-Omari and Ribak 2008; Wallis 2013). For example, mobile phones enable young Chinese migrant women – culturally constructed as "not knowing how to talk" – to have a voice, and they, as well as Palestinian girls in Israel, use phones to autonomously forge intimate and sexual relationships outside the purview of parents and in defiance of conventional gender norms (Hijazi-Omari and Ribak 2008; Wallis 2013). Within these same relationships, however, phones can be disempowering when used by intimate partners for surveillance and control. Among adolescents worldwide, one of the more recent practices that blurs issues of intimacy, empowerment, and control (as well as voice and image) is sexting. Statistics reveal that boys and girls participate nearly equally, yet girls are more likely to be victims of non-consensual sharing of images and the social shaming that accompanies the fallout (Hasinoff 2012).

Conclusion

Since the landline telephone was introduced, the gendered telephonic voice has taken on distinct meanings as a result of particular values, norms, and ideologies. This chapter has presented an overview of how this gendered voice is linked to social constructions of masculinity and femininity as well as work that is gender delineated. Such gendering has been prevalent in industry and among everyday users of telephony. In the landline era, the telephone was linked to productive and reproductive work that reinforced women's role as the predominant providers of service and care. Although teenaged girls used the telephone in ways that resisted some of these prescribed roles, their emphasis on telephony and interpersonal communication nonetheless conformed to dominant notions of gender. In the mobile era, these same patterns emerged;

that is, mobile telephony has been used in ways that affirm and challenge prior notions of the gendered voice on the line. Although western contexts were the focus of scholarly literature on the landline (in line with its pattern of diffusion), studies of mobile telephony have been global from the start. This latter body of scholarship reveals how the gendered telephonic voice has had resilience even while emerging from distinct socio-cultural contexts.

In this chapter, I used an expansive definition of "voice" in analysing gendered/gender work via mobile phones. Now, with the predominance of social media and image-based digital culture, this gendered "voice" still underlies such usage. In many settings, girls and young women have been found to be the most active users of various types of social media and the users most involved in creating content (Vermeren 2015). This, too, is a double-edged sword as it allows recurring themes of reproductive labor associated with telephony – emotional labor, relationship maintenance, intimacy, sexual exploration – that can be nurturing and empowering but also exhausting and disempowering. How to promote the former is still a topic ripe for further exploration.

References

Belt, V., Richardson, R. and Webster, J. (2000) "Women's work in the information economy: The case of telephone call centres," *Information, Communication & Society, 3*(3), pp. 366–385.

Belt, V., Richardson, R. and Webster, J. (March 2002) "Women, social skill and interactive service work in telephone call centres," *New Technology Work and Employment, 17*(1): 20–34.

Chesley, N. (2005) "Blurring boundaries? Linking technology use, spillover, individual distress, and family satisfaction," *Journal of Marriage and Family, 67*(5), pp. 1237–1248.

Cingular Wireless (2003) Guys still gab more on wireless. Cingular News Release, June 23. Retrieved November 1, 2005 from, http://cingular.mediaroom.com/index.php?s=press_releases&item=818.

Claisse, G. and Rowe, F. (1987) "The telephone in question: Questions on communication," *Computer Networks and ISDN Systems, 14*(2–5), pp. 207–219.

Dobashi, S. (2005) "The gendered use of *Keitai* in domestic contexts," in M. Ito, D. Okabe, and M. Matsuda (Eds.), *Personal, Portable, Pedestrian: Mobile Phones in Japanese Life* (pp. 219–236). Cambridge, MA: MIT Press.

Ellwood-Clayton, B. (2003) "Virtual strangers: Young love and texting in the Filipino archipelago of cyberspace," in K. Nyiri (Ed.), *Mobile Democracy: Essays on Society, Self and Politics* (pp. 225–235). Vienna: Passagen-Verlag.

Fischer, C. A. (1992) *America Calling: A Social History of the Telephone to 1940.* Berkeley: University of California Press.

Fortunati, L. (2009) "Gender and the mobile phone," in G. Goggin and L. Hjorth (Eds.), *Mobile Technologies: From Telecommunications to Media* (pp. 23–34). New York: Routledge.

Frissen, V. (1995) "Gender is calling: Some reflections on past, present and future uses of the telephone," in K. Grint and R. Gill (Eds.), *The Gender-Technology Relation: Contemporary Theory and Research* (pp. 79–94). London: Taylor & Francis.

Green, E. and Singleton, C. (2007) "Mobile selves: Gender, ethnicity and mobile phones in the everyday lives of young Pakistani-British women and men," *Information, Community and Society, 10*(4), pp. 506–526.

Green, V. (2001) *Race On the Line: Gender, Labor, and Technology in the Bell System, 1880–1980.* Durham, NC: Duke University Press.

Griggs, G. (2011) Why computer voices are mostly female. Retrieved from www.cnn.com/2011/10/21/tech/innovation/female-computer-voices/.

Hasinoff, A. A. (2012) Sexting as media production: Rethinking social media and sexuality. *New Media & Society, 15*(4), pp. 449–465.

Hijazi-Omari, H. and Ribak, R. (2008) "Playing with fire: On the domestication of the mobile phone among Palestinian teenage girls in Israel," *Information, Communication & Society, 11*(2), pp. 149–166.

Hjorth, L. (2011) "Mobile specters of intimacy: The gendered role of mobile technologies in love-past, present and future," in Rich Ling and Scott Campbell (Eds.), *Mobile Communication: Bringing Us Together and Tearing Us Apart* (pp. 37–60). New Brunswick, NJ: Transaction.

Hjorth, L. and Lim, S.S. (2012) "Mobile intimacy in an age of affective mobile media," *Feminist Media Studies, 12*, pp. 477–484.

Kearney, M.C. (2005) "Troping teenage girlhood through telephony in mid-twentieth-century US media culture," *Cultural Studies, 19*(5), pp. 568–601.

Kline, R. R. (2000) Consumers in the Country: Technology and Social Change in Rural America. Durham, NC: Johns Hopkins University Press.

Lemish, D. and Cohen, A. (2007) "On the gendered nature of mobile phone culture in Israel," *Sex Roles 52*(7), pp. 511–521.

Lim, S. S. (2014) "Women, 'double work' and mobile media: The more things change, the more they stay the same," in G. Goggin and L. Hjorth (Eds.), *The Routledge Companion to Mobile Media* (pp. 356–364). New York: Routledge.

Lim, S. S. and Soon, C. (2010) "The influence of social and cultural factors on mothers' domestication of household ICTs–experiences of Chinese and Korean women," *Telematics and Informatics, 27*(3), pp. 205–216.

Ling, R. (2005) "The sociolinguistics of SMS: An analysis of SMS use by a random sample of Norwegians," in R. Ling and P. E. Pedersen (Eds.), *Mobile Communication: Re-negotiation of the Social Sphere* (pp. 335–349). London: Springer.

Ling, R., Baron, N. S., Lenhart, A. and Campbell, S. W. (2014) "'Girls text really weird': Gender, texting and identity among teens," *Journal of Children and Media, 8*(4), pp. 423–439.

Lipartito, K. (1994) "When women were switches: Technology, work, and gender in the telephone industry, 1890–1920," *American Historical Review, 99*(4), pp. 1075–1111.

Maddox, B. (1977) "Women and the switchboard," in Ithiel de Sola Pool (Ed), *The Social Impact of the Telephone* (pp. 262–280). Cambridge, MA: MIT Press.

Madianou, M. and Miller, D. (2013) Migration and New Media: Transnational Families and Polymedia. London: Routledge.

Martin, M. (1991) "Hello, Central?" Gender, Technology, and Culture in the Formation of Telephone Systems. Montreal: McGill-Queen's University Press.

Marvin, C. (1988) *When Old Technologies Were New: Thinking About Electric Communication in the Late 19th Century.* New York: Oxford University Press.

Mayer, V. (2014) "To communicate is human; to chat is female: The feminization of US media work," in C. Carter, L. Steiner, and L. McLaughlin (Eds.), *The Routledge Companion to Gender and Media* (pp. 51–60). London: Routledge.

Moyal, A. (1995) "The feminine culture of the telephone," in N. Heap, R. Thomas, G. Einon, R. Mason, and H. Mackay (Eds.), *Information Technology and Society* (pp. 284–310). London: Sage.

Nass, C. with Yen, C. (2010) The Man Who Lied to His Laptop: What We Can Learn About Ourselves From Our Machines. New York: Penguin.

Oksman, V. and Rautiainen, P. (2003) "Extension of the hand: Children's and teenagers' relationship with the mobile phone in Finland," in L. Fortunati, J. Katz, and R. Riccini (Eds.), *Mediating the Human Body: Technology, Communication, and Fashion* (pp. 103–111). Mahwah, NJ: Lawrence Erlbaum.

Parreñas, R. (2005) "Long distance intimacy: Class, gender and intergenerational relations between mothers and children in Filipino transnational families," *Global Networks, 5*(4), pp. 317–336.

Poster, W.R. (2007) "Who's on the line? Indian call center agents pose as Americans for US-outsourced firms," *Industrial Relations: A Journal of Economy and Society, 46*(2), pp. 271–304.

Rakow, L. F. (1992) Gender on the Line: Women, the Telephone, and Community Life. Chicago, IL: University of Illinois Press.

Rakow, L. F. and Navarro, V. (1993) "Remote mothering and the parallel shift: Women meet the cellular telephone," *Critical Studies in Mass Communication, 10*(2), pp. 144–157.

Richardson, R. and Marshall, J.N. (September 1996) "The growth of telephone call centres in peripheral areas of Britain: Evidence from Tyne and Wear," *The Royal Geographical Society* (with the Institute of British Geographers), *28*(3) pp. 308–317.

Sawchuk, K. and Crow, B. (2012) "'I'm g-mom on the phone': Remote grandmothering, cell phones and inter-generational dis/connections," *Feminist Media Studies, 12*(4), pp. 496–505.

Smoreda, Z. and Licoppe, C. (2000) "Gender-specific use of the domestic telephone," *Social Psychology Quarterly, 63*(3), pp. 238–252.

Tacchi, J., Kitner, K.R. and Crawford, K. (2012) "Meaningful mobility: Gender, development and mobile phones," Feminist Media Studies, 12(4), pp. 528–537.

Vermeren, I. (2015) "Men vs. women: Who is more active on social media?" Retrieved from www.brandwatch.com/2015/01/men-vs-women-active-social-media/.

Wajcman, J., Bittman, M. and Brown, J. E. (2008) "Families without borders: Mobile phones, connectedness and work-home divisions," *Sociology, 42*(4), pp. 635–652.

Wallis, C. (2013) Technomobility in China: Young Migrant Women and Mobile Phones. New York: NYU Press.

PART VI

Introduction: sound connections

Listening across and through disciplines is integral to work in sound studies. This final section brings together scholars who work within their respective disciplines whilst reaching out to their discipline's relationship to the sonic. Organisationally and often epistemologically, scholars are frequently caught up in a Post-Enlightenment intellectual division of labour that has seen the progressive specialization and compartmentalization of knowledge and interest. This 'specialization' is often accompanied by an institutional and often personal desire for inter-disciplinarity – to reach beyond the confines of one's own specialism. So it is with this spirit of inter-disciplinarity that the following chapters discuss a variety of modes of sonic connectivity.

Historians have long written excellent work on sound. James Mansell concentrates on the ways in which historians of sound hear and not necessarily what they heard. He argues that historians of sound have tended to take a middle path between the analysis of sounds and sonic subjectivities. Historians, he argues, have been heavily influenced by the work of Murray Schafer in their use of his terminology such as soundscapes, keynote sounds and soundmarks and in terms of hearers being 'earwitnesses'. Yet Mansell also states his scepticism of Schafer's anti-urbanism as counterproductive for historians of sound.

Mansell recognises that historians typically can't use the same methods as sound scholars – field recording, ethnographies and the like as they often do not have direct access to historical sounds but rather to written records. This debate as we have seen in previous sections is alive and well. Written records often refer to a multiplicity of sonic meanings for historians and as such are often integral to the craft of the historian. Mansell takes the reader on a social shaping of hearing journey demonstrating the historian's ability to deal with historical ways of hearing. He does so through the wonderful example of an analysis of London Transport posters from 1927 indicating just how people were supposed to hear the sounds of London at that time, just as propaganda films such as *Britain Can Take it* (1940) encouraged certain forms and attitudes toward the sounds of war.

Justin St. Clair in his chapter on literature and sound interrogates the sonic nature of reading, listening and the production of texts. He points to the inherently aural nature of poetry and literature in history from ancient Greek culture to the reciting of poetry in school rooms throughout the world. But more than this he argues that the act of reading is invariably not silent, but that the reader internalises what they are reading aurally. Schafer himself acknowledges that he came to soundscapes through literature. Before the age of mechanical reproduction,

Schafer acknowledges that literature was the main source for the representation of the sonic environment. St. Clair points to the rich tradition of writing about the sonic. Modernity itself, he argues, is largely defined through the technologies that infuse everyday life – from the combustion engine to the telephone, radio and television. St. Clair argues that writers have embodied these technologies within their texts as a way of trying to understand their role and place in the development of subjectivity and culture. He argues that the novel offers a heterophonia of sounds through which subjectivities are configured.

Hudson's and Reyes pieces should be read as complementary to one another. Hudson deals with sociology and sound studies, but with a focus on the sociology of music whereas Reyes investigates the production and consumption of popular music in relation to sound studies. The issues of listening, production, cultural capital and new ways of listening come to the fore in these two chapters.

Sounds are always culturally situated and have frequently differential meanings attached to them. The sound of a police siren in the streets of New York may well engender feelings of security, fear or apprehension depending on the class, race and gender of the subject who hears. Urban sociologists have been attentive to the changing sensory nature of the city since the work of Simmel early in the 20th century. This sensory awareness coalesced around the technological tropes surrounding the understanding of 'modernism'. The sonic, on the face of it, appeared to be closely allied to aspects of the sociological. Martin Hudson in his chapter focusses primarily on the sociology of music and its relationship to sound. He begins with the work of Theodor Adorno who largely saw music production and reception as a structural product of society and as such an ideological reflection of that society. Adorno famously stated that most music:

> Takes the place of the utopia it promises. By circling people, by enveloping them – as inherent in the acoustical phenomenon – and turning them as listeners into participants, it contributes ideologically to the integration which modern society never tires of achieving in reality. It leaves no room for conceptual reflection between itself and the subject, and so it creates an illusion of immediacy in the totally mediated world, a proximity between strangers, of warmth for those who come to feel the chill of the unmitigated struggle of all against all.
>
> *(Adorno 1976: 46)*

Adorno redrew the boundaries between 'serious' music by which he meant the standard classics and 'popular' music arguing that serious music was as ideological as popular music genres heard on the radio. This led Adorno to look at the edges of music production, such as the atonality of Schonberg – for music that mirrored more accurately the dissonance of modern capitalism. In parallel to this, Adorno embraced the work of playwright Samuel Beckett for whom, he thought, words and their meanings had become increasingly redundant and fragmented. This focus led Adorno to concentrate on elements of avant-garde music through which to understand 'authentic' creativity whilst largely dismissing popular music as a harbinger for the desire of social integration with its attendant mode of passive listening. Hudson in his chapter attempts to re-interrogate the meaning attached to the sociological object – sound – in terms of a newly thought through sociological practice: He argues that the relationship between sociology and sound may express something profound about the fragmentation and complexity of identity in late modernity – that if one were to create an inventory of identity it would look more like a disparate collage than a coherent list. Hudson uses the works of Berio to construct a listening sociology – through the very act of a self-conscious fragmentary composition which itself reflects social engagement and practice rather than merely a sociological object. Hudson's chapter focusses largely on a re-evaluation of the sociology of music in relation to the aesthetics of 'sound art'.

Reyes takes on the challenge of popular music and sound studies and points out that sound studies has tended to concentrate on the works of avant-garde artists and its attendant modes of specialized listening. This is, to some extent, a replication of the work of Adorno in which difficulty in music and modes of active listening are prioritised whilst the mass of popular music is lumped into the realm of passive commodified listening practices. This was followed by the cultural studies approach which prioritised cultures of listening rather than production itself.

Reyes contends that the most active modes of listening lie precisely in the development of recording techniques that have produced new ways of listening. Yet new ways of consuming and disseminating music produce new ways of listening that can paradoxically produce what Reyes refers to as 'interpassivity' whereby the plethora of music listening opportunities produces a form of passivity or indeed the move to other visual material (via smartphones) that means that sound becomes merely a form of background Muzak. Reyes points to an academic gap in the academy when it comes to aural literacy – hence maybe the continual referral back to the work of Adorno who died fifty years ago. It is in this space between the sociology of music, popular music studies and sound studies that Reyes sees as a fertile ground of interdisciplinary study.

Tim Wall's chapter charts the mutually beneficial potentiality between radio studies and sound studies. He points to the sonic limitations of much radio research in the past arguing the need for an approach that 'integrates understanding radio's form and the experience of consuming it'. He points to the historical paradox whereby the role of radio in media studies was to some extent eclipsed with the coming of television. He argues that radio should continue to play a central role within a complex media system that is prominent in the construction of daily life for most. Wall makes a plea for popular sound to become a focus of research; in accord with the discussion surrounding sound art and the sociology of music, Wall argues that there has been an undue focus in radio sound to that which is relatively marginal, radio talk, radio drama, experimental radio as against the dominant role that music, mostly popular – plays in the production and reception of radio sound.

In our last contribution to this volume Powis and Carter takes an acoustemological approach to sporting sounds, an area largely ignored in Sport Studies. They investigate how athletes' experience of sport relates to sound through a range of topics from listening to their bodies to listening to the crack of the cricket bat. The intricacies of sporting events in practice is broadened out into a discussion of spectacular sounds within crowds and stadiums and investigate how referees might be swayed (crowds/stadiums) by noise of the crowd. Modern sport is, they argue, increasingly regulated in terms of the management of sound as an enhancement of spectatorship.

References

Adorno, T., 1976, *Introduction to the Sociology of Music*, New York: Continuum Press.

33

WAYS OF HEARING: SOUND, CULTURE AND HISTORY

James G. Mansell

In 1932 a group of social investigators based at Manchester University Settlement surveyed housing conditions in the poorest parts of their city. They reported that in the worst tenement blocks of this English industrial heartland it was not uncommon to find families living in dwellings 'the shape of a long tunnel, 41ft. long by 9ft. wide, divided into living-room and bedroom, and dimly lit by a window at each end.' Speaking to tenants, observers concluded that, 'Only those who have to live year in and year out in the old block dwellings can fully realise all that it implies.' Prominent in testimonies were complaints about 'The tramp of feet up and down the stone stairways and balconies, the running and echoing shouts of children at play in the asphalt courtyard' as well as 'the pounding of traffic' and 'the noise from the goods yard.' '"It's awful,"' one tenant complained. '"I was thankful when they took me to the hospital. The noise nearly drives you mad."' Another said, '"You long for a bit of quiet."' Life in these poorly constructed homes was one of sensory deprivation, according to the investigators: 'Without a vestige of beauty, with little privacy and constant noise, the lives of many tenants are reduced to a dull dead level from which much of the spring and interest in life has gone' (Manchester University Settlement 1932: 6–8).

Sound is there in the historical record for those ready to hear it. It has traditionally been beyond the remit of the historian to listen to the past and most historians still consider sound better left to specialists. However, a whole raft of new sound histories accompanying the wider rise of sound studies prove that historians have much to gain by routinely thinking of their historical subjects as hearing subjects. This chapter offers an overview of methodology in modern sound history, drawing on the works of some of its key practitioners, and argues that the central contribution of this subset of sound studies has been to elucidate not so much *what* but rather *how* people heard in the past. Using examples from my own research on early twentieth-century Britain, the second part of the chapter outlines an approach to sound history based on the analysis of what I describe as *ways of hearing*, a turn of phrase hinted at and sometimes used in passing in existing sound histories, but which I nevertheless take to be their core concern (for wider discussion of this approach in sensory studies see Howes & Classen 2014). My theorization of ways of hearing in this chapter is intended to offer a perspective on what it is that sound historians do and why they do it, but also to convince those engaged more broadly in history writing that they, too, should tune in to the sonic past.

Soundscapes, soundselves and ways of hearing

Historians have routinely turned to other disciplines in search of a methodology for dealing with sound. In doing so, they encounter two major options. The first is to focus on sounds themselves, on how and why particular places or things sound the way that they do and what this tells us about those places/things. The second option is to focus instead on the hearing/listening subject, the ways in which hearing and listening facilitate particular kinds of knowledges and subjectivities and situate selves in relation to environments and communities. Both come under the heading of what Bull and Back (2003) have described as 'auditory culture.' In the case of Manchester University Settlement's account of tenement sounds, an analysis might focus on the nature and effect of the noises heard by tenants: the relatively new public sound of the internal combustion engine on the city street, or the acoustic properties of poorly insulated homes. It might alternatively focus on the sonic constitution of tenement selfhoods in a wider study of domestic hearing, considering the ways in which sounds situated tenement-dwellers as tenement subjects (poor, rhythmically bound to the city and its industries, and so on) in contrast to those who lived in quieter suburbs. Sound studies scholars sometimes blend these two approaches to good effect and have actively theorized the relationship between the two, but more often one or the other predominates in their work. In this section I will argue that historians draw upon both of these methodologies, but for practical and conceptual reasons commit themselves fully to neither, finding instead their unique contribution to sound studies in the analysis of the interface between sounds and sonic subjectivities. To explain why historians have taken this medial approach, I will discuss the sound itself and the sonic-subjectivity approaches in turn before explaining why historians have settled instead on the analysis of historical ways of hearing.

As far as the study of sound itself is concerned, no influence is clearer in the work of sound historians than that of sonic ecologist R. Murray Schafer, whose concept of the 'soundscape' (Schafer 1994) appears in the titles of a range of sound histories from Picker's *Victorian Soundscapes* (2004) to Thompson's *The Soundscape of Modernity* (2004) and Birdsall's *Nazi Soundscapes* (2012). Schafer (1994: 7) described the soundscape as 'any acoustic field of study,' adding that 'We may speak of a musical composition as a soundscape or a radio program as a soundscape or an acoustic environment as a soundscape.' His argument that 'We can isolate an acoustic environment as a field of study just as we can study the characteristics of a given landscape' has proven to be particularly influential. He offered technical terms such as 'keynote' sound ('the anchor or fundamental tone' of a soundscape: the sound of motor traffic, perhaps, in our Manchester example) and 'soundmark' (like a landmark, a sound 'especially regarded or noticed' by a community, such as a church bell or a factory siren) (Schafer 1994: 9–10). He also promoted the idea that soundscapes change along with wider historical shifts such as industrialization, arguing that we should pay attention to these changes to fully understand and then, crucially, to improve our sonic environments. His theory of changing soundscapes, along with the notion of hearers as 'earwitnesses' to these changes (Schafer 1994: 8–9), has appealed to historians, who have understandably been attracted to the notion that we might be able to trace shifts in sonic epochs as a way of widening our understanding of historical categories such as modernity (Thompson 2004) or totalitarianism (Birdsall 2012). But most historians stop short of fully embracing Schafer, partly because accompanying his methodological proposals is a stark ecological message about the damage done to natural soundscapes by what he sees as the polluting influence of industrial and urban sounds. Most historians are reluctant to take such a negative *a priori* view of the sounds of modernity. In borrowing the term soundscape, as Kelman (2010) has pointed out, sound historians such as Picker (2004) use it with little of the original political context that

Schafer intended and often with much of the methodological specificity left out, too, drawing upon it much more loosely as a way of indicating their engagement with an historical world of sound, lost but recoverable.

Schafer's work has inspired a rich vein of scholarship and practical work in sonic ecology, acoustic design and sound arts which on the whole is either sympathetic to his ecological politics or otherwise committed to creating 'good' soundscapes. Such scholars and practitioners are often engaged in field recording or other forms of direct engagement with sound: they capture it, store it, measure it, create with it, and pass judgement on it. Historians do not often have this kind of direct access to sound, and even where recordings of past sounds exist, as Smith (2015) has pointed out, most historians remain skeptical about the possibility of treating these as uncomplicated evidence of what the past sounded like. Smith (2015: 56) warns against attempts to objectively re-create past soundscapes and argues that even when we have recordings, these come highly mediated both by the ear of the recordist and by our own 'epistemological preferences.' He insists that we *can* access the sounds of the past, but that this is best achieved by reading written accounts which offer 'a far more robust way to access the ways sounds and silences were understood in the past, regardless of whether they were recorded electronically' (Smith 2015: 61). Unlike Schafer, who describes earwitnesses' descriptions of sound as 'trustworthy' or 'counterfeit' in their objectivity, historians like Smith are much more apt to think in terms of a multiplicity of meanings operating in any given time or place. In Smith's case, sounds meant different things depending on which side one was on in the American Civil War, for example (Smith 2001). Although one might take issue with Smith's insistence on the primary importance of written text versus other kinds of source material (Hendy 2016 puts forward an alternative perspective), the general premise of his argument that the best sound histories deal with sound itself only in highly contextualized and contingent ways holds good. While it has been important for historians to indicate to their readers, by using the term soundscape, that they are dealing with a specific sound world, unique to its time, they have not in the end committed themselves to the empirical recovery of historical soundscapes.

The second option, to recover instead the ways in which sounds have played a role in constructing and situating selves, might at first seem to offer an ideal alternative. Connor (1997) outlines an account of a 'modern auditory I' that is persuasive and compelling. Historians have referenced 'historical acoustemology' as a method for dealing with this, drawing on the work of anthropologists of the senses. Acoustemology is a term coined by anthropologist Steven Feld which 'joins acoustics to epistemology to investigate sounding and listening as a knowing-in-action: a knowing with and knowing-through the audible' (Feld 2015: 12). Rice (2003) has further distilled the anthropological approach in referring to 'soundselves' as a way of accounting for the role that sounds play in generating selfhood. Writing specifically about the context of the hospital, Rice (2013: 22) explains that 'For those who are immersed in it…the ward soundscape can play an important role in creating and confirming a particular experience of patienthood, bringing patients to experience themselves as 'patient selves'. Moreover, he argues that sounds situate hearers as the subjects of power: in the hospital, he describes a 'panaudicon' (building on Foucault's discussion of the panopticon) in which doctors and nurses gain power/knowledge by listening to auditory signals emanating from medical technologies and patient bodies (Rice 2013: 21–37). Conversely, Cusick (2013) conducted an acoustemology with prisoners detained in the war on terror and demonstrates the extent to which solitary confinement and musical torture can erode a prisoner's sense of self, 'the destruction,' as Cusick puts it, 'of prisoners' subjectivities.' In the silence of auditory isolation and subject to the vibrational onslaught of sonic torture, prisoners lose, according to Cusick (2013: 276), 'the capacity to control the acoustical relationality that is the foundation of subjectivity.' Rice and Cusick's way of working could be extended to any number of other spatial contexts (see, for example, Gallagher 2011 on schools), and more widely to social and cultural life, and has produced profoundly important insights about the relationship between sound and subjectivity. Their method, however, based on ethnographic observation and interview, cannot easily be replicated by the historian. Certain kinds of personal testimony might allow for partial insight into how past sounds situated hearers in relation to others and in relation to structures of power, but an acoustemology of the hearing self of the kind offered by Rice is beyond the reach of all but the contemporary historian. Thus, despite gestures towards the construction of historical acoustemology as a method, this, too, is not really where sound history's contribution to sound studies is to be found.

Rather, what historians are best equipped to recover, and in practice have evolved quite sophisticated approaches to dealing with, is historical ways of hearing. In using this term, I am consciously borrowing from visual studies where Berger's famous *Ways of Seeing* (1972) is only the best-known example of a trend towards analyzing all that comes between optics on the one hand and images on the other. It is ironic, given the efforts to which some sound scholars have gone to refute the dominance of the visual in modernity, that visual studies has evolved a model well suited to overcoming the methodological dilemma that I have outlined above. In a process that Mitchell (2002) calls 'showing seeing' designed to overcome the paradox that 'vision itself is invisible,' visual culture scholars have turned their attention to how we see and concluded that between seer and seen is a realm in which perception is shaped socially. Morus (2006: 107–109) directs our attention to the extent to which eighteenth- and early nineteenth-century science depended upon a culture of visual display in which visitors to popular scientific exhibitions and demonstrations were 'taught how to see science' through both visual and verbal instruction. He concludes that 'the practice of seeing is enculturated' and that we should 'direct our attention to the mundane practices of seeing' in order to understand how people were encouraged to 'see nature' in a particular way in the eighteenth and early nineteenth century.

Bennett (2011) makes a similar point about Victorian museums. These were, he claims, laboratories for the production of 'civic seeing' where working-class visitors in particular were explicitly 'directed' in how to see in a process which he describes as 'the social organisation of vision.' He takes Henry Pitt Rivers, founder of the Pitt Rivers Museum, as a typical example of a sight director. Promoting the scientific theory of evolution, Bennett explains that for Pitt Rivers

> it was not enough to simply arrange evolutionary displays to teach the working man the lessons of progress; account had also to be taken of the specific circumstances, rooted in working-class occupations, that limited or impaired working-class vision so as to put in place a developmental program of visual instruction that would counteract those influences.
>
> *(Bennett 2011: 270–275)*

To counteract the ways of seeing 'associated with commercial forms of popular visual entertainment' and other forms of 'civically unproductive forms of visual pleasure,' museum visitors were instructed by lecturers and attendants on how to view the exhibits, creating a 'singular and fixed spectatorial position,' according to Bennett (2011: 264–277). Matthews-Jones (2011) extends this analysis to the art gallery in her work on the origins of London's Whitechapel Gallery, where founder Samuel Barnett undertook an extensive program of lectures (internally described as 'lessons in seeing') instructing working-class visitors in how to see the paintings on display, emphasizing their spiritual meaning in line with his wider evangelizing mission. Interesting, too, in these contexts, is that the 'lessons in seeing' offered by museum curators were not always fully successful and, rather than providing singular all-encompassing regimes of vision, were often resisted in whole in or in part by those who were their target (Matthews-Jones 2011; see also Hill 2005). Beyond the formal context of exhibition and display, historians Gooday (2008) and Otter (2008) have argued that we cannot understand the coming of electrical light over the late nineteenth and early twentieth centuries without taking account of the political history of liberalism and the social history of gender. They demonstrate that electrical illumination was neither a technologically determined process nor one that produced a single, neutral or uncontested way of seeing.

While they may not have reliable ways of accessing past soundscapes or past soundselves, historians do have good access to that which came between: the social shaping of hearing, captured as it is in all manner of source materials. In fact, the historical vantage point is perhaps the best position from which to understand these ways of hearing. If perception is shaped socially then we may be better placed to take a critical attitude to past than to present hearing modes. Sound history demonstrates that hearing is enculturated, to borrow Morus's term, just as seeing is. It shows that those who gain power socially also gain the power to shape ways of hearing. That shaping process is nevertheless uneven, contested, and constantly in need of maintenance. Indeed, it is precisely the need for such maintenance that makes past ways of hearing legible in the historical source material available to us.

Although they have not always explicitly theorized their work in terms of ways of hearing, sound historians are evidently engaged in the process of excavating them. Historian of technology Sterne points in this direction when he argues that 'hearing and its limits can be at once an empirical, material, and sometimes brutal reality *and also* subject to historical and personal transformation' (Sterne 2015: 72–73). Boutin (2015: 3) puts it another way in her history of hearing in nineteenth-century Paris when she argues that 'Though our ears work the same way as they did in the nineteenth century, we do not hear the same way: our sensitivity to city noise has changed.' Although Birdsall (2012: 174–178) uses the term soundscape to headline her analysis of sound in Nazi Germany, among her most important conclusions is that far from being 'immediate and intimate,' 'those who grew up during National Socialism were encouraged to perceive auditory experience in social and collective terms.' Sounds, she explains, 'were conceived as amenable tools for political appropriation.' That appropriation took place not just in the sonic qualities of music, broadcasts or sirens, but in the way people were situated as particular kinds of hearers.

Forming a counterpart to Bennett's analysis of ways of seeing in museums is Johnson's (1995) work on nineteenth-century concert hall culture. Where museums were intended to facilitate the extension of bourgeois ways of seeing to the working-class viewer, nineteenth-century concert halls, as Weber (1975) has also shown, were spaces for the establishment of sonic codes of behavior for the middle classes, including the habit of listening in silence and clapping only at the end of whole musical works rather than between movements. These codes of behavior served to form distinctions between cultivated and uncultivated hearers. A culture of cultivated concert hall listening was joined in the nineteenth century by the new modes of expert stethoscopic and telegraphic listening identified by Sterne (2003), who argues that expert listening modes like these were fundamental to the development of modern forms of science, communication and commerce. Thompson (2004) describes these as 'cultures of listening' precisely in order to *historicize* them and, like Sterne, identifies specifically modern cultures of listening particular to the late nineteenth and early twentieth centuries. Distinguishing her approach from Schafer's, Thompson (2004: 1) explicitly notes that for her purposes 'a soundscape is simultaneously a physical environment and a way of perceiving that environment; it is both a world,' she continues, 'and a culture constructed to make sense of that world.'

Historians of sound like Sterne and Thompson tend to emphasize the historicity of listening rather than hearing because they view the former as the more obviously cultural act, the more obviously situated in history. They focus on expert listeners who, over the course of the nineteenth and twentieth centuries, shaped dominant, modern, modes of knowing-through-sound. While this is undoubtedly vital terrain for historical analysis, I will argue in the next section that by explicitly shifting from a focus on expert cultures of listening to the analysis of the somewhat wider category of ways of hearing we might capture more of the contested cultural history of sound and hearing and more of its everyday dynamics.

Ways of hearing in the 'age of noise'

The Manchester tenement-dwellers who complained in the early 1930s of 'the pounding of traffic' and 'the noise from the goods yard' were far from being alone in encountering the changing world of early twentieth-century Britain through their ears. As I have argued elsewhere (Mansell 2017), Britons who lived through this period were inclined to think of themselves as living in an 'age of noise.' From the late 1920s onward, as Bijsterveld (2008) has also shown, noise became a significant problem in public discourse and public policy. In 1934, following many years of informal anti-noise campaigning, Britain gained its first organization dedicated specifically to the suppression of 'needless noise': the Anti-Noise League (Horder 1935: 46). Although the League put significant energy into lobbying government ministers, its primary goal was education of the public, via pamphlets, radio broadcasts and exhibitions, about the dangers posed to health and personal efficiency by noise, and about good ways to conduct oneself sonically. The Anti-Noise League promoted a specific way of hearing the sounds of modernity. Focusing particularly on new technological sounds such as those made by motor transport, they encouraged hearers to encounter the sounds of the modern city as unnatural, unhealthy, and uncivilized in contrast to the peaceful tranquility of the countryside, whose sonic virtues were promoted in the League's magazine *Quiet* and through undertakings such as its Second World War 'Country Residency Scheme' which took civil defense workers out of London for quiet, rural, rest breaks (Mansell 2017).

It would be easy to take the Anti-Noise League's hostility to urban noise as *the* typical attitude of the British inter-war middle classes, since as Picker (2004: 41–81) has shown, there is a much longer history of British urban 'brain workers' objecting to unruly public soundscapes. And, certainly, the majority of the Anti-Noise League's leaders were drawn from the upper echelons of professional life. However, the Anti-Noise League's anti-urban rhetoric and fixation on the ills of modern technology was only *one* of the available ways of encountering everyday urban sound at the time, and it was far from uniformly accepted, even among the middle classes. In 1907, well before the establishment of the Anti-Noise League but in the context of a longer public debate about the problem of city noise, the *Manchester Guardian* newspaper noted in an editorial that it was unconvinced not only by the medical arguments against noise but also by the social aesthetics of the growing anti-noise campaign:

> No doubt there are temperaments which find the roar and clash of the streets fatiguing, but for others they are a delight and an inspiration, nor is the taste of these last unquestionably degenerate. Noise is motion, and motion is life; and while it may not be true to say the greater the racket the intenser the humanity, to detest the clatter of our fellows is to detest sociability. The street is the voice of the city, and he who would have it gagged is no better than the morose fellow who insists upon sitting in company but requires those around him to be dumb.
>
> *(Manchester Guardian 1907: 8)*

The Anti-Noise League's deputations to government in the 1930s were often met, behind the scenes, with a similar response. Government scientists, on the whole, did not hear noise in the same way as the League's leaders, thinking of it instead as a necessary, and probably harmless, accompaniment of the modern world of trade and industry (Mansell 2017).

In early twentieth-century Britain, contest over the meaning of everyday urban noise was closely bound up with a wider contestation over the meaning, and politics, of modernity. Those who had a stake in promoting technological and urban modernity deliberately countered the anti-noise way of hearing. I have discussed elsewhere (Mansell 2011) how state-sponsored public information films of the 1930s presented noise as a productive emanation of the rhythms of social life and how these films encouraged people to hear as national and imperial subjects. In London Transport promotional materials of the same period, noise was similarly presented as inseparable from all of the benefits of modern life, part of the draw of the big city and its sensory pleasures. Such promotional materials sometimes made explicit reference to the need for hearers to take the right *attitude* to noise as in, for example, the London Underground poster 'Hearing the Riches of London' (Figure 33.1) created in 1927. The poster was part of a set of five, each encouraging people to travel into Central London to indulge one of their senses. The 'Hearing' poster demanded somewhat more of its viewer than the others, however: a woman with a finger

Figure 33.1 'Hearing the Riches of London,' an advertising poster by Frederick Charles Herrick for the Underground Electric Railway Company, London, 1927. Copyright TFL from the Transport Museum collection.

pushed to her lips in a 'shush!' motion invited sensory pleasure-seekers to hear London but, in contrast to the less complicated acts of seeing an opera, touching fine fabrics, tasting good food and smelling expensive perfumes which were depicted in the other posters, the 'shush!' gesture implied that travelers-by-Tube must take control of their hearing to appreciate the sounding metropolis. They would be rewarded, if they did so, by encountering not only London's musical pleasures, depicted below the central figure, but also the whole spectrum of the vibrating city, indicated in the poster's background by waves of color, and in the smaller illustrations by pictures of dogs barking, Big Ben chiming, and airplanes flying overhead. Each of the five figures depicted in the poster series were intended to be viewed as fashionably modern. In 'Hearing,' the woman has a bobbed haircut and a dress that matches the swirling modernist color patterns in the poster's background. She is wearing hairpins branded with the distinct modernism of London Underground's logo. The poster made explicit reference to the modernity of the 'age of noise' by including everyday sounds alongside music, but encouraged hearers to embrace these sounds as part of the excitement of urban life. In contrast to the hearer in Anti-Noise League propaganda who is encouraged to shield himself from damaging city noise, the hearer in this poster takes a *modern attitude* to sound: she is an aural pleasure-seeker who has learned to hear the sounds of modernity as invigorating rather than unnerving.

What we find in the Anti-Noise League's archive and in materials such as the London Underground poster discussed above is insight not so much into soundscapes or soundselves, but conscious efforts to wed one to the other through the encouragement of particular ways of hearing. While Sterne (2003) and Thompson (2004), for example, identify a singular sonic modernity in dominant expert cultures of listening, my suggestion is that, on the ground, the modernity of modern sound was contested, negotiated, and multiple. Sense-makers, those who had the power to influence ways of seeing or hearing, had to *actively produce* modern ways of sensing. They nevertheless had to do so in competition with one another. We should be alert, however, to the limitations of ways of sensing. For example, when government planners set about tackling the housing crisis outlined in reports such as that published by Manchester University Settlement, they focused their efforts on managing the intrusion of technological sounds into the home, drawing upon the ways of hearing that I have outlined above that focused on how to hear technology. Although some working-class hearers would have welcomed this approach to domestic acoustics (including those whose voices were presented by the Manchester settlers), social surveys produced by Mass Observation (1943: 48–49) suggest that those who were moved from slums into new council flats in the 1930s generally complained not so much about technological sounds, but about the breakdown of the sonic bonds which had held together their previous communities, and about the undesirable sounds created in their new flats by people from other social groups. The pre-occupation with technology, in other words, may not have been such a prominent feature of working-class ways of hearing, and we should remain wary of universalizing the middle-class sensory habitus.

As a number of sound studies scholars have argued, sound is affective: it prompts an embodied response that precedes cognition (Goodman 2010; see also Kane 2015). These scholars have sometimes been hostile to the auditory culture approach that I have drawn on in this chapter, arguing that sound's power lies in its materiality rather than its meaning. However, I would argue that we need not tear the two apart. Sense-makers understood the affective power of sound only too well and sought to intervene to make sound meaningful precisely because those meanings would accompany affect. Ways of hearing were not just about creating meanings for sounds, but also about the embodiment of ideology. This becomes clear in the case of the home front during the Second World War. Having previously rejected the Anti-Noise League's claims about noise's impact on health, government authorities nevertheless realized that enemy air raids were designed to cause a state of fear in civilian populations and that this fear was enacted in the air raid primarily through sound, hearing and listening (Mansell 2017). Alongside propaganda films such as *Britain Can Take It* (1940) and *Listen to Britain* (1942) which encouraged the stoical hearing of war sounds, scientists at the Medical Research Council decided to promote the use of ear plugs to save urban civilians the stress of listening out for enemy bombers at night. In other words, civilians were closely directed in how they should hear the sounds of war, and indeed when they should refrain from hearing at all. Self-help writers explicitly referred to the need to undertake 'sense training' (Hunt 1918; Hunt 1940) in order to hear the sounds of war not with fear, but with pride in the nation-at-war.

Conclusion

These brief examples I hope are enough to show that by analyzing how people heard in the past we might enrich our understanding of how they lived socially. As Sterne (2015: 72–74) and others have pointed out, we should not forget that hearing varies physically from one person to another and that it changes as we age. But, as this chapter has argued, it is also subject to historical changes that for too long have remained outside the core concerns of the historian. Those who study the past have a good deal to gain by listening.

Further Reading

Morat, D. (ed) (2014) *Sounds of Modern History: Auditory Cultures in Nineteenth and Twentieth Century Europe*, Oxford: Berghahn.

Smith, M. (ed) (2004) *Hearing History: A Reader*, Athens, GA: University of Georgia Press.

Sterne, J. (ed) (2012) *The Sound Studies Reader*, Abingdon: Routledge.

References

Bennett, T. (2011) "Civic Seeing: Museums and the Organization of Vision," in S. Macdonald (ed), *A Companion to Museum Studies*, Oxford: Blackwell.

Berger, J. (1972) *Ways of Seeing*, Harmondsworth: Penguin.

Bijsterveld, K. (2008) *Mechanical Sounds: Technology, Culture and Public Problems of Noise in the Twentieth Century*, Cambridge, MA: MIT Press.

Birdsall, C. (2012) *Nazi Soundscapes: Sound, Technology and Urban Space in Germany, 1933–1945*, Amsterdam: Amsterdam University Press.

Boutin, A. (2015) *City of Noise: Sound and Nineteenth-Century Paris*, Urbana, IL: University of Illinois Press.

Bull, M. & Back, L. (eds) (2003) *The Auditory Culture Reader*, Oxford: Berg.

Connor, S. (1997) "The Modern Auditory I," in R. Porter (ed), *Rewriting the Self: Histories from the Renaissance to the Present*, London: Routledge.

Cusick, S. (2013) "An Acoustemology of Detention in the 'Global War on Terror'," in G. Born (ed), *Music, Sound and Space: Transformations of Public and Private Experience*, Cambridge: Cambridge University Press.

Feld, S. (2015) "Acoustemology," in D. Novak & M. Sakakeeny (eds), *Keywords in Sound*, Durham, NC: Duke University Press.

Gallagher, M. (2011) "Sound, Space and Power in a Primary School," *Social & Cultural Geography*, 12(1), pp. 47–61.

Gooday, G. (2008) *Domesticating Electricity: Expertise, Uncertainty and Gender, 1880–1914*, London: Pickering & Chatto.

Goodman, S. (2010) *Sonic Warfare: Sound, Affect and the Ecology of Fear*, Cambridge, MA: MIT Press.

Hendy, D. (2016) "Distant Echoes: Evoking the Soundscapes of the Past in the Radio Documentary Series 'Noise: A Human History,'" *The New Soundtrack*, 6(1), pp. 29–49.

Hill, K. (2005) *Culture and Class in English Public Museums, 1850–1914*, Aldershot: Ashgate.

Horder, T. (1935) "Health and Noise," in Anti-Noise League, *Silencing a Noisy World: Being a Brief Report of the Conference on the Abatement of Noise*, London: Anti-Noise League.

Howes, D. & Classen, C. (2014) *Ways of Sensing: Understanding the Senses in Society*, Abingdon: Routlege.

Hunt, H. (1918) *Self-Training: The Lines of Mental Progress*, London: William Rider.

——— (1940) *How to Win the War of Nerves*, London: Rider & Co.

Johnson, J. (1995) *Listening in Paris: A Cultural History*, Berkeley, CA: University of California Press.

Kane, B. (2015) "Sound Studies Without Auditory Culture: A Critique of the Ontological Turn," *Sound Studies*, 1(1), pp. 2–21.

Kelman, A. (2010) "Rethinking the Soundscape: A Critical Genealogy of a Key Term in Sound Studies," *The Senses and Society*, 5(2), pp. 212–234.

Manchester University Settlement (1932) *Some Social Aspects of Pre-War Tenements and of Post-War Flats*, Manchester: Manchester University Settlement.

Mansell, J. (2011) "Rhythm, Modernity and the Politics of Sound," in S. Anthony & J. Mansell (eds), *The Projection of Britain: A History of the GPO Film Unit*, Basingstoke: Palgrave Macmillan.

——— (2017) *The Age of Noise in Britain: Hearing Modernity*, Urbana, IL: University of Illinois Press.

Mass Observation (1943) *An Inquiry Into People's Homes, A Report Prepared by Mass Observation for the Advertising Service Guild, the Fourth of the "Change" Wartime Surveys*, London: John Murray.

Matthews-Jones, L. (2011) "Lessons in Seeing: Art, Religion and Class in the East End of London, 1881–1898," *Journal of Victorian Culture*, 16(3), pp. 385–403.

Mitchell, W. (2002) "Showing Seeing: A Critique of Visual Culture," *Journal of Visual Culture*, 1(2), pp. 165–181.

Morus, I. (2006) "Seeing and Believing Science," *Isis*, 97(1), pp. 101–110.

Otter, C. (2008) *The Victorian Eye: A Political History of Light and Vision in Britain, 1880–1910*, Chicago, IL: University of Chicago Press.

Picker, J. (2004) *Victorian Soundscapes*, Oxford: Oxford University Press.

Rice, T. (2003) "Soundselves: An Acoustemology of Sound and Self in the Edinburgh Royal Infirmary," *Anthropology Today*, 19(4), pp. 4–9.

——— (2013) *Hearing and the Hospital: Sound, Listening, Knowledge and Experience*, Canon Pyon: Sean Kingston Publishing.

Schafer, R. (1994) *The Soundscape: Our Sonic Environment and the Tuning of the World*, Rochester, NY: Destiny Books.

Smith, M. (2001) *Listening to Nineteenth-Century America*, Chapel Hill, NC: University of North Carolina Press.

——— (2015) "Echo," in D. Novak & M. Sakakeeny (eds), *Keywords in Sound*, Durham, NC: Duke University Press.

Sterne, J. (2003) *The Audible Past: Cultural Origins of Sound Reproduction*, Durham, NC: Duke University Press.

——— (2015) "Hearing," in D. Novak & M. Sakakeeny (eds), *Keywords in Sound*, Durham, NC: Duke University Press.

Thompson, E. (2004) *The Soundscape of Modernity: Architectural Acoustics and the Culture of Listening in America, 1900–33*, Cambridge, MA: MIT Press.

Weber, W. (1975) *Music and the Middle Class: The Social Structure of Concert Life in London, Paris and Vienna*, London: Croom Helm.

34

LITERATURE AND SOUND

Justin St. Clair

From orality to aurality

In "Transmission and the Individual Remix: How Literature Works," British novelist Tom McCarthy insists that literature is governed by an "acoustic logic" (McCarthy 2012).

> My aim here, in this essay, is not to *tell* you something, but to make you *listen*: not to me, nor even to Beckett and Kafka, but to a set of signals that have been repeating, pulsing, modulating in the airspace of the novel, poem, play – in their lines, between them and around them – since each of these forms began. I want to make you listen to them, in the hope not that they'll deliver up some hidden and decisive message, but rather that they'll help attune your ear to the very pitch and frequency of its own activity – in other words, that they'll enable you to listen in on listening itself.
>
> *(McCarthy 2012)*

Literature, McCarthy contends, is constitutionally dependent on the act of listening: its transmission has always been predicated on repetition, and iterative composition "consists first and foremost of listening" (McCarthy 2012). McCarthy's proposition, while emphatic, is by no means radical. In fact, notions of literary aurality have been repeating, pulsing, and modulating in the critical airspace – to echo McCarthy's formulation – for centuries. And while some of McCarthy's particulars may be dependent on poststructuralist ideas regarding intertextuality and the role of the author (that is: the author as arranger, composer, or re-broadcaster, as opposed to Almighty Creator), the centrality of sound to the study of literature is commonsensically apparent. Assonance, consonance, dissonance, alliteration, meter, modulation, and rhyme scheme are all foundational – and fundamentally sonic – poetic devices. Much word play, moreover, from punning substitution to playful metathesis, depends upon phonological sounding. Whatever one may think of print-oriented bastardry, literature is inescapably an aural art.

A significant portion of literature's aurality certainly derives from ancient orality. The earliest narrative traditions were undeniably oral, and transmission, therefore, depended upon cultures of close listening. Within literary criticism, the most significant figure to consider the legacy of orality in the contemporary era is Walter Ong, whose *Orality and Literacy: The Technologizing of the Word* (1982) found adherents across disciplines. Ong, of course, is by no means uncontroversial.

In *The Audible Past: Cultural Origins of Sound Reproduction* (2003), Jonathan Sterne sharply criticizes Ong's theological underpinnings, arguing that however "sophisticated and iconoclastic" his Catholicism, Ong's formulations reinforce metaphysical prejudices regarding the senses that have dogged the Western philosophical tradition for centuries – from the supposed "interiority" of aurality to the persistent notion that the senses are somehow "a zero-sum game, where the dominance of one sense by necessity leads to the decline of another sense" (Sterne 2003: 16, 17). While I'm more than inclined to side with Sterne, his critique does not entirely negate several of Ong's salient observations. Foremost among these, perhaps, is an idea he lifted from Eric Havelock (1963): an insistence on the importance of aural mnemonics to oral cultures.

> In a primary oral culture, to solve effectively the problem of retaining and retrieving carefully articulated thought, you have to do your thinking in mnemonic patterns, shaped for ready oral recurrence. Your thought must come into being in heavily rhythmic, balanced patterns, in repetitions, or antitheses, in alliterations and assonances, in epithetic or other formulary expressions, … in proverbs which are constantly heard by everyone so that they come to mind readily and which themselves are patterned for retention and ready recall, or in other mnemonic form. Serious thought is intertwined with memory systems. Mnemonic needs determine even syntax.
>
> *(Ong 1982: 34)*

Whether or not one subscribes to Ong's conception of a technologically induced "secondary orality," contemporary literature – and poetry in particular – has inherited the aural legacy of patterned, acoustic mnemonics. While interest in prosody, once a mainstay of literary criticism, has waned of late, the study of sound in poetry continues to receive important attention. Over the past several decades, a number of influential essay collections have appeared, including Adalaide Morris's *Sound States: Innovative Poetics and Acoustical Technologies* (1997), Charles Bernstein's *Close Listening: Poetry and the Performed Word* (1998), and Marjorie Perloff and Craig Dworkin's *The Sound of Poetry / The Poetry of Sound* (2009).

If Ong's contributions to literary studies amplified the importance of aurality, the deconstructive work of Jacques Derrida pulled the discipline in a different direction. In *Of Grammatology* (1967, translated 1976), Derrida decries the logocentrism of Western metaphysics, which, in his estimation, has always privileged the aurality of speech over the visuality of writing. "In every case," writes Derrida, "the voice is closest to the signified, whether it is determined strictly as sense (thought or lived) or more loosely as thing" (Derrida 1976: 11). Consequently, he continues, within the Western philosophical tradition, "[a]ll signifiers, and first and foremost the written signifier, are derivative with regard to what would wed the voice indissolubly to the mind or to the thought of the signified sense, indeed to the thing itself" (Derrida 1976: 11). Derridean deconstruction, then, "can be read as an inversion of Ong's value system" (Sterne 2003: 17): not only does Derrida reject the ecclesiastical substructures of traditional criticism, but he also repudiates the notion that writing is essentially a secondary or derivative linguistic endeavor. In an era in which the literarily inclined – both artists and academics alike – felt increasingly marginalized, this theoretical valorization proved immensely satisfying. Aurality, in some senses, was but collateral damage.

Within literary criticism, Garrett Stewart can be credited, at least in part, with recuperating aurality in the face of "Derrida's frontal assault on the primacy of voice in language" (Stewart 1990: 103). In *Reading Voices: Literature and the Phonotext* (1990), Stewart develops a sophisticated theorization of the aural mechanics of reading as he attempts "to give theory back to literature by giving literature back to language" (Stewart 1990: 34). While poststructuralist criticism "might well seem to render any reading-with-the-ear a theoretically groundless pastime," Stewart responds by reconceptualizing voice as "not centered and authorial but, rather, textual, receptual" (Stewart 1990: 103). Essential to Stewart's hypothesis is the notion that so-called silent reading is never truly silent. Instead, he argues, reading is an embodied, somatic act: even when reading "quietly" to ourselves, we nonetheless engage in phonemic reading, internally evocalizing the text. The phonotext, in other words, *sounds* – even when our reading is inaudible to others.

This recognition of reading's inherent aurality better enabled literary scholars to consider what Stewart calls "a 'dyslocutionary' tension between phonemic and graphemic signification" (Stewart 1990: 5). In other words, what is silently evocalized during the embodied act of reading does not *always* correspond to that which is inscribed on the page. "The phonic," as Stewart puts it, "will not hold fast within the graphic. Or, more to the point, the phonemic will not stay put within the morphemes apparently assigned by the script" (Stewart 1990: 4–5). As every child knows, "I scream" and "ice cream" are all-but-indistinguishable when uttered aloud, and this sort of playful homophony – intentionality notwithstanding – is endemic to reading. Many phonemic soundings that fail to correspond to their graphic counterparts we simply ignore, perhaps even unconsciously. Others, however, we assimilate into our attempts at meaning-making, particularly when processing what we take to be "literary" texts. Even inexperienced readers, for example, when given Gertrude Stein's "Susie Asado," will hear "sweetie" when their eyes encounter "sweet tea." So how do we read? "The answer," Stewart insists in *Reading Voices*, "is obvious enough to elude most literary study: we listen while we read" (Stewart 1990: 37).

Acousmatic listening and audio transcription

If, historically speaking, the "how" of reading has been somewhat underappreciated in literary studies, the "where" of reading has also long been, as Stewart puts it, an "alien question" (Stewart 1990: 1). His persuasive answer is to postulate "the reading body": a "somatic locus of soundless reception" that not only "includes … the brain but" also "the organs of vocal production, from diaphragm up through throat to tongue and palate" (Stewart 1990: 1). But while an account of reading's there-ness – or, if you will, an a-where-ness of the somato-acoustic nature of literary reception – has come relatively recently to the discipline, larger locative questions have persisted for centuries. Often these have been subsumed in debates over presence, representation, authenticity, or authorial intent, all of which seem somewhat foolish in the wake of literary poststructuralism. Regardless, the relationship between literature and sound is fundamentally dislocatory: the "there" of textuality is necessarily at a remove from whatever soundscape a specific passage records, and time only amplifies the disjunction. Literature, in other words, is inherently acousmatic.

In *Treatise on Musical Objects* (1966), Pierre Schaeffer asserts the importance of acousmatic listening. He takes as his point of departure the tale of Pythagoras lecturing from behind a curtain to acolytes who, deprived of their master's image, could only attend to the sound of his voice. Sound "that one hears without seeing what causes it," Schaeffer insists, is not only endemic to the age of electronic media, but it also enables a phenomenological approach to sound: "listening itself … becomes the origin of the phenomenon to be studied" (Schaeffer 2011: 77). It should come as little surprise that this formulation sounds strikingly similar to McCarthy's assertion that literature allows us "to listen in on listening itself." Many literary scholars engaged with sound studies regard print as an audio technology, a medium that not only transcribes audio phenomena, but one that also – by very virtue of its acousmatic nature – encourages readers to attend to aurality with critical detachment, listening at a remove from whatever generative agent might be credited with the initial sounding. In short, print functions much as Schaeffer's tape recorder: "if it creates new phenomena to observe, it creates above all new conditions of observation" (Schaeffer 2011: 81). As Sam Halliday notes in *Sonic Modernity: Representing Sound in Literature, Culture and the Arts* (2013), "[t]o fully grasp the significance of sound in modern culture, it follows, we must consider visual cultures of sound and verbal cultures of sound, and see all of these in dialogue with 'sounded' cultures of sound, more self-evidently made out of sound itself" (Halliday 2013: 3). Halliday speaks for many close-listening literary scholars when he observes that

> literature … is especially well suited for revealing sound's "configured" quality, which is, again, sound's imbrication in the non- or trans-acoustic. Correlatively, literature is especially well suited for revealing such para-sonic factors as sound's social connotations, its relationship with other senses, and – perhaps most importantly of all – the qualitative dimension that means certain sounds are actually of interest to people, things they actively seek out or shun.
>
> *(Halliday 2013: 12)*

At first blush, it all might seem relentlessly paradoxical: (1) literature, read silently, still resounds; (2) its audio transcriptions – graphic, and so, constitutionally mute – decouple sound, nonetheless, from ostensible source; and (3) this literary act, literally an act of de-contextualization, enables the broader contextualization of both sound culture and sound in culture.

Unsurprisingly, many studies of sound in literature acknowledge R. Murray Schafer's *The Tuning of the World* (1977) as a singularly important antecedent. Schafer, whose approach to acousmatic listening is markedly different than Pierre Schaeffer's, refers to "the splitting of sounds from their original contexts" as schizophonia, an unfortunate neologism that deliberately pathologizes acousmatic sound by underscoring its supposed aberrance (Schafer 1994: 88). This, however, is not the basis for his appeal within literary studies. Rather, it is Schafer's insistence on the importance of interdisciplinarity and, in particular, the way he "emphatically relies on literary documents" as evidentiary material (Keskinen 2008: 13). Throughout his groundbreaking study, republished in 1994 as *The Soundscape: Our Sonic Environment and the Tuning of the World*, "Schafer calls on literature to testify to his case," a fact that has not gone unnoticed among literary scholars (Keskinen 2008: 13). In *Victorian Soundscapes* (2003), for example, John M. Picker credits Schafer as both inspiration and model, emphasizing that his conceptual innovations (that is, the earwitness: "a literary figure who records the soundscapes of his or her own time and place") have proven both predictive of later scholarly trends and particularly useful to those in narrative studies (Picker 2003: 13).

As Schafer observes, before the advent of mechanical and electro-acoustic recording technologies, literature was the primary approximative means of representing and preserving the sonic environment. "It is a special talent of novelists like Tolstoy, Thomas Hardy and Thomas Mann," he writes, "to have captured the soundscapes of their own places and times, and such descriptions constitute the best guide available in the reconstruction of soundscapes past" (Schafer 1994: 9). The field of literary studies, then, has become an important site for "performing … a kind of acoustic archaeology on the (ostensibly silent) records of the distant past" (Picker 2003: 14). Bruce R. Smith's *The Acoustic World of Early Modern England: Attending to the O-Factor* (1999) exemplifies such an approach. In this aural history, Smith uses a preponderance of musical, literary, and historical documents to reconstruct the soundscapes of 16th- and 17th-century England, arguing that acoustemology (that is: knowledge through sounded experience) was integral to the development of early modern subjectivity.

Picker's *Victorian Soundscapes* is itself another excellent example of acoustic archeology within literary studies. From Charles Dickens's *Dombey and Son* (1848) to George Eliot's *Daniel Deronda* (1876), Picker uses period literary reportage to "investigate the two major roles that hearing played in Victorian culture: as a response to a physical stimulus and as a metaphor for the communication of meaning" (Picker 2003: 7). The result is a compelling cultural history of Victorian listening practice, which

> analyzes the stages by which they sought to transform what Romantics had conceived of as a sublime *experience* into a quantifiable and marketable *object* or *thing*, a sonic commodity, in the form of a printed work, a performance, or, ultimately, an audio recording, for that most conspicuous legacy of Victorianism, the modern middle-class consumer.
>
> *(Picker 2003: 10)*

Literary art in the age of mechano-acoustic reproduction

The advent of phonography and, eventually, what we might half-jestingly call the media-consumerist complex, certainly presented a challenge to literature's cultural position. Most immediately, print lost its monopoly on audio transcription, and literature could no longer be said to represent the only method of recording the soundscapes specific to a particular time and place. However, as Douglas Kahn suggests in *Noise, Water, Meat: A History of Sound in the Arts* (1999), the invention and commercialization of mechanical recording technologies need not be read as a supersession, but can instead be understood as occasioning a dynamic state of media co-incidence. "The inscriptive attributes of phonography," he writes, "became coterminous with the legacies of writing, universal alphabets, and languages, as well as other inscriptive practices" (Kahn 1999: 16). In short, most literary scholars respond with skepticism to Friedrich A. Kittler's insistence that "[r]ecord grooves dig the grave of the author" (Kittler 1999: 83). If the author has died, it is for a set of wholly unrelated reasons (that is, a recognition of the intentional fallacy, an acknowledgement of the role that readers play in meaning-making, a poststructuralist privileging of interpretive multiplicity, etc.). Literature itself is alive and well, and media competition has only amplified its potential.

One recent examination of textual aurality in the mechano-acoustic era is Philipp Schweighauser's *The Noises of American Literature, 1890–1985: Toward a History of Literary Acoustics* (2006). In this study, Schweighauser argues that despite the ascendance of other audio media, "literary texts from the late nineteenth to the late twentieth century continue to be sites of both the cultural production and the representation of noise" (Schweighauser 2006: 19). Literary scholars, it should be noted, often have a fondness for metaphor (that is, studies of "voice" in literature, for example, are far more likely to be figurative investigations of identity projection than anything to do with aurality). From a purist's perspective, then, Schweighauser might be accused of occasionally falling prey to these tendencies as he toggles between noise as a sonic phenomenon and noise, in a systems-theory sense, as an aspect of information exchange. Nevertheless, he not only grounds many of his observations in sound theory, but he also productively attends to literature's own sonic devices. Notable among these is his notion of the audiograph: "a characterization technique that endows fictional bodies with a set of distinctive acoustic properties designed to position characters with regard to the ensemble of social facts and practices that constitute the fictional world they inhabit" (Schweighauser 2006: 71). Acoustic profiling, Schweighauser contends, is endemic to turn-of-the-century naturalism. He offers the Frank Norris novel *McTeague* (1899) as a prime example, arguing that the components of an audiograph, which "may range from characters' accents, dialects, or intonation patterns to the sounds produced by their laughter, snoring, or the acoustic impact of their footsteps," are fundamentally distinct from other descriptive minutiae "that have no other function than to make the narrative more realistic" (Schweighauser 2006: 71, 73). Ultimately, Schweighauser presents audiographic characterization as one way that literature engages "a long history of discursive struggles that involves the disparagement of the aurality of others as noise" (Schweighauser 2006: 64).

Mikko Keskinen's *Audio Book: Essays on Sound Technologies in Narrative Fiction* (2008) is another recent work of literary criticism that "deals with the ways in which the auditory – voices, sounds, noises – is represented in postphonograph narrative fiction" (Keskinen 2008: 1). Much like Schweighauser, Keskinen insists that "[l]iterature both reproduces and produces acoustical data, both represents and presents sounds" (Keskinen 2008: 5). Keskinen, however, places much of his emphasis on remediation, demonstrating that literature not only "can represent but also utilize in various ways – on levels such as diction, tropes, or narrative structure – the characteristics of … sound technologies" (Keskinen 2008: 5). While Schweighauser organizes his book around literary movements, then, Keskinen constructs his around "technologies enabling the transmission or storing of sound," including the telephone, radio, vinyl records, and magnetic tape (Keskinen 2008: 1). Keskinen's source material is eclectic, and, as its subtitle suggests, *Audio Book* is a collection of individual essays rather than a single, sustained argument. Such diversity, however, demonstrates the breadth of literature's formal engagement with other audio technologies, from Nicholson Baker's telephonic narrative structure in *Vox* (1993) to Nick Hornby's tropological use of musical recording formats in *High Fidelity* (1995).

In my own study, *Sound and Aural Media in Postmodern Literature: Novel Listening* (2013), I follow Keskinen's lead in attending to the remediative tendencies of literary fiction. For example, both Kurt Vonnegut's *Player Piano* (1999) and William Gaddis's *J R* (1993), I argue, formally remediate player piano rolls by incorporating textual lacunae. In Vonnegut's case, these take the form of "punchhole-replicating, dialogue-squelching em dashes," while Gaddis deploys ellipses as his perforator of choice (St. Clair 2013: 41). Literary engagement with nineteenth- and twentieth-century sound media, however, is not limited to the replication of formal attributes. In fact, I offer that postwar American fiction has something of an aural fixation, and that heterophonia (or: a pluralism of sound) is one of the key characteristics of the postmodern novel. Not only does such fiction record the aural complexities of the broader postwar mediascape, but it also retransmits a variety of circulating narratives concerning the cultural effects of sound media. In particular, the postmodern novel takes a special interest in background sound, suggesting that unconsidered audio – from patriotic piano ditties to mood-altering elevator music – has the potential to manipulate on a mass scale. When Vonnegut and Gaddis remediate piano rolls, then, it is part of a larger effort to bring under-attended audio streams to the foreground. As a result, my project is organized around four audio technologies capable of providing background sound: the player piano, radio, television audio, and Muzak installations. All four appear repeatedly in postmodern fiction, often figuring as vehicles for either the persuasion or the ventriloquism of the masses. While impact narratives regarding aural influence might strike the contemporary media scholar as overly simplistic, these ideas nonetheless proved quite seductive to literary practitioners worried, as they were, about the place of print in an increasingly competitive cultural marketplace. In short, literary concerns regarding the power of sound not only serve, synecdochically, as an echo of larger media anxieties, but they also allow print fiction to steal, remediatively, a bit of the competition's thunder. A dialectical engagement with media aurality, then – a simultaneous impulse to repudiate and to utilize – is often the central mechanism of heterophonic postmodernism.

Carter Mathes takes something of a different tack in *Imagine the Sound: Experimental African American Literature after Civil Rights* (2015). Rather than exploring how print fiction responds to mass-cultural sound media, Mathes investigates how African American literature attempts to leverage the countercultural potential of sound. In black writing of the postwar period, he contends, sound proliferates expressly because it "reconstitutes the political along frequencies outside of ocularcentric authoritarian containment" (Mathes 2015: 3). Using music as his point of departure, Mathes moves from the experimentation and improvisation of free jazz through the politicized literary output of the Black Arts Movement. Ultimately, he argues,

> [s]ound functions in African American literary discourse as a means of historical perception and critique, and also as a formalized 'weapon of theory' animating literary representations to suggest levels of black cultural meaning largely imperceptible to the visual registers through which race is constantly being configured in the United States.
>
> *(Mathes 2015: 13)*

Digital directions

If the advent of phonography and the development of media technologies over the course of the twentieth century presented the literary world with both challenges and opportunities, the digital advances of the early twenty-first century have certainly continued the trend. From its very inception, phonographic transcription was considered both a complement to and a replacement for print. "No sooner … was [it] invented," notes Matthew Rubery in *Audiobooks, Literature, and Sound Studies* (2011), than "the phonograph was put to use for literary ends, capturing the verse of Alfred Tennyson and Robert Browning" (Rubery 2011: 1). In fact, "many of Edison's contemporaries assumed that the phonograph would lead to the end of the printed book altogether" (Rubery 2013: 218). Perhaps most surprising in retrospect, however, is how unsentimental the Victorians were when it came to prognosticating the demise of print. This enthusiastic take on the possibilities of emerging phonographic technologies reflected not only "a culture already steeped in oral performance," but also a conviction that audio recordings might help "to democratize the book" (Rubery 2013: 228, 230). In addition, "even before the phonograph materialized as a real artifact, there was already a well-developed Victorian yearning for a technology that would make the reading experience more immediate, that would, in a sense, capture the character and subjectivity of an author without the mediation of the printed page" (Camlot 2003: 148). Victorian futurists were, of course, no more accurate in foreseeing the end of print than Edison was in 1888, when he optimistically insisted he could "put the whole of *Nicholas Nickleby* in phonogram form" onto four eight-inch cylinders (Edison 1888: 646–647). It was not until decades later – the 1930s, in fact – that "the development of the slow-speed, close-grooved record capable of playing for at least twenty minutes made it possible to record longer narratives" (Rubery 2011: 5).

The inevitable march toward miniaturization finally did facilitate full-length talking books. The LP era saw a significant uptick in literary audio, from standalone recitational records (for example, Dylan Thomas's surprisingly popular Caedmon recordings in the 1950s) to hybrid multimedia products (for example, the CBS Legacy Collection's series of soundtracked coffee-table books in the 1960s, which included titles such as *The Bullfight: A Photographic Narrative with Text by Norman Mailer* [1967]). It was the portability of the cassette tape, however, that really began to shift the paradigm. Clam-shelled sets of audiocassettes became a public library staple in the 1980s, and consumers could suddenly get their books on the go, be it via a Walkman on a weekend ramble or the car stereo during the daily commute. The CD revolution of the 1990s only increased the audience of listening readers, and, as the relatively cumbersome physical formats of the twentieth century gave way to the all-digital iterations of the early twenty-first (from mp3s to various streaming services), the audiobook began to assert itself as an important mode of literary transmission. Without a doubt, "[i]mproved ease of use is one reason why listening to audiobooks is among the minority of reading practices found to be increasing in popularity as the number of overall readers continues to decline" (Rubery 2011: 9). According to the Audio Publishers Association, "audiobook sales in 2014 totaled more than $1.47 billion," a growth of 13.5% over the previous year (APA 2015). (As a somewhat startling point of comparison: if audiobooks were a country, its GDP would rank somewhere between Djibouti and Belize.)

The audiobook, then, promises to be a central site for the intersection of sound and literary studies in the coming years. It should be noted that contemporary critics, for the most part, have not met this newly popular reading practice with the same hopeful equanimity as their Victorian counterparts. In *Audiobooks, Literature, and Sound Studies*, Rubery enumerates eight complaints leveled by skeptics of the form:

1. *Listening to an audiobook is a passive activity.*
2. *Audiobooks do not require the same level of concentration as printed books.*
3. *Audiobooks distort the original narratives though abridgement.*
4. *The pace of the audiobook is removed from a reader's control.*
5. *Reading aloud is for children.*
6. *The audiobook speaker interferes with the reader's reception of the text.*
7. *Audiobooks lack form.*
8. *Audiobooks appeal only to the ear, not the eye.*

(Rubery 2011: 10–15)

As should be clear from the list above, some of these complaints are patently absurd; others, however, raise legitimate issues regarding the formal differences between visual and aural engagement with language art. Both the codex and the audiobook offer possibilities that the other cannot duplicate; both, too, have unique limitations, and the field of literary studies will continue to explore these formal questions over the coming decade. As our lived experience becomes increasingly digital, I would predict that studies of literature and sound will necessarily turn toward other emerging trends, from the narrative possibilities of podcasting (that is, the runaway smash *Serial*) to the hybrid potential of tablet textuality (that is, the utilization of soundtracking platforms such as Booktrack). Moreover, as these new technologies and interfaces foreground the multisensory facets of reading that were always already there, we are also likely to witness a renewed interest in the phenomenology of reading: an increased attention to reading-as-sounded-practice or, as Tom McCarthy would have it, the literal enactment of listening in on listening itself.

References

Audio Publishers Association (2015). "Strong Expansion Continues for Audiobook Industry." [online] Available at: http://audiopub.org/press/Sales_Survey_APA_2015_Final.pdf [Accessed 30 Apr. 2016].
Baker, N. (1993). *Vox*, New York, NY: Vintage.
Bernstein, C. (1998). *Close Listening: Poetry and the Performed Word*, New York, NY: Oxford University Press.
Camlot, J. (2003). "Early Talking Books: Spoken Recordings and Recitation Anthologies, 1880–1920," *Book History*, 6, pp. 147–173.
Derrida, J. (1976). *Of Grammatology*, Baltimore, MD: Johns Hopkins University Press.

Dickens, C. (1848). *Dombey and Son*, London: Bradbury and Evans.

Edison, T. (1888). "The Perfected Phonograph," *North American Review*, 379, pp. 641–650.

Eliot, G. (1876). *Daniel Deronda*, Edinburgh and London: William Blackwood and Sons.

Gaddis, W. (1993). *J R*, New York, NY: Penguin.

Halliday, S. (2013). *Sonic Modernity: Representing Sound in Literature, Culture and the Arts*, Edinburgh: Edinburgh University Press.

Havelock, E. (1963). *Preface to Plato*, Cambridge: Harvard University Press.

Hornby, N. (1995). *High Fidelity*, New York, NY: Riverhead.

Kahn, D. (1999). *Noise, Water, Meat: A History of Sound in the Arts*, Cambridge, MA: MIT Press.

Keskinen, M. (2008). *Audio Book: Essays on Sound Technologies in Narrative Fiction*, Lanham, MD: Lexington Books.

Kittler, F. (1999). *Gramophone, Film, Typewriter*, Stanford, CA: Stanford University Press.

Mailer, N. (1967). *The Bullfight: A Photographic Narrative With Text by Norman Mailer*, New York, NY: CBS Legacy Collection.

Mathes, C. (2015). *Imagine the Sound: Experimental African American Literature After Civil Rights*, Minneapolis, MN: University of Minnesota Press.

McCarthy, T. (2012). *Transmission and the Individual Remix: How Literature Works*, New York, NY: Vintage. [eBook].

Morris, A. (1997). *Sound States, Innovative Poetics and Acoustical Technologies*, Chapel Hill, NC: The University of North Carolina Press.

Norris, F. (1899). *McTeague*, New York, NY: Doubleday and McClure.

Ong, W. (1982). *Orality and Literacy: The Technologizing of the Word*, New York, NY: Routledge.

Perloff, M. and Dworkin, C. (2009). *The Sound of Poetry / The Poetry of Sound*, Chicago, IL: The University of Chicago Press.

Picker, J. (2003). *Victorian Soundscapes*, New York, NY: Oxford University Press.

Rubery, M. (2011). *Audiobooks, Literature, and Sound Studies*, New York, NY: Routledge.

———. (2013). "Canned Literature: The Book after Edison," *Book History*, 16, pp. 215–245.

Schaeffer, P. (1966). *Treatise on Musical Objects: An Essay Across Disciplines*, Berkeley, CA: University of California Press.

Schaeffer, P. (2011). "Acousmatics," in C. Cox and D. Warner (eds.), *Audio Culture: Readings in Modern Music*, New York, NY: Continuum, pp. 76–81.

Schafer, R. (1994). *The Soundscape: Our Sonic Environment and the Tuning of the World*, Rochester, VT: Destiny Books.

Schweighauser, P. (2006). *The Noises of American Literature, 1890–1985: Toward a History of Literary Acoustics*, Gainesville, FL: The University Press of Florida.

Smith, B. (1999). *The Acoustic World of Early Modern England: Attending to the O-Factor*, Chicago, IL: The University of Chicago Press.

St. Clair, J. (2013). *Sound and Aural Media in Postmodern Literature: Novel Listening*, New York, NY: Routledge.

Stein, G. (1990). "Susie Asado," in C. Van Vechten (ed.), *Selected Writings of Gertrude Stein*, New York, NY: Vintage, p. 549.

Sterne, J. (2003). *The Audible Past: Cultural Origins of Sound Reproduction*, Durham, NC: Duke University Press.

Stewart, G. (1990). *Reading Voices: Literature and the Phonotext*, Berkeley, CA: University of California Press.

Vonnegut, K. (1999). *Player Piano*, New York, NY: Dial.

35

THE SOCIOLOGY OF SOUND

Martyn Hudson

To think about the sociology of sound we begin by rethinking some of the basic concepts that Adorno offered us in his philosophy and sociology of music. We then think about what sociology actually does and what is its 'work' before thinking about sound in and of itself and as something which helps us to understand social formations. Then there is a turn to the use of sounds in composition and instead of helping sociology to think about sound we think about sociology by 'thinking with' sound. In this we look specifically at the work of Luciano Berio, himself someone who tried to recompose the relationship between composition and sociology.

Adorno

To begin with: a sociology of *music* rather than sound or more specifically Adorno's sociology of music. It is the ghost of Schoenberg who haunts twentieth-century musical sociology. Literally so in the case of Theodor Adorno who would wake and in his 'dream notes' document how the composer had come to him in sleep (Adorno 2007: 11–12). Adorno's major work on the philosophy of music was written as a manifesto about advance and reaction in music – as Hullot-Kentor has said in his introduction to the work – with Schoenberg representing progress and Stravinsky the archaic and the superseded (Hullot-Kentor 2006: xix). The book was about documenting what Adorno called 'the power of the social totality' in 'such seemingly remote regions as that of music' (Hullot-Kentor 2006: 3). The darkness of the social totality of the twentieth century was one in which 'even questions of counterpoint bear witness to irreconcilable conflicts?' (Hullot-Kentor 2006: 5). Further, only the music of the 'avant-garde' truly bore witness to that darkness and negation – 'The truth of this music appears to reside in the organized absence of any meaning, by which it repudiates any meaning of organized society – if which it wants to know nothing – rather than it being capable on its own of any positive meaning. Under present conditions, music is constrained to determinate negation' (Hullot-Kentor 2006: 19). Music was simply another way in which the horror of the century was mediated.

Adorno's philosophy of music was complemented by sociological works in which he tried to delineate how the social totality was reflected or refracted through musical form. Adorno (1989) at the very beginning of this work describes music and society as having an integral relationship. In fact the very definition of musical sociology lies in understanding the relation between the production of music and the social organisation around it (1989: 1). Further, Adorno sees himself as having the legislative power to define the ideological status of a piece of music in so far as it truly reflects the social totality and its darkness or not –

> Music is not ideology pure and simple; it is ideological only insofar as it is a false con-sciousness. Accordingly, a sociology of music would have to set in at the fissures and fractures of what happens in it, unless these are attributable merely to the subjective inadequacy of the individual composer.
>
> *(Adorno 1989: 63)*

The task then of a sociology of music is to describe 'how society appears in music, how it can be read in its texture' (1989: 218). The social determination of music (Adorno 1989: 223) is about understanding the 'force of gravity of extant forms' upon music (Adorno 1989: 93) and the description of 'social structures' and their 'imprint on music' (1989: 219). In other words, understanding music means understanding the relations that structure has deposited there and that the greatest music is that which reflects the 'social totality' in its clearest non-ideological form. Further, as Adorno says, it is about understanding the 'the social complexion of music in its own interior' (1989: 70).

If Adorno's injunction against 'ideological' music is taken seriously then this leads us directly to the production of music and arts more generally which have a progressive social purpose. The whole of 'relational aesthetics' is built on this premise. As Bourriaud has said, this is 'A set of artis-tic practices which take as their theoretical and practical point of departure the whole of human relations and their social context, rather than an independent and private space' (1998: 113). The autonomy of the work of art is at once displaced by its display of social relations and then subor-dinated to social practices which totally de-centre that privileged, 'private space'. The sociology of music since Adorno continues to think through the implications of his work including the study of social and specifically social class relations within music (Dowd 2005; Roy and Dowd 2010), the social structuring and powers and effects of music (DeNora 2000, 2003, 2011), music as a semiotic system (Van Leeuwen 1998, 2012) and music as a set of social relations, practices and mediations (Looseley 2006). The fact that music is 'sign' means that 'Music can be seen as an abstract representation of social organization, as the geometry of social structure ... Music not only "represents" social relations and "signifies" ideologically crucial dichotomies, it also and simultaneously *enacts* and *rejoices* in them' (Van Leeuwen 1998: 38).

But others have felt that music is profoundly challenging to ideas of representation and sig-nification, particularly those of social relations (Nancy 2007). George Steiner has spoken of the 'radical unstranslatibility' of music (1997) whilst the composer Toru Takemitsu has said 'When sounds are possessed by ideas instead of having their own identity, music suffers' (Takemitsu 1997: 7). How far then can we translate between the dissonant and incommensurable epistemo-logical worlds of sound and 'its' society? How far does this notation of the notations of music either just replicate or evade translation? Antoine Hennion's work addresses these descriptions and notations:

> Music holds a paradoxical, unstable position with regard to the question of mediation: its objects are dynamic, elusive, always in need of interpretation. This should prevent the study of musical productions from limiting itself to those material traces that, unlike in the visual arts, never amount to the work itself. That being said, the history of music has long involved the mobilisation of material intermediaries so that it too could aspire to the status of an autonomous reality, becoming a little more object and a little less mediation and producing closed works and authors akin to literature, whilst

also attracting a solvent public: all this thanks mainly to music's transformation into written form. The history of music is not that of an art of sound counterbalancing the evolution of the visual arts, but more accurately, the story of a continuing effort on the part of musicians to make their art more visual and stable.

(Hennion 2008: 178)

The question of the object, the material intermediary and the notation and its relation to fixity and stability is of course a question of lines. That denoting and 'thinking through' questions of notation, translation and materialities means elaborating the nature of lines and what Tim Ingold calls 'unbounded entities' (Ingold 2007).

The sociology of music, then, takes three broad forms. First, the social determination of music – the ways in which society produces music and imprints itself upon its form, performance and notation. Second, music as a set of discursive formations that can be read in order that we thereby understand the society that created it. Third, understanding the determining social powers of music itself to define and shape its society and social world. Can we therefore think of a sociology of sound in the same way? As a mediator of the social formation, as discursive productions, as sonorous objects of determination? Indeed we need to understand what sociology does and what it is for.

Sociology

Classical sociology (Weber elaborating on the piano as social instrumentation, Marx on Capital and why its society could have no epic, Durkheim on tribal music, Simmel on the sonority of the city) was ultimately concerned with what we might call the relations between social formations and social phenomena: between the abstract and the individual, local and specific. Much of sociology has concerned itself with explicating and elaborating on their multiple relations and the powers of macroscopic structures and microscopic processes. Tia DeNora, in her work on Adorno, has rejected the idea that music is simply a specific, localised emanation of abstract social structures. She thinks of music as having social powers in and of itself. She also suggests that music is something that we can use to 'think with' (DeNora 2003). She argues that sociological and anthropological practice and understanding can be enhanced by a closer engagement with aesthetics without using aesthetic objects as 'data'. Yet the very concept of the sociological object is itself problematic. 'Objects' we take to be entities of study and material forms that we observe and describe and that can frustrate or make possible the interpretations that we can extract from them (Cooper 2009). Varieties of constructionism have denied the reality of objective, factually constituted objects inevitably leading to the privileging of discourse whilst realist epistemologies have challenged this, most recently in forms of 'critical' and speculative realism (Pierides and Woodman 2012). But how can those objects be identified? As Geoff Cooper has recently asked – 'What are the objects of sociology' (Cooper 2009:1)?

We know that there is and has been a sociology of music but can sound itself be a sociological object? In one sense if we see music as performing certain kinds of social functions or being expressive of social collisions then seeing music as a 'sociological object' seems an intuitive result and a worthwhile pursuit. It makes little difference whether you see music as mediation of social structure, discursive formations or itself a power of determination – music is resolutely a sociological object. It is also a psychological and an anthropological object in so far as music is entangled with human 'interiors' and social 'practices'. Indeed, musicology itself is essentially concerned with discerning the sociological object of music. So can we then think of sound as a mediation of social structure, as discursive formation or as having powers of determination? And what is it about sociological 'writing' that might make 'sound' intelligible? How far can be sociologically write up what we hear? And what does that sound actually 'mean' for our descriptions of society? Are we studying the sound for a clue to the social formation or the social formation for a clue to its sounds? Is the sound simply the docile object or container of meaning that we then use as an artefact or 'data' about the social world? Or do we just leave it, as does Jean-Luc Nancy, with a radical undecidability? That we simply listen and let the sound reverberate through our 'corps sonore', our corporeal sonorous bodies, rather than try and understand what it might mean, or signify or describe?

Sound

Let's attempt to answer those questions. So can we then think of sound as a mediation of social structure, as discursive formation or as having powers of determination? We here encounter a significant problem, that unlike music, sound is ubiquitous. It is a sensual aspect of being human. It is essentially, and again unlike music, a non-organised sonority on first encounter. For Brandon LaBelle:

> Sound is already always mine and not mine – I cannot hold it for long, nor can I arrest all its itinerant energy. Sound is promiscuous. It exists as a network that teaches us how to belong, to find place, as well as how not to belong, to drift. To be out of place, and still to search for new connection, for proximity. Auditory knowledge is non-dualistic. It is based on empathy and divergence, allowing for careful understanding and deep involvement in the present while connecting to the dynamics of mediation, displacement, and virtuality.
>
> *(LaBelle 2010: xvii)*

Sounds are phenomena in and of themselves. They are multiple and part of being in and of the world as Nancy notes above. In a simple way some sounds are of course structured by the social world and emanate from it. They can also discursively represent something to us. We hear the sound of a train, itself a product of social relationships, and we can imagine the train even if we do not see it. The sound is itself part of complex social discourses and cultures. But sounds are also part of nature, even though our responses to those sounds are cultural. We often think of the 'aesthetics' of bird song, even if those sonorities can only with reservation be perceived as 'art' or 'song' in human terms. But often sounds are dislocated from their origin, are recorded, de-contextualised, extra-territorialised in radically different and distant spaces from their genesis. They are traces of something previous, of 'dead logics' and often 'dead worlds' particularly when specific sounds are re-organised and re-structured into the new discursive formations of sound art (Hudson and Shaw 2015). In this then the sound is very clearly a sociological object. It comes from the social and natural world and can tell us about that world (as in field recordings, oral history, the sounds of machines, traditional words). But the sound does not have to signify as a sonorous object. As Nancy says, we receive sounds as part of being human, we do not need to ask for meaning or signification. And of course sound has its own social powers, to determine and to structure. In many ways, the syllables of our language structure our social identities, orality provides us with an index to who we are, the sounds of the natural world give depth to our engagement with existence. We do not just receive sound, we transmit it orally, physically and biologically, politically. Sound is part of the agonistic contestations of the world.

And what is it about sociological 'writing' that might make 'sound' intelligible? How far can we sociologically write up what we hear? And what does that sound actually 'mean' for our descriptions of society? This of course is problematic. If sound is often, but not always, a social phenomenon then why are there very few sociological descriptions of its social power? Partly this lies in the difficulties of pursuing the 'meaning' of cultural and aesthetic objects. If there is meaning inherent in the sound artefact, there is a problem with understanding that meaning or set of meanings as data without ascribing meaning to it that the object might frustrate or make untenable. Like the sociology of music the relentless search for meaning or data often evades understanding the sound object in and of itself and the morphologies and taxonomies with which it is entangled. This can rest upon the sound object itself as an aesthetic production or as simply the aural reproduction of a naturally or socially occurring activity: unprocessed 'natural' materials that are then recomposed into 'art' (Emmerson 1986: 19). Luc Ferrari for example simply viewed natural landscapes as a musical tool (Wishart 1986: 43) and as spaces and locations for sonic performance (Wishart 1996 ed: 159). Indeed Trevor Wishart has argued that 'there is no such thing as an unmusical sound object' (1996 ed: 8) whereas Leigh Landy draws the distinction between unorganised and organised sound and the use of sound objects (Landy 2007 and see LaBelle 2007). The problem of intelligibility, description and imposition essentially remains a methodological question about socially constituted and generated sound objects and how far they have an independent existence beyond our modes of sociological description.

Are we studying the sound for a clue to the social formation or the social formation for a clue to its sounds? Is the sound simply the docile object or container of meaning that we then use as an artefact or 'data' about the social world? Sociological practice concerns itself with demarcating the social and the non-social in terms of objects, often leaving the 'interiors' to psychology and the 'natural' to anthropology. Indeed any form of sociality is of concern to sociological practice including musical collectivities (Hudson 2014a). But the central issue is this idea of the docile object and not just in the sense already discussed that its docility might allow meaning to be imposed upon it. It might simply reveal what it contains as data for us to observe and see through to the things we are *really* interested in: the social structure and the social formation that have deposited the sound object to our ears. Sociological practice has to perform a different feat of listening to that of general 'human' listening. It tries to listen to what concerns it and demarcate itself off from what does not concern it. The sociological object has to have something 'social' about it. At the same time the fact that these sonorities exist in our social world means that we should attend to them as objects. This means understanding the textures, auralities, properties of the object itself rather than as something we hear through to understand something else behind it. The problem lies in the possibilities of translatability and whether we have the sociological language to describe aurality and sonority.

Brian Kane has argued for Nancy's 'allegiance to non-indexical and non-significational modes of listening' (Kane 2012: 442 and see Hudson 2014b). Kane notes that 'To make listening into something other than listening for signification or indices implies an emphasis on the sensory relationship between world and listener, a listening that begins not with the search for meanings but on the basis of the sensory qualities of sounds' (2012: 443). The displacement of the idea of the container, of the metaphor literally 'carrying over' meaning, of the sonority as data of another *thing* then begins to privilege the 'sensory qualities' of the object. This is no less sociological than the search for social 'structure' indeed it reaffirms the material entity as the privileged object of analysis. Further, its sensory qualities reveal the immediately sensual relationship between the body and the sound. As Nancy notes:

> The womb [*matrice*]-like constitution of resonance, and the resonant constitution of the womb: What is the belly of a pregnant woman, if not the space or the antrum where a new instrument comes to resound, a new *organon*, which comes to fold in on

itself, then to move, receiving from outside only sounds, which, when the day comes, it will begin to echo through its cry? ...The ear opens into the sonorous cave that we then become.

(Nancy 2007:37)

Birthed into sound, the instrumentation of the *organon*, of humans themselves, generates sonorities time and time again which echo through their being and the being of others.

Berio

Understanding the landscapes of sounds (Hudson 2015a, 2015b) entails the description of the natural and social world in which humans are enmeshed. The *organon* is itself about the logics of instrumentation: the way we used our bodies, as well as the prosthetic tools that we extend ourselves with, in order to exteriorise our sonorities. The human 'echo chamber', the *antrum* is that location which transmits and receives sound. Further, even if we receive and transmit without meaning or signification, those transmittances and listenings are essentially social. The exteriorisation of our interior will, design, imagination, projection is intimately entangled with multiple others: with other *antrums*, with the social, with civics, with politics, with history. In that spirit, rather than a sociology of sound, it is worth recomposing sociology itself with the 'sound world'. Rather than a sociology which listens, can we listen to sociology and can that listening change our sociological practice to make us more able, methodologically, to describe sonorous and aesthetic forms? Dominguez Rubio and Silva note that:

> We present artworks as more than inanimate material backdrops or inert vehicles of social meaning, organized, classified and placed in hierarchies according to the logics emerging from the struggles of agents and institutions in the field. We claim that artworks occupy a key structuring position in the field of art, and are particularly relevant within the contemporary art field, actively shaping how the field is organized, the ways its boundaries are drawn, the exercising of judgements and the enacting of field practices.
>
> *(Dominguez Rubio and Silva 2013: 162)*

The inert docile object then becomes something profoundly active and transformative. Attending to the sound might alert us to its placement in certain kinds of fields and landscapes but also how sociological practice is itself organised, where its borders and boundaries are defined and how its 'field practices' are enacted. Examining sociology in this manner also returns us to the interpretation of the sociological object or how sociology itself frames the very things it seeks to describe. As Hennion has said above and to which we return: 'Music holds a paradoxical, unstable position with regard to the question of mediation: its objects are dynamic, elusive, always in need of interpretation. This should prevent the study of musical productions from limiting itself to those material traces that, unlike in the visual arts, never amount to the work itself' (2008: 178). Indeed, in this sense what is the 'work' of sociology if the object is not the object of analytical work in terms of what it mediates? We do not sociologically labour upon the vast social structures and social formations but upon the instances and exemplars of what we presume are the hidden structures of class (taste in music indicating class position as Bourdieu has it). The sociological rather than musical 'mobilisation of material intermediaries' (Hennion 2008: 178) labours to produce the status of an 'autonomous reality', as Hennion has it, of the social structure. The objects support the materialisation and visibility of the social formation in the same way that musical notation provides a degree of fixity to the unstable and fleeting sound.

Sociology's work is then comparable to visual art practice in the way it might help notate sound and the world around it. Indeed composers like Luciano Berio saw an intimate relationship between sociological practice and musical composition and notation and employed the techniques of what would become 'performative social science'. Berio's *Sinfonia* employs as libretto a set of textual fragments from Claude Lévi-Strauss's *Le cru et le cuit* diminishing the sense of the original text (Osmond-Smith 1985: 5–6). His early work with Umberto Eco also saw the development of collaborations between social-scientific practice and the use of sound objects (see Eco 1989). In Berio's work the multiplicity of fragments, resonances, parodies of other composers, create a 'sounding together' which is allusive, repetitive, complex and devoid of any singular meaning or message. The 'juxtaposed, discontinuous fragments ... often chosen to represent salient features of the original text, developed a strikingly individual resonance in isolation and combined to generate new and sometimes unexpected meanings' (Osmond-Smith 1985: 9). This new assemblage of sounds and text repeats, fuses and experiments with multiple meanings and without being directly significatory of the 'social totality' from which it emerges. In perhaps the most sustained use of sound objects in *Visage*, Berio and Cathy Berberian forged a news sonic landscape which utterly transformed the world from which it emerged with its inventions of sound: 'These included cries, a whole gamut of different laughs, singing, a low clicking sound, isolated phonemes and syllables, and passages of nonsense language based on the phonology of English, Hebrew, and the Neapolitan dialect' (Causton 1995: 17).

Further, the relation between sociology and sound may express something profound about the fragmentation and complexity of identity in late modernity – that if one were to create an inventory of identity it would look more like a disparate collage than a coherent list. As Tim Ingold has said: 'fragmentation can be read positively in so far as it opens up passages – albeit unconventional ones – that might previously have been closed off, allowing inhabitants to find their own "ways through", and thereby to make places for themselves, amidst the ruptures of dislocation' (2007: 167). The sociology of sound can then help us rethink the question of social meaning and aesthetic objects and how far can we recompose the very nature of sociological enquiry. So to continue with some insights from Berio.

First, in terms of social meaning and the object it is possible to find all kinds of fragmented meanings in Berio's work from the use of Levi-Strauss, Samuel Beckett and Martin Luther King in the *Sinfonia* and in terms of the elements of social language in *Visage*. His work was composed and authored and although an example of 'open work' the material entities and notations of Berio create a structure, an assemblage and an intent. That intent may be to dislocate or to initiate dissonance and fragmentation but it does not mean that 'authored' meaning is absent. What it does do is radically problematize the notion that one might see his work as a module of 'social' meaning and that the artefacts and assemblages express that 'social' as if they were semiotic structures. The social leaves its detritus in the work but there is no guide to the fragmented 'social' labyrinth in the music.

Second, how far does Berio's work help us think about sociological enquiry or in what way can we perceive Berio himself as a sociologist? The distinction between aesthetic logics of production and the sociological account of objects is to some extent dissipated in Berio's work. He saw arts as enquiry, as a laboratory, as an inherently social practice but not as a way of describing the precompositional world behind it. If there is no description of the social labyrinth of modernity even as its leaves its detritus within musical form we can still elaborate and think about how humans can navigate his music, use it to orient themselves to that world and use his philosophy of musical materials and entities to think about materials and entities in the post-compositional world. The logics of Berio's aesthetic productions, collages, assemblages and structures of units alert us not just to the multitude of data-points inherent in an object, but to the layers, sedimentations and the 'routes through' the social world that they are part of. Each line of notation takes us into the very heart of the labyrinth and we have used Berio to get through, and 'think through'. This is what Tim Ingold has called a 'parliament of lines' (2007: 5) – those spaces where things, humans and notations meet in the 'lifeworld'. As Berio notates the sound, the world is elaborated: 'At the same time that the gesturing hand draws out its traces upon a surface, the observing eye is drawn into the labyrinthine entanglements of the lifeworld, yielding a sense of its forms, proportions and textures, but above all of its movements – of the generative dynamic of a world-in-formation' (Ingold 2011: 224). The logic of aesthetics is itself the logic of production of the social world and of the social totality.

References

Adorno, T.W. (1989) *Introduction to the Sociology of Music*, trans. E.B. Ashton, New York: Continuum.
Adorno, T.W. (2006) *Philosophy of New Music*, translated, edited and with an Introduction by Robert Hullot-Kentor, Minneapolis, MN: University of Minnesota Press.
Adorno, T.W. (2007) *Dream Notes*, trans. Rodney Livingstone, Cambridge: Polity.
Bourriaud, N. (1998) *Relational Aesthetics*, Dijon: Les Presses du Reel.
Causton, R. (1995) 'Berio's "Visage" and the Theatre of Electroacoustic Music', *Tempo*, 194: 15–21.
Cooper, G. (2009) 'The Objects of Sociology: An Introduction', in Cooper, G., King, A. and Rettie, R. (Eds.) *Sociological Objects: Reconfigurations of Social Theory*, Farnham: Ashgate, 1–19.
DeNora, T. (2000) *Music in Everyday Life*, Cambridge: Cambridge University Press.
DeNora, T. (2003) *After Adorno: Rethinking Music Sociology*, Cambridge: Cambridge University Press.
DeNora, T. (2011) *Music-in-Action: Selected Essays in Sonic Ecology*, Farnham: Ashgate.
Dominguez Rubio, F. and Silva, E.B. (2013) 'Materials in the Field: Object-trajectories and Object-positions in the Field of Contemporary Art', *Cultural Sociology*, 7(2): 161–178.
Dowd, T. (2005) *The Sociology of Music: Sounds, Songs and Society*, California: Sage.
Eco, U. (1989) *The Open Work*, trans. Anna Cancogni, Cambridge, MA: Harvard University Press.
Emmerson, S. (1986) 'The Relation of Language to Materials', in Emmerson, S. (Ed.) *The Language of Electroacoustic Music*, London: Macmillan, 17–39.
Hennion, A. (2008) 'The Musicalisation of the Visual Arts', *Music, Sound and the Moving Image*, 2(2): 175–182.
Hudson, M. (2014a) 'Music Collectives', in Thompson, W.F. (Ed.) *Music in the Social and Behavioral Sciences: An Encyclopedia*, London: Sage.
Hudson, M. (2014b) 'What, Am I Hearing Light?: Listening Through Jean-Luc Nancy', *HZ Journal*, 19: 1–8.
Hudson, M. (2015a) 'Archive, Sound and Landscape in Richard Skelton's Landings Sequence', *Landscapes*, 16(1): 63–78.
Hudson, M. (2015b) 'Schwitters' Ursonate and the Merz Barn Wall', *Leonardo Music Journal*, 25: 89–92.
Hudson, M. and Shaw, T. (2015) 'Dead Logics and Worlds: Sound Art and Sonorous Objects', *Organised Sound*, 20(2): 263–272.
Ingold, T. (2007) *Lines: A Brief History*, London: Routledge.
Ingold, T. (2011) *Being Alive: Essays on Movement, Knowledge and Description*, London: Routledge.
Kane, B. (2012) 'Jean-Luc Nancy and the Listening Subject', *Contemporary Music Review*, 31(5–6): 439–447.
LaBelle, B. (2007) *Background Noise: Perspectives on Sound Art*, London: Continuum.
LaBelle, B. (2010) *Acoustic Territories: Sound Culture and Everyday Life*, New York: Continuum.
Landy, L. (2007) *Understanding the Art of Sound Organization*, Cambridge, MA: MIT Press.
Looseley, D. (2006) 'Antoine Hennion and the Sociology of Music', *International Journal of Cultural Policy*, 12(3): 341–354.
Nancy, J-L. (2007) *Listening*, trans. Charlotte Mandell, New York: Fordham University Press.
Osmond-Smith, D. (1985) *Playing on Words: A Guide to Luciano Berio's Sinfonia*, London: Royal Musical Association Monographs, no. 1.
Pierides, D. and Woodman, D. (2012) 'Object-oriented Sociology and Organizing in the Face of Emergency: Bruno Latour, Graham Harman and the Material Turn', *The British Journal of Sociology*, 63(4): 662–679.

Roy, W.G. and Dowd, T.J. (2010) 'What Is Sociological about Music?', *Annual Review of Sociology*, 36: 183–203.

Steiner, G. (1997) *Errata: An Examined Life*, London: Weidenfeld and Nicolson.

Takemitsu, T. (1997) 'Nature and Music', *Terra Nova: Nature and Culture*, 2(3): 5–13.

Van Leeuwen, T. (1998) 'Music and Ideology: Notes Towards a Sociosemiotics of Mass Media Music', *Popular Music and Society*, 22(4): 25–54.

Wishart, T. (1986) 'Sound Symbols and Landscapes', in Emmerson, S. (Ed.) *The Language of Electroacoustic Music*, London: Macmillan, 41–60.

Wishart, T. (1996) *On Sonic Art*, a new and revised edition by Simon Emmerson, Amsterdam: Harwood.

36

POPULAR MUSIC AS SOUND AND LISTENING

Ian Reyes

Locating the object of music at an epistemological crossroads

"Popular music" is a form, not a style. Not to be confused with a genre—"pop music"—or whether that genre is widely liked—"popular" with listeners—it is best understood as music coming from a certain, non-art mode of production, synonymous with commercial, recorded music (Adorno, 2000; Anderson, 2006; Negus, 1996). But if the object at issue is not art, maybe not even music, how should it be understood and evaluated? This can be difficult to answer because the mediation of musical sound and listening presents a number of challenges to dominant ways of knowing and critiquing music as sound and listening.

Sakakeeny (2015) observed that music studies are a pillar of what is now called sound studies, despite the epistemological chasm between the two, across which musicological analyses and constructions of canonical works appear at odds with the more anti-canonical social, material, and political analyses of sound studies. According to Coates (2008), a major contribution of sound studies to other fields is a critical perspective on popular music as an audible phenomenon, not just as a "sound track." This comes from focusing on the audible, not just musical or semiotic aspects of popular music, framed as the outcome of industrial processes and market forces not unlike those for visual culture.

Still, Garcia Quinones (2016) found the study of music a "deaf spot" for sound studies, still underdeveloped compared to work on other sonic domains; to the extent that sound studies engage music, scholars typically prefer "experimental" art music or the more technical, studio-oriented side of popular music production. Rather than consider these emphases on experimental music and audio technologies as deaf spots, however, this chapter considers why these themes make sense with regard to the contrasting epistemologies of music and sound studies.

The crux of the matter is that traditional epistemologies of music address only particular, ideal qualities of musical sound, like pitch and rhythm. What about other aspects of sound, like timbre or spatiality? Truax (2001) argued this limit could be transcended by incorporating psychoacoustics and communication theory with musicology, thus acknowledging and building upon the listener as the center of "information exchange" between oneself and the environment, whereby sonic phenomena—sounds—are understood as the products of this listening exchange. Yet Truax (2001) also acknowledged that sounds and listeners are not independent of social and cultural forces, and that expanding music analysis to include "environmental" context is equally important as expanding what counts as the musical "text."

This, essentially, is where sound studies and popular music studies are joined today. As noted above, this is still an ongoing project, hardly the most common way to study music or the most common theme in sound studies. And there is still good reason for old, musicological episte-mologies of sound to remain strong. Limited though they may be, they have served the study of sound well. Prior to the emergence of modern acoustical sciences, many of the best tools, techniques, and vocabularies for creating, controlling, and knowing sound came from the study and practice of music. Sterne found:

> Prior to the nineteenth century, philosophies of sound usually considered their object through a particular, idealized instance such as speech or music. [...] As the notion of frequency took hold in nineteenth-century physics, acoustics, otology, and physiology, these fields broke with the older philosophies of sound. Where speech or music had been the general categories through which sound was understood, they were now special cases of the general phenomenon of sound.
>
> *(Sterne, 2003, p. 23)*

Nonetheless, this more techno-scientific understanding of sound and listening—the "tym-panic function" (Sterne, 2003) or "energy transfer model" (Truax, 2001)—was not easily bridged with old, musically oriented philosophies of sound. This is because listening to sound *as if* it were music is anathema to entrenched aesthetic and social values.

In the following, this is observed in a brief account of sound and listening as problematics in popular music studies beginning in the early 20th century. In this account, the productive friction, intellectually and materially, comes from audio media technologies and cultures. In this regard, the strength of contemporary sound studies is rigorous attention to listening. Yet the road to such attention begins roughly as critical studies of popular music listeners in the early and mid-20th century regarded the sounds of popular music and listeners who enjoyed them as suspicious, to say the least.

In the mass culture tradition (for example, T.W. Adorno, Walter Benjamin, David Riesman), music recordings were stand-ins for real, live music. Diminished though they may be, recorded substitutes were not without potential. Like any delivery system, recordings could bring the best a culture has created or it could bring insignificant trash. Ultimately, the trouble for these early scholars and their sympathizers was that the record industry decided to be agnostic on the matter, leaving modern cultural evolution in the hands of the mass market, no matter what old world elites would like.

In the cultural studies tradition (for example, Stuart Hall, Dick Hebdige, Angela McRobbie), aesthetic values are immanent to the cultures espousing them. This is not relativism, rather an attunement to social power within cultural phenomena. But this means, initially, the sounds of music recordings were of less scholarly interest than the meanings of music consumption in youth cultures. The sounds of popular music were merely aesthetic markers of underlying social processes. Later scholars would validate music fans as semiotically "active" and "productive" but how listening might be sonically active and what results from that activity requires further explanation. To begin thinking of music as listening, one must first contend with music as sound.

Music as sound: against tonal hegemony

Social and economic forces affect the differences between musical and non-musical sounds, thus these differences are historically and culturally specific (Attali, 1996). In the West, tonality is what makes music different from other sonic phenomena (Adorno, 2002; Schopenhauer, 1969;

Scruton, 2010). Think of tonality as relationships between pitched sounds, or notes—the sort of thing indicated by standard music notation. Tonality alone is not enough, however; *good* music must be *complex*, which excludes the simple, predictable, repetitive tunes of most popular music (Adorno, 2000; Scruton, 2010). Further, the corollary of complexity is *difficulty*. Good music should be difficult to write, perform, and even enjoy.

> In earlier epochs, technical virtuosity, at least, was demanded of singing stars, the castrati and prima donnas. Today, the material as such, destitute of any function, is celebrated. One need not even ask about capacity for musical performance. Even mechanical control of the instrument is no longer really expected. To legitimate the fame of its owner, a voice need only be especially voluminous or especially high.
>
> *(Adorno, 2002, p. 277)*

Because music is essentially tonal, non-tonal aspects of musical sound are non-musical (Scruton, 2010). The sound of popular music is its greatest appeal and its greatest liability. From this standpoint, it is possible to be a connoisseur of non-tonal qualities of music, but to do so is to pursue something other than music.

At worst, listening for sound is a moral failure and/or a means for social control. Therefore, musical tastes are central, not incidental, to political life. So, declining taste for complex, tonal music is related to declines in moral and political structures (Adorno, 2000; Schopenhauer, 1969; Scruton, 2010). At best—and this is the turn I aim to follow herein—this is where knowledge about musical sounds, tonal and otherwise, ground social, cultural, and economic distinctions essential for individual and collective agency (Gracyk, 2010; Hebdige, 1988; Meintjes, 2003). This is more than an alternate perspective on the sounds of popular music; this is a necessary response to a technological, social, and economic evolution of music.

Broadcasting and sound recording resulted in an ontological break, de-centering tonality. Modern systems for creating and disseminating music through audio media upset dominant ways of knowing and evaluating music. With audio recording, a reduction to pitched sounds is unnecessary for the storage, transmission, and reproduction of music. This is a fissure in the material foundation of aesthetic tradition. The music/songwriting industry gave way to the broadcasting/recording industry, and the new industry's mission to sell records by imparting social, not musical, distinction to its products would obliterate the old socio-economic bases equating musical quality with complex tonality.

Initially, phonograph marketing offered upper-class experiences to middle-class consumers (Katz, 2004; Millard, 2005; Symes, 2004). Being a cultured person, for the emerging, modern middle class, largely required consuming the right cultural objects. Even though such objects may be highly de-contextualized in form and substance—like an opera on record—the promise of listening to high fidelity sound was that, somehow, the representation of authentic concert-hall acoustics and performances might transform the listener into the sort of person who has *actual* access to such spaces and experiences, economically, socially, and culturally. Still, this means that even the consumption of good music on record is déclassé from the start, because the sounds alone lose their value when extracted from the larger gestalt of an upper-class habitus.

Eventually, by the mid-20th century, even nominal connections to such a prior social reality were unnecessary; recorded music became more of an art and world unto itself. Songwriters could be supplanted by producers, musicians by disc-jockeys. Nonetheless, pursuing production values—having "a sound"—was a suspicious adjunct to the standard market practice of substituting spectacle for substance (Anderson, 2006). This is a development that still causes anxiety to this day, as though some authentic essence of music, which is more than just sound, may be lost behind sonic smoke and mirrors. When Adorno (2002) wrote of the "fetish character in music," he was referring precisely to the dubious pleasures of listening to these sonic spectacles, which are not really music.

After the mid-20th century, many if not most popular music styles were largely simulacral, with fewer necessary references to "real" sounds as they may be in the world outside of music recordings (Doyle, 2005; Frith, 1996; Théberge, 1997). Yet sound studies, especially those orienting on science and technology, value these developments in the art of record production (for example, Greene & Porcello, 2005; Meintjes, 2003; Moorefield, 2005; Reyes, 2010; Zak, 2001). The lesson of such work is not that new technologies change traditional cultures, rather that technological design, use, and innovation are largely shaped by pre-existing cultural priorities. Popular music represents more than new sounds, it also, and more importantly, represents *new ways of listening*. Unpacking this requires putting listening first in the ontology of music.

Music as listening: towards an aural ontology of popular music

As traditional musicology affected ways of thinking about music as sound, so modern experiments in art music influenced thinking on music as listening. Broadcast and recording aside, notions of composition and performance can be saved from tonality by incorporating new noise instruments better suited to the ears of industrial-age, urban listeners (for example, F.T. Marinetti and Luigi Russolo, Pierre Schaeffer). The standout artist and work for the music-as-listening paradigm is undoubtedly John Cage's *4'33"*, the "silent piece," because of the way it positions the musically productive capacities of listening as the object of attention.

The World Soundscape Project (for example, R. Murray Schafer, Barry Truax) goes far on both of these fronts, to push the possibilities for composing with non-tonal voices, like the sounds of nature, as well as the possibilities for active listening, especially listening to the sounds of nature, as a musical practice: "Today all sounds belong to a continuous field of possibilities lying *within the comprehensive dominion of music*. Behold the new orchestra: the sonic universe!" (Schafer, 1994, p. 5, original emphasis). But, even in this expanded view, listening to popular music is still of less value because it is more passive or, simply, easier:

> The radio has actually become the bird-song of modern life, the "natural" soundscape, excluding the inimical forces from outside. To serve this function sound need not be elaborately presented, any more than wallpaper has to be painted by Michelangelo to render the drawing room attractive. Thus, the development of greater fidelity in sound reproduction ... is now canceled by a tendency to return to simpler forms of expression.
>
> *(Schafer, 1994, p. 93)*

Here, it is tonality writ large—cocooning the listener by replacing nature with music—that is too easy for the listener: "Radio was the first sound wall, enclosing the individual with the familiar and excluding the enemy" (Schafer, 1994, p. 93). Truax (2001) has similar objections to the de-contextualized and distracted listening habits enabled and encouraged by audio media. The value of difficulty comes up here, too, though now it is to be sought purely on the side of listening. Musicality, in this way, can begin to be perceived less in the arrangement of sounds and more in the activity of listening. Although most styles of popular music seem more musicologically conservative and traditional by comparison to experimental art music, they nonetheless use tonality—simple, predictable, and repetitive as it may sometimes be—as a frame for aural expression, appeal, and innovation. Doing so involves listening as a creative act.

Studying the sounds of popular music, however, comes relatively late to the academic party. Outside of musicological analyses, popular music scholarship has been dominated by sociologically influenced studies of fan cultures and literary-criticism-style studies of lyrics (for example, Hebdige, 1988; Weinstein, 2000; Rose, 1994). One reason is undoubtedly academic disciplinarity. Given how widespread is training in ethnographic observation, literary analysis, attitude surveys, and such, it is understandable that these would become standard methods for expanding music studies. Another reason is one of the basic problematics of sound studies: a general lack of listening skills and critical vocabularies for whatever those skills might reveal. Among researchers and their human subjects, this is a culturally ingrained incapacity that neither enhanced methods nor greater inter-disciplinarity can solve easily. This leaves a silence, or "deaf spot," in the study of music cultures and texts.

Research on music technologies, however, brings sound and listening to the fore. Discourses about the sounds of music technologies offer some of the most direct access to knowledge about sound and listening in music. Record production is a privileged activity because recordists are forced by the technical and collaborative nature of their work to use more precise discursive strategies to guide, shape, and manifest specific, musical sounds in the creative process (Meintjes, 2003; Porcello, 2004; Schmidt Horning, 2004; Théberge, 1997). As the outcome of such processes of critical, collaborative listening, popular music recordings are, in and of themselves, "ontologically thick" (Gracyk, 1996) "web[s] of particularity" (Zak, 2001) that document musical *listening* as well as sound.

To better grasp this perspective, consider that the essential interface for this activity is recordings.

> We generally know the music by playing tapes, albums, or compact discs. When rock music is discussed, the relevant musical work is not simply the song being performed. To employ terminology currently in vogue, we can say that recordings are the 'primary texts' of this music.
>
> *(Gracyk, 1996, p. 21)*

While some recordings may document musical performances, such is not their essence; for popular music, the sound on record is the song itself. Even when the original artist performs that song live, it is not the "real" version, rather it is a "thin" iteration of the original (recorded) song. When recordings are the primary texts for music, listening to the sounds of those recordings is how musical knowledge is (re)produced. Frith (1996) observed:

> Only when we can accept that someone is hearing what we're hearing but just doesn't value it will we cede to subjective taste and agree that there's no point to further argument. Popular cultural arguments, in other words, are not about likes and dislikes as such, but about ways of listening, about ways of hearing, about ways of being.
>
> *(Frith, 1996, p. 8)*

But how does one know that another is hearing something (in)correctly? Gracyk (2010) explained:

> understanding is not a private matter. It demands a public act that allows individuals to determine whether others have the same response. Music is objectively expressive when informed listeners can respond to it in recognizably parallel ways. The public character of that response (laughing with "D'Yer Mak'Er" or dancing in waltz time

to the verses of the Beatles' "I Me Mine" and then moving in common time to the chorus) is a defining element of our relationship to the larger community of listeners.

(Gracyk , 2010, pp. 167–168)

Yet knowing when to laugh and how to dance are hardly the only indicators of understanding. As far as public demonstrations of aural understanding go, none is more crucial to popular music than record production.

Recording is different from other ways of demonstrating understanding because the public is largely absent from the exchange. Music recordings are the sum and substance of asynchronous, aural discourses about musical value connecting private and public acts of listening. A record producer's function is to be the listener who best understands the music and demonstrates this publicly by crafting sounds that will speak to other, knowledgeable listeners (Hennion, 2000; Meintjes, 2003; Moorefield, 2005; Reyes, 2010; Zak, 2001). Gracyk's take on "D'Yer Mak'Er" as a joke hinges on the record producers' ability to communicate something that would sound ironic to the committed Led Zeppelin fan. To encode and decode the joke requires both parties to have deep, aural experience with the timbres and tonalities of far-flung references including Rosie and the Originals and roots reggae in addition to the Led Zeppelin catalog. Deep, active, knowledgeable listening on the side of production means that popular music recordings may well be engaged with equally complex, difficult listening on the side of reception. From this view, there is nothing inherent in popular music that should result in the kinds of passivity and ignorance feared by some. Yet scholars like Frith and Gracyk are responding to the activities and norms of dedicated fan cultures. While the difficult, complex listening constituting popular music recordings may welcome and reward equal aural efforts from serious fans, it also enables the opposite.

This aural ontology of popular music also suggests that certain technologies and cultures of popular music encourage (inter)passivity. Pfaller (2014) explained:

> For interpassive artworks … viewers are not required to participate; moreover, they are not even required to view. The work is there, completely finished—not only completely produced, but completely consumed as well. Contained within such works is not simply the necessary activity, but also the requisite passivity. Interpassive art absolves viewers of any necessary activity whatsoever, and also of their passivity. They can now be even more passive than passive.
>
> *(Pfaller 2014, p. 18)*

Though Pfaller looked mostly at visual media, it is possible to see how this would operate with music based on the basic concepts and practices of audio mediation. Sterne (2003), explaining the tympanic function in the work of Helmoltz, showed that audio recording devices are conceived as machines to "hear for us":

> Hearing is thereby tripled—once by the machine hearing "for us," a second time by the machine vibrating a diaphragm in reproducing the sound, and a third time in vibrating our own tympanic membranes so that the sound may be conveyed into the inner ear.
>
> *(Helmtoltz, 2003, p. 67)*

To produce a record is thus to compound music, making it "thick" by virtue of the intentional organization of listening *vis-à-vis* machines that hear for us. The reproduction of sound from a recording is a matter of reproducing an intended listening experience (Hennion, 2000; Reyes, 2010; Zak, 2001). If, even after deploying all the possible means for audio artifice afforded by today's technologies, something is "documented" or "represented" by a popular music recording, it is the critical listening of the record's producers. It is in this sense, however, that recorded music is aurally predigested, particularly compared to the kinds of listening required for live music.

Through Pfaller (2014), one can take this concept further by asking what it means for recording/duplication devices to be in the hands of everyday consumers. Audio duplication technologies, whether dual-cassette decks or bit-torrent, do more than copy sounds; they also "listen" to those sounds. Especially today, when copying and consuming music are virtually the same thing, this begins to make some sense. The engine of interpassivity is not laziness or ignorance, rather it is that listeners are overwhelmed by the cultural output of an information society. In the time that it takes to listen to a three-minute pop song, untold numbers of new recordings will come online. To comprehensively engage this material is beyond the scope of any individual listener. It may be that digital music subscription services are attractive because they skip the unnecessary step of copying music (which will not really be heard)—with a Spotify account, one may be relieved from even briefly thinking about what not to listen to.

This perspective allows the contemporary sound studies scholar to connect back to the critical priorities of earlier scholarship of the previous century. An aural ontology of popular music shows that the capacity for passivity originates in technologies that enable, capture, and reproduce active listening. This is exacerbated by the record industry, which has relieved listeners from their responsibilities as a listening public. With declining record sales and the corresponding rise of new commercial streams like social media, branding, licensing, and "360 deals," fans can be thoroughly engaged on multiple levels without ever listening to the music. Unlike the phonograph era that promised distinction by delivering the sounds of good music, today no sound is necessary for people to enjoy the social and cultural distinctions and pleasures articulated with popular music texts.

The concept of interpassivity may be a bridge too far for some scholars of sound. Nonetheless, it undoubtedly allows one to see through this theory of popular music *as* listening to its most radical end. Moreover, within the bounds of this principle, one can better appreciate that, if sound and listening continue to be rarely articulated with popular music, it may well be due to the fact that the kinds of listening prioritized by sound studies are mostly found within somewhat uncommon circles like record production, fan cultures, and experimental art music. Outside these domains, it turns out that, in an era when listeners can, technically, enjoy the greatest quality audio the world has known, culturally, most people prefer quantity and convenience over quality (Sterne, 2012).

Regarding trajectories of sound and listening in popular music studies

This chapter has been hemmed by a rather traditional emphasis on text over context. It takes a certain reverence for texts to become concerned with issues like interpassivity. Research regarding the use of these texts for extra-musical purposes, like the control of space or time (cf. Gopinath & Stanyek, 2014), suggest other possible avenues for approaching this topic from a more contextual standpoint. Still, these are exactly the non-musical uses of music that worried earlier critics. Therefore, a move towards context requires this re-conceptualization of the object of music, its construction, and its evaluation. Shifting attention from sound objects to listening subjects is the move that promises to connect text and context. But this cannot be done without contending with entrenched resistances to music as sound and listening.

The biggest is a suspicion of, sometimes aversion to, the actual sound of music, which is conceived as other to the music itself. This, alongside a general disrespect for the tastes and intellectual abilities of listeners, offers only a shaky bridge for bringing sound studies on board. Perhaps an even greater hurdle is a tradition of open hostility and disdain towards the culture industry. Targeting its products and the commercial logic behind them, distancing them from real art, obscures the critical, creative acts of listening in both production and consumption. Shining a light on these areas, one can readily find the active, knowledgeable aural cultures said to be lacking in the listening public.

Nonetheless, these may be exceptions that prove the rule. What if the listening public is as Adorno and cohort feared? The average listener may not well understand how to listen—musically or sonically—and maybe does not care to. Compared to public understanding of other media arts, particularly film, critical understandings of popular music are astoundingly inadequate. Whereas scholars, filmgoers, and the mainstream press seem to grasp the nuances of the medium and its various moving parts (for example, producers, directors, screenwriters, cinematographers) the same is not true for popular music. Scholars, audiences, and the press are relatively less sophisticated when it comes to popular music due to their inordinate interest in performers as opposed to other creative industry personnel, a situation the record industry encourages (Anderson, 2006; Zak, 2001). Lack of aural literacy, or even curiosity, is an obvious place for sound studies scholars to intervene, as many have.

Seeking better concepts, vocabularies, and techniques for popular music listening is necessary; therefore the merits of studying record production should be clear. Just as the study of music composition and performance was a key point of reference for early modern scholars of sound. Today, popular music production offers much more than examples of active listening, it also offers a remarkably useful set of terms and concepts for better understanding music as sound and listening in the context of its primary mode of production and consumption.

References

Adorno, T.W. (2000). On popular music. In S. Frith & A. Goodwin (Eds.), *On record: Rock, pop, and the written word* (pp. 301–314). London: Routledge.

Adorno, T.W. (2002). On the fetish character in music and regression of listening. In A. Arato & E. Gebhardt (Eds.), *The essential Frankfurt school reader* (pp. 270–299). New York, NY: Continuum.

Anderson, T.J. (2006). *Making easy listening.* Minneapolis, MN: University of Minnesota Press.

Attali, J. (1996). *Noise: The political economy of music.* (B. Massumi, Trans.) Minneapolis, MN: University of Minnesota Press.

Coates, N. (2008). Sound studies: missing the (popular) music for the screens? *Cinema Journal,* 48(1), pp. 123–130.

Doyle, P. (2005). *Echo and reverb: Fabricating space in popular music recording, 1900–1960.* Middletown, CT: Wesleyan University Press.

Frith, S. (1996). *Performing rites: On the value of popular music.* Cambridge, MA: Harvard University Press.

Garcia Quinones, M. (2016). Sound studies versus (popular) music studies. In J.G. Papenberg & H. Schulze (Eds.), *Sound as popular culture: A research companion* (pp. 67–76). Cambridge, MA: MIT Press.

Gopinath, S. & Stanyek, J. (Eds.) (2014). *The Oxford handbook of mobile music studies,* vol. 1. New York, NY: Oxford University Press.

Gracyk, T. (1996). *Rhythm and noise: An aesthetics of rock.* Durham, NC: Duke University Press.

_____. (2010). *Listening to popular music: Or, how I learned to stop worrying and love Led Zeppelin.* Ann Arbor, MI: University of Michigan Press.

Greene, P.D. & Porcello, T. (Eds.). (2005). *Wired for sound: Engineering and technologies in sonic cultures.* Middletown, CT: Wesleyan University Press.

Hebdige, D. (1988). *Subculture: The meaning of style.* London: Routledge.

Helmtoltz, H. (2003). *On the sensation of tone.* London: Dover Press.

Hennion, A. (2000). In S. Frith & A. Goodwin (Eds.), *On record: Rock, pop, and the written word* (pp. 185–206). London: Routledge.

Katz, M. (2004). *Capturing sound: How technology changed music*. Berkeley, CA: University of California Press.

Meintjes, L. (2003). *Sound of Africa! Making music Zulu in a South African studio*. Durham, NC: Duke University Press.

Millard, A. (2005). *America on record: A history of recorded sound*. Cambridge: Cambridge University Press.

Moorefield, V. (2005). *The producer as composer: Shaping the sounds of popular music*. Cambridge, MA: MIT Press.

Negus, K. (1996). *Popular music in theory*. Middletown, CT: Wesleyan University Press.

Pfaller, R. (2014). *On the pleasure principle in culture: Illusions without owners*. (L. Rosenblatt, Trans.) London: Verso.

Porcello, T. (2004). Speaking of sound: Language and the professionalization of recording engineers. *Social Studies of Science*, 34(5), pp. 733–758.

Reyes, I. (2010). To know beyond listening: Monitoring digital music. *The Senses & Society*, 6(2), pp. 322–338.

Rose, T. (1994). *Black noise: Rap music and black culture in contemporary America*. Middletown, CT: Wesleyan University Press.

Sakakeeny, M. (2015). Music. In D. Novak & M. Sakakeeny (Eds.), *Keywords in sound* (pp. 112–124). Durham, NC: Duke University Press.

Schafer, R.M. (1994). *The soundscape: Our sonic environment and the tuning of the world*. Rochester, VT: Destiny Books.

Schmidt Horning, S. (2004). Engineering the performance: Recording engineers, tacit knowledge and the art of controlling sound. *Social Studies of Science*, 34(5), pp. 703–731.

Schopenhauer, A. (1969). *The world as will and representation*. New York, NY: Dover Press.

Scruton, R. (2010). *Understanding Music: Philosophy and Interpretation*. New York: Continuum Press.

Sterne, J. (2003). *The audible past: Cultural origins of sound reproduction*. Durham, NC: Duke University Press.

———. (2012). *MP3: The meaning of a format*. Durham, NC: Duke University Press.

Symes, C. (2004). *Setting the record straight: A material history of classical recording*. Middletown. Wesleyan University Press

Théberge, P. (1997). *Any sound you can imagine: Making music/consuming technology*. Hanover, NH: University Press of New England.

Truax, B. (2001). *Acoustic communication* (2nd Ed.). Westport, CT: Ablex Publishing.

Weinstein, D. (2000). *Heavy metal: The music and its culture*. Cambridge, MA: Da Capo Press.

Zak, A.J. (2001). *The poetics of rock: Cutting tracks, making records*. Berkley, CA: University of California Press.

37

RADIO SOUND

Tim Wall

The field of radio studies has expanded considerably over the last two decades, building on an uneven academic engagement with the century-long history of the medium. This renaissance of radio studies has paralleled the expansion in the new field of sound studies, and the two areas have produced some mutually beneficial insights. This chapter seeks to set out the productive ways that radio has and can be studied in terms of the medium's existence as encultured sound. By this I mean understanding radio as the product of distinct national cultures at particular historical moments.

Contributing to a volume on sound studies provides an ideal opportunity to work through how we can best study radio by drawing on the fresh approaches developed within sound studies to overcome the conceptual limitations that have arisen within radio studies and use discussions of radio to rethink the confining assumptions that have emerged sound studies. The approach set out here bridges questions about the history of radio and the shifts in production practice organisation and regulatory policy, questions about the nature of specific radio texts and those about the way we listen to and experience radio as meaningful sound. I start with a critique of some of the existing approaches to understanding radio as sound, establish the historically located development of radio within the US and UK as exemplars of national radio, explore radio's dominant form and set out some ideas for grappling with radio listening as a cultural practice.

Blind-alley analysis and intellectual knot-tying in radio studies

Book-length studies of radio usually start by riffing on the idea of radio as a sound medium; often in terms of limitation or absence. Crisell (1986), for instance, states that "in radio all the signs are auditory: they consist simply of noises and silence and therefore use *time*, not space" (Crisell 1986, 43). For both (Crisell 1986, 3) and Chignell (2009, 4) radio is "blind", and for Lewis and Booth (1989) it is an "invisible medium". The need to engage a visual imagination when listening to radio is commonplace (see, for instance, (McWhinnie 1959, 21; McLeish 1978, 70). However, metaphors from our physical world take us down (forgive the pun) a number of blind alleys. It is hard to sustain the argument that the meaning or significance of radio is to be found primarily in some essence of its form, or in the minds of its listeners, however rhetorically enticing those ideas are.

We need an approach that integrates understanding radio's form and the experience of consuming it. Film and television, of course, use time as a structuring device just as much as radio and the very mobility of sound media demonstrate that consuming radio is an even more spatial experience than watching video. Jody Berland (1993) has pointed to the distinctive forms of radio time and space. Further, radio does not operate on its limitations as an audio medium, but in terms of its strengths at presenting music and the spoken word and the ease with which it can be made available over long distances. Using our inability to see radio programming as a starting point for understanding radio sound seems at best irrelevant and, while it is obviously true that we do not see radio, the recognition does not mean radio is (literally or metaphorically) invisible, nor its listeners blind.

There is a case to be made for greater attention to radio within media studies and for its place in sound studies. When television replaced radio as the main domestic medium academics somehow lost track of radio, even though this was the very moment it became ubiquitous in our social world. Radio's pervasive presence in everyday life demands more analysis, not less. Worries about television's political and moral influence, debates about state policy and legislation, and even discussions of cultural value, construct radio as a less significant medium. Sound studies, with its emphasis on the listening experience and the social-pervasiveness of sound, provides productive frames through which to understand radio.

The foundational work of radio studies, edited by Lazarsfeld and Stanton (1944), focused on social effects and regulation and established media studies as a discipline, but as the future of television increasingly dominated national policy debates and the new medium came to be perceived as the most influential, radio studies was relegated to a second division of media studies, reinforced by the contention that radio is a secondary medium. Understanding radio as a means through which other textual forms – music, speech or advertising – are consumed, or that radio consumption is undertaken while doing something else (getting up, traveling to work, cooking tea), should point us not to the marginal nature of the medium, but rather to the centrality of radio within complex media systems and its integration into everyday life.

An emphasis on radio can also contribute to developing sound studies beyond its own current limitations. Radio provides a longer history to forms of mobile listening ignored in the emphasis on new technology, and ideas of audience in radio studies enable us to explore the ways in which the listening subject can imagine themselves as part of a wider community of listeners that recontextualise work on the privatisation of sound worlds. Most importantly, radio points to the way different sound media have distinctive institutional forms, listening regimes and national characteristics.

The most unhelpful trajectory in radio studies has been an aspiration to produce a general theory of radio by isolating the essential qualities of radio. For Crisell, for instance, radio's use of sound leads him to propose that "sound is a 'natural' form of signification which exists 'out there' in the real world" and works indexically, linked to the way that sounds alert us to other physical occurrences in the real world (Crisell 1986, 43). However, radio sound is an exemplar of human invention, always mediates sound from the real world, and even the most indexical of radio sounds are not usually what they seem. Its artifice is what makes it endlessly interesting. The conventions developed over radio's history, and organised in the distinctively different national institutional form radio has taken, can only be understood with attention to the sophisticated processes of construction the medium relies on. The essentialist ideas introduced thirty years ago are still routinely set out un-interrogated in recent student textbooks (see, for instance, Crook 2012).

This essentialist misrecognition of how sound works in radio is itself rooted in a privileging of certain forms of radio sound that are marginal within the institutionalisation of radio broadcasting itself. By drawing from observations about radio talk, radio drama or even experimental forms of sound, rather than the dominant forms of music radio, authors often propose that the complexity of radio's meaning as sound can be reduced to the sound of the spoken word; that speech is radio's primary code. Crisell makes the best case for the idea on the basis that in radio the spoken word "contextualizes all other codes" (Crisell 1986, 54). Radio talk does anchor meanings, of course, and even music radio has retained presenter talk as a vital part of its form. This leads, though, to assertions about "the virtual absence of meaning in music" (Crisell 1986, 49), or the reduction of music's role to jingles, signature tunes and incidental music (Shingler and Wieringa 1998, 61–72). Given how pervasive recorded music is in the output of radio it is hard to see how this aspect of radio sound is not seen as its primary code.

Our final blind alley is the tendency, shared in both radio and sound studies, to conceive of the cultural form of sound as determined by the technologies which enabled its existence. Radio is, of course, named after its technical foundations – radio waves – and, in what is now a quaint nomenclature for its distinctive technical characteristic, was in the past called "the wireless". As Brian Winston (1998) has systematically demonstrated, such technologically determinist histories of the media marginalise the processes and forces through which media forms like radio sound acquire their distinctiveness. This is apparent in the radio timeline constructed by Shingler and Wieringa (1998, 1–13), for instance, where the majority of the seventy or so key moments they cite relate to technological innovations while only six relate to developments in radio's dominant form based upon playing music. While the innovations highlighted were vital enablers of radio sound, they did not determine that sound.

Sound studies fares no better in this area, either. Michael Bull's (2000, 2007) explorations of how people use portable music devices, to take one instance, focus our attention on the auditory, but present mobile listening as the creation of the technology, rather than the users of this technology as the agents of this mobility. The field has also been noticeably neglectful of radio. For example, Bull et al. (2015), in an otherwise impressively diverse take on sound as a subject for study, only select one aspect of radio sound – its ability to articulate nostalgia – as important enough to require a chapter of its own, and references to radio only appear a dozen times across the other thirty essays.

By engaging with radio as encultured sound we can swiftly sidestep the need to justify studying radio through discussions about absence, avoid essentialist theories and swerve around the siren voices of technological determinism. Sound studies has much to offer here as it has been much more open to the plurality of forms of sound media and the ways in which we listen. In what follows, then, I present some suggestions of how other work on radio can be used to explore the institutionalisation of a nation's radio sound at different points in its history, and how we are constructed as listeners and audiences through this institutionalisation.

Nationally institutionalised radio sound and the emergence of its dominant form

Radio sound has changed dramatically through its history. From its very beginning, as Susan J. Douglas (1987) explains, the inventor-heroes of US radio worked in emerging corporations to realise preconceived social purposes. Radio and wireless technologies were intended to create telephony – the exchange of sound messages between single users over long distances – while the wired technology that we later associated with telephone networks was first imagined as a broadcast technology. The US navy saw the value of wireless communication between individual ships, but it was the adoption of the new technology by amateur radio enthusiasts and the exploitation of complex patents that ultimately determined what radio became in the USA. From the 1920s, radio increasingly became the primary domestic medium of entertainment in the developed world. Its output was dominated by adapting the genres of other forms of public entertainment and information: drama and variety from the theater; educational lectures; and religious and political propaganda, and theater chains, universities, churches and political parties dominated early radio. Elsewhere, Douglas (1999) links late night radio listening and programming to male identity and later to the new music of jazz, while for Clifford J. Doerksen (2005), the broadcasting of jazz became a major moral and regulatory issue, and he traces the emergence of commercial radio programming forms that became radio's dominant organisational practices.

Radio swiftly adapted these entertainment genres to create its own forms – the quiz show, soap opera and comedy half-hour – as their programming staples. For Michele Hilmes (1997), these genres were the source of important national narratives aimed at imagined communities of women and of men, marked out by distinct day-time and night-time forms of institutional sound: "a social practice grounded in culture" (Hilmes 1997, xiiii). Single radio stations became absorbed into continent-wide networks and programming increasingly emerged from New York around conventional formats and scheduled programming, a mission to entertain, and all paid for by advertising sponsorship. The networks reached maturity in the difficult economic times of the 1930s. Radio sounded much like television today, but from the 1950s television took over from radio as the primary domestic medium in USA, appropriating radio's primetime audiences and programmes, and radio programmers responded by playing more commercially produced music recordings (Barnouw 1975).

As Rothenbuhler and McCourt (2002) relate, radio executives established new forms of radio sound to attract new listeners, bringing to the fore programming that had previously sat in the margins of sound broadcasting. The Top 40 format and the notion of the "total station sound", established in the mid-1940s as a soundtrack for the day-time domestic labour of the post war "housewife", were soon to became the dominant forms of US radio (Rothenbuhler and McCourt 2004). The small, mobile and cheaper transistor radios became standard in new cars and commuting suburban white-collar workers were attracted by drive-time music and information formats that emerged in response (Wall and Webber 2012). Radio stations also pursued audiences not well served by television: rural whites, poor urban African Americans and ultimately the affluent young. Country and R&B music and their hybrid, rock and roll, became characteristic of services targeted at these audiences, providing these groups a distinctive sense of identity (Malone 1985, 204–226; Cantor 1992; Barlow 1999). As early as 1947, WDIA in Memphis was aiming its programming at black urban listeners, and the format become common across all major cities during the 1950s, linked strongly to the emerging independent record companies servicing similar audiences during the period (Gillett 1971).

In Europe, radio kept to its older forms even as television became dominant in the home. Broadcasters like the BBC had a national statutory monopoly, and while radio's ability to be transmitted over borders allowed access to programming on the American model, the corporation's public service ethos produced a middle class, middle-aged version of radio's traditionally broad output. A restriction on the playing of recorded music continued even after BBC Radio One was established to play pop records in 1967, and regional commercial music radio only started in 1973 (Barnard 2000, 50–68). Advertising-funded local radio offered an alternative to the BBC, but targeted wide listenership with familiar voices and music (Wall 2000; Stoller 2010, 27–114).

Today's music radio was established in the 1990s when station formats came to determine the type of music that a station plays. As Keith Negus (1992, 101–114) shows, contemporary hits radio (CHR), an update of the Top 40 format, had the largest number of stations and scale of listeners, was organised around a highly stratified system based upon a station's ability to attract listeners, and acted as a promotional tool for the record industry. Other stations attempted to attract more specialised music tastes, and Barnes (1988) identifies eighteen music and six non-music formats which dominated US radio in its format heyday. Urban formats (black and dance music attracting young urban listeners) have now overtaken Adult Contemporary (soft rock for the middle-aged) in their ability to attract listeners, and Alternative stations (diverse music for young, white, middleclass listeners) and Country (contemporary Nashville music) attract smaller committed groups. As Barnes articulates it:

> your station convinces you, through constant repetition of slogans, that it's got more of your favourite music ... so you sit through a step set of 30 second commercials and a traffic report because you know you're going to hear your favourite song ... and if your station has done its job you will hear your favourite song.
>
> *(Barnes 1988, 50)*

Even in the internet age, music radio is intimately linked to the promotional strategies of the major record companies, and radio playlists still reflect marketing strategies: building regional hits on smaller CHR stations into a national hit; or using niche format stations to attract enough interest to "cross over" to CHR stations. As Negus (1992) notes, when record companies "get behind" a record, investing in its promotion, this attracts the attention of major stations' music programmers, increasing its airplay and so proves the "hit potential" of the record.

In smaller European countries, public service stations like BBC Radio One have far more influence. Here stations often focus on "ratings by day and credibility by night" as a way of meeting their public service obligations, and so support specialist and alternative music in the evenings and weekend (Barnard 1989, 51–62). Over the last twenty-five years, the policy of Radio One has waxed and waned between an emphasis on CHR Top 40 programming and attempts to offer a distinctive "alternative" playlist. David Hendy's (2000) analysis of Radio One in the 1990s shows the result of one dramatic moment of change when a "new music first" policy, the use of presenters with specialist music knowledge in the playlisting process, and a blurring of the "day-time pop" and "evening serious" binary created a new ecology of British radio, and possibly of popular music culture itself. Radio One moved decisively away from "international repertoire" pop to greater plays for British-produced records. Likewise, Paul Long's (2007) analysis of BBC Radio One's widely lauded music radio presenter, John Peel, is a case study of the way music acts as the primary code of radio sound and the role of presenters as taste-makers.

With all this said, as Barnard (2000) points out, this should not detract us from understanding the "over whelming allegiance to the sales charts" as the deciding playlist criteria (129–130). Computer-based scheduling is used to achieve an overall station sound that keeps listeners tuned to one station by ensuring a variety of tempo or genre and a separation of unfamiliar records. The 2,000 record plays in the weekly schedule are programmed most often using a three-level playlist system based upon information about record sales, plays on similar stations and market research into listener preferences. A list records get played once a programme, or even hourly on high rotation stations; B list records several times a day; and C list records may only get one or two plays per day. The result is a completely predictable music radio sound.

As I have shown elsewhere, national regulation of radio has been consistently used in a failed attempt to increase diversity of music played (see Wall 2000). I have also shown in other work (Wall 2006), that statutory obligations to play music from outside the national charts by stipulating which genres should be played and in what proportions, are sophisticatedly reinterpreted by commercial radio executives playing mainstream music. They justify this with the proposition that listeners who claimed they like distinctive genres of popular music actually only like pop with "a flavour" of those more specialist musics. Jody Berland (1993) has characterised such arguments as an attempt to naturalise and justify the commercial processes at work in which formats "appear to spring from and articulate a neutral marriage of musics and demographics" (Berland 1993, 107) when only certain types of music targeted at certain types of audience are catered for by commercial radio. This is an interesting example of Hotelling's (1929) economic principle of the drive of profit-maximising companies to seek the centre ground.

There is an alternative radio sound to be found in the unlicensed or non-commercial sector where, it is argued, there is a stronger link between broadcaster and popular music culture. Both Hind and Mosco (1985) and Michael Keith (1997) have pointed to the way "pirate radio" stations seldom adopt the music programming systems of licensed format stations, relying on club DJs for their shows, and usually play in music genres not often heard on mainstream radio. However, as unlicensed stations they usually have lower costs so they can afford to attract smaller audiences, and they are often as commercially orientated as licensed stations. US college radio stations, and their smaller-scale European equivalents, often display a variety of music programming not apparent in commercial music radio as a whole. Again, costs are usually kept low through the support of their host universities and the use of committed volunteers. Such stations do give airtime to specialist or new genres that make radio music far more pluralist than would otherwise be the case (Tremblay 2003; Wall 2007; Rubin 2011). The BBC's own specialist music radio programming also offers diversity. Radio One's "service remit" requires "specialist shows in the evening which operate at the forefront of new music" with "at least 40% of the schedule … devoted to specialist music or speech-based programmes" (BBC 2008), and similar service remits for the other national music radio stations produces a musical diversity not heard in the US. My own studies, with Andrew Dubber (2009), of BBC specialist music reveal the importance of the BBC for music pluralism, and the impressive experiments with online content linked to their broadcasts, even if they lag behind new music service companies and even specialist music fans online.

The access to radio sound in the twenty-first century is unrecognisable from that of the middle of the twentieth. The number of commercial radio stations within localities and at national levels has been expanding inexorably. In the UK the three music radio stations of the 1970s are matched today by over 300 AM or FM commercial music stations, as well as nearly fifty regionally based DAB multiplexed services providing a further eight regional and thirteen national stations in each area (Ofcom 2011). More significant still is the provision of internet radio-like services. When the US broadcaster CBS bought the music service Last.fm in 2007 it signaled the profound shift from over-the-air radio to internet audio distribution technologies. Last.fm, Pandora and Spotify have come to dominate the way people listen to music. The global reach and interactive nature of the internet has recast the relationship between listener and music. These services replace music programming and DJs with automated music recommendation and personalization (Wall 2016). The spread of these music services to mobile devices repositions music radio within a wider ecology of music sound, and blurs the lines between radio listening and the shuffle potential of the iPod. In this context the idea that radio needs to have a "total station sound" seems somewhat archaic.

The listener and radio sound

As we have established already, listeners to radio sound are systematically organised by the institutionalised providers of radio services into audiences. Following Raymond Williams (1976), we can examine the shifting nuances of the ideas of audience. The term first denotes the opportunity to be heard by someone with power, but is also the collective noun for those who hear, and it later became the collective noun for those who consume culture as communication; a shift from activities of speaking, to hearing, and then to an act which is simultaneously receptive, cultural and economic. To be an audience member means far more than just listening, and our status is constructed through a number of social practices which collectively constitute sound broadcasting. These, of course, are: the technical relationship between transmitter and receiver; the semiotic relationship of the meanings of radio sound to our sound world, including the address of presenters station idents, news and adverts and the programming of music; and our relationship to others who can or do listen.

The early years of radio history reveal the conflicting attempts to define a social role for the wired and wireless technologies that would enable sound broadcasting, and its final form – as professionally created and broadcast to a distant public – defined how we became known as listeners (see Hilliard 1985, 1–11; Lewis and Booth 1989, 11–29). Paddy Scannell (1989) has noted the early BBC's role in establishing a very specific mode of listening that reflected the earliest notion of audience:

> Concentrated, active listening was demanded from listeners who were brusquely informed that if they only listened with half an ear they had no right to criticise. The deliberate avoidance of continuity in and between programmes, and of fixed scheduling (apart from news bulletins) were the major ways in which programme planners sought to discourage lazy, non-stop listening.
>
> *(Scannell 1989, 332)*

By contrast the modern idea that radio listening is secondary, an accompaniment to the act of rising, working, commuting and playing phases of the industrial day, assumes a very different form of listening; one abhorred by the BBC paternalistic position with its idealised listening practices. Every aspect of the sound of modern radio, though, is premised on these abstractions.

However, we lack a sustained scholarship of how listening fits with the other aspects of everyday life. While the work of Moss and Higgins (1982) is revealing, especially in its argument that radio's address reinforces mainstream thought, their approach privileges the single radio programme over the idea that it is the sound of radio which is central to our listening (and therefore interpretative) experience. Far more productive is Jo Tacchi's (2000, 2003) work, exemplary ethnographic studies of the rich place of radio sound in our lives which demonstrate that listening is not a distinct activity, not simply structured around routine, but relates to particular psychological states as an active practice of meaning-making.

There is work on how radio professionals construct "listeners" and "listening". Helen Baehr and Michelle Ryan (1984) and Ros Gill (1993) examine how the discourse of presenters and programmers produces certain forms of gendered listener and my own work has explored the way professionals construct an idealised listener in a wider cultural field (Wall 2006). Given the scale and diversity of radio even within its mainstream forms, we need a far better picture of what constitutes the professional common-sense about radio listening and listeners, and we need to know far more about the extent and variability of professional discourse on this topic. Further, we need a way of relating these explanatory statements of radio professionals to the output of radio stations themselves.

Too often studies of radio are narrowly programme-focused and, as already noted, tend to privilege broadcast talk. That is not to say that talk is unimportant. Hugh Chignell's (2011) work on talks, news and current affairs as "public issue radio" is a vital ingredient, and David Hendy's (2007) longform study of BBC Radio Four provides the rich integration of discussion of institution programming and listeners we need for other forms of radio. Anne Karpf's (2013) suggestive exploration of the radio voice opens interesting doors about the way voice anchors, contains and sometimes pierces our domestic lives. The discourse of presenters imagine idealised individuals that create radio talk as pieces of pseudo-inter-personal communication. Montgomery's (1986) analysis of presenter talk shows how the presenter's address constructs complex relationships between the broadcaster and the implied listener. Frustratingly, though, most of these analyses deal with talk which is atypical of the general output of radio, neglecting how the talk operates within the context of the whole radio text and how this talk is made sense of by audience members. David Hendy (2000) has attempted to overcome these limitations, including use of my own work on the place of DJ talk in relation to musical intros where I demonstrate the way that DJ talk is ordered around the musical structure, rather than significant meaning in its own content.

There is an irony in the fact that, while the idealised listening that characterised the early BBC was soon replaced by the dominant idea of secondary listening, some of the best scholarship of the role of radio in our sound world comes from forms of radio that are predicated on idealised listening. Kahn and Whitehead's (1992) exploration of sound, radio and the avant-garde points to the untapped potential that radio has as a sound medium and Jennifer Doctor's (1999) examination of the BBC's broadcast of twentieth-century art music during the 1920s and 1930s highlight the determined attempts to use radio as a cultural education channel. It is, perhaps, in the study of community radio that the relationship between radio and listeners in geographic or interest communities has been explored most fruitfully. Charles Fairchild's (2012) advocacy piece refreshingly positions music broadcasting as an explicit contribution to the public sphere as the "aesthetics of democracy", and while its data is based in Australia, like most of the national studies cited in this chapter, it bears transfer to other nations.

We should finally close this section with a reflection on the long-held dreams of mobile listening. While this is most often associated with the invention of the transistor (to the point that the "transistor radio" was named after this key technical development) the concept and practice of portability and mobility in radio listening predates the invention of this miniaturising technology. In Schiffer's (1991) phrase, portability was a cultural imperative from the beginning of radio sound, important for the military, in cars from the mid-1920s and via pocket radios with ear-pieces from the late 1930s (Schiffer 1991, 17–31, 161–171). Nick Webber and I have argued in an earlier article that the transistor radio played a central part in a profound change in "cultural co-ordinates": shifting our sense of space, time and identity. In these new contexts the sound of radio was dramatically transformed. "Music on the move" becomes a significant icon of modernity in late 1950s USA, with WJR Detroit appropriately developing formats of news, travel and weather information programming aimed specifically at local car travelers in 1958 (Wall and Webber 2014). While first the Walkman and then the iPod became the focus for studies of mobile music (Bull 2005), the pocket radio established these principles from the 1960s (Schiffer 1993).

Conclusion

Radio, the first form of long-distance sound broadcasting, now fights for its place in the cacophony of the sounds of everyday life. However, it still offers a distinctive and widely encountered part of our sound world. Radio-like services are an important part of the sound experience now offered by internet platforms and radio provides an important historical perspective when trying to draw conclusions about the emerging sound experience enabled by new technologies. This chapter has pointed to the essentialist, spoken-word-privileging and technologically determinist limitations at the heart of radio studies work, and offers an integrated approach which draws on some rich and suggestive, but yet undeveloped, strands of research. The emphasis in sound studies on sound world experience and the place of radio within a wider media ecology offers significant ways forward. In return, radio studies can offer sophisticated models for understanding the distinct historical, national and media-specific ways in which sound forms emerge, and specific models to historicise our experience as listeners.

A short essay like this cannot embrace all the dimensions of radio sound and I have had to exclude important areas like fidelity, concepts of distance learning and listener community identity, and the links of radio's organisation to other media through technology, ownership and political and cultural purpose. I haven't had a chance to look at the actual and potential alternative ways of utilising radio beyond the broadcast model as the centralised production of content for distant mass audiences. These are all immensely valuable avenues for further study in which important foundational work exists. Like the work that I have examined, they show a vibrant field ready for additional study that tells us much about an important media form and cultural experience and an aspect of our social existence that can inform broader questions of the political and economic world we construct and inhabit.

References

Baehr, H. and M. Ryan (1984). Shut up and listen: women and local radio – a view from the inside. London, Comedia.

Barlow, W. (1999). Voice over: the making of black radio. Philadelphia, PA, Temple University Press.

Barnard, S. (1989). On the radio: music radio in Britain. Milton Keynes; Philadelphia, PA Open University Press.

Barnard, S. (2000). Studying radio. London, Arnold.

Barnes, K. (1988). Top 40 radio: a fragment of the imagination. Facing the music. S. Frith. New York, NY Pantheon.

Barnouw, E. (1975). Tube of plenty: the evolution of American television. New York, NY, Oxford University Press.

BBC. (2008). "Radio 1 programme policy 2008/2009," from www.bbc.co.uk/info/statements2008/radio/radio1.shtml.

Berland, J. (1993). Radio space and industrial time: the case of music formats. Rock and popular music: pollitics, policies, institutions. T. Bennett, S. Frith, L. Grossberg, J. Shepherd and G. Turner. London, Routledge: 104–118.

Bull, M. (2000). Sounding out the city: personal stereos and the management of everyday life. Oxford, Berg.

Bull, M. (2005). "No Dead Air! The iPod and the Culture of Mobile Listening." Leisure Studies 24(4): 343–355.

Bull, M. (2007). Sound moves: iPod culture and urban experience. London, Routledge.

Bull, M. and L. Back (2015). The auditory culture reader. London: Bloomsbury Publishing.

Cantor, L. (1992). Wheelin' on Beale: how WDIA Memphis became the nation's first all-black radio station and created the sound that changed America. New York, Pharos.

Chignell, H. (2009). Key concepts in radio studies. Los Angeles, CA; London, Sage.

Chignell, H. (2011). Public issue radio: talks, news and current affairs in the twentieth century. Basingstoke, Palgrave Macmillan.

Crisell, A. (1986). Understanding radio. London, Methuen.

Crook, T. (2012). The sound handbook. Abingdon, Oxon; New York, NY, Routledge.

Doctor, J. R. (1999). The BBC and ultra-modern music, 1922–1936: shaping a nation's tastes. Cambridge, Cambridge University Press.

Doerksen, C. J. (2005). American Babel: rogue radio broadcasters of the jazz age. Philadelphia, PA, University of Pennsylvania Press.

Douglas, S. J. (1987). Inventing American broadcasting, 1899–1922. Baltimore, MD, Johns Hopkins University Press.

Douglas, S. J. (1999). Listening in: radio and the American imagination, from Amos 'n' Andy and Edward R. Murrow to Wolfman Jack and Howard Stern. New York, Times Books.

Fairchild, C. (2012). Music, radio and the public sphere: the aesthetics of democracy. Basingstoke, Palgrave Macmillan.

Gill, R. (1993). "Ideology, gender and popular radio: a discourse analytical approach." Innovation 6(3): 323–339.

Gillett, C. (1971). The sound of the city: the rise of rock and roll. London, Souvenir Press.

Hendy, D. (2000). "Pop music in the public services: BBC Radio One and new music in the 1990s." Media, Culture and Society 22(6): 743–761.

Hendy, D. (2000). Radio in the global age. Cambridge, Polity.

Hendy, D. (2007). Life on air: a history of Radio Four. Oxford, Oxford University Press.

Hilliard, R. L. (1985). Radio broadcasting: an introduction to the sound medium. London, Longman.

Hilmes, M. (1997). Radio voices: American broadcasting, 1922–1952. Minneapolis, MN, University of Minnesota Press.

Hind, J. and S. Mosco (1985). Rebel radio: the full story of British pirate radio. London, Pluto Press.

Hotelling, H. (1929). "Stability in competition." Economic Journal 39: 41–57.

Kahn, D. and G. Whitehead (1992). Wireless imagination: sound, radio, and the avant-garde. Cambridge, MA; London, MIT Press.

Karpf, A. (2013). "The sound of home? Some thoughts on how the radio voice anchors, contains and sometimes pierces." Radio Journal: International Studies in Broadcast & Audio Media 11(1): 59–73.

Keith, M. C. (1997). Voices in the purple haze: underground radio and the sixties. Westport, CT; London, Praeger.

Lazarsfeld, P. F. and F. F. Stanton (1944). Radio research 1942–1943. New York, Duell, Sloan and Pearce.

Lewis, P. M. and J. Booth (1989). The invisible medium: public, commercial and community radio. Basingstoke, Macmillan Education.

Long, P. (2007). "The primary code: The meanings of John Peel, radio and popular music." Radio Journal: International Studies in Broadcast & Audio Media 4(1–2): 25–48.

Malone, B. C. (1985). Country music. U.S.A. Austin, TX, University of Texas Press.

McLeish, R. (1978). The technique of radio production: a manual for local broadcasters. London, Focal Press; New York, Focal/Hastings House.

McWhinnie, D. (1959). The art of radio. London, Faber and Faber.

Montgomery, M. (1986). "DJ talk." Media, Culture and Society 8(4): 421–440.

Moss, P. and C. Higgins (1982). Sounds real: radio in everyday life. St. Lucia, University of Queensland Press.

Negus, K. (1992). Producing pop: culture and conflict in the popular music industry. London, Edward Arnold.

Ofcom. (2011). "Radio operations formats and content regulation," available at: www.ofcom.org.uk/.

Rothenbuhler, E. and T. McCourt (2002). Radio redefines itself, 1947–1962. Radio reader: essays in the cultural history of radio. M. Hilmes and J. Loviglio. New York, Routledge: 367–388.

Rothenbuhler, E. and T. McCourt (2004). "Burnishing the brand: Todd Storz and the total station sound." Radio Journal - International Studies in Broadcast and Audio Media 2(1): 3–14.

Rubin, N. (2011). "U.S. college radio, the 'new British invasion,' and media alterity." The Radio Journal: International Studies in Broadcast & Audio Media 9(2): 127–144.

Scannell, P. (1989). "Public service broadcasting and modern public life." Media, Culture & Society 11(2): 135–166.

Schiffer, M. B. (1991). The portable radio in American life. Tucson, AZ: University of Arizona Press.

Schiffer, M. B. (1993). "Cultural imperatives and product development: the case of the shirt-pocket radio." Technology and Culture 34(1): 98–113.

Shingler, M. and C. Wieringa (1998). On air: methods and meanings of radio. New York, NY, Arnold.

Stoller, T. (2010). Sounds of your life: the rise and fall of independent radio in the UK. New Barnett, IN, John Libbey.

Tacchi, J. (2000). Gender, fantasy and radio consumption: an ethnographic case study. Women and radio. C. Mitchell. London, Routledge.

Tacchi, J. (2003). Nostalgia and radio sound. The auditory culture reader. M. Bull and L. Back. London, Bloomsbury Publishing: 281–295.

Tremblay, R. W. (2003). "A Delphi study on the future of college radio." Journal of Radio Studies 10(2): 170–185.

Wall, T. (2000). "Policy, pop, and the public: the discourse of regulation in British commercial radio." Journal of Radio Studies 7(1): 180–195.

Wall, T. (2006). "Calling the tune: resolving the tension between profit and regulation in British commercial music radio." Southern Review 39(2): 77–95.

Wall, T. (2007). "Finding an alternative: music programming in US college radio." The Radio Journal: International Studies in Broadcast & Audio Media 5(1): 35–54.

Wall, T. (2016). Music radio goes online. Music and the broadcast experience: performance, production, and audience. C. L. Baade and J. A. Deaville. New York, NY, Oxford University Press.

Wall, T. and A. Dubber (2009). Specialist music, public service and the BBC in the internet age. Radio Journal: International Studies in Broadcast & Audio Media 7(1): 27–47.

Wall, T. and N. Webber (2012). Changing cultural co-ordinates: the transistor radio and space / time / identity. Oxford Handbook of Mobile Music. S. Gopinath and J. Stanyek. New York, NY, Oxford University Press.

Wall, T. and N. Webber (2014). Changing cultural co-ordinates: the transistor radio and space / time / identity. Oxford Handbook of Mobile Music. S. Gopinath and J. Stanyek. New York, NY, Oxford University Press.

Williams, R. (1976). Keywords: a vocabulary of culture and society. London, Fontana/Croom Helm.

Winston, B. (1998). Media technology and society: a history: from the telegraph to the internet. London, Routledge.

38

SPORTING SOUNDS

Ben Powis and Thomas F. Carter

This chapter considers some of the ways that sound forms an important aspect of sport by paying attention to how the senses play roles in performance and consumption – a range of topics that is almost always taken for granted, if not actively ignored, throughout sport studies. Nevertheless, a casual perusal of sport makes it abundantly clear that even the simple act of spectating at a local sporting contest encompasses more of the sensorium than "watching sport". The auditory is a crucial element of any sporting experience. From the distinctive syncopated pattern of a table tennis rally to the visceral grunt of the front rows locking horns in a rugby scrum, the experience of playing and watching sport is made up of a number of unique sound-scapes. A soundscape is a distinct form of "auditory weather" that contributes overall to each unique sporting experience. As the acoustical environment changes, sometimes dramatically and suddenly, in a sports event, it drastically affects the overall experience and atmosphere. Thus it behoves us to push for the development of an acoustemology (Feld 1996) along the lines of meteorology, a scientific approach that explicitly addresses how "sound is central to making sense, to knowing, to experiential truth" in sporting environments.

In order to take an acoustemological approach, this chapter focuses on the sounds of sport from an expanding range of vantage points. Our approach is to start with the athletes themselves and provide an overview of the ways in which sound is acknowledged to play a role in their performance. Our initial discussion then considers the bodily production and perception of embodied sounds. These initial comments consider both how sound is used to assist athletic performance and how sound is used strategically to impede an opponent's performance. From these, we expand our auditory range to examine the relationship between the sounds found on, and emanating from, the field of competition with those found throughout the arenas of sport. In our considerations of the spatial enclosure of the field of play, the interactions between spectators and athletes become more apparent through the implementation of crowd noise both in response to athletic actions and the crowd's deliberate proactive productions of noise to impede an opponent's acts. Noise itself is one aspect; the other end of the spectrum is equally pertinent. The role of silence and its attentive norms by certain kinds of spectating crowds is also compelling. In both cases, the deliberate projection of deafening noise and music or the equally stunning use of silence to influence athlete performance forms part of the broader soundscape of any sporting spectacle. Moving further afield, we then move away from the materiality of stadia and playing fields themselves to the consumption of mediated sounds through electronic media and consider how sound transforms the consumption of sport-related entertainments.

Throughout this chapter, we draw upon a range of interdisciplinary material and our own research, including unpublished fieldnotes, that make use of the sounds of sport-related practices to demonstrate the myriad ways that the overall sporting soundscape undulates and transforms in relation to its spatial configurations. The generation of sound and its perceivers affects not only the atmosphere of an event but also the performance of the athletes as well. Thus, sound affects actual performance as well as influences the aesthetics of the spectacle.

Embodied sounds

The very breath of the athlete and its passage creates an individualized environmental experience. Listening to and identifying one's own respiratory patterns provides constant and almost instantaneous feedback (Hockey 2006). Wacquant describes such sounds of the "rhythmic puffing, hissing, sniffing, blowing, and groaning of each athlete" (2006: 71) as athletic proficiency is gained through repeated drills and sparring sessions. In sports like boxing, the guttural whoosh of forced exhalation followed by the teary-eyed gasping of having one's wind knocked out is readily apparent by an athlete's inability to immediately continue or speak due to a lack of air. Active self-evaluation of respiratory patterns is especially important for athletes who suffer with asthma (Allen-Collinson and Owton 2014). By attending to the auditory feedback during participation, in combination with previous knowledge of their condition, asthmatic athletes can recognize the early warning signs indicated through their levels of breathing. These sorts of pulmonary resonances make not only the athlete but also coaching and medical staff aware of how the athlete should be physically feeling.

These sorts of immediate corporeal sounds also provide feedback to how an athlete's current performance is going based on the timber and tone of striking an object. A boxer describes the beginnings of a training session where the sound of her fist striking the pads tells her she is using the proper technique: "After the warm-up, when we get to the padwork, I feel ready, my body's hot and ready … I hear the sounds of my technique hitting the pads – tap, tap, slam, slam, SLAM" (Allen-Collinson and Owton 2015: 260). The sound of gloves crashing into bags can grip the boxer, becoming the dominant sense of training, while also serving as an indicator for how hard their training partners are exerting themselves, thus providing the boxer with further motivation to work harder (Spencer 2014: 241–244).

Carter's research on Cuban baseball similarly reinforced his own embodied knowledge as a baseball player (2008): the "crack" of the bat in baseball tells fielders the angle and force with which the ball has been struck long before the sight of the ball's velocity and trajectory is clear. A bat's material makes all the difference: a wooden bat "cracks" while an aluminum bat "pings". Yet the tone and timber of the collision of bat and ball is deeper and more visceral than a more marginally struck ball irrespective of the material used to strike the ball. These sounds are subtle, as Sparkes makes clear as he helps his son choose the correct cricket bat (2009: 22). The reverberations of the willow differ depending on where the bat is struck and the search for the largest "sweet spot" is found through auditory testing instead of visual or tactile inspection. Sound allows the listener to "know" the depths of an object in ways that sight or touch cannot. This learned skill of "agile listening" (Bull and Back 2003) attunes the athlete to specific sounds that then shape the "correct" actions to take, including which equipment to choose.

Those subtle sounds and the knowledge of what they portend is learned through many hours of practice. The athlete's body also generates sounds due to enormous physical exertion. Grunting with effort, howling with pain, or screaming with joy all are part of sport-related milieus.

While these nonverbal vocalizations are often an unconscious secondary effect of enacted phys-ical efforts, the production of bodily noise, such as grunting, appears to increase the force with which an athlete might strike an object, whether this is a conscious decision to produce such noise or not (O'Connell et al. 2014). Furthermore, the "controversy" over "shrieking" female tennis players as being unfeminine (Geoghegan 2009) reveals more about the gendered norms of athletic comportment than it does about the effect such noise production has in masking the sorts of sounds identified in previous paragraph so as to delay an opponent's reaction to a shot. That grunting masks the sound of the ball striking the racquet's strings suggests there is a competitive advantage to be gained.

The use of sound to mask intent can also be reversed where sound is intentionally used to distract an opponent. A common form of this is the *Soto voce* insinuations and insults are a common form of this. It is a well-known activity at the bottom of a ruck or in the clinch of a scrum in rugby or a pile of athletes in American football. "Sledging" by either the wicket keeper or other fielders as a batsman returns to the crease in infamous in cricket. Similarly, a baseball catcher often talks to the batter in deliberate attempts to disrupt the batter's concentration. In all these cases some of the vitriol spewed forth is obscene, derogatory, and highly offensive, and in any other context would be considered utterly and inescapably racist, misogynist, or bigoted. "Getting in your opponent's head" is all-too-common throughout professional sports. This aspect of "gamesmanship" (Howe 2004; Evans 2007) is yet another example of how the tactical use of embodied sound can affect athletic performance. Specific sounds create potential competitive advantages.

Competitive sounds

Sound does much more than provide an immediate corporeal feedback of, or distract from, an athlete's performance. Sound actually dictates the flow of competition. A referee's whistle indi-cates the start and stoppage of play in most team sports. A starting gun fired indicates the start of the race in athletics while a klaxon and the metallic slamming of gates opening are the first signs of a horse race beginning. Through habit, experience, and training, "auditory knowledge" (Rice 2010) of a particular sport is cultivated and becomes central to understanding both the sporting environment and the individual's own performance. This is especially evident in Powis' study of visually impaired cricketers (2018).

The cricketing soundscape is made up of both linguistic and non-linguistic audio with certain players featuring prominently. Listening is an active process of attaching meaning to particular sonic landmarks that allows the players to construct the space around them and also create specific strategies to use while playing. For example, the bowler must always ask that the batsman is ready and shout "Play" as they release the ball. The wicket keeper will assist the bowler, if totally blind, in aligning the delivery by calling their name behind the stumps before they bowl. Once the ball has been hit, the (partially sighted) wicketkeeper will provide a run-ning commentary for all fielders in the path of the ball. The constant calls of the wicketkeeper are used in conjunction with the non-linguistic sounds of the ball, bat, or even thud of other player's footsteps to locate the ball when fielding. In a related fashion, a batsman uses sound to adjudicate the source, direction, and kind of delivery they can anticipate.

Such strategies necessitate an in-depth auditory knowledge of the distinctive elements of the cricketing soundscape. To the untrained ear, the sound of the bat striking the ball may only indicate the connection of the two objects but, to the visually impaired cricketer, it can indicate the type of shot played, the speed, the direction, and the amount of spin imparted on the ball.

The crack of bat, the snap of leather, the reverberations of violent collisions, shouts between athletes all manage ever shifting competitive contexts in sport. Coaches shouting instructions, referees' whistles, shouts of exultation or recrimination based on teammates' performances all contour the sporting experience whether we are discussing a small game on a village green or a professional encounter with thousands of spectators in attendance. Such sounds can reveal social relations between those involved in any given athletic performance.

Spectacular sounds

No discussion of the sounds of sport would be complete without at least a mention of the crowds. Spectators provide the "atmosphere" and that atmosphere is primarily auditory rather than visual. The visuality of a sporting spectacle is focused on the athletes themselves whereas the "atmosphere" is a sensual conjuration of communitas that can be geared towards positive feelings of belonging or abject, sometimes violent expressions of a marginalized group (Armstrong 1998; Robson 2000; Swyers 2010). The creation of atmosphere is central to a team or individual athlete benefiting from "home field advantage" and the noise generated by the crowd can be especially influential. Nevill et al. (2002) explore the effect of "home field advantage" within football and how the crowd's performance influences the referee's decision making. According to the study, a referee is much more lenient towards the home team and is clearly swayed by the presence of a noisy home support. Referees' levels of uncertainty and indecision increase the more supporters vociferously disagree with the referee's decisions. Avoiding making decisions that may displease home supporters and not being victim to their collective sonic wrath becomes a motivating factor for the officials. The collective mass of noise created in the stands, frequently described as the "twelfth man," has an effect on the performance of the players, officials, and, ultimately, the match's outcome.

Such "home field advantage" does not exist in the same way at individual events, such as professional golf and tennis (Nevill et al. 1997). The social context of crowd behavior in these sports differs considerably from the "stadium booming" of American team sports or the chanting found in the football grounds across Europe. In these instances, it is not the percussive force of thousands of voices all screaming in unison but the oppressive silence creating a pressurized environment where the absence of crowd noise accentuates the focus on the athlete's next act. Not only is silence expected, tennis umpires enforce it, demanding that the crowd restrain itself before play may resume.

Crowds strategically use sound, decisively and deliberately roaring and hushing depending on the circumstance. Carter found this acoustical interplay during fieldwork in North America that roofed stadia in particular became acoustic chambers by which the crowd alternated between torrential waves of sound and silence. During Major League Baseball playoff games between the Minnesota Twins and St. Louis Cardinals held in Minneapolis, Minnesota, the partisan crowd actively participated in events by deliberately roaring the whole time their team was at bat, but were dedicatedly quiet when the home team was in the field. When roaring, the decibel levels were louder than standing 300 yards away from 727 engines at takeoff (Kates 1992). Players sitting next to each other on the bench did not even bother to talk to one another because they couldn't hear each other (Fimrite 1987) and in the crowd Carter could not hear his companion shouting directly into his ear when the crowd was "booming" the stadium. Yet, when the home team was fielding, the noise levels dropped so that you could hear the crack of the bat from over 400 feet away. That noisemaking is part gamesmanship is widely recognized as it is frequently considered poor form to make "distracting" noises when a fly half is lining up a penalty kick in rugby union. During fieldwork in Northern Ireland in 2000, Carter observed

Ulster Rugby supporters chastising teenage members of the crowd who shrilly whistled as the opponent's fly half lined up his penalty kick.

The crowd's purposeful, conscious use of sound to support its team or attempt to directly affect the outcome of athletic actions is one motivation for spectators' vocal productions. There is more to spectators' behavior, however, than "merely" attempting to influence the outcome. There are culturally specific norms of spectator behavior involved in any sporting contest that are specific to sport and culture (Kelly 1997). Around the world, many fan groups see themselves not as passive consumers of a commoditized sporting spectacle but as active, creative participants of the overall spectacle. Their chanting and singing helps to create the energetic, enveloping atmosphere of a celebratory event. Chanting and singing are not modern phenomena and have performed a variety of functions – religious, educational, militaristic over millennia (Schoonderwoerd 2011) – yet both chanting have a number of specific characteristics in modern sport. Back (2003) discusses the importance of song in structuring a sense of feeling in football stadia where the potentially sterile steel-structured space is bestowed a sense of place and identity through communal singing and the particular lyrics being sung by the supporters. The socialised nature of collective vocalizations not only provides support for the team or athlete, it communicates a shared identity of the group. For example, the Çarşı, the principal supporter group of Beşiktaş JK, act as an "acoustic community," constructing a shared space through the use of sonic rituals such as marching and chanting (Kytö 2011). A central aspect of this strategic identity creation displayed through the fans' songs and chants is a celebration of place. The dual purpose of such chants, like "I'm Scunthorpe 'til I die!", is to identify a heartfelt connection to a given place, often the stadium, and the denizens in it while inviting the excluded others to recognize this identity (Clark 2006: 500). Liverpool's famous Kop singing "You'll Never Walk Alone" or Millwall fans more infamously chanting "No One Likes Us! We Don't Care!" are clear indications of enduring loyalty to the club but also signifies amongst supporters a public declaration of belonging to persons and place. The auditory reinforcement of identity is not only self-affirming; it is a way of creating hostility towards opposition supporters. Such aggressive "calls to arms," however, can also emphasize other racist, sexist, and homophobic aspects of shared identities (Armstrong and Young 1999; Back 2003; Caudwell 2011). However, such vocalizations need not be confrontational. Some forms of chanting may be seen as a light-hearted invitation to provoke the opposition fans into song (Granstrom 2012).

Sound competition

Spectators' creativity often generates much of the atmosphere that is so valued and lauded by a sport's authorities, the media broadcasters, and the other stakeholders in the overall spectacle. Whether through song, musical instruments, or another form of sonic act, the soundscapes created by supporters appear to influence the performance on the pitch. That energy and creativity, however, may not fit the desired sense of the spectacle's choreographers. These organic soundscapes are being forcibly altered to maintain their own ability to be heard and appreciated as a homogenizing trend feeds the global demands for sporting spectacle.

The rhythmic auditory peaks and troughs of certain events, such as cricket, are changing. Since the advent of Twenty20, a fast and furious shortened format aimed at a younger generation of fans contrasts with the placid, relaxed atmosphere of test match cricket. Nowhere have the norms of cricketing changed than in the Indian Premier League (IPL). Alongside the fireworks and the cheerleaders, the stadium's soundscape is deliberately controlled, providing an atmosphere in which loud is equated with good. Every pause in play is filled by an auditory assault, often a blast of a popular music track blasted at high decibels, that continues until the bowler is ready to deliver the next ball. If the crowd's energy begins to waver, the recording of a specific trumpet riff blares around the ground that prompts the crowd to cheer and applaud. Rather than being an organic show of collective identity, the act of vocal support is becoming something instigated by television broadcasters to make their "product" even more marketable.

The IPL's spectacularization of the cricket crowd, alongside the increasing attempts to control crowd expression in choreographed and controlled manners around the world, reflects a broader trend identified in the globalization of sport (Giulianotti and Robertson 2007; Sage 2011), although the norms of global spectacularization might be more accurately identified as the Americanization of sport spectacle but not necessarily the sport itself. Officials' increasing attempts to ensure a full-throated, full-on entertainment that does not allow for a single moment of respite also shifts spectators from active participants to passive consumers of what is put before them. Spectator participation then is to be controlled and scripted by stadia officials instead of being organic and self-generated. Fans, of course, resist such restrictions in a variety of ways and these struggles are heard in sporting venues around the world. From the Barras Bravas in Buenos Aires (Antezana 2003), to the football stands in Mexico (Magazine 2007), to the grounds of Scotland (Bradley 1998), football fans in particular resist attempts to control their expressive participation during matches. The smuggling of banners, flares, and musical instruments into facilities, as well as confrontations with stewards and police, all demonstrate that the soundscape of a sporting event is not an uncontested, choreographed performance in the manner of a theatre play. And it is not only football.

When the Belfast Giants ice hockey team began in 2000, there was no history of ice hockey in Belfast, and thus no local knowledge of how to act at a match, never mind what the sport actually was (Carter 2011: 108). Given this ethnocentric presumption that the local audience lacked any knowledge of the sport, officials ensured that there was always something stimulating happening: loud music blaring, pre-recorded videos playing, and laser lights flashing after every whistle halting play. Announcements and videos explaining rules and officiating decisions were as loud as possible. Importing a North American model of professional sport spectacles, what the Canadian-led management did not count upon was the local norms of sport spectatorship. By the mid-point of the very first season, a group of fans self-organized into a drumming group. Fans serenaded players with chanting and drum cavalcades during play and in between action on the ice, but did not try to compete with the scoreboard's video and sound system between periods. They saw themselves as enhancing the overall atmosphere. However, after several matches where they played, musical instruments were barred on "safety grounds" as Giants' management claimed the drums prevented players from hearing the referee's whistle. The public backlash forced management to engage in negotiations over the roles of spectatorship. By the next season, an agreement was in place as to who, how, where, and when fans could "contribute" to the atmosphere, complete with a designated spot for the drumming group in the arena.

The attempts at regulating the generation and deployment of spectator acoustics is not limited to club or stadia officials operating in isolation. International Sport Federations have introduced a number of pieces of legislation worldwide to restrict, control, or otherwise restrain spectators' production of sound within a venue because it affects authorities' ability to control the script and affect the soundscapes of spectacles designed more for mediated than embodied consumption, in particular. The Marleybone Cricket Club, the English institution that for years acted as the international purveyor of cricket, and the national governing body, the England and Wales Cricket Board (ECB), deliberately banned musical instruments during the 2000 West Indies cricket tour of England to ostensibly allow a better televised experience, though it was an obvious ploy to silence the distinctive calypso sounds of the away support (Gordon 2000). While that incident clearly was an act of gamesmanship, FIFA's banning of vuvuzelas, the distinctive sound-making device used during the 2010 FIFA World Cup in South Africa, at future international competitions (BBC 2010) demonstrates authorities' seriousness in controlling the auditory weather of an event. The banning of the Barmy Army's famed trumpeter, Billy Cooper, from Trent Bridge during the 2013 home Ashes series despite other cricket grounds relaxing their instrument ban (Goldstein 2013) further illustrates the (sometimes contradictory) attempts to control the sporting landscape. Sports administrators and media broadcasters are slowly accumulating the ability to shape the auditory weather of an event's atmosphere in terms of which components are permitted and at what point and what kind of spectator contributions should be made.

Concluding remarks

One of the challenges within most social scientific approaches to sport is that sport is normally addressed strictly in terms of its structural elements and that the existential actuality of the athlete is inadequately acknowledged. Soundscapes' permutations and sounds' affective reverberations clearly shape the lived experience of social reality including sport-related experiences. The specific sporting sounds that emanate from athletes, crowds, and stadia all permeate the sporting experience in myriad currents. The simple recognition that sound plays an inextricable and important role in sport is an obvious yet vital acknowledgement. From the embodied sounds of athletic exertion to the interpersonal regulation in an athletic competition, sounds form a crucial element in the overall experience of playing sport.

The embodied sounds of sport touch on phenomenological concerns, the ideas of lived experiences and ways of being, not just as an individual self but as being-in-the-world. Paying attention to the sounds produced through a body's material engagement with its surrounding environs generates fascinating, complex examples of how human beings go about becoming athletes, enact their worlds, and create social realities. The nascent concern over embodied sounds found in sporting activities raises larger questions over how sound is used to create and reinforce notions of being.

The use of sound to regulate social behavior, both on the field of competition and in the stands, points to the ways in which sporting sounds compete to be heard. The privileging of certain sensory realms over others and certain aspects of a singular sensory realm, such as sound, over other aspects are crucial questions that bear further investigation in regards to the ways in which people create and experience sport. An acoustemological approach to sport is a needed development that will, at first, necessitate its incorporation into broader theoretical and methodological approaches. The use of sound in spectacle, particularly the power relations within the politics of spectacle, is one theoretical development. Methodologically, adopting an acoustemological approach opens up new forms of knowledge directly related to ways of being and to existing power relations related to questions of identity, disability, and capability. Incorporating sound into theoretical and methodological approaches can only enhance work being done while sound-centric studies will also lead to new understandings of sport.

References

Allen-Collinson, J. & Owton, H. (2014) 'Take a Deep Breath: Asthma, Sporting Embodiment, the Senses and "Auditory Work".' *International Review for the Sociology of Sport* 49(5): 592–608.

Allen-Collinson, J. & Owton, H. (2015) 'Intense Embodiment: Senses of Heat in Women's Running and Boxing.' *Body and Society* 21(2): 245–268.

Antezana, L. H. (2003) 'Fútbol: Espáctulo e Identidad.' In P. Alabarces (ed.) *Futbologías: Fútbol, Identidad, y Violencia en América Latina*. pp. 85–98. Buenos Aires: CLASCO.

Armstrong, G. (1998) Football Hooligans: Knowing the Score. Oxford: Berg.

Armstrong, G. & Young, M. (1999) 'Fanatical Football Chants: Creating and Controlling the Carnival.' *Culture, Sport, Society* 2(3): 173–211.

Back, L. (2003) 'Sounds in the Crowd.' In M. Bull and L. Back (eds.) *The Auditory Culture Reader.* pp. 311–328. Oxford: Berg.

Back, L. & Bull, M. (2003) 'Introduction: Into Sound.' In M. Bull and L. Back (eds.) *The Auditory Culture Reader.* pp. 1–24. Oxford: Berg.

BBC (2010) 'Uefa Bans Vuvuzelas From European Matches.' Available at http://news.bbc.co.uk/sport1/hi/football/europe/8960160.stm [accessed June 16, 2015].

Bradley, J. M. (1998) '"We Shall Not Be Moved!" Mere Sport, Mere Songs?: A Tale of Scottish Football.' In A. Brown (ed) *Fanatics! Power, Identity & Fandom in Football.* pp. 203–218. London: Routledge.

Carter, T. F. (2008) The Quality of Home Runs: The Passion, Politics, and Language of Cuban Baseball. Durham, NC: Duke University Press.

Carter, T. F. (2011) In Foreign Fields: The Politics and Experiences of Transnational Sport Migration. London: Pluto Press.

Caudwell, J. (2011) '"Does Your Boyfriend Know You're Here?" The Spatiality of Homophobia in Men's Football Culture in the UK.' *Leisure Studies* 30(2): 123–138.

Clark, T. (2006) '"I'm Scunthorpe 'Til I Die": Constructing and (Re)negotiating Identity Through the Terrace Chant.' *Soccer & Society* 7(4): 494–507.

Evans, J. (2007) 'Cricket and Moral Commendation.' *Sport in Society* 10(5): 802–817.

Feld, S. (1996) 'Waterfalls of Song: An Acoustemology of Place Resounding in Bosavi, Papua New Guinea.' In K. H. Basso & S. Feld (eds.) *Senses of Place.* pp. 91–136. Santa Fe, NM: School of American Research Press.

Fimrite, R. (1987) 'A Roof-Raising Ruckus.' *Sports Illustrated* (Oct. 26). http://www.si.com/vault/1987/10/26/116473/a-roof-raising-ruckus [accessed January 25, 2016].

Geoghegan, T. (2009) 'What a Racket.' *BBC News Magazine* [online] (June 22). http://news.bbc.co.uk/1/hi/magazine/8110998.stm [accessed January 25, 2016].

Giulianotti, R. and Robertson, R., eds. (2007) *Globalization and Sport.* Chichester: Wiley-Blackwell.

Goldstein, O. (2013) 'Trent Bridge Cricket Fan Faces Brass Ban.' *The Independent.* Available at http://www.independent.co.uk/news/uk/home-news/trent-bridge-cricket-fan-faces-brass-ban-8692663.html [accessed June 15, 2015].

Gordon, O. (2000) Don't stop the music. *The Guardian* (Feb. 16). http://www.theguardian.com/sport/2000/feb/16/cricket3 [accessed June 15, 2015].

Granstrom, K. (2012) 'Cheering As an Indicator of Social Identity and Self-Regulation in Swedish Ice Hockey Supporter Groups.' *International Review for the Sociology of Sport* 47(2): 133–148.

Hockey, J. (2006) 'Sensing the Run: The Senses and Distance Running.' Sense and Society, 2: 183–201.

Howe, L. (2004) 'Gamesmanship.' *Journal of the Philosophy of Sport* 31(2): 212–225.

Kates, M. (1992) 'Metrodome Built on a Sound Basis.' *Chicago Tribune* (Jan. 20). http://articles.chicagotribune.com/1992-01-20/sports/9201060654_1_crowd-noise-noise-pollution-open-stadium [accessed December 30, 2015].

Kelly, W.W. (1997) 'An Anthropologist In the Bleachers: Cheering a Japanese Baseball Team.' *Japan Quarterly* 44(4): 66–79.

Kytö, M. (2011) 'We Are the Rebellious Voice of the Terraces, We Are Çarşı: Constructing a Football Supporter Group Through Sound.' *Soccer and Society* 1(12): 77–93

Magazine, R. (2007) Golden and Blue Like My Heart: Masculinity, Youth, and Power Among Soccer Fans in Mexico City. Tucson, AZ: University of Arizona Press.

Nevill, A. M., Balmer, N. J. & Mark Williams, A. (2002) 'The Influence of Crowd Noise and Experience Upon Refereeing Decisions in Football.' *Psychology of Sport and Exercise* 3: 261–272.

Nevill, A. M., Holder R. L., Bardsley, A., Calvert, H., and Jones, S. (1997) 'Identifying Home Advantage in International Tennis and Golf Tournaments.' *Journal of Sports Sciences* 15(4): 437–443.

O'Connell, D. G., Hinman, M. R, Hearne, K. F., Michael, Z. S., and Nixon, S. L. (2014) 'The Effects of "Grunting" on Serve and Forehand Velocities In Collegiate Tennis Players.' *Journal of Strength and Conditioning Research* 28(12): 3469–3475.

Powis, B. (2018) 'Visual Impairment, Sport and Somatic Work: The Auditory Experiences of Blind and Partially Sighted Cricket Players.' *The Senses and Society,* 13(2): 147–162.

Rice, T. (2010) 'Learning to Listen: Auscultation and the Transmission of Auditory Knowledge.' *Journal of the Royal Anthropological Institute* 16(Issue supplement s1): S41–S61.

Robson, G. (2000) 'No One Likes Us, We Don't Care': The Myth and Reality of Millwall Fandom. Oxford: Berg.

Sage, G. H. (2011) Globalizing Sport: How Organizations, Corporations, Media, and Politics Are Changing Sport. Boulder, CO: Paradigm Publishers.

Schoonderwoerd, P. (2011) '"Shall We Sing a Song For You?": Mediation, Migration and Identity in Football Chants and Fandom.' Soccer and Society 12(1): 120–141.

Sparkes, A. C. (2009) 'Ethnography and the Senses: Challenges and Possibilities.' *Qualitative Research In Sport and Exercise* 1(1): 21–35.

Spencer, D. C. (2014) 'Sensing Violence: An Ethnography of Mixed Martial Arts.' *Ethnography* 15(2): 232–254.

Swyers, H. (2010) *Wrigley Regulars: Finding Community In the Ballpark*. Urbana, IL: University of Illinois Press.

Wacquant, L. (2006) *Body & Soul: Notebooks of an Apprentice Boxer*. Oxford: Oxford University Press.

NAME INDEX

SUBJECT INDEX